THE LOEB CLASSICAL LIBRARY

FOUNDED BY JAMES LOEB 1911

EDITED BY

JEFFREY HENDERSON

DIONYSIUS OF HALICARNASSUS

CRITICAL ESSAYS

I

LCL 465

DIONYSIUS OF HALICARNASSUS

CRITICAL ESSAYS

VOLUME I

WITH AN ENGLISH TRANSLATION BY

STEPHEN USHER

HARVARD UNIVERSITY PRESS
CAMBRIDGE, MASSACHUSETTS
LONDON, ENGLAND

First published 1974

ISBN 978-0-674-99512-3

*Printed on acid-free paper and bound by
Edwards Brothers, Ann Arbor, Michigan*

CONTENTS

INTRODUCTION

Greek men of letters formed an essential part of the cultural scene at Rome from the third century B.C., and their numbers and influence increased, in spite of discouragement from Roman chauvinists and conservatives, after the conquest of the Greek world by Rome. Most of them were attached to eminent Roman families by more or less close bonds of patronage, connections having originally arisen through diplomatic or social contact before the conquest or through imprisonment and transportation to Rome after it. Over a century later, after Rome had suffered her own internal war, and Octavian, later Augustus, had reunited the East and the West of her empire, there was a renewed migration of Greeks to Rome. Dionysius of Halicarnassus arrived there late in 30 B.C. or early in 29 B.C., preceding the famous geographer Strabo by about a year and joining the historian Timagenes and the poets Parthenius and Crinagoras. He appears to have made the journey uninvited, since the gratitude he expresses for the hospitality he has received [1] is addressed to Rome at large and to no individual; but he must have known that rewarding and congenial employment awaited him in the great city. Roman education had for a long time included the learning of Greek, some boys

[1] *Antiquitates Romanae*, 1. 6. 5.

mastering it before their native tongue,[1] and many declaiming in Greek as a part of their training.[2] But more significant in the consideration of Dionysius's career is the fact that, in imperial as in republican Rome, Greek continued to enjoy a privileged position as the *lingua franca* of the literary world, so that the study of Greek language and literature at an advanced level was essential for any Roman who was to have any pretensions to wider culture, and remained so for many years to come.

But literary Greek had undergone great changes since the period of its highest achievement, the fifth and fourth centuries B.C. The greatest change accompanied the political revolution in which Philip II of Macedon, Alexander the Great and his Successors transformed the Greek world from a number of free, independent city-states into three kingdoms ruled absolutely. At the time of these conquests the Greek literary genius was expressing itself in its highest form in public oratory and political discourse, both of which depended for their inspiration upon the complete freedom of speech which the autonomous city-state provided. Athens, the home of the greatest orators and historians, came under the rule of Demetrius of Phalerum, a governor appointed by one of Alexander's successors, Cassander. In fact Demetrius himself tried to keep the Athenian literary tradition alive by writing treatises on history, politics and philosophy; but Cicero, while admiring the genuine Attic flavour of his oratory, saw in its weakness and effeminacy the beginnings of the rot.[3] In

[1] Quintilian, i. 1. 12–14.
[2] Cicero, *Brutus*, 90. 310.
[3] *Brutus*, 9. 38; 82. 285.

accordance with the political trend away from city-state orientation towards cosmopolitanism (in the limited Greek, not the modern sense), Athens ceased to be the only centre of letters and learning, and these activities themselves assumed a scholastic and academic character. The foundation of the great libraries at Alexandria and Pergamum, both at the instance of royal patrons, and the establishment of schools of rhetoric at Rhodes and elsewhere, were further steps in the sequestration of Greek literature from the world of real life. Freshness and originality were not to be expected from institutions devoted solely to criticism and recension, or to the study of techniques perfected by the great orators of the past. It is true that exceptionally gifted creative writers, like the poets Theocritus and Callimachus, overcame their environment, but their rare achievement only serves to demonstrate the relative poverty of talent in their field. History fared much better than poetry in these surroundings, however. The Greeks, unlike the earlier Romans, did not regard history as the exclusive province of the man of action: Polybius found himself in a minority when he criticised Timaeus of Tauromenium for spending all his time in libraries [1] instead of travelling, as he himself had done, and seeing history in action: Timaeus survived these criticisms and remained, from the shelter of the dusty shelves, one of the most popular of all the Greek historians. Of his immediate predecessors Ephorus of Cyme was at once one of the most popular and one of the least notable for any active participation in the events from which history is made. Polybius himself, however, came under heavy criticism for

[1] xii. 25f.

what was regarded by most readers as a worse fault in a historian than remoteness from events and lack of political experience—the inability to write in an attractive style. It was mainly from this standpoint that the historians attracted, and in some cases almost monopolised, the attention of the literary critics. It was a historian, Hegesias of Magnesia, who became for our own Dionysius the personification of "Asiatic" bad taste. Oratory and philosophy are virtually unrepresented in this early Hellenistic period.

Details of the activities of Greek rhetorical schools in the Hellenistic period are meagre and incoherent. Aeschines is said to have retired to Rhodes on finding his political career in ruins after his duel with Demosthenes over the Crown, and to have founded a school of rhetoric there which may have retained some of the features of the best Athenian oratory [1] and so established an Attic tradition. In the hands of teachers of less imagination, like Artamenes, Aristocles, Philagrion and perhaps even Cicero's teacher Molon,[2] the Attic style lost its more colourful features, because these were more difficult to imitate, and became conservative and aridly academic. Rival centres grew up on the Asiatic mainland: Caria, Mysia and Phrygia are three areas in which the new style was practised.[3] Cicero distinguished two kinds of Asiatic style, an earlier epigrammatic style, practised by Hierocles and Menecles of Alabanda, and a modern style which was ample, fluent and ornate,[4]

[1] Plutarch, *Lives of the Ten Orators*, 840D.
[2] Dionysius, *Dinarchus*, 8.
[3] Cicero, *Brutus*, 95. 325; Dionysius, *On the Ancient Orators*, Introd. 1.
[4] *ibid.*

whose exponents included Aeschylus of Cnidus and Aeschines of Miletus. The absence of comparable information concerning developments in the Attic tradition illustrates the advantage which the new style had over the old. It was untramelled by rules, precedents and preconceptions, and could develop in whatever direction its masters chose, always providing novelty and change. Atticism, on the other hand, became synonymous with conformity and restraint, with study and imitation rather than spontaneous creativity and originality: such, at least, are its characteristics when it emerges from obscurity in Roman literary controversy in the first century B.C. The subject will arise again in the course of the following discussion of individual influences on Dionysius.

Now rhetoric, as Plato knew, was too important a subject to be left to rhetoricians. His pupil Aristotle, a practical philosopher who found his master's theoretical and moral objections to rhetoric unconvincing, set out in his *Rhetoric* to present the sum of rhetorical teaching up to his own time, and many ideas of his own which answered Plato's objections and followed lines of enquiry adumbrated by him.[1] Dionysius was thoroughly familiar with the *Rhetoric* of Aristotle. In the *First Letter to Ammaeus* he refutes an assertion of an unknown Peripatetic that Demosthenes learned his oratorical technique from the *Rhetoric*, and in the course of his argument quotes from all three books. Again, his critical essays are replete with technical terms and statements which are to be found in Aristotle's great treatise. But these occasional points of contact between Aristotle

[1] See Grube, *The Greek and Roman Critics*, pp. 92–3.

and Dionysius in the details of their rhetorical teaching are overshadowed by the fundamental difference of purpose, not to say of mental powers, of the two men. Aristotle's training and cast of mind, and in particular his biologist's interest in analysis, analogy and classification, led him to construct an elaborate and wholly admirable rhetorical system based on the work and the experience of earlier practitioners, but defining their terms and differentiating between types of evidence and the other materials of persuasion. His is an ideal system: the practical orators of the fourth century were both less systematic and less inventive than the sources provided by Aristotle would have enabled them to be. On the other hand, in the matter of style, to which Aristotle devotes only one of his three books, the Attic orators provide models which are superior to any system which even Aristotle could have provided; and it is with style that Dionysius is concerned in most of his critical writing. Thus it is not surprising to find no explicit reference to the *Rhetoric* in Dionysius's essays on the Attic Orators.

But Theophrastus, Aristotle's pupil, is quoted four times in these essays and once in the *De Compositione Verborum.* He wrote a treatise On Style (περὶ λέξεως) in which he elaborated upon his master's teaching that lucidity (τὸ σαφές) was the essential virtue of style, and that the application of this principle should be regulated by the criterion of appropriateness.[1] Theophrastus, whose system is reproduced by Cicero,[2] derived four virtues of style from this simple Aristotelian concept: purity of language

[1] *Rhetoric* iii. 2.
[2] *Orator*, 79.

(ἑλληνισμός), lucidity (τὸ σαφές), appropriateness (τὸ πρέπον) and ornament (κατασκευή), the latter being subdivided into choice of words (ἐκλογὴ ὀνομάτων), arrangement (ἁρμονία) and the use of figures of speech (σχήματα). Most of these terms, or terms derived from the concepts underlying them, are used by Dionysius in his critical essays. The concept of purity was of especial relevance to Atticism. Aristotle uses it to try to differentiate between the language of poetry and the language of prose. In Dionysius we find a different distinction: his idea of Attic purity is that of a literary language which was based on the everyday language of Athens in the late fifth and fourth centuries B.C. It is tempting to trace this idea back to Theophrastus, but evidence is lacking. Theophrastus's other "virtues" were considerably elaborated, either by Dionysius himself or by an unknown intervening critic, and were divided into "essential" (ἀναγκαῖαι) and "additional" (ἐπίθετοι). Theophrastus's systematisation of virtues has led to the unwarranted assumption that he also devised the more important and far-reaching system of three "styles," "grand," "middle" and "plain," which Dionysius uses in the essay on Demosthenes and in the *De Compositione Verborum*. The earliest extant reference to it is in the *Rhetorica ad Herennium* (iv. 8–11), but the identity of its inventor seems likely to remain obscure. The only other subjects treated by Dionysius which may be traced back to the work of Theophrastus are prose rhythm and figures of speech. The former is discussed in general terms by Aristotle (*Rhetoric* iii. 8), but Dionysius's discussion of the effects of various rhythms in *De Compositione Verborum* 18 is much more

comprehensive; and Cicero tells us that Theophrastus discussed prose-rhythm more thoroughly than Aristotle.[1] Regarding figures of speech, both Theophrastus and Dionysius use the word σχήματα in that sense whereas Aristotle does not. This at least makes Theophrastus an original source for the concept as used by Dionysius.

With Hermagoras of Temnos we return to professional rhetoricians. Closer to Dionysius in time than Aristotle and Theophrastus (he taught at Athens around the middle of the second century B.C.), he reaffirmed the view of the earliest rhetoricians, Corax and Tisias, and the sophists Protagoras and Prodicus, that rhetoric was a complex technique (τέχνη) which could be taught on its own without reference to philosophical or moral principles. He devised his own complete rhetorical system, embracing all types of oratory and all the conventional parts of the speech, from the point of view of both style and subject matter. He analysed different types of subject-matter, dividing it into general (θέσεις) and particular (ὑποθέσεις) questions, and defined the different standpoints of an argument (στάσεις). This probably represents the most original part of his work, and was of fundamental importance in the development of practical oratory under the Republic and of declamatory oratory under the empire. Dionysius's debt to Hermagoras might have been greater if his purpose had been to train practical orators from first principles. But, as with other predecessors, his purpose and his methods are different. In Dionysius discussion centres upon ready-made models. In the course of these discussions, however, Dionysius uses a

[1] *Orator*, 172; *De Oratore* iii. 184.

number of technical terms which may ultimately derive from Hermagoras, particularly those which describe various aspects of the division of a speech, e.g. *κρίσις, διαίρεσις, ἔφοδος, ἐξεργασία, μερισμός*.

Attempts to find predecessors who influenced Dionysius thus succeed only in underlining his apparent isolation and originality. His mission as an Atticist and the obscurity of the early history of that movement (if it can be given so definite a form), account for this isolation in some measure. It is natural to seek the origin of Atticism in the libraries of Alexandria and Pergamum, where part of the librarians' work was to identify the authors of manuscripts of unknown provenance. Such work would involve the consideration of dialect as well as of chronological evidence, and it is interesting to find Dionysius doing this as a part of his own work. Librarians were also concerned with acquiring the works of the best authors of the Classical period, and the ability to identify Attic style was necessary if errors were to be avoided. It is therefore not surprising to hear that the first librarian at Pergamum, Crates of Mallos, made a study of the Attic dialect. The proximity of Pergamum to the cities in which the Asianic style was born may have led it to assume an early importance in the preservation of Attic standards. But the terms of the controversy were probably dictated at all times as much by the personal caprice of individual critics and teachers as by absolute stylistic standards; and the transference of the controversy to Rome did nothing to change this.

If no Greek predecessor is to be closely identified with Dionysius's Attic crusade, there is yet one whose life and work was devoted to increasing the beneficial

influence of the spoken and the written word. Isocrates wrote and taught in the fourth century, and was one of those who contributed most to making that period most productive of the best Attic prose. He gathered around him a select circle of able pupils and taught them a special kind of literary discourse, claiming that education based upon this teaching would produce citizens whose counsels would confer the greatest benefits upon the state. Such democratic possibilities no longer existed in the imperial Rome under which Dionysius lived, but the underlying principle, that the study and composition of artistic prose was the finest medium of education and moral training was wholly consonant with his position and his work in the city. Though he could not boast a Timotheus, and so rival Isocrates in the training of men of action, Dionysius could point to pupils who distinguished themselves as historians, like the Isocrateans Ephorus and Theopompus. Both men valued the practical application to life and to educative literature of their own special form of rhetoric, "philosophic rhetoric."[1] Dionysius wrote a treatise, now lost, on "Political Philosophy,"[2] and he invariably uses the terms "philosophy" and "philosophic" with reference to the practical life of man as a political animal (as Isocrates does)[3] rather than to abstract speculation. Isocrates was also an attractive and influential precursor from the point of view of style in that he was (after Demosthenes) the most successful exponent of the middle style, which Diony-

[1] Dionysius, *On the Ancient Orators*, Introduction, 1; Isocrates, *Against the Sophists*, 16–18.

[2] *Thucydides*, 2.

[3] *Antidosis*, 184–5, 271; *Panathenaicus*, 28–30; *Helen*, 5.

sius pronounces to be the best.[1] Dionysius's criticisms of the style of Isocrates, and in particular of his excessive addiction to parallelism and assonance, arise partly out of his enthusiasm for Demosthenes; and his own style shows closer affinities with that of Isocrates than with that of Demosthenes. Regarding content, on which a "philosophic rhetorician" might be expected to be judged by the highest standards, Dionysius's verdict on Isocrates is unreservedly favourable: he states that readers of his discourses cannot fail to be imbued with feelings of pride, patriotism, justice and responsibility.[2] He agrees with Isocrates that a rhetorical training is the best preparation for public life,[3] and saw in the subjects on which he discoursed the ideal material for great literature, better for the education of future writers than the narrowly specialised speeches of forensic orators, even when one of the forensic orators is Lysias.[4]

Returning to Dionysius's Roman environment, we are faced with the complexity of two vigorous literary cultures living side-by-side in a city itself torn by political tumult. The late republic was a turbulent period, but also a fruitful one for literature. Native Roman talent abounded in all media: in poetry Lucretius, Catullus, Propertius, Tibullus, Horace and Virgil, and in prose Caesar, Cicero, Sallust and Livy realised to the full the potential of Latin as a literary

[1] *Demosthenes*, 34.

[2] *Isocrates*, 5–9.

[3] *Antidosis*; 30. 306–309. Dionysius, *On the Ancient Orators*, Introd. 1: *ἑτέρα δέ τις . . . τὰς τιμὰς καὶ τὰς προστασίας τῶν πόλεων, ἃς ἔδει τὴν φιλόσοφον ἔχειν, εἰς ἑαυτὴν ἀνηρτήσατο.*

[4] *Isocrates*, 12.

language and created a Golden Age of Latin literature which rivalled the Attic period of Greece. The attendant upsurge of Roman confidence in Latin as a literary language led to a change of emphasis both in the more esoteric discussions of the literary côteries and in curricular education. In the latter, Latin played a more prominent part in its literary role than hitherto, while in the former, discussions of fundamental questions, like that of the ideal style, were conducted in the terms of early Greek controversy (in the above case, Atticism and Asianism), but with Latin and not Greek as the subject. The models are both Greek and Roman orators, but since the latter—accomplished speakers like Gaius Gracchus, Crassus, Antonius, Galba and Carbo—had done the vital spadework of adapting Greek theory to Roman practice, it was relatively easy and natural for Cicero's contemporaries to discuss Latin style in the general aesthetic terms which may be permitted only to mature critics of a mature language. In the hands of Hortensius, Cicero, Calvus and Caesar, Roman oratory attained heights comparable with those achieved by Greek oratory in the age of Demosthenes, and under political conditions of similar stress. Nothing popularises an art so much as great performers. In the case of oratory, performance without practical purpose had always been a part of training: both the teacher and his pupils declaimed in the classroom, the former to show how it should be done, the latter in order to perfect his technique. The teacher also opened his school to the outside world and gave public hearings in order to advertise his school. From this practice in Greece, and more especially in Rome, declamation developed into one of the most

popular forms of entertainment, rivalling the theatre. But its very popularity with the Roman public promoted Latin still further at the expense of Greek, for the average Roman was not sufficiently fluent in Greek to enjoy listening to a prolonged discourse in that language. Nor would he feel constrained to by cultural deference, for Latin was now the equal of Greek as a medium of great literature. It is therefore hardly surprising to find no evidence for the practice of public declamation in Greek at Rome in Dionysius's time of residence there.

Apart from learning the Latin language in order to study sources for his *Antiquitates Romanae*, Dionysius confined himself strictly to his Greek microcosm, an island populated by a few learned Hellenes in a vast ocean seething with cultural activity of an alien kind. In spite of his expressed gratitude to Rome, he felt no apparent affinity even with men of similar literary interests to his own, like Cicero and Horace: at all events he mentions neither, nor any other important Roman writer. His small circle of friends and pupils (hardly a school), shared his interest in maintaining the status of Greek as a literary language, especially for the writing of history and antiquities. Their discussions centred mainly upon topics of narrow literary interest, and on occasion smack of academic quibbling. They represent his esoteric world: his wider audience was catered for by the *Antiquitates Romanae*, which were addressed, like the *Histories* of Polybius, to the cultured Mediterranean world at large. It has been assumed, I think rightly, that the composition of this work occupied most of Dionysius's working hours at Rome. The absence of the name of a dedicatee suggests that, if it was commissioned, the com-

missioner may have been none other than the Princeps himself, who wished to lay a cloak of anonymity over his part in a work whose purpose was to reconcile the Greek world to the supremacy of Rome.[1] It is difficult to explain his long and apparently comfortable residence in Rome except by assuming patronage and assured financial support. His circle of friends and pupils was small, and he shows no special attachment to any one of them; so that it seems unlikely that he was able to support himself on his teaching alone, which was in any case, as has been said, his secondary occupation.

It is not uncommon, however, even for scholars to derive more pleasure from secondary occupations than from the work which earns them their bread and butter. At all events, Dionysius's extant rhetorical works constitute the largest body of Ancient Greek literary criticism by a single author, and contain many vigorous and colourful passages which betray the authors' enthusiasm for the subject, a quality less easy to discover in the *Antiquitates Romanae*. These critical works also show a wide range of intellectual quality, suggesting more than one level of academic purpose. Acquaintance is assumed throughout with the standard material of the rhetorical handbooks: Dionysius assumes that his readers know what he means when he uses terms like *προκατασκευή*, *ἔφοδος*, *μερισμός*[2] and, like Isocrates, he considers that the discussion of the technical *minutiae* of rhetoric is the business of the writers of practical handbooks, not of teachers of "philosophic" rhetoric like himself.

[1] See Cary's Introduction to his text and translation in the Loeb series, Vol. I, pp. xii–xv.
[2] *Isaeus*, 3.

This is his attitude in all the essays on individual authors. In the *De Compositione Verborum*, on the other hand, he deals thoroughly and minutely with the basic tools of two trades—that of the creative writer and that of the literary critic—and includes poetry in his discussion to an even greater extent than prose, showing that both are subject to the same natural phonetic and rhythmic laws.

Dionysius thus wages his Atticist campaign on a wide front. The study of literary composition from first principles was an important part of his teaching, but it seems likely, from the proportion of his extant output devoted to it, that the examination of Attic models for the purpose of imitation was the central discipline to which he subjected his pupils. It is interesting to note that, in spite of his frequent references to his pupils as connoisseurs,[1] he finds it necessary to quote whole passages from the orators, the historians and Plato. It would seem that the charge often laid against modern students by their teachers, that they read too much about literature and too little of the literature itself, may not be without its ancient parallels. To correct this tendency was vital to Dionysius's purpose, which was to confront his pupils with the texts of the finest Attic models, and to draw their attention to the qualities in which each excelled. With the paramount importance of the text itself thus established, it was inevitable that the criticism, at least in the early essays with which the present volume begins, should be of a somewhat cut-and-dried character. Dionysius's main message in each case was " Read the orator ": these essays were intended to guide the reader to those parts of the

[1] e.g. *Lysias*, 20; *Isaeus*, 14; *Demosthenes*, 42, 46; 50 (*sub. fin.*).

speeches of Lysias, Isocrates and Isaeus in which he might expect to find their best qualities exhibited. The essays on Demosthenes and Thucydides are more analytical and more specialised. Demosthenes's singular genius was ultimately inimitable, so that the critic's most useful service to his readers was, Dionysius thought, to show in what respects Demosthenes was superior to his nearest rivals. On Thucydides, Dionysius writes not only as a literary critic, but as one practical historian addressing another, the dedicatee Q. Aelius Tubero. He concludes that although Thucydides had many admirers, and was in some ways the greatest Attic historian, his obscurity both in style and in the arrangement of his material disqualified him as a model. Finally, an Atticist needed to be a detective. Dionysius's essay on Dinarchus, the last of the Attic orators, is largely concerned with establishing the identity of that orator's speeches. There is also a discussion on the subject of ascription in the essay on Lysias.

A total of ten critical essays, treatises and letters have come down to us, and these comprise the bulk of Dionysius's rhetorical writing. It is likely that he planned to write more than he actually completed, and there is evidence that much of what he did write was written in some haste. In addition to stating on a number of occasions that he is pressed for time,[1] Dionysius sometimes repeats words, phrases and even whole passages from one work in another. He is also guilty, much to the translator's discomfort, of an occasional imprecise use of words which might, with a little more thought, have been avoided. The only

[1] *Lysias*, 10; *Isocrates*, 20; *Isaeus*, 15; *Demosthenes*, 14, 32.

rhetorical[1] work which he is known for certain to have written, and which is lost except for some fragments, is the treatise *On Imitation*. It is possible that he wrote an essay on Demosthenes's treatment of subject matter as a companion to the extant essay on his style; but there is little evidence to suggest that he completed the projected essays on Aeschines and Hyperides.

The starting-point to an investigation of the likely order of the rhetorical works of Dionysius is the concluding sentence of the Introduction to the essays on the Attic Orators. In it Dionysius says that he intends to treat six orators in two separate groups of essays, in the first group Lysias, Isocrates and Isaeus, and in the second Demosthenes, Hyperides and Aeschines. There are enough cross-references in the first three essays to show that they were written in that order[2]; and the use of the aorist participle γραφείσης in the Introduction to refer to them suggests that it was composed after them. That the incomplete essay on Demosthenes which we have belongs to this series and is not an independent work, in spite of its much greater scale, is proved by a quotation from it in the Letter to Pompeius, ch. 2, where it is referred to as a part of his " work on the Attic Orators " (πραγματεία περὶ τῶν Ἀττικῶν ῥητόρων); and by a reference in the essay itself (ch. 2) to the *Lysias* as already composed.[3] But the *Demosthenes* also contains references to an already completed treatise *On Literary Composition* (περὶ

[1] Ignoring his treatise *On Political Philosophy*.

[2] *Isocrates*, 1 (*sub. init.*); 2, 3, 4; *Isaeus*, later than Lysias: *passim*; later than *Isocrates*: 19.

[3] ἐν τῇ πρὸ ταύτης δεδήλωται γραφῆς.

Συνθέσεως Ὀνομάτων, *De Compositione Verborum*) (chs. 49, 50). The essay on Thucydides contains a reference to a work on Demosthenes which Dionysius has set aside in order to write the present essay (ch. 1), but it is uncertain whether this is the essay on Demosthenes' style which we have or its companion on his treatment of subject-matter, which he promised at the end of that essay. In ch. 18 of the *De Compositione Verborum*, however, there is a criticism of Plato's choice of language which corresponds with that made in the *Demosthenes* (chs. 5–7), and to which he appears to refer with the words *ἑτέρωθί μοι δηλοῦται σαφέστερον*. If the present tense is taken to describe continuous contemporaneous action, as it normally does, it will be concluded that the two treatises occupied their author over approximately the same period, but that he finished the *De Compositione Verborum* before completing the *Demosthenes*. No abrupt internal division of the *Demosthenes* seems satisfactory,[1] and it is not possible to show any point in either work where it was set aside in order to write the other. On the other hand, it is perfectly in accord with what is known of Dionysius's working methods to conceive that he may have been working on two or more treatises at the same time.

Of the three Letters, the *Letter to Pompeius* may be safely placed soon after the *Demosthenes*, since it owes its composition to its recipient's objection to Dionysius's criticisms of Plato in that treatise.[2] The *First Letter to Ammaeus* was written to refute a suggestion that Demosthenes used Aristotle's *Rhetoric* to guide

[1] *Pace* Bonner, *The Literary Treatises of Dionysius of Halicarnassus*. (Cambridge, 1939) pp. 31–3.
[2] ch. 1; cf. *Demosthenes*, 5–7.

him in the composition of his speeches. Its first sentence contains some verbal echoes of the Introduction to the essays on Lysias, Isocrates and Isaeus,[1] which was written soon after these. It is also natural to link discussion of the influences upon Demosthenes with the *Isaeus*, and this orator is mentioned in this connection in both works.[2] The most natural point to place this letter in the order is therefore after the Introduction, and probably before the *Demosthenes*. The *Second Letter to Ammaeus* was written after the essay on Thucydides,[3] which in turn occupied Dionysius while he was writing either the extant *Demosthenes* or the essay which he subsequently wrote [4] on Demosthenes's treatment of subject-matter.

Two books of the lost treatise *On Imitation* had been composed when Dionysius wrote ch. 3 of the *Letter to Pompeius*, and the final book was at that time unfinished. That the first two books preceded the essays on the Attic Orators is strongly suggested by the inclusion in the second book of Lycurgus among the orators suitable for imitation, and the exclusion of Isaeus, whose importance as the most influential forerunner of Demosthenes is strongly argued in the *Isaeus*. Almost nothing is known about the contents of the third book of the treatise *On Imitation*, but it may have been published before the essay on Thucydides if it can be assumed that the opening sentence of that essay refers to all three books.[5] The three

[1] e.g. τῷ καθ' ἡμᾶς χρόνῳ . . . ἄλλων μέν τινων . . . οὐχ ἥκιστα δὲ and πολλῶν μετ' ἀλλων . . . ὁ καθ' ἡμᾶς χρόνος . . . ἓν δέ τι καὶ τοῦτο . . .

[2] *Isaeus*, 1, 3, 4, 13, 14; *First Letter to Ammaeus*, 2 *sub. fin.*

[3] ch. 1.

[4] *Demosthenes*, 58 *fin.*

[5] An assumption not strictly warranted by the words: ἐν τοῖς προεκδοθεῖσι περὶ τῆς μιμήσεως ὑπομνηματισμοῖς.

books were concerned respectively with principles, models and methods, and the second contained a wide-ranging survey of poets and prose authors whose styles might be studied for purposes of imitation.

The first sentence of the essay on Dinarchus shows that it was one of his later rhetorical works. This sentence refers to the two groups of essays mentioned in the Introduction as having been completed. Criticisms of Thucydides which are similar to those found in the *Thucydides* [1] but are not found in the *Demosthenes* may point to the completion of the *Thucydides* before the *Dinarchus*, but it is once more equally possible that Dionysius was engaged on the two essays at the same time.

It is clear from the evidence presented that an order of composition for individual works cannot be established beyond the three early essays on the Attic orators and their Introduction. These works, together with the *First Letter to Ammaeus*, may be assigned to an early period. To a middle period may be assigned the *De Compositione*, the first two books *On Imitation*, the *Demosthenes* and the *Letter to Pompeius*, and to a late period the *Thucydides*, the *Second Letter to Ammaeus*, the *Dinarchus* and the third book *On Imitation*. The treatise *On Political Philosophy*, of whose contents nothing is known but the name, was composed before the *Thucydides*.

The individual merits and shortcomings of the essays will be considered briefly in the introductions to each. In assessing the achievement of the whole the reader must take into account a variety of critical purposes and the contending claims of rhetoric and pure literary aesthetic. There is good reason to

[1] Dinarchus, 8.

believe that the analysis of Attic models and the isolation of qualities for imitation is a technique which Dionysius pioneered. As to his championing of Demosthenes as the finest Attic prose author, his choice may not have been original, but the technique of comparison with other rivals which he uses in the *Demosthenes* probably was. It is less easy to assess his originality in the *Thucydides*, since it is clear that controversy about that author and his methods had been raging for some time. The *De Compositione Verborum* owed something to the work of earlier grammarians and rhetoricians, but the high level of aesthetic percipience shown in it can but reflect a very cultivated and lively critical mind, surpassed in these qualities only by the unknown author of the noble treatise *On the Sublime*.

THE TEXT

The Teubner edition of Hermann Usener and Ludwig Radermacher forms the basis of the text of both the two present volumes. Their division of labour resulted in the *Thucydides* falling to Usener and the remaining treatises in this volume to his pupil. Radermacher's text bears many signs of his teacher's hand, and the debt of both to earlier editors and commentators, inevitable in view of the attention which the treatises attracted, is evident throughout. Sylburg (1586), Holwell (1766), Reiske (1774–7), Krüger (1823), Dobree (1831–3), van Herwerden (1861), Sadée (1878), Weil (1889) and Sauppe (1863) are the most important of these. But Usener and Radermacher have applied the principle of *lectio difficilior potior* to good effect, and have thus preserved many readings which others have sought to emend. I have carried this principle a stage further in a few places, bearing in mind the occasional carelessness and inconsistency of Dionysius.

The manuscripts, in probable order of authority, are as follows:

F	Florentinus Laurentianus LIX 15	(12th Century)
M	Ambrosianus D 119 sup.	(15th Century)
P	Vaticanus Palatinus 58	(15th Century)

THE TEXT

A	Parisiensis 1657	(15th Century)
B	Parisiensis 1742	(15th–16th Century)
C	Parisiensis 1800	(16th Century)
G	Guelferbytanus 806	(16th Century)
a	Editio Aldina Manutia (editio princeps, 1502–1508)	
s	Stephanorum (R. and H.) Editiones. (1546–1554)	

The text of the treatises in the present volume suffers somewhat from their absence from the oldest and most authoritative manuscript, *Parisiensis* 1741 (11th Century). M, P and B are thought by Usener and Radermacher to be derived from a single lost archetype (S), which may deserve equal status with F for the *Lysias*, *Isocrates* and *Isaeus* and the *Introduction*. I have generally followed Radermacher against Sadée in preferring the manuscript of greater antiquity (F) when it differs from M, P and B, in spite of the fact that it contains many corrupt, and occasionally nonsensical readings. A is derived from P. C contains only the *Introduction* and the first five lines of the *Lysias* of the treatises in this volume, but supplies one reading which is surely to be preferred: μεταβάλλοντι (μεταβαλόντι BA) (ch. 4 *init.*). G contains only the *Lysias* of our essays, and has been shown by Radermacher not to deserve the faith placed in it by Desrousseaux and Egger in their edition of that treatise (1890). Nevertheless it supplies the following readings: ἀπολογίαν (ἀπώλειαν FMPB) (ch. 12); λάβωσιν (λάβητε FMPB) (ch. 33). In the *Isocrates* I have followed Radermacher's policy of preferring the readings of the editions of Isocrates only when the received Dionysian reading is plainly in-

ferior. By this procedure possible alternatives are preserved. (This choice of readings does not arise in the *Lysias* and the *Isaeus*, as the passages which Dionysius quotes from these orators are not preserved elsewhere.)

For the *Demosthenes* we are dependent upon M, B and P and, for the opening quotation from Gorgias's *Epitaphios*, upon Syrianus (p. 90, 12R). The absence of early manuscripts is reflected in the many uncertainties of the text. In these circumstances greater weight has been attached to readings from the editions of Demosthenes, Thucydides, Isocrates and Plato than in the *Isocrates*. Usener and Radermacher have added to the list of lacunae noted by earlier editors. Some are beyond restoration, while others have tested the present editor's ingenuity, though to less effect, it must be confessed, than that of his illustrious predecessors. The *Thucydides* presents comparable problems. The fact that it is not contained in B is partly compensated for by the presence of a number of useful scribes' emendations in M and P. The greater uncertainty of the received text of Thucydides compared with that of Demosthenes has made it seem advisable to show greater reluctance to prefer its readings to those of Dionysius.

No attempt has been made in the present edition to provide an exhaustive *apparatus criticus*, for which readers may refer to Usener–Radermacher (Teubner, 1899–1905–1929). Textual notes are confined in the main to the conjectures and emendations of editors.

SELECT BIBLIOGRAPHY

Modern Editions:

A. Desrousseaux–M. Egger: *Denys d' Halicarnasse, Jugement sur Lysias.* Paris, 1890.

W. R. Roberts: *Dionysius of Halicarnassus, the Three Literary Letters.* Cambridge, 1901.

W. R. Roberts: *Dionysius of Halicarnassus, On Literary Composition.* London, 1910.

G. Pavano: *Dionisio d'Alicarnasso, Saggio su Tucidide.* Palermo, 1952.

Other Publications:

F. Blass: *Die Griechische Beredsamkeit in dem Zeitraum von Alexander bis auf Augustus.* Berlin, 1865.

A. Kiessling: *Zu den rhetorischen Schriften des Dionysios von Halikarnass.* Rheinisches Museum 1868, 248–54.

L. Sadée: *Zu Dionysios von Halicarnasos.* Neue Jahrbuch für Philologie und Pädagogik 1888, 549–55.

G. Ammon: *De Dionysii Halicarnassensis Librorum Rhetoricorum Fontibus.* Munich, 1889.

M. Mille: *Le Jugement de Denys d'Halicarnasse sur Thucydide.* Annales de la Faculté des Lettres de Bordeaux, 1889.

J. Denis: *Denys d'Halicarnass, Jugement sur Lysias.* Faculté des Lettres de Caen, Bulletin Mensuel, 1890.

W. R. Roberts: *The Literary Circle of Dionysius of Halicarnassus.* Classical Review 1900, 439–42.

M. Egger: *Denys d' Halicarnasse.* Paris, 1902.

L. Radermacher: in Pauly-Wissowa *Realencyclopädie* V.i (1903), 961–71.

E. Kremer: *Über das rhetorische System des Dionys von Halikarnass.* Strassburg, 1907.

R. H. Tukey: *A Note on Dionysius.* Classical Review 1909, 187–9.

The Composition of the De Oratoribus Antiquis of Dionysius. Classical Philology 1909, 390–404.

H. M. Hubbell: *The Influence of Isocrates on Cicero, Dionysius and Aristides.* Yale, 1914, 41–53.

J. D. Denniston: *Greek Literary Criticism.* London, 1924. Ch. 5.

E. Kalinka: *Die Arbeitsweise des Rhetors Dionys.* Wiener Studien 1924, 157–68; 1925, 46–68.

W. R. Roberts: *Greek Rhetoric and Literary Criticism.* London and New York, 1928. Ch. 4.

J. W. H. Atkins: *Literary Criticism in Antiquity.* Vol. II, 1934. Ch. 3.

J. F. Lockwood: *The Metaphorical Terminology of Dionysius of Halicarnassus.* Classical Quarterly 1937, 192–203.

S. F. Bonner: *Dionysius of Halicarnassus and the Peripatetic Mean of Style.* Classical Philology 1938, 257–66.

S. F. Bonner: *The Literary Treatises of Dionysius of Halicarnassus.* Cambridge, 1939; repr. Amsterdam, 1969.

S. F. Bonner: *Three Notes on the Scripta Rhetorica of*

Dionysius of Halicarnassus. Classical Review 1940, 183–4.

G. M. A. Grube: *Dionysius of Halicarnassus on Thucydides.* Phoenix 1950, 95–110.

G. M. A. Grube: *Thrasymachus, Theophrastus and Dionysius of Halicarnassus.* American Journal of Philology 1952, 251–67.

G. P. Goold: *A Greek Professorial Circle.* Transactions of the American Philological Association 1961, 168–92.

G. M. A. Grube: *The Greek and Roman Critics.* London, 1965. Ch. 13.

D. A. Russell and M. Winterbottom: *Ancient Literary Criticism: the principal texts in new translations.* Oxford, 1972.

ACKNOWLEDGMENT

The translator's problems are many, and they are multiplied in an author like Dionysius, whose rhetorical works combine technical and aesthetic criticism, and whose thought processes can be erratic and unpredictable, whether because of the haste with which he wrote these *parerga*, or through a native imprecision wedded to an overactive imagination. Attempts to overcome these problems by applying Caesarian standards of purity, whereby a given word is always translated by the same English word, lead simply to mistranslation, as, for example in the case of nouns like *λέξις* and *προαίρεσις* and in the case of adjectives like *θεατρικός*, which are used in both a pejorative and a laudatory sense. Faced with this constant necessity to search for the right word to fit the particular occasion, the translator sometimes fails to hit upon it each time, and often misses it even after mature reflection. A fresh mind is needed to renew the search. My friend and ex-colleague Professor Hugh Tredennick lent me his most generously, reading through the whole of my translation and making many corrections and improvements. Such felicities

as it possesses are due in large measure to his vigilance and sense of style. I am solely responsible for any faults which remain.

March 1972 Stephen Usher

ON THE ANCIENT ORATORS

INTRODUCTION

In these introductory chapters to his essays on the individual orators, Dionysius touches with tantalising allusiveness on two important topics. The first is the decline of literary taste, which he dates from the death of Alexander the Great, and its subsequent revival, which he relates to the conquest of the world by Rome. The process was marked by controversy: when a work of art has been broken down, there will be more than one opinion as to how it should be restored to its former glory. In Dionysius's version of the controversy (which incidentally gives us a foretaste of his vigorous, figurative and exuberant style), two rival Rhetorics form the subjects of a *prosopopoeia* which recalls the visual arts. The sober and chaste Attic Muse, who is like a model of 5th-Century Athenian womanhood, and the wanton Asiatic harlot, form an unharmonious *maison-à-trois* with their master (the literary world?), who is unable to decide between their claims until Rome has restored his sanity. This colourful allegory enables Dionysius to disguise or conceal two embarrassing realities. The first was a delicate matter of politics. The real reason for the initial decline of literature, and particularly of oratory, was the demise of freedom; and this was not a subject

which a privileged visitor could raise in Augustan Rome without appearing to abuse the emperor's hospitality. The second concerns the literary debate personified by the two ladies above—the recent wrangle between the Atticists and the Asianists. This was scarcely less perplexing for the honest critic, for by Dionysius's time this protean debate had become so confused and bedevilled by personalities that it was utterly impossible to say, with any degree of objectivity, what constituted Attic and what Asiatic style. The controversy was further complicated by the fact that its most vigorous participants in recent times had been Romans, a fact which Dionysius indirectly acknowledges by referring to Rome's leaders as discerning men of culture who have educated public taste.[1]

The second topic is his own contribution to this literary revival, and especially his method. This may be described as eclectic imitation. It involved the careful study of the finest Attic Orators and historians and the selection of the best qualities from each. Dionysius is scrupulously honest in making no absolute claim to originality, but so far as is known he is the first critic to employ this particular method. The imitation of models in a more general way may have been advocated by Theophrastus,[2] and it can scarcely be doubted that it played an important part

[1] See Introduction to this vol., pp. xvii–xix.

[2] One of the requirements of good style was purity of language (ἑλληνισμός), according to Theophrastus. The decline of literary Attic had already begun in his lifetime (witness Cicero's verdict on the style of his contemporary Demetrius of Phalerum in *Brutus*, 9. 38), so that the maintenance of ancient standards of purity depended upon the constant use of classical models.

in the teaching of the rhetorical schools at Rhodes and elsewhere. It is also implicit in many of the discussions of style in Cicero's oratorical treatises. Dionysius's contemporary Caecilius of Calacte wrote a treatise, now lost, *On the Style of the Ten Attic Orators*,[1] the purpose of which can only have been to demonstrate to readers who shared his revivalist zeal the variety of forms which Attic writing assumed in the hands of ten classical orators of differing but approximately equal talents. Here too the intention to imitate is implied. But Dionysius leads his readers more strongly and autocratically than his predecessors. He does not recognise Caecilius's canon of Ten Attic orators, choosing only six: and it soon becomes clear that he admires one more than the others.

[1] On Caecilius, see W. Rhys Roberts in *American Journal of Philology* 18 (1897) pp. 302–312.

ΔΙΟΝΥΣΙΟΥ ΑΛΙΚΑΡΝΑΣΕΩΣ ΠΕΡΙ ΤΩΝ ΑΡΧΑΙΩΝ ΡΗΤΟΡΩΝ

1 Πολλὴν χάριν ἦν εἰδέναι τῷ καθ᾿ ἡμᾶς χρόνῳ δίκαιον, ὦ κράτιστε Ἀμμαῖε, καὶ ἄλλων μέν τινων ἐπιτηδευμάτων ἕνεκα νῦν κάλλιον ἀσκουμένων ἢ πρότερον, οὐχ ἥκιστα δὲ τῆς περὶ τοὺς πολιτικοὺς λόγους ἐπιμελείας οὐ μικρὰν ἐπίδοσιν πεποιημένης ἐπὶ τὰ κρείττω. ἐν γὰρ δὴ τοῖς πρὸ ἡμῶν χρόνοις ἡ μὲν ἀρχαία καὶ φιλόσοφος ῥητορικὴ προπηλακιζομένη καὶ δεινὰς ὕβρεις ὑπομένουσα κατελύετο, ἀρξαμένη μὲν ἀπὸ τῆς Ἀλεξάνδρου τοῦ Μακεδόνος τελευτῆς ἐκπνεῖν καὶ μαραίνεσθαι κατ᾿ ὀλίγον, ἐπὶ δὲ τῆς καθ᾿ ἡμᾶς ἡλικίας μικροῦ δεήσασα εἰς τέλος ἠφανίσθαι· ἑτέρα δέ τις ἐπὶ τὴν ἐκείνης παρελθοῦσα τάξιν, ἀφόρητος ἀναιδείᾳ[1] θεατρικῇ καὶ ἀνάγωγος καὶ οὔτε φιλοσοφίας οὔτε ἄλλου παιδεύματος οὐδενὸς μετειληφυῖα ἐλευθερίου, λαθοῦσα καὶ παρακρουσαμένη τὴν τῶν

[1] ἀναιδείᾳ θεατρικῇ Sylburg: ἀναίδεια θεατρικὴ codd.

THE CRITICAL ESSAYS OF DIONYSIUS OF HALICARNASSUS

1. THE ANCIENT ORATORS

We ought to acknowledge a great debt of gratitude 1
to the age in which we live, my most accomplished Ammaeus, for an improvement in certain fields of serious study, and especially for the considerable revival in the practice of civil oratory.[1] In the epoch preceding our own, the old philosophic Rhetoric was so grossly abused and maltreated that it fell into a decline. From the death of Alexander of Macedon it began to lose its spirit and gradually wither away, and in our generation had reached a state of almost total extinction. Another Rhetoric stole in and took its place, intolerably shameless and histrionic, ill-bred and without a vestige either of philosophy or of any other aspect of liberal education. Deceiving the mob and exploiting its ignorance, it not only came to

[1] See Introduction pp. xviii–xix.

ὄχλων ἄγνοιαν, οὐ μόνον ἐν εὐπορίᾳ [1] καὶ τρυφῇ καὶ μορφῇ πλείονι τῆς ἑτέρας διῆγεν, ἀλλὰ καὶ τὰς τιμὰς καὶ τὰς προστασίας τῶν πόλεων, ἃς ἔδει τὴν φιλόσοφον ἔχειν, εἰς ἑαυτὴν ἀνηρτήσατο καὶ ἦν φορτική τις πάνυ καὶ ὀχληρὰ καὶ τελευτῶσα παραπλησίαν ἐποίησε γενέσθαι τὴν Ἑλλάδα ταῖς τῶν ἀσώτων καὶ κακοδαιμόνων οἰκίαις. ὥσπερ γὰρ ἐν ἐκείναις ἡ μὲν ἐλευθέρα καὶ σώφρων γαμετὴ κάθηται μηδενὸς οὖσα τῶν αὑτῆς κυρία, ἑταίρα δέ τις ἄφρων ἐπ' ὀλέθρῳ τοῦ βίου παροῦσα πάσης ἀξιοῖ τῆς οὐσίας ἄρχειν, σκυβαλίζουσα καὶ δεδιττομένη τὴν ἑτέραν· τὸν αὐτὸν τρόπον ἐν πάσῃ πόλει καὶ οὐδεμιᾶς ἧττον ἐν ταῖς εὐπαιδεύτοις (τουτὶ γὰρ ἁπάντων τῶν κακῶν ἔσχατον) ἡ μὲν Ἀττικὴ μοῦσα καὶ ἀρχαία καὶ αὐτόχθων ἄτιμον εἰλήφει σχῆμα, τῶν ἑαυτῆς ἐκπεσοῦσα ἀγαθῶν, ἡ δὲ ἔκ τινων βαράθρων τῆς Ἀσίας ἐχθὲς καὶ πρῴην ἀφικομένη, Μυσὴ [2] ἢ Φρυγία τις ἢ Καρικόν τι κακόν, Ἑλληνίδας ἠξίου διοικεῖν πόλεις ἀπελάσασα τῶν κοινῶν τὴν ἑτέραν, ἡ ἀμαθὴς τὴν φιλόσοφον καὶ ἡ μαινομένη τὴν σώφρονα.

2 ἀλλὰ γὰρ οὐ μόνον "ἀνδρῶν δικαίων χρόνος σωτὴρ ἄριστος" κατὰ Πίνδαρον, ἀλλὰ καὶ τεχνῶν

[1] εὐπορίᾳ Usener: εὐπορία M²: ἀπορία codd.
[2] Μυσὴ Kiessling: μοῦσα codd.

---

[1] For the Atticism–Asianism controversy see pp. x–xi, xv, xviii. The personification and the colourful language of this highly wrought passage partly conceals an inconsistency in its argument. On the one hand, the death of Alexander is rightly chosen as the starting-point of the gradual decline, while on the other hand, the usurper is described as an upstart

enjoy greater wealth, luxury and splendour than the other, but actually made itself the key to civic honours and high office, a power which ought to have been reserved for the philosophic art. It was altogether vulgar and disgusting, and finally made the Greek world resemble the houses of the profligate and the abandoned: just as in such households there sits the lawful wife, freeborn and chaste, but with no authority over her domain, while an insensate harlot, bent on destroying her livelihood, claims control of the whole estate, treating the other like dirt and keeping her in a state of terror; so in every city, and in the highly civilised ones as much as any (which was the final indignity), the ancient and indigenous Attic Muse, deprived of her possessions, had lost her civic rank, while her antagonist, an upstart that had arrived only yesterday or the day before from some Asiatic death-hole,[1] a Mysian or Phrygian or Carian creature, claimed the right to rule over Greek cities, expelling her rival from public life. Thus was wisdom driven out by ignorance, and sanity by madness.

But it is not only "of just men" that Pindar's 2
saying "Time is the best champion" holds good:[2]

who seized control suddenly. Dionysius has been carried away by his desire to dramatise; but in referring to the hostile Asianic Rhetoric as "arrived only yesterday" he has left the way open for an interpretation which accords with the historical facts: that the controversy itself was of recent origin at the time of writing. The first Attic revivalists began to purify literary Greek towards the middle of the first century B.C.; but in fairness to Dionysius it should be said that the earliest authors criticised as Asianic by him (see esp. *De Compositione Verborum* 4, 18) and his fellow-Atticists belong to the early Hellenistic period immediately following the death of Alexander.

[2] Frag. 159 Bergk.

νὴ Δία καὶ ἐπιτηδευμάτων γε καὶ παντὸς ἄλλου σπουδαίου χρήματος. ἔδειξε δὲ ὁ καθ' ἡμᾶς χρόνος, εἴτε θεῶν τινος ἄρξαντος εἴτε φυσικῆς περιόδου τὴν ἀρχαίαν τάξιν ἀνακυκλούσης εἴτε ἀνθρωπίνης ὁρμῆς ἐπὶ τὰ ὅμοια πολλοὺς ἀγούσης, καὶ ἀπέδωκε τῇ μὲν ἀρχαίᾳ καὶ σώφρονι ῥητορικῇ τὴν δικαίαν τιμήν, ἣν καὶ πρότερον εἶχε καλῶς, ἀπολαβεῖν, τῇ δὲ νέᾳ καὶ ἀνοήτῳ παύσασθαι δόξαν οὐ προσήκουσαν καρπουμένῃ καὶ ἐν ἀλλοτρίοις ἀγαθοῖς τρυφώσῃ. καὶ οὐ καθ' ἓν ἴσως τοῦτο μόνον ἐπαινεῖν τὸν παρόντα χρόνον καὶ τοὺς συμφιλοσοφοῦντας ἀνθρώπους ἄξιον, ὅτι τὰ κρείττω τιμιώτερα ποιεῖν τῶν χειρόνων ἤρξαντο (καίτοι μέρος γε τοῦ παντὸς ἥμισυ ἀρχὴ λέγεταί τε καὶ ἔστιν), ἀλλ' ὅτι καὶ ταχεῖαν τὴν μεταβολὴν καὶ μεγάλην τὴν ἐπίδοσιν αὐτῶν παρεσκεύασε γενέσθαι. ἔξω γὰρ ὀλίγων τινῶν Ἀσιανῶν πόλεων, αἷς δι' ἀμαθίαν βραδεῖά ἐστιν ἡ τῶν καλῶν μάθησις, αἱ λοιπαὶ πέπαυνται τοὺς φορτικοὺς καὶ ψυχροὺς καὶ ἀναισθήτους ἀγαπῶσαι λόγους, τῶν μὲν πρότερον μέγα ἐπ' αὐτοῖς φρονούντων αἰδουμένων ἤδη καὶ κατὰ μικρὸν ἀπαυτομολούντων πρὸς τοὺς ἑτέρους, εἰ μή τινες παντάπασιν ἀνιάτως ἔχουσι, τῶν δὲ νεωστὶ τοῦ μαθήματος ἁπτομένων εἰς καταφρόνησιν ἀγόντων τοὺς λόγους καὶ γέλωτα ποιουμένων τὴν ἐπ' αὐτοῖς σπουδήν.

3 αἰτία δ' οἶμαι καὶ ἀρχὴ τῆς τοσαύτης μεταβολῆς

---

[1] Cf. Plato, *Politicus*, 269C–D. The idea of a cyclic order of the universe is Pythagorean.

[2] A common ancient aphorism, attributed to Pythagoras by

for Time does the same for the arts, of course, and also for practical pursuits and for every other worthwhile activity. Our own age has demonstrated this. Whether at the instance of some god, or by the return of the old order of things in accordance with a natural cycle,[1] or through the human urge that draws many towards the same activities: for whatever reason, the ancient, sober Rhetoric has thereby been restored to her former rightful place of honour, while the brainless new Rhetoric has been restrained from enjoying a fame which it does not deserve and from living in luxury on the fruits of another's labours. And this is perhaps not the only reason for praising the present age and the men who guide its culture—that they were pioneers in the promotion of good taste over bad (though it is rightly said that the beginning is a half of the whole) [2]—but equally to be commended is the rapidity with which they have brought about this change and the measure of the improvement. Apart from a few Asian cities, where the progress of culture is impeded by ignorance, the world has ceased to admire vulgar, frigid and banal oratory. Some of those who formerly used to glory in this style are now recovering their sense of decorum and are gradually deserting to the other camp, except for a few totally incurable cases,[3] while those who are newly embarking on their studies despise this form of oratory and ridicule the cult of it.

I think that the cause and origin of this great 3

Iamblichus (*Vita Pythagorae*, 29), and to Hesiod by Lucian (*Hermotimus*, 3), who perhaps confused it with *Works and Days*, 40. It may well have been earlier than either of these. Cf. Plato, *Laws*, 753E.

[3] An echo of Demosthenes, *De Corona*, 324.

ἐγένετο ἡ πάντων κρατοῦσα Ῥώμη πρὸς ἑαυτὴν ἀναγκάζουσα τὰς ὅλας πόλεις ἀποβλέπειν καὶ ταύτης δὲ [1] αὐτῆς οἱ δυναστεύοντες κατ' ἀρετὴν καὶ ἀπὸ τοῦ κρατίστου τὰ κοινὰ διοικοῦντες, εὐπαίδευτοι πάνυ καὶ γενναῖοι τὰς κρίσεις γενόμενοι, ὑφ' ὧν κοσμούμενον τό τε φρόνιμον τῆς πόλεως μέρος ἔτι μᾶλλον ἐπιδέδωκεν καὶ τὸ ἀνόητον ἠνάγκασται νοῦν ἔχειν. τοιγάρτοι πολλαὶ μὲν ἱστορίαι σπουδῆς ἄξιαι γράφονται τοῖς νῦν, πολλοὶ δὲ λόγοι πολιτικοὶ χαρίεντες ἐκφέρονται φιλόσοφοί τε συντάξεις οὐ μὰ Δία εὐκαταφρόνητοι ἄλλαι τε πολλαὶ καὶ καλαὶ πραγματεῖαι καὶ Ῥωμαίοις καὶ Ἕλλησιν εὖ μάλα διεσπουδασμέναι προεληλύθασί τε καὶ προελεύσονται κατὰ τὸ εἰκός. καὶ οὐκ ἂν θαυμάσαιμι τηλικαύτης μεταβολῆς ἐν τούτῳ τῷ βραχεῖ χρόνῳ γεγενημένης, εἰ μηκέτι χωρήσει προσωτέρω μιᾶς γενεᾶς ὁ ζῆλος ἐκεῖνος τῶν ἀνοήτων λόγων· τὸ γὰρ ἐκ παντὸς εἰς ἐλάχιστον συναχθὲν ῥᾴδιον ἐξ ὀλίγου μηδὲν εἶναι.

4 ἀλλὰ γὰρ τὸ μὲν εὐχαριστεῖν τῷ μεταβάλλοντι τὰ πράγματα χρόνῳ καὶ τὸ τοὺς τὰ κράτιστα προαιρουμένους ἐπαινεῖν καὶ τὸ τὰ μέλλοντα ἐκ τῶν γεγονότων εἰκάζειν καὶ πάντα τὰ παραπλήσια τούτοις, ἃ κἂν ὁ τυχὼν εἰπεῖν δύναιτο, ἀφήσω, ἐξ ὧν δ' ἂν ἔτι μείζω λάβοι τὰ κρείττονα ἰσχύν, ταῦτα πειράσομαι λέγειν, ὑπόθεσιν τοῦ λόγου κοινὴν καὶ φιλάνθρωπον καὶ πλεῖστα δυναμένην

[1] δὲ Usener: τε codd.

---

[1] Cf. *Antiquitates Romanae*, 1. 3. 3–5.
[2] As is clear from ch. 1, Dionysius is interested only in Greek

revolution has been the conquest of the world by Rome, who has thus made every city focus its entire attention upon her.[1] Her leaders are chosen on merit, and administer the state according to the highest principles. They are thoroughly cultured and in the highest degree discerning, so that under their ordering influence the sensible section of the population has increased its power and the foolish have been compelled to behave rationally. This state of affairs has led to the composition of many worthwhile works of history by contemporary writers, and the publication of many elegant political tracts and many by no means negligible philosophical treatises; and a host of other fine works, the products of well-directed industry, have proceeded from the pens of both Greeks and Romans,[2] and will probably continue to do so. And since this great revolution has taken place in so short a time, I should not be surprised if that craze for a silly style of oratory fails to survive another single generation; for what has been reduced from omnipotence to insignificance can soon easily be wiped out altogether.

But I shall stop expressing gratitude to Time for effecting these changes, and praising those writers who are choosing the best style; nor shall I speculate upon the future in the light of the past or indulge in any similar game which anyone could play. It will be my task to show how still further strength can be given to the winning cause; and the subject I have chosen for my discourse is one of general interest and 4

literature; but he is here obliged to mention Roman literature also not only from courtesy to his hosts but by the slightly embarrassing historical fact that Atticism in its practical form began as a Roman movement.

ὠφελῆσαι λαβών. ἔστι δὲ ἥδε, τίνες εἰσὶν ἀξιολογώτατοι τῶν ἀρχαίων ῥητόρων τε καὶ συγγραφέων καὶ τίνες αὐτῶν ἐγένοντο προαιρέσεις τοῦ τε βίου καὶ τῶν λόγων [1] καὶ τί παρ' ἑκάστου δεῖ λαμβάνειν ἢ φυλάττεσθαι, καλὰ θεωρήματα καὶ ἀναγκαῖα τοῖς ἀσκοῦσι [2] τὴν πολιτικὴν φιλοσοφίαν καὶ οὐ δήπου μὰ Δία κοινὰ οὐδὲ καθημαξευμένα τοῖς πρότερον. ἐγὼ γοῦν οὐδεμιᾷ τοιαύτῃ περιτυχὼν οἶδα γραφῇ, πολλὴν ζήτησιν αὐτῶν ποιησάμενος. οὐ μέντοι [3] διαβεβαιοῦμαί γε ὡς δὴ καὶ σαφῶς εἰδώς· τάχα γὰρ ἂν εἶέν τινες αἱ ἐμὲ διαλανθάνουσαι τοιαῦται γραφαί, τὸ δὲ τῆς ἁπάντων ἱστορίας ὅρον ἑαυτὸν ποιεῖν καὶ περὶ τοῦ μὴ γεγονέναι τι τῶν δυνατῶν γενέσθαι λέγειν αὔθαδες πάνυ καὶ οὐ πόρρω μανίας. περὶ μὲν οὖν τούτων οὐδὲν ἔχω, καθάπερ ἔφην, διαβεβαιοῦσθαι. τῶν δὲ ῥητόρων τε καὶ συγγραφέων, ὑπὲρ ὧν ὁ λόγος, πολλῶν πάνυ ὄντων καὶ ἀγαθῶν τὸ μὲν ὑπὲρ ἁπάντων γράφειν μακροῦ λόγου δεόμενον ὁρῶν ἐάσω, τοὺς δὲ χαριεστάτους ἐξ αὐτῶν προχειρισάμενος κατὰ τὰς ἡλικίας ἐρῶ περὶ ἑκάστου, νῦν μὲν περὶ τῶν ῥητόρων, ἐὰν δὲ ἐγχωρῇ, καὶ περὶ τῶν ἱστορικῶν. ἔσονται δὲ οἱ παραλαμβανόμενοι ῥήτορες τρεῖς μὲν ἐκ τῶν πρεσβυτέρων, Λυσίας Ἰσοκράτης Ἰσαῖος, τρεῖς δ' ἐκ τῶν ἐπακμασάντων τούτοις, Δημοσθένης Ὑπερείδης Αἰσχίνης, οὓς ἐγὼ τῶν ἄλλων ἡγοῦμαι κρατίστους, καὶ διαιρεθήσεται μὲν εἰς δύο συντάξεις

[1] τῶν λόγων Reiske: τοῦ λόγου codd.
[2] ἀσκοῦσι Reiske: ἀκούουσι codd.
[3] μέντοι Sadée: μὲν δὴ codd.

great potential benefit to mankind. It is this. Who are the most important of the ancient orators and historians? What manner of life and style of writing did they adopt? Which characteristics of each of them should we imitate, and which should we avoid? These are worthy subjects, which students of political thought must examine, yet they have certainly not become commonplace or hackneyed through the attentions of earlier writers. I cannot myself recall ever having come across any treatise on this subject, in spite of exhaustive research: though I do not affirm this with positive certainty, for there may be such works which have escaped my notice; and it would be utterly arbitrary, to the point of madness, to set oneself up as an authority on every subject of research, especially to the extent of saying that something does not exist when it is possible that it does.[1] Concerning such works, therefore, as I said, I can make no positive statement. As to my own subject, I realise that there are so many good orators and historians that to write about all of them would be a long task. I shall not attempt to do this, but shall select the most elegant of them and examine them chronologically, beginning with the present work on the orators and then proceeding to the historians, if I have the time. The orators to be compared will be three from the earlier generation, Lysias, Isocrates and Isaeus, and three from those who flourished after these, Demosthenes, Hyperides and Aeschines.[2] These I consider to be the best orators. My work

[1] Dionysius's claim to originality in his choice of subject seems irrefutable on the evidence now available.

[2] No treatise by Dionysius on either Hyperides or Aeschines survives.

ἡ πραγματεία, τὴν δὲ ἀρχὴν ἀπὸ ταύτης λήψεται τῆς ὑπὲρ τῶν πρεσβυτέρων γραφείσης. προειρημένων δὴ τούτων ἐπανάγειν καιρὸς ἐπὶ τὰ προκείμενα.

will be divided into two sections, the first dealing with the older orators. With these prefatory remarks, the time has come to return to the subject itself.

LYSIAS

INTRODUCTION

The first and most substantial of the three early essays is devoted to an orator who played an important part in the Atticist–Asianist controversy. The Roman Atticists Brutus and Calvus made him their model, and Caecilius of Calacte was said to have written a treatise on Lysias in which he compared him favourably with Plato.[1] This presented Dionysius with a dilemma. Lysias possessed many of the virtues which both he and his predecessors Aristotle and Theophrastus admired, and which met the primary requirements of Atticism: purity of dialect, the standard vocabulary of prose, lucidity and brevity. He possessed the further qualities of vividness, moral characterisation, propriety and finally a certain charm which is wholly individual and defies description. Dionysius must have found it difficult not to follow others, and to look no further for his ideal

[1] The treatise *On the Sublime*, 32. 8.

model. But he commands our full agreement, not to say our admiration for his critical acumen, when he finds Lysias somewhat weak in portraying emotion, especially in his proofs and perorations, and therefore a suitable model only for introduction, narrative and technical sections of the proof. We later read in the Isocrates that Lysias's virtual confinement to the field of forensic oratory rendered him inferior to that orator in his general treatment of subject-matter, simply because he lacked the practice of writing about noble subjects.[1] Thus we see the eclectic process in operation.

A chapter is devoted to each of the required qualities, and the orator's performance in each is recorded. The rather rigid schematisation which this method of criticism entails serves Dionysius quite well in this treatise, since it enables him to give a clear and comprehensive description of the archetype of pure Attic style, which furnishes a basis for the examination of subsequent models. Lysias was the most suitable model for all but the most elevated style of oratory. Again, although the critic mentions his individual "charm" and warns us that his apparent artlessness conceals art,[2] Lysias is otherwise the most imitable of

[1] *Isocrates*, 4.
[2] *Lysias*, 16.

the orators because he lacks a distinctive personality, at least in Dionysius's estimation. This may be inferred from the brevity of the biographical sketch with which the essay begins, and which contains little of the promised[1] information about the orator's "chosen manner of life," and leaves the last thirty years or so of it untouched. Lysias's ability to adapt his style to his client's personality[2] provides the student with a variety of styles and at the same time introduces him to a colourful portrait-gallery of types not unlike the *Characters* of Theophrastus. But in drawing attention to Lysias's indefinable "charm" Dionysius introduces into his criticism an element whose importance would be difficult to exaggerate: it is instinctive criticism based on pure perception devoid of reason (ἄλογος αἴσθησις). This introduction of higher aesthetic ideals, which presuppose in the critic a literary inspiration almost as great as that of the creative writer whom he is criticising, into a treatise which is otherwise noteworthy for its systematic and somewhat mechanical treatment of its subject, gives the *Lysias* a Janus-like quality, looking inwards to the earlier systems of the ancient rhetori-

[1] In *Introd.*, 4.

[2] On this aspect of Lysias's style, see S. Usher in *Eranos* 63 (1965) pp. 99–119.

cians, of Theophrastus and Hermagoras, and outwards to the later intuitive criticism of Dionysius in the *De Compositione Verborum*, and of the author of the treatise *On the Sublime*.

ΛΥΣΙΑΣ ΣΥΡΑΚΟΥΣΙΟΣ ΠΑΤΡΟΘΕΝ

1 Λυσίας ὁ Κεφάλου Συρακουσίων μὲν ἦν γονέων, ἐγεννήθη δὲ Ἀθήνησι μετοικοῦντι τῷ πατρὶ καὶ συνεπαιδεύθη τοῖς ἐπιφανεστάτοις Ἀθηναίων. ἔτη δὲ πεντεκαίδεκα γεγονὼς εἰς Θουρίους ᾤχετο πλέων σὺν ἀδελφοῖς δυσίν, κοινωνήσων τῆς ἀποικίας, ἣν ἔστελλον Ἀθηναῖοί τε καὶ ἡ ἄλλη Ἑλλὰς δωδεκάτῳ πρότερον ἔτει τοῦ Πελοποννησιακοῦ πολέμου, καὶ διετέλεσεν αὐτόθι πολιτευόμενος ἐν εὐπορίᾳ πολλῇ καὶ ⟨παιδευόμενος παρὰ Τισίᾳ τε καὶ Νικίᾳ⟩ [1] μέχρι τῆς συμφορᾶς τῆς κατασχούσης Ἀθηναίους ἐν Σικελίᾳ. μετ᾽ ἐκεῖνο δὲ τὸ πάθος στασιάσαντος τοῦ δήμου ἐκπίπτει σὺν ἄλλοις τριακοσίοις ἀττικισμὸν ἐγκληθείς. καὶ παραγενόμενος αὖθις εἰς Ἀθήνας κατὰ ἄρχοντα Καλλίαν, ἕβδομον καὶ τετταρακοστὸν ἔτος ἔχων, ὡς ἄν τις εἰκάσειεν, ἐξ ἐκείνου τοῦ χρόνου διετέλεσε τὰς διατριβὰς ποιούμενος Ἀθήνησι. πλείστους δὲ γράψας λόγους εἰς δικαστήριά τε καὶ βουλὰς καὶ πρὸς ἐκκλησίας εὐθέτους,

[1] παιδευόμενος . . . Νικίᾳ supplevit Usener ex Vitis X Oratorum 835d.

LYSIAS

Lysias was the son of Syracusan parents, but he was 1
born at Athens, where his father Cephalus was living as a resident alien, and he received the same education as the most illustrious citizens.[1] At the age of fifteen he sailed away to Thurii with his two brothers [2] to join in the foundation of a colony there, a Panhellenic venture promoted by the Athenians in the twelfth year before the Peloponnesian War.[3] He continued to reside there as a citizen in considerable prosperity, and received further teaching from Tisias and Nicias, until the ill-fated Athenian expedition to Sicily. After that disaster there was a revolution, and he was exiled along with three hundred others on the charge of pro-Athenian sympathies. Returning to Athens in the archonship of Callias,[4] when his age was presumably forty-seven, he lived and worked for the remainder of his life at Athens. He wrote many speeches for the lawcourts, and for debates in the Council and the Assembly, each well-adapted to its

[1] Dionysius here reproduces uncritically facts recorded by earlier biographers. Cf. *First Letter to Ammaeus*, 3.

[2] Polemarchus and Euthydemus.

[3] 443/2 B.C., making 459 or 458 the date of Lysias's birth. Acceptance of this date entails serious difficulties. See Dover, *Lysias and the Corpus Lysiacum* (1968) pp. 40–3, who prefers a later date. Thurii was founded near Sybaris in Italy.

[4] 412–411 B.C.

πρὸς δὲ τούτοις πανηγυρικούς, ἐρωτικούς, ἐπιστολικούς, τῶν μὲν ἔμπροσθεν γενομένων ῥητόρων ἢ κατὰ τὸν αὐτὸν χρόνον ἀκμασάντων ἠφάνισε τὰς δόξας, τῶν δὲ ἐπιγινομένων οὔτε πολλοῖς τισι κατέλιπεν ὑπερβολὴν οὔτ' ἐν ἁπάσαις ταῖς ἰδέαις τῶν λόγων [1] καὶ μὰ Δί' οὔ τί γε ταῖς φαυλοτάταις. τίνι δὲ κέχρηται χαρακτῆρι λόγων καὶ τίνας ἀρετὰς εἰσενήνεκται τίνι τε κρείττων ἐστὶ τῶν μεθ' ἑαυτὸν ἀκμασάντων καὶ πῇ καταδεέστερος καὶ τί δεῖ λαμβάνειν παρ' αὐτοῦ, νῦν ἤδη πειράσομαι λέγειν.

2 καθαρός ἐστι τὴν ἑρμηνείαν πάνυ καὶ τῆς Ἀττικῆς γλώττης ἄριστος κανών, οὐ τῆς ἀρχαίας, ᾗ κέχρηται Πλάτων τε καὶ Θουκυδίδης, ἀλλὰ τῆς κατ' ἐκεῖνον τὸν χρόνον ἐπιχωριαζούσης, ὡς ἔστι τεκμήρασθαι τοῖς τε Ἀνδοκίδου λόγοις καὶ τοῖς Κριτίου καὶ ἄλλοις συχνοῖς. κατὰ τοῦτο μὲν δὴ τὸ μέρος, ὅ πέρ ἐστι πρῶτόν τε καὶ κυριώτατον ἐν λόγοις, λέγω δὲ τὸ καθαρεύειν τὴν διάλεκτον, οὐθεὶς τῶν μεταγενεστέρων αὐτὸν ὑπερεβάλετο, ἀλλ' οὐδὲ μιμήσασθαι πολλοὶ δύναμιν ἔσχον ὅτι μὴ μόνος Ἰσοκράτης· καθαρώτατος γὰρ δὴ τῶν ἄλλων μετὰ Λυσίαν ἐν τοῖς ὀνόμασιν οὗτος ἔμοιγε δοκεῖ γενέσθαι ὁ ἀνήρ. μίαν μὲν δὴ ταύτην ἀρετὴν ἀξίαν ζήλου καὶ μιμήσεως εὑρίσκω παρὰ τῷ ῥήτορι καὶ παρακελευσαίμην ἂν τοῖς βουλομένοις καθαρῶς γράφειν ἢ λέγειν ἐκεῖνον τὸν ἄνδρα ποιεῖσθαι παράδειγμα ταύτης τῆς ἀρετῆς.

3 ἑτέραν δὲ καὶ οὐδὲν ἐλάττονα ταύτης, ἣν πολλοὶ μὲν ἐζήλωσαν τῶν κατὰ τὸν αὐτὸν χρόνον ἀκμασάντων, οὐδεὶς δὲ βεβαιότερον ἀπεδείξατο· τίς δ'

medium; also panegyric and amatory discourses, and discourses in the epistolary style. With these he eclipsed the fame of his predecessors and of contemporary orators, and left few of his successors with the opportunity of improving upon his performance in any of these media, indeed, not even in the most trivial. What type of style did he employ? What qualities did he originate? In what respects is he superior to his successors, and in what respects inferior? Which of his qualities should be adopted? I shall now try to answer these questions.

He is completely pure in his vocabulary, and is the perfect model of the Attic dialect—not the archaic dialect used by Plato and Thucydides, but that which was in general currency in his day, as exemplified in the speeches of Andocides, Critias and many other orators. In this matter of pure language, which is of cardinal importance in oratory, none of his successors surpassed him: few, in fact, had the ability even to emulate him; only Isocrates did so, and I therefore regard him as the purest of Lysias's successors in his choice of words. This, then, is one quality I find in our orator which deserves to be studiously imitated; and I should urge those who seek purity in either the spoken or the written word to make this orator their model for this quality. 2

He displays a second quality no less important than this. Many of his contemporaries strove to attain it, but none displayed it more consistently than he. 3

---

[1] Lacunam indicavit Radermacher verbis huiusmodi supplendam: ἀλλ' ἔν τισι καὶ πρωτεύει.

ἔστιν αὕτη; ἡ διὰ τῶν κυρίων τε καὶ κοινῶν καὶ ἐν μέσῳ κειμένων ὀνομάτων ἐκφέρουσα τὰ νοούμενα ⟨ἑρμηνεία⟩.[1] ἥκιστα γὰρ ἄν τις εὕροι Λυσίαν τροπικῇ φράσει χρησάμενον. καὶ οὐκ ἐπὶ τούτῳ μόνον ἐπαινεῖν αὐτὸν ἄξιον. ἀλλ' ὅτι καὶ σεμνὰ καὶ περιττὰ καὶ μεγάλα φαίνεσθαι τὰ πράγματα ποιεῖ τοῖς κοινοτάτοις χρώμενος ὀνόμασι καὶ ποιητικῆς οὐχ ἁπτόμενος κατασκευῆς. τοῖς δὲ προτέροις οὐχ αὕτη ἡ δόξα ἦν, ἀλλὰ[2] βουλόμενοι κόσμον τινὰ προσεῖναι τοῖς λόγοις[3] ἐξήλλαττον τὸν ἰδιώτην καὶ κατέφευγον εἰς τὴν ποιητικὴν φράσιν, μεταφοραῖς τε πολλαῖς χρώμενοι καὶ ὑπερβολαῖς καὶ ταῖς ἄλλαις τροπικαῖς ἰδέαις, ὀνομάτων τε γλωττηματικῶν καὶ ξένων χρήσει καὶ τῶν οὐκ εἰωθότων σχηματισμῶν τῇ διαλλαγῇ καὶ τῇ ἄλλῃ καινολογίᾳ καταπληττόμενοι τὸν ἰδιώτην. δηλοῖ δὲ τοῦτο Γοργίας τε ὁ Λεοντῖνος, ἐν πολλοῖς πάνυ φορτικήν τε καὶ ὑπέρογκον ποιῶν τὴν κατασκευὴν καὶ "οὐ πόρρω διθυράμβων τινῶν" ἔνια φθεγγόμενος, καὶ τῶν ἐκείνου συνουσιαστῶν οἱ περὶ Λικύμνιόν τε καὶ Πῶλον. ἥψατο δὲ καὶ τῶν Ἀθήνησι ῥητόρων ἡ ποιητική τε καὶ τροπικὴ φράσις, ὡς μὲν Τίμαιός φησι, Γοργίου ἄρξαντος ἡνίκ' Ἀθήναζε πρεσβεύων κατεπλήξατο τοὺς ἀκούοντας τῇ δημηγορίᾳ, ὡς

[1] ἑρμηνεία supplevit Usener.
[2] ἀλλὰ Usener: ἀλλ' οἱ codd.
[3] λόγοις Victorius: ὅλοις codd.

What is it? It is the expression of ideas in standard, ordinary, everyday language: Lysias is rarely to be found employing metaphorical expressions. And his claim for admiration rests not upon this alone, but also upon his success in making his subjects seem dignified, extraordinary and grand while describing them in the commonest words without recourse to artificial devices. His predecessors have no such claim to praise: whenever they wished to add colour to their speeches, they abandoned ordinary language and resorted to artificial expression. They used a plethora of metaphors, exaggerations and other forms of figurative language, and further confused the ordinary members of their audiences by using recondite and exotic words, and by resorting to unfamiliar figures of speech and other novel modes of expression. Gorgias of Leontini is a case in point. He wrote many of his speeches in a quite vulgar, inflated style, using language which was sometimes "not far removed from dithyrambic verse."[1] His pupils Lycymnius and Polus[2] and their associates wrote in the same manner. According to Timaeus,[3] it was Gorgias who first made artificial and metaphorical expression catch the imagination of Athenian orators, when he came as an ambassador to the city and astounded the Assembly

[1] Plato, *Phaedrus* 238D. Gorgias's arrival at Athens in 427 B.C. may have revolutionised Athenian spoken oratory, but his direct influence on literary oratorical style did not last long because of the excesses which Dionysius mentions.

[2] Lycymnius was said to have been Polus's teacher, and to have studied the formation, classification and usage of words. Polus appears as a professional rhetorician in Plato's *Gorgias*, where Socrates makes fun of his penchant for coining new rhetorical terms.

[3] FGH IIIB LXIX, frag. 137 (Jacoby). Cf. Diodorus Siculus xii. 53. 4.

δὲ τἀληθὲς ἔχει, τὸ καὶ παλαιότερον αἰεί τι θαυμαζομένη. Θουκυδίδης γοῦν ὁ [1] δαιμονιώτατος τῶν συγγραφέων ἔν τε τῷ ἐπιταφίῳ καὶ ἐν ταῖς δημηγορίαις ποιητικῇ κατασκευῇ χρησάμενος ἐν πολλοῖς ἐξήλλαξε τὴν ἑρμηνείαν εἰς ὄγκον ἅμα καὶ κόσμον ὀνομάτων ἀηθέστερον. Λυσίας δὲ τοιοῦτον οὐδὲν ἤσκησεν ἔν γ' οὖν τοῖς σπουδῇ γραφομένοις δικανικοῖς λόγοις καὶ συμβουλευτικοῖς ποιῆσαι, πλὴν εἴ τι μικρὸν ἐν τοῖς πανηγυρικοῖς· περὶ γὰρ δὴ τῶν ἐπιστολικῶν αὐτοῦ καὶ ἑταιρικῶν καὶ τῶν ἄλλων, οὓς μετὰ παιδιᾶς ἔγραψεν, οὐδὲν δέομαι λέγειν. ὁμοίως δὲ τοῖς ἰδιώταις διαλέγεσθαι δοκῶν πλεῖστον ὅσον ἰδιώτου διαφέρει καὶ ἔστι ποιητὴς κράτιστος λόγων, λελυμένης ἐκ τοῦ μέτρου λέξεως ἰδίαν τινὰ εὑρηκὼς ἁρμονίαν, ᾗ τὰ ὀνόματα κοσμεῖ τε καὶ ἡδύνει μηδὲν ἔχοντα ὀγκῶδες μηδὲ φορτικόν. ταύτην δευτέραν τὴν ἀρετὴν κελεύω παρὰ τοῦ ῥήτορος τούτου λαμβάνειν, εἴ τινες ἀξιοῦσι τὸν αὐτὸν ἐκείνῳ διαλέγεσθαι τρόπον. ἐγένοντο μὲν οὖν πολλοὶ τῆς προαιρέσεως ταύτης ζηλωταὶ συγγραφεῖς τε καὶ ῥήτορες, ἔγγιστα δὲ αὐτῆς μετὰ Λυσίαν ἥψατο τῶν πρεσβυτέρων νέος ἐπακμάσας Ἰσοκράτης, καὶ οὐκ ἂν ἔχοι τις εἰπεῖν προσωτέρω τούτων σκοπῶν ἑτέρους ῥήτορας ἰσχὺν καὶ δύναμιν τοσαύτην ἐν ὀνόμασι κυρίοις καὶ κοινοῖς ἀποδειξαμένους.

[1] θαυμαζομένη. Θουκυδίδης γοῦν ὁ Desrousseaux: θαυμαζομένη Θουκυδίδης τοὔνομα codd.

with his rhetoric. The truth is, however, that this style had a continuous following even in earlier time.[1] Thucydides, for instance, that most inspired historian, used artificial expressions both in his Funeral Oration and in his deliberative speeches,[2] frequently imposing an elevated tone upon the style and at the same time embellishing it with rather unusual words. Lysias did not follow this practice, at least in the serious speeches which he wrote for the law-courts and for the assembly, and did so only to a limited extent in his epideictic discourses; while I need say nothing about his letters, his amatory discourses or the other works which he wrote for amusement.

Yet, although he seems to use the language of ordinary conversation, Lysias's style is as different from it as it could be. He is a most accomplished literary artist who has invented a uniquely melodious style that is yet free from metre, in which he makes his language beautiful and attractive without bombast or vulgarity. I advise those who wish to discourse in the same style as Lysias to imitate this second quality of his. In fact this style which he chose found many imitators among the historians and the orators, and the man who came nearest to achieving it among the earlier writers was his successor Isocrates in his early career; but on looking ahead beyond these two one would not be able to find any later writer than these who displayed comparable force and power while using only standard and ordinary words.

[1] A salutary note of caution, as any perceptive reader of Herodotus would appreciate.

[2] Thucydides wrote most of his history, including the speeches, after his exile in 424 B.C.

4 τρίτην ἀρετὴν ἀποφαίνομαι περὶ τὸν ἄνδρα τὴν σαφήνειαν οὐ μόνον τὴν ἐν τοῖς ὀνόμασιν, ἀλλὰ καὶ τὴν ἐν τοῖς πράγμασιν· ἔστι γάρ τις καὶ πραγματικὴ σαφήνεια οὐ πολλοῖς γνώριμος. τεκμαίρομαι δέ, ὅτι τῆς μὲν Θουκυδίδου λέξεως καὶ Δημοσθένους, οἳ δεινότατοι πράγματα ἐξειπεῖν ἐγένοντο, πολλὰ δυσείκαστά ἐστιν ἡμῖν καὶ ἀσαφῆ καὶ δεόμενα ἐξηγητῶν. ἡ δὲ Λυσίου λέξις ἅπασά ἐστι φανερὰ καὶ σαφὴς καὶ τῷ πάνυ πόρρω δοκοῦντι πολιτικῶν ἀφεστάναι λόγων. καὶ εἰ μὲν δι' ἀσθένειαν δυνάμεως ἐγίνετο τὸ σαφές, οὐκ ἄξιον ἦν αὐτὸ ἀγαπᾶν, νῦν δὲ ὁ πλοῦτος τῶν κυρίων ὀνομάτων ἐκ πολλῆς αὐτῷ περιουσίας ἀποδείκνυται ταύτην τὴν ἀρετήν. ὥστε καὶ τὴν σαφήνειαν αὐτοῦ ζηλοῦν ἄξιον. καὶ μὴν τό γε βραχέως ἐκφέρειν τὰ νοήματα μετὰ τοῦ σαφῶς, χαλεποῦ πράγματος ὄντος φύσει τοῦ συναγαγεῖν ἄμφω ταῦτα καὶ κεράσαι μετρίως, ᾗ μάλιστα οὐδενὸς ἧττον τῶν ἄλλων ἀποδείκνυται Λυσίας, ὅς γε οὐδὲν τοῖς διὰ χειρὸς ἔχουσι τὸν ἄνδρα οὔτε ἀκυρολογίας οὔτε ἀσαφείας δόξειεν ἂν λαβεῖν. τούτου δὲ αἴτιον, ὅτι οὐ τοῖς ὀνόμασι δουλεύει τὰ πράγματα παρ' αὐτῷ, τοῖς δὲ πράγμασιν ἀκολουθεῖ τὰ ὀνόματα, τὸν δὲ κόσμον οὐκ ἐν τῷ διαλλάττειν τὸν ἰδιώτην, ἀλλ' ἐν τῷ μιμήσασθαι λαμβάνει.

5 καὶ οὐκ ἐπὶ μὲν τῆς ἑρμηνείας τοιοῦτός ἐστιν, ἐν δὲ τοῖς πράγμασιν ἄκαιρός τις καὶ μακρός, συνέστραπται δὲ εἴ τις καὶ ἄλλος καὶ πεπύκνωται

The third quality I assign to our orator is lucidity.[1] 4 He displays it not only in his language but also in his subject-matter, for there is such a thing as lucidity of subject-matter, though not many people realise it. For example, Thucydides and Demosthenes were brilliant narrators, but much of what they say is enigmatic and obscure, and requires an interpreter. Lysias's style, however, is uniformly clear and lucid, even to a reader who is supposed to be totally removed from the sphere of political debate. Now if this lucidity were the consequence of a lack of energy, it would deserve no admiration; but in the event, what produces this quality is the wealth and superabundance of standard words which he uses. His kind of lucidity is therefore another quality which is worthy of imitation. Then there is his ability to combine this lucidity with brevity of expression,[2] two ingredients which are naturally difficult to blend in due proportion. Lysias manages this combination much more successfully than any other writer, and anyone who reads him will testify to his avoidance of both inexact and obscure language. The reason for this success is that he does not make his subject the slave of his words, but makes the words conform to the subject; and he achieves elegance not by changing the language of everyday life, but by reproducing it.

This latter quality is not confined to style, leaving 5 his treatment of subject-matter ill-balanced and long-winded; on the contrary, there is no author who

[1] A primary requirement of oratory, according to Aristotle (*Rhetoric* iii. 2. 1).

[2] Another Aristotelian requirement (*Rhetoric* iii. 6. 1), but of especial importance to Dionysius because of its central position in the Atticism–Asianism controversy.

τοῖς νοήμασι, καὶ τοσούτου δεῖ τῶν οὐκ ἀναγκαίων τι λέγειν, ὥστε καὶ πολλὰ καὶ τῶν χρησίμων ἂν δόξειε παραλιπεῖν, οὐ μὰ Δία ἀσθενείᾳ εὑρέσεως αὐτὸ ποιῶν, ἀλλὰ συμμετρήσει τοῦ χρόνου, πρὸς ὃν ἔδει γενέσθαι τοὺς λόγους. βραχύς γε μὴν οὗτος, ὡς μὲν ἰδιώτῃ δηλῶσαι βουλομένῳ τὰ πράγματα ἀποχρῶν, ὡς δὲ ῥήτορι περιουσίαν δυνάμεως ἐνδείξασθαι ζητοῦντι οὐχ ἱκανός. μιμητέον δὴ καὶ τὴν βραχύτητα τὴν Λυσίου· μετριωτέρα γὰρ οὐκ ἂν εὑρεθείη παρ᾽ ἑτέρῳ ῥήτορι.

6 μετὰ ταύτας ἀρετὴν εὑρίσκω παρὰ Λυσίᾳ πάνυ θαυμαστήν, ἧς Θεόφραστος μέν φησιν ἄρξαι Θρασύμαχον, ἐγὼ δ᾽ ἡγοῦμαι Λυσίαν· καὶ γὰρ τοῖς χρόνοις οὗτος ἐκείνου προέχειν ἔμοιγε δοκεῖ (λέγω δ᾽ ὡς ἐν ἀκμῇ κοινῇ βίου γενομένων ἀμφοῖν), καὶ εἰ μὴ τοῦτο δοθείη, τῷ γέ τοι περὶ τοὺς ἀληθινοὺς ἀγῶνας ἐκείνου μᾶλλον τετρῖφθαι. οὐ μέντοι διαβεβαιοῦμαί γε, ὁπότερος ἦρξε τῆς ἀρετῆς ταύτης, κατὰ τὸ παρόν, ἀλλ᾽ ὅτι Λυσίας μᾶλλον ἐν αὐτῇ διήνεγκεν, τοῦτο θαρρῶν ἂν ἀποφηναίμην. τίς δ᾽ ἐστὶν ἥν φημι ἀρετήν; ἡ συστρέφουσα τὰ νοήματα καὶ στρογγύλως ἐκφέρουσα λέξις, οἰκεία πάνυ καὶ ἀναγκαία τοῖς δικανικοῖς λόγοις καὶ παντὶ ἀληθεῖ ἀγῶνι. ταύτην ὀλίγοι μὲν ἐμιμήσαντο, Δημοσθένης δὲ καὶ ὑπερεβάλετο πλὴν οὐχ οὕτως γε λευκῶς [1] οὐδὲ ἀφελῶς ὥσπερ Λυσίας

[1] οὕτως γε λευκῶς Radermacher: οὕτως τελευκῶς codd. οὕτως γε λεπτῶς Bonner CR (1940) 183.

---

[1] Theophrastus, *Frag.* 3 Schmidt.

[2] This assumption depends on Dionysius's early dating of Lysias's birth (see note 3, p. 21), as Thrasymachus was a con-

expresses his ideas with greater terseness and concentration. Far from introducing inessential material, he may sometimes appear to have omitted much that might have helped his case; but of course he does this not through poverty of invention, but in order to keep within the time allowed for the delivery of his speeches. The short amount of time available was adequate for the ordinary citizen to explain his case, but insufficient for an orator who was anxious to display his rhetorical powers. Thus the brevity of Lysias is a further quality to be imitated, for no other orator will be found to use it more judiciously.

The next quality I find in Lysias is a quite remark- 6
able one, and I consider him to be its inventor, though Theophrastus says that Thrasymachus was.[1] Assuming that both reached their prime at the same age, I believe that Lysias was the senior of the two;[2] and even if this view is not accepted, I assert that Lysias engaged in more live contests than Thrasymachus. Nevertheless I do not press the argument concerning priority in that quality: for present purposes I need only to affirm that Lysias excelled in the quality, and I can do this with confidence. But to what quality am I referring? It is a manner of expression in which ideas are reduced to their essentials and expressed tersely, a style most appropriate, and indeed necessary in forensic speeches and every other form of practical oratory. Very few have attempted this style, but Demosthenes excelled in it; yet the effects that he produced with it were laboured and harsh[3]

temporary of Gorgias, and was probably in his prime at the time of the visit of the Leontinian embassy, of which Gorgias was a member, to Athens in 427 B.C.

[3] An echo of Aeschines, *In Ctesiphontem*, 229.

χρησάμενος αὐτῇ, ἀλλὰ περιέργως καὶ πικρῶς· λεγέσθω γάρ, ὥς ἐμοὶ φαίνεται. ὑπὲρ ὧν κατὰ τὸν οἰκεῖον διαλέξομαι καιρόν.

7 ἔχει δὲ καὶ τὴν ἐνάργειαν πολλὴν ἡ Λυσίου λέξις. αὕτη δ' ἐστὶ δύναμίς τις ὑπὸ τὰς αἰσθήσεις ἄγουσα τὰ λεγόμενα, γίγνεται δ' ἐκ τῆς τῶν παρακολουθούντων λήψεως. ὁ δὴ προσέχων τὴν διάνοιαν τοῖς Λυσίου λόγοις οὐχ οὕτως ἔσται σκαιὸς ἢ δυσάρεστος ἢ βραδὺς τὸν νοῦν, ὃς οὐχ ὑπολήψεται γινόμενα τὰ δηλούμενα ὁρᾶν καὶ ὥσπερ παροῦσιν οἷς ἂν ὁ ῥήτωρ εἰσάγῃ προσώποις ὁμιλεῖν. ἐπιζητήσει τε οὐθέν, οἷον εἰκὸς τοὺς μὲν ἂν δρᾶσαι, τοὺς δὲ παθεῖν,[1] τοὺς δὲ διανοηθῆναι, τοὺς δὲ εἰπεῖν. κράτιστος γὰρ δὴ πάντων ἐγένετο ῥητόρων φύσιν ἀνθρώπων κατοπτεῦσαι καὶ τὰ προσήκοντα ἑκάστοις ἀποδοῦναι πάθη τε καὶ ἤθη καὶ ἔργα.

8 ἀποδίδωμί τε οὖν αὐτῷ καὶ τὴν εὐπρεπεστάτην ἀρετήν, καλουμένην δὲ ὑπὸ πολλῶν ἠθοποιΐαν. ἁπλῶς γὰρ οὐδὲν [2] εὑρεῖν δύναμαι παρὰ τῷ ῥήτορι τούτῳ πρόσωπον οὔτε ἀνηθοποίητον οὔτε ἄψυχον. τριῶν τε ὄντων, ἐν οἷς καὶ περὶ ἃ τὴν ἀρετὴν εἶναι ταύτην συμβέβηκε, διανοίας τε καὶ λέξεως καὶ τρίτης τῆς συνθέσεως, ἐν ἅπασι τούτοις αὐτὸν ἀποφαίνομαι κατορθοῦν. οὐ γὰρ διανοουμένους μόνον ὑποτίθεται χρηστὰ καὶ ἐπιεικῆ καὶ μέτρια τοὺς λέγοντας, ὥστε εἰκόνας εἶναι δοκεῖν τῶν

[1] ἂν δρᾶσαι τοὺς δὲ παθεῖν Markland: ἄνδρας αἰτοῦσα εἰ ταθείη F G.
[2] οὐδὲν Sylburg: οὐδὲ codd.

compared with Lysias's limpid simplicity. This may be taken as my present view; but I shall discuss these matters in their appropriate place.

7 Vividness is a quality which the style of Lysias has in abundance. This consists in a certain power he has of conveying the things he is describing to the senses of his audience,[1] and it arises out of his grasp of circumstantial detail.[2] Nobody who applies his mind to the speeches of Lysias will be so obtuse, insensitive or slow-witted that he will not feel that he can see the actions which are being described going on and that he is meeting face-to-face the characters in the orator's story. And he will require no further evidence of the likely actions, feelings, thoughts or words of the different persons. He was the best of all the orators at observing human nature and ascribing to each type of person the appropriate emotions, moral qualities and actions.

8 I also ascribe to Lysias that most pleasing quality, which is generally called characterisation.[3] I am quite unable to find a single person in this orator's speeches who is devoid of character or vitality. There are three departments or aspects in which this quality manifests itself: thought, language and composition; and I declare him to be successful in all three. For not only are the thoughts he ascribes to his clients worthy, reasonable and fair, so that their words seem to reflect their good moral character, but he also makes them speak in a style which is appropriate to

[1] Cf. Aristotle, *Rhetoric* iii. 11. 1–3.
[2] Cf. Demetrius, *On Style*, 209–210.
[3] *i.e.* favourable characterisation, portraying the moral qualities which will win the audience's good will, e.g. ἐπιείκεια (Aristotle, *Rhetoric* i. 2. 4). ἠθοποιία never means individual or personal characterisation.

ἠθῶν τοὺς λόγους, ἀλλὰ καὶ τὴν λέξιν ἀποδίδωσι τοῖς ἤθεσιν οἰκείαν, ᾗ πέφυκεν αὐτὰ ἑαυτῶν κράτιστα δηλοῦσθαι, τὴν σαφῆ καὶ κυρίαν καὶ κοινὴν καὶ πᾶσιν ἀνθρώποις συνηθεστάτην· ὁ γὰρ ὄγκος καὶ τὸ ξένον καὶ τὸ ἐξ ἐπιτηδεύσεως ἅπαν ἀνηθοποίητον. καὶ συντίθησί γε αὐτὴν ἀφελῶς πάνυ καὶ ἁπλῶς, ὁρῶν ὅτι οὐκ ἐν τῇ περιόδῳ καὶ τοῖς ῥυθμοῖς, ἀλλ' ἐν τῇ διαλελυμένῃ λέξει γίνεται τὸ ἦθος. καθόλου δέ, ἵνα καὶ περὶ ταύτης εἴπω τῆς ἀρετῆς, οὐκ οἶδ' εἴ τις ἄλλος ῥητόρων τῶν γε τῇ ὁμοίᾳ κατασκευῇ χρησαμένων τοῦ λόγου εἴτε ἥδιον συνέθηκεν εἴτε πιθανώτερον. δοκεῖ μὲν γὰρ ἀποίητός τις εἶναι καὶ ἀτεχνίτευτος ὁ τῆς ἁρμονίας αὐτοῦ χαρακτὴρ καὶ οὐ θαυμάσαιμ' ἄν, εἰ πᾶσι μὲν τοῖς ἰδιώταις, οὐκ ὀλίγοις δὲ καὶ τῶν φιλολόγων, ὅσοι μὴ μεγάλας ἔχουσι τριβὰς περὶ λόγους, τοιαύτην τινὰ παράσχοι δόξαν. ὅτι ἀνεπιτηδεύτως καὶ οὐ κατὰ τέχνην, αὐτομάτως δέ πως καὶ ὡς ἔτυχε σύγκειται. ἔστι δὲ παντὸς μᾶλλον ἔργου τεχνικοῦ κατεσκευασμένος. πεποίηται γὰρ αὐτῷ τοῦτο τὸ ἀποίητον καὶ δέδεται τὸ λελυμένον καὶ ἐν αὐτῷ τῷ μὴ δοκεῖν δεινῶς κατεσκευάσθαι τὸ δεινὸν ἔχει. τὴν ἀλήθειαν οὖν τις ἐπιτηδεύων καὶ φύσεως μιμητὴς γίνεσθαι βουλόμενος οὐκ ἂν ἁμαρτάνοι τῇ Λυσίου συνθέσει χρώμενος· ἑτέραν γὰρ οὐκ ἂν εὕροι ταύτης ἀληθεστέραν.

9 οἴομαι δὲ καὶ τὸ πρέπον ἔχειν τὴν Λυσίου λέξιν οὐθενὸς ἧττον τῶν ἀρχαίων ῥητόρων, κρατίστην ἁπασῶν ἀρετὴν καὶ τελειοτάτην, ὁρῶν αὐτήν πρός τε τὸν λέγοντα καὶ πρὸς τοὺς ἀκούοντας καὶ πρὸς

these qualities, and which by its nature displays them in their best light—clear, standard, ordinary speech which is thoroughly familiar to everyone. All forms of pompous, outlandish and contrived language are foreign to characterisation. As to his composition, it is absolutely simple and straightforward. He sees that characterisation is achieved not by periodic structure and the use of rhythms, but by loosely constructed sentences. As a further general comment on this quality, I may say that I do not know of any other orator—at least any who employs a similar sentence-structure—with greater charm or persuasiveness. The distinctive nature of its melodious composition seems, as it were, not to be contrived or formed by any conscious art, and it would not surprise me if every layman, and even many of those scholars who have not specialised in oratory, should receive the impression that this arrangement has not been deliberately and artistically devised, but is somehow spontaneous and fortuitous. Yet it is more carefully composed than any work of art. For this artlessness is itself the product of art: the relaxed structure is really under control, and it is in the very illusion of not having been composed with masterly skill that the mastery lies. Therefore the student of realism and naturalism would not go wrong if he were to follow Lysias in his composition, for he will find no model who is more true to life.

I think that in propriety,[1] too—the most important and crowning virtue—Lysias's style yields to that of 9
none of the other ancient orators; for I observe that he has adapted it satisfactorily to the speaker, the

[1] Cf. Aristotle, *Rhetoric* iii. 2. 1; 7. 1.

τὸ πρᾶγμα (ἐν τούτοις γὰρ δὴ καὶ πρὸς ταῦτα τὸ πρέπον) ἀρκούντως ἡρμοσμένην.[1] καὶ γὰρ ἡλικίᾳ καὶ γένει καὶ παιδείᾳ καὶ ἐπιτηδεύματι καὶ βίῳ καὶ τοῖς ἄλλοις, ἐν οἷς διαφέρει τῶν προσώπων πρόσωπα, τὰς οἰκείας ἀποδίδωσι φωνὰς πρός τε τὸν ἀκροατὴν συμμετρεῖται τὰ λεγόμενα οἰκείως, οὐ τὸν αὐτὸν τρόπον δικαστῇ καὶ ἐκκλησιαστῇ καὶ πανηγυρίζοντι διαλεγόμενος ὄχλῳ. διαφοράς τε αὐτῷ λαμβάνει κατὰ τὰς ἰδέας τῶν πραγμάτων ἡ λέξις· ἀρχομένῳ μὲν γάρ ἐστι καθεστηκυῖα καὶ ἠθική, διηγουμένῳ δὲ πιθανὴ κἀπερίεργος, ἀποδεικνύντι δὲ στρογγύλη καὶ πυκνή, αὔξοντι δὲ καὶ παθαινομένῳ σεμνὴ καὶ ἀληθινή, ἀνακεφαλαιουμένῳ δὲ διαλελυμένη καὶ σύντομος. ληπτέον δὴ καὶ τὸ πρέπον τῆς λέξεως παρὰ Λυσίου.

10 ὅτι μὲν γὰρ πιθανὴ καὶ πειστικὴ πολὺ τὸ φυσικὸν ἐπιφαίνουσα καὶ πάνθ᾽ ὅσα τῆς τοιαύτης ἰδέας ἔχεται, πρὸς εἰδότας οὐδὲν ἴσως δεῖ λέγειν· δι᾽ ὄχλου γὰρ ἤδη τοῦτό γε καὶ οὐδείς ἐστιν ὃς οὐχὶ καὶ πείρᾳ καὶ ἀκοῇ μαθὼν ὁμολογεῖ πάντων ῥητόρων αὐτὸν εἶναι πιθανώτατον. ὥστε καὶ ταύτην τὴν ἀρετὴν ληπτέον παρὰ τοῦ ῥήτορος.

πολλὰ καὶ καλὰ λέγειν ἔχων περὶ τῆς Λυσίου λέξεως, ἣν λαμβάνων καὶ μιμούμενος ἄν τις ἀμείνων γένοιτο τὴν ἑρμηνείαν, τὰ μὲν ἄλλα τοῦ χρόνου στοχαζόμενος ἐάσω, μίαν δὲ ἀρετὴν ἔτι τοῦ ῥήτορος ἀποδείξομαι, κρίνας καλλίστην τε καὶ κυριωτάτην[2] καὶ μόνην αὐτὴν μάλιστα τῶν ἄλλων

[1] ἡρμοσμένην Matthiae: ἡρμοσμένη FPB.
[2] κυριωτάτην Markland: κοινοτάτην codd.

audience and the subject, and it is in these, and in relation to these, that propriety is found. For characters differ from one another in age, family background, education, occupation, way of life and in other respects:[1] Lysias puts words in their mouths which suit their several conditions. Similarly, with regard to his audiences, his words are gauged to suit their several dispositions: he does not address a jury, a political assembly and a festival audience in the same style. He also varies his style according to the different parts of the speech: his introductions have a firm moral tone, his narratives are persuasive and economical, his proofs terse and concentrated, his amplifications and appeals to the emotions are dignified and sincere, and his concluding summaries are relaxed and concise. Thus propriety of diction is yet another quality to be taken from Lysias.

Perhaps it is unnecessary, when addressing con- 10
noisseurs, to say that his style is persuasive and convincing, is natural to a high degree and displays all the qualities that are derived from this naturalness: for this is already common knowledge, and there is nobody who does not agree, both from what he has been told and from personal experience, that Lysias is the most persuasive of all the orators. Hence this is another quality which is to be taken from the orator.

I could mention many other fine qualities of Lysias's style which would improve the expressive powers of anyone who adopted and imitated them. But I shall keep my eye on the time, and confine myself to mentioning one more, which I consider to be his finest and most important quality, and the one

[1] These are analysed at length by Aristotle (*Rhetoric* ii. 12–17).

τὸν Λυσίου χαρακτῆρα δυναμένην βεβαιῶσαι, ἣν ὑπερεβάλετο μὲν οὐδεὶς τῶν ὕστερον, ἐμιμήσαντο δὲ πολλοὶ καὶ παρ' αὐτὸ τοῦτο κρείττους ἑτέρων ἔδοξαν εἶναι τὴν ἄλλην δύναμιν οὐθὲν διαφέροντες· ὑπὲρ ὧν, ἂν ἐγχωρῇ, κατὰ τὸν οἰκεῖον διαλέξομαι τόπον. τίς δ' ἐστὶν ἥδε ἡ ἀρετή; ἡ πᾶσιν[1] ἐπανθοῦσα τοῖς ὀνόμασι κἀπ' ἴσης χάρις, πρᾶγμα παντὸς κρεῖττον λόγου καὶ θαυμασιώτερον. ῥᾷστον[2] μὲν γάρ ἐστιν ὀφθῆναι καὶ παντὶ ὁμοίως ἰδιώτῃ τε καὶ τεχνίτῃ φανερόν, χαλεπώτατον δὲ λόγῳ δηλωθῆναι καὶ οὐδὲ τοῖς κράτιστα εἰπεῖν δυναμένοις εὔπορον.

11 ὥστε εἴ τις ἀξιοίη λόγῳ διδαχθῆναι ταύτην τὴν δύναμιν, ἥ τίς ποτ' ἐστίν, οὐκ ἂν φθάνοι καὶ ἄλλων πολλῶν καὶ καλῶν πραγμάτων δυσεκλαλήτων ἀπαιτῶν λόγον· λέγω δὲ ἐπὶ κάλλους μὲν σωμάτων, τί δή ποτε τοῦτ' ἐστίν, ὃ καλοῦμεν ὥραν, ἐπὶ κινήσεως δὲ μελῶν καὶ πλοκῆς φθόγγων, τί λέγεται τὸ εὐάρμοστον, ἐπὶ συμμετρίας δὲ χρόνων, τίς ἡ τάξις καὶ τί τὸ εὔρυθμον, καὶ ἐπὶ παντὸς δὲ συλλήβδην ἔργου τε καὶ πράγματος, τίς ὁ λεγόμενος καιρὸς καὶ ποῦ τὸ μέτριον. αἰσθήσει γὰρ τούτων ἕκαστον καταλαμβάνεται καὶ οὐ λόγῳ. ὥσθ' ὅπερ οἱ μουσικοὶ παραγγέλλουσι ποιεῖν τοῖς βουλομένοις ἀκούειν ἀκριβῶς ἁρμονίας, ὥστε μηδὲ τὴν ἐλαχίστην ἐν τοῖς διαστήμασι[3] δίεσιν ἀγνοεῖν, τὴν ἀκοὴν ἐθίζειν καὶ μηδὲν ἄλλο ταύτης ἀκριβέστερον

[1] ἡ πᾶσιν Sylburg: ἥτις πᾶσιν codd.
[2] ῥᾷστον Taylor: ἄριστον codd.
[3] διαστήμασι Sylburg: διηγήμασι codd.

above all which enables us to establish his peculiar character. None of his successors excelled him in it, but many of those who aspired to it were considered superior to their rivals on the strength of this alone, not because they had greater general ability. But I shall discuss these authors in their proper place, if I have the opportunity. What is this quality? It is his charm, which blossoms forth in every word he writes, a quality which is beyond description and too wonderful for words. It is very easy and plain for layman and expert alike to see, but to express it in words is very difficult, nor is it easy even for those with exceptional descriptive powers.

Therefore anyone who demands to learn what this 11
quality is should start straight away by seeking definitions of many other fine qualities which are difficult to express in words. In regard to physical beauty, what in the world is that quality which we call "youth?" In the movement of any song and the texture of vocal sounds, what constitutes good melody?[1] In verse composition, what constitutes good arrangement and good rhythm? In short, in every field of activity, how are we to define what is called "timeliness?" And where do we find the mean? In each case it is our senses and not our reason that provide the key. The advice which teachers of music give to those wishing to acquire an accurate sense of melody and thus be able to discern the smallest tone-interval in the musical scale, is that they should simply cultivate the ear, and seek no more

[1] Not "harmony" in the sense used in modern music: in Greek music ἁρμονία describes the relation of single notes (φθόγγοι) to one another *in series*, not when played simultaneously. So too below.

ζητεῖν κριτήριον, τοῦτο κἀγὼ τοῖς ἀναγινώσκουσι τὸν Λυσίαν καὶ τίς ἡ παρ' αὐτῷ χάρις ἐστὶ βουλομένοις μαθεῖν ὑποθείμην ἂν ἐπιτηδεύειν, χρόνῳ πολλῷ καὶ μακρᾷ τριβῇ καὶ ἀλόγῳ πάθει τὴν ἄλογον συνασκεῖν αἴσθησιν. ταύτην μέντοι κρατίστην τε ἀρετὴν καὶ χαρακτηρικωτάτην τῆς Λυσίου λέξεως ἔγωγε τίθεμαι, εἴτε φύσεως αὐτὴν δεῖ καλεῖν εὐτυχίαν εἴτε πόνου καὶ τέχνης ἐργασίαν εἴτε μικτὴν ἐξ ἀμφοῖν ἕξιν ἢ δύναμιν, ᾗ πάντας ὑπερέχει τοὺς λοιποὺς ῥήτορας. καὶ ὅταν διαπορῶ περί τινος τῶν ἀναφερομένων εἰς αὐτὸν λόγων καὶ μὴ ῥᾴδιον ᾖ μοι διὰ τῶν ἄλλων σημείων τἀληθὲς εὑρεῖν, ἐπὶ ταύτην καταφεύγω τὴν ἀρετὴν ὡς ἐπὶ ψῆφον ἐσχάτην. ἔπειτα ἂν μὲν αἱ χάριτες αἱ τῆς λέξεως ἐπικοσμεῖν δοκῶσί μοι τὴν γραφήν, τῆς Λυσίου ψυχῆς αὐτὴν τίθεμαι καὶ οὐδὲν ἔτι πορρωτέρω ταύτης σκοπεῖν ἀξιῶ. ἐὰν δὲ μηδεμίαν ἡδονὴν μηδὲ ἀφροδίτην ὁ τῆς λέξεως χαρακτὴρ ἔχῃ, δυσωπῶ καὶ ὑποπτεύω μήποτ' οὐ Λυσίου ὁ λόγος καὶ οὐκ ἔτι βιάζομαι τὴν ἄλογον αἴσθησιν, οὐδ' ἐὰν πάνυ δεινὸς εἶναι τὰ γοῦν ἄλλα μοι δοκῇ καὶ περιττῶς ἐξειργασμένος ὁ λόγος, τὸ μὲν εὖ γράφειν πολλοῖς οἰόμενος ὑπάρχειν κατά τινας καὶ ἄλλους ἰδίους λέξεως [1] χαρακτῆρας (πολυειδὲς γὰρ τοῦτο), τὸ δ' ἡδέως καὶ κεχαρισμένως καὶ ἐπαφροδίτως Λυσίᾳ.

12 τεκμηρίῳ γ' οὖν οὐκ ἄλλῳ τινὶ κρείττονι χρώμενος ἢ τῷ καθ' ἡδονὴν ἑρμηνεύεσθαι τὰ ὑπὸ τούτου λεγόμενα [ᾧ] [2] πολλοὺς ἤδη τῶν ἀναφε-

accurate standard of judgment than this. My advice also would be the same to those readers of Lysias who wish to learn the nature of his charm: to banish reason from the senses and train them by patient study over a long period to feel without thinking. This charm, then, I am persuaded is the most important and characteristic virtue of Lysias's style, (whether we are to call it a natural gift or the product of application and skill, or whether it is a condition or faculty which has been acquired through the mixture of these two), and one in which he surpasses all other orators. Whenever I am uncertain as to the genuineness of any speech that is attributed to him, and find it difficult to arrive at the truth by means of the other available evidence, I resort to this criterion to cast the final vote. Then, if the writing seems to be graced with those additional qualities of charm, I deem it to be a product of Lysias's genius, and consider it unnecessary to investigate further. But if the style is devoid of grace and beauty, I view the speech with a jaundiced and suspicious eye, and conclude that it could never be by Lysias. I do not strain my instinctive feeling beyond this, even though in other respects I may think the speech very effective and exceptionally well executed. For I believe that many authors have the ability to write well in regard to certain particular characteristics of style (for many factors contribute to good writing), but grace, charm and beauty are peculiar to Lysias.

Using, then, as my main criterion simply that the 12
speeches of Lysias are composed in a pleasing style,

---

[1] λέξεως Taylor: ἕξεως codd.
[2] ᾧ seclusit Markland.

ρομένων εἰς αὐτὸν λόγων καὶ πεπιστευμένων ὑπὸ τοῦ πλήθους, ὡς εἰσὶν ἐν τοῖς πάνυ γνησίοις Λυσίου, καὶ τά γε ἄλλα οὐκ ἀτόπως ἔχοντας, ὅτι τὴν χάριν οὐ προσβάλλουσι τὴν Λυσιακὴν οὐδὲ τὴν εὐστομίαν ἔχουσιν ἐκείνης τῆς λέξεως, ὑποπτεύσας τε καὶ βασανίσας εὗρον οὐκ ὄντας Λυσίου. ὧν ἐστι καὶ ὁ περὶ τῆς Ἰφικράτους εἰκόνος, ὃν οἶδ' ὅτι πολλοὶ καὶ χαρακτῆρα ἡγήσαιντο ἂν καὶ κανόνα τῆς ἐκείνου δυνάμεως. οὗτος μέντοι ὁ λόγος ὁ καὶ τοῖς ὀνόμασιν ἡρμηνεῦσθαι δοκῶν ἰσχυρῶς καὶ τοῖς ἐνθυμήμασιν εὑρῆσθαι [1] περιττῶς καὶ ἄλλας πολλὰς ἀρετὰς ἔχων ἄχαρίς ἐστι καὶ πολλοῦ δεῖ τὸ Λυσιακὸν ἐπιφαίνειν στόμα. μάλιστα δ' ἐγένετό μοι καταφανὴς ὅτι οὐχ ὑπ' ἐκείνου τοῦ ῥήτορος ἐγράφη, τοὺς χρόνους ἀναλογισαμένῳ. εἰ γὰρ ὀγδοηκονταετῆ γενόμενον θήσει τις τελευτῆσαι Λυσίαν ἐπὶ Νίκωνος ἢ ἐπὶ Ναυσινίκου ἄρχοντος, ἑπτὰ ἔτεσιν ὅλοις ἂν εἴη προτεροῦσα τῆς γραφῆς τοῦ ψηφίσματος ἡ τελευτὴ τοῦ ῥήτορος. μετὰ γὰρ Ἀλκισθένην ἄρχοντα, ἐφ' οὗ τὴν εἰρήνην Ἀθηναῖοί τε καὶ Λακεδαιμόνιοι καὶ βασιλεὺς ὤμοσαν, ἀποδοὺς τὰ στρατεύματα Ἰφικράτης ἰδιώτης γίνεται καὶ τὸ περὶ τῆς εἰκόνος ἦν τότ' ἔτεσιν ἑπτὰ πρότερον τετελευτηκότος τῆς γραφῆς Λυσίου, πρὸ τοῦ συντάξασθαι τοῦτον τὸν ἀγῶνα Ἰφικράτει. ὁμοίως δὲ καὶ τὴν ἀπολογίαν τοῦ ἀνδρὸς καὶ αὐτὴν εἰς Λυσίαν ἀναφερομένην οὔτε τοῖς πράγμασιν ἀτόπως ἔχουσαν οὔτε τοῖς ὀνόμασιν ἀσθενῶς δι' ὑποψίας ἔλαβον οὐκ ἐπανθούσης τῇ λέξει τῆς Λυσιακῆς χάριτος· καὶ

[1] εὑρῆσθαι Dobree: εἰρῆσθαι codd.

I have come to suspect many of the speeches which have been commonly regarded as genuine. I put them to the test and found them spurious, not because there was anything wrong with them in a general way, but because they did not strike me with that characteristic Lysianic charm or with the euphony of that style. One of these is the speech about the statue of Iphicrates,[1] which I know many would regard as a typical example and model of his art. Certainly the language of this speech seems forceful, and its arguments full of invention, and it has many other virtues; yet it is devoid of charm, and does not at all display the eloquence of Lysias. But the blatancy of its spuriousness only forced itself upon me when I came to calculate its date. If one assumes that Lysias died in his eighty-first year during the archonship of Nicon or Nausinicus, the consequence would be that the orator died fully seven years before the bill was formulated: for it was after the archonship of Alcisthenes, during whose year of office the Athenians, the Spartans and the Persian King made their treaty,[2] that Iphicrates retired from his military commands and became a private citizen. It was then that the question of the statue was raised, Lysias having died seven years before the bill, and before this speech was composed for Iphicrates. I applied the same process to the speech defending this man, which is attributed to Lysias. The material is by no means ineptly handled

[1] *c.* 415–353 B.C. Athenian general in the best tradition of 4th-century professionalism. See Xenophon, *Hellenica* vi. 2. 29–31. Centuries later Pausanias (Att. 1. 24.7) saw this *εἰκών*, which could mean "painting" or "portrait" but "statue" is to be preferred.

[2] 372–371 B.C.

παραθεὶς τοὺς χρόνους οὐκ ὀλίγοις ἔτεσιν εὗρον ὑστεροῦσαν τῆς τελευτῆς τοῦ ῥήτορος ἀλλὰ καὶ εἴκοσιν ὅλοις. ἐν γὰρ τῷ συμμαχικῷ πολέμῳ τὴν εἰσαγγελίαν Ἰφικράτης ἠγώνισται καὶ τὰς εὐθύνας ὑπέσχηκε τῆς στρατηγίας, ὡς ἐξ αὐτοῦ γίνεται τοῦ λόγου καταφανές· οὗτος δὲ ὁ πόλεμος πίπτει κατὰ Ἀγαθοκλέα καὶ Ἐλπίνην ἄρχοντας. ὅτου[1] μὲν οὖν εἰσι λόγοι ῥήτορος ⟨οἱ⟩[2] περί τε τῆς εἰκόνος καὶ τῆς προδοσίας, οὐκ ἔχω βεβαίως εἰπεῖν. ὅτι δὲ ἑνὸς ἀμφότεροι, πολλοῖς τεκμηρίοις ἔχοιμ' ἂν εἰπεῖν· ἡ γὰρ αὐτὴ προαίρεσίς τε καὶ δύναμις ἐν ἀμφοτέροις, ὑπὲρ ὧν οὐ καιρὸς ἐν τῷ παρόντι διασκοπεῖν. εἰκάζω δὲ Ἰφικράτους εἶναι αὐτούς· καὶ γὰρ τὰ πολέμια δεινὸς ὁ ἀνὴρ καὶ ἐν λόγοις οὐκ εὐκαταφρόνητος, ἥ τε λέξις ἐν ἀμφοῖν πολὺ τὸ φορτικὸν καὶ στρατιωτικὸν ἔχει καὶ οὐχ οὕτως ἐμφαίνει ῥητορικὴν ἀγχίνοιαν ὡς στρατιωτικὴν αὐθάδειαν καὶ ἀλαζονείαν. ἀλλ' ὑπὲρ μὲν τούτων ἑτέρωθι δηλωθήσεται διὰ πλειόνων.

13 ἀνιτέον δέ, ὅθεν ἐξέβημεν εἰς ταῦτα. ὅτι[3] κράτιστόν ἐστι τῶν Λυσίου ἔργων καὶ χαρακτηρικώτατον τῆς δυνάμεως ἡ κοσμοῦσά τε καὶ ἀνθίζουσα τὴν λέξιν αὐτοῦ χάρις, ἣν οὐθ' ὑπερεβάλετο τῶν ἐπιγινομένων οὐθεὶς οὔτε εἰς ἄκρον ἐμιμήσατο. καὶ τὰ μὲν περὶ τὴν ἑρμηνείαν ἀγαθὰ

[1] ὅτου Sylburg: ὅτι codd.
[2] οἱ inseruit Sauppe.
[3] ὅτι Usener: τὸ codd.

and the language is not without power; but I came to suspect it when I noted the absence of the bloom of Lysianic charm from its style. And when I came to compare dates, I found that it was written after the orator's death—not a few years after, but all of twenty; for it was during the *War of the Allies* that Iphicrates faced impeachment and submitted his military command to an official scrutiny.[1] This becomes clear from the speech itself; and this war falls during the archonships of Agathocles and Elpines. As to the authorship of the speeches concerning the statue and the charge of treason, I can make no positive assertion; but I can say that both are by the same author, and have ample evidence to support this statement. They display the same turn of mind and are written with the same power; but now is not the time to look into these matters. I surmise that they are the work of Iphicrates himself, who was certainly a brilliant general, and was also by no means to be despised as an orator. Moreover, the style in both speeches contains much vulgar army slang, and reveals not so much the nimble wits of the rhetorician as the headstrong and boastful character of the soldier. But I shall illustrate this at greater length elsewhere.[2]

But I must return to the point from which I 13
digressed so far. That was the statement that the most important of Lysias's qualities, and the one which most characterises his art, is the charm which lends adornment and colour to his style. None of his successors surpassed him in this, nor indeed imitated him with complete success. I shall now summarise

[1] 356–355 B.C.
[2] Not in any extant work.

τοῦ ῥήτορος ταῦτα· συγκεφαλαιώσομαι γὰρ τὰ ῥηθέντα· τὸ καθαρὸν τῶν ὀνομάτων, ἡ ἀκρίβεια τῆς διαλέκτου, τὸ διὰ τῶν κυρίων καὶ μὴ τροπικῶν κατασκευῶν ἐκφέρειν τὰ νοήματα, ἡ σαφήνεια, ἡ συντομία, τὸ συστρέφειν τε καὶ στρογγυλίζειν τὰ νοήματα, τὸ ὑπὸ τὰς αἰσθήσεις ἄγειν τὰ δηλούμενα, τὸ μηδὲν ἄψυχον ὑποτίθεσθαι πρόσωπον μηδὲ ἀνηθοποίητον, ἡ τῆς συνθέσεως τῶν ὀνομάτων ἡδονὴ μιμουμένης [1] τὸν ἰδιώτην, τὸ τοῖς ὑποκειμένοις προσώποις καὶ πράγμασι τοὺς πρέποντας ἐφαρμόττειν λόγους, ἡ πιθανότης καὶ τὸ πειστικὸν καὶ ἡ χάρις καὶ ὁ πάντα μετρῶν καιρός. ταῦτα παρὰ Λυσίου λαμβάνων ἄν τις ὠφεληθείη. ὑψηλὴ δὲ καὶ μεγαλοπρεπὴς οὐκ ἔστιν ἡ Λυσίου λέξις οὐδὲ καταπληκτικὴ μὰ Δία καὶ θαυμαστὴ οὐδὲ τὸ πικρὸν ἢ τὸ δεινὸν ἢ τὸ φοβερὸν ἐπιφαίνουσα οὐδὲ ἁφὰς ἔχει καὶ τόνους ἰσχυροὺς οὐδὲ θυμοῦ καὶ πνεύματός ἐστι μεστὴ οὐδ', ὥσπερ ἐν τοῖς ἤθεσίν ἐστι πιθανή, οὕτως ἐν τοῖς πάθεσιν ἰσχυρὰ οὐδ' ὡς ἡδῦναι καὶ πεῖσαι καὶ χαριεντίσασθαι δύναται, οὕτω βιάσασθαί τε καὶ προσαναγκάσαι. ἀσφαλής τε μᾶλλόν ἐστιν ἢ παρακεκινδυνευμένη καὶ οὐκ ἐπὶ τοσοῦτον ἰσχὺν ἱκανὴ δηλῶσαι τέχνης, ἐφ' ὅσον ἀλήθειαν εἰκάσαι φύσεως.

14 καὶ θαυμάζειν ἄξιον, τί δή ποτε παθὼν ὁ Θεόφραστος τῶν φορτικῶν καὶ περιέργων αὐτὸν οἴεται ζηλωτὴν γενέσθαι λόγων καὶ τὸ ποιητικὸν διώκειν μᾶλλον ἢ τὸ ἀληθινόν. ἐν γοῦν τοῖς περὶ λέξεως γραφεῖσι τῶν τε ἄλλων καταμέμφεται τῶν περὶ τὰς ἀντιθέσεις καὶ παρισώσεις καὶ παρομοιώσεις καὶ τὰ παραπλήσια τούτοις σχήματα διεσπου-

the virtues of style which I have assigned to him: purity of language, correct dialect, the presentation of ideas by means of standard, not figurative expressions; clarity, brevity, concision, terseness, vivid representation, the investment of every person with life and character, the pleasing arrangement of words after the manner of ordinary speech, the choice of arguments to suit the persons and the circumstances of the case, the ability to win over and persuade, charm and a sense of timing which regulates everything else. Anyone who learned these qualities from Lysias would improve his own style. But there is nothing sublime or imposing about the style of Lysias. It certainly does not excite us or move us to wonder, nor does it portray pungency, intensity or fear; nor again does it have the power to grip the listener's attention, and to keep it in rapt suspense; nor is it full of energy and feeling, or able to match its moral persuasiveness with an equal power to portray emotion, and its capacity to entertain, persuade and charm with an ability to force and compel his audience. It is a conservative style rather than an adventurous one, and is suited not so much to the display of rhetorical power as to the portrayal of the realities of human nature.

We may well wonder what has happened to Theo- 14
phrastus's judgment when he expresses the view that Lysias aimed at vulgarity and laboured expression in his speeches, and sought artificiality rather than realism. In fact, in his treatise *On Style*,[1] he even includes Lysias among a number of writers whom he

[1] Frag. 2 Schmidt.

---

[1] *μιμουμένης* Usener: *μιμουμένη* codd.

δακότων καὶ δὴ καὶ τὸν Λυσίαν ἐν τούτοις κατηρίθμηκε, τὸν ὑπὲρ Νικίου τοῦ στρατηγοῦ τῶν Ἀθηναίων λόγον, ὃν εἶπεν ἐπὶ Συρακουσίων αἰχμάλωτος ὤν, ὡς ὑπὸ τούτου γεγραμμένον τοῦ ῥήτορος παρατιθείς. κωλύσει δ' οὐδὲν ἴσως καὶ τὴν λέξιν αὐτὴν θεῖναι τὴν Θεοφράστου. ἔστι δὲ ἥδε· "ἀντίθεσις δ' ἐστὶ τριττῶς, ὅταν τῷ αὐτῷ τὰ ἐναντία ἢ τῷ ἐναντίῳ τὰ αὐτὰ ἢ τοῖς ἐναντίοις ἐναντία προσκατηγορηθῇ.[1] τοσαυταχῶς γὰρ ἐγχωρεῖ συζευχθῆναι. τούτων δὲ τὸ μὲν ἴσον καὶ τὸ ὅμοιον παιδιῶδες καὶ καθαπερεὶ ποίημα· διὸ καὶ ἧττον ἁρμόττει τῇ σπουδῇ. φαίνεται γὰρ ἀπρεπὲς σπουδάζοντα τοῖς πράγμασι τοῖς ὀνόμασι παίζειν καὶ τὸ πάθος τῇ λέξει περιαιρεῖν· ἐκλύει γὰρ τὸν ἀκροατήν. οἷον ὡς ὁ Λυσίας ἐν τῇ τοῦ Νικίου ἀπολογίᾳ βουλόμενος ἔλεον ποιεῖν· "Ἑλλήνων κλαίω ἀμάχητον καὶ ἀναυμάχητον ὄλεθρον . . . ἱκέται μὲν αὐτοὶ τῶν θεῶν καθίζοντες, προδότας δὲ τῶν ὅρκων ὑμᾶς[2] ἀποφαίνοντες . . . ἀνακαλοῦντές τε συγγένειαν, εὐμένειαν."" ταῦτα γὰρ εἰ μὲν τῷ ὄντι Λυσίας ἔγραψε, δικαίως ἂν ἐπιτιμήσεως ἀξιοῖτο χαριεντιζόμενος ἐν οὐ χαρίεντι καιρῷ. εἰ δὲ ἑτέρου τινός ἐστιν ὁ λόγος, ὥς περ ἔστιν, ὁ κατηγορῶν, ἃ μὴ προσῆκε, τοῦ ἀνδρὸς μεμπτότερος. ὅτι δὲ οὐκ ἔγραψε Λυσίας τὸν ὑπὲρ Νικίου λόγον οὐδ' ἔστιν οὔτε τῆς ψυχῆς οὔτε τῆς λέξεως ἐκείνης

[1] προσκατηγορηθῇ Sylburg: προσκατηγορηθείη F: προκατηγορηθείη G.

[2] ὑμᾶς Tournier: ἡμᾶς codd.

criticises for their addiction to antithesis, symmetry, assonance and related figures of language. He gives the speech on behalf of Nicias, which that Athenian general spoke before the Syracusans as a prisoner of war, as an example of our orator's work. I suppose that there will be no objection if I quote the actual words of Theophrastus. They are as follows:

" There are three forms of antithesis: when a single statement is contrasted with its unlike opposites, when like statements are contrasted with a single opposite, and when a number of unlike statements are contrasted with another number of unlike statements. That is the total number of possible combinations. But equal quantity and similar sound in such clauses is puerile and makes them resemble verse, and therefore ill accords with a serious purpose. It is inappropriate for a speaker who is concerned with matters of importance to indulge in word-play, and to destroy the emotional effect by the style, since in doing so he loses his hold on his audience. This is what Lysias does in his defence of Nicias,[1] when he is trying to elicit pity: " I grieve that the slaughter of the Greeks should have been in a battle which was neither on sea nor on land . . . suppliants to the gods are we, while we expose you as betrayers of your oaths . . . to ties of blood appealing and to kind feeling." If this had really been written by Lysias, he might justly be thought deserving of censure for introducing felicities at an infelicitous time. But if the speech is by someone else, which it is, it is the unfair critic who deserves blame, not Lysias. That Lysias did not write the speech for Nicias, and that it is written neither in his spirit nor in his style, I can

[1] Frag. 99 Scheibe.

τὸ γράμμα, πολλοῖς πάνυ τεκμηρίοις ἀποδεῖξαι δυνάμενος οὐκ ἔχω καιρὸν ἐν τῷ παρόντι λόγῳ. ἰδίαν δὲ περὶ τοῦ ῥήτορος πραγματείαν συντταττόμενος, ἐν ᾗ τά τε ἄλλα δηλωθήσεταί μοι καὶ τίνες εἰσὶν αὐτοῦ λόγοι γνήσιοι, τὴν ἀκρίβειαν ἐν ἐκείνοις καὶ περὶ τοῦδε ἀποδοῦναι πειράσομαι τοῦ λόγου.

15 νυνὶ δὲ περὶ τῶν ἑξῆς διαλέξομαι, τίς ὁ πραγματικός ἐστι Λυσίου χαρακτήρ, ἐπειδὴ τὸν ὑπὲρ τῆς λέξεως ⟨λόγον⟩ [1] ἀποδέδωκα· τουτὶ γὰρ ἔτι λείπεται τὸ μέρος. εὑρετικὸς γάρ ἐστι τῶν ἐν τοῖς πράγμασιν ἐνόντων λόγων ὁ ἀνήρ, οὐ μόνον ὧν ἅπαντες ἂν εὕροιμεν, ἀλλὰ καὶ ὧν μηθείς. οὐδὲν γὰρ ἁπλῶς Λυσίας παραλείπει τῶν στοιχείων, ἐξ ὧν οἱ λόγοι,[2] οὐ τὰ πρόσωπα, οὐ τὰ πράγματα, οὐκ αὐτὰς τὰς πράξεις, οὐ τρόπους τε καὶ αἰτίας αὐτῶν, οὐ καιρούς, οὐ χρόνους, οὐ τόπους, οὐ τὰς ἑκάστου τούτων διαφορὰς ἄχρι τῆς εἰς ἐλάχιστον τομῆς, ἀλλ' ἐξ ἁπάσης θεωρίας καὶ παντὸς μερισμοῦ τὰς οἰκείας ἀφορμὰς ἐκλέγει. δηλοῦσι δὲ μάλιστα τὴν δεινότητα τῆς εὑρέσεως αὐτοῦ οἵ τε ἀμάρτυροι τῶν λόγων καὶ οἱ περὶ τὰς παραδόξους συνταχθέντες ὑποθέσεις, ἐν οἷς πλεῖστα καὶ κάλλιστα ἐνθυμήματα λέγει καὶ τὰ πάνυ δοκοῦντα τοῖς ἄλλοις ἄπορα εἶναι καὶ ἀδύνατα εὔπορα καὶ δυνατὰ φαίνεσθαι ποιεῖ. κριτικὸς ὧν δεῖ λέγειν καὶ ὅτε μὴ πᾶσιν ἐξῆν χρῆσθαι τοῖς εὑρεθεῖσι, τῶν κρατίστων δὲ καὶ κυριωτάτων ἐκλεκτικός, εἰ μὴ

prove by an abundance of evidence; but the present treatise does not afford me the opportunity to do so. I am in the process of composing a monograph on the orator in which, among other things, I shall show which are his genuine speeches, and in that context I shall try to give a detailed account of this speech and its claims to authenticity.

Now that I have dealt with Lysias's style, I shall 15
proceed to discuss the characteristics of his treatment of subject-matter, which is the remaining question to consider. Our orator is adept at discovering the arguments inherent in a situation, not only those which any of us could discover, but also those which would be beyond anyone else's imagination. He omits absolutely none of the elements that constitute an argument: neither persons, nor situations, nor the actions themselves, nor the manner of their occurrence, nor their causes; nor opportunities, nor times and places, nor discrepancies between them, up to the last detail; and from every examination and analysis he extracts the appropriate material for his arguments. The cleverness of his invention is best exemplified in those speeches in which there is no direct evidence and those composed upon extraordinary themes. In these he furnishes a great many excellent arguments and makes cases regarded by everyone else as hopeless and impossible seem easy and practicable. For he is a good judge of what ought to be said; and when it has not been possible to make use of all the arguments that he has discovered, he is equal, if not superior to other orators in his

[1] λόγον addidit Krüger.
[2] οἱ λόγοι Usener: ὁμολογεῖ codd.

καὶ μάλιστα τῶν ἄλλων ῥητόρων, οὐδενός γε ἧττον. τάξει δὲ ἁπλῇ τινι κέχρηται τῶν πραγμάτων καὶ τὰ πολλὰ ὁμοειδεῖ, καὶ περὶ τὰς ἐξεργασίας τῶν ἐπιχειρημάτων ἀφελής τις καὶ ἀπερίεργός ἐστιν· οὔτε γὰρ προκατασκευαῖς οὔτ᾽ ἐφόδοις οὔτε μερισμοῖς οὔτε ποικιλίαις σχημάτων οὔτε ταῖς ἄλλαις ταῖς τοιαύταις πανουργίαις εὑρίσκεται χρώμενος, ἀλλ᾽ ἔστιν ἀπέριττός τις ἐλευθέριός τε καὶ ἀπόνηρος οἰκονομῆσαι τὰ εὑρεθέντα. ἐκ δὴ τούτων παρακελεύομαι τοῖς ἀναγινώσκουσιν αὐτὸν τὴν μὲν εὕρεσιν τῶν ἐνθυμημάτων καὶ τὴν κρίσιν [1] ζηλοῦν, τὴν δὲ τάξιν καὶ τὴν ἐργασίαν αὐτῶν, ἐνδεεστέραν οὖσαν τοῦ προσήκοντος, μὴ ἀποδέχεσθαι [2] τοῦ ἀνδρός, ἀλλὰ παρ᾽ ἑτέρων, οἳ κρείττους οἰκονομῆσαι τὰ εὑρεθέντα ἐγένοντο, περὶ ὧν ὕστερον ἐρῶ, τοῦτο τὸ στοιχεῖον λαμβάνειν.

16 ἀποδεδωκὼς δὲ τὸν ὑπὲρ τῶν ἀρετῶν τε καὶ στοιχείων λόγον, ἐρῶ νῦν καὶ περὶ τοῦ γένους τῶν ἀμφισβητημάτων ἐν οἷς ἔστι θεωρήμασιν ἡ πολιτικὴ τέχνη. τριχῇ δὲ νενεμημένου τοῦ ῥητορικοῦ λόγου καὶ τρία περιειληφότος διάφορα τοῖς τέλεσι γένη, τό τε δικανικὸν καὶ τὸ συμβουλευτικὸν καὶ τὸ καλούμενον ἐπιδεικτικὸν ἢ πανηγυρικόν, ἐν ἅπασι μὲν τούτοις ἐστὶν ὁ ἀνὴρ λόγου ἄξιος, μάλιστα δὲ ἐν τοῖς δικανικοῖς ἀγῶσι. κἀν τούτοις δὲ αὐτοῖς ἀμείνων ἐστὶ τὰ μικρὰ καὶ παράδοξα καὶ ἄπορα εἰπεῖν καλῶς, ἢ τὰ σεμνὰ καὶ μεγάλα καὶ εὔπορα δυνατῶς. ὁ βουλόμενος δὴ τὴν Λυσίου δύναμιν ἀκριβῶς καταμαθεῖν ἐκ τῶν δικανικῶν αὐτὴν μᾶλλον λόγων ἢ ἐκ τῶν πανηγυρικῶν τε καὶ

[1] κρίσιν Sadée: σύγκρισιν codd.

ability to select the most cogent and the most important. His arrangement of material is simple and for the most part uniform, and his development of arguments straightforward and uncomplicated. You do not find him using anticipations or insinuations or analyses or elaborate rhetorical figures or any other such unscrupulous devices, but his arrangement is unaffected, open and ingenuous. Now of these qualities the ones which I recommend readers of Lysias to imitate are his invention and selection of arguments; whereas, since his ordering and development are less effective than they should be, he should not be their model for these, but they should draw these elements from certain other orators who were his superiors in the arrangement of the material they have invented. I shall speak of these later.

16 Having completed my discussion of the virtues and the elements of Lysias's style, I shall now consider him in relation to the forms of debate which must be studied by an aspirant to public life. Oratory is divided into three kinds which have three different objects—forensic, deliberative and the genre called epideictic or ceremonial oratory.[1] Lysias has made his mark in each of these forms, but especially in forensic contests. In this type of oratory, as in the others, he is more capable of speaking well on small, unexpected or difficult matters than of speaking forcefully on weighty, important or straightforward subjects. The student who wishes to make an accurate assessment of Lysias's ability should look for it in his

[1] Aristotle, *Rhetoric* i. 3. 3.

---

[2] μὴ ἀποδέχεσθαι Usener: μὴ ἀπό γε codd.

συμβουλευτικῶν σκοπείτω. ἵνα δὲ καὶ περὶ τῶν ἰδεῶν ἐγγένηταί μοι τὰ προσήκοντα εἰπεῖν, ἐάσω τε ταῦτα περί τε προοιμίων καὶ διηγήσεων καὶ τῶν ἄλλων μερῶν τοῦ λόγου καὶ διαλέξομαι καὶ δηλώσω, ποῖός τίς ἐστιν ἐν ἑκάστῃ τῶν ἰδεῶν ὁ ἀνήρ. διαιρήσομαι δὲ αὐτάς, ὡς Ἰσοκράτει τε καὶ τοῖς κατ' ἐκεῖνον τὸν ἄνδρα κοσμουμένοις ἤρεσεν, ἀρξάμενος ἀπὸ τῶν προοιμίων.

17 φημὶ δὴ πάντων δεξιώτατον εἶναι τὸν ῥήτορα κατὰ τὰς εἰσβολὰς τῶν λόγων καὶ χαριέστατον, ἐννοούμενος, ὅτι ἄρξασθαι μὲν καλῶς οὐ ῥᾴδιόν ἐστιν, εἰ δή [1] τις τῇ προσηκούσῃ χρῆσθαι βούλοιτο ἀρχῇ καὶ μὴ τὸν ἐπιτυχόντα λόγον εἰπεῖν (οὐ γὰρ τὸ πρῶτον ῥηθέν, ἀλλ' ὃ τοῦ προτεθέντος λόγου μηδαμοῦ μᾶλλον ἢ ἐπὶ πρώτου [2] ὠφελήσειε, τοῦτο ἀρχή τε καὶ προοίμιον), ὁρῶν δὲ τὸν ῥήτορα πᾶσι κεχρημένον, οἷς τέχναι τε παραγγέλλουσι καὶ τὰ πράγματα βούλεται. τότε μὲν γὰρ ἀπὸ τοῦ ἰδίου ἐπαίνου λέγων αὐτὸς [3] ἄρχεται, τότε δὲ ἀπὸ τῆς διαβολῆς τοῦ ἀντιδίκου, εἰ δὲ τύχοι αὐτὸς προδιαβληθείς, τὰς αἰτίας πρῶτον ἀπολύεται τὰς καθ' αὑτοῦ· τότε δὲ τοὺς δικαστὰς ἐπαινῶν καὶ θεραπεύων οἰκείους ἑαυτῷ τε καὶ τῷ πράγματι καθίστησι, τότε δὲ τὴν ἀσθένειαν τὴν ἰδίαν καὶ τὴν πλεονεξίαν τὴν τοῦ ἀντιδίκου καὶ τὸ μὴ περὶ τῶν ἴσων ἀμφοτέροις εἶναι τὸν ἀγῶνα ὑποδείκνυσι· τότε δὲ ὡς κοινὰ τὰ πράγματα καὶ ἀναγκαῖα πᾶσι καὶ οὐκ ἄξια ὑπὸ τῶν ἀκουόντων ἀμελεῖσθαι λέγει, τότε δὲ ἄλλο τι κατασκευάζεται τῶν δυναμένων

[1] εἰ δή Matthiae: εἰ μή codd.
[2] ἐπὶ πρώτου Usener: ἐπ' αὐτοῦ codd.

forensic rather than in his ceremonial or deliberative speeches. In order to furnish myself with appropriate examples of the different forms of his oratory, I shall conclude the present discussion and go on to talk about the introduction, narrative and other parts of the speech, and to demonstrate the orator's characteristics in each part. I shall divide them up according to the arrangement favoured by Isocrates and his school, beginning with the introduction.

I pronounce Lysias the most skilful and elegant of 17
the orators as he embarks on his speeches. I realise that it is not easy to make a good beginning, assuming that the speaker is aiming to make the right start and not merely to say the first thing that occurs to him: for the beginning of the introduction proper of a proposed speech is not the first sentence, but that part which could be nowhere more effectively placed than at the beginning. I also observe that Lysias employs all the themes which the handbooks recommend for the introduction, and which the circumstances of his case require. Sometimes he begins in the first person with self-praise; at other times he begins with his opponent's accusation, first refuting the charges against himself if he happens to have been attacked first. Sometimes he makes the jury sympathetic to himself and his case by praise and flattery; at other times he suggests that he is in a vulnerable position, while his opponent is at an advantage, and that the stakes for which they are contending are unequal. Sometimes he says that his case is of universal importance and concern and deserving of the jury's attention, and in general

---

[3] αὐτὸς Markland: αὐτὸ codd.

αὐτὸν μὲν ὠφελῆσαι, τὸν δὲ ἀντίδικον ἐλαττῶσαι. ταῦτα δὲ συντόμως καὶ ἀφελῶς διανοίαις τε χρησταῖς καὶ γνώμαις εὐκαίροις καὶ ἐνθυμήμασι μετρίοις περιλαβὼν ἐπὶ τὴν πρόθεσιν ἐπείγεται, δι' ἧς τὰ μέλλοντα ἐν ταῖς ἀποδείξεσι λέγεσθαι προειπὼν καὶ τὸν ἀκροατὴν παρασκευάσας εὐμαθῆ πρὸς τὸν μέλλοντα λόγον ἐπὶ τὴν διήγησιν καθίσταται· καὶ ἔστι μεθόριον αὐτῷ ἑκατέρας τῶν ἰδεῶν ὡς τὰ πολλὰ ἡ πρόθεσις, ἤδη δέ ποτε καὶ ἀπὸ μόνης ταύτης ἤρξατο. καὶ ἀπροοιμιάστως ποτὲ εἰσέβαλε τὴν διήγησιν ἀρχὴν λαβών. καὶ οὐκ ἄψυχος οὐδ' ἀκίνητός ἐστι περὶ ταύτην τὴν ἰδέαν· μάλιστα δ' ἂν τις αὐτοῦ θαυμάσειε τὴν ἐν τοῖς προοιμίοις δύναμιν, ἐνθυμηθεὶς ὅτι διακοσίων οὐκ ἐλάττους δικανικοὺς γράψας λόγους ἐν οὐδενὶ πέφηνεν οὔτε ἀπιθάνως προοιμιαζόμενος οὔτε ἀπηρτημένῃ τῶν πραγμάτων ἀρχῇ χρώμενος, ἀλλ' οὐδὲ τοῖς ἐνθυμήμασιν ἐπιβέβληκε τοῖς αὐτοῖς οὐδ' ἐπὶ τὰς αὐτὰς κατενήνεκται διανοίας. καίτοι γε τοῦτο καὶ οἱ λόγους ὀλίγους γράψαντες εὑρίσκονται πεπονθότες, λέγω δὲ τὸ τοῖς αὐτοῖς ἐπιβαλεῖν τόποις· ἐῶ γὰρ ὅτι καὶ τὰ παρ' ἑτέροις εἰρημένα λαμβάνοντες ὀλίγου δεῖν πάντες οὐκ ἐν αἰσχύνῃ τίθενται τὸ ἔργον. οὑτοσὶ δὲ καινὸς ὁ ῥήτωρ ἐστὶ καθ' ἕκαστον τῶν λόγων κατά γε οὖν τὰς εἰσβολὰς καὶ τὰ προοίμια καὶ δυνατός, ὃ βούλοιτο, διαπράξασθαι· οὔτε γὰρ εὔνοιαν κινῆσαι βουλόμενος οὔτε προσοχὴν οὔτε εὐμάθειαν ἀτυχή-

devises any argument which can assist his case and weaken that of his opponent. These themes he presents concisely and simply, investing them with noble sentiments, apt sayings and reasonable arguments, and then hastens on to his statement of the case, in which he gives a preview of the arguments to be used in the proof. Having thus prepared his audience to listen intelligently to what he is going to say he proceeds to his narrative. This statement of the case is, in Lysias, usually a no-man's-land between the introduction and the narrative; but some of his speeches begin with this statement alone. Again, on occasion, he embarks immediately upon the narrative, making that his starting-point and dispensing with the introduction. But his introductions have plenty of life and movement; and the power he displays in them is especially remarkable when we consider that he wrote no fewer than two hundred forensic speeches,[1] and yet in none has he been found writing an unconvincing introduction or using an irrelevant starting-point, or even having recourse to the same arguments or taking refuge in the same ideas. Yet this fault of using the same commonplaces is found in orators who have written only a few speeches; and I need not add that nearly all of them are not ashamed to indulge in plagiarism. But Lysias is completely original in every speech, at any rate as regards the beginning and the introduction, and he is able to achieve whatever effect he desires; whether he is trying to excite sympathy, or secure his audience's attention, or make them receptive to his arguments,[2] he could never fail in his purpose.

[1] Cf. [Plutarch] *Lives of the Ten Orators*, 836A.
[2] Aristotle, *Rhetoric* iii. 14. 6–8.

σειεν ἄν ποτε τοῦ σκοποῦ. κατὰ μὲν δὴ ταύτην τὴν ἰδέαν ἢ πρῶτον ἢ οὐδενὸς δεύτερον αὐτὸν ἀποφαίνομαι.

18 ἐν δὲ τῷ διηγεῖσθαι τὰ πράγματα, ὅπερ οἶμαι μέρος πλείστης δεῖται φροντίδος καὶ φυλακῆς, ἀναμφιλόγως ἡγοῦμαι κράτιστον αὐτὸν εἶναι πάντων ῥητόρων, ὅρον τε καὶ κανόνα τῆς ἰδέας ταύτης αὐτὸν ἀποφαίνομαι. οἴομαι δὲ [1] καὶ τὰς τέχνας τῶν λόγων, ἐν αἷς εἴρηταί ⟨τι⟩ περὶ διηγήσεως ἀξιόλογον, οὐκ ἐξ ἄλλων τινῶν μᾶλλον ἢ τῶν ὑπὸ Λυσίου γραφεισῶν εἰληφέναι τὰ παραγγέλματα καὶ τὰς ἀφορμάς. καὶ γὰρ τὸ σύντομον μάλιστα αὗται ἔχουσιν αἱ διηγήσεις καὶ τὸ σαφὲς ἡδεῖαί τέ εἰσιν ὡς οὐχ ἕτεραι καὶ πιθαναὶ καὶ τὴν πίστιν ἅμα λεληθότως συνεπιφέρουσιν, ὥστε μὴ ῥᾴδιον εἶναι μήθ' ὅλην διήγησιν μηδεμίαν μήτε μέρος αὐτῆς ψευδὲς ἢ ἀπίθανον εὑρεθῆναι· τοσαύτην ἔχει πειθὼ καὶ ἀφροδίτην τὰ λεγόμενα καὶ οὕτως λανθάνει τοὺς ἀκούοντας εἴτ' ἀληθῆ ὄντα εἴτε πεπλασμένα. ὥσθ' ὅπερ Ὅμηρος ἐπαινῶν τὸν Ὀδυσσέα ὡς πιθανὸν εἰπεῖν καὶ πλάσασθαι τὰ μὴ γενόμενα εἴρηκε, τοῦτό μοι δοκεῖ κἂν ἐπὶ Λυσίου τις εἰπεῖν·

εἶσκεν ψεύδεα πολλὰ λέγων ἐτύμοισιν ὁμοῖα.

πᾶσί τε καὶ παντὸς μάλιστα τοῦτο παρακελευσαίμην ⟨ἂν⟩ [2] ἀσκεῖν τὸ μέρος ἐν τοῖς Λυσίου παραδείγμασι ποιουμένους τὰς γυμνασίας. κράτιστα γὰρ ⟨ἄν⟩ [3] ἀποδείξαιτο ταύτην τὴν ἰδέαν ὁ μάλιστα τοῦτον τὸν ἄνδρα μιμησάμενος.

[1] οἴομαι δὲ Sylburg: οἴομαί τε codd.
[2] ἂν addidit Krüger.

Therefore in this part of the speech I pronounce him to be the equal of any and superior to most.

In the narration of the facts, which I regard as the section requiring the most thought and care, Lysias is in my opinion unquestionably the best of all the orators. I pronounce him to be the standard and the model of excellence in this form of oratory. I consider that those rhetorical treatises which have anything worthwhile to say about narrative draw their precepts and materials more from Lysianic examples than from others. These narratives of his possess the virtues of conciseness and clarity to a high degree:[1] they are moreover singularly agreeable, while their persuasive powers are such that they smuggle conviction unnoticed past the listener's senses. It is thus difficult to find a narrative that appears false and unconvincing, either in whole or in part, such is the persuasive charm of the story as he tells it, and his power to deceive his audience as to whether it is true or fictitious. So I think one might apply to Lysias the words with which Homer praised Odysseus's powers of persuasion and his ability to fabricate fictions:[2] 18

He spoke many falsehoods and made them sound true.

This above all is the part of the speech which I should advise all students to practise in their training from Lysianic examples; for the one who imitates this orator most closely will make the best showing in this kind of oratory.

I shall now discuss how Lysias handles the proof of facts.

[1] See note 1, p. 29

[2] *Odyssey*, xix. 203.

---

[3] ἂν addidit Krüger.

ἐν δὲ τῷ πιστοῦσθαι τὰ πράγματα [1] τοιοῦτός τις
19 ὁ ἀνήρ ἐστιν. ἄρξομαι δὲ ἀπὸ τῶν καλουμένων ἐντέχνων πίστεων καὶ χωρὶς ὑπὲρ ἑκάστου μέρους διαλέξομαι. τριχῇ δὴ νενεμημένων τούτων εἴς τε τὸ πρᾶγμα καὶ τὸ πάθος καὶ τὸ ἦθος τὰ μὲν ἐκ τοῦ πράγματος οὐδενὸς χεῖρον εὑρεῖν τε καὶ ἐξειπεῖν δύναται Λυσίας. καὶ γὰρ τοῦ εἰκότος ἄριστος ὁ ἀνὴρ εἰκαστὴς [2] καὶ τοῦ παραδείγματος, πῇ τε ὅμοιον εἶναι πέφυκε καὶ πῇ διαφέρον, ἀκριβέστατος κριτὴς τά τε σημεῖα διελεῖν τὰ παρεπόμενα τοῖς πράγμασι καὶ εἰς τεκμηρίων δόξαν ἀγαγεῖν δυνατώτατος. καὶ τὰς ἐκ τῶν ἠθῶν γε πίστεις ἀξιολόγως πάνυ κατασκευάζειν ἔμοιγε δοκεῖ. πολλάκις μὲν γὰρ ἐκ τοῦ βίου καὶ τῆς φύσεως, πολλάκις δ' ἐκ τῶν προτέρων πράξεων καὶ προαιρέσεων ἀξιόπιστα κατασκευάζει τὰ ἤθη. ὅταν δὲ μηδεμίαν ἀφορμὴν τοιαύτην λάβῃ παρὰ τῶν πραγμάτων, αὐτὸς ἠθοποιεῖ καὶ κατασκευάζει τὰ πρόσωπα τῷ λόγῳ πιστὰ καὶ χρηστά, προαιρέσεις τε αὐτοῖς ἀστείας ὑποτιθεὶς καὶ πάθη μέτρια προσάπτων καὶ λόγους ἐπιεικεῖς ἀποδιδοὺς καὶ ταῖς τύχαις ἀκόλουθα φρονοῦντας εἰσάγων καὶ ἐπὶ μὲν τοῖς ἀδίκοις ἀχθομένους καὶ λόγοις καὶ ἔργοις, τὰ δὲ δίκαια προαιρουμένους ποιῶν καὶ πάντα ⟨τὰ⟩ [3] παραπλήσια τούτοις, ἐξ ὧν ἐπιεικὲς ἂν καὶ μέτριον ἦθος φανείη, κατασκευάζων. περὶ

[1] ἐν δὲ τῷ πιστοῦσθαι τὰ πράγματα Sylburg: ἔν γε τῷ πιστοῦσθαι τὸν ἄνδρα τὰ πράγματα codd.

[2] ἄριστος ὁ ἀνὴρ εἰκαστὴς Markland: ἄριστος δικαστὴς ὁ ἀνὴρ codd.

[3] τὰ inseruit Sadée.

I shall begin with what are called rhetorical proofs, 19
dealing with each of the three kinds that are distinguished, the factual, the emotional and the moral.[1] In drawing conclusions from the facts Lysias is second to none either in invention or exposition; for he is excellent at exploring the scope of argument from probability [2] and at using examples,[3] and is a very accurate judge of natural similarities and differences; he is masterly, too, at distinguishing the evidence which actions leave behind them,[4] and elevating it to the status of positive proof. He also seems to me to show very notable skill in constructing proofs from character. He often makes us believe in his client's good character by referring to the circumstances of his life and his parentage, and often again by describing his past actions and the principles governing them. And when the facts fail to provide him with such material, he creates his own moral tone, making his characters seem by their speech to be trustworthy and honest. He credits them with civilised dispositions and attributes controlled feelings to them; he makes them voice appropriate sentiments, and introduces them as men whose thoughts befit their status in life, and who abhor both evil words and evil deeds. He represents them as men who always choose the just course, and ascribes to them every other related quality that may reveal a respectable and moderate character.[5] But he is somewhat weak

[1] Aristotle, *Rhetoric* i. 2. 3–6.
[2] Aristotle, *Rhetoric* i. 2. 15.
[3] Aristotle, *Rhetoric* i. 2. 8–9; ii. 20.
[4] Aristotle, *Rhetoric* i. 2. 16–18.
[5] See note 3, p. 33. Dionysius underestimates Lysias's ability at individual characterisation. See Usher, *Eranos* 1965, 99–119.

δὲ τὰ πάθη μαλακώτερός ἐστι καὶ οὔτε αὐξήσεις οὔτε δεινώσεις οὔτε οἴκτους οὐθ' ὅσα τούτοις ἐστὶ παραπλήσια νεανικῶς πάνυ καὶ ἐρρωμένως κατασκευάσαι δυνατός. οὐ δεῖ δὴ ταῦτα ἐπιζητεῖν παρὰ Λυσίου. κἀν τοῖς ἐπιλόγοις δὲ τὸ μὲν ἀνακεφαλαιωτικὸν τῶν ῥηθέντων μέρος μετρίως τε καὶ χαριέντως ἀπαριθμεῖ, τὸ δὲ παθητικὸν ἐκεῖνο, ἐν ᾧ παράκλησίς τε καὶ ἔλεος καὶ δέησις καὶ τὰ τούτοις ἀδελφὰ ἔνεστι, τοῦ προσήκοντος ἐνδεεστέρως ἀποδίδωσι.

20 τοιοῦτος μὲν δή ἐστιν ὁ Λυσίου χαρακτήρ, ὡς ἐγὼ δόξης ἔχω περὶ αὐτοῦ. εἰ δέ τις ἄλλα παρὰ ταῦτα ἔγνωκεν, λεγέτω· κἂν ᾖ πιθανώτερα, πολλὴν αὐτῷ χάριν εἴσομαι. ἵνα δὲ βέλτιον τῷ βουλομένῳ ἐγγένηται [1] μαθεῖν, εἴτε ὀρθῶς ἡμεῖς ταῦτα καὶ προσηκόντως πεπείσμεθα εἴτε καὶ διημαρτήκαμεν τὴν κρίσιν, τὴν ἐξέτασιν ἐπὶ τῶν ὑπ' ἐκείνου γραφέντων ποιήσομαι προχειρισάμενός τε ἕνα [2] λόγον (οὐ γὰρ ἐγχωρεῖ πολλοῖς χρῆσθαι παραδείγμασιν) ἐξ ἐκείνου τήν τε προαίρεσιν καὶ τὴν δύναμιν τοῦ ἀνδρὸς ἐπιδείξομαι, ἀποχρῆν οἰόμενος ψυχαῖς εὐπαιδεύτοις καὶ μετρίαις μικρά τε μεγάλων καὶ ὀλίγα πολλῶν γενέσθαι δείγματα. ἔστι δὲ ὁ λόγος ἐκ τῶν ἐπιτροπικῶν, ἐπιγραφόμενος κατὰ Διογείτονος, ὑπόθεσιν δὲ ἔχων τοιάνδε·

21 Διόδοτος, εἷς τῶν μετὰ Θρασύλλου καταλεγέντων ἐν τῷ Πελοποννησιακῷ πολέμῳ, μέλλων ἐκπλεῖν εἰς τὴν Ἀσίαν ἐπὶ Γλαυκίππου ἄρχοντος, ἔχων νήπια παιδία, διαθήκας ἐποιήσατο καταλιπὼν

[1] ἐγγένηται Sadée: γένηται codd.
[2] τε ἕνα Sadée: τινα codd.

at portraying emotion, and lacks the final degree both of youthful vigour and of mature strength to amplify and exaggerate, or to arouse pity and its kindred emotions. Therefore such qualities are not to be sought in Lysias. In his perorations, too, he recites his summary of the main points moderately and pleasingly, but when he passes to the emotional appeal, which includes pleas for help, prayers for mercy, entreaties and kindred themes, the effect he produces is less forceful than it should be.

These, then, are the characteristics which in my 20
opinion distinguish the style of Lysias. If anyone has formed different conclusions, let him state them; and if they are more convincing than mine, I shall be very grateful to him. But in order to give anyone who requires it a better opportunity to decide whether my conclusions are correct and fair, or whether my judgment is at fault, I shall turn my examination to his actual writings, selecting a single speech (for there is not time to employ many examples). I shall use this speech to illustrate the orator's approach and his power of execution, on the assumption that men of culture and discrimination will find a few short examples sufficient to demonstrate characteristics which occur prominently and frequently in his oratory. The speech I have chosen is one of those concerned with guardianship, and is entitled *Against Diogeiton.*[1] The argument is as follows:

" Diodotus was one of those enrolled to serve under 21
Thrasyllus in the Peloponnesian War. When he was about to sail to Asia during the archonship of Glaucippus, as he had young children, he made a will in which

[1] Oration 32 (O.C.T.), as here preserved by Dionysius.

αὐτοῖς ἐπίτροπον τὸν ἑαυτοῦ μὲν ἀδελφὸν Διογείτονα, τῶν δὲ παιδίων θεῖόν τε καὶ πάππον ἀπὸ μητρός. αὐτὸς μὲν οὖν ἐν Ἐφέσῳ μαχόμενος ἀποθνήσκει, Διογείτων δὲ πᾶσαν τὴν οὐσίαν τῶν ὀρφανῶν διαχειρισάμενος καὶ ἐκ πολλῶν πάνυ χρημάτων οὐδὲν ἀποδείξας αὐτοῖς, ἔτι περιὼν κατηγορεῖται πρὸς ἑνὸς τῶν μειρακίων δοκιμασθέντος κακῆς ἐπιτροπῆς. λέγει δὲ κατ' αὐτοῦ τὴν δίκην ὁ τῆς ἐκείνου μὲν θυγατριδῆς τῶν δὲ μειρακίων ἀδελφῆς ἀνήρ.

22 προὔλαβον δὲ τὴν ὑπόθεσιν, ἵνα μᾶλλον γένηται καταφανές, εἰ μετρίᾳ καὶ προσηκούσῃ ἀρχῇ κέχρηται·

23 "Εἰ μὲν μὴ μεγάλα ἦν τὰ διαφέροντα, ὦ ἄνδρες δικασταί, οὐκ ἄν ποτε εἰς ὑμᾶς εἰσελθεῖν τούτους εἴασα, νομίζων αἴσχιστον εἶναι πρὸς τοὺς οἰκείους διαφέρεσθαι, εἰδὼς ὅτι οὐ μόνον οἱ ἀδικοῦντες χείρους ὑμῖν εἶναι δοκοῦσιν, ἀλλὰ καὶ οἵτινες ἂν ἔλαττον ὑπὸ τῶν προσηκόντων ἔχοντες ἀνέχεσθαι μὴ δύνωνται. ἐπειδὴ μέντοι, ὦ ἄνδρες δικασταί, πολλῶν χρημάτων ἀπεστέρηνται καὶ πολλὰ καὶ δεινὰ πεπονθότες ὑφ' ὧν ἥκιστα ἐχρῆν ἐπ' ἐμὲ κηδεστὴν ὄντα κατέφυγον, ἀνάγκη μοι γεγένηται εἰπεῖν ὑπὲρ αὐτῶν. ἔχω δὲ τούτων μὲν ἀδελφὴν Διογείτονος δὲ θυγατριδῆν· καὶ πολλὰ δεηθεὶς ἀμφοτέρων τὸ μὲν πρῶτον ἔπεισα αὐτοὺς τοῖς φίλοις [1] ἐπιτρέψαι δίαιταν, περὶ πολλοῦ ποιούμενος τὰ τούτων πράγματα μηδένα τῶν

he left as their guardian his own brother Diogeiton, who was their maternal grandfather in addition to being their uncle. Now Diodotus was killed in a battle at Ephesus, but Diogeiton, having gained control of the whole of the orphans' estate, rendered them a void account from what had been a very large sum of money, and survived to be charged with abusing his guardianship by one of the young heirs who had attained his majority. The case against him is conducted by the husband of his daughter's daughter, who is also the young men's sister."

I have given the argument first in order to make it 22
easier to see clearly whether the opening that he uses is reasonable and appropriate:

"If the matters at issue were not important, 23
gentlemen of the jury, I should never have allowed these persons to appear before you; for I regard a family dispute as a most discreditable thing, and I know that you disapprove not only of those who do wrong, but also of anyone who cannot stand being overreached by a relative. But, gentlemen, since they have been robbed of a large sum of money and, after suffering many indignities at the hands of those who ought to have been the last to behave in such a way, have fled to me, their brother-in-law, for protection, I have found myself obliged to speak on their behalf. I am married to their sister, who is the daughter of Diogeiton's daughter; and in the first instance, after many entreaties, I persuaded both parties to submit the case to mutual friends for arbitration, because I thought it highly desirable that

---

[1] ἔπεισα αὐτοὺς τοῖς φίλοις Sylburg: ἔπεισα τοὺς φίλους FMPB.

ἄλλων εἰδέναι. ἐπειδὴ δὲ Διογείτων, ἃ φανερῶς ἔχων ἐξηλέγχετο, περὶ τούτων οὐδενὶ τῶν αὑτοῦ φίλων ἐτόλμα πείθεσθαι, ἀλλ' ἠβουλήθη καὶ φεύγειν δίκας καὶ μὴ οὔσας διώκειν καὶ ὑπομεῖναι τοὺς ἐσχάτους κινδύνους μᾶλλον ἢ τὰ δίκαια ποιήσας ἀπηλλάχθαι τῶν πρὸς τούτους ἐγκλημάτων, ὑμῶν δέομαι, ἐὰν μὲν ἀποδείξω οὕτως αἰσχρῶς αὐτοὺς ἐπιτετροπευμένους ὑπὸ τοῦ πάππου, ὡς οὐδεὶς πώποτε ὑπὸ τῶν οὐδὲν προσηκόντων ἐν τῇ πόλει, βοηθεῖν αὐτοῖς τὰ δίκαια· εἰ δὲ μή, τούτῳ μὲν ἅπαντα πιστεύειν, ἡμᾶς δὲ εἰς τὸν λοιπὸν χρόνον ἡγεῖσθαι χείρους εἶναι. ἐξ ἀρχῆς δ' ὑμᾶς περὶ αὐτῶν διδάξαι πειράσομαι."

24 τοῦτο τὸ προοίμιον ἁπάσας ἔχει τὰς ἀρετάς, ὅσας δεῖ τὸ προοίμιον ἔχειν. δηλώσουσι δὲ οἱ κανόνες αὐτῷ παρατεθέντες οἱ τῶν τεχνῶν. ἅπαντες γὰρ δή που παραγγέλλουσιν οἱ συνταξάμενοι τὰς τέχνας, ὅταν πρὸς οἰκείους ὁ ἀγών, σκοπεῖν ὅπως μὴ πονηροὶ μηδὲ φιλοπράγμονες οἱ κατήγοροι φανήσονται. κελεύουσίν τε πρῶτον μὲν τὴν αἰτίαν εἰς τοὺς ἀντιδίκους περιιστάναι καὶ τοῦ ἐγκλήματος καὶ τοῦ ἀγῶνος καὶ λέγειν, ὅτι μεγάλα τἀδικήματα [1] καὶ οὐκ ἐνῆν αὐτὰ μετρίως ἐνεγκεῖν καὶ ὅτι ὑπὲρ ἀναγκαιοτέρων προσώπων ὁ ἀγὼν καὶ ἐρήμων καὶ ἧττον ὑπεροφθῆναι ἀξίων, οἷς μὴ βοηθοῦντες κακίους ἂν ἐφάνησαν· καὶ ὅτι προκαλούμενοι τοὺς ἀντιδίκους εἰς διαλλαγὰς καὶ φίλοις τὰ πράγματα ἐπιτρέποντες καὶ τὰ δυνατὰ ἐλατ-

[1] τἀδικήματα Markland: ἀδικήματα codd.

their affairs should not be known to anyone else. But since Diogeiton would not risk taking the advice of any of his friends regarding the property which he was plainly convicted of holding, but preferred to face prosecution and even to file suits if they were not brought against him, and to undergo the utmost dangers rather than do the just thing and so be rid of all their charges, I ask you, if I now prove that the guardianship has been more shamefully mismanaged by their grandfather than any in the city before, including those in which the guardian was not a relative, to give them the help to which they are entitled: otherwise, believe all that this man has said and discredit the rest of our case. I shall now try to inform you of the facts from the beginning."

This introduction has all the virtues that an intro- 24
duction ought to have, as a comparison with the rules in the handbooks will show.[1] For all the writers of handbooks recommend that when the defendants in a case are relatives of the plaintiffs, the latter should take care not to appear malicious or vexatious. They advise that the blame for both the charge and the lawsuit should be placed at the opponent's door at the outset; that the plaintiff should say that the wrongs committed are great and beyond what could reasonably be tolerated, and that the parties he is supporting are more closely related to him than the accused and are without support and therefore more deserving of his aid, while he would have incurred a loss of face if he had failed to come to their assistance. He should also say that they have invited the other side to make a private settlement, but have been unable to obtain

[1] In this chapter Dionysius preserves a number of rules from early handbooks which are not found elsewhere.

τοῦσθαι ὑπομένοντες οὐδενὸς ἠδυνήθησαν τυχεῖν τῶν μετρίων. ταῦτα μὲν δὴ παραγγέλλουσι ποιεῖν οἱ τεχνογράφοι, ἵνα τὸ ἦθος τοῦ λέγοντος ἐπιεικέστερον εἶναι δόξῃ. δύναται δὲ αὐτοῖς εὔνοιαν τοῦτο ποιεῖν καὶ ἔστι κράτιστον τῆς κατασκευῆς μέρος. ταῦθ' ὁρῶ πάντα διὰ τοῦ προοιμίου τοῦδε γεγονότα. καὶ μὴν εἴς γε τὸ εὐμαθεῖς τοὺς ἀκροατὰς ποιῆσαι κελεύουσι συστρέψαντας εἰπεῖν τὸ πρᾶγμα, ἵνα μὴ ἀγνοῶσι τὴν ὑπόθεσιν οἱ δικασταί, καὶ οἷά περ ἂν ᾖ τὰ μέλλοντα λέγεσθαι, τοιοῦτο καὶ τὸ προοίμιον ὑποτίθεσθαι ἀπ' ἀρχῆς καὶ δεῖγμα τοῦ πράγματος ποιουμένους κατευθὺ ἀπ' ἐνθυμημάτων πειρᾶσθαι ἄρχεσθαι. ἔχει δὴ καὶ ταῦτα τὸ προοίμιον. ἔτι περὶ τῆς προσοχῆς ὧδέ πως τεχνολογοῦσιν, ὅτι δεῖ τὸν προσεκτικοὺς μέλλοντα ποιεῖν τοὺς ἀκροατὰς καὶ λέγειν θαυμαστὰ καὶ παράδοξα καὶ δεῖσθαι τῶν δικαστῶν ἀκοῦσαι. φαίνεται δὴ καὶ ταῦτα πεποιηκὼς ὁ Λυσίας. καὶ πρόσεστι [1] τούτοις τὸ λεῖον τῆς ἑρμηνείας καὶ τὸ ἀφελὲς τῆς κατασκευῆς, ὧν μάλιστα δεῖ τοῖς ὑπὲρ οἰκείων [2] προοιμιαζομένοις. ἄξιον δὲ καὶ τὴν διήγησιν ὡς ᾠκονόμηται καταμαθεῖν. ἔχει δὲ οὕτως·

" Ἀδελφοὶ ἦσαν, ὦ ἄνδρες δικασταί, Διόδοτος καὶ Διογείτων ὁμοπάτριοι καὶ ὁμομήτριοι. καὶ τὴν μὲν ἀφανῆ οὐσίαν ἐνείμαντο, τῆς δὲ φανερᾶς ἐκοινώνουν. ἐργασαμένου δὲ Διοδότου κατ' ἐμπο-

[1] πρόσεστι Krüger: πρὸς ἔτι FM, προσέτι PBG.

a fair deal even after appointing friends to arbitrate and being prepared to make all possible concessions. These are the themes recommended by the rhetorical theorists in order to make the litigant appear more fair-minded than his opponent; for this can secure the goodwill of the jury, which is the most important function of the argument here. I find all these themes occurring in the course of this introduction. Again, they advise that the facts be stated concisely in order that the jury should understand them easily, and to ensure that they know what the dispute is about; and that the orator should try to make the introduction, from its very beginning, contain arguments which foreshadow those which are to be used later and which describe the case. Lysias's introduction fulfils this requirement also. As to the question of the jury's attentiveness, the advice of the rhetoricians is to the effect that the orator who aims to win his audience's attention must say remarkable and unexpected things and beg the jury to listen to him. Lysias has manifestly done this too. They further recommend smoothness of expression and simplicity of composition, qualities which those who are introducing a speech on behalf of relatives should certainly display. It is worthwhile now to consider how the narrative is managed. It runs as follows:

"Diodotus and Diogeiton, gentlemen of the jury, 25
were brothers born of the same father and mother, and they had divided between them the personal estate, but held the real property jointly. When Diodotus had made a large fortune in commerce,

[2] ὑπὲρ οἰκείων scripsi post Usener ὑπ' οἰκείων: ὑπὲρ ἐκείνων MPB: ὑπ' ἐκείνων FGv.

ρίαν πολλὰ χρήματα πείθει αὐτὸν Διογείτων λαβεῖν τὴν ἑαυτοῦ θυγατέρα, ἥ περ ἦν αὐτῷ μόνη. καὶ γίνονται αὐτῷ υἱοὶ δύο καὶ θυγάτηρ. χρόνῳ δὲ ὕστερον καταλεγεὶς Διόδοτος μετὰ Θρασύλλου τῶν ὁπλιτῶν, καλέσας τὴν ἑαυτοῦ γυναῖκα ἀδελφιδῆν οὖσαν καὶ τὸν ἐκείνης μὲν πατέρα αὐτοῦ δὲ κηδεστὴν καὶ ἀδελφὸν [ὁμοπάτριον],[1] πάππον δὲ τῶν παιδίων καὶ θεῖον, ἡγούμενος διὰ ταύτας τὰς ἀναγκαιότητας οὐδενὶ μᾶλλον προσήκειν δικαίῳ περὶ τοὺς αὐτοῦ παῖδας [2] γενέσθαι, διαθήκην αὐτῷ δίδωσι καὶ πέντε τάλαντα ἀργυρίου παρακαταθήκην, ναυτικὰ [3] δὲ ἀπέδειξεν ἐκδεδομένα ἑπτὰ τάλαντα καὶ τετταράκοντα μνᾶς, ...[4] δισχιλίας δὲ ὀφειλομένας ἐν Χερρονήσῳ. ἐπέσκηψε δέ, ἐάν τι πάθῃ, τάλαντον μὲν ἐπιδοῦναι τῇ γυναικὶ καὶ τὰ ἐν τῷ δωματίῳ δοῦναι, τάλαντον δὲ τῇ θυγατρί. κατέλιπε ⟨δὲ⟩ [5] καὶ εἴκοσι μνᾶς τῇ γυναικὶ καὶ τριάκοντα στατῆρας Κυζικηνούς. ταῦτα δὲ πράξας καὶ οἴκοι ἀντίγραφα καταλιπὼν ᾤχετο στρατευσόμενος μετὰ Θρασύλλου. ἀποθανόντος δὲ ἐκείνου ἐν Ἐφέσῳ Διογείτων τὴν μὲν θυγατέρα ἔκρυπτε τὸν θάνατον τοῦ ἀνδρὸς καὶ τὰ γράμματα λαμβάνει, ἃ κατέλιπε σεσημασμένα, φάσκων τὰ ναυτικὰ χρήματα δεῖν ἐκ τούτων τῶν γραμματείων κομίσασθαι. ἐπειδὴ [6] δὲ χρόνῳ ἐδήλωσε τὸν θάνατον αὐτοῖς καὶ ἐποίησαν τὰ νομιζόμενα, τὸν μὲν πρῶτον ἐνιαυτὸν ἐν Πειραιεῖ διῃτῶντο· ἅπαντα γὰρ αὐτοῦ κατελέλειπτο τὰ ἐπιτήδεια. ἐκείνων

[1] ὁμοπάτριον seclusit Herwerden.

[2] δικαίῳ περὶ τοὺς αὐτοῦ παῖδας Sauppe: καὶ ὥσπερ τοῦ αὐτοῦ παῖδας FMPB.

Diogeiton persuaded him to marry his only daughter, and two sons and a daughter were born to him. Some time later when Diodotus was enrolled for infantry service with Thrasyllus, he summoned his wife, who was his niece, and her father, who was also his father-in-law and his brother, and grandfather and uncle of the children, since he felt that with these bonds of kinship there was nobody more bound to act justly by his children. He then gave him a will and five talents of silver in deposit, and he also produced a record of his loans on bottomry, amounting to seven talents and forty minae . . . and two thousand drachmae invested in the Chersonese. He instructed him, in case anything should happen to himself, to give his wife and his daughter each a dowry of one talent, and to give his wife the contents of their modest house. He also bequeathed to his wife twenty minae and thirty Cyzicean staters. Having made these dispositions and left a copy of the will in his house, he went to serve abroad with Thrasyllus. He was killed at Ephesus. For a time Diogeiton concealed from his daughter the death of her husband, and took possession of the will which he had left under seal, alleging that these documents were needed for the recovery of the money lent on bottomry. When he finally informed them of his death, and they had performed the customary rites, they lived on in the Piraeus for the first year, as all their possessions had been left there. But as money began to run short,

---

3 ναυτικὰ Markland: αὐτίκα codd.
4 lacunam statuit Sauppe.
5 δὲ inseruit Reiske.
6 ἐπειδὴ Fuhr : ἐπεὶ codd.

δ' ἐπιλειπόντων[1] τοὺς μὲν παῖδας εἰς ἄστυ ἀναπέμπει, τὴν δὲ μητέρα αὐτῶν ἐκδίδωσιν ἐπιδοὺς πεντακισχιλίας δραχμάς, χιλίαις ἔλαττον ὧν ὁ ἀνὴρ αὐτῆς ἔδωκεν. ὀγδόῳ δ' ἔτει δοκιμασθέντος μετὰ ταῦτα τοῦ πρεσβυτέρου τοῖν μειρακίοιν καλέσας αὐτοὺς εἶπε Διογείτων, ὅτι καταλείποι αὐτοῖς ὁ πατὴρ εἴκοσι μνᾶς ἀργυρίου καὶ τριάκοντα στατῆρας. ἐγὼ οὖν πολλὰ τῶν ἐμαυτοῦ δεδαπάνηκα εἰς τὴν ὑμετέραν τροφήν. καὶ ἕως μὲν εἶχον, οὐδέν μοι διέφερεν· νυνὶ δὲ καὶ αὐτὸς ἀπόρως διάκειμαι. σὺ οὖν, ἐπειδὴ δεδοκίμασαι καὶ ἀνὴρ γεγένησαι, σκόπει αὐτὸς ἤδη, πόθεν ἕξεις τὰ ἐπιτήδεια. ταῦτ' ἀκούσαντες, ἐκπεπληγμένοι καὶ δακρύοντες ᾤχοντο πρὸς τὴν μητέρα καὶ παραλαβόντες ἐκείνην ἧκον πρὸς ἐμέ, οἰκτρῶς ὑπὸ τοῦ πάθους διακείμενοι καὶ ἀθλίως ἐκπεπτωκότες, κλαίοντες καὶ παρακαλοῦντές με μὴ περιιδεῖν αὐτοὺς ἀποστερηθέντας τῶν πατρῴων μηδ' εἰς πτωχείαν καταστάντας, ὑβρισμένους ὑφ' ὧν ἥκιστα ἐχρῆν, ἀλλὰ βοηθῆσαι καὶ τῆς ἀδελφῆς ἕνεκα[2] καὶ σφῶν αὐτῶν. πολλὰ ἂν εἴη λέγειν, ὅσον πένθος ἐν τῇ ἐμῇ οἰκίᾳ ἦν ἐν ἐκείνῳ τῷ χρόνῳ. τελευτῶσα δὲ ἡ μήτηρ αὐτῶν ἠντιβόλει με καὶ ἱκέτευσε συναγαγεῖν αὐτῆς τὸν πατέρα καὶ τοὺς φίλους, εἰποῦσα ὅτι, εἰ καὶ μὴ πρότερον εἴθισται λέγειν ἐν ἀνδράσι, τὸ μέγεθος αὐτὴν ἀναγκάσει τῶν συμφορῶν περὶ τῶν σφετέρων κακῶν δηλῶσαι πάντα πρὸς ἡμᾶς. ἐλθὼν δ' ἐγὼ ἠγανάκτουν μὲν πρὸς Ἡγήμονα τὸν ἔχοντα τὴν

[1] ἐπιλειπόντων Reiske: ὑπολειπόντων codd.
[2] ἕνεκα Dobson: οὕνεκα codd.

he sent the children up to the city, and gave their mother in marriage with a dowry of five thousand drachmae—a thousand less than her husband had given her. Seven years later the elder boy was certified to be of age. Diogeiton summoned them, and said that their father had left them twenty minae of silver and thirty staters, adding, 'Now I have spent a great deal of my own money on your upbringing: so long as I had the means I did not mind; but at this moment I am in difficulties myself. You, therefore, since you have been certified and have attained manhood, must henceforth look to providing for yourself.' On hearing these words they were astounded, and went weeping to their mother, and brought her along with them to me. It was pitiful to see how they suffered from the blow: the poor creatures, thrown out on to the streets, wept aloud and begged me not to allow them to be deprived of their patrimony and reduced to beggary by the last persons who should have abused them so, but to help them both for their sister's sake and their own.

" It would take a long time to describe the mourning that filled my house at that time. In the end, their mother implored and supplicated me to assemble her father and friends together, saying that even though she had not before been accustomed to speak in the presence of men, the magnitude of their misfortunes would force her to give us a full account of their hardships. I went and expressed my indignation to Hegemon, the husband of this man's daughter;

τούτου θυγατέρα, λόγους δ' ἐποιούμην πρὸς τοὺς ἄλλους ἐπιτηδείους, ἠξίουν δὲ τοῦτον εἰς ἔλεγχον ἰέναι περὶ τῶν πραγμάτων. Διογείτων δὲ τὸ μὲν πρῶτον οὐκ ἤθελε, τελευτῶν δὲ ὑπὸ τῶν φίλων ἠναγκάσθη. ἐπειδὴ δὲ συνήλθομεν, ἤρετο αὐτὸν ἡ γυνή, τίνα ποτὲ ψυχὴν ἔχων ἀξιοῖ περὶ τῶν παίδων τοιαύτῃ γνώμῃ χρῆσθαι, ἀδελφὸς μὲν ὢν τοῦ πατρὸς αὐτῶν, πατὴρ δ' ἐμός, θεῖος δὲ αὐτοῖς καὶ πάππος. καὶ εἰ μηδένα ἀνθρώπων ᾐσχύνου, τοὺς θεοὺς ἐχρῆν σε, φησί, δεδιέναι, ὃς ἔλαβες μέν, ὅτ' ἐκεῖνος ἐξέπλει,[1] πέντε τάλαντα παρ' αὐτοῦ παρακαταθήκην, καὶ περὶ τούτων ἐγὼ θέλω τοὺς παῖδας παραστησαμένη καὶ τούτους καὶ τοὺς ὕστερον ἐμαυτῇ γενομένους ὀμόσαι, ὅπου ἂν οὗτος λέγῃ· καίτοι οὐχ οὕτως ἐγώ εἰμι ἀθλία οὐδ' οὕτω περὶ πολλοῦ ποιοῦμαι χρήματα ὥστ' ἐπιορκήσασα κατὰ τῶν παίδων τῶν ἐμαυτῆς τὸν βίον καταναλίσκειν, ἀδίκως δὲ ἀφελέσθαι τὴν τοῦ πατρὸς οὐσίαν. ἔτι τοίνυν ἐξήλεγχεν αὐτὴ ἑπτὰ τάλαντα κεκομισμένον ναυτικὰ [2] καὶ τετρακισχιλίας δραχμὰς καὶ τούτων τὰ γράμματ' ἀπέδειξεν. ἐν γὰρ τῇ διοικίσει,[3] ὅτ' ἐκ Κολλυτοῦ διῳκίζετο εἰς τὴν Φαίδρου οἰκίαν, τοὺς παῖδας ἐπιτυχόντας ἐκβεβλημένῳ βιβλίῳ ἐνεγκεῖν πρὸς αὐτήν.[4] ἀπέφηνε δ' αὐτὸν ἑκατὸν μνᾶς κεκομισμένον ἐγγείῳ [5] ἐπὶ τόκῳ δεδανεισμένας καὶ ἑτέρας δισχιλίας δραχμὰς καὶ ἔπιπλα πολλοῦ ἄξια, φοιτᾶν δὲ καὶ σῖτον αὐτοῖς ἐκ Χερρονήσου καθ' ἕκαστον ἐνιαυτόν. ἔπειτα σὺ ἐτόλμησας, ἔφη, εἰπεῖν, ἔχων τοσαῦτα

[1] ἐξέπλει Taylor: ἐξέλιπε codd.
[2] ναυτικὰ Markland: αὐτίκα codd.

I spoke too with the other relations; then I called upon the defendant himself to allow his handling of the money to be investigated. Diogeiton at first refused, but finally he was compelled by his friends. When we came together, the mother asked him what heart he could have to contemplate such treatment of the children, 'when you are their father's brother,' she said, 'and my father, and their uncle and grandfather. Even if you felt no shame before any man, you ought to have feared the gods: for you received from him, when he sailed on the campaign, five talents in deposit. I offer to swear the truth of this by the lives of my children, both these and those since born to me, in any place that you yourself may name. Yet I am not so abject, or so fond of money, as to leave this life after perjuring myself on the lives of my own children, and to appropriate unjustly my father's estate.' And she proved further that he had recovered seven talents and four thousand drachmae from loans on bottomry, and produced the documents to prove this: for she showed that in the course of his removal from Collytus to the house of Phaedrus, the children had come across the register, which had been mislaid, and had brought it to her. She also proved that he had recovered a hundred minae which had been lent at interest on land mortgages, and also two thousand drachmae and some furniture of great value; and that corn came in to them every year from the Chersonese. 'After that,' she said, 'you had the temerity to say, when you had so much money in your

---

[3] διοικίσει Matthiae: διοικήσει codd.
[4] πρὸς αὐτήν Markland: πρὸς ταύτην codd.
[5] ἐγγείῳ Naber: ἐγγείους codd.

χρήματα, ὡς δισχιλίας δραχμὰς ὁ τούτων πατὴρ κατέλιπε καὶ τριάκοντα στατῆρας; ἅ περ ἐμοὶ καταλειφθέντα ἐκείνου τελευτήσαντος ἐγώ σοι ἔδωκα· καὶ ἐκβάλλειν τούτους ἠξίωκας θυγατριδοῦς ὄντας ἐκ τῆς οἰκίας τῆς αὑτῶν ἐν τριβωνίοις, ἀνυποδήτους, οὐ μετὰ ἀκολούθου, οὐ μετὰ στρωμάτων, οὐ μετὰ ἱματίων, οὐ μετὰ τῶν ἐπίπλων, ἃ ὁ πατὴρ αὐτοῖς κατέλιπεν, οὐδὲ μετὰ τῶν παρακαταθηκῶν, ἃς ἐκεῖνος παρὰ σοὶ κατέθετο. καὶ νῦν τοὺς μὲν ἐκ τῆς μητρυιᾶς τῆς ἐμῆς παιδεύεις ἐν πολλοῖς χρήμασιν εὐδαίμονας ὄντας (καὶ ταῦτα μὲν καλῶς ποιεῖς), τοὺς δ' ἐμοὺς ἀδικεῖς, οὓς ἀτίμους ἐκ τῆς οἰκίας ἐκβαλὼν ἀντὶ πλουσίων πτωχοὺς ἀποδεῖξαι προθυμεῖ. καὶ ἐπὶ τοιούτοις ἔργοις οὔτε τοὺς θεοὺς φοβεῖ οὔτε ἐμὲ τὴν συνειδυῖαν αἰσχύνῃ οὔτε τοῦ ἀδελφοῦ μέμνησαι, ἀλλὰ πάντας ἡμᾶς περὶ ἐλάττονος ποιεῖ χρημάτων. τότε μὲν οὖν, ὦ ἄνδρες δικασταί, πολλῶν καὶ δεινῶν ὑπὸ τῆς γυναικὸς ῥηθέντων οὕτω διετέθημεν πάντες οἱ παρόντες ὑπὸ τῶν τούτῳ πεπραγμένων καὶ τῶν λόγων τῶν ἐκείνης, ὁρῶντες μὲν τοὺς παῖδας οἷα ἦσαν πεπονθότες, ἀναμιμνησκόμενοι δὲ τοῦ ἀποθανόντος, ὡς ἀνάξιον τῆς οὐσίας τὸν ἐπίτροπον κατέλιπεν, ἐνθυμούμενοι δέ, ὡς χαλεπὸν ἐξευρεῖν ὅτῳ χρὴ περὶ τῶν ἑαυτοῦ πιστεῦσαι· ὥστε, ὦ ἄνδρες δικασταί, μηδένα τῶν παρόντων δύνασθαι φθέγξασθαι, ἀλλὰ καὶ δακρύοντας μὴ ἧττον τῶν πεπονθότων ἀπιόντας οἴχεσθαι σιωπῇ."

26 ἵνα δὲ καὶ ὁ τῶν ἀποδείξεων χαρακτὴρ καταφανὴς γένηται, θήσω καὶ τὰ ἐπὶ τούτοις λεγόμενα.

possession, that their father bequeathed them two thousand drachmae and thirty staters—just the amount that was bequeathed to me, and that I gave you after he died! And you thought fit to turn these, the children of your daughter, out of their own house, in rough clothes, unshod, without an attendant, without bedding and without a cloak; without the furniture which their father left to them, and without the money he had deposited with you. And now you are bringing up the children you have had by my stepmother in all the comforts of wealth. You are quite right to do that: but you are doing wrong to my children, whom you ejected from the house in dishonour, and whom you are intent on turning from persons of ample means into beggars. And in committing such outrages you feel neither fear of the gods nor shame before me who know what you have done, nor are you mindful of your brother, but value money more highly than all of us.' Thereupon, gentlemen of the jury, when we had heard all these shocking accusations from the mother, we who were present were all so affected by this man's conduct and by her account of it—when we saw how the children had been treated, and recalled the dead man to mind and how unworthy was the guardian he had left in charge of his estate, and reflected how difficult it is to find a person who can be trusted with one's affairs—that none of our company was able to utter a word: we could only weep as sadly as the victims, and go our ways in silence."

In order to illustrate his style in the proof section 26
also, I shall quote the sequel to the above passage.

τὰς μὲν οὖν ἰδίας πίστεις, ὡς οὐ πολλῶν ἔτι λόγων δεομένας, δι' αὐτῶν βεβαιοῦται τῶν μαρτύρων οὐδὲν ἕτερον ἢ τοῦτο εἰπών· "Πρῶτον μὲν οὖν τούτων ἀνάβητέ μοι μάρτυρες." τὰ δὲ τοῦ ἀντιδίκου δίκαια διχῇ νείμας, ὡς τὰ μὲν ὁμολογήσαντος αὐτοῦ λαβεῖν καὶ εἰς τὰς τροφὰς τῶν ὀρφανῶν ἀνηλωκέναι σκηψαμένου, τὰ δὲ ἐξάρνου γενηθέντος εἰληφέναι κἄπειτα ἐλεγχθέντος, ὑπὲρ ἀμφοτέρων ποιεῖται τὸν λόγον τὰς [δὲ] δαπάνας οὐχ ἃς ἐκεῖνος ἀπέφηνε γενέσθαι λέγων καὶ περὶ τῶν ἀμφιβόλων τὰς πίστεις ἀποδιδούς·

27 "Ἀξιῶ τοίνυν, ὦ ἄνδρες δικασταί, τῷ λογισμῷ προσέχειν τὸν νοῦν, ἵνα τοὺς μὲν νεανίσκους διὰ τὸ μέγεθος τῶν συμφορῶν ἐλεήσητε, τοῦτον δ' ἅπασι τοῖς πολίταις ἄξιον ὀργῆς ἡγήσησθε. εἰς τοσαύτην γὰρ ὑποψίαν Διογείτων πάντας ἀνθρώπους πρὸς ἀλλήλους καθίστησιν, ὥστε μήτε ζῶντας μήτε[1] ἀποθνήσκοντας μηδὲν μᾶλλον τοῖς οἰκειοτάτοις ἢ τοῖς ἐχθίστοις πιστεύειν· ὃς ἐτόλμησε τῶν μὲν ἔξαρνος γενέσθαι, τὰ δὲ τελευτῶν ὁμολογήσας ἔχειν[2] εἰς δύο παῖδας καὶ ἀδελφὴν λῆμμα καὶ ἀνάλωμα ἐν ὀκτὼ ἔτεσιν ἑπτὰ τάλαντα ἀργυρίου καὶ ἑπτακισχιλίας δραχμὰς ἀποδεῖξαι. καὶ εἰς τοῦτο ἦλθεν ἀναισχυντίας, ὥστε οὐκ ἔχων, ὅποι[3] τρέψειε τὰ χρήματα, εἰς ὄψον μὲν δυοῖν παιδίοιν καὶ ἀδελφῇ πέντε ὀβολοὺς τῆς ἡμέρας ἐλογίζετο, εἰς ὑποδήματα δὲ καὶ εἰς γναφεῖον ⟨καὶ εἰς⟩[4] ἱμάτια καὶ εἰς κουρέως κατὰ μῆνα οὐκ ἦν

[1] μήτε—μήτε Bekker: μηδὲ—μηδὲ codd.
[2] ἔχειν Reiske: ἑλεῖν codd.
[3] ὅποι τρέψειε Conte: ὅπου στρέψειε codd.

The evidence as to what was transacted in private among the parties requires little argument, so he establishes it by the words of the witnesses themselves, simply with the formula " First, will the witnesses come forward to confirm my statement." He then divides the opponent's case into two parts, his admission that he had received some of the money and his allegation that he had spent it on the children's upbringing, and his denial that he had received other monies, which was subsequently refuted. He examines both these lines of defence, saying that the defendant has misrepresented his expenditure, and furnishing proof of the discrepancy:

" Now, gentlemen of the jury, I ask you to pay due 27
attention to this calculation, in order that you may take pity on the young people for the magnitude of their misfortune, and may consider that this man deserves the anger of everyone in the city. For Diogeiton is rendering all men so suspicious towards their fellows that neither in life nor in death can they place any more confidence in their nearest relatives than in their bitterest enemies; since he has had the effrontery to deny one part of his debt and, after finally confessing the rest, to make out that he has received and spent a sum of seven talents of silver and seven thousand drachmae on the upbringing of two boys and their sister during eight years. So gross is his impudence that, not knowing under what heading to enter the sums spent, he reckoned for the young boys' and their sister's food five obols a day; for shoes, laundry and hairdressing he kept no monthly or yearly account, but he shows it as a lump sum, for

---

[4] καὶ εἰς addidit Frohberger.

αὐτῷ οὐδὲ κατ' ἐνιαυτὸν γεγραμμένα, συλλήβδην δὲ παντὸς τοῦ χρόνου πλεῖον ἢ τάλαντον ἀργυρίου. εἰς δὲ τὸ μνῆμα τοῦ πατρὸς οὐκ ἀναλώσας πέντε καὶ εἴκοσι μνᾶς ἐκ πεντακισχιλίων δραχμῶν, τὸ μὲν ἥμισυ αὐτῷ τίθησι τὸ δὲ τούτοις λελόγισται. εἰς Διονύσια τοίνυν, ὦ ἄνδρες δικασταί (οὐκ ἄτοπον γάρ μοι δοκεῖ καὶ περὶ τούτου μνησθῆναι), ἑκκαίδεκα δραχμῶν ἀπέφηνεν ἐωνημένον ἀρνίον καὶ τούτων τὰς ὀκτὼ δραχμὰς ἐλογίζετο τοῖς παισίν. ἐφ' ᾧ [1] ἡμεῖς οὐχ ἥκιστα ὠργίσθημεν. οὕτως, ὦ ἄνδρες, ἐν ταῖς μεγάλαις ζημίαις ἐνίοτε οὐχ ἧττον τὰ μικρὰ λυπεῖ τοὺς ἀδικουμένους· λίαν γὰρ φανερὰν τὴν πονηρίαν τῶν ἀδικούντων ἐπιδείκνυσιν. εἰς τοίνυν τὰς ἄλλας ἑορτὰς καὶ θυσίας ἐλογίσατο αὐτοῖς πλέον ἢ τετρακισχιλίας δραχμὰς ἀνηλωμένας ἕτερά τε παμπληθῆ, ἃ πρὸς τὸ κεφάλαιον συνελογίζετο· ὥσπερ διὰ τοῦτο ἐπίτροπος τῶν παιδίων καταλειφθείς, ἵνα γράμματ' αὐτοῖς ἀντὶ τῶν χρημάτων ἀποδείξειεν καὶ πενεστάτους ἀντὶ πλουσίων ἀποφήνειε καὶ ἵνα, εἰ μέν τις αὐτοῖς πατρικὸς ἐχθρὸς ἦν, ἐκείνου μὲν ἐπιλάθωνται, τῷ δ' ἐπιτρόπῳ [2] τῶν πατρῴων ἀπεστερημένοι πολεμῶσι. καίτοι εἰ ἠβούλετο δίκαιος εἶναι περὶ τοὺς παῖδας, ἐξῆν αὐτῷ κατὰ τοὺς νόμους, οἳ κεῖνται περὶ τῶν ὀρφανῶν καὶ τοῖς ἀδυνάτοις τῶν ἐπιτρόπων καὶ τοῖς δυναμένοις, μισθῶσαι τὸν οἶκον ἀπηλλαγμένον [3] πολλῶν πραγμάτων ἢ γῆν πριάμενον ἐκ τῶν προσιόντων τοὺς παῖδας τρέφειν, καὶ ὁπότερα τούτων ἐποίησεν,

[1] ἐφ' ᾧ Sylburg: ἐφ' ὧν codd.
[2] ἐπιτρόπῳ Frohberger: ἐπὶ codd.

the whole period, as more than a talent of silver. For their father's tomb, though he did not spend twenty-five minae of the five thousand drachmae shown, he charges half this sum to himself, and has entered half against them. Then for the Dionysia, gentlemen of the jury—and I do not think it irrelevant to mention this also—he showed sixteen drachmae as the price of a lamb, and charged eight of these drachmae to the children: this entry especially aroused our anger. And this is how it is, gentlemen: when there has been a heavy loss, the victims of injustice sometimes find small wrongs no less grievous than great ones, for these expose in so very clear a light the wickedness of the wrongdoer. Then for the other festivals and sacrifices he charged to their account an expenditure of more than four thousand drachmae; and he added a host of things which he included to make up his total, as though he had been named in the will as the guardian of the children merely in order that he might show them the figures instead of the money, and reduce them from wealth to utter poverty, and that they might forget whatever ancestral enemy they might have and wage war on their guardian for stripping them of their patrimony! And yet if he had wished to act justly by the children, he was free to act in accordance with the laws which deal with orphans for the guidance of incapable as well as capable guardians: he might have farmed out the estate and so got rid of a load of liabilities, or purchased land and used the income for the children's support; whichever course he had taken, they would

---

[3] *ἀπηλλαγμένον* Dobree: *ἀπηλλαγμένοις* codd.

οὐδενὸς ἂν ἧττον Ἀθηναίων πλούσιοι ἦσαν. νῦν δέ μοι δοκεῖ οὐδεπώποτε διανοηθῆναι ὡς φανερὰν καταστήσων τὴν οὐσίαν, ἀλλ' ὡς αὐτὸς ἕξων τὰ τούτων, ἡγούμενος δεῖν τὴν αὐτοῦ πονηρίαν κληρονόμον εἶναι τῶν τοῦ τεθνεῶτος χρημάτων. ὃ δὲ πάντων δεινότατον, ὦ ⟨ἄνδρες⟩ [1] δικασταί· οὗτος γὰρ συντριηραρχῶν Ἀλέξιδι τῷ Ἀριστοδίκου, φάσκων δυοῖν δεούσας πεντήκοντα μνᾶς ἐκείνῳ συμβάλλεσθαι, τὸ ἥμισυ τούτοις [2] ὀρφανοῖς οὖσι λελόγισται, οὓς ἡ πόλις οὐ μόνον παῖδας ὄντας ἀτελεῖς ἐποίησεν, ἀλλὰ καὶ ἐπειδὰν δοκιμασθῶσιν, ἐνιαυτὸν ἀφῆκεν ἁπασῶν τῶν λειτουργιῶν. οὗτος δὲ πάππος ὢν παρὰ τοὺς νόμους τῆς ἑαυτοῦ τριηραρχίας παρὰ τῶν θυγατριδῶν τὸ ἥμισυ πράττεται. καὶ ἀποπέμψας εἰς τὸν Ἀδρίαν ὁλκάδα δυοῖν ταλάντοιν, ὅτε μὲν ἀπέστελλεν, ἔλεγε πρὸς τὴν μητέρα αὐτῶν, ὅτι τῶν παίδων ὁ κίνδυνος εἴη. ἐπεὶ δὲ ἐσώθη καὶ ἐδιπλασίασεν, αὑτοῦ τὴν ἐμπορίαν φάσκει εἶναι. καίτοι εἰ μὲν τὰς ζημίας τούτων ἀποδείξει, τὰ δὲ σωθέντα τῶν χρημάτων αὐτὸς ἕξει, ὅποι μὲν ἀνήλωται τὰ χρήματα οὐ χαλεπῶς εἰς τὸν λόγον ἐγγράψει, ῥᾳδίως δὲ ἐκ τῶν ἀλλοτρίων αὐτὸς πλουτήσει. καθ' ἕκαστον μὲν οὖν, ὦ ⟨ἄνδρες⟩ δικασταί, πολὺ ἂν ἔργον εἴη πρὸς ὑμᾶς λογίζεσθαι. ἐπειδὴ δὲ μόλις παρ' αὐτοῦ παρέλαβον τὰ γράμματα, μάρτυρας ἔχων ἠρώτων Ἀριστόδικον τὸν ἀδελφὸν τὸν Ἀλέξιδος (αὐτὸς γὰρ ἐτύγχανε τετελευτηκώς), εἰ ὁ λόγος αὐτῷ εἴη τῆς τριηραρχίας. ὁ δὲ

[1] ἄνδρες inseruit Herwerden.

have been as rich as anyone in Athens. But the fact is, in my opinion, that at no time has he had any intention of turning their fortune into real estate, but has meant to keep their property for himself, assuming that his own wickedness should be the heir of the dead man's money. But the most monstrous thing of all, gentlemen of the jury, is his assertion that in sharing with Alexis, son of Aristodicus, the duty of equipping a trireme, he paid him a contribution of forty-eight minae, and has entered half of this against these orphan children, whom the state has not only exempted during their childhood, but has freed from all public services for a year after they have been certified to be of age. Yet their grandfather illegally exacts from his daughter's children one half of his expenses in equipping a trireme. Again, he despatched to the Adriatic a cargo valued at two talents, and told their mother, at the time of its departure, that it was sailing at the children's risk. But when it arrived safely and the value was doubled, he declared that the cargo was his. But if he is to lay the losses to their charge and keep the money from the preserved merchandise to himself, he will have no difficulty in making the account show on what the money has been spent, while he will find it easy to enrich himself from the money of others. To set the figures before you in detail, gentlemen of the jury, would be a lengthy task; but when with some difficulty I had extracted the balance-sheet from him, in the presence of witnesses I asked Aristodicus, brother of Alexis—the latter now being dead—whether he had the account for the equipment of the trireme. He told

[2] τούτοις Dobree: τούτων τοῖς codd.

ἔφασκεν εἶναι. καὶ ἐλθόντες οἴκαδε εὕρομεν Διογείτονα τέτταρας καὶ εἴκοσι μνᾶς ἐκείνῳ συμβεβλημένον εἰς τὴν τριηραρχίαν. οὗτος δὲ ἐπέδειξε δυοῖν δεούσας πεντήκοντα μνᾶς ἀνηλωκέναι· ὥστε τούτοις λελογίσθαι, ὅσον περ ὅλον τὸ ἀνάλωμα αὐτῷ γεγένηται. καίτοι τί αὐτὸν οἴεσθε πεποιηκέναι περὶ ὧν αὐτῷ οὐδεὶς σύνοιδεν, ἀλλ' αὐτὸς μόνος διεχείριζεν, ὅς, ἃ δι' ἑτέρων ἐπράχθη καὶ οὐ χαλεπὸν ἦν περὶ τούτων πυθέσθαι, ἐτόλμησε ψευσάμενος τέτταρσι καὶ εἴκοσι μναῖς τοὺς αὑτοῦ θυγατριδοῦς ζημιῶσαι; καί μοι ἀνάβητε τούτων μάρτυρες."—⟨μάρτυρες.⟩—"τῶν μὲν μαρτύρων ἀκηκόατε, ὦ ⟨ἄνδρες⟩ [1] δικασταί. ἐγὼ δ' ὅσα τελευτῶν ὡμολόγησεν ἔχειν αὐτὸς χρήματα, ἑπτὰ τάλαντα καὶ τετταράκοντα μνᾶς, ἐκ τούτων αὐτῷ λογιοῦμαι πρόσοδον μὲν οὐδεμίαν ἀποφαίνων, ἀπὸ δὲ τῶν ὑπαρχόντων ἀναλίσκων, καὶ θήσω, ὅσον οὐδεὶς πώποτ' ἐν τῇ πόλει, εἰς δύο παῖδας καὶ ἀδελφὴν καὶ παιδαγωγὸν καὶ θεράπαιναν χιλίας δραχμὰς ἑκάστου ἐνιαυτοῦ, μικρῷ ἔλαττον ἢ τρεῖς δραχμὰς τῆς ἡμέρας. ἐν ὀκτὼ αὗται ἔτεσιν γίγνονται ὀκτακισχίλιαι δραχμαί . . . ἓξ τάλαντα περιόντα τῶν ἑπτὰ ταλάντων, καὶ εἴκοσι μναῖ ⟨τῶν τετταράκοντα μνῶν⟩. [2] οὐ γὰρ ἂν δύναιτο ἀποδεῖξαι οὔθ' ὑπὸ λῃστῶν ἀπολωλεκὼς οὔτε ζημίαν εἰληφὼς οὔτε χρήσταις ἀποδεδωκώς." . . .

28 ἐν μὲν δὴ τοῖς δικανικοῖς λόγοις ⟨τοιοῦτός τις ὁ ἀνήρ ἐστιν, ἐν δὲ τοῖς ἐπιδεικτικοῖς⟩ [3] μαλακώτερος, ὥσπερ ἔφην. βούλεται μὲν γὰρ ὑψηλότερος

[1] ἄνδρες inseruit Herwerden.
[2] τῶν τετταράκοντα μνῶν addidit Markland.

me that he had, and we went to his house and found that Diogeiton had paid Alexis a contribution of twenty-four minae towards equipping a trireme. But the expenditure that he showed was forty-eight minae, so that the children have been charged exactly the total of what he has spent. Now, what do you think he has done in cases which nobody else knew about, but he managed the transactions alone, when in those which were conducted through others and of which information could easily be obtained he did not shrink from falsehood in mulcting his own daughter's children to an amount of twenty-four minae? Will the witnesses come forward to confirm my statement?

WITNESSES

You have heard the witnesses, gentlemen of the jury. I shall now base my reckoning against him on the sum which he eventually confessed to holding—seven talents and forty minae. Not counting in any income, I shall stipulate, as spent out of capital, a larger amount than anyone in the city has ever spent —for two boys and their sister, an attendant and a maid, a thousand drachmae a year, a little less than three drachmae a day. For eight years, that amounts to eight thousand drachmae; and we can show a balance of six talents and twenty minae. He will not be able to show that he has either suffered losses through piracy or met with failure or paid off debts. . . ."

Such are Lysias's qualities as a forensic orator. In 28
ceremonial oratory he is less forceful, as I have said. For he tries to be more lofty and impressive, and

[3] lacunam supplevit Krüger.

εἶναι καὶ μεγαλοπρεπέστερος καὶ τῶν γε καθ' ἑαυτὸν ἢ πρότερον ῥητόρων ἀκμασάντων οὐθενὸς ἂν δόξειεν εἶναι καταδεέστερος, οὐ διεγείρει δὲ τὸν ἀκροατὴν ὥσπερ Ἰσοκράτης ἢ Δημοσθένης. θήσω δὲ καὶ τούτων παράδειγμα.

29 ἔστι δή τις αὐτῷ πανηγυρικὸς λόγος, ἐν ᾧ πείθει τοὺς Ἕλληνας ἀγομένης Ὀλυμπίασι τῆς πανηγύρεως ἐκβάλλειν Διονύσιον τὸν τύραννον ἐκ τῆς ἀρχῆς καὶ Σικελίαν ἐλευθερῶσαι ἄρξασθαί τε τῆς ἔχθρας αὐτίκα μάλα, διαρπάσαντας τὴν τοῦ τυράννου σκηνὴν χρυσῷ τε καὶ πορφύρᾳ καὶ ἄλλῳ πλούτῳ πολλῷ κεκοσμημένην. ἔπεμψε γὰρ δὴ θεωροὺς εἰς τὴν πανήγυριν ὁ Διονύσιος ἄγοντας θυσίαν τῷ θεῷ, μεγαλοπρεπής τε καταγωγὴ τῶν θεωρῶν ἐγένετο ἐν τῷ τεμένει καὶ πολυτελής, ἵνα θαυμασθείη μᾶλλον ὁ τύραννος ὑπὸ τῆς Ἑλλάδος. ταύτην λαβὼν τὴν ὑπόθεσιν τοιαύτην πεποίηται τὴν ἀρχὴν τοῦ λόγου·

30 "Ἄλλων τε πολλῶν καὶ καλῶν ἔργων ἕνεκα, ὦ ἄνδρες, ἄξιον Ἡρακλέους μεμνῆσθαι καὶ ὅτι τόνδε τὸν ἀγῶνα πρῶτος συνήγειρε δι' εὔνοιαν τῆς Ἑλλάδος. ἐν μὲν γὰρ τῷ τέως χρόνῳ ἀλλοτρίως αἱ πόλεις πρὸς ἀλλήλας διέκειντο, ἐπειδὴ δὲ ἐκεῖνος τοὺς τυράννους ἔπαυσε καὶ τοὺς ὑβρίζοντας ἐκώλυσεν, ἀγῶνα μὲν σωμάτων ἐποίησε, φιλοτιμίαν ⟨δὲ⟩ πλούτῳ, γνώμης δ' ἐπίδειξιν ἐν τῷ καλλίστῳ τῆς Ἑλλάδος, ἵνα τούτων ἁπάντων ἕνεκα εἰς τὸ αὐτὸ συνέλθωμεν, τὰ μὲν ὀψόμενοι, τὰ δ' ἀκουσόμενοι. ἡγήσατο γὰρ τὸν ἐνθάδε σύλλογον ἀρχὴν γενήσεσθαι [1] τοῖς Ἕλλησι τῆς πρὸς ἀλλήλους φιλίας. ἐκεῖνος μὲν οὖν ταῦθ' ὑφηγήσατο. ἐγὼ

indeed he should probably not be considered inferior to any of his predecessors or contemporaries; but he does not arouse his audience as powerfully as Isocrates and Demosthenes do theirs. I shall give an example of his ceremonial oratory.

There is a festival speech of his, in which he 29
addresses the Greeks at the Olympic games,[1] and exhorts them to cast the tyrant Dionysius from his throne and free Sicily, starting their mission of hatred there and then by despoiling the royal tent of its gold, its purple finery and its many other riches. Dionysius had actually sent delegates to attend the festival and to make offerings to the god. Their arrival in the temple precinct had been staged on an impressive and lavish scale in order to enhance the tyrant's reputation among the Greeks. It was against this background that Lysias began his speech in the following words:

"Among many noble deeds, gentlemen, for which 30
Heracles deserves to be remembered, we ought to recall the fact that he was the first to convene this contest, because he felt affection for the Greeks. Before that time the cities were estranged from one another; but he, when he had crushed the tyrants and put a stop to outrage, founded a contest of physical strength, a challenge of wealth, and a display of intelligence in the fairest part of Greece, so that we might come together in the same place for all these enjoyments, to see some and to hear others; for he thought that our meeting here would be the beginning of mutual friendship among the Greeks. His,

[1] Oration 33 (O.C.T.). 384 B.C. Dionysius I was tyrant 405–367 B.C. Dionysius is the sole source for this speech.

---

[1] γενήσεσθαι Markland: γενέσθαι codd.

δὲ ἥκω οὐ μικρολογησόμενος οὐδὲ περὶ τῶν ὀνομάτων μαχούμενος· ἡγοῦμαι γὰρ ταῦτα ἔργα μὲν εἶναι σοφιστῶν [1] λίαν ἀχρήστων [2] καὶ σφόδρα βίου δεομένων, ἀνδρὸς δὲ ἀγαθοῦ καὶ πολίτου πολλοῦ ἀξίου περὶ τῶν μεγίστων συμβουλεύειν, ὁρῶν οὕτως αἰσχρῶς διακειμένην τὴν Ἑλλάδα καὶ πολλὰ μὲν αὐτῆς ὄντα ὑπὸ τῷ βαρβάρῳ, πολλὰς δὲ πόλεις ὑπὸ τυράννων ἀναστάτους γεγενημένας. καὶ ταῦτα εἰ μὲν δι' ἀσθένειαν ἐπάσχομεν, στέργειν ἂν ἦν ἀνάγκη τὴν τύχην, ἐπειδὴ δὲ διὰ στάσιν καὶ τὴν πρὸς ἀλλήλους φιλονεικίαν, πῶς οὐκ ἄξιον τῶν μὲν παύσασθαι, τὰ δὲ κωλῦσαι, εἰδότας ὅτι φιλονεικεῖν μέν ἐστιν εὖ πραττόντων, γνῶναι δὲ τὰ βέλτιστ' ἀγωνιώντων; ὁρῶμεν γὰρ τοὺς κινδύνους καὶ μεγάλους καὶ πανταχόθεν περιεστηκότας. ἐπίστασθε δὲ ὅτι ἡ μὲν ἀρχὴ τῶν κρατούντων τῆς θαλάττης, τῶν δὲ χρημάτων βασιλεὺς ταμίας, τὰ δὲ τῶν Ἑλλήνων σώματα τῶν δαπανᾶσθαι δυναμένων, ναῦς δὲ πολλὰς αὐτὸς κέκτηται, πολλὰς δ' ὁ τύραννος τῆς Σικελίας. ὥστε ἄξιον τὸν μὲν πρὸς ἀλλήλους πόλεμον καταθέσθαι, τῇ δ' αὐτῇ γνώμῃ χρωμένους τῆς σωτηρίας ἀντέχεσθαι καὶ περὶ μὲν τῶν παρεληλυθότων αἰσχύνεσθαι, περὶ δὲ τῶν μελλόντων ἔσεσθαι δεδιέναι καὶ πρὸς τοὺς προγόνους μιμεῖσθαι, οἳ τοὺς μὲν βαρβάρους ἐποίησαν τῆς ἀλλοτρίας ἐπιθυμοῦντας τῆς σφετέρας αὐτῶν στερεῖσθαι, τοὺς δὲ τυράννους ἐξελάσαντες κοινὴν ἅπασι τὴν ἐλευθερίαν κατέστησαν. θαυμάζω δὲ Λακεδαιμονίους πάντων μάλιστα, τίνι ποτὲ γνώμῃ χρώμενοι καιομένην τὴν "Ἑλλάδα περιορῶσιν

then was the original idea; and so I have not come here to talk trivialities or to indulge in verbal wrangling. I take that to be the business of utterly futile sophists who are living on their last mite; but I think that a worthy man and a good citizen ought to be giving counsel on the most important questions, when I see Greece in this shameful plight, with many parts of her held in subjection by the barbarian, and many of her cities ravaged by tyrants. Now if these troubles were due to weakness, it would be necessary to accept our fate: but since they are due to faction and mutual rivalry, surely we ought to desist from the one and put a stop to the other, realising that if rivalry befits the prosperous, the most prudent counsels befit those suffering misfortune. For we see both the gravity of our dangers and their imminence on every side: you know that empire belongs to those who command the sea, that the Persian King has control of the money, that Greek manpower is for sale to those who can pay for it, that the King has many ships and that the tyrant of Sicily has many also. We should therefore abandon our internecine war, and with a single aim in our minds secure our safety; to feel shame for past events and fear for those that lie in the future, and to compete with our ancestors, who caused the foreigner to be deprived of his own land when he grasped at the land of others, and who expelled the tyrants and established freedom for all alike. But I am surprised most of all at the Lacedaemonians: what can be their purpose in allowing Greece to be devastated, when they are leaders of the

[1] σοφιστῶν Markland: σοφὰ τῶν codd.
[2] ἀχρήστων Markland: χρηστῶν codd.

ἡγεμόνες ὄντες τῶν Ἑλλήνων οὐκ ἀδίκως καὶ διὰ τὴν ἔμφυτον ἀρετὴν καὶ διὰ τὴν περὶ [1] τὸν πόλεμον ἐπιστήμην, μόνοι δὲ οἰκοῦντες ἀπόρθητοι καὶ ἀτείχιστοι καὶ ἀστασίαστοι καὶ ἀήττητοι καὶ τρόποις [2] ἀεὶ τοῖς αὐτοῖς χρώμενοι· ὧν ἕνεκα ἐλπὶς ἀθάνατον τὴν ἐλευθερίαν αὐτοὺς κεκτῆσθαι καὶ ἐν τοῖς παρεληλυθόσι κινδύνοις σωτῆρας γενομένους τῆς Ἑλλάδος περὶ τῶν μελλόντων προορᾶσθαι. οὐ τοίνυν ὁ ἐπιὼν καιρὸς τοῦ παρόντος βελτίων· οὐ γὰρ ἀλλοτρίας δεῖ τὰς τῶν ἀπολωλότων συμφορὰς νομίζειν ἀλλ' οἰκείας, οὐδ' ἀναμεῖναι, ἕως ἂν ἐπ' αὐτοὺς ἡμᾶς αἱ δυνάμεις ἀμφοτέρων ἔλθωσιν, ἀλλ' ἕως ἔτι ἔξεστι, τὴν τούτων ὕβριν κωλῦσαι. τίς γὰρ οὐκ ἂν ⟨ἀγανακτήσει⟩εν [3] ὁρῶν ἐν τῷ πρὸς ἀλλήλους πολέμῳ μεγάλους αὐτοὺς γεγενημένους; ὧν οὐ μόνον αἰσχρῶν ὄντων ἀλλὰ καὶ δεινῶν τοῖς μὲν μεγάλα ἡμαρτηκόσιν ἐξουσία γεγένηται τῶν πεπραγμένων, τοῖς δὲ Ἕλλησιν οὐδεμία αὐτῶν τιμωρία."

31 ἑνὸς ἔτι παράδειγμα θήσω λόγου συμβουλευτικοῦ, ἵνα καὶ τούτου τοῦ γένους τῶν λόγων [4] ὁ χαρακτὴρ γένηται σαφής.

32 ὑπόθεσιν δὲ περιείληφε τὴν περὶ τοῦ μὴ καταλῦσαι τὴν πάτριον πολιτείαν Ἀθήνησι. τοῦ γὰρ δήμου κατελθόντος ἐκ Πειραιῶς καὶ ψηφισαμένου διαλύσασθαι πρὸς τοὺς ἐν ἄστει καὶ μηδενὸς τῶν γενομένων μνησικακεῖν, δέους δὲ ὄντος μὴ πάλιν τὸ πλῆθος ἐς τοὺς εὐπόρους

[1] *περὶ* Fuhr: *πρὸς* codd.
[2] *τρόποις* Markland: *τόποις* codd.
[3] Hiatum indicavit et supplevit Baiter.

Greeks by the just claims both of their inborn valour and of their knowledge of war, and when they alone have their homes unravaged, their cities unwalled and live free from civil strife and defeat in war, always maintaining the same institutions. This would lead to the expectation that the liberty which they possess will never die, and that having been the saviours of Greece in her past dangers they are providing against those that are to come. Now the future will bring no better opportunity than the present. We ought to view the misfortunes of those who have been ruined not as the concern of others, but as our own. Let us not wait for the forces of both our enemies to advance upon us, but while there is still time let us curb their arrogance. For who would not be angered to see how strong they have grown through our internecine warfare? Those quarrels, which are not only shameful but dangerous, have enabled those who have wronged us grievously to do what they have done, and have prevented the Greeks from taking revenge for their crimes. . . ."

I shall give one further example, this time from a 31
deliberative speech, in order to illustrate clearly his characteristic style in this kind of oratory also.

He has taken as his subject the proposition that the 32
ancestral constitution at Athens should not be abolished. The democrats have returned from the Piraeus and voted for reconciliation with the party of the city and a general amnesty.[1] But there was some fear that, when the people had recovered their

[1] 403 B.C.

---

[4] τῶν λόγων Usener: τοῦ λόγου codd.

ὑβρίζῃ τὴν ἀρχαίαν ἐξουσίαν κεκομισμένον καὶ πολλῶν ὑπὲρ τούτου γινομένων λόγων Φορμίσιός τις τῶν συγκατελθόντων μετὰ τοῦ δήμου γνώμην εἰσηγήσατο τοὺς μὲν φεύγοντας κατιέναι, τὴν δὲ πολιτείαν μὴ πᾶσιν, ἀλλὰ τοῖς [τὴν] [1] γῆν ἔχουσι παραδοῦναι, βουλομένων ταῦτα γενέσθαι καὶ Λακεδαιμονίων. ἔμελλον δὲ τοῦ ψηφίσματος τούτου κυρωθέντος πεντακισχίλιοι σχεδὸν Ἀθηναίων ἀπελαθήσεσθαι τῶν κοινῶν. ἵνα δὴ μὴ τοῦτο γένοιτο, γράφει τὸν λόγον τόνδε ὁ Λυσίας τῶν ἐπισήμων τινὶ καὶ πολιτευομένων. εἰ μὲν οὖν ἐρρήθη τότε, ἄδηλον· σύγκειται γοῦν ὡς πρὸς ἀγῶνα ἐπιτηδείως. ἔστι δὲ ὅδε·

33 "Ὅτε ἐνομίζομεν, ὦ ⟨ἄνδρες⟩ [2] Ἀθηναῖοι, τὰς γεγενημένας συμφορὰς ἱκανὰ μνημεῖα τῇ πόλει καταλελεῖφθαι, ὥστε μηδ᾽ ἂν τοὺς ἐπιγινομένους ἑτέρας πολιτείας ἐπιθυμεῖν, τότε δὴ οὗτοι τοὺς κακῶς πεπονθότας καὶ ἀμφοτέρων πεπειραμένους ἐξαπατῆσαι ζητοῦσι τοῖς αὐτοῖς ψηφίσμασιν, οἷσπερ καὶ πρότερον δὶς ἤδη. καὶ [3] τούτων μὲν οὐ θαυμάζω, ὑμῶν δὲ τῶν ἀκροωμένων, ὅτι πάντων ἐστὲ [4] ἐπιλησμονέστατοι ἢ πάσχειν ἑτοιμότατοι κακῶς ὑπὸ τοιούτων ἀνδρῶν, οἳ τῇ μὲν τύχῃ τῶν Πειραιεῖ πραγμάτων μετέσχον, τῇ δὲ γνώμῃ τῶν ἐξ ἄστεως. καίτοι τί ἔδει φεύγοντας κατελθεῖν, εἰ χειροτονοῦντες ὑμᾶς αὐτοὺς καταδουλώσεσθε; ἐγὼ μὲν οὖν, ὦ ἄνδρες Ἀθηναῖοι, ⟨οὔτε οὐσίᾳ τῆς πολιτείας⟩ [5] οὔτε γένει ἀπελαυνόμενος,

[1] τὴν seclusit Baiter.
[2] ἄνδρες inseruit Usener.
[3] δὶς ἤδη. καὶ Dobree: διὸ δὴ καὶ codd.

former power, they might do violence to the wealthy citizens. During much discussion of the problem, Phormisius, one of the restored democrats, advocated the recall of exiles and the conferment of citizenship not upon all, but only upon the owners of land, a proposal which also met with Spartan approval. But if this proposal had passed into law almost five thousand Athenians would have been disenfranchised. It was in order to prevent this from happening that Lysias wrote this speech for one of the prominent politicians. It is unknown whether it was ever delivered: at all events, it is composed in a suitable style for an actual debate. Here it is:[1]

"When we were actually thinking, men of Athens, that the disasters that have befallen the city have left behind them sufficient reminders to her to prevent even our descendants from desiring a change of constitution, these men are seeking to deceive us, after our dreadful sufferings and our experience of both systems, with the very same proposals as those with which they tricked us twice before. They do not surprise me, but you do when you listen to them: you are either the most forgetful of mankind, or else the readiest to suffer injury from such men as these; for they shared by mere chance in the operations at the Piraeus, when their feelings were with the party of the city. What, I ask you, was your purpose in returning from exile, if by your votes you are going to enslave yourselves? Now I, men of Athens, do not face disenfranchisement either for reasons of

[1] Oration 34 (O.C.T.), from Dionysius.

---

[4] ἐστὲ Taylor: εἰσὶν codd.
[5] οὔτε οὐσίᾳ τῆς πολιτείας supplevit Usener.

ἀλλ᾽ ἀμφότερα τῶν ἀντιλεγόντων πρότερος ὧν ἡγοῦμαι ταύτην μόνην σωτηρίαν εἶναι τῇ πόλει, ἅπασιν Ἀθηναίοις τῆς πολιτείας μετεῖναι· ἐπεὶ ὅτε καὶ τὰ τείχη καὶ τὰς ναῦς καὶ τὰ χρήματα καὶ συμμάχους ἐκτησάμεθα, οὐχ ὅπως [1] τινὰ Ἀθηναῖον ἀπώσομεν [2] διενοούμεθα, ἀλλὰ καὶ Εὐβοεῦσιν ἐπιγαμίαν ἐποιούμεθα· νῦν δὲ καὶ τοὺς ὑπάρχοντας πολίτας ἀπελῶμεν; [3] οὔκ, ἂν ἔμοιγε πείθησθε, οὐδὲ μετὰ τῶν τειχῶν καὶ ταῦτα ἡμῶν αὐτῶν περιαιρησόμεθα, ὁπλίτας πολλοὺς καὶ ἱππέας καὶ τοξότας· ὧν ὑμεῖς ἀντεχόμενοι βεβαίως δημοκρατήσεσθε, τῶν δὲ ἐχθρῶν πλέον ἐπικρατήσετε, ὠφελιμώτεροι δὲ τοῖς συμμάχοις ἔσεσθε. ἐπίστασθε γὰρ ταῖς ἐφ᾽ ἡμῶν ὀλιγαρχίαις γεγενημέναις [καὶ] [4] οὐ τοὺς γῆν κεκτημένους ἔχοντας τὴν πόλιν, ἀλλὰ πολλοὺς μὲν αὐτῶν ἀποθανόντας, πολλοὺς δ᾽ ἐκ τῆς πόλεως ἐκπεσόντας· οὓς ὁ δῆμος καταγαγὼν ὑμῖν μὲν τὴν ὑμετέραν ἀπέδωκεν, αὐτὸς δὲ ταύτης οὐκ ἐτόλμησε μετασχεῖν. ὥστ᾽ ἐὰν [5] ἔμοιγε πείθησθε, οὐ τοὺς εὐεργέτας, καθὸ δύνασθε, τῆς πατρίδος ἀποστερήσετε οὐδὲ τοὺς λόγους πιστοτέρους τῶν ἔργων οὐδὲ τὰ μέλλοντα τῶν γεγενημένων νομιεῖτε ἄλλως τε καὶ μεμνημένοι τῶν περὶ τῆς ὀλιγαρχίας μαχομένων, οἳ τῷ μὲν λόγῳ τῷ δήμῳ πολεμοῦσι, τῷ δὲ ἔργῳ τῶν ὑμετέρων ἐπιθυμοῦσιν, ἅπερ κτήσονται,[6] ὅταν ὑμᾶς ἐρήμους συμμάχων λάβωσιν, εἶτα τοιούτων [7]

[1] ὅπως H. Stephanus: οὕτως codd.
[2] ἀπώσομεν Baiter: ποιήσωμεν codd.
[3] ἀπελῶμεν Bekker: ἀπολοῦμεν codd.
[4] καὶ seclusi.

wealth or birth, but in both respects I have the advantage of my opponents; and I consider that the only hope of salvation for the city lies in allowing all Athenians to share the citizenship. For when we possessed our walls, our ships, our money and our allies, far from proposing to exclude any Athenian, we actually granted the right of marriage to the Euboeans. Shall we today exclude even our present citizens? Not if you accept my advice; nor, after losing our walls, shall we denude ourselves of our forces—large numbers of our infantry, our cavalry and our archers—for if you hold fast to these you will make your democracy secure, you will increase your superiority over your enemies, and will be more useful to your allies. You are well aware that in the previous oligarchies of our time it was not the owners of land who controlled the city: many of them were put to death, and many were expelled from the city; and the people, after recalling them, restored your city to you, but did not dare to share in its administration themselves. Thus, if you take my advice, you will not be depriving your benefactors of their native land, as far as you are able, nor be placing more confidence in words than in deeds, in the future than in the past, especially if you remember the champions of oligarchy, who in speech make war upon the people, but in fact are aiming at your property; and this they will acquire when they catch you without allies. And then they ask us, when we are in this plight, what

---

[5] *ὥστε ἐὰν* Usener: *ὥστε ἂν* codd.
[6] *ἅπερ κτήσονται* H. Stephanus: *ἀποκτήσονται* codd.
[7] *τοιούτων* Baiter: *τοῖς τῶν* codd.

ἡμῖν ὑπαρχόντων ἐροῦσι,[1] τίς ἔσται σωτηρία τῇ πόλει, εἰ μὴ ποιήσομεν, ἃ Λακεδαιμόνιοι κελεύουσιν; ἐγὼ δὲ τούτους εἰπεῖν ἀξιῶ, τίς τῷ πλήθει περιγενήσεται, εἰ ποιήσομεν, ἃ ἐκεῖνοι προστάττουσιν; εἰ δὲ μή, πολὺ κάλλιον μαχομένοις[2] ἀποθνήσκειν ἢ φανερῶς ἡμῶν αὐτῶν θάνατον καταψηφίσασθαι. ἡγοῦμαι γάρ, ἐὰν μὲν πείσω,[3] ἀμφοτέροις εἶναι κοινὸν ⟨τὸν⟩ κίνδυνον . . . ὁρῶ δὲ καὶ Ἀργείους καὶ Μαντινέας τὴν αὐτὴν ἔχοντας γνώμην τὴν αὐτῶν οἰκοῦντας, τοὺς μὲν ὁμόρους ὄντας Λακεδαιμονίοις, τοὺς δ' ἐγγὺς οἰκοῦντας, καὶ τοὺς μὲν οὐδὲν ἡμῶν πλείους, τοὺς δὲ οὐδὲ τρισχιλίους ὄντας. ἴσασι γὰρ ⟨Λακεδαιμόνιοι⟩[4] ὅτι, κἂν πολλάκις εἰς τὴν τούτων ἐμβάλωσι, πολλάκις αὐτοῖς ἀπαντήσονται ὅπλα λαβόντες, ὥστε οὐ καλὸς αὐτοῖς ὁ κίνδυνος δοκεῖ εἶναι, ἐὰν μὲν νικήσωσι, τούτους ⟨οὐδὲ⟩[5] καταδουλώσασθαί[6] γ', ἐὰν[7] δὲ ἡττηθῶσι, σφᾶς αὐτοὺς τῶν ὑπαρχόντων ἀγαθῶν ἀποστερῆσαι. ὅσῳ δ' ἂν ἄμεινον πράττωσι, τοσούτῳ ⟨ἧττον⟩[8] ἐπιθυμοῦσι κινδυνεύειν. εἴχομεν δέ, ὦ ἄνδρες Ἀθηναῖοι, καὶ ἡμεῖς ταύτην τὴν γνώμην, ὅτε τῶν Ἑλλήνων ἤρχομεν, καὶ ἐδοκοῦμεν καλῶς βουλεύεσθαι, περιορῶντες μὲν τὴν χώραν τεμνομένην, οὐ νομίζοντες δὲ χρῆναι περὶ αὐτῆς διαμάχεσθαι. ἄξιον γὰρ ἦν ὀλίγων ἀμελοῦντας πολλῶν ἀγαθῶν φείσασθαι. νῦν δὲ ἐπεὶ ἐκείνων μὲν ἁπάντων μάχῃ ἐστερήμεθα, ἡ δὲ πατρὶς ἡμῖν λέγειπται, ἴσμεν ὅτι ὁ κίνδυνος

[1] ἐροῦσι Desrousseaux: ἐρῶσι codd.
[2] μαχομένοις Usener: μαχόμενοι codd.
[3] πείσω Usener: πείθω codd.

salvation there can be for the city, unless we do what the Lacedaemonians demand. But I call upon them to tell us, what will be left for the people if we obey their orders? If we do not, it will be far nobler to die fighting than to pass a clear sentence of death upon ourselves; for I believe that if I can persuade you, the danger will be common to both sides. . . . And I observe the same attitude in both the Argives and the Mantineans, each inhabiting their own land—the former bordering on the Lacedaemonians, the latter dwelling near them; in the one case, their number is no greater than ours, in the other it is less than three thousand. The Lacedaemonians know that however often they may invade the territories of these people, they will always march out to oppose them under arms. Hence they see no glory in the venture: if they should win, they could not enslave them, and if they should lose, they must deprive themselves of the advantages that they already possess. The more they prosper, the less is their appetite for risk. We also, men of Athens, held this opinion, when we ruled over the Greeks; and we thought it a wise course to allow our land to be ravaged without feeling obliged to fight in its defence, because our interest lay in neglecting a few things in order to preserve many advantages. But today, when the fortune of battle has deprived us of all these things, and our country is all that we have left, we know that this enterprise is

---

4 Λακεδαιμόνιοι inseruit Usener.
5 οὐδὲ inseruit Usener.
6 καταδουλώσασθαι Sylburg: καταδουλώσεσθαι codd.
7 γ' ἐὰν Usener: γε ἂν codd.
8 ἧττον inseruit Reiske.

οὗτος μόνος ἔχει τὰς ἐλπίδας τῆς σωτηρίας. ἀλλὰ γὰρ χρὴ ἀναμνησθέντας, ὅτι ἤδη καὶ ἑτέροις ἀδικουμένοις βοηθήσαντες ἐν τῇ ἀλλοτρίᾳ πολλὰ τρόπαια τῶν πολεμίων ἐστήσαμεν, ἄνδρας ἀγαθοὺς περὶ τῆς πατρίδος καὶ ἡμῶν αὐτῶν γίγνεσθαι, πιστεύοντας μὲν τοῖς θεοῖς καὶ ἐλπίζοντας ἐπὶ τὸ δίκαιον μετὰ τῶν ἀδικουμένων ἔσεσθαι· δεινὸν γὰρ ἂν εἴη, ὦ ἄνδρες Ἀθηναῖοι, εἰ, ὅτε μὲν ἐφεύγομεν, ἐμαχόμεθα Λακεδαιμονίοις, ἵνα κατέλθωμεν, κατελθόντες δὲ φευξόμεθα, ἵνα μὴ μαχώμεθα. οὐκοῦν αἰσχρόν, εἰ εἰς τοῦτο κακίας ἥξομεν, ὥστε οἱ μὲν πρόγονοι καὶ ὑπὲρ τῆς τῶν ἄλλων ἐλευθερίας διεκινδύνευον, ὑμεῖς δὲ οὐδὲ ὑπὲρ τῆς ὑμετέρας αὐτῶν τολμᾶτε πολεμεῖν;"

34 ἀλλ' ἅλις ἤδη παραδειγμάτων, ἵνα καὶ περὶ τῶν λοιπῶν ῥητόρων τὸν αὐτὸν διαλεχθῶμεν τρόπον. ἕπεται δὲ τῷ ῥήτορι τούτῳ κατὰ τὴν τάξιν τῶν χρόνων Ἰσοκράτης. περὶ δὴ τούτου λεκτέον ἐφεξῆς ἑτέραν ἀρχὴν λαβοῦσιν.

the only thing that holds out hopes of salvation for us. But surely we ought to remember that on previous occasions we have gone to the aid of other victims of injustice and set up many trophies over our enemies on alien soil. So now we ought to act as valiant defenders of our country and of ourselves. Let us trust in the gods, and hope that they will stand for justice on the side of the injured. It would indeed be terrible, men of Athens, if after fighting the Lacedaemonians during our exile in order to return, we should go into exile after our return in order to avoid fighting. And will it not be disgraceful if we sink to such a depth of baseness that, whereas our ancestors risked everything for the freedom of their neighbours, you do not even dare to make war for your own . . .?

We now have enough examples, if I am to discuss 34
the remaining orators on the same scale. The one who follows Lysias in chronological order is Isocrates. I must make a fresh start and consider him next.

ISOCRATES

INTRODUCTION

The *Lysias* concludes with three illustrative passages on which no comment is made. The discourses of Isocrates receive analytical treatment because their subject-matter has a special interest for Dionysius.[1] The biographical introduction is correspondingly fuller than that of the *Lysias*, and in it allusions are made to passages in the discourses which state Isocrates's aims in his own words, thus implying Dionysius's approval of them. Not only does the essay end with continuous illustrative passages, but also parts of the *Panegyricus*, *Philippus*, *On the Peace*, *Areopagiticus* and *Antidosis* are summarised and praised for their noble sentiments. In both choice and handling of subject-matter he is judged to be Lysias's superior, the former being dictated by his "philosophic purpose."[2]

Isocrates's style also receives a more analytical treatment than that of Lysias. Although only four chapters are devoted to style, chs. 2–3 and 13–14, the

[1] See *General Introduction* pp. xvi–xvii. For the subject of the influence of Isocrates on Dionysius, see H. M. Hubbell, *The Influence of Isocrates on Cicero, Dionysius and Aristides*. Yale, 1913, pp. 41–53.

[2] ch. 12.

latter chapter contains a critical analysis of the stylistic defects of a passage of the *Panegyricus* (75ff.). Dionysius disapproves of the excessive elaboration and artificiality of Isocrates's periodic style, and his addiction to parallelism and assonance. These faults deprive his style of some of the emotional power with which his noble themes might have been treated, and render his discourses more suitable for private reading than for declamation.[1] These criticisms of Isocrates are not original, as Dionysius admits,[2] but the critical analysis has no known antecedents. In spite of it, however, and of the resultant overall impression of a balanced and judicious critique of the author, Dionysius's enthusiasm for Isocrates's ideals has resulted in a less complete picture of Isocrates's style than is found in the *Lysias*. The *Isocrates* is chiefly important for the fact that it contains the first example of the technique of critical analysis which pervades Dionysius's later works; but for a more balanced estimate of Isocrates's style we must turn to the *Demosthenes*.

[1] ch. 2.
[2] ch. 13.

ΙΣΟΚΡΑΤΗΣ ΑΘΗΝΑΙΟΣ

1 Ἰσοκράτης Ἀθηναῖος ἐγεννήθη μὲν ἐπὶ τῆς ὀγδοηκοστῆς καὶ ἕκτης Ὀλυμπιάδος ἄρχοντος Ἀθήνησι Λυσιμάχου πέμπτῳ πρότερον ἔτει τοῦ Πελοποννησιακοῦ πολέμου, δυσὶ καὶ εἴκοσιν ἔτεσι νεώτερος Λυσίου, πατρὸς δὲ ἦν Θεοδώρου, τινὸς τῶν μετρίων πολιτῶν, θεράποντας αὐλοποιοὺς κεκτημένου καὶ τὸν βίον ἀπὸ ταύτης ἔχοντος τῆς ἐργασίας. ἀγωγῆς δὲ τυχὼν εὐσχήμονος καὶ παιδευθεὶς οὐδενὸς Ἀθηναίων χεῖρον, ἐπειδὴ τάχιστα ἀνὴρ ἐγένετο, φιλοσοφίας ἐπεθύμησε. γενόμενος δὲ ἀκουστὴς Προδίκου τε τοῦ Κείου καὶ Γοργίου τοῦ Λεοντίνου καὶ Τισίου τοῦ Συρακουσίου, τῶν τότε μέγιστον ὄνομα ἐν τοῖς Ἕλλησιν ἐχόντων ἐπὶ σοφίᾳ, ὡς δέ τινες ἱστοροῦσι, καὶ Θηραμένους τοῦ ῥήτορος, ὃν οἱ τριάκοντα ἀπέκτειναν δημοτικὸν εἶναι δοκοῦντα, σπουδὴν

---

[1] 436–435 B.C. Cf. [Plutarch] *Lives of the Ten Orators*, 837F.

[2] A sophist of the generation immediately following Protagoras, he may have been one of those chiefly responsible for the standardisation and precision of the language of literary prose.

[3] One of the two pioneers of Sicilian, and hence of Greek rhetoric, the other being Corax. Tisias probably applied the

ISOCRATES

Isocrates was an Athenian. He was born in the eighty-sixth Olympiad during the archonship of Lysimachus at Athens, four years before the Peloponnesian War,[1] and was thus twenty-two years younger than Lysias. His father Theodorus was a citizen of moderate persuasion who owned a staff of slaves who made reed-pipes, and earned his livelihood from this trade. Isocrates was decently brought up, and received an education as good as that of any other Athenian. As soon as he reached manhood, he was strongly attracted to the study of philosophy. He attended the lectures of Prodicus of Ceos,[2] Gorgias of Leontini and Tisias of Syracuse,[3] the men who enjoyed the highest reputation for wisdom [4] in Greece at that time. Some also say that he was a pupil of Theramenes, the politician who was killed for alleged democratic sympathies by the Thirty.[5] He con- 1

techniques which Corax had devised for political oratory to forensic oratory. He wrote a handbook in which the technique of argument from probability was illustrated.

[4] "Wisdom" in the sense found in Isocrates's own writings, connoting an understanding of the arts of civilisation. He uses "philosophia" in the same sense of a desire to understand those arts. See Jaeger, *Paideia* III, p. 49.

[5] Cf. the story in [Plutarch] *Lives of the Ten Orators*, 836F–837A, in which Isocrates is said to have tried to defend Theramenes against his enemies at the time of his arrest.

μὲν ἐποιεῖτο πράττειν τε καὶ λέγειν τὰ πολιτικά, ὡς δὲ ἡ φύσις ἠναντιοῦτο, τὰ πρῶτα καὶ κυριώτατα [1] τοῦ ῥήτορος ἀφελομένη, τόλμαν τε καὶ φωνῆς μέγεθος, ὧν χωρὶς οὐχ οἷόν τε ἦν ἐν ὄχλῳ λέγειν, ταύτης μὲν ἀπέστη τῆς προαιρέσεως· ἐπιθυμῶν δὲ δόξης καὶ τοῦ πρωτεῦσαι παρὰ τοῖς Ἕλλησιν ἐπὶ σοφίᾳ, καθάπερ αὐτὸς εἴρηκεν, ἐπὶ τὸ γράφειν ἃ διανοηθείη κατέφυγεν, οὐ περὶ μικρῶν τὴν προαίρεσιν ποιούμενος οὐδὲ περὶ τῶν ἰδίων συμβολαίων οὐδὲ ὑπὲρ ὧν ἄλλοι τινὲς τῶν τότε σοφιστῶν, περὶ δὲ τῶν Ἑλληνικῶν καὶ βασιλικῶν ⟨καὶ πολιτικῶν⟩ [2] πραγμάτων, ἐξ ὧν ὑπελάμβανε τάς τε πόλεις ἄμεινον οἰκήσεσθαι καὶ τοὺς ἰδιώτας ἐπίδοσιν ἕξειν πρὸς ἀρετήν. ταῦτα γὰρ ἐν τῷ Παναθηναϊκῷ λόγῳ περὶ αὐτοῦ γράφει. πεφυρμένην τε παραλαβὼν τὴν ἄσκησιν τῶν λόγων ὑπὸ τῶν περὶ Γοργίαν καὶ Πρωταγόραν σοφιστῶν πρῶτος ἐχώρησεν ἀπὸ τῶν ἐριστικῶν τε καὶ φυσικῶν ἐπὶ τοὺς πολιτικοὺς καὶ περὶ αὐτὴν σπουδάζων τὴν ἐπιστήμην διετέλεσεν, ἐξ ἧς, ὥς φησιν αὐτός, τὸ βουλεύεσθαι καὶ λέγειν καὶ πράττειν τὰ συμφέροντα παραγίνεται τοῖς μαθοῦσιν. ἐπιφανέστατος δὲ γενόμενος τῶν κατὰ τὸν αὐτὸν ἀκμασάντων χρόνον καὶ τοὺς κρατίστους τῶν Ἀθήνησί τε καὶ ἐν τῇ ἄλλῃ Ἑλλάδι νέων παιδεύσας, ὧν οἳ μὲν ἐν τοῖς δικανικοῖς ἐγένοντο ἄριστοι

[1] *κυριώτατα* Sylburg: *κυριώτερα* codd.
[2] *καὶ πολιτικῶν* ex Isocrate addidit Radermacher.

---

[1] Isocrates, *Panathenaicus*, 10; *Philippus*, 81; *Ep*. I. 9; VIII. 7.
[2] Isocrates, *Panathenaicus*, 11.

ceived the ambition to become an active politician, but his constitution thwarted him: he lacked the first and most important qualities of a public speaker, self-confidence and a strong voice, without which it is impossible to address a crowd.[1] He therefore abandoned this purpose, but retained his desire for renown: as he himself admits,[2] he wished to be regarded as the wisest man in Greece, and it was with this end in view that he took to setting down his opinions in writing. The subjects which he chose were not trivial issues, nor private cases, nor those treated by certain contemporary sophists, but Hellenic and royal [3] affairs and constitutional matters, the study of which he believed would enable cities to manage better, and individuals to improve their characters. This is what he says about himself in the *Panathenaicus*. Gorgias, Protagoras [4] and their associates had reduced the study of oratory to a state of confusion. Isocrates took it over from them and was the first to set it on a new course, turning away from treatises on dialectic and natural philosophy and concentrating on writing political discourses and on political science itself which, to use his own words, confers upon its students the ability to benefit their state by counsel, word and deed.[5] He became the outstanding figure among the famous men of his day, and the teacher of the most eminent men at Athens and in Greece at large, both the best forensic orators,

[3] "Hellenic" here refers to matters affecting the relation of the Greek cities with one another, and "royal" refers to that of Greece to Persia and her king.

[4] See p. xiv.

[5] This proposition is not stated in these words anywhere in Isocrates, but they summarise views stated in many places, e.g. *Antidosis*, 175, 255 ff., 276; *Nicocles*, 7–8.

λόγοις, οἱ δ' ἐν τῷ πολιτεύεσθαι καὶ τὰ κοινὰ πράττειν διήνεγκαν, καὶ ἄλλοι δὲ τὰς κοινὰς τῶν Ἑλλήνων τε καὶ βαρβάρων πράξεις ἀνέγραψαν, καὶ τῆς Ἀθηναίων πόλεως εἰκόνα ποιήσας τὴν ἑαυτοῦ σχολὴν κατὰ τὰς ἀποικίας τῶν λόγων, πλοῦτον ὅσον οὐδεὶς τῶν ἀπὸ φιλοσοφίας χρηματισαμένων περιποιησάμενος, ἐτελεύτα τὸν βίον ἐπὶ Χαιρωνίδου ἄρχοντος ὀλίγαις ἡμέραις ὕστερον τῆς ἐν Χαιρωνείᾳ μάχης δυεῖν δέοντα βεβιωκὼς ἑκατὸν ἔτη, γνώμῃ χρησάμενος ἅμα τοῖς ἀγαθοῖς τῆς πόλεως συγκαταλῦσαι τὸν ἑαυτοῦ βίον, ἀδήλου ἔτι ὄντος, πῶς χρήσεται τῇ τύχῃ Φίλιππος παραλαβὼν τὴν ἀρχὴν τῶν Ἑλλήνων. τὰ μὲν οὖν ἱστορούμενα περὶ αὐτοῦ κεφαλαιωδῶς ταῦτ' ἐστίν.

2 ἡ δὲ λέξις, ᾗ κέχρηται, τοιοῦτόν τινα χαρακτῆρα ἔχει. καθαρὰ μέν ἐστιν οὐχ ἧττον τῆς Λυσίου καὶ οὐδὲν εἰκῇ τιθεῖσα ὄνομα τήν τε διάλεκτον ἀκριβοῦσα ἐν τοῖς πάνυ τὴν κοινὴν καὶ συνηθεστάτην. καὶ γὰρ αὕτη πέφευγεν ἀπηρχαιωμένων καὶ σημειωδῶν ὀνομάτων τὴν ἀπειροκαλίαν, κατὰ δὲ τὴν τροπικὴν φράσιν ὀλίγον τι διαλλάττει τῆς Λυσίου καὶ κέκραται συμμέτρως, τό τε σαφὲς ἐκείνῃ παραπλήσιον ἔχει καὶ τὸ ἐναργές, ἠθική τέ ἐστι καὶ πιθανὴ καὶ ⟨πρέπουσα⟩.[1] στρογγύλη δὲ οὐκ ἔστιν, ὥσπερ ἐκείνη, καὶ συγκεκροτημένη καὶ πρὸς ἀγῶνας δικανικοὺς εὔθετος, ὑπτία δέ ἐστι μᾶλλον καὶ κεχυμένη πλουσίως, οὐδὲ δὴ σύντομος οὕτως, ἀλλὰ καὶ κατασκελὴς καὶ βραδυτέρα τοῦ μετρίου. δι' ἣν δὲ αἰτίαν τοῦτο πάσχει, μετὰ μικρὸν ἐρῶ. οὐδὲ τὴν σύνθεσιν ἐπιδείκνυται τὴν

[1] *πρέπουσα* addidit Radermacher.

and those who distinguished themselves in politics and public life. Historians, too, were among his pupils, both those who wrote of Greek affairs and those who included the outside world, and his school came to represent Athens herself in the eyes of literate men abroad.[1] He made more money from academic work than anyone else, and passed away in the archonship of Chaeronidas, a few days after the battle of Chaeronea, at the age of ninety-eight, having decided to end his life with his city's heroes, when it was still uncertain how Philip would use his good fortune now that he had succeeded to the leadership of Greece. Such, then, in brief is the tradition concerning Isocrates.

His style has the following characteristics: it is as 2
pure as that of Lysias; not a word is used at random; and the language conforms closely to the most ordinary and familiar usage. Like its predecessor, it avoids the banality of archaic and obscure words, but uses figurative language somewhat more than Lysias, achieving a happy balance in this respect. In the matter of lucidity and vividness it is similar to that of Lysias; it is also moral and convincing in tone and appropriate to its subject. On the other hand, it is not a compact, closely-knit style like the other, and is therefore ill-suited to forensic purposes: it sprawls and overflows with its own exuberance. Again, it is not so concise, but seems to drag its feet and move too slowly. (I shall explain the reason for this fault shortly.) Nor again does it display a natural, simple

[1] A colourful expression which may ultimately derive from Thucydides ii. 41, though there seems to be no parallel to this metaphorical use of ἀποικία.

φυσικὴν καὶ ἀφελῆ καὶ ἐναγώνιον, ὥσπερ ἡ Λυσίου, ἀλλὰ πεποιημένην μᾶλλον εἰς σεμνότητα πομπικὴν καὶ ποικίλην καὶ πῇ μὲν εὐπρεπεστέραν ἐκείνης πῇ δὲ περιεργοτέραν. ὁ γὰρ ἀνὴρ οὗτος τὴν εὐέπειαν ἐκ παντὸς διώκει καὶ τοῦ γλαφυρῶς λέγειν στοχάζεται μᾶλλον ἢ τοῦ ἀφελῶς. τῶν τε γὰρ φωνηέντων τὰς παραλλήλους θέσεις ὡς ἐκλυούσας[1] τὰς ἁρμονίας τῶν ἤχων καὶ τὴν λειότητα τῶν φθόγγων λυμαινομένας περιίσταται, περιόδῳ τε καὶ κύκλῳ περιλαμβάνειν τὰ νοήματα πειρᾶται ῥυθμοειδεῖ πάνυ καὶ οὐ πολὺ ἀπέχοντι τοῦ ποιητικοῦ μέτρου, ἀναγνώσεώς τε μᾶλλον οἰκειότερός ἐστιν ἢ χρήσεως. τοιγάρτοι τὰς μὲν ἐπιδείξεις τὰς ἐν ταῖς πανηγύρεσι καὶ τὴν ἐκ χειρὸς θεωρίαν φέρουσιν αὐτοῦ οἱ λόγοι, τοὺς δὲ ἐν ἐκκλησίαις καὶ δικαστηρίοις ἀγῶνας οὐχ ὑπομένουσι. τούτου δὲ αἴτιον, ὅτι πολὺ τὸ παθητικὸν ἐν ἐκείνοις εἶναι δεῖ· τοῦτο δὲ ἥκιστα δέχεται περίοδος. αἵ τε παρομοιώσεις[2] καὶ παρισώσεις καὶ τὰ ἀντίθετα καὶ πᾶς ὁ τῶν τοιούτων σχημάτων κόσμος πολύς ἐστι παρ᾽ αὐτῷ καὶ λυπεῖ πολλάκις τὴν ἄλλην κατασκευὴν προσιστάμενος ταῖς ἀκοαῖς.

3 καθόλου δὲ τριῶν ὄντων, ὥς φησι Θεόφραστος, ἐξ ὧν γίνεται τὸ μέγα καὶ σεμνὸν καὶ περιττὸν ἐν λέξει, τῆς τε ἐκλογῆς τῶν ὀνομάτων καὶ τῆς ἐκ τούτων ἁρμονίας καὶ τῶν περιλαμβανόντων αὐτὰ σχημάτων, ἐκλέγει μὲν εὖ πάνυ καὶ τὰ κράτιστα τῶν ὀνομάτων τίθησιν, ἁρμόττει δὲ αὐτὰ περιέργως,

[1] ἐκλυούσας Sylburg: λυούσας codd.
[2] παρομοιώσεις Sylburg: γὰρ ὁμοιώσεις codd.

and vigorous arrangement of words like that of Lysias: rather it is designed to create an effect of ceremonious and ornate dignity, so that it may at times be more attractive, but at other times it seems laboured. For this orator seeks beauty of expression by every means, and aims at polish rather than simplicity. He avoids hiatus,[1] on the ground that this breaks the continuity of utterance and impairs the smoothness of the sounds. He tries to express his ideas within the framework of the rounded period, using strong rhythms which are not far removed from those of verse, thus rendering his work more suitable for reading than for practical use. For the same reason his speeches will bear recitation on ceremonial occasions, and private study, but cannot stand up to the stresses of the assembly or the law-courts. This is because such occasions demand intensity of feeling, and this is what the period is least capable of expressing. Clauses ending with similar sounds and having equal length, antithesis and the whole array of figures of this kind,[2] are found in Isocrates in great numbers, and often spoil the rest of his artistry by obtruding themselves upon the ear.

There are altogether three means, according to 3
Theophrastus,[3] by which grandeur, dignity and impressiveness are achieved: the choice of words, their melodious arrangement and the figures of speech in which they are set. Isocrates chooses his words very well, and uses the best possible; but his arrangement

[1] One of the precepts found among the fragments of a handbook ascribed to him (Syrianus, *In Hermogenem* I, p. 28).

[2] The "Gorgianic" figures of parallelism and assonance. See note 1, p. 137; p. 253.

[3] Frag. 5 Schmidt.

τὴν εὐφωνίαν ἐντείνων μουσικήν, σχηματίζει τε φορτικῶς καὶ τὰ πολλὰ γίνεται ψυχρὸς ἢ τῷ πόρρωθεν λαμβάνειν ἢ τῷ μὴ πρέποντα εἶναι τὰ σχήματα τοῖς πράγμασι διὰ τὸ μὴ κρατεῖν τοῦ μετρίου. ταῦτα μέντοι καὶ μακροτέραν αὐτῷ ποιεῖ τὴν λέξιν πολλάκις, λέγω δὲ τό τε εἰς περιόδους ἐναρμόττειν ἅπαντα τὰ νοήματα καὶ τὸ τοῖς αὐτοῖς τύποις τῶν σχημάτων τὰς περιόδους περιλαμβάνειν καὶ τὸ διώκειν ἐκ παντὸς τὴν εὐρυθμίαν. οὐ γὰρ ἅπαντα δέχεται οὔτε μῆκος τὸ αὐτὸ οὔτε σχῆμα τὸ παραπλήσιον οὔτε ῥυθμὸν τὸν ἴσον. ὥστε ἀνάγκη παραπληρώμασι λέξεων οὐδὲν ὠφελουσῶν χρῆσθαι καὶ ἀπομηκύνειν πέρα τοῦ χρησίμου τὸν λόγον. λέγω δὲ οὐχ ὡς διαπαντὸς αὐτοῦ ταῦτα ποιοῦντος (οὐχ οὕτως μαίνομαι· καὶ γὰρ συντίθησί ποτε ἀφελῶς τὰ ὀνόματα καὶ λύει τὴν περίοδον εὐγενῶς καὶ τὰ περίεργα σχήματα καὶ φορτικὰ φεύγει καὶ μάλιστα ἐν τοῖς συμβουλευτικοῖς τε καὶ δικανικοῖς λόγοις), ἀλλ᾽ ὡς ἐπὶ τὸ πολὺ τῷ ῥυθμῷ δουλεύοντος καὶ τῷ κύκλῳ τῆς περιόδου καὶ τὸ κάλλος τῆς ἀπαγγελίας ἐν τῷ περιττῷ τιθεμένου κοινότερον εἴρηκα περὶ αὐτοῦ. κατὰ δὴ ταῦτά φημι τὴν Ἰσοκράτους λέξιν λείπεσθαι τῆς Λυσίου καὶ ἔτι κατὰ τὴν χάριν. καίτοι γε ἀνθηρός ἐστιν, εἰ καί τις ἄλλος, καὶ ἐπαγωγὸς ἡδονῇ τῶν ἀκροωμένων Ἰσοκράτης, ἀλλ᾽ οὐκ ἔχει τὴν αὐτὴν χάριν ἐκείνῳ. τοσοῦτον δὲ αὐτοῦ λείπεται κατὰ ταύτην τὴν ἀρετήν, ὅσον τῶν φύσει καλῶν σωμάτων τὰ συνερανιζόμενα κόσμοις ἐπιθέτοις. πέφυκε γὰρ ἡ Λυσίου λέξις ἔχειν τὸ χαρίεν, ἡ δὲ Ἰσοκράτους βούλεται.

of them is laboured because he is striving after musical effect. His use of figures is crude, and its effect is usually frigid: they are either far-fetched or inappropriate to their subject-matter, both faults being the result of his failure to achieve artistic moderation. A further factor often leads to longwindedness—I mean his habit of arranging all his ideas in periodic form, framing them in the same kinds of figures, and striving by every means after rhythmic cadence. But not every subject may be treated at the same length, nor are the same figures suited to all, or the same rhythm. He is therefore compelled to pad his sentences with words that contribute nothing, and to extend his speech beyond its effective length. I do not mean to imply that he invariably does this (I am not so mad as to do that: for there are times, especially in his political and forensic speeches, when he tastefully relieves the periodic structure and avoids the excessive and vulgar use of figures, and composes in the plain style). But in making out that for most of the time he is the slave of rhythm and the rounded period, and identifies beauty of expression with the creation of effect, I have given a somewhat generalised account. Thus I say that Isocrates's style is inferior to that of Lysias in these respects, and also in respect of charm. Isocrates is indeed as colourful as any orator, and wins over his audiences by the pleasure he gives; but he does not possess charm to the degree that Lysias does. He is as inferior to Lysias in this quality as a body that is a hotch-potch of applied cosmetics is inferior to one which has natural beauty. Lysias possesses charm naturally; Isocrates is always looking for it. Such, in my opinion at least, are the qualities in which

ταύταις μὲν δὴ ταῖς ἀρεταῖς ὑστερεῖ Λυσίου κατὰ γοῦν τὴν ἐμὴν γνώμην. προτερεῖ δέ γε ἐν ταῖς μελλούσαις λέγεσθαι· ὑψηλότερός ἐστιν ἐκείνου κατὰ τὴν ἑρμηνείαν καὶ μεγαλοπρεπέστερος μακρῷ καὶ ἀξιωματικώτερος. θαυμαστὸν γὰρ δὴ καὶ μέγα τὸ τῆς Ἰσοκράτους κατασκευῆς ὕψος, ἡρωϊκῆς μᾶλλον ἢ ἀνθρωπίνης φύσεως οἰκεῖον. δοκεῖ δή μοι μὴ ἀπὸ σκοποῦ τις ἂν εἰκάσαι τὴν μὲν Ἰσοκράτους ῥητορικὴν τῇ Πολυκλείτου τε καὶ Φειδίου τέχνῃ κατὰ τὸ σεμνὸν καὶ μεγαλότεχνον καὶ ἀξιωματικόν, τὴν δὲ Λυσίου τῇ Καλάμιδος καὶ Καλλιμάχου τῆς λεπτότητος ἕνεκα καὶ τῆς χάριτος. ὥσπερ γὰρ ἐκείνων οἳ μὲν ἐν τοῖς ἐλάττοσι καὶ ἀνθρωπικοῖς ἔργοις εἰσὶν ἐπιτυχέστεροι τῶν ἑτέρων, οἳ δ' ἐν τοῖς μείζοσι καὶ θειοτέροις δεξιώτεροι, οὕτως καὶ τῶν ῥητόρων ὃ μὲν ἐν τοῖς μικροῖς ἐστι σοφώτερος, ὃ δ' ἐν τοῖς μεγάλοις περιττότερος, τάχα μὲν γὰρ καὶ τῇ φύσει μεγαλόφρων τις ὤν, εἰ δὲ μή, τῇ γε προαιρέσει πάντως τὸ σεμνὸν καὶ θαυμαστὸν διώκων. ταῦτα μὲν οὖν περὶ τῆς λέξεως τοῦ ῥήτορος.

4 τὰ δὲ ἐν τῷ πραγματικῷ τόπῳ [1] θεωρήματα τὰ μὲν ὅμοια τοῖς Λυσίου, τὰ δὲ κρείττονα. ἡ μὲν εὕρεσις ἡ τῶν ἐνθυμημάτων ἡ πρὸς ἕκαστον ἁρμόττουσα πρᾶγμα πολλὴ καὶ πυκνὴ καὶ οὐδὲν

[1] τόπῳ Wolf: τρόπῳ codd.

---

[1] For similar comparisons with sculpture and painting see Cicero, *Brutus*, 70, *De Oratore*, iii. 26; Quintilian xii. 10.

[2] Argive sculptor, younger contemporary of Pheidias, greatest representative of the 5th-Century Peloponnesian tradition.

Isocrates is inferior to Lysias. In the following ways, however, he is superior: he is capable of expressing himself in a more lofty manner, being much more impressive and dignified. Indeed, this lofty quality of Isocrates's artistry is a great and wonderful thing, and has a character more suited to demigods than to men. I think one would not be wide of the mark in comparing [1] the oratory of Isocrates, in respect of its grandeur, its virtuosity and its dignity, with the art of Polyclitus [2] and Phidias,[3] and the style of Lysias, for its lightness and charm, with that of Calamis [4] and Callimachus; [5] for just as the latter two sculptors are more successful than their rivals in portraying lesser human subjects, where the former two are cleverer at treating grander and superhuman subjects, so with the two orators: Lysias has the greater skill with small subjects, while Isocrates is the more impressive with grand subjects. This is perhaps because he is naturally of a noble cast of mind; or, if this is not the case, it is at least because his mind is wholly set upon grand and admirable designs. So much for the orator's style.

Turning to subject-matter, we find that his treatment is sometimes similar to that of Lysias, and at other times better. His invention of arguments [6] to suit particular situations is fertile and rich, and in no 4

[3] Famous Athenian sculptor and designer of the marble sculptures of the Parthenon (447–432 B.C.).

[4] fl. *c.* 480–450.

[5] Reputedly the inventor of the Corinthian capital *c.* 440 B.C., which would account for Dionysius's ascription to him of the qualities of lightness and charm.

[6] For possible influence of Hermagoras in this chapter see Introd. pp. xiv–xv.

ἐκείνης λειπομένη. καὶ κρίσις ὡσαύτως ἀπὸ μεγάλης φρονήσεως γινομένη. τάξις δὲ καὶ μερισμοὶ τῶν πραγμάτων καὶ ἡ κατ' ἐπιχείρημα ἐξεργασία καὶ τὸ διαλαμβάνεσθαι τὴν ὁμοείδειαν[1] ἰδίαις μεταβολαῖς καὶ ξένοις ἐπεισοδίοις τά τε ἄλλα ὅσα περὶ τὴν πραγματικὴν οἰκονομίαν ἐστὶν ἀγαθὰ πολλῷ μείζονά ἐστι παρ' Ἰσοκράτει καὶ κρείττονα, μάλιστα δ' ἡ προαίρεσις ἡ τῶν λόγων, περὶ οὓς ἐσπούδαζε, καὶ τῶν ὑποθέσεων τὸ κάλλος, ἐν αἷς ἐποιεῖτο τὰς διατριβάς. ἐξ ὧν οὐ λέγειν δεινοὺς μόνον ἀπεργάσαιτ' ἂν τοὺς προσέχοντας αὐτῷ τὸν νοῦν, ἀλλὰ καὶ τὰ ἤθη σπουδαίους, οἴκῳ τε καὶ πόλει καὶ ὅλῃ τῇ Ἑλλάδι χρησίμους. κράτιστα γὰρ δὴ παιδεύματα πρὸς ἀρετὴν ἐν τοῖς Ἰσοκράτους ἔστιν εὑρεῖν λόγοις. καὶ ἔγωγέ φημι χρῆναι τοὺς μέλλοντας οὐχὶ μέρος τι τῆς πολιτικῆς δυνάμεως ἀλλ' ὅλην αὐτὴν κτήσασθαι τοῦτον ἔχειν τὸν ῥήτορα διὰ χειρός. καὶ εἴ τις ἐπιτηδεύει τὴν ἀληθινὴν φιλοσοφίαν, μὴ τὸ θεωρητικὸν αὐτῆς μόνον ἀγαπῶν ἀλλὰ καὶ τὸ πρακτικόν, μηδ' ἀφ' ὧν αὐτὸς ἄλυπον ἕξει βίον, ταῦτα προαιρούμενος, ἀλλ' ἐξ ὧν πολλοὺς ὠφελήσει, παρακελευσαίμην ἂν αὐτῷ τὴν ἐκείνου τοῦ ῥήτορος μιμεῖσθαι προαίρεσιν.

5 τίς γὰρ οὐκ ἂν γένοιτο φιλόπολίς τε καὶ φιλόδημος ἢ τίς οὐκ ἂν ἐπιτηδεύσειε τὴν πολιτικὴν καλοκἀγαθίαν ἀναγνοὺς αὐτοῦ τὸν Πανηγυρικόν; ἐν ᾧ διεξιὼν τὰς τῶν ἀρχαίων ἀρετὰς φησίν, ὡς οἱ τὴν Ἑλλάδα ἐλευθερώσαντες ἀπὸ τῶν βαρβάρων οὐ τὰ πολέμια

way inferior to that of Lysias. The same applies to his selection of material, which is the choice of a noble mind. And the arrangement and division of topics, their development by means of argumentation, the relief of monotony by varying the treatment of the different elements of the subject itself and by introducing digressions from external sources, and all other techniques concerned with the disposition of subject-matter, are found to a greater degree and to greater effect in Isocrates. But most significant of all are the themes upon which he chose to concentrate, and the nobility of the subjects which he spent his time in studying. The influence of these would make anyone who applied himself to his works not only good orators, but men of sterling character, of positive service to their families, to their state and to Greece at large. The best possible lessons in virtue are to be found in the discourses of Isocrates: I therefore affirm that the man who intends to acquire ability in the whole field of politics, not merely a part of that science, should make Isocrates his constant companion. And anyone who is interested in true philosophy, and enjoys studying its practical as well as its speculative branches, and is seeking a career by which he will benefit many people, not one which will give him a carefree life, would be well advised to follow the principles which this orator adopts.

Who could fail to become a patriotic supporter of 5
democracy and a student of civic virtue after reading his *Panegyricus*? In this discourse, as he enumerates the virtues of the men of old, he remarks that the liberators of Greece from the barbarians were not only

[1] ὁμοείδειαν Krüger: ὁμοειδίαν FP.

δεινοὶ μόνον ἦσαν, ἀλλὰ καὶ τὰ ἤθη γενναῖοι καὶ φιλότιμοι καὶ σώφρονες, οἵ γε τῶν μὲν κοινῶν μᾶλλον ἐφρόντιζον ἢ τῶν ἰδίων, τῶν δὲ ἀλλοτρίων ἧττον ἐπεθύμουν ἢ τῶν ἀδυνάτων καὶ τὴν εὐδαιμονίαν οὐ πρὸς ἀργύριον ἔκρινον ἀλλὰ πρὸς εὐδοξίαν, μέγαν οἰόμενοι τοῖς παισὶ καταλείψειν πλοῦτον καὶ ἀνεπίφθονον τὴν παρὰ τοῖς πλήθεσι τιμήν· κρείττονα δὲ ἡγοῦντο τὸν εὐσχήμονα θάνατον ἢ τὸν ἀκλεῆ βίον, ἐσκόπουν δὲ οὐχ ὅπως οἱ νόμοι καλῶς καὶ ἀκριβῶς αὐτοῖς ἕξουσιν, ἀλλ' ὡς ἡ τῶν καθ' ἡμέραν ἐπιτηδευμάτων μετριότης μηθὲν ἐκβήσεται τῶν πατρίων· οὕτως δὲ εἶχεν αὐτοῖς τὰ πρὸς ἀλλήλους φιλοτίμως καὶ πολιτικῶς, ὥστε καὶ τὰς στάσεις ἐποιοῦντο πρὸς ἀλλήλους, πότεροι πλείω τὴν πόλιν ἀγαθὰ ποιήσουσιν, οὐχ οἵτινες τοὺς ἑτέρους ἀπολέσαντες τῶν λοιπῶν αὐτοὶ ἄρξουσι. τῇ δὲ αὐτῇ προθυμίᾳ χρώμενοι καὶ πρὸς τὴν Ἑλλάδα τῷ θεραπεύειν προσήγοντο τὰς πόλεις καὶ τῷ πείθειν ταῖς εὐεργεσίαις μᾶλλον ἢ τῷ βιάζεσθαι τοῖς ὅπλοις κατεῖχον, πιστοτέροις χρώμενοι τοῖς λόγοις ἢ νῦν τοῖς ὅρκοις, καὶ ταῖς συνθήκαις ἀξιοῦντες μᾶλλον ἐμμένειν ἢ ταῖς ἀνάγκαις, τοιαῦτα δὲ περὶ τῶν ἡττόνων ἀξιοῦντες γινώσκειν, οἷα περὶ σφῶν αὐτῶν τοὺς κρείττους ἂν ἠξίωσαν φρονεῖν, οὕτω δὲ παρεσκευασμένοι τὰς γνώμας, ὡς ἰδίᾳ μὲν ἔχοντες τὰς ἑαυτῶν πόλεις, κοινὴν δὲ πατρίδα τὴν Ἑλλάδα οἰκοῦντες.

---

[1] 81. [2] 76.
[3] 77. [4] 78.

formidable warriors, but also men of noble character, who combined a desire for honour with self-control,[1] who took thought for the common good rather than for personal advantage,[2] who were less covetous of the possessions of others than men of inferior ability, and who measured their happiness not according to their wealth but according to their good name, because they considered that the greatest heritage they could leave to their children, and the least invidious, was the esteem of the people. They regarded a noble death as preferable to an inglorious life.[3] They were less concerned with maintaining a fair and explicit legal code than with ensuring that the moderation with which their ancestors had conducted their daily affairs should continue to be observed.[4] Their political rivalry took the form of a contest to decide not who should destroy their opponents and themselves gain control of the rest, but which should confer the greatest benefits on the state.[5] They brought the same constructive spirit to their dealings with other Greek cities, winning them over by kindness and maintaining their influence by rendering them service instead of constraining them with armed force.[6] They kept their word more faithfully than men today keep their oath, and regarded free agreements as more binding than those entered into under compulsion, because they thought it their duty to take the same view of the rights of their inferiors as they would have expected their superiors to take of their own rights. Having assumed this attitude of mind, they had come to look upon their several cities as their individual homes, but thought of Greece as their common fatherland and home.[7]

[5] 79. [6] 80. [7] 81.

6 τίς δ' οὐκ ἂν ἀγαπήσειε μέγεθος ἔχων ἀνὴρ καὶ δυνάμεώς τινος ἡγούμενος, ἃ πρὸς Φίλιππον αὐτῷ τὸν Μακεδόνα γέγραπται; ἐν οἷς ἀξιοῖ στρατηγὸν ἄνδρα καὶ τηλικαύτης ἐξουσίας κύριον διαλλάττειν μὲν τὰς διαφερομένας πόλεις ἀλλὰ μὴ συγκρούειν πρὸς ἀλλήλας, τὴν δὲ Ἑλλάδα μεγάλην ἐκ μικρᾶς ποιεῖν, ὑπεριδόντα ⟨τε⟩ [1] τῆς περὶ τὰ μικρὰ φιλοτιμίας τοῖς τοιούτοις ἐπιχειρεῖν ἔργοις, ἐξ ὧν κατορθώσας τε πάντων ἡγεμόνων ἐπιφανέστατος ἔσται καὶ ἀποτυχὼν τήν γε εὔνοιαν τὴν παρὰ τῶν Ἑλλήνων κτήσεται· ἧς οἱ τυχόντες πολλῷ μᾶλλόν εἰσι ζηλωτότεροι τῶν μεγάλας πόλεις καὶ πολλὰς χώρας καταστρεψαμένων. ἔτι δὲ παρακελεύεται μιμεῖσθαι τὴν Ἡρακλέους τε προαίρεσιν καὶ τῶν ἄλλων ἡγεμόνων, ὅσοι μετὰ τῶν Ἑλλήνων ἐπὶ τοὺς βαρβάρους ἐστράτευσαν, καί φησι χρῆναι τοὺς ἑτέρων διαφέροντας προαιρεῖσθαι μὲν τὰς μέγεθος ἐχούσας πράξεις, ἐπιτελεῖν δὲ αὐτὰς μετ' ἀρετῆς, ἐνθυμουμένους, ὅτι τὸ μὲν σῶμα θνητὸν ἔχομεν, ἀθάνατοι δὲ γιγνόμεθα δι' ἀρετήν, καὶ τοῖς μὲν πρὸς ἄλλο τι τῶν ἀγαθῶν ἀπλήστως διακειμένοις ἀχθόμεθα, τοὺς δὲ τιμὴν μείζω τῆς ὑπαρχούσης ἀεὶ κτωμένους ἐπαινοῦμεν, καὶ ὅτι τῶν μὲν ἄλλων, ἐφ' οἷς εἰσιν ἀνθρώπιναι σπουδαί,[2] πλούτου καὶ ἀρχῆς καὶ δυναστείας, πολλάκις τοὺς ἐχθροὺς συμβαίνει γίγνεσθαι κυρίους, τῆς δὲ ἀρετῆς καὶ τῆς παρὰ τοῖς πλήθεσιν εὐνοίας τοὺς οἰκείους ἑκάστου κληρονομεῖν. πολλὴ γὰρ ἀνάγκη τοὺς

What man in high office and power would not 6
delight in his letter to Philip of Macedon? In this letter he urges the king to use his position as general and his great authority to reconcile the warring cities instead of setting them against one another, and to raise Greece from insignificance to greatness;[1] and, despising petty ambition, to engage in enterprises which, if he is successful, will make him the most renowned leader among the Greeks, while even if he fails he will at least have won their good will, which is a more enviable possession than mighty cities captured and great tracts of land conquered.[2] He further urges him to follow the course chosen by Heracles[3] and the other leaders who marched with the Greeks against the barbarians,[4] and says that men of exceptional ability should undertake great enterprises and follow them through with courage,[5] reflecting that our bodies are mortal, but that we attain immortality through valour;[6] that we regard with resentment those who are insatiably greedy for the other good things in life, but with approval those who are constantly adding to the honour that they already possess;[7] and that whereas the other prizes to which men aspire—wealth, eminence and power—often fall into the hands of our enemies, honour and popular esteem are a heritage which the families of each of us can enjoy.[8] Any potentate reading this letter is

[1] *Philippus*, 30. [2] 68.
[3] 109–115. [4] 90–92; 119.
[5] 41. [6] 134.
[7] 135. [8] 136.

---

[1] τε inclusit Holwell.
[2] ἐφ' οἷς εἰσιν ἀνθρώπιναι σπουδαί Usener–Radermacher: ἐφ' οἷς ἐὰν ἀνθρωπίν[α]ις τοῦ δὲ F.

ἀναγιγνώσκοντας ταῦτα δυνάστας φρονήματός τε μείζονος ὑποπίμπλασθαι καὶ μᾶλλον ἐπιθυμεῖν τῆς ἀρετῆς.

7 τίς δὲ ἂν μᾶλλον ἐπὶ τὴν δικαιοσύνην καὶ τὴν εὐσέβειαν προτρέψαιτο καθ' ἕκαστόν τε ἄνδρα ἰδίᾳ καὶ κοινῇ τὰς πόλεις ὅλας τοῦ Περὶ τῆς εἰρήνης λόγου; ἐν γὰρ δὴ τούτῳ πείθει τοὺς Ἀθηναίους τῶν μὲν ἀλλοτρίων μὴ ἐπιθυμεῖν, ἐπὶ δὲ τοῖς παροῦσι στέργειν, καὶ τῶν μὲν μικρῶν πόλεων ὡσπερανεὶ κτημάτων φείδεσθαι, τοὺς δὲ συμμάχους ⟨εὐνοίᾳ⟩ τε [1] καὶ εὐεργεσίαις πειρᾶσθαι κατέχειν, ἀλλὰ μὴ ταῖς ἀνάγκαις μηδὲ ταῖς βίαις. τῶν δὲ προγόνων μιμεῖσθαι μὴ τοὺς πρὸ τῶν Δεκελεικῶν γενομένους, οἳ μικροῦ ἐδέησαν ἀπολέσαι τὴν πόλιν, ἀλλὰ τοὺς πρὸ τῶν Περσικῶν, οἳ καλοκἀγαθίαν ἀσκοῦντες διετέλεσαν. ἐπιδείκνυταί τε ὡς οὐχ αἱ πολλαὶ τριήρεις οὐδ' οἱ μετὰ βίας ἀρχόμενοι Ἕλληνες μεγάλην ποιοῦσι τὴν πόλιν, ἀλλ' αἱ δίκαιαί τε προαιρέσεις καὶ τὸ τοῖς ἀδικουμένοις βοηθεῖν. παρακαλεῖ τε τὴν τῶν Ἑλλήνων εὔνοιαν οἰκείαν ποιεῖν τῇ πόλει, μεγίστην ἡγουμένους [2] μερίδα πρὸς εὐδαιμονίαν, καὶ πολεμικοὺς μὲν εἶναι ταῖς παρασκευαῖς καὶ ταῖς μελέταις, εἰρηνικοὺς δὲ τῷ μηδένα μηδὲν ἀδικεῖν, διδάσκων ὡς οὔτε πρὸς πλοῦτον οὔτε πρὸς δόξαν οὔθ' ὅλως πρὸς εὐδαιμονίαν οὐθὲν ἂν συμβάλοιτο τηλικαύτην δύναμιν, ὅσην ἀρετὴ καὶ τὰ μέρη ταύτης· καὶ τοῖς μὴ ταῦτα ὑπειληφόσιν ἐπιτιμῶν, οἳ τὴν μὲν ἀδικίαν κερδαλέαν ἡγοῦντο καὶ πρὸς τὸν βίον τὸν

[1] εὐνοίᾳ τε Wolf: γε codd.
[2] ἡγουμένους Krüger: ἡγούμενος codd.

absolutely bound to become imbued with a nobler spirit and a greater desire to achieve excellence.

What greater exhortation to justice and piety could 7
there be, for individuals singly and collectively for whole communities, than the discourse *On the Peace*? In this speech he tries to persuade the Athenians not to covet the land of others, but to be content with what they have;[1] to be as considerate in their treatment of small cities as if they were their own possessions; and to secure the loyalty of their allies by good will and acts of kindness and not by coercion and acts of violence.[2] He urges them to model themselves on their ancestors—not the generation preceding the Decelean War, who all but destroyed the 413 B.C.
city, but those who lived before the Persian Wars, 490–479 B.C.
who had an unbroken record of noble conduct.[3] He shows that neither a large fleet of warships nor a Hellenic empire ruled by force can make Athens great, but a policy based on justice and succour for the wronged.[4] He urges them to make the good will of the Greek world their peculiar possession, regarding this as the foundation of the city's prosperity.[5] He advises them to be warlike in their preparations and their exercises, but to be peaceable in committing no act of aggression against anybody.[6] He teaches them that nothing in the world can promote wealth, fame and happiness in general as potently as virtue in its various aspects; and he criticises those who have not grasped these principles, and have thought injustice profitable and advantageous in everyday

[1] *On the Peace*, 7.
[2] 134.
[3] 74–76.
[4] 29; 64; 137.
[5] 135.
[6] 136.

καθ' ἡμέραν συμφέρουσαν, τὴν δὲ δικαιοσύνην ἀλυσιτελῆ καὶ μᾶλλον ἑτέροις ἢ τοῖς ἔχουσιν ὠφέλιμον. τούτων γὰρ οὐκ οἶδ' εἴ τις ἂν ἢ βελτίους ἢ ἀληθεστέρους ἢ μᾶλλον πρέποντας φιλοσοφίᾳ δύναιτο λόγους εἰπεῖν.

8 τίς δὲ τὸν Ἀρεοπαγιτικὸν ἀναγνοὺς λόγον οὐκ ἂν γένοιτο κοσμιώτερος, ἢ τίς οὐκ ἂν θαυμάσειε τὴν ἐπιβολὴν τοῦ ῥήτορος; ὃς ἐτόλμησε διαλεχθῆναι περὶ πολιτείας Ἀθηναίοις ἀξιῶν μεταθέσθαι μὲν τὴν τότε καθεστῶσαν δημοκρατίαν ὡς μεγάλα βλάπτουσαν τὴν πόλιν, ὑπὲρ ἧς τῶν δημαγωγῶν οὐθεὶς ἐπεχείρει λέγειν, θεωρῶν εἰς τοσαύτην αὐτὴν προεληλυθυῖαν ἀκοσμίαν, ὥστε μηδὲ τοὺς ἄρχοντας ἔτι τῶν ἰδιωτῶν κρατεῖν, ἀλλ' ἕκαστον, ὅ τι καθ' ἡδονὴν αὐτῷ γίνοιτο, καὶ ποιοῦντα καὶ λέγοντα. καὶ τὴν ἄκαιρον παρρησίαν δημοτικὴν ἐξουσίαν ὑπὸ πάντων νομιζομένην, ἀνασώσασθαι δὲ τὴν ὑπὸ Σόλωνός τε καὶ Κλεισθένους κατασταθεῖσαν πολιτείαν. ἧς τὴν προαίρεσιν καὶ τὰ ἤθη[1] διεξιὼν δεινότερον μὲν ἡγεῖσθαί φησι τοὺς τότε ἀνθρώπους τὸ τοῖς πρεσβυτέροις ἀντειπεῖν ἢ ⟨λοιδορήσασθαι ἢ νῦν περὶ τοὺς γονέας ἐξαμαρτεῖν⟩[2] δημοκρατίαν δὲ αὐτοὺς νομίζειν οὐ τὴν ἀκολασίαν, ἀλλὰ τὴν σωφροσύνην. τὸ δὲ ἐλεύθερον οὐκ ἐν τῷ καταφρονεῖν τῶν ἀρχόντων ἀλλ' ἐν τῷ τὰ κελευόμενα ποιεῖν τίθεσθαι, ἐξουσίαν τε οὐθενὶ τῶν ἀκολάστων ἐπιτρέπειν, ἀλλὰ τοῖς βελτίστοις ἀνατιθέναι τὰς ἀρχάς, τοιούτους ἔσεσθαι τοὺς ἄλλους

[1] ἤθη Holwell: ἔθη codd.
[2] λοιδορήσασθαι—ἐξαμαρτεῖν inclusi ex Isocrate.

[1] 32. [2] *Areopagiticus*, 20.

dealings, and justice unprofitable and less beneficial to those who practice it than to those who do not.[1] I doubt whether one could adduce any better or more valid arguments than these, or any that are more fitting to a philosopher.

Who would not become a more responsible citizen 8
after reading the *Areopagiticus*? Or who would not admire the orator's enterprise in daring to discuss their constitution with the Athenians and recommending that the established democracy be changed because of the harm it was doing to the city? This was a subject which no politician was prepared to broach; but Isocrates saw that she had reached such a state of disorder that even the magistrates no longer exercised control over private citizens, but every individual man was doing and saying just what he pleased, and all were equating the rash use of free speech with the exercise of democratic power.[2] He recommended the restoration of the constitution of 594 ff., 508 ff. B.C.
Solon and Cleisthenes.[3] In describing the purpose and the moral basis of this constitution he says that the men of that age considered it a worse crime to contradict their elders ⟨or to commit slander than those of today regard acts committed against parents⟩;[4] and they equated democracy not with licence, but with self-control. He says that they considered freedom to consist not in contempt for authority but in obedience to its commands;[5] and they did not confer power upon incorrigible men, but entrusted the offices of state to the most worthy, in the expectation that the rest of the citizens would model their conduct on that of their administrators.[6]

[3] 16.
[4] 49.
[5] 20.
[6] 22.

ὑπολαμβάνοντας, οἷοί περ ἂν ὦσιν οἱ τὴν πόλιν διοικοῦντες. ἀντὶ δὲ τοῦ τὰς ἰδίας οὐσίας ἐκ τῶν δημοσίων ἐπανορθοῦν τοὺς ἰδίους πλούτους εἰς τὰ κοινὰ καταχορηγεῖν.[1] χωρὶς δὲ τούτων πλείω τὴν ἐπιμέλειαν ποιεῖσθαι τοὺς πατέρας τῶν υἱῶν ἀνδρῶν γενομένων ἢ παίδων ὄντων ἐποιοῦντο, ἐνθυμουμένους, ὡς οὐκ ἐξ ἐκείνης τῆς παιδείας ἀλλ' ἐκ ταύτης τῆς σωφροσύνης μᾶλλον ὠφελεῖται τὸ κοινόν. κρείττονά τε ὑπολαμβάνειν τὰ χρηστὰ ἐπιτηδεύματα τῆς ἀκριβοῦς νομοθεσίας, σκοποῦντας οὐχ ὅπως ταῖς τιμωρίαις τοὺς ἁμαρτάνοντας ἀνείρξουσιν, ἀλλ' ὡς μηδὲν ἄξιον ζημίας ἕκαστον ⟨παρασκευάσουσιν⟩ [2] ἐπιτηδεύειν, καὶ τὴν μὲν πατρίδα δεῖν οἰομένους ἐν ἐξουσίᾳ διάγειν μεγάλῃ, τοῖς δ' ἰδιώταις μηδὲν ἐξεῖναι ποιεῖν, ὅ τι ἂν οἱ νόμοι κωλύωσι. καρτερεῖν δὲ τὰ δεινὰ καὶ μὴ ἐκπλήττεσθαι ταῖς συμφοραῖς.

9 τίς δ' ἂν μᾶλλον πείσειε καὶ πόλιν καὶ ἄνδρας τοῦ ῥήτορος πολλαχῇ μὲν καὶ ἄλλῃ, μάλιστα δ' ἐν τῷ πρὸς Λακεδαιμονίους γραφέντι λόγῳ, ὃς ἐπιγράφεται μὲν Ἀρχίδαμος, ὑπόθεσιν δὲ περιείληφε τὴν περὶ τοῦ μὴ προέσθαι Μεσσήνην Βοιωτοῖς μηδὲ ποιεῖν τὸ προσταττόμενον ὑπὸ τῶν ἐχθρῶν; ἠτύχητο γὰρ δὴ τοῖς Λακεδαιμονίοις ἥ τε περὶ Λεῦκτρα μάχη καὶ πολλαὶ μετ' ἐκείνην ἕτεραι, καὶ τὰ μὲν Θηβαίων πράγματα ἤνθει τε καὶ εἰς μέγεθος ἀρχῆς προεληλύθει, τὰ δὲ τῆς Σπάρτης ταπεινὰ καὶ ἀνάξια τῆς ἀρχαίας ἡγεμονίας γεγόνει. τελευτῶσα γοῦν, ἵνα τύχῃ τῆς εἰρήνης ἡ πόλις, ἐβουλεύετο εἰ χρὴ Μεσσηνίας ἀποστῆναι,

[1] καταχορηγεῖν Corais: καταχορηγήσειν codd.

Instead of reimbursing themselves at the state's expense, they used up their private resources to defray the cost of public services.[1] Furthermore, fathers in those days supervised their sons with greater care after they had grown up than during their boyhood, because they thought that the common good would be served better by their later self-restraint than by their earlier education.[2] They also believed that a good code of behaviour is better than punctilious legislation, and aimed not to constrain wrongdoers by punishment but to dispose them individually not to engage in any activity that merited it.[3] They thought that their city should continue to exercise great power, but that its private citizens should do nothing that was forbidden by the law; and that they should be steadfast in the face of adversity and undaunted by disasters.

There are many examples of Isocrates's unrivalled 9
power to persuade men and states, but what better one could there be than the speech addressed to the Spartans, entitled *Archidamus*? The purpose of this 366 B.C.
speech is to persuade the Spartans not to comply with the demand of their Boeotian enemies to cede Messene to them. Now the Spartans had suffered defeats at Leuctra and in several subsequent battles. 371 *and later* B.C.
The Thebans were at the height of their power and had advanced to imperial greatness, while the fortunes of Sparta had declined and were unworthy of her past leadership. Finally, in order to obtain peace, Sparta was considering whether to withdraw

[1] 24. [2] 37.
[3] 39; 40; 42; 48.

---

[2] παρασκευάσουσιν supplevit Radermacher ex Isocrate.

ταύτην ἐπιτιθέντων αὐτῇ Βοιωτῶν τὴν ἀνάγκην. ὁρῶν οὖν αὐτὴν ἀνάξια πράττειν μέλλουσαν τῶν προγόνων τόνδε τὸν λόγον συνετάξατο Ἀρχιδάμῳ νέῳ μὲν ὄντι καὶ οὔπω βασιλεύοντι, ἐλπίδας δὲ πολλὰς ἔχοντι ταύτης τεύξεσθαι τῆς τιμῆς. ἐν ᾧ διεξέρχεται πρῶτον μέν, ὡς δικαίως ἐκτήσαντο Μεσσήνην Λακεδαιμόνιοι, παραδόντων τε αὐτὴν τῶν Κρεσφόντου παίδων ὅτε ἐξέπεσον ἐκ τῆς ἀρχῆς, καὶ τοῦ θεοῦ προστάξαντος δέχεσθαι καὶ τιμωρεῖν τοῖς ἀδικουμένοις, πρὸς δὲ τούτοις ἐπικυρώσαντος μὲν τὴν κτῆσιν τοῦ πολέμου, κάτοχον δὲ καὶ βέβαιον πεποιηκότος τοῦ χρόνου. διδάσκει δέ, ὡς οὐ Μεσσηνίοις τοῖς οὐκέτ' οὖσιν ἀλλὰ δούλοις καὶ εἵλωσιν ὁρμητήριον καὶ καταφυγὴν παρέξουσι τὴν πόλιν. διεξέρχεταί τε τοὺς κινδύνους τῶν προγόνων, οὓς ὑπέμειναν ἕνεκα τῆς ἡγεμονίας, καὶ τῆς δόξης ὑπομιμνήσκει τῆς παρὰ τοῖς Ἕλλησιν ὑπαρχούσης περὶ αὐτῶν παραινεῖ τε μὴ συγκαταπίπτειν ταῖς τύχαις μηδ' ἀπογιγνώσκειν τὰς μεταβολάς, ἐνθυμουμένους ὅτι πολλοὶ μὲν ἤδη μείζω δύναμιν ἔχοντες ἢ Θηβαῖοι ὑπὸ τῶν ἀσθενεστέρων ἐκρατήθησαν, πολλοὶ δὲ εἰς πολιορκίαν κατακλεισθέντες καὶ δεινότερα ἢ Λακεδαιμόνιοι πάσχοντες διέφθειραν τοὺς ἐπιστρατεύσαντας. καὶ παράδειγμα ποιεῖται τὴν Ἀθηναίων πόλιν, ἥτις ἐκ πολλῆς εὐδαιμονίας ἀνάστατος γενομένη τοὺς ἐσχάτους ὑπέστη κινδύνους, ἵνα μὴ τοῖς βαρβάροις ποιῇ τὸ προσταττόμενον. παρακελεύεται δὲ καὶ καρτερεῖν ἐπὶ τοῖς παροῦσι καὶ θαρρεῖν περὶ τῶν μελλόντων, ἐπισταμένους ὅτι τὰς τοιαύτας συμφορὰς αἱ πόλεις

from Messenia, which was the condition being imposed on her by the Boeotians. Seeing that the Spartans were about to act in a manner unworthy of their ancestors, Isocrates composed this speech on behalf of the young Archidamus, who had not yet come to the throne, but had high hopes of achieving this honour. In the speech he describes how the Spartans acquired Messene by just means, having been given it by the sons of Cresphontes, when they were deposed,[1] and had been instructed by the god to accept the gift and avenge the wronged;[2] and how, in addition, the subsequent war had legalised the acquisition, and time had confirmed and consolidated it. He then points out that by ceding the city they would be providing a base and a refuge not for the Messenians, who were by now no longer in existence, but for slaves and Helots.[3] He then describes the perils which their ancestors faced in order to preserve their hegemony, then reminds them of their existing reputation in the Greek world, and urges them not to yield to misfortunes or to abandon the new situation as hopeless, but to recall that many more powerful states than Thebes have been overcome by weaker states before, and that many beleaguered garrisons in a worse plight than the Spartans have destroyed their attackers.[4] He illustrates this by the example of the Athenian state, which, after enjoying great prosperity, was evacuated and underwent extreme danger rather than obey the orders of a foreign 480 B.C.
power.[5] He then exhorts the Spartans to endure their present misfortunes and be optimistic for the

[1] *Archidamus*, 16.
[2] 23.
[3] 28.
[4] 40.
[5] 42.

ἐπανορθοῦνται πολιτείᾳ χρηστῇ καὶ πολέμων ἐμπειρίαις, ἐν οἷς προεῖχεν ἡ Σπάρτη τῶν ἄλλων πόλεων. οἴεται δὲ δεῖν οὐ τοὺς[1] κακῶς πράττοντας εἰρήνης ἐπιθυμεῖν, οἷς ἐκ τῆς καινουργίας ἐπὶ τὸ κρεῖττον μεταβάλλειν τὰ πράγματα ἐλπίς, ἀλλὰ τοὺς εὐτυχοῦντας· ἐν γὰρ τἀκινδύνῳ τὴν τῶν παρόντων ἀγαθῶν εἶναι φυλακήν. πολλὰ δὲ καὶ ἄλλα πρὸς τούτοις διεξελθών, ὅσα καὶ κοινῇ καὶ ἰδίᾳ τοῖς ἐπιφανεστάτοις αὐτῶν ἐπράχθη κατὰ τοὺς πολέμους λαμπρὰ ἔργα, καὶ ὅσης αἰσχύνης ἄξια δράσουσι, καὶ ὡς καὶ διαβληθήσονται παρὰ τοῖς Ἕλλησιν, ἐπιλογισάμενος καὶ ὅτι πάντοθεν αὐτοῖς ἐπικουρία τις ἔσται τὸν ἀγῶνα ποιουμένοις καὶ παρὰ θεῶν καὶ παρὰ συμμάχων καὶ παρὰ πάντων ἀνθρώπων, οἷς ἐπίφθονος ἡ Θηβαίων δύναμις αὐξομένη, καὶ τὴν κατέχουσαν ἀκοσμίαν καὶ ταραχὴν τὰς πόλεις ἐπιτροπευόντων τῆς Ἑλλάδος Βοιωτῶν ἐπιδειξάμενος, τελευτῶν, εἰ καὶ μηθὲν τούτων μέλλοι γίνεσθαι μηδ' ὑπολείποιτό τις ἄλλη σωτηρίας ἐλπίς, ἐκλιπεῖν κελεύει τὴν πόλιν, διδάσκων αὐτούς, ὡς χρὴ παῖδας μὲν καὶ γυναῖκας καὶ τὸν ἄλλον ὄχλον εἴς τε Σικελίαν ἐκπέμψαι καὶ Ἰταλίαν καὶ τἄλλα χωρία τὰ φίλια, αὐτοὺς δὲ καταλαβομένους τόπον, ὅστις ἂν ὀχυρώτατος ᾖ καὶ πρὸς τὸν πόλεμον ἐπιτηδειότατος, ἄγειν καὶ φέρειν τοὺς πολεμίους καὶ κατὰ γῆν καὶ κατὰ θάλατταν. οὐδεμίαν γὰρ ἀξιώσειν δύναμιν ὁμόσε χωρεῖν ἀνδράσι κρατίστοις μὲν τὰ

[1] *οὐ τοὺς* F, Reiske: *αὐτοὺς* codd.

---

[1] 48. [2] 50.

future, in the knowledge that states recover from such disasters if they have good institutions and military experience, in both of which Sparta once led the Greek world.[1] He considers that a desire for peace is not to be expected from those who are suffering ill-fortune, for such men will look to revolutionary action to produce a change for the better, but from the fortunate,[2] who find protection for their present position in the avoidance of danger.[3] He further describes many brilliant exploits of Sparta's most famous sons in war,[4] both public and private, and contrasts these with the shame their proposed action will incur,[5] and also the abuse they will suffer at the hands of the Greeks. Help, he argues, will pour in from every source if they take up the struggle—from the gods, from their allies, from all men—for the rise of Thebes is viewed with odium by the whole Greek world,[6] which he shows to owe its present state of disorder and confusion to Boeotian administration.[7] Finally he proposes that, should none of these possibilities be realised and no other hope of saving the city remain, they should abandon their city,[8] and he explains that they must transport their women and children and the rest of the population to Sicily, Italy and other friendly lands,[9] and themselves occupy the strongest position from which they can conduct the war to the greatest effect, and then plunder and harass the enemy by land and sea.[10] No force would dare to join battle with the best warriors in Greece when they have been driven desperate to the point of sui-

[3] 104.
[4] 52–53.
[5] 57.
[6] 59.
[7] 64–69.
[8] 70.
[9] 73.
[10] 74.

πολέμια τῶν Ἑλλήνων, ἀπονενοημένως δὲ πρὸς τὸ ζῆν διακειμένοις, δικαίαν δὲ ὀργὴν καὶ πρόφασιν εὐπρεπῆ τῆς ἀνάγκης ἔχουσι. ταῦτα γὰρ οὐ Λακεδαιμονίοις μόνοις συμβουλεύειν φαίην ἂν αὐτὸν ἔγωγε ἀλλὰ καὶ τοῖς ἄλλοις Ἕλλησι καὶ πᾶσιν ἀνθρώποις πολλῷ κρεῖττον ἁπάντων φιλοσόφων, οἳ τέλος ποιοῦνται τοῦ βίου τὴν ἀρετὴν καὶ τὸ καλόν.

10 ἔχων δὲ πολλοὺς αὐτοῦ καὶ ἄλλους διεξιέναι λόγους πρὸς πόλεις τε καὶ δυνάστας καὶ ἰδιώτας γραφέντας, ὧν οἱ μὲν εἰς ὁμόνοιαν καὶ σωφροσύνην τὰ πλήθη παρακαλοῦσιν, οἱ δὲ εἰς μετριότητα καὶ νόμιμον ἀρχὴν τοὺς δυνάστας προάγουσιν, οἱ δὲ κοσμίους τῶν ἰδιωτῶν ἀπεργάζονται τοὺς βίους, ἃ δεῖ πράττειν ἕκαστον ὑποτιθέμενοι, δεδοικὼς μὴ πέρα τοῦ δέοντος ὁ λόγος ἐκμηκυνθῇ μοι, ταῦτα μὲν ἐάσω, τοῦ δ' εὐπαρακολούθητα γενέσθαι μοι μᾶλλον τὰ πρόσθεν εἰρημένα, καὶ τῆς διαφορᾶς ἕνεκα, ᾗ διαλλάττει Λυσίου, τὰς ἀρετὰς αὐτῶν εἰς βραχύτερον συναγαγὼν λόγον ἐπὶ τὰ παραδείγματα μεταβήσομαι.

11 πρώτην μὲν τοίνυν ἔφην ἀρετὴν εἶναι λόγων τὴν καθαρὰν ἑρμηνείαν, ἐν ᾗ διαλλαγὴν οὐδεμίαν εὕρισκον παρ' οὐδετέρῳ. ἔπειτα τὴν ἀκρίβειαν τὴν διαλέκτου τῆς τότε συνήθους· καὶ ταύτην ἑώρων ὁμοίαν παρ' ἀμφοτέροις. μετὰ ταῦτα ἐπελογιζόμην, ὅτι τοῖς κυρίοις καὶ συνήθεσι καὶ κοινοῖς ὀνόμασιν ἀμφότεροι κέχρηνται, ἡ δὲ Ἰσοκράτους λέξις προσλαβοῦσά τι τῆς τροπικῆς κατασκευῆς μέχρι τοῦ μὴ λυπῆσαι προῆλθεν. τῆς σαφηνείας καὶ τῆς ἐναργείας ἀμφοτέρους κρατεῖν

cide, and are fortified by righteous indignation and the compelling motive of necessity.[1] I should suggest that Isocrates was giving this advice not to the Spartans alone but to all Greeks and all men; and it is much more effective advice than that given by all those philosophers who assert that the purpose of life is to pursue what is good and noble.

I could describe many other discourses which Iso- 10
crates addressed to states, to potentates and to private citizens. Some of these call upon the people to foster harmony and moderation; others advise princes to rule temperately and according to the laws; others try to induce private citizens to lead an orderly life: in each case the proper course of action is suggested. But I shall leave this subject here for fear that my treatise may become too long; and in order to make my previous remarks easier to follow,[2] and to bring out the differences which contrast his style with that of Lysias, I shall summarise its qualities in a briefer account than before, and then proceed to some examples.

I said that purity of expression was a primary virtue 11
in oratory, and could find no difference between the two orators in this.[3] I also found them similar in their scrupulous conformity with the dialect of their day. Next I noted that they both use standard, familiar and ordinary language, but that Isocrates has occasional recourse to metaphorical expression, though to an unexceptionable degree. I pronounced both to be masters of lucidity and vividness, but

[1] 75.
[2] Cf. Aristotle, *Nicomachean Ethics* ii. 7. 11.
[3] ch. 11 is a summary of chs. 2 and 3.

ἀπεφηνάμην, ἐν δὲ τῷ συντόμως ἐκφέρειν τὰ νοήματα Λυσίαν μᾶλλον ἡγούμην ἐπιτυγχάνειν. περὶ τὰς αὐξήσεις Ἰσοκράτη κατορθοῦν ἄμεινον ἐδόκουν. ἐν τῷ συστρέφειν τὰ νοήματα καὶ στρογγύλως ἐκφέρειν ὡς πρὸς ἀληθινοὺς ἀγῶνας ἐπιτήδειον Λυσίαν ἀπεδεχόμην. ἐν ταῖς ἠθοποιΐαις ἀμφοτέρους εὕρισκον δεξιούς, τῆς δὲ χάριτος καὶ τῆς ἡδονῆς ἀναμφιλόγως ἀπεδίδουν τὰ πρωτεῖα Λυσίᾳ. τὸ μεγαλοπρεπὲς ἑώρων [1] παρ' Ἰσοκράτει. τοῦ πιθανοῦ καὶ πρέποντος οὐδέτερον ἐδόκουν ἀπολείπεσθαι. ἐν τῇ συνθέσει τῶν ὀνομάτων Λυσίαν μὲν ἀφελέστερον ἔκρινον, Ἰσοκράτην δὲ περιεργότερον, καὶ τὸν μὲν τῆς ἀληθείας πιθανώτερον [2] εἰκαστήν, τὸν δὲ τῆς κατασκευῆς ἀθλητὴν ἰσχυρότερον.

12 ταῦτα ἔφην περὶ τῆς λέξεως τῆς ἑκατέρου. τῶν δὲ πραγμάτων ποιούμενος ⟨τὴν⟩ [3] ἐξέτασιν, τὴν μὲν εὕρεσιν θαυμαστὴν παρ' ἀμφοῖν κατελαβόμην καὶ ἔτι τὴν κρίσιν. τῇ δὲ τάξει τῶν ἐνθυμημάτων καὶ τοῖς μερισμοῖς τῶν ἐπιχειρημάτων καὶ τῇ καθ' ἕκαστον εἶδος ἐξεργασίᾳ τοῖς τε ἄλλοις ἅπασι τοῖς ἐν τῷ πραγματικῷ τόπῳ θεωρήμασι παρὰ πολὺ προτερεῖν ἡγούμην Ἰσοκράτην Λυσίου, κατὰ δὲ τὴν λαμπρότητα τῶν ὑποθέσεων καὶ τὸ φιλόσοφον τῆς προαιρέσεως πλεῖον διαφέρειν ἢ παιδὸς ἄνδρα, ὡς ὁ Πλάτων εἴρηκεν, εἰ δὲ χρὴ τἀληθὲς εἰπεῖν, καὶ τῶν ἄλλων ἁπάντων ῥητόρων, ὅσοι φιλοσόφως τοῦ μαθήματος τούτου προέστησαν. τῆς μέντοι ἀγωγῆς τῶν περιόδων τὸ κύκλιον καὶ

[1] ἑώρων Kiessling: ἡρῷον codd.
[2] πιθανώτερον Sylburg: πιθανότερον codd.

found Lysias the more successful in the concise expression of ideas, and Isocrates the superior at rhetorical amplification. In view of his ability to reduce ideas to their essentials and to express them tersely, I acknowledged Lysias to be a suitable orator for actual lawsuits. In the portrayal of moral qualities I found both equally skilful, but I had no hesitation in giving the prize for charm and grace to Lysias, and that for impressiveness to Isocrates. I thought that neither was deficient in persuasiveness and propriety. I judged Lysias to be the simpler in sentence-structure and Isocrates the more elaborate; the former more convincing in creating the illusion of truth, the latter the more powerful master of technique.

Such were my comments on the style of each 12
orator. When I came to examine subject-matter, I found the invention and also the division to be admirable in both, but in the arrangement of individual arguments and the partition of rhetorical proofs, and generally in the development of each form of statement, and in all other aspects of the treatment of subject-matter, I thought Isocrates far superior to Lysias,[1] to tell the truth, while in the brilliance of his themes and his philosophic purpose his superiority to all other orators, not only to Lysias but to all other orators who have won professional eminence in this branch of learning, is greater than (to use Plato's words) that of a grown man to a boy.[2] I did not, however, approve of his cyclic construction of the

[1] ch. 12 thus far is a summary of ch. 4.
[2] *Phaedrus*, 279A.

---

[3] τὴν inseruit Radermacher.

τῶν σχηματισμῶν τῆς λέξεως τὸ μειρακιῶδες οὐκ ἐδοκίμαζον. δουλεύει γὰρ ἡ διάνοια πολλάκις τῷ ῥυθμῷ τῆς λέξεως καὶ τοῦ κομψοῦ λείπεται τὸ ἀληθινόν. κράτιστον δὲ[1] ἐπιτήδευμα ἐν διαλέκτῳ πολιτικῇ καὶ ἐναγωνίῳ τὸ ὁμοιότατον τῷ κατὰ φύσιν. βούλεται δὲ ἡ φύσις τοῖς νοήμασιν ἕπεσθαι τὴν λέξιν, οὐ τῇ λέξει τὰ νοήματα. συμβούλῳ δὲ δὴ περὶ πολέμου καὶ εἰρήνης λέγοντι καὶ ἰδιώτῃ τὸν περὶ ψυχῆς τρέχοντι κίνδυνον ἐν δικασταῖς τὰ κομψὰ καὶ θεατρικὰ καὶ μειρακιώδη ταῦτα οὐκ οἶδα ἥντινα δύναιτο ἂν παρασχεῖν ὠφέλειαν, μᾶλλον δὲ οἶδα ὅτι καὶ βλάβης ἂν αἴτια γένοιτο. χαριεντισμὸς γὰρ πᾶς ἐν σπουδῇ καὶ κακοῖς[2] γινόμενος ἄωρον πρᾶγμα καὶ πολεμιώτατον ἐλέῳ.

13 οὗτος δὲ οὐκ ἐμὸς ὁ λόγος πρώτου μὰ Δία, ἐπεὶ πολλοὶ καὶ τῶν παλαιῶν ταύτην εἶχον ὑπὲρ αὐτοῦ τὴν δόξαν. Φιλόνικος μὲν γὰρ ὁ διαλεκτικὸς τὴν ἄλλην κατασκευὴν τῆς λέξεως ἐπαινῶν τἀνδρὸς μέμφεται τῆς κενότητός τ' αὐτῆς καὶ τοῦ φορτικοῦ ἐοικέναι τέ φησιν αὐτὸν ζωγράφῳ ταῖς αὐταῖς ἐσθῆσι[3] καὶ τοῖς αὐτοῖς σχήμασι πάσας ἐπικοσμοῦντι τὰς γραφάς· "ἅπαντας γοῦν εὕρισκον τοὺς λόγους αὐτοῦ τοῖς αὐτοῖς τρόποις τῆς λέξεως κεχρημένους, ὥστ' ἐν πολλοῖς τεχνικῶς τὰ καθ' ἕκαστα ἐξεργαζόμενον τοῖς ὅλοις ἀπρεπῆ παντελῶς φαίνεσθαι διὰ τὸ μὴ προσηκόντως τοῖς ὑποκειμένοις τῶν ἠθῶν φράζειν." Ἱερώνυμος δὲ ὁ φιλό-

[1] δὲ Krüger: τε codd.
[2] καὶ κακοῖς Casaubon: καὶ καλῶς codd.
[3] ἐσθῆσι Ammon: ἐσθήσεσι codd.

[1] See chs. 2–3. [2] See ch. 2; *Lysias*, 3.

period and his juvenile use of figures of speech, whereby the thought often becomes slave to the rhythm of the words, and realism is sacrificed to elegance.[1] The most effective style to cultivate in political and forensic oratory is that which most resembles natural speech;[2] and nature demands that the words should follow the thought, not *vice versa.* I certainly doubt whether these affected, histrionic and juvenile devices could be of any assistance either to a politician advising on matters of war and peace or to a defendant whose life is at stake in a law-court; on the contrary, I am sure that they could cause considerable damage. Preciosity is always out of place in serious discussion and in unhappy situations, and tends to destroy all sympathy for the speaker.

This judgment of mine is not, of course, original:[3] 13
many earlier critics have held the same view regarding Isocrates. Philonicus the grammarian,[4] while in general praising the artistry of his style, criticises its lack of substance and of taste, and says that he is like a painter who portrays all his subjects wearing the same clothes and adopting the same pose. He says: "I found the same figures of speech used in all his speeches, so that although in many individual cases the treatment was skilful, the overall effect was completely incongruous because the language did not accord with the underlying nature of his characters." Hieronymus the philosopher[5] says that one could

[3] Euripides, Frag. 488 Nauck.

[4] In view of Dionysius's use of the word διαλεκτικός, perhaps a Stoic grammarian. He was a Megarian. See Blass, *Die Attische Beredsamkeit*, ii. p. 120.

[5] Philosopher and literary historian, *c.* 290–230 B.C. Trained as a Peripatetic, but founded a school of his own at Athens. Cf. Philodemus, *Rhetorica*, Sudhaus p. 198.

σοφός φησιν ἀναγνῶναι μὲν ἄν τινα δυνηθῆναι τοὺς λόγους αὐτοῦ καλῶς, δημηγορῆσαι δὲ τήν τε φωνὴν καὶ τὸν τόνον ἐπάραντα καὶ ἐν ταύτῃ τῇ κατασκευῇ μετὰ τῆς ἁρμοττούσης ὑποκρίσεως εἰπεῖν οὐ παντελῶς. τὸ γὰρ μέγιστον καὶ κινητικώτατον τῶν ὄχλων παρεῖσθαι,[1] τὸ παθητικὸν καὶ ἔμψυχον· δουλεύειν γὰρ αὐτὸν τῇ λειότητι διαπαντός, τὸ δὲ κεκραμένον καὶ παντοδαπὸν ἐπιτάσει τε καὶ ἀνέσει καὶ τὸ ταῖς παθητικαῖς ὑπερθέσεσι[2] διειλημμένον ἀποβεβληκέναι.[3] καθόλου δέ φησιν αὐτὸν εἰς ἀναγνώστου παιδὸς φωνὴν καταδύντα μήτε τόνον μήτε πάθος μήτε ὑπόκρισιν δύνασθαι φέρειν. πολλοῖς δὲ καὶ ἄλλοις ταῦτα καὶ παραπλήσια τούτοις εἴρηται, περὶ ὧν οὐδὲν δέομαι γράφειν. ἐξ αὐτῆς γὰρ ἔσται τῆς Ἰσοκράτους λέξεως τεθείσης καταφανὴς ὅ τε τῶν περιόδων ῥυθμὸς ἐκ παντὸς διώκων τὸ γλαφυρὸν καὶ τῶν σχημάτων τὸ μειρακιῶδες περὶ τὰς ἀντιθέσεις καὶ παρισώσεις καὶ παρομοιώσεις κατατριβόμενον. καὶ οὐ τὸ γένος μέμφομαι τῶν σχημάτων (πολλοὶ γὰρ αὐτοῖς ἐχρήσαντο καὶ συγγραφεῖς καὶ ῥήτορες, ἀνθίσαι βουλόμενοι τὴν λέξιν), ἀλλὰ τὸν πλεονασμόν.

14 τῷ γὰρ μὴ ἐν καιρῷ γίνεσθαι μηδὲ ἐν ὥρᾳ ταῦτα τὰ σχήματα[4] προσίστασθαί φημι ταῖς ἀκοαῖς. ἐν γοῦν τῷ πανηγυρικῷ τῷ περιβοήτῳ λόγῳ πολύς

[1] παρεῖσθαι Philod.: παραιτεῖσθαι codd.
[2] ὑπερθέσεσιν Philod.: ὑποθέσεσι codd.
[3] ἀποβεβληκέναι Philod.: ὑπερβεβηκέναι codd.
[4] ταῦτα τὰ σχήματα supplevi lacunam a Radermachero significatam.

read his discourses effectively, but to declaim them in public with modulation of the volume and the pitch of the voice, and with the appropriate techniques of delivery that are used in live oratory, would be quite impossible; for he has neglected the orator's most important instrument for arousing the emotions of a crowd—animation and intensity of feeling. He is always the slave of smoothness, and has sacrificed the advantages of the moderation and variety that are achieved by the increase and relaxation of tension, and has not divided up his speeches by means of emotional climaxes. He concludes that the reader of Isocrates's prose must assume the monotonous voice of a child, because it cannot accommodate inflection, expression or animated delivery. Many other critics have passed this and similar judgments, and there is no need for me to comment on these. An actual example will clearly display both the rhythmic nature of the periods, which aims at a polished effect by every means, and the juvenile affectation of his figures, which exhausts itself with its antitheses and clauses of equal length and with rhyming endings.[1] I have no fault to find with this type of figure, which many historians and orators have used from a desire to add colour to their style; but I consider that he has overdone their use.

I say, then, that he offends the ear by the untimely 14
and unseasonable use of these figures. Even in his

[1] *Antithesis*: clauses or phrases containing contrasting subject-matter, whether or not contrived.
Parisosis: parallel clauses or phrases having corresponding words and approximately equal length.
Paromoeosis: parallel clauses or phrases with the same syllables in corresponding places, resulting in assonance and, when occurring at the ends, in rhyme.

ἐστιν ἐν τοῖς τοιούτοις· "πλείστων μὲν οὖν ἀγαθῶν αἰτίους καὶ μεγίστων ἐπαίνων ἀξίους ἡγοῦμαι"· ἐνταῦθα γὰρ οὐ μόνον τῷ κώλῳ τὸ κῶλον ἴσον, ἀλλὰ καὶ τὰ ὀνόματα τοῖς ὀνόμασι, τῷ μὲν πλείστων τὸ μεγίστων, τῷ δ' ἀγαθῶν τὸ ἐπαίνων,[1] τῷ δὲ αἰτίους τὸ ἀξίους. καὶ αὖθις· "οὐδὲ ἀπέλαυον μὲν ὡς ἰδίων, ἠμέλουν δὲ ὡς ἀλλοτρίων"· τό τε γὰρ κῶλον τὸ δεύτερον τῷ κώλῳ πάρισον καὶ τῶν ὀνομάτων τῷ μὲν ἀπέλαυον τὸ ἠμέλουν ἀντίθετον, τῷ δὲ ἰδίων τὸ ἀλλοτρίων. οἷς ἐπιτίθησιν· "ἀλλὰ ἐκήδοντο μὲν ὡς οἰκείων, ἀπείχοντο δὲ ὥσπερ χρὴ τῶν μηδὲν προσηκόντων." ἀντίκειται [γὰρ][2] δὴ πάλιν κἀνταῦθα τῷ μὲν ἐκήδοντο τὸ ἀπείχοντο, τῷ δὲ οἰκείων τὸ μηδὲν προσηκόντων. καὶ οὔπω ταῦθ' ἱκανά, ἀλλ' ἐν τῇ μετὰ ταῦτα περιόδῳ πάλιν ἀντιστρέφει τῷ μὲν "αὐτός τε μέλλοι μάλιστα εὐδοκιμήσειν" τὸ ἐπιφερόμενον "καὶ τοῖς παισὶ μεγάλην δόξαν καταλείψειν," τῷ δὲ "οὐδὲ τὰς θρασύτητας τὰς ἀλλήλων ἐζήλουν" τὸ συναπτόμενον αὐτῷ "οὐδὲ τὰς τόλμας τὰς αὑτῶν ἤσκουν." καὶ οὐδὲ μικρὸν διαλιπὼν ἐπιφέρει τούτοις· "ἀλλὰ δεινότερον μὲν ἐνόμιζον εἶναι κακῶς ὑπὸ τῶν πολιτῶν ἀκούειν ἢ καλῶς ὑπὲρ τῆς πατρίδος ἀποθνήσκειν." οὐκοῦν καὶ δεύτερον τῷ μὲν καλῶς τὸ κακῶς ἀντίστροφον, τῷ δὲ ἀκούειν τὸ ἀποθνήσκειν πάρισον. εἰ μέτριος εἴη[3] μέχρι δεῦρο, ἀνεκτός, ἀλλ' οὐκ ἀνήσει. πάλιν γοῦν ἐν τῇ μετ' αὐτὴν περιόδῳ τίθησιν·

[1] τῷ μὲν πλείστων τὸ μέγιστων, τῷ δ' ἀγαθῶν τὸ ἐπαίνων Wolf: τῷ μὲν πλείστῳ τὸ μέγιστον· τῷ δὲ ἀγαθῷ τὸν ἔπαινον codd.

renowned *Panegyricus* there are many examples of the following kind:[1] " I consider that those who conferred the greatest benefactions and deserved the highest commendations . . ." Here not only are the clauses equal in length, but even the words correspond—" greatest " with " highest," " benefactions " with " commendations," and " conferred " with " deserved." And again, in ". . . nor did they enjoy them as their own concern, and neglect them as if the concern of others," the second clause is the same length as the first, and there is contrast between " enjoyed " and " neglected " and between " own " and " others." This is followed by " . . . but they cared for the public revenues as for their private property, and yet abstained from them as one must from the property of others," in which " cared for " is balanced by " abstained from," and " private property " by " property of others." And, as if this is not enough, in the following period, ". . . would himself win the greatest fame " is balanced by the following " and would leave to his children the greatest name," and " neither did they emulate one another in rashness " with its continuation " nor did they cultivate recklessness in themselves." And after a short interval he comes up with this: ". . . but they thought it a more terrible thing to have a bad name with their countrymen than to die a noble death for their country." Here again we have a contrast, between " bad " and " noble," and " name " and " death " are balanced. If he were to show moderation and leave it at that, it would be tolerable; but he will not stop.

[1] 75 ff.

[2] γὰρ seclusit Radermacher. [3] εἴη Sadée: εἰ codd.

"ὅτι τοῖς ἀγαθοῖς [1] τῶν ἀνθρώπων οὐδὲν δεήσει πολλῶν γραμμάτων ἀλλ' ὀλίγων συνθημάτων, καὶ περὶ τῶν κοινῶν καὶ περὶ τῶν ἰδίων ὁμονοήσουσιν." οὐκοῦν τὸ γραμμάτων καὶ συνθημάτων πάρισον καὶ τὸ πολλῶν καὶ ὀλίγων καὶ κοινῶν καὶ ἰδίων ἀντίθετα. ἔπειθ' ὥσπερ οὐδὲν εἰρηκὼς τοιοῦτον ἀθρόαις ἐπικλύσει ταῖς παρισώσεσιν, ἐπιφέρων ταυτί· "καὶ [2] τὰ τῶν ἄλλων διῴκουν θεραπεύοντες ἀλλ' οὐχ ὑβρίζοντες τοὺς Ἕλληνας καὶ στρατηγεῖν οἰόμενοι δεῖν αὐτῶν ἀλλὰ μὴ τυραννεῖν αὐτῶν καὶ μᾶλλον ἐπιθυμοῦντες ἡγεμόνες ἢ δεσπόται προσαγορεύεσθαι καὶ σωτῆρες ἀλλὰ μὴ λυμεῶνες ἀποκαλεῖσθαι, τῷ ποιεῖν εὖ προσαγόμενοι τὰς πόλεις ἀλλ' οὐ βίᾳ καταστρεφόμενοι, πιστοτέροις μὲν τοῖς λόγοις ἢ νῦν τοῖς ὅρκοις χρώμενοι, ταῖς δὲ συνθήκαις ὥσπερ ἀνάγκαις ἐμμένειν ἀξιοῦντες." καὶ τί δεῖ τὰ καθ' ἕκαστα διεξιόντα μηκύνειν; ὀλίγου γὰρ ἅπας ὁ λόγος ὑπὸ τῶν τοιούτων αὐτῷ κεκόμψευται σχημάτων. οἱ μέντοι γε ἐπὶ τελευτῇ τοῦ βίου γραφέντες λόγοι ἧττόν εἰσι μειρακιώδεις, ὡς ἂν οἶμαι τελείαν ἀπειληφότες τὴν φρόνησιν παρὰ τοῦ χρόνου. καὶ περὶ μὲν τούτων ἱκανὰ ταῦτα.

15 ὥρα δὲ ἂν εἴη καὶ τῶν παραδειγμάτων ἅψασθαι καὶ δεῖξαι τούτοις τίς ἐστιν [3] τοῦ ῥήτορος ἰσχύς. ἅπαντα μὲν οὖν τὰ γένη τῶν προβλημάτων καὶ πάσας τὰς ἰδέας τῶν λόγων ἀμήχανον ἐν ὀλίγῳ δηλῶσαι, ἀρκεῖ δὲ μία τε δημηγορία παραληφθεῖσα

[1] καλοῖς κἀγαθοῖς Isoc.
[2] ἐπιφέρων ταυτί καὶ Holwell: ἐπιφέρων ταὐτίκα codd.

In the very next period he writes: ". . . that for good men there will be no need of many written laws, but only of a few agreements, and they will be of one mind in both public and private matters." Here "law" and "agreements" are balanced, "many" is contrasted with "few" and "public" with "private." After this, as if he had not used these figures before, he will again inundate us with floods of parallelisms, beginning the assault thus: ". . . and they conducted their relations with other Greeks in a spirit of conciliation, not of insolence, considering that they should command them in the field but not tyrannise over them, and desiring to be addressed as leaders rather than as masters, and rather to be greeted as saviours than reviled as destroyers; they won over the Greek cities by kindness instead of subduing them by force, keeping their word more faithfully than men today keep their oath, and considering their agreements as binding as necessity itself." What need is there to give a long list of individual examples? He has bedizened nearly the whole of the speech with figures of this kind. But the speeches which he wrote towards the end of his life are less juvenile in this respect, I suppose because time may have brought him a maturer mentality. But enough of this subject.

I think it may now be time to turn to examples, 15
and to show through these where our orator's strength lies. It is impossible in a short space to illustrate every class of subject which he treated or every form of oratory in which he wrote. It is enough to quote from one of his political discourses and one

---

[3] δεῖξαι τούτοις τίς ἐστιν Wolf: δεῖξαι τίς ἐστι τούτοις codd.

καὶ λόγος εἷς ἐκ ⟨τῶν⟩ [1] δικανικῶν. ὁ μὲν οὖν συμβουλευτικὸς λόγος ἔστω,[2] ἐν ᾧ παρακαλεῖ τοὺς Ἀθηναίους διαλύσασθαι μὲν τὸν συμμαχικὸν κληθέντα πόλεμον, ὃν ἐπολέμουν πρὸς αὐτοὺς Χῖοί τε καὶ Ῥόδιοι καὶ οἱ τούτων σύμμαχοι, παύσασθαι δὲ πλεονεκτοῦντας καὶ τῆς κατὰ γῆν καὶ κατὰ θάλατταν ἐπιθυμοῦντας ἀρχῆς· διδάσκων ὡς ἔστιν οὐ μόνον κρείττων ἡ δικαιοσύνη τῆς ἀδικίας ἀλλὰ καὶ ὠφελιμωτέρα. τὸ μὲν οὖν ὕπτιον καὶ ἀναβεβλημένον τῆς ἀγωγῆς καὶ τῶν περιόδων ὁ χαριεντισμὸς ἔνεστι κἀν τούτοις, τὰ δὲ θεατρικὰ τῶν σχημάτων τεταμιευμένως παρείληπται. ταῦτα μὲν δὴ παρορᾶν δεῖ τοὺς ἀναγιγνώσκοντας καὶ μὴ ἄξια ἡγεῖσθαι σπουδῆς, ὥσπερ ⟨καὶ⟩ [3] κατ' ἀρχὰς ἔφην, τοῖς δὲ ἄλλοις πάνυ προσέχειν τὸν νοῦν. ἄρχεται δὲ ὁ λόγος ἐντεῦθεν·

16 "Ἅπαντες μὲν εἰώθασιν οἱ παριόντες ἐνθάδε ταῦτα μέγιστα φάσκειν εἶναι καὶ μάλιστα σπουδῆς ἄξια τῇ πόλει, περὶ ὧν αὐτοὶ μέλλουσι συμβουλεύειν. οὐ μὴν ἀλλ' εἰ καὶ περὶ ἄλλων τινῶν πραγμάτων ἥρμοσε τοιαῦτα προειπεῖν, δοκεῖ μοι πρέπειν καὶ περὶ τῶν νῦν παρόντων ἐντεῦθεν ποιήσασθαι τὴν ἀρχήν. ἥκομεν γὰρ ἐκκλησιάσοντες περί τε πολέμου καὶ εἰρήνης, ἃ μεγίστην ἔχει δύναμιν ἐν τῷ βίῳ τῷ τῶν ἀνθρώπων καὶ περὶ ὧν ἀνάγκη τοὺς ὀρθῶς βουλευσαμένους ἄμεινον τῶν ἄλλων πράττειν. τὸ μὲν οὖν μέγεθος ὑπὲρ ὧν συνεληλύθαμεν τηλικοῦτόν ἐστιν. ὁρῶ δὲ ὑμᾶς οὐκ ἐξ ἴσου τῶν λεγόντων τὴν ἀκρόασιν

[1] τῶν inclusit Wolf.
[2] ἔστω Krüger: ἐστὶν codd.

of his forensic speeches. The political discourse is to be the one in which he calls upon the Athenians to put an end to the so-called War of the Allies, which the Chians, the Rhodians and their allies were waging against them, and to abandon their expansionist policy and their aspirations to territorial and maritime empire.[1] He shows that justice is superior to injustice not only on moral but also on practical grounds. His leisurely, suspended clausal structure and the elegance of his periods are found even in this speech, but the more histrionic figures are used sparingly. The reader should ignore these latter features, regarding them as unworthy of imitation, as I said at the beginning. But he should pay close attention to its other qualities. The speech begins with these words:[2]

"All those who come forward here to address you 16
usually claim that the subjects on which they are themselves about to advise you are of the greatest importance and worthy of serious consideration by the state. Still, I think, if it was ever appropriate to introduce the discussion of any subject with such words, the subject now before us deserves to be so introduced. For we are assembled here to deliberate about war and peace, which hold the greatest power over the life of man, and are subjects on which those who are correctly advised must inevitably fare better than other men. Such, then, is the importance of the question which brings us to this assembly.

"I see, however, that you do not listen with equal

[1] The discourse *On the Peace*. (355 B.C.).
[2] 1–17.

---

[3] καὶ inseruit Sadée.

ποιουμένους, ἀλλὰ τοῖς μὲν προσέχοντας τὸν νοῦν, τῶν δὲ οὐδὲ τῆς φωνῆς ἀνεχομένους. καὶ θαυμαστὸν οὐδὲν ποιεῖτε. καὶ γὰρ τὸν ἄλλον χρόνον εἰώθατε τοὺς ἄλλους ἅπαντας ἐκβάλλειν πλὴν τοὺς συναγορεύοντας ταῖς ἐπιθυμίαις ὑμῶν. οἷς καὶ δικαίως ἄν τις ἐπιτιμήσειεν, ὅτι συνειδότες πολλοὺς καὶ μεγάλους οἴκους ὑπὸ τῶν κολακευόντων ἀναστάτους γεγενημένους καὶ μισοῦντες ἐπὶ τῶν ἰδίων τοὺς ταύτην ἔχοντας τὴν τέχνην ἐπὶ τῶν κοινῶν οὐχ ὁμοίως διάκεισθε πρὸς αὐτούς, ἀλλὰ κατηγοροῦντες τῶν προσιεμένων καὶ χαιρόντων τοῖς τοιούτοις αὐτοὶ μᾶλλον φαίνεσθε τούτοις πιστεύοντες ἢ τοῖς ἄλλοις πολίταις. καὶ γάρ τοι πεποιήκατε τοὺς ῥήτορας μελετᾶν καὶ φιλοσοφεῖν οὐ τὰ μέλλοντα τῇ πόλει συνοίσειν, ἀλλ᾿ ὅπως ἀρέσκοντας ὑμῖν λόγους ἐροῦσιν· ἐφ᾿ οὓς καὶ νῦν τὸ πλῆθος αὐτῶν ἐρρύηκεν. ἅπασι γὰρ ἦν φανερόν, ὅτι μᾶλλον ἡσθήσεσθε [1] τοῖς παρακαλοῦσιν ὑμᾶς ἐπὶ τὸν πόλεμον ἢ τοῖς περὶ τῆς εἰρήνης συμβουλεύουσιν. οἱ μὲν γὰρ προσδοκίαν ἐμποιοῦσιν, ὡς τὰς κτήσεις τὰς ἐν ταῖς πόλεσι κομιούμεθα καὶ τὴν δύναμιν ἀναληψόμεθα πάλιν, ἣν πρότερον ἐτυγχάνομεν ἔχοντες, οἱ δ᾿ οὐδὲν τοιοῦτον ὑποτείνουσιν, ἀλλ᾿ ὡς ἡσυχίαν ἔχειν δεῖ καὶ μὴ μεγάλων ἐπιθυμεῖν παρὰ τὸ δίκαιον, ἀλλὰ στέργειν τοῖς παροῦσιν,[2] ὃ χαλεπώτατον πάντων τοῖς πλείστοις τῶν ἀνθρώπων ἐστίν. οὕτω γὰρ ἐξηρτήμεθα τῶν ἐλπίδων καὶ πρὸς τὰς δοκούσας εἶναι πλεονεξίας ἀπλήστως ἔχομεν, ὥστ᾿ [3] οὐδὲ οἱ κεκτημένοι τοὺς

[1] ἡσθήσεσθε Radermacher ex Isocrate: ἥσθησθε codd.
[2] τοῖς παροῦσιν Radermacher ex Isocrate: τὸ ἴσον codd.

favour to those who address you, but that, while paying attention to some, you do not even allow the voices of others to be heard. And it is not surprising that you do this: for in the past it has been your custom to drive from the rostrum all the orators except those who support your desires. One might justly criticise you for this because, although you are fully aware that many great families have been ruined by flatterers, and although in your private affairs you hate those who practise this art, in your public affairs your attitude to them is different: while denouncing those who seek and enjoy the society of such men, you yourselves show clearly that you place greater confidence in them than in the rest of your fellow-citizens.

"Indeed, you have caused the orators to practise and study not what will be advantageous to the state, but how they may say things which will please you. And at the present time this is the kind of discourse that most of them have hastened to employ, for they have all realised that you will be more pleased with those who summon you to war than with those you advise peace; for the former put into your minds the expectation both of recovering our possessions in the several states and of regaining the power which we formerly enjoyed, whereas the latter hold forth no such hope, but insist rather that we must have peace and not desire great possessions contrary to justice, but be content with those we have—a position which the great majority of mankind finds most difficulty in adopting. We depend so much upon our hopes, and cannot forbear to seize what seems to be our advantage, that even those with the greatest riches are un-

---

[3] ὥστ' Radermacher ex Isocrate: ὡς codd.

μεγίστους πλούτους μένειν ἐπὶ τούτοις ἐθέλουσιν, ἀλλ' ἀεὶ τοῦ πλείονος ὀρεγόμενοι περὶ τῶν ὑπαρχόντων κινδυνεύουσι. διόπερ ἄξιόν ἐστι δεδιέναι, μὴ καὶ νῦν ἡμεῖς ἔνοχοι γενώμεθα ταύταις ταῖς ἀνοίαις. λίαν γάρ τινές μοι δοκοῦσιν ὡρμῆσθαι πρὸς τὸν πόλεμον, ὥσπερ οὐ τῶν τυχόντων συμβεβουλευκότων ἀλλὰ τῶν θεῶν ἀκηκοότες, ὅτι κατορθώσομεν ἅπαντα καὶ ῥᾳδίως κρατήσομεν τῶν ἐχθρῶν. χρὴ δὲ τοὺς νοῦν ἔχοντας περὶ μὲν ὧν ἴσασι μὴ βουλεύεσθαι (περίεργον γάρ), ἀλλὰ πράττειν ὡς ἐγνώκασι, περὶ ὧν δ' ἂν βουλεύωνται, μὴ νομίζειν εἰδέναι τὸ συμβησόμενον, ἀλλ' ὡς δόξῃ μὲν χρωμένους, ὅ τι δὲ ἂν τύχῃ γενησόμενον, οὕτω διανοεῖσθαι περὶ αὐτῶν. ὧν ὑμεῖς οὐδέτερον τυγχάνετε ποιοῦντες, ἀλλ' ὡς οἷόν τε ταραχωδέστατα διάκεισθε. συνεληλύθατε γὰρ ὡς δέον ὑμᾶς ἐξ ἁπάντων τῶν ῥηθέντων ἐκλέξασθαι τὸ βέλτιστον,[1] ὥσπερ δ' ἤδη σαφῶς εἰδότες ὃ πρακτέον ἐστὶν οὐ θέλετε ἀκούειν πλὴν τῶν πρὸς ἡδονὴν δημηγορούντων.[2] καίτοι προσῆκεν ὑμᾶς, εἴπερ ἐβούλεσθε ζητεῖν τὸ τῇ πόλει συμφέρον, μᾶλλον τοῖς ἐναντιουμένοις ταῖς ὑμετέραις γνώμαις προσέχειν τὸν νοῦν ἢ τοῖς χαριζομένοις, εἰδότας ὅτι τῶν ἐνθάδε παριόντων οἱ μὲν ἃ βούλεσθε λέγοντες ῥᾳδίως ἐξαπατᾶν δύνανται· τὸ γὰρ πρὸς χάριν ῥηθὲν ἐπισκοτεῖ τῷ καθορᾶν τὸ βέλτιστον.

[1] ἐκλέξασθαι τὸ βέλτιστον Radermacher ex Isocrate: ἐκλέξαι τὸ βέλτιον codd.

willing to rest content with them, but are always grasping after more and so risking the loss of what they have. Therefore we ought duly to be cautious not to be subject to this madness in the present situation: for some of us seem to me to be too strongly attracted to the idea of war, as if they had heard, not from chance advisers but from the gods, that we shall succeed in all our campaigns and easily conquer our enemies.

"But men of intelligence, when dealing with matters of which they have certain knowledge, ought not to take advice (for this is superfluous), but should act as men who have already decided what to do; whereas in matters about which they take advice, they ought not to think that they know what the outcome will be, but to view these contingencies as men who indeed exercise judgment, but do not know what chance will hold for them in the future. You, however, do neither the one thing nor the other, but are in as confused a mental state as you could be. You have come together as if your duty were to select the best course from all those proposed, but you will not listen to any except those who orate for your gratification, as if you had made up your minds what must be done. And yet, if you really wished to find out what is to the state's advantage, you ought to give more attention to those who oppose your views than to those who wish to flatter you, knowing well that of the orators who come before you here, those who say what you desire are able to delude you easily—since what is said in order to win favour clouds your vision

---

[2] *πρὸς ἡδονὴν δημηγορούντων* Radermacher ex Isocrate: *εἰς ἡδονὴν κατηγορούντων* codd.

ὑπὸ δὲ τῶν μὴ πρὸς ἡδονὴν συμβουλευόντων οὐδὲν ἂν πάθοιτε τοιοῦτον. οὐ γάρ ἐστιν ὅπως ἂν μεταπεῖσαι δυνηθεῖεν ⟨ὑμᾶς μὴ φανερὸν τὸ συμφέρον ποιήσαντες. χωρὶς δὲ τούτων πῶς ἂν ἄνθρωποι δυνηθεῖεν⟩ καλῶς ἢ κρῖναι περὶ τῶν γεγενημένων ἢ βουλεύεσθαι περὶ τῶν μελλόντων, εἰ μὴ τοὺς μὲν λόγους τοὺς τῶν ἐναντιουμένων παρ' ἀλλήλους ἐξετάζοιεν, αὐτοὶ δ' αὑτοὺς κοινοὺς ἀμφοτέροις ἀκροατὰς παράσχοιεν; θαυμάζω δὲ τὰ τῶν πρεσβυτέρων, εἰ μηκέτι μνημονεύουσι, καὶ τῶν νεωτέρων, εἰ μηδενὸς ⟨ἀκηκόασιν, ὅτι⟩ [1] διὰ μὲν γὰρ τοὺς παραινοῦντας ⟨ἀντέχεσθαι⟩ [2] τῆς εἰρήνης οὐδὲν πώποτε ⟨κακὸν⟩ [3] ἐπάθομεν, διὰ δὲ τοὺς ῥᾳδίως πολεμεῖν αἱρουμένους ⟨πολλαῖς ἤδη καὶ⟩ μεγάλαις συμφοραῖς περιεπέσομεν. ὧν ἡμεῖς οὐδεμίαν ποιούμεθα μνείαν, ἀλλ' ἑτοίμως ἔχομεν μηδὲν εἰς τὸ πρόσθεν ἡμῖν αὐτοῖς πράττοντες τριήρεις πληροῦν καὶ χρημάτων εἰσφορὰς ποιεῖσθαι καὶ βοηθεῖν καὶ πολεμεῖν, ὥσπερ ἂν τύχωμεν ἐν ἀλλοτρίᾳ τῇ πόλει κινδυνεύοντες. τούτων δ' αἴτιόν ἐστιν, ὅτι προσῆκον ὑμᾶς ὁμοίως τῶν κοινῶν ὥσπερ τῶν ἰδίων σπουδάζειν, οὐ τὴν αὐτὴν γνώμην ἔχετε περὶ αὐτῶν, ἀλλ' ὅταν μὲν ὑπὲρ τῶν ἰδίων βουλεύησθε, ζητεῖτε συμβούλους τοὺς ἄμεινον φρονοῦντας ὑμῶν αὐτῶν, ὅταν δ' ὑπὲρ τῆς πόλεως ἐκκλησιάζητε, τοῖς μὲν τοιούτοις ἀπιστεῖτε καὶ φθονεῖτε, τοὺς δὲ πονηροτάτους τῶν ἐπὶ τὸ βῆμα παριόντων ἐπαινεῖτε καὶ νομίζετε δημοτικωτέρους

[1] ἀκηκόασιν ὅτι Radermacher lacunam supplevit ex Isocrate.
[2] ἀντέχεσθαι supplevit Radermacher ex Isocrate.
[3] κακὸν Radermacher lacunam supplevit ex Isocrate.

of what is best—whereas those who advise you without regard to your pleasure can affect you in no such way, since they could not convert you to their way of thinking until they have first made clear what is to your advantage. But, apart from these considerations, how can men form sound judgment on past events or take wise counsel for the future unless they examine and compare the arguments of opposing speakers, themselves giving an equal hearing to both sides?

" But I am surprised that our older men no longer remember, and our younger men have not yet been told by anyone, that the orators who urge us to hold on to peace have never caused us to suffer any misfortune, whereas those who readily opt for war have already embroiled us in many great disasters. Yet we have no memory for these facts, but are always ready, without in the least advancing our own welfare, to man triremes, to levy war-taxes, and to lend aid to the campaigns of others or wage war against them, as chance may determine, as if we were incurring dangers as if the city we were living in was not our own. And the reason for this condition of affairs is that, although you ought to be as much concerned about the business of the commonwealth as about your own, you do not feel the same interest in the one as in the other; on the contrary, whenever you take counsel regarding your private business, you look to men who are superior to you in intelligence to advise you, but when you deliberate on affairs of state you distrust and dislike men of that kind and look to the most depraved of the orators who come before you on this rostrum. You regard speakers who are drunk as better friends of the people than those who are sober,

εἶναι τοὺς μεθύοντας τῶν νηφόντων καὶ τοὺς νοῦν οὐκ ἔχοντας τῶν εὖ φρονούντων καὶ τοὺς τὰ τῆς πόλεως διανεμομένους τῶν ἐκ τῆς ⟨ἰδίας⟩ οὐσίας ὑμῖν λειτουργούντων. ὥστ' ἄξιον θαυμάζειν, εἴ τις ἐλπίζει τὴν πόλιν τοιούτοις συμβούλοις χρωμένην ἐπὶ τὸ βέλτιον ἐπιδώσειν. ἐγὼ δ' οἶδα μέν, ὅτι πρόσαντές ἐστιν ἐναντιοῦσθαι ταῖς ὑμετέραις διανοίαις καὶ διότι δημοκρατίας οὔσης οὐκ ἔστι παρρησία πλὴν ἐνθάδε μὲν τοῖς ἀφρονεστάτοις καὶ μηδὲν ὑμῶν φροντίζουσιν, ἐν δὲ τοῖς θεάτροις τοῖς κωμῳδοδιδασκάλοις. ὃ καὶ πάντων ἐστὶ δεινότατον, ὅτι τοῖς μὲν ἐκφέρουσιν εἰς τοὺς ἄλλους Ἕλληνας ⟨τὰ⟩ τῆς πόλεως ἁμαρτήματα τοσαύτην ἔχετε χάριν, ὅσην οὐδὲ τοῖς εὖ ποιοῦσι, πρὸς δὲ τοὺς ἐπιπλήττοντας καὶ νουθετοῦντας ὑμᾶς οὕτω διατίθεσθε δυσκόλως, ὥσπερ πρὸς τοὺς κακόν τι τὴν πόλιν ἐργαζομένους. ὅμως δὲ καὶ τούτων ὑπαρχόντων οὐκ ἂν ἀποσταίην ὧν διενοήθην. παρελήλυθα γὰρ οὐ χαριούμενος ὑμῖν οὐδὲ χειροτονίαν μνηστεύσων ἀλλ' ἀποφανούμενος ἃ τυγχάνω γιγνώσκων, πρῶτον μὲν περὶ ὧν ὁ πρύτανις προτίθησιν, ἔπειτα περὶ τῶν ἄλλων τῶν τῆς πόλεως πραγμάτων. οὐδὲν γὰρ ὄφελος ἔσται τῶν νῦν περὶ [1] τῆς εἰρήνης γνωσθέντων, ἂν μὴ περὶ τῶν λοιπῶν ὀρθῶς βουλευσώμεθα. φημὶ δ' οὖν χρῆναι ποιεῖσθαι τὴν εἰρήνην μὴ μόνον πρὸς Χίους τε καὶ Ῥοδίους καὶ Βυζαντίους καὶ Κῴους ἀλλὰ πάντας ἀνθρώπους, καὶ χρῆσθαι ταῖς συνθή-

and prefer those who are witless to those who are wise, and those who dole out public money to those who perform public services at their own expense. Consequently it is surprising that anyone should expect a state which employs such counsellors to prosper.

"But I know that it is hazardous to oppose your views and that, although this is a free government, there is no freedom of speech, except that which is enjoyed in this assembly by the most brainless orators, who care nothing for your welfare, and in the theatre by the producers of comedies. And, what is most outrageous of all, you show greater favour to those who advertise the failings of Athens to the rest of Greece than you show even to those who benefit the city, while you are as ill-disposed to those who rebuke and admonish you as you are to men who do injury to the state. Nevertheless, in spite of these conditions, I shall not shrink from saying what I intended to say. For I have come before you not to seek your favour nor to solicit your votes, but to make known the views I happen to hold, first regarding the proposals which have been put before you by the Presidents of the Council, and second, regarding the other interests of the state; for no good will come of the resolutions which have now been made regarding the peace unless we are well advised also regarding the future.

"I say, then, that we should make peace, not only with the men of Chios, Rhodes, Byzantium and Cos, but with all men, and that we should accept not the terms of peace which certain parties have recently drawn up, but those we entered into with the King

---

[1] *νῦν περὶ* Radermacher ex Isocrate: *ὑπὲρ* codd.

καις μὴ ταύταις, αἷς νῦν τινες γεγράφασιν, ἀλλὰ ταῖς γενομέναις μὲν πρὸς βασιλέα καὶ Λακεδαιμονίους, προσταττούσαις δὲ τοὺς Ἕλληνας αὐτονόμους εἶναι καὶ τὰς φρουρὰς ἐκ τῶν ἀλλοτρίων πόλεων ἐξιέναι καὶ τὴν αὑτῶν ἔχειν ἑκάστους. τούτων γὰρ οὔτε δικαιοτέρας εὑρήσομεν οὔτε μᾶλλον τῇ πόλει συμφερούσας."

17 ταῦτα προειπὼν καὶ οὕτω διαθεὶς τοὺς ἀκούοντας πρὸς τὸν μέλλοντα λόγον ἐπιτηδείως ἐγκώμιόν τε κάλλιστον τῆς δικαιοσύνης διαθέμενος καὶ τὰ καθεστηκότα πράγματα μεμψάμενος ἐπιτίθησι τούτοις τὴν σύγκρισιν τῶν τότε ἀνθρώπων πρὸς τοὺς προγόνους· "Τούτου δὲ ἕνεκα ταῦτα προεῖπον, ὅτι περὶ τῶν λοιπῶν οὐδὲν ὑποστειλάμενος ἀλλὰ παντάπασιν ἀνειμένως μέλλω τοὺς λόγους ποιεῖσθαι πρὸς ὑμᾶς. τίς γὰρ ἂν ἄλλοθεν ἐπελθὼν καὶ μὴ συνδιεφθαρμένος ἡμῖν, ἀλλ' ἐξαίφνης ἐπιστὰς τοῖς γιγνομένοις οὐκ ἂν μαίνεσθαι καὶ παραφρονεῖν ἡμᾶς νομίσειεν, οἳ φιλοτιμούμεθα μὲν ἐπὶ τοῖς τῶν προγόνων ἔργοις καὶ τὴν πόλιν ἐκ τῶν τότε πραχθέντων ἐγκωμιάζειν ἀξιοῦμεν, οὐδὲν δὲ τῶν αὐτῶν ἐκείνοις πράττομεν, ἀλλὰ πᾶν τοὐναντίον; οἳ μὲν γὰρ ὑπὲρ τῶν Ἑλλήνων τοῖς βαρβάροις πολεμοῦντες διετέλεσαν, ἡμεῖς δὲ τοὺς ἐκ τῆς Ἀσίας τὸν βίον ποριζομένους ἐκεῖθεν ἀναστήσαντες ἐπὶ τοὺς Ἕλληνας ἠγάγομεν. κἀκεῖνοι μὲν ἐλευθεροῦντες τὰς πόλεις τὰς Ἑλληνίδας καὶ βοηθοῦντες αὐταῖς τῆς ἡγεμονίας ἠξιώθησαν, ἡμεῖς δὲ καταδουλούμενοι καὶ τἀναντία τοῖς τότε πράττοντες ἀγανακτοῦμεν, εἰ μὴ τὴν αὐτὴν τιμὴν ἐκείνοις ἕξομεν, οἳ τοσοῦτον ἀπολελείμμεθα καὶ τοῖς

of Persia and the Lacedaemonians, which lay down that the Greeks should be independent, that foreign garrisons be removed from the several states, and that each people should retain its own territory. We shall not find terms of peace that are more just than these nor more expedient for our city."

With this introduction he has prepared his audience suitably for the main argument that follows. He has at the same time composed a most noble encomium of justice and has outlined his criticisms of the existing state of affairs. He follows this with a comparison between the Athenians of his day and their ancestors:[1] 17

" I have said these things by way of a preface because for the rest of my discourse I am going to speak without reserve and with complete frankness to you. Suppose that a stranger from some other country were to come to Athens, having had no time to become tainted with our depravity, but coming suddenly face-to-face with what goes on here, would he not think that we were mad and beside ourselves when we pride ourselves on the deeds of our ancestors and think fit to praise our city by recounting the deeds of their time, and yet behave in no way like them, but in the very opposite way? For while they waged war ceaselessly against the barbarian on behalf of the Greeks, we drove from their homes those who derive their livelihood from Asia and led them against the Greeks; and whereas they liberated the cities of Greece and lent them their aid, and so were adjudged worthy of the leadership, we try to enslave these cities and pursue a completely opposite policy to theirs and then feel aggrieved that we are not held in

[1] 41–53.

ἔργοις καὶ ταῖς διανοίαις τῶν κατ' ἐκεῖνον τὸν χρόνον γενομένων, ὅσον οἱ μὲν ὑπὲρ τῆς [1] . . .

. . . .

. . . .

. . . .

φροντίζομεν· ἓν γὰρ ἀκούσαντες γνώσεσθε καὶ περὶ τῶν ἄλλων· ὡς θανάτου τῆς ζημίας ἐπικειμένης, ἤν [2] τις ἁλῷ δεκάζων,[3] τοὺς τοῦτο φανερώτατα ποιοῦντας στρατηγοὺς χειροτονοῦμεν καὶ τὸν πλείστους διαφθεῖραι δυνηθέντα τῶν πολιτῶν τοῦτον ἐπὶ τὰ μέγιστα τῶν πραγμάτων καθίσταμεν. σπουδάζοντες δὲ περὶ τὴν πολιτείαν οὐχ ἧττον ἢ περὶ τὴν σωτηρίαν ὅλης τῆς πόλεως καὶ τὴν δημοκρατίαν εἰδότες ἐν μὲν ταῖς ἡσυχίαις καὶ ταῖς ἀσφαλείαις αὐξομένην καὶ διαμένουσαν, ἐν δὲ τοῖς πολέμοις δὶς ἤδη καταλυθεῖσαν, πρὸς μὲν τοὺς τῆς εἰρήνης ἐπιθυμοῦντας ὡς πρὸς ὀλιγαρχικοὺς ὄντας δυσκόλως ἔχομεν, τοὺς δὲ τὸν πόλεμον ἀγαπῶντας ὡς τῆς δημοκρατίας κηδομένους εὔνους εἶναι νομίζομεν. ἐμπειρότατοι δὲ λόγων καὶ πραγμάτων ὄντες οὕτως ἀλογίστως ἔχομεν, ὥστε περὶ τῶν αὐτῶν τῆς αὐτῆς ἡμέρας οὐ ταὐτὰ γινώσκομεν, ἀλλ' ὧν πρὶν εἰς τὴν ἐκκλησίαν ἀναβῆναι κατηγοροῦμεν, ταῦτα συνελθόντες [4] χειροτονοῦμεν, οὐ πολὺν δὲ χρόνον διαλιπόντες τοῖς ψηφισθεῖσιν, ἐπειδὰν ἀπίωμεν, πάλιν ἐπιτιμῶμεν. προσποιούμενοι δὲ σωφρονέστατοι τῶν Ἑλλήνων εἶναι, τοιούτοις χρώμεθα συμβούλοις, ὧν οὐκ ἔστιν ὅστις οὐκ ἂν καταφρονήσειε, καὶ τοὺς

[1] Exciderunt Isoc. *De. Pace* cap. 44–49.
[2] ἤν Radermacher ex Isocrate: εἰ codd.

equal honour with them—we who fall so far short of those who lived in those days both in our deeds and in our thoughts, that whereas they, on behalf of . . . . . . but we care so little about them (for if I give you a single instance you will be able to judge the others as well), that although we have prescribed the penalty of death for anyone who is convicted of bribery, we elect men who are most palpably guilty of this crime as our generals, and we select the man who has succeeded in corrupting the greatest number of our citizens and place him in charge of our most important affairs. We are as concerned about our constitution as about the safety of the whole state, and we know that our democracy flourishes and endures in times of peace and security while in times of war it has twice already been overthrown; but we are hostile to those who desire peace, regarding them like oligarchic sympathisers, while we are friendly towards those who advocate war, as if assured thereby that they are devoted to democracy. We are the most experienced of men in debate and in politics, but we are so devoid of reason that we do not hold the same views about the same question on the same day; on the contrary, the things which we condemn before we enter the assembly are the very things which we vote for when we are in session, and again a little later when we depart for our homes we disapprove of the things which we resolved upon here. We pose as the wisest of the Greeks, but we employ the kind of advisers that nobody could fail to despise, and we

411 B.C., 404 B.C.

[3] *δεκάζων* Radermacher ex Isocrate: *δὲ καὶ ζῶν* codd.
[4] *συνελθόντες* Radermacher ex Isocrate: *ἐλθόντες* codd.

αὐτοὺς τούτους κυρίους ἁπάντων τῶν κοινῶν καθίσταμεν, οἷς οὐδεὶς οὐδὲν ἂν τῶν ἰδίων ἐπιτρέψειε."

18 τοιοῦτος μὲν δή τις ἐν τοῖς συμβουλευτικοῖς λόγοις ὁ ἀνήρ. ἐν δὲ τοῖς δικανικοῖς τὰ μὲν ἄλλα πάνυ ἀκριβὴς καὶ ἀληθινὸς καὶ τῷ Λυσίου χαρακτῆρι ἔγγιστα μὲν προσεληλυθώς, ἐν δὲ τῇ συνθέσει τῶν ὀνομάτων τὸ λεῖον ἐκεῖνο καὶ εὐπρεπὲς ἔχων, ἔλαττον μὲν ἢ ἐν τοῖς ἄλλοις λόγοις, οὐ μὴν ἀλλὰ ἔχων γε. μηθεὶς δ' ἀγνοεῖν ⟨μ'⟩ [1] ὑπολάβῃ μήθ' [2] ὅτι Ἀφαρεὺς ὁ πρόγονός τε καὶ εἰσποίητος Ἰσοκράτει γενόμενος ἐν τῷ πρὸς Μεγακλείδην περὶ τῆς Ἀντιδόσεως λόγῳ διορίζεται μηδεμίαν ὑπὸ τοῦ πατρὸς ὑπόθεσιν εἰς δικαστήριον γεγράφθαι, μήθ' [3] ὅτι δέσμας πάνυ πολλὰς δικανικῶν λόγων Ἰσοκρατείων περιφέρεσθαί φησιν ὑπὸ τῶν βυβλιοπωλῶν Ἀριστοτέλης. ἐπίσταμαι γὰρ ταῦτα ὑπὸ τῶν ἀνδρῶν ἐκείνων λεγόμενα, καὶ οὔτε Ἀριστοτέλει πείθομαι ῥυπαίνειν τὸν ἄνδρα βουλομένῳ οὔτ' Ἀφαρεῖ τούτου γ' ἕνεκα λόγον εὐπρεπῆ πλαττομένῳ συντίθεμαι. ἱκανὸν δὲ ἡγησάμενος εἶναι τῆς ἀληθείας βεβαιωτὴν τὸν Ἀθηναῖον Κηφισόδωρον, ὃς καὶ συνεβίωσεν Ἰσοκράτει καὶ γνησιώτατος ἀκουστὴς ἐγένετο καὶ τὴν ἀπολογίαν τὴν ὑπὲρ αὐτοῦ τὴν πάνυ θαυμαστὴν ἐν ταῖς πρὸς Ἀριστοτέλην ἀντιγραφαῖς ἐποιήσατο, πιστεύω γεγράφθαι λόγους τινὰς ὑπὸ τοῦ ἀνδρὸς εἰς δικαστήρια οὐ μέντοι πολλούς, καὶ

[1] μ' inseruit Wolf.
[2] μήθ' Krüger: μηδ' codd.
[3] μήθ' Krüger: μηδ' codd.

place these very same men in control of all our public interests, to whom nobody would entrust a single one of his private affairs."

18 Such, then, are the orator's characteristics in his political discourses. In his forensic speeches his style is in general full of precision and realism, and closely resembles that of Lysias, yet showing his familiar smoothness and elegance in the arrangement of words, to a lesser degree certainly than in his other oratory, but showing it nevertheless. Nobody must think that I do not know of the letter which my ancestor Aphareus, who was an adoptive son of Isocrates,[1] wrote in reply to Megaclides concerning the *Antidosis*, in which he affirms that his father wrote no speeches for the law-courts. I am also aware of the statement of Aristotle that the itinerant booksellers carry around with them many bundles of Isocrates's forensic speeches.[2] I know of these men's statements, and disbelieve Aristotle because he is trying to besmirch Isocrates; while I find Aphareus no more convincing because he is trying to fabricate a specious story to counter him. But I regard Cephisodorus the Athenian [3] as a sufficiently reliable authority, since he lived with Isocrates and was his most reputable pupil, and wrote a very remarkable defence of Isocrates in his counterblast to the accusations of Aristotle. Following a statement of his, I believe that Isocrates wrote some speeches for the law-courts, but not many. There is no time to quote more than one

[1] Cf. [Plutarch], *Lives of the Ten Orators*, 838B–C; 839B–C.

[2] Frag. 140. See Dover, *Lysias and the Corpus Lysiacum*, p. 25.

[3] In addition to his writing(s) against Aristotle in defence of his teacher, Cephisodorus wrote a history of the Sacred War in 12 books.

χρῶμαι παραδείγματι ἐξ αὐτῶν ἑνί (οὐ γὰρ ἐγχωρεῖ πλείοσι) τῷ Τραπεζιτικῷ λεγομένῳ, ὃν ἔγραψε ξένῳ τινὶ τῶν μαθητῶν κατὰ Πασίωνος τοῦ τραπεζίτου. ἔστι δὲ ὁ λόγος οὗτος·

19 "Ὁ μὲν ἀγών μοι μέγας ἐστίν, ὦ ἄνδρες δικασταί· οὐ γὰρ μόνον περὶ πολλῶν χρημάτων κινδυνεύω, ἀλλὰ καὶ περὶ τοῦ μὴ δοκεῖν ἀδίκως τῶν ἀλλοτρίων ἐπίθυμεῖν· ὃ ἐγὼ περὶ πλείστου ποιοῦμαι· οὐσία γάρ μοι ἱκανὴ καταλειφθήσεται καὶ τούτων στερηθέντι. εἰ δὲ δόξαιμι μηδὲν προσῆκον τοσαῦτα χρήματα ἐγκαλέσαι, διαβληθείην ἂν τὸν ἅπαντα βίον. ἔστι δέ, ὦ ἄνδρες δικασταί, πάντων χαλεπώτατον τοιούτων ἀντιδίκων τυχεῖν. τὰ μὲν γὰρ συμβόλαια πρὸς τοὺς ἐπὶ ταῖς τραπέζαις ἄνευ μαρτύρων γίνεται, τοῖς ἀδικουμένοις δὲ πρὸς τοιούτους ἀνάγκη κινδυνεύειν, οἳ καὶ φίλους πολλοὺς κέκτηνται καὶ χρήματα ⟨πολλὰ⟩ [1] διαχειρίζουσι καὶ πιστοὶ διὰ τὴν τέχνην δοκοῦσιν εἶναι. ὅμως δὲ καὶ τούτων ὑπαρχόντων ἡγοῦμαι φανερὸν πᾶσι ποιήσειν, ὅτι ἀποστεροῦμαι τοσούτων χρημάτων ὑπὸ Πασίωνος. ἐξ ἀρχῆς δὲ ὑμῖν, ὅπως ἂν δύνωμαι, διηγήσομαι τὰ πεπραγμένα. ἐμοὶ γάρ, ὦ ἄνδρες δικασταί, πατὴρ μέν ἐστι Σωπαῖος,[2] ὃν οἱ πλέοντες εἰς τὸν Πόντον ἅπαντες ἴσασιν οὕτως οἰκείως πρὸς Σάτυρον διακείμενον, ὥστε πολλῆς μὲν χώρας ἄρχειν, ἁπάσης δὲ τῆς δυνάμεως ἐπιμελεῖσθαι τῆς ἐκείνου. πυνθανόμενος δὲ καὶ περὶ τῆσδε τῆς πόλεως καὶ περὶ τῆς ἄλλης Ἑλλάδος ἐπεθύμησ' ἀποδημῆσαι. ἐμπλήσας δὲ

[1] πολλὰ ex Isocrate Stephanorum editiones.

example from these, and the speech I have chosen is the one called *Trapeziticus*, which he wrote for one of his pupils from abroad against Pasion the banker. This is the speech:[1]

"This trial, gentlemen of the jury, is an important 19
one for me, for I have at stake not only a large sum of money, but also I am in danger of suffering the reputation of coveting what justly belongs to another; and this is a matter of great concern to me. For I shall have enough property left even if I am defrauded of this sum; but if I should be thought to be laying claim to so large a sum of money without just cause, I should have an evil reputation for the rest of my life. The greatest difficulty of all, gentlemen of the jury, is that I have opponents of the character of the defendants. For contracts with bankers are entered into without witnesses, and anyone who is wronged by them is obliged to bring a suit against men who have many friends, handle much money, and have a reputation for honesty because of their profession. In spite of these difficulties I think I shall make it clear that I have been defrauded of all that money by Pasion.

"I shall tell you the facts from the beginning as well as I can. My father, gentlemen of the jury, is Sopaeus; all who sail to the Pontus know that his relations with Satyrus are so intimate that he is ruler of an extensive territory and has charge of that ruler's entire forces. Having heard reports both of this state and of other lands where Greeks live, I desired to travel abroad. Therefore my father loaded two

[1] 1–12.

---

[2] Σωπαῖος Isoc.: Σινωπεύς codd.

ὁ πατήρ μου δύο ναῦς σίτου καὶ χρήματα δοὺς ἐξέπεμψεν ἅμα κατ' ἐμπορίαν καὶ θεωρίαν. συστήσαντος δέ μοι Πυθοδώρου τοῦ Φοίνικος Πασίωνα ἐχρώμην τῇ τούτου τραπέζῃ. χρόνῳ δ' ὕστερον διαβολῆς πρὸς Σάτυρον γενομένης, ὡς καὶ ὁ πατὴρ οὑμὸς ἐπιβουλεύοι τῇ ἀρχῇ κἀγὼ τοῖς φυγάσι συγγενοίμην, τὸν μὲν πατέρα μου συλλαμβάνει, ἐπιστέλλει δὲ τοῖς ἐνθάδε ἐπιδημοῦσιν ἐκ τοῦ Πόντου, τὰ χρήματα παρ' ἐμοῦ παραλαβεῖν καὶ αὐτὸν εἰσπλεῖν κελεύειν, ἐὰν δὲ τούτων μηδὲν ποιῶ, παρ' ὑμῶν ἐξαιτεῖν. ἐν τοσούτοις δὲ κακοῖς ὤν, ὦ ἄνδρες δικασταί, λέγω πρὸς Πασίωνα τὰς ἐμαυτοῦ συμφοράς. οὕτω γὰρ οἰκείως πρὸς αὐτὸν διεκείμην, ὥστε μὴ μόνον περὶ τῶν χρημάτων ἀλλὰ καὶ περὶ τῶν ἄλλων τούτῳ μάλιστα πιστεύειν. ἡγούμην δέ, εἰ μὲν προοίμην ἅπαντα τὰ χρήματα, κινδυνεύσειν, εἴ τι πάθοι ἐκεῖνος, στερηθεὶς καὶ τῶν ἐνθάδε καὶ τῶν ἐκεῖ πάντων ἐνδεὴς γενήσεσθαι, εἰ δ' ὁμολογῶν εἶναι ἐπιστείλαντος Σατύρου μὴ παραδοίην, εἰς τὰς μεγίστας διαβολὰς ἐμαυτὸν καὶ τὸν πατέρα καταστήσειν πρὸς Σάτυρον. βουλευομένοις οὖν ἡμῖν ἐδόκει βέλτιστον εἶναι τὰ μὲν φανερὰ τῶν χρημάτων παραδοῦναι, περὶ δὲ τῶν παρὰ τούτῳ κειμένων μὴ μόνον ἔξαρνον εἶναι, ἀλλὰ καὶ ὀφείλοντά με καὶ τούτῳ καὶ ἑτέροις [1] ἐπὶ τόκῳ φαίνεσθαι καὶ πάντα ποιεῖν, ἐξ ὧν ἐκεῖνοι μάλιστα ἤμελλον πεισθήσεσθαι μὴ εἶναί μοι χρήματα. τότε μὲν οὖν, ὦ ἄνδρες δικασταί, ἐνόμιζόν μοι Πασίωνα δι' εὔνοιαν ἅπαντα ταῦτα

[1] καὶ τούτῳ καὶ ἑτέροις Radermacher ex Isoc.: καὶ τούτῳ καθάπερ εἴ γε F.

ships with grain, gave me money and sent me off on a trading voyage and at the same time to see the world. Pythodorus the Phoenician introduced me to Pasion and I opened an account in his bank. Some time later, as a result of the slander which reached Satyrus to the effect that my father was plotting against the throne and that I was associating with the exiles, Satyrus arrested my father and sent orders to citizens of Pontus in residence here in Athens to take possession of my money and order me to return and, if I refused to obey, to demand of you my extradition. When I found myself in such embarrassing difficulties, gentlemen of the jury, I told Pasion of my troubles; for I was on such intimate terms with him that I had the greatest confidence in him, not only in matters of money, but in everything else as well. I thought that, if I should lose control of all my money, I should run the risk, if my father met with misfortune, after being deprived of my money both here in Athens and at home, of becoming completely destitute; and that, if I should acknowledge the existence of money here, yet fail to surrender it at Satyrus's command, I should incur the most serious charges against myself and my father at Satyrus's hands. On consideration we decided that it would be best to agree to comply with all Satyrus's demands and to surrender the money whose existence was known, but as for the funds on deposit with Pasion, we should not only deny their existence, but also make it appear that I had borrowed at interest both from Pasion and from others, and do everything which was likely to make them believe that I had no money.

" At that time, gentlemen of the jury, I thought that Pasion was giving me all this advice because of

συμβουλεύειν. ἐπειδὴ δὲ ταῦτα πρὸς τοὺς περὶ Σάτυρον διεπραξάμην, ἔγνων αὐτὸν ἐπιβουλεύοντα τοῖς ἐμοῖς. βουλομένου γὰρ ἐμοῦ κομίσασθαι τἀμαυτοῦ καὶ πλεῖν εἰς Βυζάντιον, ἡγησάμενος οὗτος [1] κάλλιστον καιρὸν αὐτῷ παραπεπτωκέναι· τὰ μὲν γὰρ χρήματα πολλὰ εἶναι τὰ παρ᾽ αὐτῷ κείμενα καὶ ἄξια ἀναισχυντίας, ἐμὲ δὲ πολλῶν ἀκουόντων ἔξαρνον γεγενῆσθαι μηδὲν κεκτῆσθαι πᾶσί τε φανερὸν ἀπαιτούμενον καὶ ἑτέροις ὁμολογοῦντα ὀφείλειν· καὶ πρὸς τούτοις, ὦ ἄνδρες δικασταί, νομίζων, εἰ μὲν αὐτοῦ μένειν ἐπιχειροίην, ἐκδοθήσεσθαί με ὑπὸ τῆς πόλεως Σατύρῳ, εἰ δ᾽ ἄλλοσέ ποι τραποίμην, οὐδὲν αὐτῷ μελήσειν τῶν ἐμῶν λόγων, εἰ δ᾽ εἰσπλευσοίμην εἰς τὸν Πόντον, ἀποθανεῖσθαί με μετὰ τοῦ πατρός· ταῦτα διαλογιζόμενος διενοεῖτό με ἀποστερεῖν τὰ χρήματα καὶ πρὸς μὲν ἐμὲ προσεποιεῖτο ἀπορεῖν ἐν τῷ παρόντι καὶ οὐκ ἂν ἔχειν ἀποδοῦναι. ἐπειδὴ δ᾽ ἐγώ, βουλόμενος εἰδέναι τὸ πρᾶγμα, προσπέμπω Φιλόμηλον αὐτῷ καὶ Μενέξενον ἀπαιτήσοντας, ἔξαρνος γίνεται πρὸς αὐτοὺς μηδὲν ἔχειν τῶν ἐμῶν. πανταχόθεν δέ μοι τοσούτων κακῶν προσπεπτωκότων τίνα οἴεσθέ με γνώμην ἔχειν; ᾧ γε ὑπῆρχε σιωπῶντι μὲν ὑπὸ τούτου ἀποστερῆσθαι τῶν χρημάτων, λέγοντι δὲ ταῦτα μὲν μηδὲν μᾶλλον κομίσασθαι, πρὸς Σάτυρον δὲ εἰς τὴν μεγίστην διαβολὴν ἐμαυτὸν καὶ τὸν πατέρα καταστῆσαι. κράτιστον οὖν ἡγησάμην ἡσυχίαν ἄγειν. μετὰ ταῦτα, ὦ ἄνδρες δικασταί, ἀφικνοῦν-

[1] οὗτος Radermacher ex Isoc.: αὐτὸς codd.

good will towards me; but when I had arranged these matters with the representatives of Satyrus, I realised that he had designs on my property. For when I wished to recover my money and sail to Byzantium, Pasion thought a most favourable opportunity had come his way; for the sum of money on deposit with him was large and of sufficient value to warrant a shameless act, and I, in the presence of many listeners, had denied that I possessed anything, and everybody had seen that money was being demanded of me and that I was acknowledging that I was indebted to others also. Moreover, gentlemen of the jury, he was of the opinion that if I attempted to remain here, the city would hand me over to Satyrus, and if I should go anywhere else, he would be indifferent to my complaints, and if I should sail to the Pontus, I should be put to death along with my father. It was on the strength of these calculations that Pasion decided to defraud me of my money. And although to me he pretended that for the moment he was short of funds and would not be able to repay me, yet when I, wishing to ascertain the truth exactly, sent Philomelus and Menexenus to him to demand my property, he denied to them that he had anything belonging to me. Thus beset with such terrible misfortunes on every side, what do you think was my state of mind? If I kept silent, I should be defrauded of my money by Pasion here; if I should make this complaint, I was no more likely to recover it and I should bring myself and my father into the greatest disrepute with Satyrus. I therefore thought that the wisest course was to keep silent.

"After this, gentlemen of the jury, messengers arrived with the news that my father had been

ταί μοι ἀπαγγέλλοντες, ὅτι ὁ πατὴρ ἀφεῖται καὶ Σατύρῳ οὕτων ἁπάντων μεταμέλει τῶν πεπραγμένων, ὥστε πίστεις τε τὰς μεγίστας αὐτῷ δεδωκὼς εἴη καὶ τὴν ἀρχὴν ἔτι μείζω πεποιηκὼς ἧς εἶχε πρότερον καὶ τὴν ἀδελφὴν τὴν ἐμὴν γυναῖκα τῷ ἑαυτοῦ υἱεῖ εἰληφώς. πυθόμενος δὲ ταῦτα Πασίων καὶ εἰδὼς ὅτι φανερῶς ἤδη πράξω ⟨περὶ⟩ [1] τῶν ἐμαυτοῦ, ἀφανίζει τὸν παῖδα, ὃς συνῄδει ⟨περὶ⟩ [2] τῶν χρημάτων. ἐπειδὴ δὲ ἐγὼ προσελθὼν ἐπεζήτουν αὐτόν, ἡγούμενος ἔλεγχον ἂν τοῦτον [3] σαφέστατον γενέσθαι περὶ ὧν ἐνεκάλουν, λέγει λόγον δεινότατον, ὡς ἐγὼ καὶ Μενέξενος διαφθείραντες καὶ πείσαντες τὸν ἐπὶ τῇ τραπέζῃ καθήμενον ἓξ τάλαντα ἀργυρίου λάβοιμεν παρ' αὐτοῦ. ἵνα δὲ μηδεὶς ἔλεγχος μηδὲ βάσανος γένοιτο περὶ αὐτῶν, ἔφασκεν ἡμᾶς ἀφανίσαντας τὸν παῖδα ἀντεγκαλεῖν αὐτῷ καὶ ἐξαιτεῖν τοῦτον, ὃν αὐτοὶ ἠφανίσαμεν. καὶ ταῦτα λέγων καὶ ἀγανακτῶν καὶ δακρύων εἷλκέ με πρὸς τὸν πολέμαρχον, ἐγγυητὰς αἰτῶν, καὶ οὐ πρότερον ἀφῆκεν, ἕως αὐτῷ κατέστησα ἓξ ταλάντων ἐγγυητάς. καί μοι ἀνάβητε τούτων μάρτυρες."

20 ταῦθ' ὅτι μὲν ὅλῳ τῷ γένει διαφέρει τῶν ἐπιδεικτικῶν τε καὶ συμβουλευτικῶν κατὰ [4] τὸν χαρακτῆρα τῆς λέξεως, οὐθείς ἐστιν ὃς οὐκ ἂν ὁμολογήσειεν. οὐ μέντοι παντάπασί γε τὴν Ἰσοκράτειον ἀγωγὴν ἐκβέβηκεν, ἀκαρῆ δέ τινα διασῴζει

[1] περὶ inseruit Radermacher.
[2] περὶ inseruit Radermacher.
[3] ἔλεγχον ἂν τοῦτον Radermacher ex Isoc.: ἔλεγεν αὐτοῦ τὸ F.
[4] κατὰ Wolf: καὶ codd.

released and that Satyrus was so repentant of all that had occurred that he had proffered my father pledges of his confidence of the strongest kind, and had offered to make him master of even more land than he formerly possessed and had conferred his son upon my sister in marriage. When Pasion heard this and realised that I would now bring action openly about my property, he arranged the disappearance of his slave Cittus, who had knowledge of our financial transactions. And when I went to him and demanded the surrender of Cittus, because I believed that this slave could furnish the clearest proof of my claim, Pasion made the most outrageous charge, that Menexenus and I had corrupted him as he sat at his banking-table and received six talents of silver from him. And that there might be neither examination nor torture on these matters, he asserted that it was we who had caused the slave's disappearance and had brought the counter-charge against himself with a demand that this slave, whom we had caused to disappear, be produced. And while he was making this plea and protesting and weeping, he dragged me before the Polemarch with a demand for guarantors, and he did not release me until I had furnished bail to the sum of six talents. Will the witnesses to these facts please come forward?"

Everyone would agree that the style of this speech 20
is in a wholly different category from that of the ceremonial and deliberative speeches. Yet he has not entirely abandoned the Isocratean manner,[1] but preserves some brief arguments that recall the

[1] A misleading statement, since the *Trapeziticus* was an early speech and was composed at a time when Isocrates's epideictic style had not yet developed.

τῆς κατασκευῆς τε καὶ σεμνολογίας ἐκείνης ἐνθυμήματα καὶ ποιητικώτερα μᾶλλόν ἐστιν ἢ ἀληθινώτερα. οἷον ὅταν φῇ· "ἡγούμην δέ, εἰ μὲν προείμην τὰ χρήματα, κινδυνεύσειν." τὸ γὰρ ἀποίητόν τε καὶ ἀφελὲς τοιοῦτον· "ἡγούμην δὲ [μὴ] [1] παραδοὺς τὰ χρήματα κινδυνεύσειν." ἔτι ἐκεῖνο· "καὶ πρὸς τούτοις, ὦ ἄνδρες δικασταί, νομίζων, εἰ μὲν αὐτοῦ μένειν ἐπιχειροίην, ἐκδοθήσεσθαί με ὑπὸ τῆς πόλεως Σατύρῳ, εἰ δὲ ἄλλοσέ ποι τραποίμην, οὐδὲν αὐτῷ μελήσειν τῶν ἐμῶν λόγων, εἰ δὲ εἰσπλευσοίμην εἰς τὸν Πόντον, ἀποθανεῖσθαί με μετὰ τοῦ πατρός." ἥ τε γὰρ περίοδος ἐκμηκύνεται καὶ . . . [2] πέρα τοῦ δικανικοῦ τρόπου καὶ ἡ σύνθεσις ἔχει τι τοῦ ποιητικοῦ τό τε σχῆμα τῆς λέξεως ἐκ τῶν ἐπιδεικτικῶν εἴληπται παρισώσεων καὶ παρομοιώσεων. τό τε οὖν ἐπιχειροίην καὶ τραποίμην καὶ εἰσπλευσοίμην ἐν ἑνὶ χωρίῳ κείμενα καὶ τῶν κώλων τριῶν ὄντων τὸ μῆκος ἴσον ὑπάρχον τεκμήρια τῆς Ἰσοκράτους κατασκευῆς ἐστι. καὶ τὰ τούτοις ἐπιφερόμενα· "διενοεῖτό με ἀποστερεῖν τὰ χρήματα καὶ πρὸς μὲν ἐμὲ προσεποιεῖτο ἀπορεῖν καὶ οὐκ ἂν ἔχειν" παρόμοιά τε καὶ παραπλήσια ἀλλήλοις ἐστίν. καὶ πρὸς τούτοις, ἃ μετ᾽ ὀλίγον ἐπιτίθησιν· "ὥστε πίστεις τε ⟨τὰς⟩ μεγίστας αὐτῷ δεδωκὼς εἴη καὶ τὴν ἀρχὴν ἔτι μείζω πεποιηκὼς ἧς εἶχε πρότερον καὶ τὴν ἀδελφὴν τὴν ἐμὴν γυναῖκα τῷ ἑαυτοῦ υἱεῖ εἰληφώς." καὶ γὰρ ἐνταῦθα πάλιν τὸ δεδωκὼς καὶ πεποιηκὼς καὶ εἰληφὼς παρόμοιον καὶ ⟨τὸ⟩ [3] τὴν ἀρχὴν καὶ τὴν ἀδελφήν. ἔχοι δὲ ἄν τις καὶ ἄλλα πρὸς τούτοις

familiar artistry and dignity, and these are expressed in a form which is artificial rather than natural. When he says " I thought that, if I should lose control of all my money, I should run the risk . . ." it would have been simpler and more natural to say " I thought that in handing over the money I should run the risk . . ." And again, " Moreover, gentlemen of the jury, he was of the opinion that if I attempted to remain here, the city would hand me over to Satyrus, and if I should go anywhere else, he would be indifferent to my complaints, and if I should sail to the Pontus, I should be put to death along with my father." The period is spun out to a length which is excessive for a forensic speech, and the form of the language, with its balanced, rhyming clauses, has been taken from his epideictic oratory. The position of " attempted," " should go," " should sail " at corresponding points in three clauses of equal length is characteristic of Isocrates's arrangement. And the sequel " He decided to defraud me of my money, and although he pretended to me that he was short of funds and would not be able to repay me " contains assonance and corresponding phrases. A little later, he writes " that he had proffered to my father pledges of the strongest kind, and had offered to make him master of even more land than he formerly possessed and had conferred his son upon my sister in marriage. Here again, " proffered," " offered " and " conferred " form assonances, as do

---

[1] μὴ seclusit Fuhr.

[2] Lacuna καλλωπίζεται, ὑπάγεται, σχηματίζεται ex *De Demos.* 4, 8 supplenda.

[3] τὸ inseruit Usener.

λέγειν, ἐξ ὧν ὁ χαρακτὴρ τοῦ ῥήτορος ἔσται καταφανής, ἀνάγκη δὲ ἴσως στοχάζεσθαι τοῦ χρόνου.

" master " and " sister." One could cite additional examples to these to illustrate the orator's style, but I should perhaps keep my eye on the time.

ISAEUS

INTRODUCTION

Isaeus specialised in the branch of forensic oratory concerned with inheritance, and wrote in a style similar in many respects to that of Lysias. Dionysius therefore has to explain his decision to include him when he has omitted at least one orator with stronger claims to originality—Antiphon, the first of the Attic Orators. He does so neatly in his opening words: Isaeus was Demosthenes's teacher. The pseudo-Plutarchian *Lives* of Isaeus and Demosthenes enlarge on this statement by saying that Isaeus lived in Demosthenes's house for a time as his private tutor. Dionysius's aim in this essay is to establish Isaeus's position as a link between the earlier forensic style, of which Lysias was the best representative, and the mature eloquence of the supreme master of

Attic oratory. But Isaeus's oratory is in no sense represented as occupying a half-way position: he has been firmly assigned to the early period,[1] and Dionysius devotes most of the essay to a comparison of passages from Isaeus and Lysias (chs. 3–12). Lysias remains the standpoint from which the later orator is judged: he shows that Isaeus excelled Lysias in the invention and presentation of arguments, and bequeathed these qualities to his more famous pupil; but he also points out that rhetorical brilliance often defeats its own purpose, and arouses suspicions of dishonesty even when these are unjustified.[2]

The first three pairs of passages analysed are *prooemia* from the two earlier orators. The relation of Isaeus to Demosthenes is brought out by comparison of passages from the proof sections of their speeches. In particular, Isaeus's style in these sections is characterised by the use of questions,[3] a technique which Demosthenes perfected. Isaeus also observes the conventional divisions into *pro-*

[1] *Introd.*, 4.
[2] ch. 16.
[3] ch. 13 *init.*

oemion, *narrative*, *proof* and *epilogue* with less rigidity than his predecessor. He also employs a more exhaustive and elaborate form of argument than had been used hitherto.[1] The examples are well chosen, and Dionysius's main contention, that Isaeus is distinguished by technical brilliance and a relentless pursuit of rhetorical effect, is reflected in the considerable amount of technical vocabulary in the treatise. It is also worth noting that it contains no injunctions to pupils to imitate this or that quality of the author. This is perhaps to be explained by the fact that Isaeus's specialisation in cases of inheritance rendered him an unsuitable model for the broader literary purposes of Dionysius's teaching. It also seems probable that Dionysius considered that Demosthenes did everything that Isaeus did, but better. The treatise thus occupies a peculiar but important position in the corpus of Dionysius's critical treatises. It establishes the comparison of examples as a permanent feature, replacing the earlier system of virtues; and by ending with the

[1] See note 2, pp. 212–213.

statement that Demosthenes is the perfect orator, it leads the student irreversibly away from the mechanical imitation of individual traits towards an altogether higher plane of critical and aesthetic appreciation.

ΙΣΑΙΟΣ ΑΘΗΝΑΙΟΣ

1 Ἰσαῖος δὲ ὁ Δημοσθένους καθηγησάμενος καὶ διὰ τοῦτο μάλιστα γενόμενος περιφανής, ὡς μέν τινες ἱστοροῦσιν, Ἀθηναῖος ἦν τὸ γένος, ὡς δ' ἕτεροι γράφουσι, Χαλκιδεύς. ἤκμασε δὲ μετὰ τὸν Πελοποννησιακὸν πόλεμον, ὡς ἐκ λόγων αὐτοῦ τεκμαίρομαι, καὶ μέχρι τῆς Φιλίππου δυναστείας παρεξέτεινε. γενέσεως δὲ καὶ τελευτῆς τοῦ ῥήτορος ἀκριβῆ χρόνον εἰπεῖν οὐκ ἔχω οὐδὲ δὴ περὶ τοῦ βίου τἀνδρός, οἷός τις ἦν, οὐδὲ περὶ τῆς προαιρέσεως τῶν πολιτευμάτων οὐδέν, ἀρχὴν εἰ προείλετό τινα ἢ πολιτείαν, οὐδ' ὅλως περὶ τῶν τοιούτων οὐδενὸς διὰ τὸ μηδεμιᾷ[1] τοιαύτῃ περιτυγχάνειν ἱστορίᾳ. οὐδὲ γὰρ ὁ τοὺς Ἰσοκράτους μαθητὰς ἀναγράψας Ἕρμιππος, ἀκριβὴς ἐν τοῖς ἄλλοις γενόμενος, ὑπὲρ τοῦδε τοῦ ῥήτορος οὐδὲν εἴρηκεν ἔξω δυεῖν τούτων, ὅτι διήκουσε μὲν Ἰσοκράτους καθηγήσατο δὲ Δημοσθένους.

2 λείπεται δὴ περὶ τῆς προαιρέσεως καὶ δυνάμεως αὐτοῦ καὶ τίνι κέχρηται χαρακτῆρι λέγειν. γένους

[1] μηδεμιᾷ Krüger: μηδὲ codd.

---

[1] The tradition of Isaeus's Athenian origins is attributed to Hermippus, see note 2, p. 175, and that of Chalcidian origins to

ISAEUS

Isaeus was the teacher of Demosthenes and became 1
famous chiefly for that reason. According to some his family was Athenian, while others record that it was Chalcidian.[1] I deduce from his speeches that he was in his prime after the Peloponnesian war, and lived on into the years of Philip's hegemony. I am unable to give precise dates for the orator's birth, or to describe the kind of life he led. His political persuasion is likewise unknown to me: I do not know whether he preferred absolute or constitutional government, and am completely unable to answer all questions of this kind because I have not come upon any such information. Even Hermippus,[2] the biographer of the pupils of Isocrates who is accurate in other matters, supplies only two facts about Isaeus, that he studied for some time under Isocrates and was Demosthenes's teacher.

It remains to describe the style in which he chose 2
to write, to assess its effectiveness, and to distinguish

Demetrius of Magnesia, by Harpocration (s.v. Ἰσαῖος). [Plutarch], *Lives of the Ten Orators*, 839E mentions only his Chalcidian origin, and calls him Isaeus of Chalcis in the Life of Demosthenes, 844B.

[2] Born at Smyrna probably during the 3rd Century B.C. Peripatetic biographer who was a major source for Plutarch, Diogenes Laertius and others.

μὲν δὴ λόγων ἑνὸς ἀσκητὴς ἐγένετο τοῦ δικανικοῦ καὶ περὶ τοῦτο μάλιστα ἐσπούδασε. χαρακτῆρα δὲ τὸν Λυσίου κατὰ τὸ πλεῖστον ἐζήλωσε καὶ εἰ μή τις ἔμπειρος πάνυ τῶν ἀνδρῶν εἴη καὶ τριβὰς ἀξιολόγους ἀμφοῖν ἔχων, οὐκ ἂν διαγνοίη ῥᾳδίως πολλοὺς τῶν λόγων, ὁποτέρου τῶν ῥητόρων εἰσίν, ἀλλὰ παρακρούσεται ταῖς ἐπιγραφαῖς ⟨οὐχ⟩ [1] οὕτως ἀκριβῶς ἐχούσαις, ὡς διὰ μιᾶς δηλοῦταί μοι γραφῆς. οὐ μὴν ἀπαράλλακτός γέ ἐστιν ἡ τοῦ χαρακτῆρος ὁμοιότης, ἀλλὰ ἔχουσα διαφοράς τινας οὐ μικρὰς οὐδὲ ὀλίγας καὶ κατὰ τὴν ἑρμηνείαν καὶ κατὰ τὰ πράγματα, περὶ ὧν καιρὸς ἂν εἴη λέγειν, ὡς ἡμεῖς ὑπειλήφαμεν. ἐπειδὴ δὲ κατὰ τὴν λέξιν μᾶλλον ἔοικε τῷ Λυσίᾳ, τὴν ἀρχὴν ἀπὸ ταύτης ποιησάμενος τὰς ὁμοιότητάς τι καὶ τὰς διαφοράς, ἃς ἔχει πρὸς ἐκείνην, ἐρῶ.

3 καθαρὰ μὲν καὶ ἀκριβὴς καὶ σαφὴς κυρία τε καὶ ἐναργὴς καὶ σύντομος, πρὸς δὲ τούτοις πιθανή τε καὶ πρέπουσα τοῖς ὑποκειμένοις στρογγύλη τε καὶ δικανικὴ οὐχ ἧττόν ἐστιν ἡ Ἰσαίου λέξις τῆς Λυσίου, καὶ κατὰ μὲν ταῦτα οὐκ ἄν τις αὐτὴν διαγνοίη. διαφέρειν δὲ ἐκείνης δόξειεν ἂν ἐν τοῖσδε· ἣ μὲν γὰρ ἀφελής τε καὶ ἠθικὴ μᾶλλόν ἐστι σύγκειταί τε φυσικώτερον καὶ ἐσχημάτισται ἁπλούστερον ἡδονῇ τε καὶ χάριτι πολλῇ κεχορήγηται. ἡ δὲ Ἰσαίου τεχνικωτέρα δόξειεν ἂν εἶναι καὶ ἀκριβεστέρα τῆς Λυσίου τήν τε σύνθεσιν

[1] οὐχ inseruit Hudson.

---

[1] In fact the eleven surviving complete speeches and the fragment preserved in this treatise all concern inheritance,

its individual qualities. He became a specialist in a single branch of oratory, forensic, and devoted his energies chiefly to this.[1] In most respects he modelled his style upon that of Lysias,[2] and anyone who was unfamiliar with the two orators and had not spent a considerable amount of time in studying their speeches would find many of them difficult to assign to the right author, and would be deceived by the ascriptions on their title-pages, some of which are not very accurate, as I have shown in one of my treatises. As a matter of fact, their styles are not so similar as to be indistinguishable: some of the differences are considerable, and there are many of them, involving both language and subject-matter. It would seem to be time for me to give my views on both of these aspects, but since Isaeus's resemblance to Lysias is more pronounced in the matter of language, I shall begin my examination of the points of similarity and difference between them with that aspect.

The language of Isaeus is pure, precise, clear, stan- 3
dard, vivid and concise, and also persuasive, appropriate to the subject and suitable for use in the law-courts in the same degree as that of Lysias;[3] and in all these respects is indistinguishable from it. It would seem to differ, however, in the following ways: the language of Lysias is plainer and has a stronger moral flavour; its composition is more natural and the figures which it contains are simpler;[4] and it is generously endowed with grace and charm.[5] That of

though it is known that he wrote for other kinds of lawsuit.

[2] Cf. [Plutarch], *Lives of the Ten Orators*, 839E.

[3] Cf. *Lysias*, 13.

[4] Cf. *Lysias*, 8.

[5] Cf. *Lysias*, 10.

περιεργοτέρα τις καὶ σχηματισμοῖς διειλημμένη ποικίλοις, ὅσον τε ἀπολείπεται τῆς χάριτος ἐκείνης, τοσοῦτον ὑπερέχει τῇ δεινότητι τῆς κατασκευῆς καὶ πηγή τις ὄντως ἐστὶ τῆς Δημοσθένους δυνάμεως. τὴν μὲν οὖν λέξιν οὕτως ἄν τις διαγνοίη, ἐν δὲ τοῖς πράγμασι τοιαύτας τινὰς εὑρήσει διαφοράς. παρὰ Λυσίᾳ μὲν οὐ πολλὴν τὴν ἐπιτέχνησιν οὔτ' ἐν τοῖς μερισμοῖς τῶν πραγμάτων οὔτ' ἐν τῇ τάξει τῶν ἐνθυμημάτων οὔτ' ἐν ταῖς ἐξεργασίαις αὐτῶν ὄψεται· ἁπλοῦς γὰρ ὁ ἀνήρ. παρ' Ἰσαίῳ δὲ ⟨ἀκριβέστερον⟩ [1] καὶ τεχνικώτερον ἤδη γινόμενα ταῦτα εὑρήσει. καὶ γὰρ ἐφόδοις χρῆται καὶ προκατασκευαῖς καὶ μερισμοῖς τεχνικωτέροις καὶ † τίθησιν ἐν οἷς δίδωσι χωρίον ἕκαστον [2] † καὶ μέχρι πολλοῦ προάγει τὰς τῶν ἐπιχειρημάτων [3] ἐξεργασίας σχημάτων τε μεταβολαῖς ἐναγωνίων καὶ παθητικῶν ποικίλλει τοὺς λόγους. καὶ πρὸς μὲν τὸν ἀντίδικον διαπονηρεύεται, τοὺς δὲ δικαστὰς καταστρατηγεῖ, τοῖς δὲ πράγμασιν, ὑπὲρ ὧν ὁ λόγος, ἐκ παντὸς πειρᾶται βοηθεῖν.

4 ἵνα δὲ μᾶλλον ἡ διαφορὰ τῶν ἀνδρῶν γένηται καταφανής, εἰκόνι χρήσομαι τῶν ὁρατῶν τινι. εἰσὶ δή τινες ἀρχαῖαι γραφαί, χρώμασι μὲν εἰργασμέναι ἁπλῶς καὶ οὐδεμίαν ἐν τοῖς μίγμασιν

[1] ἀκριβέστερον inseruit Sadée.
[2] τίθησιν ἐν οἷς δίδωσι χωρίον ἕκαστον lectio plane corrupta: τίθησιν οἷς δίδωσι χωρίον ἐν χωρίῳ ἕκαστον scribendum esse censeo sensum secutus.
[3] ἐπιχειρημάτων Krüger: ἐγχειρημάτων codd.

---

[1] διαίρεσις in Aristotle (*Rhetoric*, ii. 23. 10), *partitio* in *Ad*

Isaeus would seem to suggest more technical skill and attention to detail than that of Lysias: its structure is more elaborate and interspersed with a variety of figures. It compensates for its lack of Lysianic charm by that brilliant artistic resource which makes it the real spring from which the rhetorical power of Demosthenes flows. Such are the differences by which their language may be distinguished. In their treatment of subject-matter the following differences will be found: with Lysias there is not much artifice in the division of topics [1] and the arrangement of arguments,[2] nor in their development, for Lysias is a straightforward man. But the reader of Isaeus will find these handled with more precision and technical skill. He uses insinuations [3] and anticipations [4] and analyses of a more contrived kind, assigning a place to each when he uses them. He carries the development of his arguments [5] to great length and gives variety to his speeches by alternating devices of debate with emotional appeal. He blackens his opponent's character, outgenerals the jury with his stratagems and tries by every means to help his client's case.

In order to clarify further the difference between 4
the two men, I shall use a simile from the visual arts. There are some old paintings which are worked in simple colours without any subtle blending of tints

Herennium (iii. 9. 19), Cicero (*De Partitione Oratoria passim*, *De Oratore* 2. 52. 209–210), Quintilian iv. 5.

[2] See note 5.

[3] For illustration see Spengel, *Rhetores Graeci* II p. 50.

[4] For illustration see *Rhetorica ad Alexandrum*, 18.

[5] In this passage the word "argument" is used to translate both *ἐνθύμημα* and *ἐπιχείρημα*. Dionysius distinguishes between the two in ch. 16. See note 2, pp. 212–213.

ἔχουσαι ποικιλίαν, ἀκριβεῖς δὲ ταῖς γραμμαῖς καὶ πολὺ τὸ χαρίεν ἐν ταύταις ἔχουσαι. αἱ δὲ μετ᾽ ἐκείνας εὔγραμμοι μὲν ἧττον, ἐξειργασμέναι δὲ μᾶλλον, σκιᾷ τε καὶ φωτὶ ποικιλλόμεναι καὶ ἐν τῷ πλήθει τῶν μιγμάτων τὴν ἰσχὺν ἔχουσαι. τούτων μὲν δὴ ταῖς ἀρχαιοτέραις ἔοικεν ὁ Λυσίας κατὰ τὴν ἁπλότητα καὶ τὴν χάριν, ταῖς δὲ ἐκπεπονημέναις τε καὶ τεχνικωτέραις ὁ Ἰσαῖος. ἦν δὲ περὶ αὐτοῦ δόξα παρὰ τοῖς τότε γοητείας καὶ ἀπάτης, ὡς δεινὸς ἀνὴρ [1] τεχνιτεῦσαι λόγους ἐπὶ τὰ πονηρότερα, καὶ εἰς τοῦτο διεβάλλετο. δηλοῖ δὲ τοῦτο τῶν ἀρχαίων τις ῥητόρων ἐν τῇ Δημοσθένους κατηγορίᾳ Πυθέας, ὡς ἐμοὶ δοκεῖ. πονηρίαν γὰρ τῷ Δημοσθένει καὶ κακίαν τὴν ἐξ ἀνθρώπων πᾶσαν ἐνοικεῖν φήσας,[2] κατὰ τόδε τὸ μέρος οἷον εἰς διαβολὴν ἐπιτίθησιν, ὅτι τὸν Ἰσαῖον ὅλον καὶ τὰς τῶν λόγων ἐκείνου τέχνας σεσίτισται. καὶ μὰ Δία οὐκ ἀπὸ σκοποῦ τὴν διαβολὴν ταύτην εἶχεν ἑκάτερος. ἐμοὶ γοῦν οἱ μὲν Ἰσαίου τε καὶ Δημοσθένους λόγοι, κἂν περὶ ἀληθεῖς καὶ δικαίας συνταχθῶσιν ὑποθέσεις,[3] ὕποπτοι δοκοῦσιν εἶναι τῆς πολλῆς ἐπιτεχνήσεως ἕνεκα, οἱ δὲ Ἰσοκράτους καὶ Λυσίου παντὸς μάλιστα δίκαιοί τε καὶ ἀληθεῖς, κἂν μὴ τοιαῦτα τὰ πράγματα ἐν αὐτοῖς, ὅτι κακοῦργον οὐδὲν ἐπιφαίνουσιν ἐπὶ τῆς κατασκευῆς, ἀλλ᾽ εἰσὶν ἐλεύθεροί τινες καὶ ἀφελεῖς.

[1] ἀνὴρ Krüger: ἀνὴρ codd.
[2] φήσας Sylburg: φῆσαι F: φησὶ MBP.
[3] κἂν περὶ ἀληθεῖς καὶ δικαίας συνταχθῶσιν ὑποθέσεις Blass: καὶ περὶ ἀληθείας καὶ δικαίας συντάξεως αἱ ὑποθέσεις codd.

but clear in their outline, and thereby possessing great charm; whereas the later paintings are less well-drawn but contain greater detail and a subtle interplay of light and shade, and are effective because of the many nuances of colour which they contain. Now Lysias resembles the older paintings by his simplicity and charm, and Isaeus their more elaborate and more skilfully wrought successors. Isaeus had a reputation among his contemporaries for chicanery and deception, and for being clever at devising speeches for the worse cause, and was accused of doing so. This charge is proved, in my opinion, by Pytheas,[1] one of the early orators, in his prosecution of Demosthenes. After saying that all the villainy of the human race resided in that orator, he confirms his point by adding, as a further jibe, that Demosthenes had digested the whole of Isaeus, including his rhetorical technique. And indeed this charge was not wide of the mark in the case of both these orators: for even when the cases they are presenting are genuine and just, the speeches of Isaeus and Demosthenes seem to me at least to be suspect because of their great rhetorical skill; whereas those of Isocrates and Lysias seem the most genuine and just of all, even when the facts of the case suggest otherwise, because they display nothing malicious in their presentation, but are straightforward and simple.

[1] A younger contemporary of Demosthenes, who failed to achieve inclusion in the Canon of Ten because his style was ill-disciplined, θρασὺς καὶ διεσπασμένος (Suda, s.v.). Responsible for the famous criticism of Demosthenes's oratory, that it "smelt of the lamp" (Plut. *Dem.* 8). See Blass III², pp. 283–288.

5 ταυτί μοι τὰ διαλλάττοντα ἔδοξεν εἶναι, ἐξ ὧν ἄν τις οὐ χαλεπῶς διαγνῶναι τοὺς Λυσίου τε καὶ Ἰσαίου λόγους δυνηθείη. εἰ δὲ ὀρθῶς ὑπείληφα, ἐξέσται τῷ βουλομένῳ σκοπεῖν ⟨ἐπ᾿ αὐτῶν τῶν παραδειγμάτων ποιουμένῳ⟩[1] τὴν ἐξέτασιν. ἄρξομαι δὲ ἀπὸ τῶν περὶ τὴν λέξιν θεωρημάτων. ἔστι δή τις Ἰσαίου λόγος ὑπὲρ Εὐμάθους, μετοίκου τινὸς τῶν τραπεζιτευόντων Ἀθήνησιν, ὃν εἰς δουλείαν ἀγόμενον ὑπὸ τοῦ κληρονομήσαντος τὸν ἀπηλευθερωκότα τῶν ἀστῶν τις ἀφαιρεῖται καὶ τὴν ἀπολογίαν ποιεῖται περὶ αὐτοῦ. τὸ προοίμιον δέ ἐστι τοῦ λόγου τοιόνδε· "Ἄνδρες δικασταί, ἐγὼ καὶ πρότερον Εὐμάθει τούτῳ ἐγενόμην χρήσιμος δικαίως καὶ νῦν, εἴ τι ἔστι κατ᾿ ἐμέ, πειράσομαι συσσῴζειν αὐτὸν μεθ᾿ ὑμῶν. μικρὰ δέ μου ἀκούσατε, ἵνα μηδεὶς ὑπολάβῃ ὑμῶν, ὡς ἐγὼ προπετείᾳ ἢ ἄλλῃ τινὶ ἀδικίᾳ πρὸς τὰ Εὐμάθους πράγματα προσῆλθον. τριηραρχοῦντος γάρ μου ἐπὶ Κηφισοδότου ἄρχοντος καὶ λόγου ἀπαγγελθέντος πρὸς τοὺς οἰκείους, ὡς ἄρα τετελευτηκὼς εἴην ἐν τῇ ναυμαχίᾳ, οὔσης μοι παρακαταθήκης παρ᾿ Εὐμάθει τούτῳ, μεταπεμψάμενος τοὺς οἰκείους καὶ φίλους τοὺς ἐμοὺς Εὐμάθης ἐνεφάνισε τὰ χρήματα, ἃ ἦν μοι παρ᾿ αὐτῷ, καὶ ἀπέδωκε πάντα ὀρθῶς καὶ δικαίως. ἀνθ᾿ ὧν ἐγὼ σωθεὶς ἐχρώμην τε αὐτῷ ἔτι μᾶλλον καὶ κατασκευαζομένῳ τὴν τράπεζαν εἰσευπόρησα ἀργυρίου. καὶ μετὰ ταῦτα ἄγοντος αὐτὸν Διονυσίου ἐξειλόμην εἰς ἐλευθερίαν

These seemed to me to be the differences by which 5
the speeches of Lysias and Isaeus could be distinguished without difficulty. Anyone can test the correctness of my judgment by examining actual examples. I shall begin with my views about his language. There is a speech of Isaeus for Eumathes, one of the resident aliens who was engaged in banking at Athens. The heir of the man who has liberated him is trying to re-enslave him, and an Athenian citizen is asserting his freedom and pleading in his defence. The introduction of the speech is as follows:[1]

"Gentlemen of the jury, on a former occasion I rendered a service to the defendant Eumathes, as was right, and I shall try now, by whatever means I can, to help to save him with your aid. Listen to a brief explanation from me, so that none of you may suppose that I interfered in Eumathes's affairs in a spirit of petulance or from any other wrong motive. When I was trierarch in the archonship of Cephisodotus[2] and news was brought to my relatives that I had died in the sea-battle, Eumathes here, with whom I had deposited some money, sent for my relatives and friends and declared the money that he had belonging to me, and handed over the whole amount with scrupulous honesty. As a result of this, when I returned home safely, I became more friendly with him, and when he established his bank, I contributed capital to it; and afterwards, when Dionysius tried to enslave him, I asserted his liberty, being aware

[1] Frag. 18.
[2] 358–357 B.C.

[1] Lacunam supplevit Krüger

εἰδὼς ἀφειμένον ἐν τῷ δικαστηρίῳ ὑπὸ Ἐπιγένους. ἀλλὰ περὶ μὲν τούτων ἐπισχήσω."[1]

6 ἔστι δὴ καὶ παρὰ τῷ Λυσίᾳ τις ὑπὲρ ἀνδρὸς ξένου δίκην φεύγοντος περὶ κλήρου ποιούμενος τὴν ἀπολογίαν. τοῦτον ἐπιγράφει τὸν λόγον Καλλίμαχος "περὶ Φερενίκου ὑπὲρ τοῦ Ἀνδροκλείδου κλήρου" καὶ ἔστι πολλοῖς πρότερον ἠγωνισμένος ἔτεσι θατέρου. ἐν ᾧ τὴν αἰτίαν πρῶτος ἐπιδείκνυσιν ὁ περὶ τοῦ ξένου ποιούμενος τοὺς λόγους ὥσπερ ὁ τὸν μέτοικον ἐξαιρούμενος εἰς ἐλευθερίαν. ἔστι δὲ τὸ προοίμιον τοῦ λόγου τόδε· "Ἀναγκαῖόν μοι δοκεῖ εἶναι, ὦ ἄνδρες δικασταί, περὶ τῆς φιλίας τῆς ἐμῆς καὶ τῆς Φερενίκου πρῶτον εἰπεῖν πρὸς ὑμᾶς, ἵνα μηδεὶς ὑμῶν θαυμάσῃ, ὅτι ὑπὲρ οὐδενὸς ὑμῶν πώποτε εἰρηκὼς πρότερον ὑπὲρ τούτου νυνὶ λέγω. ἐμοὶ γάρ, ὦ ἄνδρες δικασταί, ξένος ἦν Κηφισόδοτος ὁ τούτου πατήρ, καὶ ὅτε ἐφεύγομεν, ἐν Θήβαις παρ' ἐκείνῳ κατηγόμην καὶ ἐγὼ καὶ ἄλλος Ἀθηναίων ὁ βουλόμενος, καὶ πολλὰ καὶ ἀγαθὰ καὶ ἰδίᾳ καὶ δημοσίᾳ παθόντες ὑπ' αὐτοῦ εἰς τὴν ἡμετέραν αὐτῶν κατήλθομεν. ἐπεὶ δ' οὖν οὗτοι ταῖς αὐταῖς τύχαις ἐχρήσαντο καὶ φυγάδες Ἀθήναζε ἀφίκοντο, ἡγούμενος τὴν μεγίστην αὐτοῖς ὀφείλειν χάριν οὕτως οἰκείως αὐτοὺς ὑπεδεξάμην, ὥστε μηδένα γνῶναι τῶν εἰσιόντων, εἰ μή τις πρότερον ἠπίστατο, ὁπότερος ἡμῶν ἐκέκτητο τὴν οἰκίαν. οἶδε μὲν οὖν καὶ Φερένικος, ὦ ἄνδρες δικασταί, ὅτι πολλοὶ λέγειν εἰσὶν ἐμοῦ δεινότεροι καὶ

[1] ἐπισχήσω Sylburg: ὑποσχήσω codd.

that he had been proclaimed a free man by Epigenes in open court. But I shall say no more of this."

Lysias also wrote a speech in defence of an alien facing a charge involving an inheritance. Callimachus[1] entitles this speech *Concerning the Claim of Pherenicus to the Estate of Androclides*, and the case was fought many years before that of Eumathes. In it the citizen speaking on the alien's behalf begins by giving his reason for doing so, as does the defender of the metic's freedom. Here is the introduction of the speech:[2] 6

" I think it necessary, gentlemen of the jury, to speak to you first about the friendship between Pherenicus and myself, so that none of you may be surprised that I, who have never previously spoken in defence of any of you, should now be speaking on behalf of this man. Cephisodotus, the defendant's father, was a guest-friend of mine, gentlemen, and when we were in exile, I and any other Athenian who wished to, enjoyed his hospitality in Thebes, and received many favours at his hands in public and in private before returning to our own city. Now that these gentlemen have suffered the same misfortunes as we, and have come in exile to Athens, realising that I have a huge debt of gratitude to repay, I have taken them so completely into my family that no visitor without prior knowledge would know which of us was the owner of the house. Pherenicus, too, knows that there are many cleverer speakers than I, gentlemen,

[1] Poet and librarian at Alexandria during the third century B.C. (he died around 240 B.C.). In addition to his extensive literary activities, his work involved him in problems of ascription and identification. See Dover, *Lysias and the Corpus Lysiacum*, ch. 2.

[2] Frag. 120 Scheibe.

μᾶλλον τοιούτων πραγμάτων ἔμπειροι, ἀλλ' ὅμως ἡγεῖται τὴν ἐμὴν οἰκειότητα πιστοτάτην εἶναι. αἰσχρὸν οὖν μοι δοκεῖ εἶναι κελεύοντος τούτου καὶ δεομένου τὰ δίκαια αὐτῷ βοηθῆσαι περιιδεῖν αὐτόν, καθ' ὅσον οἷός τ' εἰμὶ ἐγώ, τῶν ὑπ' Ἀνδροκλείδου δεδομένων στερηθῆναι."

7 τί δὴ ταῦτα τὰ προοίμια ἀλλήλων διαφέρει; παρὰ Λυσίᾳ μὲν ἡδεῖά[1] ἐστιν ἡ εἰσβολὴ καὶ δι' οὐδὲν ἄλλο μᾶλλον ἢ ὅτι φυσικῶς πως εἴρηται καὶ ἀφελῶς· "ἀναγκαῖόν μοι δοκεῖ εἶναι, ὦ ἄνδρες δικασταί, περὶ τῆς φιλίας τῆς ἐμῆς καὶ τῆς Φερενίκου πρῶτον εἰπεῖν πρὸς ὑμᾶς." καὶ τὸ ἐπιλεγόμενον τούτῳ ἔτι μᾶλλον ἀκατάσκευον φαίνεται εἶναι καί, ὡς ἂν ἰδιώτης τις εἰπεῖν δύναιτο, τὸ εἰρημένον· "ἵνα μηδεὶς ὑμῶν θαυμάσῃ, ὅτι ὑπὲρ οὐδενὸς ὑμῶν πώποτε εἰρηκὼς πρότερον ὑπὲρ τούτου νῦν λέγω." παρὰ δὲ Ἰσαίῳ κατεσκεύασται τὸ δοκοῦν εἶναι ἀφελὲς καὶ οὐ λέληθεν, ὅτι ἐστὶ ῥητορικόν· "ἐγὼ καὶ πρότερον Εὐμάθει τούτῳ ἐγενόμην χρήσιμος δικαίως καὶ νῦν, εἴ τι ἔστι κατ' ἐμέ, πειράσομαι συσσῴζειν αὐτόν." ὑψηλότερά τε ⟨γάρ⟩[2] ἐστι καὶ ἧττον ἐκείνων ἀφελέστερα, καὶ ἔτι μᾶλλον τὰ ἐπιφερόμενα· "μικρὰ δέ μου ἀκούσατε, ἵνα μηδεὶς ὑπολάβῃ ὑμῶν, ὡς ἐγὼ προπετείᾳ ἢ ἄλλῃ τινὶ ἀδικίᾳ πρὸς τὰ Εὐμάθους πράγματα προσῆλθον." ἥ τε γὰρ προπέτεια καὶ ἡ ἀδικία καὶ τὸ πρὸς τὰ Εὐμάθους πράγματα προσελθεῖν πεποιημένοις[3] μᾶλλον ἔοικεν

and many with more experience in this kind of case, and yet he chooses to rely completely upon my friendship. Since he calls upon me and begs me to assist him in securing justice, it seems to me shameful not to do all I can to see that he is not deprived of his inheritance from Androclides."

What are the points of difference between these 7 introductions? Lysias's opening words are pleasant, and the main reason for this is that they are natural and simple: "I think it necessary, gentlemen of the jury, to speak to you first about the friendship between Pherenicus and myself." And what follows seems even more unaffected and like the words any ordinary man would use: ". . . in order that none of you should be surprised that I, who have never previously spoken in defence of any of you, should now be speaking on behalf of this man." In Isaeus, however, apparently simple concepts are elaborated, and their rhetorical treatment is plain to see: "On a former occasion I rendered a service to the defendant Eumathes, as was right, and I shall try now, by whatever means I can, to help to save him with your aid." This is more elevated and less simple than the other, qualities which are even more marked in what follows: "Listen to a brief explanation from me, so that none of you may suppose that I interfered in Eumathes's affairs in a spirit of petulance or from any other wrong motive." "Spirit of petulance," "wrong motive" and "interfered in Eumathes's affairs" seem to have been artificially rather than

---

1 ἡδεῖά Reiske: ἰδία codd.
2 γάρ inseruit Sylburg.
3 πεποιημένοις Sylburg: πεποιημέναις codd.

ἢ αὐτοφυέσι. καὶ αὖθίς γε παρὰ μὲν τῷ Λυσίᾳ ἡ πρόφασις λέγεται ἀνεπιτηδεύτως· "ἐμοὶ γάρ, ὦ ἄνδρες δικασταί, ξένος ἦν Κηφισόδοτος ὁ τούτου πατήρ, καὶ ὅτε ἐφεύγομεν, ἐν Θήβαις παρ' ἐκείνῳ κατηγόμην καὶ ἐγὼ καὶ ἄλλος Ἀθηναίων ὁ βουλόμενος." ἡδέως τε καὶ ἀφοριστικῶς τὰ μετὰ ταῦτα ἐπιτίθεται· "καὶ πολλὰ καὶ ἀγαθὰ καὶ ἰδίᾳ καὶ δημοσίᾳ παθόντες ὑπ' αὐτοῦ εἰς τὴν ἡμετέραν αὐτῶν κατήλθομεν." παρὰ δὲ τῷ Ἰσαίῳ πέφρασται περιεργότερον καὶ οὐ μακρὰν ἀπέχει τῆς Δημοσθένους κατασκευῆς· "τριηραρχοῦντος γάρ ⟨μου⟩ ἐπὶ Κηφισοδότου ἄρχοντος καὶ λόγου ἀπαγγελθέντος πρὸς τοὺς οἰκείους, ὡς ἄρα τετελευτηκὼς εἴην ἐν τῇ ναυμαχίᾳ, οὔσης μοι παρακαταθήκης παρ' Εὐμάθει τούτῳ." τό τε γὰρ λόγου ἀπαγγελθέντος καὶ τὸ ὡς ἄρα τετελευτηκὼς εἴην καὶ τὸ οὔσης ἐμοὶ παρακαταθήκης οὐκ ἂν φαίην ἔγωγε ἀφελῶς εἰρῆσθαι. ἐκείνως γὰρ λεγόμενα μᾶλλον ἀποίητα· "ὅτε γὰρ ἐτριηράρχουν καὶ ἀπηγγέλη τοῖς ἐνθάδε, ὡς ἄρα τετελευτηκὼς εἴην, ἔχων μου παρακαταθήκην Εὐμάθης οὑτοσί."

8 καὶ τὰ λοιπὰ δὲ τῶν προοιμίων μέρη παρ' ᾧ μὲν ἀφελέστερον ἄν τις εὕροι λεγόμενα, παρ' ᾧ δὲ ῥητορικώτερον. ἐν ἑτέρῳ δὲ [1] ἀγῶνι πάλιν ὁ μὲν Ἰσαῖος ἐπιτρόπῳ τινὶ συντάξας ἀπολογίαν ὑπὸ τοῦ ἰδίου ἀδελφιδοῦ κρινομένῳ τοιαύτῃ κέχρηται ⟨τῇ⟩ [2] ἀρχῇ· "Ἐβουλόμην μέν, ὦ ἄνδρες δικασταί, μὴ λίαν οὕτως Ἁγνόθεον πρὸς χρήματ' [3] ἔχειν αἰσχρῶς, ὥστε τοῖς ἀλλοτρίοις ἐπιβουλεύειν καὶ

[1] δὲ Reiske: τὲ M: τε FBP.
[2] τῇ inseruit Sadée.

spontaneously introduced. And again, in Lysias, the explanation is introduced artlessly, " Cephisodotus, the defendant's father, was a guest-friend of mine, gentlemen, and when we were in exile, I and any other Athenian who wished to, enjoyed his hospitality in Thebes "; and what follows this is expressed with an agreeable conciseness: " . . . and received many favours at his hands in public and in private before returning to our own city." In Isaeus the structure is more elaborate, and approaches that of Demosthenes: " When I was trierarch in the archonship of Cephisodotus and news was brought to my relatives that I had died in the sea-battle, Eumathes here, with whom I had deposited some money . . ." The clauses " news was brought " and " that I had died " and " with whom I had deposited some money " hardly make the structure simple, in my opinion. A more straightforward way of saying this would have been: " When I was trierarch and it was reported home that I had died, Eumathes here, who had some money which I had deposited with him . . ."

The remaining portions of their introductions will 8
be found to be expressed more simply, in the one case, and more rhetorically in the other. And again, in another lawsuit, Isaeus composed a speech in defence of a trustee who was being accused by his nephew, which begins as follows:[1]

" I should have wished, gentlemen of the jury, that Hagnotheus did not have such a shameful passion for money as to plot against the property of others and

[1] Frag. 1.

---

[3] πρὸς χρήματ' Bekker: προσχήματα codd.

δίκας τοιαύτας λαγχάνειν, ἀλλ' ὄντα γε οὖν[1] ἀδελφιδοῦν ἐμὸν καὶ κύριον τῆς πατρῴας οὐσίας οὐ μικρᾶς ἀλλ' ἱκανῆς ὥστε καὶ λειτουργεῖν, ὑφ' ἡμῶν αὐτῷ[2] παραδοθείσης, ταύτης ἐπιμελεῖσθαι, τῶν δ' ἐμῶν μὴ ἐπιθυμεῖν· ἵνα βελτίων τ' ἐδόκει πᾶσιν εἶναι σῴζων αὐτὴν καὶ πλείω ποιῶν χρησιμώτερον ὑμῖν πολίτην παρεῖχεν ἑαυτόν. ἐπεὶ δὲ τὴν μὲν ἀνήρηκε καὶ πέπρακε καὶ αἰσχρῶς καὶ κακῶς διολώλεκεν, ὡς οὐκ ἂν ἐβουλόμην, πιστεύων δ' ἑταιρίαις καὶ λόγων παρασκευαῖς ἐπὶ τὴν ἐμὴν ἐλήλυθεν, ἀνάγκη, ὡς ἔοικε, συμφορὰν μὲν εἶναι νομίζειν, ὅτι τοιοῦτός ἐστιν οἰκεῖος ὤν, ἀπολογεῖσθαι δὲ περὶ ὧν ἐγκέκληκε καὶ ἔξω με τοῦ πράγματος διαβέβληκεν ὡς ἂν οὖν δυνώμεθα προθυμότατα πρὸς ὑμᾶς." ὁ δὲ Λυσίας ἀνδρὶ ὑπὸ τῶν ἀδελφῶν τῆς ἑαυτοῦ γυναικὸς ἐγκαλουμένῳ κακῆς ἐπιτροπῆς συγγράψας λόγον τοιούτῳ κέχρηται τῷ προοιμίῳ· "Οὐχ ἱκανόν, ὦ ἄνδρες δικασταί, τοῖς ἐπιτρόποις, ὅσα πράγματα διὰ τὴν ἐπιτροπείαν ἔχουσιν, ἀλλὰ καὶ διασῴζοντες τὰς τῶν φίλων οὐσίας συκοφαντοῦνται ὑπὸ τῶν ὀρφανῶν πολλοί. ὅπερ κἀμοὶ νῦν συμβέβηκεν. ἐγὼ γάρ, ὦ ἄνδρες δικασταί, καταλειφθεὶς ἐπίτροπος τῶν Ἱπποκράτους χρημάτων καὶ διαχειρίσας ὀρθῶς καὶ δικαίως τὴν οὐσίαν καὶ παραδοὺς τοῖς υἱοῖς δοκιμασθεῖσι τὰ χρήματα, ὧν ἐπίτροπος κατελείφθην, συκοφαντοῦμαι νῦν ὑπ' αὐτῶν ἀδίκως."

9 οὐ πολλῶν οἶμαι δεῖν λόγων, ὅτι τοῦτο μὲν ἀφελῶς καὶ ἡδέως εἴρηται ἦθός τε οὐ πεπλασμένον

[1] ἀλλ' ὄντα γε οὖν Dobree: ἀλλ' οὐ τό γε οὖν codd.
[2] αὐτῷ Reiske: αὐτῶν codd.

file lawsuits like the present one. Since he is my nephew and the master of a considerable inheritance, ample for the discharge of public services, and handed over to him by us, he should have devoted his attention to it instead of coveting mine, so that by conserving his own wealth he might have enjoyed a better reputation, and by increasing it might have shown himself a more valuable member of your community. But since he had squandered, sold and shamefully and wickedly lost it all—conduct which no one deplores more than I—and now, relying on the support of his political henchmen and trumped-up charges, has attacked my property, it seems that I am forced to regard it as a misfortune that I have such a man as a relative, and to make my defence before you against the charges he has brought, and his entirely irrelevant accusations, with all the energy at my command."

Lysias, in a speech composed for a man accused by his wife's brothers of breach of guardianship, begins with these words:[1]

"Gentlemen of the jury, guardians do not only have to endure the trouble involved in their guardianship, but many, even when they hand over their friends' property intact, are often falsely accused by their wards. This is what has now happened to me. I was left trustee of the estate of Hippocrates. I managed the money that had been left in my care in an upright and fair manner, and when his sons came of age I handed over to them the money of which I had been left the trustee. Now they are accusing me unjustly."

I do not think that much discussion is needed to 9
show that this is a simple and pleasing statement, and

[1] Frag. 62 Scheibe.

ἀλλὰ φυσικὸν ἐπιφαίνει. τὸ γάρ· "οὐχ ἱκανόν, ὦ ἄνδρες δικασταί, τοῖς ἐπιτρόποις, ὅσα πράγματα διὰ τὴν ἐπιτροπείαν ἔχουσιν' οὐδεὶς ἂν εἴποι ῥήτορος εἶναι, ἀλλὰ παντὸς ἰδιώτου καταστάντος εἰς ἀγῶνα ἄδικον. τὸ δ' Ἰσαίου πεποιῆσθαι ῥητορικῶς καὶ κεκαλλιλογῆσθαι [1] σεμνότερον ἅπαντες ἂν φήσειαν, τὸ γάρ· "ἐβουλόμην μέν, ὦ ἄνδρες δικασταί, μὴ λίαν οὕτως Ἁγνόθεον πρὸς χρήματα ἔχειν αἰσχρῶς, ὥστε τοῖς ἀλλοτρίοις ἐπιβουλεύειν." καὶ ἔτι μᾶλλον παρὰ Λυσίᾳ μὲν χαριέντως πάνυ καὶ ἀφελῶς εἰρῆσθαι τό· "ἐγὼ γάρ, ὦ ἄνδρες δικασταί, καταλειφθεὶς ἐπίτροπος τῶν Ἱπποκράτους χρημάτων καὶ διαχειρίσας ὀρθῶς καὶ δικαίως τὴν οὐσίαν καὶ παραδοὺς τοῖς υἱοῖς δοκιμασθεῖσι τὰ χρήματα." θάτερον δὲ τρανότερον καὶ οὐχ ὡς ἂν ἰδιώτης συνέθηκεν· "ἀλλ' ὄντα γε οὖν ἀδελφιδοῦν ἐμὸν καὶ κύριον τῆς πατρῴας οὐσίας οὐ μικρᾶς ἀλλ' ἱκανῆς, ὥστε καὶ λειτουργεῖν, ὑφ' ἡμῶν αὐτῷ παραδοθείσης, ταύτης ἐπιμελεῖσθαι." ἑνὸς δ' ἔτι μνησθήσομαι γένους, ἐξ οὗ μάλιστα ἡ διαφορὰ τῶν ἀνδρῶν ἔσται καταφανής.

10 ὑποτίθεται δὲ ἑκάτερος ἰδιώτην ἄνδρα καὶ ἀπράγμονα καὶ νέον παρὰ τὴν ἑαυτοῦ προαίρεσίν τε καὶ φύσιν ἠναγκασμένον ἐν δικαστηρίῳ λέγειν, ὁ μὲν Λυσίας ἐν τῷ πρὸς Ἀρχεβιάδην λόγῳ τὸν τρόπον τοῦτον· "Ἐπειδὴ τάχιστα ἔλαχέ μοι ταύτην τὴν δίκην Ἀρχεβιάδης, ὦ ἄνδρες δικασταί, προσῆλθον αὐτῷ λέγων, ὅτι νέος καὶ ἄπειρος

[1] κεκαλλιλογῆσθαι Sylburg: καλλιλογίσασθαι codd.

it has a natural, uncontrived moral flavour. Nobody could say that " Gentlemen of the jury, guardians do not only have to endure the trouble involved in their guardianship " is a rhetorical expression, but only that it is the language of any ordinary person who is exposed to unjust litigation. But everyone would agree that the passage of Isaeus has been rhetorically composed and elegantly phrased in a grander manner, when he says, " I should have wished, gentlemen of the jury, that Hagnotheus did not have such a shameful passion for money as to plot against the property of others." They would agree even more readily that Lysias's words are quite simple and charming when he says: " I was left trustee of the estate of Hippocrates. I managed the money that had been left in my care in an upright and fair manner, and when his sons came of age I handed the money over to them." Isaeus expresses himself more explicitly, and not as an ordinary man would have done: " Since he is my nephew and the master of a considerable inheritance, ample for the discharge of public services, and handed over to him by us, he should have devoted his attention to it." I shall mention one further aspect which will illustrate the difference between them in the clearest light.

Each orator represents his client as an ordinary 10
man, self-effacing, young and forced to speak in court contrary to his inclination and nature. Lysias does this in his speech *Against Archebiades* in the following way: [1]

" As soon as Archebiades filed this suit against me, gentlemen of the jury, I went to him and said that I was young and inexperienced in public life, and had

[1] Frag. 19 Scheibe.

εἴην [1] πραγμάτων καὶ οὐδὲν δεόμενος εἰσιέναι εἰς δικαστήριον. ἐγὼ οὖν σε ἀξιῶ μὴ εὕρεμα ἡγεῖσθαι τὴν ἡλικίαν τὴν ἐμήν, ἀλλὰ παραλαβόντα τοὺς ἐμοὺς φίλους καὶ τοὺς σαυτοῦ διηγήσασθαι περὶ τοῦ χρέως,[2] ὅθεν γεγένηται. κἂν δόξῃς ἀληθῆ λέγειν ἐκείνοις, οὐδέν σοι δεήσει πραγμάτων, ἀλλὰ λαβὼν ἄπει [3] τὰ σαυτοῦ. δίκαιος δὲ εἶ [3] μηδὲν παραλιπεῖν, ἀλλ' εἰπεῖν ἅπαντα, ἐπειδὴ νεώτερός εἰμι τοῦ συμβολαίου,[4] ἵνα ἀκούσαντες, περὶ ὧν οὐκ ἴσμεν, βουλευσώμεθα περὶ ὧν σὺ λέγεις· ἐάν πως φανερὸν γένηται, πότερον ἀδίκως τῶν ἐμῶν ἐφίεσαι ἢ δικαίως τὰ σεαυτοῦ ζητεῖς κομίσασθαι. ταῦτ' ἐμοῦ προκαλουμένου οὐδεπώποτ' ἠθέλησε συνελθεῖν οὐδὲ λόγον περὶ ὧν ἐνεκάλει [5] ποιήσασθαι οὐδὲ δίαιταν ἐπιτρέψαι, ἕως ὑμεῖς τὸν νόμον τὸν περὶ τῶν διαιτητῶν ἔθεσθε." ὁ δὲ Ἰσαῖος ἐν ἀμφισβητήσει χωρίου τοῦ ὑπὸ τῶν δημοτῶν κατεσχημένου,[6] οἷς τὸ χωρίον ὑπέκειτο, ταύτῃ χρώμενον εἰσάγει [7] τῇ ἀρχῇ· "Μάλιστα μὲν ἐβουλόμην, ὦ ἄνδρες δικασταί, μηδ' ὑφ' ἑνὸς ἀδικεῖσθαι τῶν πολιτῶν, εἰ δὲ μή, τοιούτων ἀντιδίκων τυχεῖν, πρὸς οὓς οὐδὲν ἂν ἐφρόντιζον διαφερόμενος. νῦν δέ μοι πάντων πραγμάτων λυπηρότατον συμβέβηκεν. ἀδικοῦμαι γὰρ ὑπὸ τῶν δημοτῶν, οὓς περιορᾶν μὲν ἀποστεροῦντας οὐ ῥᾴδιον, ἀπέχθεσθαι δὲ ἀηδές,[8] μεθ' ὧν ἀνάγκη καὶ

[1] εἴην Franz: codd.
[2] χρέως Scheibe: χρέους codd.
[3] ἄπει Reiske: ἐπὶ codd. εἶ Reiske: εἰμὶ codd.
[4] συμβολαίου Emperius: συμβουλεύειν codd.
[5] ἐνεκάλει Bekker: ἐνεκαλεῖτο codd.

no desire to go to court. 'I therefore ask you not to take advantage of my youth, but assemble my friends and yours together and tell them how I came to be in your debt. If they decide that you are telling the truth, further proceedings will not be necessary, but for you to take your dues and go. You ought to leave no detail unmentioned, but you should tell the whole story, for the contract was made before I was born. We shall then be able to hear what we do not at present know and consider your version of the case; then perhaps it will become clear whether you are unjustly aiming to procure what is mine or legitimately seeking to recover what is yours.' I challenged him to do this, but he would never agree to a meeting or a discussion of his charges, nor to submit to arbitration until you passed the arbitration law."

But Isaeus, in a dispute about a piece of land held by the fellow-parishioners of his client, who had mortgaged it to them, introduces the subject with these opening words:[1]

"I should have greatly preferred, gentlemen of the jury, never to suffer injustice at the hands of any of my fellow-citizens; or, if that were impossible, to find adversaries with whom I can quarrel without feeling concern. As it is, the most painful thing possible has happened to me: I am being wronged by my fellow-demesmen, whose robbery I cannot easily overlook, yet with whom it is unpleasant to be at enmity, since

[1] Frag. 6.

---

[6] *χωρίου τοῦ—κατεσχημένου* Sylburg: acc. codd.
[7] *εἰσάγει* Sylburg: *εἰσαγαγεῖν* codd.
[8] *δὲ ἀηδές* Sylburg: *δὲ ἡδέως* codd.

⟨συνθύειν καὶ⟩ [1] συνουσίας κοινὰς ποιεῖσθαι. πρὸς μὲν οὖν πολλοὺς χαλεπὸν ἀντιδικεῖν· μέγα γὰρ μέρος συμβάλλεται ⟨τὸ⟩ [2] πλῆθος αὐτοῖς πρὸς τὸ δοκεῖν ἀληθῆ λέγειν· ὅμως δὲ διὰ τὸ πιστεύειν τοῖς πράγμασι, πολλῶν μοι καὶ δυσκόλων συμπιπτόντων οὐχ ἡγούμην δεῖν κατοκνῆσαι δι' ὑμῶν πειρᾶσθαι τυγχάνειν τῶν δικαίων. δέομαι οὖν ὑμῶν συγγνώμην ἔχειν, εἰ καὶ νεώτερος ὢν λέγειν ἐπὶ δικαστηρίου τετόλμηκα· διὰ γὰρ τοὺς ἀδικοῦντας ἀναγκάζομαι παρὰ τὸν ἐμαυτοῦ τρόπον τοιοῦτόν τι ποιεῖν. πειράσομαι δ' ὑμῖν ἐξ ἀρχῆς, ὡς ἂν δύνωμαι, διὰ βραχυτάτων εἰπεῖν περὶ τοῦ πράγματος."

11 τίς ἂν οὖν οὐκ ἂν ὁμολογήσειε τὸν μὲν Λυσίου νέον καὶ ἰδιώτην καὶ ἀπράγμονα ἀρχέτυπόν τινα εἶναι τῆς ἀληθείας διαφέροντα ἐκείνης οὐδ' ὁτιοῦν, τὸν ἕτερον δὲ ἀπόγραφόν τινα καὶ οὐ λανθάνοντα ὅτι πέπλασται ῥητορικῇ τέχνῃ; καὶ γὰρ αἱ λέξεις καὶ τὰ νοήματα παρ' ἐκείνῳ μὲν τὸ αὐτοφυές, παρὰ δὲ τούτῳ τὸ κατασκευαστὸν ἀποφαίνουσιν. ὃ μέν γε ἀρχῇ κέχρηται, ὅτι νέος τε καὶ ἄπειρος εἴη πραγμάτων καὶ οὐδὲν δεόμενος εἰς δικαστήριον εἰσιέναι. καὶ ἐπιφέρει πάνυ ἠθικῶς· "ἐγὼ οὖν σε ἀξιῶ μὴ εὕρεμα ἡγεῖσθαι τὴν ἡλικίαν τὴν ἐμήν." καὶ τὸ μετὰ τοῦτο, ὡς φύσιν εἶχε γενέσθαι τε καὶ ῥηθῆναι, λέγει· ὡς ἐπὶ διαιτητὰς ἠξίου ⟨τοὺς⟩ [3] κοινοὺς ἐλθεῖν φίλους "κἂν δόξῃς ἀληθῆ λέγειν ἐκείνοις, οὐδέν σοι

[1] *συνθύειν καὶ* inseruit Sauppe.
[2] *τὸ* inseruit Sylburg.
[3] *τοὺς* inseruit Radermacher.

I am obliged to share their sacrifices and attend their common gatherings. It is difficult to reply to the charges of a large number of adversaries; for their very number adds a large measure of credibility to their statements. Nevertheless, since I have confidence in the facts, though many difficulties beset me, I have not thought it necessary to shrink from trying to obtain justice from your hands. I beg you, therefore, to excuse me, if at my early age I have ventured to address a court of law: it is those who are wronging me who force me to act in this manner, which is alien to my natural character. I shall try to tell you my story from the beginning in the fewest possible words."

Who would not recognise Lysias's client as the 11
original type of young, ordinary, retiring citizen, differing in no way from the well-known reality; whereas the other speaker is a sort of copy, a manifest fiction of the rhetorician's art. The former's words and thoughts reveal spontaneity, the latter's contrivance. The former begins by saying that he is young and inexperienced in public life and not at all anxious to become involved in litigation.[1] And he adds, very much in character, " I therefore ask you not to take advantage of my youth . . . ," and he reports what followed as it was natural for it to happen and to be described, that he proposed that they should submit the case to arbitrators chosen from among their mutual friends: ". . . and if they decide that you are telling the truth, further proceedings will not be necessary, but for you to take your

[1] These are commonplaces intended to elicit the jury's good will. Cf. Antiphon, *On the Murder of Herodes*, 1, 7; [Demosthenes], *Against Boeotus*, 1.

δεήσει πραγμάτων, ἀλλὰ λαβὼν ἄπει τὰ σαυτοῦ." καὶ τὰ λοιπὰ ἐν ἤθει χρηστῷ διεξελθὼν τελευτῶν ἐπιτίθησι· "ταῦτ' ἐμοῦ προκαλουμένου οὐδεπώποτε ἠθέλησε συνελθεῖν." ὁ δὲ Ἰσαῖος τουτὶ μὲν τὸ μέρος τὸ· "παρὰ τὴν ἑαυτοῦ [1] γνώμην ἠναγκάσθαι λέγειν ἐν δικαστηρίῳ νέον ὄντα" ἐπὶ τελευτῇ τοῦ προοιμίου τίθησιν. ἄρχεται δὲ ἀπὸ διανοίας οὐ φαύλης μὰ Δία οὐδὲ ἰδιωτικῆς, ἀνιαρότερον εἶναι λέγων πρὸς τοιούτους ἀπέχθεσθαι, μεθ' ὧν ἀνάγκην εἶναι τῶν τιμιωτάτων κοινωνεῖν. ἔπειτα ἀπολύεταί τι τῶν μελλόντων αὐτὸν λυπεῖν, τὸ δὴ πολλοὺς ὄντας τοὺς δημότας πρὸς αὐτὸν ἀντιδικεῖν.[2] συντίθησί τε τὰ ὀνόματα οὐ φαύλως μὰ Δία οὐδ' ὡς ἂν ἰδιώτης· "ἀδικοῦμαι γὰρ ὑπὸ τῶν δημοτῶν," φησίν, "οὓς περιορᾶν μὲν οὐ ῥᾴδιον ἀποστεροῦντας, ἀπέχθεσθαι δ' ἀηδές,[3] μεθ' ὧν ἀνάγκη καὶ ⟨συνθύειν καὶ⟩ συνουσίας κοινὰς ποιεῖσθαι." ἡ γὰρ ἀηδὴς ἀπέχθεια καὶ αἱ κοιναὶ συνουσίαι τεχνικώτερον σύγκεινται μᾶλλον ἢ ἀφελέστερον, καὶ ἔτι τὸ "πολλῶν μοι καὶ δυσκόλων συμπιπτόντων οὐχ ἡγούμην δεῖν κατοκνῆσαι δι' ὑμῶν πειρᾶσθαι τυγχάνειν τῶν δικαίων." ἥκιστα γὰρ ἰδιώτης ἂν οὕτως· "οὐχ ἡγούμην δεῖν κατοκνῆσαι" οὐδέ γε τὸ "δι' ὑμῶν πειρᾶσθαι τυγχάνειν τῶν δικαίων," ἀλλ' ἐκείνως πως μᾶλλον· "τοσούτων γέ μοι συμπιπτόντων δυσκόλων ἐφ' ὑμᾶς ἠνάγκασμαι καταφυγεῖν, ἵνα τῶν δικαίων τύχω δι' ὑμῶν."

1 ἑαυτοῦ Reiske: ἐμαυτοῦ codd.
2 ἀντιδικεῖν Sylburg: ἀδικεῖν codd.
3 ἀηδές Sylburg: ἂν ἡδέως codd.

dues and go." After telling the rest of the story like an honest man he finally adds: "I challenged him to do this, but he would never agree to a meeting." Isaeus, on the other hand, places his reference to his youth and to his having been forced into litigation against his will at the end of his introduction. The sentiment with which he begins is by no means ineffective or such as an ordinary man would have expressed, when he says that he finds it the more painful to be at enmity with men with whom he must share the most cherished common possessions. Then he demolishes one of the arguments that are most likely to cause him difficulty, that his opponents, who are his fellow-demesmen, are numerous. The way in which he puts his words together is certainly not ineffective or like that which an ordinary speaker would have used: "I am being wronged by my fellow-demesmen, he says, whose robbery I cannot easily overlook, yet with whom it is unpleasant to be at enmity, since I am obliged to share their sacrifices and attend their common gatherings." The expressions "unpleasant enmity" and "common gatherings" are artificially contrived rather than simple, as also is the sentence ". . . though many difficulties beset me, I have not thought it necessary to shrink from trying to obtain justice from your hands." An ordinary speaker would be most unlikely to have said "I have not thought it necessary to shrink," or indeed ". . . from trying to obtain justice from your hands," but would rather have expressed himself in the following way: "Since so many difficulties are besetting me, I have been forced to seek your help in order to secure justice through you."

12 οἶμαι μὲν οὖν καὶ ἐκ τούτων οὐκ ἄδηλον εἶναι τὴν τῶν ἀνδρῶν διαφοράν. οὐ μὴν ἀλλὰ καὶ ἐκ τῶν μελλόντων λέγεσθαι μᾶλλον ἔσται καταφανὴς καὶ μάλιστα ἐκ τῶν ἀποδεικτικῶν καὶ παθητικῶν λόγων, ἐν οἷς ὁ μὲν Λυσίας ἁπλούστερός τίς ἐστι καὶ κατὰ τὴν σύνθεσιν τῶν ὀνομάτων καὶ κατὰ τὴν κοινότητα τῶν σχημάτων, οὑτοσὶ δὲ ποικιλώτερος. πολλὰ γὰρ ἄν τις ἰδὼν εὕροι παρ' αὐτῷ ὡς ἐν τούτῳ· "πόθεν χρὴ πιστεύεσθαι τὰ εἰρημένα πρὸς θεῶν; οὐκ ἐκ τῶν μαρτύρων; οἴομαί γε. πόθεν δὲ τοὺς μάρτυρας; οὐκ ἐκ τῶν βασάνων; εἰκός γε. πόθεν δέ γε ἀπιστεῖσθαι τοὺς λόγους τοὺς τούτων; οὐκ ἐκ τοῦ φεύγειν τοὺς ἐλέγχους; ἀνάγκη μεγάλη. φαίνομαι τοίνυν ἐγὼ μὲν διώκων ταῦτα καὶ τὰ πράγματα εἰς βασάνους ἄγων, οὗτος δὲ ἐπὶ διαβολὰς καὶ λόγους καθιστάς, ὅπερ ἄν τις πλεονεκτεῖν βουλόμενος ποιήσειεν.[1] ἐχρῆν δὲ αὐτόν, εἴπερ τι δίκαιον ἐφρόνει[2] καὶ μὴ παρακρούσασθαι[3] τὰς ὑμετέρας γνώμας ἐζήτει,[4] μὴ μὰ Δία ταῦτα ποιεῖν, ἀλλ' ἐπὶ τὸν λογισμὸν μετὰ μαρτύρων ἐλθεῖν καὶ ἐξετάζειν ἕκαστα τῶν ἐν τῷ λόγῳ τοῦτον τὸν τρόπον παρ' ἐμοῦ πυνθανόμενον· εἰσφορὰς λογίζῃ πόσας;[5] τόσας· κατὰ πόσον[6] ἀργύριον εἰσενηνεγμένας;[7] κατὰ τόσον καὶ τόσον· κατὰ ποῖα[8] ψηφίσματα; ταυτί· ταύτας

[1] ποιήσειεν Schoemann: ἐποίησεν codd.
[2] ἐφρόνει Reiske: φρόνει codd.
[3] παρακρούσασθαι Sylburg: παρακρούσεσθαι codd.
[4] ἐζήτει Reiske: ζήτει codd.
[5] πόσας; Reiske: πρὸς codd.
[6] κατὰ πόσον Reiske: καὶ πόσον codd.
[7] εἰσενηνεγμένας Sylburg: εἰσενηνεγμένης codd.
[8] ποῖα Reiske: πόσα codd.

Well, I think that the difference between the two 12
orators is plain even from these examples. But it will be made more obvious still by the following passages, especially those containing argument and emotional appeal.[1] In these Lysias is the simpler in his composition, and he uses the commoner figures of speech, while Isaeus is the more varied. Many figures are to be found in Isaeus like the following:

"Tell me, why should we believe these statements? Isn't it on the evidence of witnesses? I certainly think so. But why should you believe the witnesses? Surely because they were examined under torture? It is only reasonable. And why should you disbelieve the story of my opponents? Surely because they refuse to be examined? This is an inevitable conclusion. It is quite obvious, then, that I am adopting this line of prosecution and bringing the case to the test of examination under torture, while my opponent makes it an occasion for slander and argument, as a man would do when he was trying to gain an advantage. If he had any thought for justice and were not seeking to mislead your judgment, he ought not, by Heaven, to be acting in this way but should proceed to an exact reckoning supported by witnesses and examine every item in the accounts, interrogating me in the following manner: 'How much do you reckon for contributions?' 'So much.' 'On what basis were you paid?' 'On such and such a basis.' 'In accordance with what decrees?' 'These.' 'Who have received the contributions?' 'These men.' And he ought to

[1] Argument and emotional appeal are two of the three forms of proof, according to Aristotle; the other being character (ἦθος) (*Rhetoric* i. 2. 3).

εἰλήφασι τίνες;[1] οἶδε· καὶ ταῦτα μαρτυρόμενον σκέψασθαι τὰ ψηφίσματα, τὸ πλῆθος τῶν εἰσφορῶν, τὰ εἰσενηνεγμένα, τοὺς λαβόντας, καὶ εἰ μὲν εὖτε . . ., τῷ λόγῳ πιστεύειν, εἰ δὲ μή, νῦν παρασχέσθαι μάρτυρας, εἴ τι ψεῦδος ἦν ὧν ἐλογισάμην αὐτοῖς."[2]

13 ταυτὶ μὲν διαλελυμένα καὶ ἐξ ἐπερωτήσεως. οἷς ὁ Λυσίας μὲν ἥκιστα κέχρηται, Δημοσθένης δὲ ὁ παρὰ τουτουὶ τὰς ἀφορμὰς λαβὼν ἀφειδέστερον, οἷον· " οὐκ οὖν σὺ μισθοφορὰν λέγεις; φήσει τις.[3] καὶ παραχρῆμά γε τὴν αὐτὴν σύνταξιν ἁπάντων, ὦ ἄνδρες Ἀθηναῖοι, ἵνα τῶν κοινῶν τὸ μέρος λαμβάνων ἕκαστος, ὅτου δέοιτο ἡ πόλις, τοῦτο παρέχοι. ἔξεστιν ἄγειν ἡσυχίαν; οἴκοι μένων βελτίων εἶ, τοῦ δι' ἔνδειαν ἀνάγκῃ τι ποιεῖν αἰσχρὸν ἀπηλλαγμένος. συμβαίνει τι τοιοῦτον, οἷα καὶ τὰ νῦν; στρατιώτης αὐτὸς ὑπάρχων ἀπὸ τῶν αὐτῶν τούτων λημμάτων, ὥσπερ ἐστὶ δίκαιον ὑπὲρ τῆς πατρίδος. ἔστι τις ἔξω τῆς ἡλικίας ἡμῶν; ὅσα οὗτος ἀτάκτως νῦν λαμβάνων οὐκ ὠφελεῖ, ταῦτα ἐν ἴσῃ τάξει παραλαμβάνων πάντ' ἐφορῶν καὶ διοικῶν, ἃ χρὴ πράττεσθαι. ὅλως δὲ οὔτε ἀφελὼν οὔτε προσθεὶς πλήν τι μικρῷ τὴν ἀταξίαν ἀνελών, εἰς τάξιν ἤγαγον τὴν πόλιν, τὴν αὐτὴν τοῦ λαβεῖν, τοῦ στρατεύεσθαι, τοῦ δικάζειν, τοῦ ποιεῖν τοῦθ', ὅ τι καθ' ἡλικίαν ἕκαστος ἔχοι καὶ ὅτου καιρὸς εἴη, τάξιν ποιήσας." ἐκεῖνα[4] δὲ κατὰ συστροφὴν καὶ παρακεκινδυνευ-

[1] τίνες Reiske: τινες codd.
[2] αὐτοῖς Sylburg: αὐτῆς codd.
[3] φήσει τις ex Dem.: φήσεις codd.

scrutinize my evidence on these points—the decrees, the number of contributions, the sums paid, and the receivers of them—and if everything were exact and in order, he ought to trust my reckoning; and if not, he ought now to produce witnesses regarding any false entries in the accounts which I submitted to them."

Here the construction is disjunctive and interroga- 13
tive in form. This style is used very little by Lysias; but Demosthenes, who drew his inspiration from Isaeus, uses it more freely:[1]

"What? someone will ask: do you mean mercenary service? Yes, and forthwith the same arrangement for all, Athenians, so that each man, drawing his share of pay from common funds, may provide what service the state requires of him. Is peace to be had? You are better off at home, under no compulsion to do anything dishonourable through poverty. Is there such an emergency as the present? Better to be a soldier, as you ought, in your country's cause, maintained by that very pay. Is any one of you too old for service? What he now irregularly takes without doing service, let him take by just regulation, superintending and transacting all necessary business. Thus, without detracting from or adding to our political system, only reducing its irregularity to some small degree, I have brought it into order, establishing a uniform rule for receiving money, for serving in the army, for sitting on juries, for doing what each according to his age can do and what the occasion requires."

Then there is a style which is condensed and bold in

[1] *Olynth.* iii. 34–35.

[4] ἐκεῖνα Victorius: ἐκείνῳ codd.

μένα τῷ τε βραχέως καὶ ἀγκύλως καὶ ἐκ παραδόξου συντίθεσθαι, καὶ οὐχ ἅπασιν οὐδὲ ἐκ προχείρου γνωριζόμενα· "καὶ οὗτος ὁ πάντων ἀνθρώπων σχετλιώτατος, οὐ παρεχομένων αὐτῶν μάρτυρας, ὧν ἐναντίον ἡμῖν ἀποδοῦναι φασίν, ἐκείνοις πιστεύειν προσποιεῖται μᾶλλον, ὡς ἀποδεδώκασιν ἡμῖν, ἢ ⟨ἡμῖν⟩,[1] ὡς οὐκ ἀπειλήφαμεν. καίτοι πᾶσι φανερόν, ὡς ἔοικεν, ⟨οἳ καὶ⟩ [2] τὸν τούτου πατέρα ἀπεστέρουν [3] ὄντα ἐπίτιμον, ὅτι ἡμῖν ἑκόντες οὐκ ἂν ἀπέδοσαν, εἰσπράξασθαι ⟨δὲ⟩ οὕτως ἔχοντες οὐκ ἂν ἐδυνήθημεν." καὶ γὰρ τοῦτό ἐστι τὸ σχῆμα, ᾧ πολλάκις Δημοσθένης κέχρηται· "εἶτ' οἴεσθε, οἳ μὲν αὐτὸν οὐδὲν ⟨ἂν⟩ [4] ἠδυνήθησαν ποιῆσαι κακόν, αὐτοὶ δὲ μὴ παθεῖν ἐφυλάξαντ' ἂν ἴσως, τούτους μὲν [5] ἐξαπατᾶν αἱρεῖσθαι μᾶλλον ἢ προλέγοντα βιάζεσθαι, ὑμῖν δὲ ἐκ προρρήσεως πολεμῆσαι;" καὶ ἔτι γε τὰ τοιαῦτα· "ᾧ γάρ, ἃ μὲν ὑπῆρχεν ἔξω τῶν ἀποτιμηθέντων, κατελελειτούργητο,[6] δανειζομένῳ δ' οὐδεὶς ἂν ἔδωκεν ἐπ' αὐτοῖς ἔτι πλέον οὐδέν, ἀποδεδωκότι τὰς μισθώσεις ἔχειν ἐμοὶ προσῆκον ἀναμφισβητήτως ⟨ἐκεῖνα⟩,[7] οὗτοι τηλικαύτην δίκην λαχόντες καὶ σφέτερα αὐτῶν εἶναι φάσκοντες ἐκώλυσάν μ' [8] ἐξ αὐτῶν ποιήσασθαι τὴν ἐπισκευήν." καὶ τί δεῖ τὰ πλείω παρατιθέντα μηκύνειν; πολλὰ

[1] ἡμῖν inseruit Reiske.
[2] οἳ καὶ addidit Radermacher.
[3] ἀπεστέρουν Bekker: ἀποστέρουν codd.
[4] ἂν inseruit Radermacher.
[5] τούτους μὲν Reiske: τοὺς μὲν codd.
[6] κατελελειτούργητο Buermann: καταλελειτουργηκότα codd.
[7] ἐκεῖνα inseruit Buermann.

the brevity, succinctness and unorthodoxy of its composition and which is not universally or readily understood:[1]

"And this most wicked of all men, though they do not produce any witnesses in whose presence they allege they paid us, expects you to believe their statement that they paid us, and not ours that we have received no payment. Yet it seems obvious to all that men who defrauded my client's father when he was in full possession of civic rights, would not have paid us voluntarily, and that our situation would not have allowed us to recover it."

This is the figure often used by Demosthenes:[2]

"Then do you think that, whereas he chose to deceive rather than give prior warning of his attack to men who could not have done him any active harm, but might have adopted measures of defence, in your case he would declare war before opening hostilities?"

Again, Isaeus writes passages like this:[3]

"For whereas all I possessed, except property which had been mortgaged, had been spent on state services, and if I had tried to borrow on it, no one would have lent me any more, as I had alienated the revenue from it, though I have an undoubted right to have it my opponents, by bringing so serious a suit against me and alleging that the property is theirs, prevented me from using the money to carry out repairs."

Why prolong the discussion by multiplying examples? Many passages can be found in Isaeus

[1] *Frag.* 45.1. [2] *Phil.* iii. 13. [3] *Frag.* 45.2.

[8] ἐκώλυσάν με Reiske: ἐκώλυσαν μὲν codd.

γὰρ ἄν τις εὕροι τῶν Ἰσαίου ⟨καὶ⟩ κατὰ[1] τὴν σύνθεσιν καὶ κατὰ τοὺς σχηματισμοὺς ἐξηλλαγμένα μὲν τῆς Λυσίου λέξεως, ἐοικότα δὲ τῇ Δημοσθένους δεινότητι.

14 εἰρηκὼς δὲ καὶ περὶ τῶν πραγμάτων ὅτι δεινότερός ἐστιν οἰκονομῆσαι Λυσίου καὶ ὅλους τοὺς λόγους καὶ τὰ μέρη αὐτῶν καὶ οὐδὲν ἔξω ποιῶν τῆς τέχνης, ᾗ μετὰ ταῦτα πολλῇ ὁ Δημοσθένης ἐχρήσατο, βούλομαι καὶ τὰς ὑπὲρ τούτων παρασχέσθαι πίστεις. ἔσται δὲ κεφαλαιώδης τε καὶ ὡς πρὸς ἀνεγνωκότας τὸν ἄνδρα ὁ λόγος· οὐ γὰρ ἐγχωρεῖ[2] παραδείγματα πάντων τιθέναι. αὐτίκα τὰς διηγήσεις τότε μὲν ἀπροκατασκευάστους καὶ συντόμους καὶ οὐδὲν προκαταλαμβανούσας τῶν ἀποδεικτικῶν ἐν τῇ προσηκούσῃ τίθησι χώρᾳ, καθάπερ ἐν τῷ[3] πρὸς Μέδοντα ποιεῖ λόγῳ καὶ ἐν τῷ πρὸς Ἁγνόθεον καὶ ἐν τῇ πρὸς τοὺς δημότας ἀμφισβητήσει περὶ τοῦ χωρίου καὶ ἐν ἄλλοις συχνοῖς. τότε δὲ μερίσας αὐτὰς κατὰ κεφάλαια καὶ παρ᾽ ἕκαστον αὐτῶν τὰς πίστεις παρατιθεὶς ἐκμηκύνει τε μᾶλλον καὶ ἐκβαίνει τὸ τῆς διηγήσεως σχῆμα, τῷ συμφέροντι χρώμενος. ταύτης ἐστὶ τῆς ἰδέας ἥ τε πρὸς Ἕρμωνα ὑπὲρ τῆς ἐγγύης ἀπολογία καὶ ἡ πρὸς Εὐκλείδην ἀμφισβήτησις ὑπὲρ τῆς τοῦ χωρίου λύσεως καὶ ἡ ὑπὲρ Εὐφιλήτου πρὸς τὸν Ἐρχιέων δῆμον ἔφεσις. ἐν γὰρ δὴ τοῖς λόγοις τούτοις μακροτέρας τὰς διηγήσεις οὔσας οὐχ ἅμα τίθησιν

[1] καὶ inseruit Radermacher.
[2] ἐγχωρεῖ Sadée: ἐνεχώρει codd.
[3] ἐν τῷ Sauppe: ἐφ᾽ ᾧ codd.

which, both in composition and in the use of figures, are quite different from the language of Lysias and resemble the brilliance of Demosthenes.

As I have also said that Isaeus is cleverer in his arrangement of subject-matter than Lysias, with regard both to the speech as a whole and its parts, and that he writes nothing without using this technique, which Demosthenes later largely adopted, I should now like to furnish proof of these statements. My observations will be of a summary nature, and I shall assume that the student has read the speeches of Isaeus, for there is not space to quote examples of everything. To begin with, we may say that some of his narratives have no preparatory section, are concise, occupy their correct position in the speech and contain nothing that anticipates the material of the proof section. These qualities are found in his speeches against Medon and Hagnotheus and the speech in which his client is prosecuting his fellow-demesman over a piece of land,[1] and in many others. In certain other speeches, he divides his narratives into sections and subjoins a proof to each section, thus prolonging them and departing from the conventional form of the narrative to suit his purpose. This is the form adopted in the defence against Hermon concerning a surety, the dispute with Euclides regarding the redemption of a plot of land[2] and the appeal on behalf of Euphiletus against the deme of Ercheia.[3] In these speeches the narrative material is longer, and he does not present it in a continuous passage, but 14

[1] None of these is extant.
[2] Neither of these is extant.
[3] Part of the proof-section of this speech is given in ch. 17.

ὅλας, ἀλλὰ κατὰ μέρη διαλαμβάνων ἐφ᾽ ἑκάστῳ κεφαλαίῳ τούς τε μάρτυρας ἐπάγεται καὶ τὰς ἄλλας παρέχεται πίστεις, δεδοικώς, παρ᾽ ὅσα [1] γοῦν ἐμοὶ δοκεῖ, μὴ δυσπαρακολούθητος γένηται διὰ τὸ πλῆθος τῶν κεφαλαίων ὁ λόγος καὶ πελαγίσῃ,[2] αἵ τε πίστεις εἰς ἓν χωρίον ἅπασαι συναχθεῖσαι, πολλαὶ καὶ περὶ πολλῶν οὖσαι πραγμάτων, μὴ συνταράξωσι τὴν σαφήνειαν. τοιγάρτοι μετὰ τὰς διηγήσεις τὰς οὕτως ᾠκονομημένας οὐκ ἔτι τὰς προηγουμένας ἀποδείξεις πολλοῖς βεβαιοῦται λόγοις οὐδ᾽ ἔστιν ὅμοιος τοῖς νέοις τεχνογράφοις, ἀλλὰ τὰς τῶν ἀντιδίκων πίστεις ἀναιρεῖν οἴεται δεῖν.

τότε δὲ προκατασκευάζεταί τινα πρὸ τῶν διηγήσεων πράγματα καὶ προλαμβάνει τὰ μέλλοντα πιστοτέρας αὐτὰς ἢ κατ᾽ ἄλλο τι χρησιμωτέρας ποιήσειν οἰόμενος,[3] ὡς ἐν τῇ λήξει [4] τῇ πρὸς Ἀριστογείτονα καὶ Ἄρχιππον εὑρίσκεται πεποιηκώς, ἐν ᾗ κλήρου τις ἀμφισβητῶν, ἀδελφὸς ὢν τοῦ τελευτήσαντος, προκαλεῖται [5] τὸν ἔχοντα τἀφανῆ χρήματα εἰς ἐμφανῶν [6] κατάστασιν, ὁ δὲ τοῦ κλήρου κρατῶν παραγράφεται τὴν κλῆσιν, δεδόσθαι λέγων ἑαυτῷ τὰ χρήματα κατὰ διαθήκας. διττῆς δὲ τῆς ἀμφισβητήσεως ὑπαρχούσης, τῆς μὲν περὶ τοῦ γεγονέναι τὰς διαθήκας ἢ μή, τῆς δέ, τῶν διαθηκῶν ἀμφισβητουμένων ἤδη, τίνα δεῖ τοῦ κλήρου κρατεῖν, πρῶτον ἀποδοὺς τὸν ὑπὲρ τῶν νόμων λόγον καὶ ⟨κατὰ⟩ τοῦτο [7] ἀποδείξας τὸ

[1] παρ᾽ ὅσα γ᾽ Reiske: γὰρ ὅσα γ᾽ FM.
[2] πελαγίσῃ Usener: πολλάκις codd.
[3] οἰόμενος seclusit Krüger.

divides it into sections, introducing the witnesses and other evidence for each topic as it is stated. He does this, so far as I can judge, because he is afraid that the speech may become difficult to follow and the jury be inundated with a sea of topics; while if the proofs are all assembled in one place, their number and the diversity of the topics they deal with may impair the clarity of the whole. The result of this arrangement of his narratives is that the main points of the preceding proof no longer need to be confirmed at length. He also differs from modern theorists in insisting on the refutation of the opponent's arguments.

On occasion he presents some of his material before 15
the narrative and anticipates events, hoping by doing so to render the narrative more credible and more effective for some other purpose. This is what he is found to have done in the action against Aristogeiton and Archippus,[1] in which the claimant to the estate, being the brother of the deceased, summons the holder of the undisclosed part of the estate to disclose it, while the possessor of the estate files a demurrer, alleging that the property has been left to him in the will. Two points are in dispute: first, whether a will was made or not, and secondly, if the will itself is challenged, which party ought to possess the estate. The speaker, having first dealt with the issue at law, and having shown that from this point of view an estate

[1] Only the following argument is preserved.

---

[4] *λήξει* Valesius: *λύσει* codd.
[5] *προκαλεῖται* Sylburg: *προσκαλεῖται* codd.
[6] *ἐμφανῶν* Reiske: *ἐμφανῆ*.
[7] *καὶ κατὰ τοῦτο* Sadée post Sauppe: *καὶ ταῦτα* codd.

μέρος, ὡς οὐ δεῖ τὸν ἐπίδικον κρατεῖσθαι κλῆρον πρὸ δίκης, οὕτως ἐπὶ τὴν διήγησιν ἔρχεται, δι' ἧς ἀποδείκνυσιν οὐδὲ[1] γεγενημένας ὑπὸ τοῦ τετελευτηκότος τὰς διαθήκας. καὶ οὐδὲ ταύτην τὴν διήγησιν ἁπλῶς πως συστρέψας καὶ ἀκατασκευάστως τίθησιν, ἀλλὰ καὶ ταύτην μακροτέραν οὖσαν ἀποτομαῖς τισι διαλαμβάνει καὶ καθ' ἕκαστον εἶδος μάρτυρας ἀναβιβάζεται καὶ προκλήσεις ἀναγινώσκει καὶ συνθήκας παρέχεται τεκμηρίοις τε καὶ σημείοις καὶ τοῖς ἐκ τῶν εἰκότων ἐλέγχοις ἅπασι χρῆται. πολλὰς δ' ἂν ἔχοιμι καὶ ἄλλας παρασχέσθαι διηγήσεις, πρὸς τὸ συμφέρον ᾠκονομημένας ὑπὸ τοῦ ῥήτορος προκατασκευαῖς, παρασκευαῖς, μερισμοῖς, χωρίων ἀλλαγαῖς, πραγμάτων μεταγωγαῖς, τῷ τὰ κεφάλαια ἀνεστράφθαι, τῷ μὴ κατὰ τοὺς χρόνους τὰ πραχθέντα εἰρῆσθαι, τῷ [ὡς][2] μὴ πάντα μηδ' ἅμ' ὡς φύσιν εἶχε πραχθῆναι μηδ' ὡς ἂν ἰδιώτης τις εἴποι λέγεσθαι, μυρίοις ἄλλοις τοιούτοις τρόποις. ἀλλ' οὔτε χρόνον ἱκανὸν ἔχω περὶ πασῶν λέγειν, ἐκδιηγούμενος εὐθὺς ἐφ' ἑκάστης τὴν τέχνην, ὡς ἐβουλόμην ἄν, οὔθ' ὁ πρὸς τοὺς ἐπισταμένους τὰ πράγματα λόγος ἐν τῷ πλήθει τῶν παραδειγμάτων τὸ πιστὸν ἔχει ἀλλ' ἀρκεῖ τοῖς τοιούτοις καὶ ἡ βραχεῖα δήλωσις.

16 ἐρῶ δὲ καὶ κεφαλαιωδῶς περὶ ταύτης τῆς ἰδέας ἣν ἐγὼ δόξαν ἔχω καὶ τίνι διαφέρειν οἴομαι τὸν Ἰσαῖον τοῦ Λυσίου. τοῦ Λυσίου μὲν δή[3] τις ἀναγινώσκων τὰς διηγήσεις οὐδὲν ἂν ὑπολάβοι[4] λέγεσθαι κατὰ τέχνην ἢ πονηρίαν, ἀλλ' ὡς ἡ

[1] οὐδὲ Sylburg: οὔτε codd.

which is the subject of litigation should not be in the possession of one of the parties before a legal decision has been made, then proceeds to his narrative, in the course of which he demonstrates that the will was not even made by the deceased. Even this narrative is not set out in a simple, concise and straightforward manner, but because of its length he divides it into sections and for each point produces witnesses, reads out challenges, furnishes contracts, uses evidence and indications and all forms of argument from probability. I could show you many other narratives which the orator has furnished with prefaces for effect, others with anticipations, set pieces, divisions, and the rearrangement of the parts, with transposition of subject-matter, change in the order of topics, with the description of events piecemeal and at different times, and without regard to their natural sequence or to the layman's way of recounting them. But I have not the time to discuss all these variations and to give a detailed appraisal of the skill he deploys in each case, as I should like to do. Anyone who understands the subject does not need a host of examples to convince him: even a brief demonstration is enough for such a person.

I shall now briefly summarise my views on this 16
aspect of Isaeus's oratory and indicate in what respects I think he differs from Lysias. Any reader of Lysias's narratives would suppose that no art or dishonesty had gone into their composition, but that they are written in accordance with nature and

---

[2] ὡς seclusit Sylburg.
[3] δή Sadée: ἄν codd.
[4] ὑπολάβοι Krüger: ὑπολάβῃ codd.

φύσις καὶ ἡ ἀλήθεια φέρει, αὐτὸ τοῦτο ἀγνοῶν τῆς τέχνης, ὅτι τὸ μιμήσασθαι τὴν φύσιν αὐτῆς μέγιστον ἔργον ἦν. ἐπὶ δὲ τῶν Ἰσαίου διηγημάτων τοὐναντίον ἂν πάθοι,[1] μηδὲν ὑπολαβεῖν αὐτοφυῶς καὶ ἀπραγματεύτως [2] λέγεσθαι μηδ' εἴ τινα ὡς ἔτυχε γενόμενα εἴρηται, ἐκ κατασκευῆς δὲ πάντα καὶ μεμηχανημένα [3] πρὸς ἀπάτην ἢ ἄλλην τινὰ κακουργίαν. καὶ τῷ μὲν ἂν καὶ τὰ ψευδῆ λέγοντι πιστεύσειεν ἄν, τῷ δὲ μηδ' ἂν ἀληθεύῃ, χωρὶς ὑποψίας προσέξει.[4]

ἐν δὲ τοῖς ἀποδεικτικοῖς [5] διαλλάττειν ἂν δόξειεν Ἰσαῖος Λυσίου τῷ τε μὴ κατ' ἐνθύμημά τι [6] λέγειν ἀλλὰ κατ' ἐπιχείρημα καὶ τῷ μὴ βραχέως ἀλλὰ διεξοδικῶς μηδὲ ἁπλῶς ἀλλ' ἀκριβῶς αὔξειν τε μᾶλλον καὶ δεινότερα ποιεῖν τὰ πράγματα καὶ τὰ πάθη ποιεῖν γεννικώτερα.[7] ἐν γὰρ δὴ τούτοις οὐχ ἧττόν ἐστι φανερὸς τῇ Δημοσθένους τέχνῃ

[1] πάθοι Sadée: παθεῖν codd.
[2] ἀπραγματεύτως Reiske: αὐτοπραγματεύτως codd.
[3] μεμηχανημένα Usener: μεμηχανευμένα codd.
[4] προσέξει Sadée: προσέξειν codd.
[5] ἀποδεικτικοῖς Sylburg: ἐπιδεικτικοῖς codd.
[6] ἐνθύμημά τι Victorius: ἐνθυμήματι F^1 ἐνθύμημα F^2MBP.
[7] γεννικώτερα Usener: γενικώτερον codd.

---

[1] Cf. *Lysias*, 18.

[2] Aristotle defines the enthymeme as a "rhetorical demonstration" (ῥητορικὴ ἀπόδειξις) (*Rhetoric* i. 1. 11), the counterpart in rhetoric of the syllogism in logic; but he uses the term *epicheireme* in an entirely different sense (*Topics*. viii. 11. 12). The present passage is the first extant one in which the distinction is drawn, but Theophrastus is known to have used the term *epicheireme*, and Diogenes Laertius (5. 45) attributes two books to him on the subject. That rhetoricians after Aristotle

truth. He would not know that this illusion is itself the product of an art whose greatest achievement was to imitate nature.[1] In the case of Isaeus's narratives he would receive the opposite impression, that not a single statement was spontaneous or unconsidered, not even when it described something as it actually happened, but that everything was artfully designed and contrived to mislead, or for some other sinister purpose. Thus a mendacious client of Lysias might be believed, whereas a client of Isaeus, even if he speaks the truth, will not be heard without suspicion.

In his proofs Isaeus would appear to differ from Lysias in his use of the epichireme and the enthymeme,[2] of thorough exposition instead of brevity, of detail rather than outline, of greater amplification and exaggeration of the facts; and in making the emotions seem more noble. It is through these qualities as much as through any others that he clearly emerges as the source of Demosthenes's technique,

felt the need for a more thorough and rigorous form of argument than the Aristotelian enthymeme, in which premisses were often taken for granted or assimilated into a single statement, is clear from the discussions in the early Latin treatises on rhetoric, the *Ad Herennium* (2. 28) and Cicero *De Inventione*, i. 35. 61 and i. 37. 67. But neither of these uses the term *epicheireme*, which appears in Latin for the first time in Quintilian, v. 10. 1, and he may well have taken it from Dionysius. His discussion of it in v. 14. 6, however, seems to owe more to Aristotle than to Dionysius, which makes the present passage of particular importance. The underlying principle of complexity, elaboration and precision rather than brevity and simplicity is probably to be traced to Isocrates, but his main concern was with epideictic oratory. For the idea that the use of the epicheireme rather than the enthymeme involved *expatiation*, see Dionysius, *Dinarchus*, 6, where Hyperides is the subject. See also *Isocrates* 4.

τὰς ἀφορμὰς δεδωκώς, ἀλλ' οὐ τὴν Λυσίου διώκων ἀφέλειαν,[1] ὡς ἐκ πολλῶν [2] ἔστι λόγων, μᾶλλον δὲ ἐκ πάντων τῶν γραφέντων ὑπ' αὐτοῦ τεκμήρασθαι. εἰ δέ τι δεῖ καὶ παραδείγμασι χρῆσθαι, μή τις ἀναπόδεικτα δόξῃ λέγειν ἡμᾶς, ποιήσω καὶ τοῦτο, προχειρισάμενος τὸν ὑπὲρ Εὐφιλήτου λόγον, ἐν ᾧ τὸν Ἐρχιέων δῆμον εἰς τὸ δικαστήριον προσκαλεῖταί τις τῶν ἀποψηφισθέντων ὡς ἀδίκως τῆς πολιτείας ἀπελαυνόμενος. ἐγράφη γὰρ δή τις ὑπὸ τῶν Ἀθηναίων νόμος ἐξέτασιν γενέσθαι τῶν πολιτῶν κατὰ δήμους, τὸν δὲ ἀποψηφισθέντα ὑπὸ τῶν δημοτῶν τῆς πολιτείας μὴ μετέχειν, τοῖς δὲ ἀδίκως ἀποψηφισθεῖσιν ἔφεσιν εἰς τὸ δικαστήριον εἶναι, προσκαλεσαμένοις [3] τοὺς δημότας, καὶ ἐὰν τὸ δεύτερον ἐξελεγχθῶσι, πεπρᾶσθαι αὐτοὺς καὶ τὰ χρήματα εἶναι δημόσια. κατὰ τοῦτον τὸν νόμον ὁ Εὐφίλητος προσκαλεσάμενος τοὺς Ἐρχιέας ὡς ἀδίκως καταψηφισαμένους αὐτοῦ τὸν ἀγῶνα τόνδε διατίθεται. προείρηται μὲν δὴ τὰ πράγματα ταῦτ' ἀκριβῶς καὶ πεπίστωται διὰ τῶν μαρτύρων, οἷς δὲ βεβαίας βούλεται ποιῆσαι τὰς μαρτυρίας, τάδε ἐστίν, ὡς μὲν ἐγὼ δόξης ἔχω, πάντ' ἀκριβῶς ἐξειργασμένα. κρινέτω δὲ ὁ βουλόμενος, εἰ τὰ προσήκοντα ἔγνωκα περὶ αὐτῶν·

17 "ὅτι μὲν τοίνυν, ὦ ἄνδρες δικασταί, ἀδελφὸς ἡμῖν ἐστιν οὑτοσὶ Εὐφίλητος, οὐ μόνον ἡμῶν ἀλλὰ καὶ τῶν συγγενῶν ἁπάντων ἀκηκόατε μαρτυρούντων. σκέψασθε δὲ πρῶτον τὸν πατέρα ἡμῶν,

[1] ἀφέλειαν Sylburg: ἀσφάλειαν codd.
[2] πολλῶν Krüger: τε ἄλλων codd.

and not an imitator of the simple style of Lysias; and many, or rather all of the speeches that he wrote confirm this impression. If it is necessary to supply examples to satisfy anyone who thinks that I cannot prove my assertion, I have one to hand and will give it forthwith. It is the speech for Euphiletus, in which the litigant, a disenfranchised man, summons the demesmen of Ercheia to court, claiming that they have unjustly deprived him of his political rights. A law had been passed by the Athenians ordering that a review be made of the citizens listed according to demes, and that anyone who was rejected by the votes of his fellow-demesmen should no longer enjoy the rights of citizenship; but that those who were unjustly rejected had the right to appeal to a court by summoning the members of the deme, and, if they were again excluded, they were to be sold as slaves and their property confiscated. It was under this law that Euphiletus, having summoned the demesmen of Ercheia on the ground that they had unjustly expelled him, instituted this case. The facts have already been skilfully set forth and confirmed by witnesses. The whole of the following passage, in which the orator seeks to confirm the evidence, is composed, in my opinion, with thoroughness and great attention to detail; but the reader must decide for himself whether my judgment of it is correct.[1]

17 " Gentlemen of the jury, you have heard evidence not only from us but from all our kinsmen that Euphiletus here is our brother. Now consider,

[1] The fragment of the 12th speech, preserved here by Dionysius.

---

[3] προσκαλεσαμένοις Reiske: προκαλεσαμένοις codd.

τίνος ἕνεκεν ἂν ψεύδοιτο καὶ τοῦτον μὴ ὄντα αὐτοῦ υἱὸν εἰσεποιεῖτο. πάντας γὰρ εὑρήσετε τοὺς τὰ τοιαῦτα πράττοντας ἢ οὐκ ὄντων αὐτοῖς γνησίων παίδων ἢ διὰ πενίαν ἀναγκαζομένους ξένους ἀνθρώπους εἰσποιεῖσθαι, ὅπως ὠφελῶνταί τι ἀπ' αὐτῶν δι' αὐτοὺς Ἀθηναίων γεγονότων. τῷ τοίνυν πατρὶ τούτων οὐδέτερον ὑπάρχει. γνήσιοι μὲν γὰρ αὐτῷ ἡμεῖς δύο υἱεῖς ἐσμεν· ὥστε οὐκ ἄν γε δι' ἐρημίαν τοῦτον εἰσεποιεῖτο. ἀλλὰ μὴν οὐδὲ τροφῆς τε καὶ εὐπορίας τῆς παρὰ τούτου δεόμενος. ἔστι γὰρ αὐτῷ ⟨βίος⟩ [1] ἱκανὸς καὶ χωρὶς τούτου μεμαρτύρηται ὑμῖν τοῦτον ἐκ παίδων τρέφων καὶ ἀσκῶν καὶ εἰς ⟨τοὺς⟩ [2] φράτερας εἰσάγων· καὶ ταῦτα οὐ μικρὰ δαπανήματά ἐστιν. ὥστε τόν τε πατέρα ἡμῶν οὐκ εἰκός ἐστιν, ὦ ἄνδρες δικασταί, μηδὲν ὠφελούμενον οὕτως ἀδίκῳ πράγματι ἐπιχειρῆσαι. ἀλλὰ μὴν οὐδ' ἐμέ γε οὐθεὶς ἀνθρώπων οὕτως τελέως ἂν ἄφρονα ὑπολάβοι, ὥστε τούτῳ μαρτυρεῖν τὰ ψευδῆ, ὅπως τὰ πατρῷα διὰ πλειόνων διανείμωμαι. καὶ γὰρ οὐδ' ἀμφισβητῆσαί μοι ἐξουσία γένοιτ' ἂν ὕστερον, ὡς οὐκ ἔστιν ἀδελφὸς οὗτος. ἐμοῦ γὰρ οὐθεὶς ἂν ὑμῶν τὴν φωνὴν ἀνάσχοιτ' ἂν ἀκούων, ⟨εἰ⟩ [3] νῦν μὲν ὑπόδικον ἐμαυτὸν καθιστὰς μαρτυρῶ, ὡς ἔστιν ἀδελφὸς ἡμέτερος, ὕστερον δὲ φαινοίμην τούτοις ἀντιλέγων. οὐ μόνον τοίνυν ἡμᾶς, ὦ ἄνδρες δικασταί, εἰκός ἐστι τἀληθῆ μεμαρτυρηκέναι ἀλλὰ καὶ τοὺς ἄλλους συγγενεῖς. ἐνθυμήθητε γὰρ πρῶτον μέν, ὅτι τὰς ἀδελφὰς

[1] βίος inseruit Reiske.
[2] τοὺς inseruit Schoemann.

firstly what motive our father could have for lying and having adopted Euphiletus as his son, if he was not so. You will find that all those who do such things either have no legitimate children of their own or else are forced by poverty to adopt aliens in order that they may receive some assistance from them, because they are indebted to them for their Athenian citizenship. Our father had neither of these motives, for in us he has two legitimate sons, so that he would never have adopted Euphiletus because he lacked an heir. Nor again is he in need of any material support or comfort which Euphiletus could give him; for he has sufficient resources, and further evidence has been given to you that he brought up Euphiletus and educated him from childhood and introduced him to members of his ward—all of which represents a considerable outlay. It is therefore unlikely, gentlemen of the jury, that my father committed so wicked a crime for no advantage. Again, as for myself, no one could imagine me to be so completely insane as to bear false witness in favour of Euphiletus with the result that I should have to share my patrimony with a larger number of heirs: for after this I should never be at liberty to plead that Euphiletus is not my brother, since none of you would listen to me for a moment if, after now bearing witness that he is my brother and making myself liable to the penalties of the law, I should later openly contradict this assertion. Thus, gentlemen of the jury, the probabilities are in favour of my having given true evidence, and the same applies to the other relatives. For consider firstly, that the husbands of our sisters would never

[3] εἰ supplevit Sylburg.

ἡμῶν ἔχοντες οὐκ ἄν ποτε ἐμαρτύρουν περὶ τούτου τὰ ψευδῆ. μητρυιὰ γὰρ ἡ τούτου μήτηρ ἐγεγένητο ταῖς ἡμετέραις ἀδελφαῖς. εἰώθασι δέ πως ὡς ἐπὶ τὸ πολὺ διαφέρεσθαι ἀλλήλαις αἵ τε μητρυιαὶ καὶ αἱ πρόγονοι. ὥστε εἰ οὗτος ἐξ ἄλλου τινὸς ἀνδρὸς ἦν τῇ μητρυιᾷ καὶ οὐκ ἐκ τοῦ ἡμετέρου πατρός, οὐκ ἄν ποτε, ὦ ἄνδρες δικασταί, τοὺς ἑαυτῶν ἄνδρας αἱ ἀδελφαὶ μαρτυρεῖν ἐπέτρεψαν. καὶ μὴν οὐδ' [1] ἂν ὁ θεῖος πρὸς μητρὸς ἡμῖν ὤν, τούτῳ δὲ οὐδὲν προσήκων δήπου τῇ τούτου μητρὶ ἠθέλησεν ἄν, ὦ ἄνδρες δικασταί, μαρτυρῆσαι ψευδῆ μαρτυρίαν, δι' ἣν ἡμῖν γίνεται βλάβη περιφανής, εἴπερ ξένον ὄντα τοῦτον εἰσποιοῦμεν ἀδελφὸν ἡμῖν αὐτοῖς. ἔτι τοίνυν, ὦ ἄνδρες δικασταί, πρὸς τούτοις πῶς ἄν τις ὑμῶν [2] καταγνοίη ψευδομαρτυριῶν [3] Δημαράτου τουτουὶ καὶ Ἡγήμονος καὶ Νικοστράτου; οἳ πρῶτον μὲν οὐδὲν αἰσχρὸν οὐδέποτε φανήσονται ἐπιτηδεύσαντες, εἶτα δ' οἰκεῖοι ὄντες ἡμῖν καὶ εἰδότες ἡμᾶς ἅπαντας [4] μεμαρτυρήκασιν Εὐφιλήτῳ τούτῳ τὴν αὑτοῦ συγγένειαν ἕκαστος. ὥστε ἡδέως κἂν τῶν ἀντιδικούντων ἡμῖν τοῦ σεμνοτάτου πυθοίμην, εἰ ἄλλοθέν ποθεν ἔχοι ἂν ἐπιδεῖξαι αὑτὸν Ἀθηναῖον ἢ ἐκ τούτων, ὧν καὶ ἡμεῖς Εὐφίλητον ἐπιδείκνυμεν, ἐγὼ μὲν γὰρ οὐκ οἶμαι ἄλλο τι ἂν αὐτὸν ⟨εἰπεῖν⟩ [5] ὅτι ἡ μήτηρ ἀστή τέ ἐστι καὶ γαμετὴ καὶ ἀστὸς ὁ πατήρ· καὶ ὡς ταῦτ' ἀληθῆ λέγει, παρέχοιτ' ἂν αὐτῷ τοὺς συγγενεῖς μάρτυρας· εἶτα, ὦ ἄνδρες

[1] οὐδ' Bekker: οὐκ codd.
[2] ὑμῶν Sylburg: ἡμῶν codd.
[3] ψευδομαρτυρίων Schoemann: ψευδομαρτυρίαν codd.

have given false evidence in favour of Euphiletus: for his mother had become stepmother to our sisters, and it is normal for stepmothers and the daughters of a previous marriage to be on bad terms; so that, if their stepmother had borne Euphiletus to any man other than our father, our sisters would never have allowed their husbands to give evidence in their favour. Again, our uncle, a relative on our mother's side and not a kinsman of Euphiletus, would never have agreed, gentlemen of the jury, to give in favour of Euphiletus's mother evidence which was clearly against our interests, if Euphiletus were an alien whom we are attempting to introduce into the family as our own brother. Furthermore, gentlemen of the jury, how could any of you convict of perjury Demaratus here and Hegemon and Nicostratus, who, in the first place, will never be shown to have engaged in any shameful undertaking, and who, secondly, being our kinsmen and knowing us all, have each borne witness to his own relationship to Euphiletus? I should therefore like to hear from the most respectable of our opponents, whether he can produce any other sources of evidence to prove his own Athenian citizenship than those which we are employing in support of Euphiletus. I do not think he could urge any plea except that his mother was a citizen and a married woman and his father a citizen, and he could produce his kinsmen to bear witness that he was telling the truth. Then, gentlemen of the jury, if it were our opponents who were on trial, they would demand that you should believe the evidence of their kinsmen

---

[4] ἅπαντας Reiske: ἅπαντα codd.
[5] εἰπεῖν inseruit Sauppe.

δικασταί, εἰ μὲν οὗτοι ἐκινδύνευον, ἠξίουν ἂν τοῖς αὑτῶν οἰκείοις ὑμᾶς πιστεύειν μαρτυροῦσι μᾶλλον ἢ τοῖς κατηγόροις. νυνὶ δὲ ἡμῶν πάντα ταῦτα παρεχομένων ἀξιώσουσιν ὑμᾶς [1] τοῖς αὑτῶν πείθεσθαι λόγοις μᾶλλον ἢ τῷ πατρὶ τῷ Εὐφιλήτου καὶ ἐμοὶ καὶ τῷ ἀδελφῷ καὶ τοῖς φράτορσι καὶ πάσῃ τῇ ἡμετέρᾳ συγγενείᾳ; καὶ μὴν οὗτοι μὲν οὐδὲν οὐδενὶ κινδυνεύοντες ἰδίας ἔχθρας ἕνεκα ⟨ταῦτα⟩ [2] ποιοῦσιν, ἡμεῖς δὲ πάντας ὑποδίκους ἡμᾶς [3] αὐτοὺς καθιστάντες μαρτυροῦμεν. καὶ πρὸς ταῖς μαρτυρίαις, ὦ ἄνδρες δικασταί, πρῶτον μὲν ἡ τοῦ Εὐφιλήτου μήτηρ, ἣν οὗτοι ὁμολογοῦσιν ἀστὴν εἶναι, ὅρκον ὀμόσαι ἐπὶ τοῦ διαιτητοῦ ἐβούλετο ἐπὶ Δελφινίῳ, ἦ μὴν τουτονὶ Εὐφίλητον εἶναι ἐξ αὑτῆς καὶ τοῦ ἡμετέρου πατρός. καίτοι τίνα προσῆκε μᾶλλον αὐτῆς ἐκείνης τοῦτ' εἰδέναι; ἔπειτα, ὦ ἄνδρες δικασταί, ὁ πατὴρ ὁ ἡμέτερος, ὃν εἰκός ἐστι μετὰ τὴν τούτου μητέρα ἄριστα τὸν [4] αὑτοῦ υἱὸν γιγνώσκειν, [5] οὗτος καὶ τότε καὶ νυνὶ βούλεται ὀμόσαι, ἦ μὴν [6] Εὐφίλητον τοῦτον τοῦτον υἱὸν εἶναι αὑτοῦ ἐξ ἀστῆς καὶ γαμετῆς γυναικός. πρὸς τούτοις τοίνυν, ὦ ἄνδρες δικασταί, ἐγὼ ἐτύγχανον μὲν τρισκαιδεκαετὴς ὤν, ὥσπερ καὶ πρότερον εἶπον, ὅτε οὗτος ἐγένετο, ἕτοιμος δέ εἰμι ὀμόσαι, ἦ μὴν [7] Εὐφίλητον τουτονὶ ἀδελφὸν εἶναι ἐμαυτοῦ ὁμοπάτριον. ὥστε, ὦ ἄνδρες δικασταί, δικαίως ἂν καὶ τοὺς ἡμετέρους ὅρκους πιστοτέρους νομίζοιτε ἢ τοὺς τούτων λόγους. ἡμεῖς μὲν γὰρ ἀκριβῶς εἰδότες ὀμόσαι περὶ

[1] ὑμᾶς Sylburg: ἡμᾶς codd.
[2] ταῦτα Reiske inseruit.

rather than their accusers; and now, when we produce all these proofs, are they going to demand that you should believe what they say, rather than Euphiletus's father and me and my brother and the members of the ward and all our family? Furthermore, our opponents are acting out of personal spite without exposing themselves to any risk, while we are all rendering ourselves liable to the penalties of the law in giving evidence. And in addition to the depositions, gentlemen of the jury, in the first place, the mother of Euphiletus, who is admitted by our opponents to be a citizen, expressed before the arbitrators her willingness to swear an oath in the sanctuary of Delphinian Apollo that Euphiletus here was the issue of herself and our father; and who had better means of knowing than she? Secondly, judges, our father, who naturally is better able to recognise his own son than anyone else except his mother, was ready on the former occasion, and is ready now, to swear that Euphiletus here is his son by a mother who is a citizen and legally married. In addition to this, gentlemen of the jury, I was thirteen years old, as I have already said, when he was born, and am ready to swear that Euphiletus here is my brother by the same father. You would therefore be justified, gentlemen of the jury, in regarding our oaths as more worthy of credence than the statements of our opponents; for we, knowing all the facts, are willing to swear oaths concerning them, while they are

---

[3] *ὑποδίκους ἡμᾶς* Victorius: *ὑποδιημᾶς* F[1]: *ὑποδίκους* F[2]MPB.
[4] *ἄριστα τὸν* Reiske: *ἄριστον* codd.
[5] *γιγνώσκειν* Sylburg: *ἐγίνωσκεν* codd.
[6] *ἦ μὴν* Sylburg: *ἡμῖν* MBF: *ὑμῖν* P.
[7] *ἦ μὴν* Sylburg: *ἡμὶν* P: *ὑμῖν* FMB.

αὐτοῦ θέλομεν, οὗτοι δὲ ταῦτα ἀκηκοότες παρὰ τῶν τούτου διαφόρων ἢ αὐτοὶ πλάττοντες λέγουσι. πρὸς δὲ τούτοις, ὦ ἄνδρες δικασταί, ἡμεῖς μὲν τοὺς συγγενεῖς μάρτυρας καὶ ἐπὶ τῶν διαιτητῶν καὶ ἐφ' ὑμῶν παρεχόμεθα, οἷς οὐκ ἄξιον ἀπιστεῖν, οὗτοι δέ, ἐπειδὴ ἔλαχεν Εὐφίλητος τὴν δίκην τὴν προτέραν τῷ κοινῷ τῶν δημοτῶν καὶ τῷ τότε δημαρχοῦντι, ὃς νῦν τετελεύτηκε, δύο ἔτη τοῦ διαιτητοῦ τὴν δίαιταν ἔχοντος οὐκ ἠδυνήθησαν οὐδεμίαν μαρτυρίαν εὑρεῖν, ὡς οὑτοσὶ ἄλλου τινὸς πατρός ἐστιν ἢ τοῦ ἡμετέρου. τοῖς δὲ διαιτῶσι μέγιστα ⟨ταῦτα⟩ [1] σημεῖα ἦν τοῦ ψεύδεσθαί τούτους καὶ κατεδιῄτησαν αὐτῶν ἀμφότεροι. καί μοι λαβὲ [2] τῆς προτέρας διαίτης τὴν μαρτυρίαν.—Μαρτυρία.—Ὡς μὲν τοίνυν καὶ τότε ὦφλον [3] τὴν δίαιταν, ἀκηκόατε. ἀξιῶ δέ, ὦ ἄνδρες δικασταί, ὥσπερ οὗτοι μέγα [4] τοῦτ' ἂν [5] ἔφασαν εἶναι σημεῖον, ὡς οὐκ ἔστιν Ἡγησίππου, εἰ οἱ διαιτηταὶ αὐτῶν ἀπεδιῄτησαν, οὕτω τὸ νῦν ἡμῖν τοιοῦτον εἶναι μαρτύριον ὅτι ἀληθῆ λέγομεν, ἐπεὶ ἔδοξαν αὐτοὶ ἀδικεῖν τοῦτον Ἀθηναῖον ὄντα καὶ κυρίως πρῶτον ἐγγραφέντα ὕστερον ἐξαλείψαντες. ὅτι μὲν οὖν ἀδελφὸς ἡμῶν ἐστιν οὑτοσὶ Εὐφίλητος καὶ πολίτης ὑμέτερος καὶ ἀδίκως ὑβρίσθη ὑπὸ τῶν

[1] ταῦτα inseruit Reiske.
[2] λαβὲ Reiske: λάβετε codd.
[3] ὦφλον Holwell: ὤφειλον codd.
[4] μέγα Reiske: μετὰ codd.
[5] τοῦτ' ἂν Schoemann: ταῦτα codd.

repeating statements which they have heard from his enemies or making up their own story. Furthermore, gentlemen of the jury, we are producing before you our kinsmen, as we produced them before the arbitrators, as witnesses whom there is no reason for you to disbelieve; whereas our opponents, when Euphiletus brought his former case against the community of demesmen and the demarch then in office, who has since died, though the case was before the arbitrator for two years, could never find a single piece of evidence to show that Euphiletus was the son of any other father than ours. In the opinion of the arbitrators this was the strongest indication that our opponents were lying, and they both gave their verdict against them. Please take the deposition about the earlier arbitration.

DEPOSITION

You have now heard that my opponents lost their case before the arbitrators on that occasion also. I claim, gentlemen of the jury, that, just as they have declared, if the arbitrators had decided in their favour, that this was a strong proof that Euphiletus is not the son of Hegesippus, so now you should regard as equally strong evidence of the truth of our contention the fact that they were considered by the arbitrators to be doing Euphiletus an injury in having subsequently deleted his name, though he was a citizen and had before been legally enrolled. You have, I think, now heard enough, gentlemen of the jury, to convince you that Euphiletus here is our brother and your fellow-citizen, and that he has been

ἐν τῷ δήμῳ συστάντων, ἱκανῶς οἴομαι ὑμᾶς, ὦ ἄνδρες δικασταί, ἀκηκοέναι."

18 οὗτος ὁ χαρακτὴρ τῶν Ἰσαίου λόγων καὶ ταῦτα τὰ διαλλάττοντα παρὰ τὴν Λυσίου ἀγωγήν. οὐθὲν δὲ κωλύει καὶ κεφαλαιωδῶς περιλαβόντα δι' ἐλαχίστης δηλώσεως τὰ φανερώτατα εἰπεῖν, ὅτι μοι δοκεῖ Λυσίας μὲν τὴν ἀλήθειαν διώκειν μᾶλλον, Ἰσαῖος δὲ τὴν τέχνην, καὶ ὅ μὲν στοχάζεσθαι τοῦ χαριέντως, ὃ δὲ τοῦ δεινῶς. εἰ δέ τις παραθεωροίη ταῦτα ὡς μικρὰ καὶ φαῦλα, οὐκ ἂν ἔτι γένοιτο ἱκανὸς αὐτῶν κριτής.[1] ἀλλὰ γὰρ αἱ ὁμοιότητες συνταράξουσιν αὐτοῦ τὴν γνώμην, ὥστε μὴ διαγνῶναι τὸν ἴδιον ἑκατέρου χαρακτῆρα. καὶ περὶ μὲν τούτων ὡς ἔχω δόξης δεδήλωταί μοι.

19 βούλομαι δὲ ἤδη καὶ περὶ τῶν ἄλλων ῥητόρων ἀποδοῦναι τὸν λόγον, ἵνα μή τις ἀγνοίᾳ με δόξῃ παραλιπεῖν αὐτοὺς ἐπιφανεῖς ὄντας καὶ ὀνόματος ἠξιωμένους οὐ μετρίου ἢ φυγῇ τοῦ πόνου τὸ ῥᾷστον αἱρούμενον τῶν ἔργων τὴν περὶ αὐτῶν ἀφεικέναι σκέψιν. ἐγὼ γὰρ οὔτε ἠγνόουν, οὓς ἅπαντες ἴσασιν, οὔτε ὤκνουν ⟨ἂν⟩ [2] ὑπὲρ αὐτῶν γράφειν, εἴ τι χρήσιμον ἔμελλεν ἐξοίσειν ἡ γραφή. ἐνθυμούμενος δέ, ὅτι τὴν μὲν ποιητικὴν κατασκευὴν καὶ τὸ μετέωρον δὴ τοῦτο καὶ πομπικὸν εἰρημένον οὐδεὶς Ἰσοκράτους ἀμείνων ἐγένετο, παρέλιπον ἑκών, οὓς ᾔδειν ἧττον ἐν ταῖς ἰδέαις ταύταις κατορθοῦντας, Γοργίαν μὲν τὸν Λεοντῖνον ἐκπίπτοντα τοῦ μετρίου καὶ πολλαχοῦ παιδαριώδη γιγνόμενον ὁρῶν, Ἀλκιδάμαντα δὲ τὸν ἀκουστὴν

[1] κριτής Krüger: κρατῆσαι codd.

unjustly insulted by those who have conspired against him in the deme."

Those are the characteristics of the speeches of Isaeus, and the qualities which distinguish them from the style of Lysias. But there is nothing against my summarising the most obvious difference in the briefest possible way by saying that I think Lysias aims more at realism, and Isaeus at artistic effect; that the object of the first is charm, that of the second forcefulness. But if anyone is inclined to discount these differences as small and trifling, he can give up all hope of becoming a competent critic of the two orators. In fact, the similarities will only confuse his judgment and prevent him from discerning the individual characteristics of each. I have now made my opinion on these matters clear. 18

I now wish to give an account of the other orators, so that nobody may think that, although their renown deserves more than passing acclaim, I have passed over them through ignorance, or have chosen the easiest course through laziness and neglected to study them. Orators who were familiar to everyone else were not unknown to me; nor should I hesitate to write about them if the resulting treatise were likely to serve a useful purpose. But I considered that none of them was better than Isocrates at the elaborate, elevated and "ceremonial" style, and therefore deliberately passed them over, knowing that they were less successful than he was in these forms of oratory. I observed that Gorgias of Leontini exceeds the bounds of moderation and frequently lapses into puerility; that the diction of Alcidamas 19

[2] ἂν inseruit Holwell.

αὐτοῦ παχύτερον ὄντα τὴν λέξιν καὶ κενότερον,[1] Θεόδωρον δὲ τὸν Βυζάντιον ἀρχαῖόν τινα καὶ οὔτε ἐν ταῖς τέχναις ἀκριβῆ οὔτε ἐξέτασιν ἱκανὴν ἐν τοῖς ἐναγωνίοις δεδωκότα λόγοις, Ἀναξιμένην δὲ τὸν Λαμψακηνὸν ἐν ἁπάσαις μὲν ταῖς ἰδέαις τῶν λόγων τετράγωνόν τινα εἶναι βουλόμενον (καὶ γὰρ ἱστορίας γέγραφε καὶ περὶ τοῦ ποιητοῦ συντάξεις καταλέλοιπε καὶ τέχνας ἐξενήνοχεν, ἧπται δὲ καὶ συμβουλευτικῶν καὶ δικανικῶν ἀγώνων), οὐ μέντοι τέλειόν γε ἐν οὐδεμιᾷ τούτων τῶν ἰδεῶν ἀλλ' ἀσθενῆ καὶ ἀπίθανον ὄντα ἐν ἁπάσαις θεωρῶν. οὐ δὴ δεῖν ᾠόμην Ἰσοκράτους ἐν ἅπασι πάντων τούτων ὑπερέχοντος λόγον τινὰ ποιεῖσθαι περὶ ἐκείνων οὐδέ γε περὶ τῶν συμβιωσάντων Ἰσοκράτει καὶ τὸν χαρακτῆρα τῆς ἑρμηνείας ἐκείνου ἐκμιμησαμένων οὐθενός, Θεοδέκτου λέγω καὶ Θεοπόμπου καὶ Ναυκράτους Ἐφόρου τε καὶ Φιλίσκου καὶ Κηφισοδώρου καὶ ἄλλων συχνῶν. οὐδὲ γὰρ ἐκεῖνοι κρίνεσθαι πρὸς τὴν Ἰσοκράτους δύναμίν εἰσιν ἐπιτήδειοι.

[1] κενότερον Krüger: κοινότερον codd.

---

[1] Remembered chiefly as the champion of impromptu speaking, and opponent of Isocrates and the literary discourse. See H. Ll. Hudson-Williams, *Political and Forensic Oratory* CQ 1951.

[2] Rhetorician, contemporary of Gorgias, who was noted chiefly for his work on the division of speeches (Plato, *Phaedrus*, 266D). Dionysius's criticism contradicts the main body of the tradition, which rather implies that he was pedantically overelaborate. See Radermacher, *Artium Scriptores*, pp. 106–111.

[3] A pupil of Zoilus (see note 5, p. 229) and teacher of Alexander. The *Rhetorica ad Alexandrum* is probably to be attributed to him.

[4] An important literary figure (*c.* 375–334 B.C.), pupil of

his pupil [1] is at once rather heavy and lacking in content; that Theodorus of Byzantium [2] is rather old-fashioned, and his technical works lack precision, while his forensic oratory does not provide sufficient quantity for examination. There is Anaximenes of Lampsacus also,[3] who wishes to be an all-round performer in every branch of literature (he has indeed written history and has left us treatises on poetry, has published rhetorical handbooks and has tried his hand at political debates and lawsuits); but in my view he falls short of perfection in all these genres, and is indeed weak and unconvincing in all of them. It has therefore seemed unnecessary to me, since Isocrates was superior to all of these writers in every genre, to write a separate critique of each, or indeed of any of his contemporaries who closely imitated his individual style—I refer to Theodectes,[4] Theopompus,[5] Naucrates,[6] Ephorus,[7] Philiscus,[8] Cephisodorus [9] and many others—for these writers do not deserve to be compared with the genius of Isocrates.

Plato, Isocrates and Aristotle. Wrote plays in addition to rhetorical works and speeches.

[5] Pupil of Isocrates; he wrote history, *Hellenica* and *Philippica*, in a strong vein of moral censure, showing the influence of his rhetorical training. Dionysius expresses admiration for both his style and his treatment of subject-matter in his *Letter to Pompeius*, ch. 6.

[6] Another pupil of Isocrates who apparently practised as an orator and followed his master's principles closely. (See Cicero, *De Oratore*, iii. 44. 173.)

[7] Perhaps the most famous of the literary pupils of Isocrates. His *Universal History* was one of the main sources used by Diodorus Siculus. See G. L. Barber, *The Historian Ephorus*.

[8] A rhetorician who began his career as a reed-pipe player before attending Isocrates's school.

[9] See note 3, p. 157.

20 τῶν μὲν δὴ κατὰ ταύτην τὴν ἀγωγὴν κοσμουμένων ἐκεῖνον τὸν ἄνδρα διαφορώτατον ἡγησάμενος, οὐκ ἔτι περὶ τῶν ἄλλων ἠξίωσα μακρολογεῖν καὶ δαπανᾶν εἰς οὐδὲν ἀναγκαῖον τὸν χρόνον. τῶν δὲ τοὺς ἀκριβεῖς προαιρουμένων λόγους καὶ πρὸς τὴν ἐναγώνιον ἀσκούντων ῥητορικήν, ὧν ἐγένετο Ἀντιφῶν τε ὁ Ῥαμνούσιος καὶ Θρασύμαχος ὁ Καλχηδόνιος καὶ Πολυκράτης ὁ Ἀθηναῖος Κριτίας τε ὁ τῶν τριάκοντα ἄρξας καὶ Ζωΐλος ὁ τὰς καθ' Ὁμήρου συντάξεις καταλιπὼν καὶ ἄλλοι τοιοῦτοί τινες, οὐδένα ἡγούμενος οὔτε ἀκριβέστερον οὔτε χαριέστερον γεγονέναι Λυσίου· Ἀντιφῶν γε μὴν τὸ αὐστηρὸν ἔχει μόνον καὶ ἀρχαῖον, ἀγωνιστὴς δὲ λόγων οὔτε συμβουλευτικῶν οὔτε δικανικῶν ἐστι, Πολυκράτης δὲ κενὸς μὲν ἐν τοῖς ἀληθινοῖς, ψυχρὸς δὲ καὶ φορτικὸς ἐν τοῖς ἐπιδεικτικοῖς, ἄχαρις δὲ ἐν τοῖς χαριεντισμοῦ δεομένοις ἐστί, Θρασύμαχος δὲ καθαρὸς μὲν καὶ λεπτὸς καὶ δεινὸς εὑρεῖν τε καὶ εἰπεῖν στρογγύλως καὶ περιττῶς, ὃ βούλεται, πᾶς δέ ἐστιν ἐν τοῖς τεχνογραφικοῖς καὶ ἐπιδεικτικοῖς, δικανικοὺς δὲ [ἢ συμβουλευτικοὺς] οὐκ ἀπολέλοιπε λόγους, τὰ δὲ αὐτὰ καὶ περὶ Κριτίου καὶ περὶ Ζωΐλου τις

---

[1] The first of the Canon of Ten Attic Orators. Prominent oligarch (Thucydides viii. 68), master-mind behind the Revolution of 411 B.C. Best representative of the early grand style in Attic oratory.

[2] See note 2, pp. 30–31; pp. 247–253.

[3] Fourth-century rhetorician in the Gorgianic tradition, whose exercises were criticised by Isocrates for their triviality (*Busiris*, 1, 48). An encomium of Thrasybulus attributed to him (*Schol. ad Ar. Rhet.* p. 150R) suggests democratic sym-

Because I regarded Isocrates as the most distinguished exponent of this ornate style, I did not think it worthwhile to give an extended account of these other writers, thereby spending time unnecessarily. As for those who preferred factual discourses and practical rhetoric designed for the lawcourts, like Antiphon of Rhamnus,[1] Thrasymachus of Calchedon,[2] Polycrates of Athens,[3] Critias the leader of the Thirty,[4] Zoilus who left the studies criticising Homer[5] and other writers of this character, I found none more incisive or more charming than Lysias. As for Antiphon, he cultivates only the severe, old-fashioned style, and does not engage personally either in political debates or in lawsuits. Polycrates is ineffectual in his speeches for actual lawsuits, frigid and vulgar in his display-speeches and lacking in charm when charm is required. Thrasymachus is pure, subtle and inventive, and able at will to speak either with terseness or with an abundance of words; but he devoted himself to writing handbooks and display-speeches, and has left no forensic speeches. One might say the same about Critias and 20

pathies, which might also account for his hostility towards Socrates.

[4] The most prominent and extreme of the Thirty oligarchs who ruled Athens for less than a year after her defeat by Sparta in 404 B.C. A forceful and persuasive orator, he also wrote poetry and, like other political men of his day, tracts on constitutional theory. He admired the Spartan way of life. See S. Usher in JHS 88 (1968) pp. 128–135.

[5] Pupil of Polycrates who earned the nickname of Scourge of Homer (Ὁμηρόμαστιξ), and whom Dionysius names as the archetypal censorious critic (*Letter to Pompeius*, 1). But his work was also characterised by attention to detail, in regard to both style and subject-matter. See Blass, *op. cit.* ii, pp. 375–378.

ἂν εἰπεῖν ἔχοι πλὴν ὅσον τοῖς χαρακτῆρσι τῆς ἑρμηνείας διαλλάττουσιν ἀλλήλων· τούτων δή, φημί, τῶν ἀνδρῶν καὶ τῶν παραπλησίων τούτοις διαφέρειν οἰόμενος Λυσίαν καὶ ὥσπερ ἀρχέτυπον ἀπογράφων [1] ὑπερέχειν, ἐκεῖνον τὸν ἄνδρα ταύτης τῆς προαιρέσεως τῶν λόγων ἐποιησάμην κανόνα. τὸν δὲ δὴ τρίτον Ἰσαῖον εἴ τις ἔροιτό με τίνος ἕνεκα προσεθέμην, Λυσίου δὴ ζηλωτὴν ὄντα, ταύτην ἂν αὐτῷ φαίην τὴν αἰτίαν, ὅτι μοι δοκεῖ τῆς Δημοσθένους δεινότητος, ἣν οὐθείς ἐστιν ὃς οὐ τελειοτάτην ἁπασῶν οἴεται γενέσθαι, τὰ σπέρματα καὶ τὰς ἀρχὰς οὗτος ὁ ἀνὴρ παρασχεῖν. διὰ μὲν δὴ ταύτας τὰς αἰτίας τούσδε τοὺς ἄνδρας μόνους παρέλαβον. εἰ δὲ περὶ πάντων ἠξίουν γράφειν, εἰς κενότητας ἄν μοι ὁ λόγος ἐξέπιπτε καὶ πρὸς τῷ μηθὲν ἢ μὴ πολὺ τὸ χρήσιμον ἔχειν εἰς ἀπέραντόν τινα καὶ οὐ σύμμετρον ἐξεμηκύνθη γραφήν. καὶ περὶ τούτων μὲν ἅλις. ἑτέραν δὲ ἀρχὴν ποιήσομαι τοῦ λόγου περί τε Δημοσθένους καὶ Ὑπερείδου καὶ τρίτου λέγων Αἰσχίνου. ἡ γὰρ δὴ τελειοτάτη ῥητορικὴ καὶ τὸ κράτος τῶν ἐναγωνίων λόγων ἐν τούτοις τοῖς ἀνδράσιν ἔοικεν εἶναι.

[1] ἀπογράφων Reiske: ὑπογράφων codd.

Zoilus, except in so far as they differ from one another in the individual characteristics of their styles. I think Lysias is superior to these men and to others in the same way as the original is superior to the copy. I have therefore made him the standard of this type of oratory. As for the third orator, Isaeus, if anyone were to ask why I have included him, since he is an imitator of Lysias, I should give as my reason that it is in him that we find the seeds and the beginnings of the genius of Demosthenes, which everyone agrees to be oratory in its most perfect form. These, then, are my reasons for choosing these three orators, and no more. If I decided to write about all these other orators, my work would lose all its substance, and in addition to containing little or nothing that is useful would have been spun out to an ill-defined and disproportionate length. But enough of this explanation. I shall make a fresh start to my treatise, dealing with Demosthenes and Hyperides, and thirdly with Aeschines: for it was probably in these men that oratory reached its highest point of perfection, and forensic eloquence found its most accomplished exponents.

DEMOSTHENES

INTRODUCTION

The original length of the *Demosthenes* is unknown, for the first part is lost; but what remains is still longer than any of his other extant critical works except the *De Compositione Verborum*. This is altogether appropriate in view of Demosthenes's special position in Dionysius's scheme of Attic models. But the treatise proves to be much more than a critique of Demosthenes's style. We join it some way through an illustrated discussion of the grand style. This is followed by a briefer discussion of the plain style, without examples. Thucydides is a model for the former, Lysias for the latter. The scale of the next discussion of the intermediate or middle style corresponds with Dionysius's stated opinion [1] that it is the best style, combining the qualities of the other two. Hence the particular importance of the comparison between Isocrates and Plato on the one hand and Demosthenes on the other. Dionysius's purpose in the first part of the treatise (chs. 1–34) is to show that the authors who have come to be regarded by

[1] ch. 34.

many as masters of a particular style are inferior to Demosthenes because they have exaggerated the qualities of that style and excluded qualities from other styles which would have given them a more flexible and attractive medium through which to express their thought. Thus in Demosthenes's hands the plain style retains the desirable Lysianic qualities, but is more vigorous and intense;[1] Thucydides, the leading exponent of the grand style, is criticised for his tortuous indirectness and unnatural obscurity,[2] faults which Demosthenes eschews, while retaining the essential exotic qualities of that style. But it is against Isocrates and Plato, who are both widely admired for their mastery of the middle style, that the greatest weight of criticism is aimed. With regard to Isocrates Dionysius reproduces in a refined form much of what he wrote in the earlier treatise: in particular his comparison of the Isocratean period with a meandering river is a happy critical stroke. He also analyses a passage from the discourse *On the Peace* (41–50), and offers a version of it which serves to underline his criticisms. He follows this with a passage from Demosthenes (*Olynthiacs* III, 23–32) which he considers to be superior.

To judge from his method of dealing with Plato, the philosopher presented a graver threat to Dionysius's position as champion of Demosthenes than Isocrates. Like Thucydides, he made genuine lovers of litera-

[1] ch. 13. [2] ch. 9–10.

ture, both Greek and Roman, feel instinctively that they were in the presence of a towering intellect whose style they could recognise as the medium through which profound thought was being expressed, even when they could not always fully understand the latter; while others, the poseurs and the *dilettanti*, liked to cultivate the appearance of enjoying the recondite, the archaic and the intractable. Elsewhere Dionysius shows a proper appreciation of Plato's style:[1] in this treatise he is at times both unfair and so obtuse as to fail to detect Plato's characteristic irony with regard to style, whereby he deliberately exaggerates certain aspects of the diction, and even writes whole passages in a consciously contrived manner. This is less true of the first passage which he criticises, the opening chapters of the *Phaedrus*, than of the passages against which the main body of criticism is directed. In this (23–30), after attempting to disarm possible opposition, he plumbs the depths of partisanship by choosing a passage from the *Menexenus*, a work which few even of his contemporaries can have read as a representative example of Plato's style, or even as a dialogue of serious intent. As if this were not enough, he chooses for comparison what is arguably the finest passage in the whole of Demosthenes, chs. 199–209 of the *De Corona*. In the face of this we can only deplore the folly of excessive adulation.

[1] e.g. *De Compositione Verborum* 18; 42.

What he has to say about Demosthenes himself, however, shows an important advance on earlier criticism. Demosthenes is found to conform to no single style, but to have selected the best qualities from all three styles and all authors, and to have developed an individual style which could be adapted to all needs. He has thus in a sense done the critic's work for him: he is himself the ideal eclectic which Dionysius has urged his pupils to aim to be. Having established this, he turns to examine word-order and sentence-structure.[1] Those who have found the essay repetitive and wanting in unity have argued that the following chapters serve only to confuse what has been said earlier about the three categories of style. It has also been noted that they repeat much of what has already been written in the *De Compositione Verborum*. These criticisms are not without substance; and the introduction of individual styles into the earlier discussion, indispensable as it is for eclectic imitation, has blurred distinctions and added to the confusion. Isocrates and Plato are named as exponents of the middle style, yet it is obvious that their styles are different, and both contain qualities that are to be found in neither of the two extremes. When Dionysius comes to discuss word-order and sentence-structure these qualities—smoothness, balance and melodiousness—are assigned to a new extreme form of style, the counterpart of the grand,

[1] ch. 34.

rough, archaic and austere style; and the third style is intermediate between these two. What has happened is that, although the discussion in the earlier part of the essay was mainly about *language*,[1] Dionysius found it impossible to exclude from it, when examining the style of Isocrates, consideration of his use of figures (σχήματα), and this in turn involved him in discussion of that orator's addiction to balanced clauses and periodic structure. It is here that the preserves of language (λέξις) and structure (ἁρμονία, σύνθεσις) overlap. In the later discussion, which follows chs. 22–24 of the *De Compositione Verborum* closely, the intermediate style represents a true mean, not a third distinct category. It combines the best qualities of the other two, and Demosthenes is its finest exponent. In his descriptions of the three ἁρμονίαι Dionysius shows full awareness of the need for a critic of literature some three centuries old to awaken and educate his pupils' senses to the subtleties of which their language was capable in its prime and in the hands of the classical masters. He shows an admirable understanding of the value of analysing the mechanical means by which effects are achieved. It is also excellent criticism to stress the emotional effect which fine oratory wrought upon ancient audiences; and refreshingly honest to include a section on delivery, and thus to admit the limitations of

[1] See Grube in *American Journal of Philology* 73 (1952) pp. 261–6.

purely academic criticism removed from the din of the popular assembly or the dramatic tension of the law-court. Even allowing for their common ground with the *De Compositione Verborum*, these later chapters (35–end) display the full range of Dionysius's critical equipment. Demosthenes is set in the broader context of the whole literary pantheon, the special features of his style are analysed in the minutest detail, his critic Aeschines is silenced and the pupil is left to reflect on the limits of emulation, and to feel that admiration and aesthetic pleasure are all that he may allow himself when he reads the speeches of Demosthenes.

ΔΙΟΝΥΣΙΟΥ ΑΛΙΚΑΡΝΑΣΕΩΣ
ΠΕΡΙ ΤΗΣ ΔΗΜΟΣΘΕΝΟΥΣ ΛΕΞΕΩΣ

1 . . . .
δικανικοῖς μὲν οὖν οὐ περιέτυχον αὐτοῦ λόγοις, δημηγορικοῖς δὲ ὀλίγοις καί τισι καὶ τέχναις, τοῖς δὲ πλείοσιν ἐπιδεικτικοῖς. τῆς δὲ ἰδέας αὐτοῦ τῶν λόγων τοιοῦτος ὁ χαρακτήρ, ἐγκωμιάζει δὲ τοὺς ἐν πολέμοις ἀριστεύσαντας Ἀθηναίων· "Τί γὰρ ἀπῆν τοῖς ἀνδράσι τούτοις, ὧν δεῖ ἀνδράσι προσεῖναι; τί δὲ προσῆν, ὧν δεῖ ἀπεῖναι; εἰπεῖν δυναίμην, ἃ βούλομαι, βουλοίμην δέ, ἃ δεῖ, λαθὼν μὲν τὴν θείαν νέμεσιν, φυγὼν δὲ τὸν ἀνθρώπινον φθόνον. οὗτοι γὰρ ἐκέκτηντο ἔνθεον μὲν τὴν ἀρετήν, ἀνθρώπινον δὲ τὸ θνητόν, πολλὰ μὲν δὴ τὸ παρὸν ἐπιεκὲς τοῦ αὐθάδους δικαίου προκρίνοντες, πολλὰ δὲ νόμου ἀκριβείας λόγων ὀρθότητα, τοῦτον νομίζοντες θειότατον καὶ κοινότατον νόμων τὸ δέον ἐν τῷ δέοντι καὶ λέγειν καὶ σιγᾶν καὶ ποιεῖν, καὶ δισσὰ ἀσκήσαντες μάλιστα ὧν δεῖ, γνώμην ⟨καὶ ῥώμην⟩,[1] τὴν μὲν βουλεύοντες τὴν δ' ἀποτελοῦντες, θεράποντες μὲν τῶν ἀδίκως δυστυχούντων, κολασταὶ δὲ τῶν ἀδίκως εὐτυχούντων,

[1] καὶ ῥώμην addidit Foss.

---

[1] We join the essay some way through a discussion of the

ON THE STYLE OF DEMOSTHENES

. . . Thus I[1] have not come across any forensic speeches by him:[2] apart from a few political speeches and some handbooks, most of those which I have read are epideictic. The following passage shows the characteristic qualities of his speeches in the genre. He is celebrating the valour of the Athenians who distinguished themselves in war in the words:[3] 1

"What did these men lack that men should have, or what did they have that men should lack? May I be able to speak as I wish, and to wish as I ought, escaping the wrath of the gods and evading the envy of men. For these men were endowed with a valour that was divine, but a mortality that was human, and they far preferred practical equity to rigid justice, and integrity of speech to the exactitude of the law, considering that the most divine and universal law is to speak, to be silent and to act, each rightly and at the right time. They cultivated the two most necessary qualities—strength of mind and strength of body—the first for counsel, the second for action. Helpers of the undeservedly unfortunate, chasteners of the undeservedly fortunate, uncompromising towards

Grand Style, which has presumably been preceded by an introduction.

[2] Gorgias of Leontini. See *Lysias*, 3 and note *ad. loc.*

[3] Dionysius here preserves a fragment of Gorgias's *Epitaphios*. Its historical circumstances, if any, are unknown.

αὐθάδεις πρὸς τὸ συμφέρον, εὐόργητοι πρὸς τὸ πρέπον, τῷ φρονίμῳ τῆς γνώμης παύοντες τὸ ἄφρον, ὑβρισταὶ εἰς τοὺς ὑβρίζοντας, κόσμιοι εἰς τοὺς κοσμίους, ἄφοβοι εἰς τοὺς ἀφόβους, δεινοὶ ἐν τοῖς δεινοῖς. μαρτύρια δὲ τούτων τρόπαια ἐστήσαντο τῶν πολεμίων Διὸς μὲν ἀγάλματα τούτων δὲ ἀναθήματα, οὐκ ἄπειροι οὔτε ἐμφύτου Ἄρεως οὔτε νομίμων ἐρώτων οὔτε ἐνοπλίου ἔριδος οὔτε φιλοκάλου εἰρήνης, σεμνοὶ μὲν πρὸς τοὺς θεοὺς τῷ δικαίῳ, ὅσιοι δὲ πρὸς τοὺς τοκέας τῇ θεραπείᾳ, δίκαιοι δὲ πρὸς τοὺς ἀστοὺς τῷ ἴσῳ, εὐσεβεῖς δὲ πρὸς τοὺς φίλους τῇ πίστει. τοιγαροῦν αὐτῶν ἀποθανόντων ὁ πόθος οὐ συναπέθανεν, ἀλλ' ἀθάνατος ἐν οὐκ ἀθανάτοις σώμασι ζῇ οὐ ζώντων." . . . .

. . . .

⟨" ἐστασίαζέ τε οὖν τὰ τῶν πόλε⟩ων, καὶ τὰ ἐφυστερίζοντά που πύστει [1] τῶν προγενομένων πολὺ ἐπέφερε τὴν ὑπερβολὴν τοῦ [2] καινοῦσθαι τὰς διανοίας τῶν τ' ἐπιχειρήσεων περιτεχνήσει καὶ τῶν τιμωριῶν ἀτοπίᾳ. καὶ τὴν εἰωθυῖαν ἀξίωσιν τῶν ὀνομάτων ἐς τὰ ἔργα ἀντήλλαξαν τῇ δικαιώσει. τόλμα μὲν γὰρ ἀλόγιστος ἀνδρία φιλέταιρος ἐνομίσθη, μέλλησις δὲ προμηθὴς δειλία εὐπρεπής, τὸ δὲ σῶφρον τοῦ ἀνάνδρου πρόσχημα. καὶ τὸ

[1] πύστει Thuc.: πύστα B: πείστει P.
[2] τοῦ Thuc.: ἐς τὸ codd.

---

[1] After perhaps further examples of the Grand Style, bridging the gap between its uses in purely epideictic oratory and in practical oratory, Dionysius comes to Thucydides. He chooses as his example the famous description of the spirit of revolution

mere expediency, but kindly disposed towards fair dealing, they curbed foolishness with their good sense, answered violence with violence, orderliness with orderliness, fearlessness with fearlessness; and were formidable in formidable situations. They set up as testimonials to these qualities trophies captured from the enemy, and these serve both as offerings to the gods and as tributes to their own courage. Not unversed either in belligerence (for Ares is their native god), or in lawful love, in armed strife or in the arts of peace, they showed reverence for the gods by observing justice and filial piety towards their parents by caring for them; integrity towards their fellow-citizens by their equity, and loyalty towards their friends by their good faith. So it is that, though they have died, our loving memory of those who live no more has not died with them, but lives on immortal in our mortal bodies."

(*Lacuna*) [1]

"Revolution thus ran its course throughout the states, and those which experienced it later anywhere, having heard what had been done before, carried to a still greater excess the invention of new ideas through the elaborate ingenuity of their enterprises and the atrocity of their reprisals. They changed the normal meaning of words, as they thought fit, to suit their actions. Reckless bravado came to be regarded as the courage of a loyal ally; provident hesitation as specious cowardice; modera-

in iii. 82. 3 ff., a passage which he later criticises in his essay on Thucydides for its tortuous obscurity (29–33). It becomes evident from the present essay that Dionysius's preferences lie with the Middle Style, which combines the best qualities of the Grand and the Plain Style. But see introd. pp. xvi–xvii.

πρὸς ἅπαν ξυνετὸν ἐπίπαν ἀργόν, τὸ δ' ἐμπλήκτως ὀξὺ ἀνδρὸς μοίρᾳ προσετέθη, ἀσφάλειᾳ δὲ τὸ ἐπιβουλεύσασθαι, ἀποτροπῆς πρόφασις εὔλογος. καὶ ὁ μὲν χαλεπαίνων πιστὸς ἀεί, ὁ δὲ ἀντιλέγων αὐτῷ ὕποπτος. ἐπιβουλεύσας δέ τις τυχών τε ξυνετὸς καὶ ὑπονοήσας ἔτι δεινότερος. προβουλεύσας δέ, ὅπως μηδὲν αὐτῷ δεήσει, τῆς τε ἑταιρίας διαλυτὴς καὶ τοὺς ἐναντίους ἐκπεπληγμένος. ἁπλῶς δὲ ὁ φθάσας τὸν μέλλοντα κακόν τι δρᾶν ἐπῃνεῖτο καὶ ὁ ἐπικελεύσας τὸν μὴ διανοούμενον. καὶ μὴν καὶ τὸ ξυγγενὲς τοῦ ἑταιρικοῦ ἀλλοτριώτερον ἐγένετο, διὰ τὸ ἑτοιμότερον εἶναι ἀπροφασίστως τολμᾶν. οὐ γὰρ μετὰ τῶν κειμένων νόμων ὠφελείας αἱ τοιαῦται ξύνοδοι, ἀλλὰ παρὰ τοὺς καθεστῶτας πλεονεξίᾳ. καὶ τὰς ἐς σφᾶς αὐτοὺς πίστεις οὐ τῷ θείῳ καὶ νομίμῳ μᾶλλον ἐκρατύνοντο ἢ τῷ κοινῇ τι παρανομῆσαι· τά τε ἀπὸ τῶν ἐναντίων καλῶς λεγόμενα ἐνεδέχοντο ἔργων φυλακῇ, εἰ προὔχοιεν, καὶ οὐ γενναιότητι. ἀντιτιμωρήσασθαί τε τινα περὶ πλείονος ἦν ἢ αὐτὸν μὴ προπαθεῖν. καὶ ὅρκοι εἴ που ἄρα γένοιντο ξυναλλαγῆς, ἐν τῷ αὐτίκα πρὸς τὸ ἄπορον ἑκατέρῳ διδόμενοι ἴσχυον οὐκ ἐχόντων ἄλλοθεν δύναμιν." ἡ μὲν οὖν ἐξηλλαγμένη καὶ περιττὴ καὶ ἐγκατάσκευος καὶ τοῖς ἐπιθέτοις κόσμοις ἅπασι συμπεπληρωμένη λέξις, ἧς ὅρος καὶ κανὼν ὁ Θουκυδίδης, ὃν οὐθεὶς οὔθ' ὑπερεβάλετο τῶν ἐπιγι-

tion as a cloak for unmanliness; ability to understand all as inability to act in any. Frantic violence became the attribute of a man, plotting as a mere means of self-preservation and a reasoned excuse for withdrawal. The advocate of extreme policies was always trusted, and his opponent suspected. The successful conspirator was deemed clever, the man who disclosed a plot even more brilliant; but the man who planned to avoid having to do either was accused of destroying his party and being afraid of his opponents. In short, both the man who anticipated another in some evil deed and the man who suggested a crime to one who had no such idea were equally praised. Moreover, ties of kinship became less binding than those of party, because the latter induced a greater readiness for unstinted action. For such associations are created not to benefit from the support of established laws, but to oppose them and so win greater advantages. The mutual trust of their members for each other derived its strength not from any religious or human sanction, but rather from the consciousness of some common act of crime. The fair proposals of their opponents were accepted by the stronger party with precautionary action, not in a spirit of generosity. Revenge upon another was also considered more desirable than avoidance of original wrong oneself. As for oaths of reconciliation, in the few cases they were exchanged, they held good only while immediate difficulties obtained and no other source offered support."

This passage illustrates the striking, elaborate style which is remote from normality and is full of every kind of accessory embellishment. Thucydides is the standard and pattern of this style, and no subse-

νομένων οὔτε ⟨εἰς ἄκρον⟩ [1] ἐμιμήσατο, τοιαύτη τις ἦν.

2 ἡ δὲ ἑτέρα λέξις ἡ λιτὴ καὶ ἀφελὴς καὶ δοκοῦσα κατασκευήν τε καὶ ἰσχὺν τὴν πρὸς ἰδιώτην ἔχειν λόγον [καὶ] [2] ὁμοιότητα πολλοὺς μὲν ἔσχε καὶ ἀγαθοὺς ἄνδρας προστάτας συγγραφεῖς τε καὶ φιλοσόφους καὶ ῥήτορας. καὶ γὰρ οἱ τὰς γενεαλογίας ἐξενέγκαντες καὶ οἱ τὰς τοπικὰς ἱστορίας πραγματευσάμενοι καὶ οἱ τὰ φυσικὰ φιλοσοφήσαντες καὶ οἱ τῶν ἠθικῶν διαλόγων ποιηταί, ὧν ἦν τὸ Σωκρατικὸν διδασκαλεῖον πᾶν ἔξω Πλάτωνος, καὶ οἱ τοὺς δημηγορικοὺς ἢ δικανικοὺς συνταττόμενοι λόγους ὀλίγου δεῖν πάντες ταύτης ἐγένοντο τῆς προαιρέσεως. ἐτελείωσε δ' αὐτὴν καὶ εἰς ἄκρον ἤγαγε τῆς ἰδίας ἀρετῆς Λυσίας ὁ Κεφάλου, κατὰ τοὺς αὐτοὺς χρόνους Γοργίᾳ τε καὶ Θουκυδίδῃ γενόμενος. τίς δὲ ἦν ἡ προαίρεσις αὐτοῦ καὶ τίς ἡ δύναμις, ἐν τῇ πρὸ ταύτης δεδήλωται γραφῇ καὶ οὐδὲν δεῖ νῦν πάλιν ὑπὲρ τῶν αὐτῶν λέγειν. ἀρκέσει δὲ τοσοῦτο μόνον εἰπεῖν, ὅτι τὴν διαπασῶν ἁρμονίαν οὗτοι πρὸς ἀλλήλους οἱ ἄνδρες ἡρμόσαντο, τὰς ἀκρότητας ἀμφοτέρας τῆς λέξεως, αἳ πλεῖστον ἀλλήλων ἀπέχουσι, δαιμονίᾳ σπουδῇ προελόμενοί τε καὶ τελειώσαντες. καὶ ὅνπερ ἡ νήτη πρὸς ὑπάτην ἐν μουσικῇ λόγον ἔχει, τοῦτον ἡ Λυσίου λέξις ἐν πολιτικῇ διαλέκτῳ πρὸς τὴν Θουκυδίδου. ἣ μὲν γὰρ καταπλήξασθαι δύναται τὴν διάνοιαν, ἣ δὲ ἡδῦναι, καὶ ἣ μὲν συστρέψαι καὶ συντεῖναι τὸν νοῦν, ἣ δὲ ἀνεῖναι καὶ μαλάξαι, καὶ εἰς πάθος

[1] *εἰς ἄκρον* inseruit Kiessling.
[2] *καὶ* seclusi.

quent writer employed it to greater effect or imitated him with complete success.

The second kind of style is plain and simple. Its 2
artistry and power seem to consist in its resemblance to the language of ordinary speech.[1] This style had many successful exponents among the historians, the philosophers and the orators. Indeed, it was the style chosen by the genealogists, those who dealt with local history, the natural philosophers and the moral philosophers who wrote dialogues, including the entire Socratic School except Plato; and almost all those who composed political and forensic speeches chose this style. The man who perfected it and realised its potential as a distinct style was Lysias the son of Cephalus, a contemporary of Gorgias and Thucydides. I have explained what his theory was and with what success he put it into practice in my earlier treatise, and there is no need to go over the same ground again. It will be sufficient to say this only, that among themselves these men covered the whole musical scale of style with inspired zeal, choosing and perfecting the extreme and the most widely contrasted forms of it. The style of Lysias in deliberative oratory bears the same relation to that of Thucydides as the lowest to the highest note on the musical scale.[2] The latter has the power to startle the mind, the former to soothe it; the one can induce tension and strain, the other relaxation and relief; the one can express violent emotion, the other can con-

[1] Cf. *Lysias*, 2–3; 5.

[2] νήτος and ὕπατος are used to describe the position on the instrument of the string which sounded the note; and since the top string (ὑπάτη) was the longest, and the bottom string (νήτη) the shortest, they were, respectively, the lowest and the highest in pitch.

ἐκείνη προαγαγεῖν, εἰς δὲ ἦθος αὕτη καταστῆσαι. πλὴν ἀλλὰ καὶ τὸ μὲν βιάσασθαι καὶ προσαναγκάσαι τι τῆς Θουκυδίδου λέξεως ἴδιον, τὸ δ' ἀπατῆσαι καὶ κλέψαι τὰ πράγματα τῆς Λυσίου. καὶ ἡ μὲν νεωτεροποιία καὶ τὸ τολμηρὸν τῆς τοῦ συγγραφέως οἰκεῖον ἰδέας, ἡ δ' ἀσφάλεια καὶ τὸ ἀκίνδυνον τῆς τοῦ ῥήτορος. . . . . ὅτι οὐκ ἐν ἐπιτηδεύσει φαίνεται . . . . ἀνεπιτήδευτον εἶναι θέλει. κατεσκεύασται μὲν οὖν ἑκατέρα καὶ εἰς ἄκρον γε ἥκει τῆς ἰδίας κατασκευῆς· ῥέπει δὲ ἣ μὲν ἐπὶ τὸ μᾶλλον ἢ πέφυκεν εἶναι δοκεῖν, ἣ δὲ τὸ ἧττον. παραδειγμάτων δὲ καὶ ταύτης τῆς λέξεως οὐθὲν ἐν τῷ παρόντι οἶμαι δεῖν. δύο μὲν δὴ χαρακτῆρες οὗτοι λέξεως, τοσοῦτον ἀλλήλων διάφοροι κατὰ τὰς ἀγωγάς, καὶ ἄνδρες οἱ πρωτεύσαντες ἐν αὐτοῖς, οὓς διεξῆλθον, δεινοὶ μὲν ἐν τοῖς αὑτῶν ἔργοις ἀμφότεροι, καθ' ὃ δὲ ἴσοι ἀλλήλων ἦσαν, ἀτελεῖς.

3 τρίτη λέξεως ⟨ἰδέα⟩[1] ἦν ἡ μικτή τε καὶ σύνθετος ἐκ τούτων τῶν δυεῖν, ἣν ὁ μὲν πρῶτος ἁρμοσάμενος καὶ καταστήσας εἰς τὸν νῦν ὑπάρχοντα κόσμον εἴτε Θρασύμαχος ὁ Καλχηδόνιος ἦν, ὡς οἴεται Θεόφραστος, εἴτε ἄλλος τις, οὐκ ἔχω λέγειν. οἱ δὲ ἐκδεξάμενοι καὶ ἀναθρέψαντες καὶ οὐ πολὺ ἀποσχόντες τοῦ τελειῶσαι ῥητόρων μὲν Ἰσοκράτης ὁ Ἀθηναῖος ἐγένετο, φιλοσόφων δὲ

duce to moral character.[1] I need hardly say more; but further properties of Thucydides's style, however, are forcefulness and compulsion, while that of Lysias can deceive the listener and conceal the facts from him.[2] Again, Thucydides's style is characterised by daring originality,[3] whereas the orator is conventional and conservative. ⟨Thucydides's style is overtly recherché, elaborate and artificial⟩, whereas that of Lysias is apparently unstudied . . .[4] an illusion which the orator deliberately fosters. In fact both styles are artistically contrived, and each achieves perfection of its kind, the one tending to depict things as larger, the other as smaller than life-size. Here again I think that there is no need for examples at present. We have these two individual styles, so different in their effects, and I have described their most distinguished exponents, both brilliant when judged on their individual specialities, but imperfect in respect of those qualities which they possess in common.

The third kind of style was a mixture formed by 3
combining the other two. Whether the person who united them and reduced the product to its present form was Thrasymachus of Calchedon,[5] as Theophrastus thinks, or somebody else, I cannot say. But those of his successors who took this style over, developed it and virtually perfected it were Isocrates the Athenian among the orators and Plato the

1 Cf. *Lysias*, 8.
2 Cf. *Lysias*, 18.
3 Cf. Thuc. I. 102. 3.
4 Cf. *Lysias*, 8; *Isaeus*, 3; 7.
5 See note 2, pp. 31–32; p. 229.

---

1 ἰδέα inserui post Sylburg.

Πλάτων ὁ Σωκρατικός· τούτων γὰρ ἀμήχανον εὑρεῖν τῶν ἀνδρῶν ἑτέρους τινὰς ἔξω Δημοσθένους ἢ τἀναγκαῖα καὶ χρήσιμα κρεῖττον ἀσκήσαντας ἢ τὴν καλλιλογίαν καὶ τὰς ἐπιθέτους κατασκευὰς βέλτιον ἀποδειξαμένους.[1] ἡ μὲν οὖν Θρασυμάχου λέξις, εἰ δὴ[2] πηγή[3] τις ἦν ὄντως τῆς μεσότητος, αὐτὴν τὴν προαίρεσιν ἔοικεν ἔχειν σπουδῆς ἀξίαν· κέκραται γὰρ εὖ πως καὶ αὐτὸ τὸ χρήσιμον εἴληφεν ἑκατέρας. δυνάμει δὲ[4] ὡς οὐκ ἴσῃ ⟨τῇ⟩[5] βουλήσει κέχρηται, παράδειγμα ἐξ ἑνὸς τῶν δημηγορικῶν λόγων τόδε· "Ἐβουλόμην μέν, ὦ ἄνδρες Ἀθηναῖοι, μετασχεῖν ἐκείνου τοῦ χρόνου τοῦ παλαιοῦ καὶ τῶν πραγμάτων, ἡνίκα σιωπᾶν ἀπέχρη τοῖς νεωτέροις, τῶν τε πραγμάτων οὐκ ἀναγκαζόντων ἀγορεύειν καὶ τῶν πρεσβυτέρων ὀρθῶς τὴν πόλιν ἐπιτροπευόντων. ἐπειδὴ δ' εἰς τοιοῦτον ἡμᾶς ἀνέθετο χρόνον ὁ δαίμων, ὥστε ⟨ἑτέρων μὲν ἀρχόντων⟩[6] τῆς πόλεως ἀκούειν ,τὰς δὲ συμφορὰς ⟨ὑπέχειν⟩[7] αὐτοὺς καὶ τούτων τὰ μέγιστα μὴ θεῶν ἔργα εἶναι μηδὲ τῆς τύχης ἀλλὰ τῶν ἐπιμεληθέντων, ἀνάγκη λέγειν. ἢ γὰρ ἀναίσθητος ἢ καρτερικώτατός[8] ἐστιν, ὅστις ἐνεξαμαρτάνειν[9] ἑαυτὸν ἔτι παρέξει τοῖς βουλομένοις καὶ τῆς ἑτέρων ἐπιβουλῆς τε καὶ κακίας αὐτὸς ὑποσχήσει τὰς αἰτίας. ἅλις γὰρ ἡμῖν ὁ παρελθὼν χρόνος καὶ ἀντὶ μὲν εἰρήνης ἐν πολέμῳ γενέσθαι

[1] ἀποδειξαμένους Sylburg: ἀποδεξάμενος codd.
[2] εἰ δὴ Schenkl: ἢ codd.
[3] πηγή Sadée: λοιπή codd.
[4] δυνάμει δὲ ὡς Sauppe: δυναμέως · ὡς δὲ codd.
[5] τῇ inseruit Reiske.
[6] ἑτέρων μὲν ἀρχόντων lacunam supplevi.

Socratic among the philosophers: it is impossible to find any other writers, except Demosthenes, who practised the essential and ancillary virtues of this style to greater effect, or who expressed themselves in more beautiful language and adorned it more skilfully with additional touches of artistry. The style of Thrasymachus, if it was really a source of the middle type, appears to possess its peculiar qualities to an admirable degree: for it contains a happy blend of the actual merits of the other two. But performance falls short of ambition, as is seen in the following passage from one of his public speeches:[1]

"Gentlemen, I would have preferred to share in the political life of old, when young men were expected to remain silent, because their participation in debate was unnecessary and their elders managed the state's affairs efficiently. But since fate has assigned me to an age in which others rule the city and we obey them, but we ourselves suffer the disastrous consequences of their rule (for the worst of these are not the work of gods or of chance, but of human ministers), I am forced to speak. For a man who will allow himself to be continually exploited by anyone who wishes to, and will take the blame for other men's treachery and cowardice, is either a fool or a model of patient forbearance. We have had enough of the past and the change from peace to the

[1] For a stylistic appreciation of this passage, see Denniston, *Greek Prose Style*, pp. 14–15.

---

[7] *ὑπέχειν* supplevi sensum secutus.
[8] *καρτερικώτατός* Usener: *καρτερώτατός* codd.
[9] *ἐνεξαμαρτάνειν* Reiske: *ἐξαμαρτάνειν* codd.

καὶ κινδύνῳ, εἰς τόνδε τὸν χρόνον τὴν μὲν παρελθοῦσαν ἡμέραν ἀγαπῶσι, τὴν δ' ἐπιοῦσαν δεδιόσιν, ἀντὶ δ' ὁμονοίας εἰς ἔχθραν καὶ ταραχὰς πρὸς ἀλλήλους ἀφικέσθαι. καὶ τοὺς μὲν ἄλλους τὸ πλῆθος τῶν ἀγαθῶν ὑβρίζειν τε ποιεῖ καὶ στασιάζειν, ἡμεῖς δὲ μετὰ μὲν τῶν ἀγαθῶν ἐσωφρονοῦμεν, ἐν δὲ τοῖς κακοῖς ἐμάνημεν, ἃ τοὺς ἄλλους σωφρονίζειν εἴωθεν. τί δῆτα μέλλοι τις ἂν γιγνώσκειν ἢ εἰπεῖν,[1] ὅτῳ γε ⟨λείπεται τὸ⟩ [2] λυπεῖσθαι ἐπὶ τοῖς παροῦσι καὶ νομίζειν ἔχειν τι τοιοῦτον, ὡς μηδὲν ἔτι τοιοῦτον ἔσται; πρῶτον μὲν οὖν τοὺς διαφερομένους πρὸς ἀλλήλους καὶ τῶν ῥητόρων καὶ τῶν ἄλλων ἀποδείξω γε παρὰ λόγον [3] πεπονθότας πρὸς ἀλλήλους, ὅπερ ἀνάγκη τοὺς ἄνευ γνώμης φιλονικοῦντας πάσχειν· οἰόμενοι γὰρ ἐναντία λέγειν ἀλλήλοις ἀλλήλοις οὐκ αἰσθάνονται τὰ αὐτὰ πράττοντες οὐδὲ τὸν τῶν ἑτέρων λόγον ἐν τῷ σφετέρῳ[4] λόγῳ ἐνόντα. σκέψασθε γὰρ ἐξ ἀρχῆς, ἃ ζητοῦσιν ἑκάτεροι. πρῶτον μὲν ἡ πάτριος πολιτεία ταραχὴν αὐτοῖς παρέχει ῥᾴστη [5] γνωσθῆναι καὶ κοινοτάτη τοῖς πολίταις οὖσα πᾶσιν. ὁπόσα μὲν οὖν ἐπέκεινα [6] τῆς ἡμετέρας γνώμης ἐστίν, ἀκοὴν [7] ἀνάγκη λέγειν τῶν παλαιοτέρων, ὁπόσα δ' αὐτοὶ ἐπεῖδον οἱ πρεσβύτεροι, ταῦτα [δὲ] [8] παρὰ τῶν εἰδότων πυνθάνεσθαι." τοιαύτη μὲν οὖν τις ἡ Θρασυμάχειος ἑρμηνεία, μέση τοῖν δυεῖν καὶ εὔκρατος καὶ

[1] γιγνώσκειν ἢ εἰπεῖν Reiske: γιγνώσκειν εἰπεῖν codd.
[2] λείπεται τὸ inseruit Radermacher.
[3] παρὰ λόγον Usener: προλέγων codd.
[4] σφετέρῳ Cobet: ἑτέρῳ codd.

danger of war: up to now we have constantly been hankering after yesterday and dreading tomorrow. Enough, too, of the change from concord to mutual hostility and turbulence. While everyone else is made arrogant and seditious by an excess of good fortune, this had a sobering effect upon us; but we have lost our heads when faced with misfortunes, which usually have a sobering effect upon others. What, therefore, is a man going to conclude or say when he is left to contemplate the present state of affairs with dismay, while at the same time thinking that he knows how to prevent its continuance into the future? The first thing I shall point out is that those politicians and others who are engaged in argument stand in a paradoxical relationship to one another, as is inevitable when men indulge in thoughtless wrangling. For, thinking that they express opposing views, they do not see that their policies are identical and that their opponents' speeches contain the same arguments as their own. Consider from the beginning the aims of both parties. The first object of contention is the ancestral constitution, that possession which all citizens hold most in common and which is very easy to find out about. Now for events which are beyond our knowledge we must rely on accounts provided by our ancestors; as to events which our senior citizens have actually witnessed, we must learn of these from their own lips."

Such is the style of Thrasymachus, a well-blended

---

[5] ῥᾴστῃ Sylburg: ῥᾴστην codd.
[6] ἐπέκεινα Reiske: ἐκείνων codd.
[7] ἀκοὴν scripsi: ἀκούειν codd.
[8] δὲ delevi.

εἰς ⟨ἀμφο⟩τέρους [1] τοὺς χαρακτῆρας ἐπίκαιρον ἀφετήριον.

4 ⟨ἡ δὲ Ἰσο⟩κράτους [2] λέξις, ὃς μέγιστον ὄνομα ἐν τοῖς Ἕλλησιν ⟨ἐκτήσατο ἐπὶ σοφίᾳ⟩,[3] ἀγῶνα μὲν οὔτ᾽ ἴδιον οὔτε δημόσιον οὐδένα ⟨πώποτε τἀνδρὸς ἀγω⟩νισαμένου[4] γραφὰς δὲ συνταξαμένου πολλὰς καὶ καλὰς εἰς ἅπασαν ἰδέαν λόγων, ὅντινα χαρακτῆρα ἔχειν ἐφαίνετό μοι, διὰ πλειόνων μὲν ἐδήλωσα πρότερον. οὐθὲν δὲ κωλύσει καὶ νῦν ἐπὶ κεφαλαίων αὐτὰ τὰ ἀναγκαιότατα εἰπεῖν· ὅτι τῆς μὲν Λυσιακῆς λέξεως τὸ καθαρὸν ἔχει καὶ τὸ ἀκριβές· οὔτε γὰρ ἀρχαίοις οὔτε πεποιημένοις οὔτε γλωττηματικοῖς ὀνόμασιν ἀλλὰ τοῖς κοινοτάτοις καὶ συνηθεστάτοις κέχρηται. ἠθική τε καὶ πιθανὴ καὶ ἡδεῖά ἐστι καὶ πέφευγε τὴν τροπικήν, ὥσπερ ἐκείνη, φράσιν, τῆς δὲ Θουκυδίδου καὶ Γοργίου τὴν μεγαλοπρέπειαν καὶ σεμνότητα καὶ καλλιλογίαν εἴληφε. καὶ εἰς μὲν τὸ διδάξαι τὸν ἀκροατὴν σαφέστατα, ὅ τι βούλοιτο, τὴν ἁπλῆν καὶ ἀκόσμητον ἑρμηνείαν ἐπιτηδεύει τὴν Λυσίου, εἰς δὲ τὸ καταπλήξασθαι τῷ κάλλει τῶν ὀνομάτων σεμνότητά τε καὶ μεγαληγορίαν περιθεῖναι τοῖς πράγμασι τὴν ἐπίθετον καὶ κατεσκευασμένην φράσιν τῶν περὶ Γοργίαν ἐκμέμακται.[5] ἁμαρτάνει δὲ ἐν οἷς ὡραΐζεταί ποτε, τοὺς Γοργίου νεαροὺς σχηματισμοὺς ζηλοῦσα (τὰ γὰρ ἀντίθετά τε καὶ πάρισα καὶ τὰ παραπλήσια τούτοις οὔτε μετριάζοντα οὔτ᾽ ἐν [6] καιρῷ γινόμενα καταισχύνει τὴν μεγαλοπρέπειαν αὐτῆς), καὶ ἔτι μᾶλλον ἐν

[1] lacunam supplevit Sylburg.
[2] lacunam supplevit Sylburg.

mixture of the two extremes, and an appropriate starting-point for the study of both.

Isocrates acquired a very high reputation in Greece 4
for his intellectual ability. He was not a practical orator either in the law-courts or in the assembly, but composed many fine works in every medium of oratory. I have already described at some length the characteristics of his style, as I conceived them, but it will not be amiss to summarise its essential features at this point. It has the Lysianic qualities of purity and clarity, employing no archaic, poetical or recondite words but only the commonest and the most familiar.[1] It has moral tone, is persuasive and pleasant, and, like that of Lysias, avoids metaphorical expressions. It has also adopted the splendour, the dignity and the beautiful language of Thucydides and Gorgias. To instruct his hearers upon any desired subject he wishes with the greatest lucidity he employs the simple, unadorned style of Lysias; but when he wishes to astound them with the beauty of his words and to invest his theme with dignity and grandiloquence, he casts his style in the artificial and elaborate mould of the Gorgianic School. And sometimes the ornamentation is overdone when Gorgias's immature figures are imitated (for the excessive and untimely use of antithesis, balanced clauses and the like, detracts from the stately quality of the style). He is even more at fault when, in his pursuit of beauty

[1] Cf. *Isocrates*, 2.

---

[3] lacunam supplevit Radermacher.
[4] lacunam supplevit Radermacher.
[5] *ἐκμέμακται* Krüger: *ἐκμέμακεν* codd.
[6] *οὔτ' ἐν* Sadée: *οὔτε* codd.

οἷς τὴν εὐέπειαν διώκουσα καὶ τὴν εὐρυθμίαν δι' εὐλαβείας μὲν λαμβάνει τὸ συγκροῦσαι τὰ φωνήεντα τῶν γραμμάτων δι' εὐλαβείας δὲ ποιεῖται τὸ χρήσασθαί τινι τῶν τραχυνόντων. διώκει δ' ἐκ παντὸς τρόπου τὴν περίοδον οὐδὲ ταύτην στρογγύλην καὶ πυκνὴν ἀλλ' ὑπαγωγικήν τινα καὶ πλατεῖαν καὶ πολλοὺς ἀγκῶνας, ὥσπερ οἱ μὴ κατ' εὐθείας ῥέοντες ποταμοὶ ποιοῦσιν, ἐγκολπιζομένην. ταῦτα μέντοι πολλαχῇ μακροτέραν τε αὐτὴν ποιεῖ κἀναληθεστέραν ἀπαθῆ τε καὶ ⟨ἄψυχον⟩ [1] καὶ πανηγυρικὴν μᾶλλον ἢ ἐναγώνιον. τοῖς δὲ παραδείγμασιν ὀλίγον ὕστερον, ὅταν ὁ καιρὸς ἀπαιτῇ, χρήσομαι.

5 ἡ δὲ δὴ Πλατωνικὴ διάλεκτος βούλεται μὲν εἶναι καὶ αὐτὴ μῖγμα ἑκατέρων τῶν χαρακτήρων, τοῦ τε ὑψηλοῦ καὶ ἰσχνοῦ, καθάπερ εἴρηταί μοι πρότερον, πέφυκε δ' οὐχ ὁμοίως πρὸς ἀμφοτέρους τοὺς χαρακτῆρας εὐτυχής. ὅταν μὲν οὖν τὴν ἰσχνὴν καὶ ἀφελῆ καὶ ἀποίητον ἐπιτηδεύῃ φράσιν, ἐκτόπως ἡδεῖά ἐστι καὶ φιλάνθρωπος. καθαρὰ γὰρ ἀποχρώντως γίνεται καὶ διαυγής, ὥσπερ τὰ διαφανέστατα τῶν ναμάτων, ἀκριβής τε καὶ λεπτὴ παρ' ἡντινοῦν ἑτέραν τῶν [εἰς] τὴν αὐτὴν διάλεκτον εἰργασμένων. τήν τε κοινότητα διώκει τῶν ὀνομάτων καὶ τὴν σαφήνειαν ἀσκεῖ, πάσης ὑπεριδοῦσα κατασκευῆς ἐπιθέτου. ὅ τε πίνος αὐτῇ ὁ τῆς ἀρχαιότητος ἠρέμα καὶ λεληθότως ἐπιτρέχει χλοερόν τέ τι καὶ τεθηλὸς καὶ μεστὸν ὥρας ἄνθος ἀναδίδωσι. καὶ ὥσπερ ἀπὸ τῶν εὐωδεστάτων λειμώνων αὖρά τις ἡδεῖα ἐξ αὐτῆς φέρεται. καὶ οὔτε τὸ λιγυρὸν ἔοικεν ἐμφαίνειν

of sound and rhythm he carefully avoids the clashing of vowels and the use of words containing rough consonants.[1] He cultivates the period as much as possible, not the terse, compact kind, but one which follows a broad and leisurely course like a meandering river, with many curves and inlets. This often produces a tedious and unconvincing effect, robbing the speech of all feeling and life, and makes it more suited to ceremonial than to forensic oratory. I shall give examples of this style a little later, when the occasion demands.

Plato's style, too, purports to be a mixture of the 5
grand and the plain style, as I have said before,[2] but his nature did not render him equally effective in both styles. Thus when he expresses himself in plain, simple and unartificial language, his style is extraordinarily agreeable and pleasant; it becomes altogether pure and transparent, like the most pellucid of streams, and compares well in finely-drawn precision with that of any other writing in this style. It aims to use standard vocabulary and cultivates clarity, spurning all superfluous artifice; and it betrays its old-fashioned quality only by the almost imperceptible patina of age that gently steals over and imparts to it a certain verdant, burgeoning bloom full of vigour. A sweet breeze emanates from it, as from the most fragrant of meadows. Its piercing clarity seems not to give rise to garrulity, nor its

[1] See *De Compositione Verborum*, 14; 22.

[2] Chs. 5 and 6 are reproduced in the *Letter to Pompeius*, 2, so that his advocacy of Demosthenes against Plato was evidently an abiding occupation.

---

[1] ἄψυχον: lacunam supplevit Sadée.

λάλον οὔτε τὸ κομψὸν θεατρικόν. ὅταν δὲ εἰς τὴν περιττολογίαν καὶ τὸ καλλιεπεῖν, ὃ πολλάκις εἴωθε ποιεῖν, ἄμετρον ὁρμὴν λάβῃ, πολλῷ χείρων ἑαυτῆς γίνεται· καὶ γὰρ ἀηδεστέρα τῆς ἑτέρας καὶ κάκιον ἑλληνίζουσα καὶ παχυτέρα φαίνεται μελαίνει τε τὸ σαφὲς καὶ ζόφῳ ποιεῖ παραπλήσιον ἕλκει τε μακρὸν ἀποτείνασα τὸν νοῦν, συστρέψαι δέον ἐν ὀνόμασιν ὀλίγοις. ἐκχεῖται δ' εἰς ἀπειροκάλους περιφράσεις πλοῦτον ὀνομάτων ἐπιδεικνυμένη κενόν, ὑπεριδοῦσά τε τῶν κυρίων καὶ ἐν τῇ κοινῇ χρήσει κειμένων τὰ πεποιημένα ζητεῖ καὶ ξένα καὶ ἀρχαιοπρεπῆ. μάλιστα δὲ χειμάζεται περὶ τὴν τροπικὴν φράσιν, πολλὴ μὲν ἐν τοῖς ἐπιθέτοις, ἄκαιρος δ' ἐν ταῖς μετωνυμίαις, σκληρὰ δὲ καὶ οὐ σῴζουσα τὴν ἀναλογίαν ἐν ταῖς ⟨μεταφοραῖς⟩.[1] ἀλληγορίας τε περιβάλλεται πολλὰς ⟨καὶ μακράς⟩, οὔτε μέτρον ἐχούσας οὔτε καιρόν. σχήμασί τε ποιητικοῖς ἐσχάτην προσβάλλουσιν ἀηδίαν καὶ μάλιστα τοῖς Γοργιείοις ἀκαίρως καὶ μειρακιωδῶς ἐναβρύνεται. καὶ πολὺς ὁ τελέτης[2] ἐν τοῖς τοιούτοις παρ' αὐτῷ ὡς καὶ Δημήτριος ὁ Φαληρεὺς εἴρηκέ που καὶ ἄλλοι συχνοὶ πρότερον. οὐ γὰρ ἐμὸς ὁ μῦθος.

6 μηδεὶς δέ με τὰ τοιαῦτα ὑπολάβῃ λέγειν ἁπάσης καταγινώσκοντα τῆς ἐξηλλαγμένης καὶ ἐγκατασκεύου λέξεως, ᾗ κέχρηται Πλάτων· μὴ γὰρ δὴ[3] οὕτω σκαιὸς μηδ' ἀναίσθητος ἐγὼ γενοίμην, ὥστε ταύτην τὴν δόξαν ὑπὲρ ἀνδρὸς τηλικούτου λαβεῖν, ἐπεὶ πολλὰ περὶ πολλῶν οἶδα μεγάλα καὶ θαυμαστὰ

[1] μεταφοραῖς lacunam supplevit Radermacher.
[2] πολὺς ὁ τελέτης Usener: πολυτέλειά τις codd.

elegance to mere show. But when, as often, he launches unrestrainedly into impressive and decorated language, he does himself far less than full justice: for this style is less pleasing than the other, since it lacks its purity of dialect and transparency of texture. It darkens what is clear and reduces it almost to obscurity. It conveys its meaning in a long-drawn-out way when concision and brevity are called for. It abandons itself to tasteless circumlocutions and an empty show of verbal exuberance and, in defiance of correct usage and standard vocabulary, seeks artificial, exotic and archaic forms of expression. It is in figurative speech that it founders decisively: it abounds in appositions, is inopportune in its metonymies and harsh and inaccurate in its metaphors. It also admits allegories whose frequency and length are governed by no considerations of measure or occasion, and revels inappropriately and in a juvenile manner in the conceits of artificial expression, and especially in the Gorgianic figures, which can arouse the utmost displeasure. Indeed, he is quite the hierophant in these matters, as Demetrius of Phalerum and several of his predecessors said; for "the saying is not mine."[1]

But no one should suppose that in making these 6
criticisms I am condemning all the forms of unconventional and ornate style which Plato employs. I hope that I should not be so obtuse and insensitive[2] as to take this view of such a great man, for I know that he has produced many works on a variety of sub-

[1] Euripides Frag. 488 Nauck.
[2] An echo of Demosthenes, *De Corona*, 120.

---

[3] δὴ Cobet: ἂν codd.

καὶ ἀπὸ τῆς ἄκρας δυνάμεως ἐξενηνεγμένα ὑπ' αὐτοῦ· ἀλλ' ἐκεῖνο ἐνδείξασθαι βουλόμενον ὅτι τὰ τοιαῦτα ἁμαρτήματα ἐν ταῖς κατασκευαῖς εἴωθεν ἁμαρτάνειν καὶ χείρων μὲν αὐτὸς αὑτοῦ γίνεται, ὅταν τὸ μέγα διώκῃ καὶ περιττὸν ἐν τῇ φράσει, μακρῷ δέ τινι ἀμείνων, ὅταν τὴν ἰσχνὴν καὶ ἀκριβῆ καὶ δοκοῦσαν μὲν ἀποίητον εἶναι κατεσκευασμένην δ' ἀμωμήτῳ καὶ ἀφελεῖ κατασκευῇ διάλεκτον εἰσφέρῃ. ἢ γὰρ οὐδὲν ἁμαρτάνει καθάπαξ ἢ βραχύ τι κομιδῇ καὶ οὐκ ἄξιον κατηγορίας. ἐγὼ δὲ ἠξίον τηλικοῦτον ἄνδρα πεφυλάχθαι πᾶσαν ἐπιτίμησιν. ταὐτὰ [1] μέντοι καὶ οἱ κατ' αὐτὸν ἐκεῖνον γενόμενοι ὡς ἁμαρτάνοντι τῷ ἀνδρὶ ἐπιτιμῶσιν, ὧν τὰ ὀνόματα οὐθὲν δέομαι λέγειν, καὶ αὐτὸς ἑαυτῷ· τοῦτο γὰρ δὴ τὸ λαμπρότατον. ᾔσθετο γάρ, ὡς ἔοικεν, τῆς ἰδίας ἀπειροκαλίας καὶ ὄνομα ἔθετο αὐτῇ τὸ διθύραμβον, ὃ νῦν ἂν ᾐδέσθην ἐγὼ λέγειν ἀληθὲς ὄν. τοῦτο δὲ παθεῖν ἔοικεν, ὡς μὲν ἐγὼ νομίζω, τραφεὶς μὲν ἐν τοῖς Σωκρατικοῖς διαλόγοις ἰσχνοτάτοις ⟨οὖσι⟩ καὶ ἀκριβεστάτοις, οὐ μείνας δ' ἐν αὐτοῖς ἀλλὰ τῆς Γοργίου καὶ Θουκυδίδου κατασκευῆς ἐρασθείς. ὥστ' οὐθὲν ἔξω τοῦ εἰκότος ἔμελλε πείσεσθαι σπάσας τινὰ καὶ τῶν ἁμαρτημάτων ἅμα τοῖς ἀγαθοῖς, ὧν ἔχουσιν οἱ τῶν ἀνδρῶν ἐκείνων χαρακτῆρες.

7 παράδειγμα δὲ ποιοῦμαι τῆς γε ὑψηλῆς λέξεως ἐξ ἑνὸς βυβλίου τῶν πάνυ περιβοήτων, ἐν ᾧ τοὺς ἐρωτικοὺς διατίθεται λόγους ὁ Σωκράτης πρὸς ἕνα τῶν γνωρίμων Φαῖδρον, ἀφ' οὗ τὴν ἐπιγραφὴν εἴληφε τὸ βυβλίον. ἐν γὰρ δὴ τῷ συγγράμματι

jects that are great and admirable and show the highest ability. I only wish to show that he is apt to commit errors of this kind in his more elaborate passages and that he falls below his own standards when he strives to express himself in a grand and extraordinary manner, but is far better when he uses language that is plain and precise and appears natural, but really contains a certain degree of simple and unexceptionable artifice. Then he is either completely blameless or but slightly and venially at fault. But I should have expected such a great writer to have insured himself against all forms of criticism. In point of fact, contemporaries of his whose names I need not mention reproach him with this very fault; and the most striking thing is that he acknowledges it himself. He apparently noticed his own tendency towards banality, and called it his " dithyrambic " style, a term which I should have been ashamed to introduce myself at this point, apt though it is. This fault seems to me to be due to the fact that, although he was brought up on the rigorous plainness and precision of the Socratic dialogues, he did not remain constant to these, but fell in love with the artificial styles of Gorgias and Thucydides; so that it was predictable that he should absorb some of the faults of these authors' styles along with their virtues.

I am taking as an example of the elevated style a 7
passage from one of his most celebrated dialogues, in which Socrates addresses his discourse on love to one of his friends, Phaedrus, from whom the dialogue derives its title. Now this work shows him at the

[1] ταὐτὰ Usener: ταῦτα codd.

τούτῳ πολλὴν μὲν ὥραν ἔχει καὶ χαρίτων ἐστὶ μεστὰ τὰ πρῶτα ταυτί· "Ὦ φίλε Φαῖδρε, ποῖ δὴ καὶ πόθεν; Παρὰ Λυσίου, ὦ Σώκρατες, τοῦ Κεφάλου. πορεύομαι δὴ πρὸς περίπατον ἔξω τείχους. συχνὸν γὰρ ἐκεῖ διέτριψα χρόνον καθήμενος ἐξ ἑωθινοῦ" μέχρι τῆς ἀναγνώσεως τοῦ Λυσιακοῦ λόγου καὶ μετὰ τὴν ἀνάγνωσιν ἕως τινός. εἶθ', ὥσπερ ἐξ ἀέρος εὐδίου καὶ σταθεροῦ πολὺς ἄνεμος καταρραγείς, ταράττει τὸ καθαρὸν τῆς φράσεως ἐς ποιητικὴν ἐκφέρων ἀπειροκαλίαν, ἐνθένδ' ἀρξάμενος· "Ἄγετε δή, Μοῦσαι, εἴτε δι' ᾠδῆς εἶδος λίγειαι εἴτε διὰ γένος τὸ Λιγύων μουσικὸν ταύτην ἔσχετε τὴν ἐπωνυμίαν, ξύμ μοι λάβεσθε τοῦ μύθου." ὅτι δὲ ψόφοι ταῦτ' εἰσὶ καὶ διθύραμβοι, κόμπον ὀνομάτων πολὺν νοῦν δὲ ὀλίγον ἔχοντες, αὐτὸς ἐρεῖ. διεξιὼν γάρ, ἀφ' ἧς αἰτίας ἔρως ἐτίθη τῷ πάθει τοὔνομα, καὶ τῇδε χρησάμενος· "Ἡ γὰρ ἄνευ λόγου δόξης ἐπὶ τἀγαθὸν ὁρμώσης κρατήσασα ἐπιθυμία, πρὸς ἡδονὴν ἄγουσα κάλλους καὶ τῶν ἑαυτῆς συγγενῶν ἐπιθυμιῶν, ἐπὶ σωμάτων κάλλος ἐρρωμένως ῥωσθεῖσα νικήσασα ἀγωγὴ ἀπ' αὐτῆς τῆς ῥώμης ἐπωνυμίαν λαβοῦσα ἔρως ἐκλήθη" καὶ τοσαύτην ἐκμηκύνας περίφρασιν ὀλίγοις τοῖς ὀνόμασι δυναμένου περιληφθῆναι πράγματος ἐπιλαμβάνεται τῆς ἀκαιρίας τῆς αὐτὸς αὑτοῦ καί φησι· "Σιγῇ τοίνυν μου ἄκουε. τῷ ὄντι γὰρ θεῖος εἶναι ἔοικεν ὁ

---

[1] Plato, *Phaedrus*, 237A.
[2] Plato, *Phaedrus*, 238B–C.
[3] Plato, *Phaedrus*, 238D.

height of his powers, and it thus begins with a passage of infinite grace and charm:

"My dear Phaedrus, where are you going and where have you been?"

"With Lysias the son of Cephalus, Socrates; and I'm going for a walk outside the wall, as I've been sitting with him the whole morning long."

It continues up to the reading of Lysias's speech and a short way beyond. Then, like a violent wind bursting out of the calm, still air, he shatters the purity of the expression by resorting to tasteless artificiality, beginning at this point:[1]

"Come now, ye clear-voiced ('*ligeiai*') Muses, either from the nature of your song so called, or named after the musical race of the Ligurians, aid me as I tell my tale."

That this is mere high-sounding bombast, a fulsome show of words without much content, he himself will shortly admit. Having explained how the name "love" came to be used to denote "passion," in the following words:[2]

"When irrational desire has conquered the belief that impels us towards virtue, and leads us, like the force it is, towards the enjoyment of beauty and of desires which are akin to itself, this force, in drawing us strongly ("*errōmenōs*") towards physical beauty, gains strength from its own power, and so acquires its name, Love ("*Erōs*").

Using such a long circumlocution to describe a quality which could be defined in a few words, he takes himself to task for his own want of taste, saying:[3]

"Then be quiet and listen to me: for there really does seem to be a divine presence in this spot, so that

τόπος. ὥστ' ἐὰν ἄρα πολλάκις νυμφόληπτος γένωμαι προϊόντος τοῦ λόγου, μὴ θαυμάσῃς. τὰ νῦν γὰρ ⟨οὐκέ⟩τι[1] πόρρω διθυράμβων τινῶν φθέγγομαι." ⟨τάδ' οὐχ ὑ⟩π'[2] ἄλλων, ἀλλὰ τοῖς αὑτῶν λόγοις ἁλισκόμεσθα ⟨κατὰ τὴν τραγῳδί⟩αν,[2] δαιμονιώτατε Πλάτων, διθυράμβων ψόφους καὶ λήρους ἠγαπηκότες. ἃ δ' ἐν τῇ παλινῳδίᾳ τὸν ἔρωτα ἀφοσιούμενος αὖθις ὁ Σωκράτης εἴρηκεν ἐνθένδε ἀρξάμενος· "Ὁ μὲν δὴ μέγας ἡγεμὼν ἐν οὐρανῷ Ζεὺς ἐλαύνων πτηνὸν ἅρμα, πρῶτος πορεύεται διακοσμῶν πάντα καὶ ἐπιμελούμενος. τῷ δ' ἕπεται στρατιὰ θεῶν καὶ δαιμόνων κατὰ ἕνδεκα μέρη κεκοσμημένη. μένει γὰρ Ἑστία ἐν θεῶν οἴκῳ μόνη. τῶν δ' ἄλλων, ὅσοι ἐν τῷ τῶν δώδεκα θεῶν ἀριθμῷ τεταγμένοι θεοὶ ἄρχοντες ἡγοῦνται κατὰ τάξιν, ἣν ἕκαστος ἐτάχθη. πολλαὶ μὲν οὖν καὶ μακάριαι θέαι τε καὶ ἔξοδοι ἐντὸς οὐρανοῦ, ἃς θεῶν γένος εὐδαιμόνων ἐπιστρέφεται, πράττων ἕκαστος δι' αὑτοῦ τὰ αὑτῶν. ἕπεται δ' αἰεὶ ὁ θέλων τε καὶ δυνάμενος· φθόνος γὰρ ἔξω θείου χοροῦ ἵσταται." ταῦτα καὶ τὰ ὅμοια τούτοις, ἃ πολλά ἐστιν, εἰ λάβοι μέλη καὶ ῥυθμοὺς ὥσπερ οἱ διθύραμβοι καὶ τὰ ὑπορχήματα, τοῖς Πινδάρου ποιήμασιν ἐοικέναι δόξειεν ἂν τοῖς εἰς τὸν ἥλιον εἰρημένοις, ὥς γ' ἐμοὶ φαίνεται· "Ἀκτὶς ἀελίου, τί πολύσκοπ' ἐμήσω θοῶν[3] μᾶτερ[4] ὀμμάτων; ἄστρον ὑπέρτατον, ἐν

[1] lacunam supplevit Sylburg.
[2] lacunas supplevit Porson.
[3] θοῶν Bergk: θεῶ codd.
[4] μᾶτερ Boissonade: μ'ἅτερ M μ'ἀτερ B μ'ἅτερ P.

you must not be surprised if, as my discourse proceeds, I frequently become as one possessed; for my language is already not far removed from that of dithyrambic poetry."

> "Thus not by others' voices, but our own,
> Are we convicted"

—as the poet said,[1] divine Plato, of being infatuated with high-sounding but idle noises. Socrates begins his recantation, in which he repudiates love, with these words:[2]

"And behold, there is the great leader in heaven, Zeus, driving his winged chariot. Everything comes under his ordering and tending hand as he proceeds at the head of the host of gods and daemons, marshalled in eleven companies: for Hestia tarries alone in their heavenly abode. Of the rest, all who rank among the twelve sovereign gods lead their several companies, each according to his appointed position. There are many happy spectacles and processions to be seen in heaven, in which the blessed gods pass to and fro, each going about his work. And any who will and can may follow; for envy has no place in the divine choir."

In my opinion, this and many other similar passages, if given metrical rhythm and accompanied by music like the dithyrambs and choral odes of poetry, would resemble the poem which Pindar addressed to the Sun:[3]

"Ray of the Sun, mother of swift Sight, far-seeing one, what plan have you devised? Mightiest of the

[1] Aeschylus Frag. 135 Nauck.
[2] Plato, *Phaedrus*, 246E–247A.
[3] Frag. 107 Bergk.

ἁμέρᾳ κλεπτόμενον ἔθηκας ἀμάχανον ἰσχὺν πτανὸν ἀνδράσι καὶ σοφίας ὁδόν, ἐπίσκοτον ἀτραπὸν ἐσσυμένα. ἐλαύνεις τι νεώτερον ἢ πάρος; ἀλλά σε πρὸς Διὸς ἱπποσόα θοάς, ἱκετεύω, ἀπήμονα ἐς οἶμον [1] τινὰ τράποιο [2] Θήβαις, ὦ πότνια, πάγκοινον τέρας. πολέμου δ' εἰ σᾶμα [3] φέρεις τινὸς ἢ καρποῦ φθίσιν ἢ νιφετοῦ σθένος ὑπέρφατον ἢ στάσιν οὐλομέναν ἢ πόντου κενεῶσιν ἀμ πέδον ἢ παγετὸν χθονὸς ἢ νότιον θέρος ὕδατι ζακότῳ διερὸν [4] ἢ γαῖαν κατακλύσαισα [5] θήσεις [6] ἀνδρῶν νέον ἐξ ἀρχᾶς [7] γένος, ὀλοφύ⟨ρομαι οὐ⟩δὲν [8] ὅ,τι πάντων μέτα πείσομαι." [9] κἀνταῦθα οὐ⟨κ ἄκαιρος ἡ ἀλ⟩ληγορία, [10] ὡς παρὰ Πλάτωνι;

8 ἀλλὰ γάρ, ἵνα μὴ ⟨πέρα τοῦ δέοντος⟩ [11] ὁ λόγος μοι προβῇ, Πλάτωνα μὲν ἐάσω, πορεύσομαι δ' ἐπὶ τὸν Δημοσθένην, οὗ δὴ χάριν τούς τε χαρακτῆρας τῆς λέξεως, οὓς ἡγούμην εἶναι κρατίστους, καὶ τοὺς δυναστεύσαντας ἐν αὐτοῖς κατηριθμησάμην, οὐχ ἅπαντας· Ἀντίφων γὰρ δὴ καὶ Θεόδωρος καὶ Πολυκράτης Ἰσαῖός τε καὶ Ζωίλος καὶ Ἀναξιμένης καὶ οἱ κατὰ τοὺς αὐτοὺς γενόμενοι τούτοις χρόνους οὐθὲν οὔτε καινὸν οὔτε περιττὸν ἐπετήδευσαν, ἀλλὰ ἀπὸ τούτων τῶν χαρακτήρων καὶ παρὰ τούτους τοὺς κανόνας τὰς ἑαυτῶν λέξεις

[1] οἶμον Hermann: ὄλβον codd.
[2] τράποιο Sylburg: τρόποιο codd.
[3] δ' εἰ σᾶμα Hermann: δὶς ἅμα codd.
[4] διερὸν Sylburg: ἱερὸν codd.
[5] κατακλύσαισα Boeckh: κατακλύσασα M.
[6] θήσεις Barnes: θήσει codd.
[7] ἀρχᾶς Boeckh: ἀρχῆς codd.
[8] lacunam supplevit Hermann.
[9] μέτα πείσομαι Hermann: μεταπείσομαι codd.

stars, stealing away by day you have rendered your fantastic power elusive to men and deprived them of the way to knowledge as you rush along your darkened course. Art thou bringing upon us some disaster unknown? Yet, by Zeus, I beg thee, thou swift driver of steeds, turn the world-wide portent along some path that brings no pain to Thebes. But if thou art bringing a sign of some war, or of a blight to crops, or of an unspeakably violent snowstorm, or a destructive civil war, or again of emptying of sea over land, or earth-binding frost, or the hot south wind saturated with raging rain; or if thou wilt flood the earth and place upon it a new race of men to begin again, I lament for nothing that I shall suffer with the rest of mankind."

In this, as in the Plato passage, is not the imagery inappropriate?

But I must not prolong my essay unduly. I shall 8
therefore leave Plato and proceed to Demosthenes, since it is on his account that I have enumerated the individual types of style which I considered to be the cardinal ones, and their most able exponents. The list was not exhaustive: I excluded men like Antiphon,[1] Theodorus,[2] Polycrates,[3] Isaeus, Zoilus [4] and Anaximenes [5] and their contemporaries because they did not cultivate any new or striking features but fashioned their styles according to these types and

[1] See note 1, p. 228.
[2] See note 2, p. 226.
[3] See note 3, p. 228.
[4] See note 5, p. 229.
[5] See note 3, p. 226.

---

[10] lacunam supplevit Radermacher.
[11] lacunam supplevit Sadée post Krüger.

κατεσκεύασαν. τοιαύτην δὴ καταλαβὼν τὴν πολιτικὴν λέξιν ὁ Δημοσθένης οὕτω κεκινημένην ποικίλως, καὶ τηλικούτοις ἐπεισελθὼν ἀνδράσιν ἑνὸς μὲν οὐθενὸς ἠξίωσε γενέσθαι ζηλωτὴς οὔτε χαρακτῆρος οὔτε ἀνδρός, ἡμιέργους τινὰς ἅπαντας οἰόμενος εἶναι καὶ ἀτελεῖς, ἐξ ἁπάντων δ' αὐτῶν ὅσα κράτιστα καὶ χρησιμώτατα ἦν, ἐκλεγόμενος συνύφαινε καὶ μίαν ἐκ πολλῶν διάλεκτον ἀπετέλει, μεγαλοπρεπῆ λιτήν, περιττὴν ἀπέριττον, ἐξηλλαγμένην συνήθη, πανηγυρικὴν ἀληθινήν, αὐστηρὰν ἱλαράν, σύντονον ἀνειμένην, ἡδεῖαν πικράν, ἠθικὴν παθητικήν, οὐδὲν διαλλάττουσαν τοῦ μεμυθευμένου παρὰ τοῖς ἀρχαίοις ποιηταῖς Πρωτέως, ὃς ἅπασαν ἰδέαν μορφῆς ἀμογητὶ μετελάμβανεν, εἴτε θεὸς ἢ δαίμων τις ἐκεῖνος ἄρα ἦν παρακρουόμενος ὄψεις τὰς ἀνθρωπίνας εἴτε διαλέκτου ποικίλον τι χρῶμα ἐν ἀνδρὶ σοφῷ, πάσης ἀπατηλὸν ἀκοῆς, ὃ μᾶλλον ἄν τις εἰκάσειεν, ἐπειδὴ ταπεινὰς καὶ ἀσχήμονας ὄψεις οὔτε θεοῖς οὔτε δαίμοσι προσάπτειν ὅσιον. ἐγὼ μὲν ⟨δὴ⟩ [1] τοιαύτην τινὰ δόξαν ὑπὲρ τῆς Δημοσθένους λέξεως ἔχω καὶ τὸν χαρακτῆρα τοῦτον ἀποδίδωμι αὐτῷ τὸν ἐξ ἁπάσης μικτὸν ἰδέας.

9 εἰ δὲ τὰ προσήκοντα ἔγνωκα, πάρεστι τῷ βουλομένῳ σκοπεῖν ἐπ' αὐτῶν ποιουμένῳ [2] τῶν παραδειγμάτων τὴν ἐξέτασιν. ἃ μὲν οὖν παρὰ τὸν Θουκυδίδου χαρακτῆρα κατεσκεύασται τῷ ῥήτορι, τοιάδε τινά ἐστιν· "Πολλῶν, ὦ ἄνδρες Ἀθηναῖοι, λόγων γινομένων ὀλίγου δεῖν καθ'

[1] δὴ inseruit Sadée.
[2] ποιουμένῳ Sylburg: ποιουμένων codd.

the rules governing them. Thus political oratory had gone through a variety of changes when Demosthenes came on the scene. He found himself following in the footsteps of some illustrious men, but refused to make any single orator or any single style his model, for he considered every one to be incomplete and imperfect. Instead he selected the best and most useful elements from all of them, weaving them together to make a single, perfect, composite style embracing the opposite qualities of grandeur and simplicity, the elaborate and the plain, the strange and the familiar, the ceremonial and the practical, the serious and the light-hearted, the intense and the relaxed, the sweet and the bitter, the sober and the emotional. It thus has a character not at all unlike that of Proteus as portrayed by the mythological poets, who effortlessly assumed every kind of shape, being either a god or superhuman, with the power to deceive human eyes, or a clever man with the power to vary his speech and so beguile every ear: the latter alternative seeming the more likely, since it is irreverent to attribute mean and unbecoming appearances to gods and superhuman beings. This, then, is my opinion of Demosthenes's diction, and I ascribe to him a style which is a mixture of every form.

If I have formed a proper judgment of him, the student can learn about the style of Demosthenes simply by studying examples. The following passage illustrates the Thucydidean elements in his composition:[1] 9

" Many speeches, Athenians, are made in all but every assembly about the outrages which Philip has

[1] *Phil.* iii. 110.

ἑκάστην ἐκκλησίαν περὶ ὧν Φίλιππος, ἀφ᾽ οὗ τὴν εἰρήνην ἐποιήσατο, οὐ μόνον ὑμᾶς ἀλλὰ καὶ τοὺς ἄλλους ⟨Ἕλληνας⟩ [1] ἀδικεῖ, καὶ πάντων εὖ οἶδ᾽ ὅτι φησάντων γ᾽ ἄν, εἰ καὶ μὴ ποιοῦσι τοῦτο, καὶ λέγειν δεῖν καὶ πράττειν, ὅπως ἐκεῖνος παύσεται τῆς ὕβρεως καὶ δίκην δώσει, εἰς τοῦτο ὑπηγμένα πάντα τὰ πράγματα καὶ προειμένα ὁρῶ, ὥστε δέδοικα, μὴ βλάσφημον μὲν εἰπεῖν ἀληθὲς δὲ ᾖ· εἰ καὶ λέγειν ἅπαντες ἐβούλοντο οἱ παριόντες καὶ χειροτονεῖν ὑμεῖς, ἐξ ὧν ὡς φαυλότατα τὰ πράγματα ἤμελλεν ἕξειν, οὐκ ἂν ἡγοῦμαι δύνασθαι χεῖρον ἢ νῦν διατεθῆναι." κατὰ τί δὴ ταύτην ἡγοῦμαι τὴν λέξιν ἐοικέναι τῇ Θουκυδίδου; καθ᾽ ὃ κἀκείνην πείθομαι μάλιστα διαφέρειν τῶν ἄλλων. τουτὶ δ᾽ ἔστι τὸ μὴ κατ᾽ εὐθεῖαν ἑρμηνείαν ἐξενηνέχθαι τὰ νοήματα μηδ᾽, ὡς ἔστι τοῖς ἄλλοις σύνηθες λέγειν, ἁπλῶς καὶ ἀφελῶς, ἀλλὰ ἐξηλλάχθαι καὶ ἀπεστράφθαι τὴν διάλεκτον ἐκ τῶν ἐν ἔθει καὶ κατὰ φύσιν εἰς τὰ μὴ συνήθη τοῖς πολλοῖς μηδ᾽ ὡς ἡ φύσις ἀπαιτεῖ. ὃ δὲ λέγω, τοιοῦτόν ἐστιν. ἁπλῶς ἂν ὁ λόγος ἦν [2] καὶ κατ᾽ εὐθεῖαν ἑρμηνείαν ἐκφερόμενος, εἴ τις οὕτως κατεσκεύασεν αὐτόν· "πολλῶν, ὦ ἄνδρες Ἀθηναῖοι, λόγων γιγνομένων καθ᾽ ἑκάστην σχεδὸν ἐκκλησίαν, περὶ ὧν ἀδικεῖ Φίλιππος ὑμᾶς τε καὶ τοὺς ⟨ἄλλους⟩ [3] Ἕλληνας, ἀφ᾽ οὗ τὴν εἰρήνην ἐποιήσατο." νυνὶ δὲ τό τε ὀλίγου δεῖν παραληφθὲν ἀντὶ τοῦ σχεδὸν καὶ τὸ ἀδικεῖ Φίλιππος διαιρεθὲν καὶ διὰ μακροῦ τὴν ἀκολουθίαν κομισάμενον καὶ τὸ οὐ μόνον ὑμᾶς

[1] Ἕλληνας inseruit Sylburg ex Demosthene.
[2] ἦν Sylburg: ἐστὶ codd.

been committing not only against you but against the rest of Greece ever since he made peace with us; and I am sure that everyone would have said though they do not actually do so, that our counsels and our actions should be directed towards curbing his arrogance and exacting requital from him. Yet I see that all our affairs have been so half-heartedly and negligently conducted, that I fear it is a harsh truth to say, that if all your speakers had wished to propose, and you to approve, measures designed to weaken our power as much as possible, we could not, I think, be worse off than we are now."

In what respect do I consider this style to resemble that of Thucydides? In that which I believe most distinguishes Thucydides's style from others: the expression of thought by indirect means, not simply and plainly, as is the normal practice of other writers, but in language removed and divorced from what is customary and natural and containing instead expressions which are unfamiliar to most people and not what nature demands. This is what I mean. A simple arrangement of the sentence, which would convey its meaning directly, would have been as follows:

"There have been many speeches, Athenians, at almost every meeting of this assembly on the subject of Philip's outrages against you and the rest of Greece ever since he made peace with us."

In Demosthenes's version "all but" has been preferred to "almost" and the clause referring to Philip's outrages has been broken up and the sequence of thought delayed for some time; and phrase "not

---

[3] ἄλλους inseruit Sylburg.

ἀλλὰ καὶ τοὺς ἄλλους Ἕλληνας, δυνάμενον καὶ χωρὶς ἀποφάσεως διὰ τῆς συπλοκῆς μόνης τὸ πρᾶγμα δηλῶσαι, τοῦ συνήθους ἐξηλλαγμένην καὶ περίεργον πεποίηκε τὴν λέξιν. ὁμοίως δὲ καὶ ⟨τὸ⟩ [1] ἐπιλεγόμενον τούτῳ, εἰ μὲν ἁπλῶς καὶ ἀπεριέργως ἔδει ῥηθῆναι, τοῦτον ἂν δή που τὸν τρόπον ἀπήγ⟨γελτο· "κ⟩αὶ [2] πάντων λεγόντων, καὶ εἴ τινες τοῦτο μὴ ποιοῦσιν, ὅτι δεῖ καὶ λέγειν καὶ πράττειν ταῦτα, ἐξ ὧν ἐκεῖνος παύσεται τῆς ὕβρεως καὶ δίκην δώσει." οὕτω δὲ ἐξενεχθέν· "καὶ πάντων εὖ οἶδ' ὅτι φησάντων γ' ἄν" οὐ σῴζει τὴν εὐθεῖαν τῆς λέξεως ὁδόν. τό τε γὰρ οἶδ' ὅτι χώραν οὐκ ἀναγκαίαν εἶχε, καὶ τὸ φησάντων γ' ἂν ἀντὶ τοῦ φασκόντων παρειλημμένον οὐ τὴν ἀφελῆ διάλεκτον ἀλλὰ τὴν ἐξηλλαγμένην καὶ περίεργον ἐμφαίνει. ὅμοια δὲ τούτοις ἐστὶ κἀκεῖνα· "εἶτ' οἴεσθε, οἳ μὲν οὐδὲν ἂν αὐτὸν ἠδυνήθησαν ποιῆσαι κακόν, αὐτοὶ δὲ μὴ παθεῖν ἐφυλάξαντο ἂν ἴσως, τούτους μὲν ἐξαπατᾶν αἱρεῖσθαι μᾶλλον ἢ προλέγοντα βιάζεσθαι;" ἐνταυθοῖ γὰρ οὐθὲν ἂν εἶχε περίεργον ἡ λέξις οὐδὲ σκολιόν, εἰ τοῦτον ἐξήνεγκε τὸν τρόπον· "εἶτ' οἴεσθε αὐτόν, οὓς μὲν ἑώρα μηδὲν δυναμένους αὐτὸν διαθεῖναι κάκιον, φυλαξαμένους δὲ ἂν ἴσως μὴ παθεῖν, τούτους μὲν ἐξαπατᾶν αἱρεῖσθαι μᾶλλον ἢ προλέγοντα βιάζεσθαι;" ἐναλλαγείσης δὲ τῆς πτώσεως καὶ τῶν συνδέσμων πολλῶν εἰς βραχὺ συναχθέντων, οἶμαι, περίεργός τε καὶ ἀσυνήθης καὶ ἐξηλλαγμένη γέγονεν ἡ διάλεκτος. ἔτι κἀκεῖνα

[1] τὸ inseruit Sylburg.
[2] lacunam supplevit Sylburg.

only against you but against the rest of Greece" could express the sense without the negative, by means of a simple conjunction. These devices have made the diction unfamiliar and laboured. So too with the sequel: the way to express it in a simple and uncomplicated manner would have been:

"And everyone is saying, even if some do not act upon their words, that our counsels and our actions should be aimed towards making him stop behaving violently and pay for his misdeeds."

Demosthenes's rendering, "I am sure that everyone," fails to convey the sense directly: "I am sure" need not be there; and "would have said" instead of "says" produces a strange and laboured expression instead of a simple one. What follows is similar:[1]

"Then do you think that the people who would have been unable to do him any harm, and would presumably have taken care to avoid trouble themselves, would be the ones he chooses to trick rather than declare war upon them first?"

There would have been nothing laboured or tortuous about this sentence if it had been written in this way:

"Then do you think that the people who he saw were unable to damage his position and would be presumably concerned to avoid trouble, would be the ones he chooses to trick rather than declare war upon them first?"

By changing the case of the relative and cramming a lot of connectives into a narrow space he has, I think, made the style laboured, unfamiliar and strange. The same characteristics are to be found in this passage:[2]

[1] *Phil.* iii. 13. [2] *Against Midias*, 69.

τῆς αὐτῆς ἐστιν ἰδέας· "νῦν δὲ τοῦτο μὲν οὐκ ἐποίησεν, ἐν ᾧ τὸν δῆμον ἐτίμησεν ἄν, οὐδ' ἐνεανιεύσατο τοιοῦτον οὐδέν. ἐμοὶ δέ, ὅς, εἴτε τις, ὦ ἄνδρες Ἀθηναῖοι, βούλεται νομίσαι μανίαν (μανία γὰρ ἴσως ἐστὶν ὑπὲρ δύναμίν τι ποιεῖν), εἴτε καὶ φιλοτιμίαν, χορηγὸς ὑπέστην, οὕτω φανερῶς ⟨καὶ μιαρῶς⟩ ἐπηρεάζων παρηκολούθησεν, ὥστε μηδὲ τῶν ἱερῶν ἱματίων μηδὲ τοῦ χοροῦ μηδὲ τοῦ σώματος τὼ χεῖρε τελευτῶν ἀποσχέσθαι μου." τί δὴ πάλιν ἐστὶν ἐν τούτοις τὸ συντάραττον τὴν κατὰ φύσιν ἀπαγγελίαν; πρῶτον μὲν τό, πρὶν ἀπαρτίσαι τὸ ἡγούμενον εἴτε νόημα χρὴ λέγειν εἴτε κῶλον, ἕτερον παρεμβαλεῖν καὶ μηδὲ τοῦ δευτέρου τέλος ἔχοντος τὸ τρίτον ἐπιζεῦξαι, εἶτα τὴν τοῦ δευτέρου νοήματος ἀκολουθίαν ἐπὶ τῷ τρίτῳ τέλος εἰληφότι θεῖναι, κἄπειτα ἐπὶ πᾶσιν, ὃ τοῦ πρώτου μέρος ἦν, διὰ μακροῦ καὶ οὐκέτι τῆς διανοίας αὐτὸ προσδεχομένης ἀποδοῦναι. Ἐμοὶ δὲ ὃς—οὔπω τοῦτο τέλος ἔχει—εἴτε τις, ὦ ⟨ἄνδρες⟩ Ἀθηναῖοι, βούλεται νομίσαι μανίαν—ἕτερον τοῦτο κεχωρισμένον τοῦ προτέρου ἀτελὲς καὶ αὐτό—μανία γὰρ ἴσως ἐστὶν ὑπὲρ δύναμίν τι ποιεῖν—οὐδετέρου τοῦτο πάλιν τῶν προειρημένων μέρος ἀλλ' αὐτὸ καθ' αὑτό· κεφαλαιώδης γάρ τίς ἐστιν ἀπόφασις—ἢ φιλοτιμίαν [1] τοῦτο δὲ τοῦ δευτέρου μέρος ἦν τοῦ εἴτε τις βούλεται νομίσαι μανίαν. τὸ δ' ἐπὶ τούτοις λεγόμενον ἅπασι [2] τὸ χορηγὸς ὑπέστην τοῦ πρώτου μέρος ἦν τοῦ ἐμοὶ δέ, ὅς. μυρία τοιαῦτά ἐστι παρὰ Δημοσθένει καὶ μάλιστα ἐν τοῖς κατὰ Φιλίππου λόγοις, μᾶλλον δὲ ⟨ὀλίγα μὲν ἐν τοῖς

" But in the event he did not do what the people would have honoured him for, nor make any such impulsive promise; but my footsteps, Athenians, when I had undertaken the duty of choregus—whether you like to call it madness (since it is madness, I suppose, to attempt something beyond one's powers), or ambition—he dogged with such blatant and foul persecution that in the end he could not keep his hands off my sacred robes, the chorus or my person."

What is it that destroys the natural expression in this as before? In the first place, before rounding off the first idea (or clause if it should be so called), a second idea is introduced; then a third is subjoined before the second is complete, and material belonging to the second is tacked on after the third has been completed; and at the very end the remains of the first subject, after a long interval, are added when the sense can no longer accommodate it. The phrase " my footsteps, Athenians, . . ." is incomplete; " whether you like to call it madness " is a new idea, separated from the first and itself incomplete; then " since it is madness, I suppose, to attempt something beyond one's powers again is not related to either of the preceding ideas but is isolated, a sort of aphoristic statement. Then " ambition " belongs to the second idea, " whether you like to call it madness." The sequel to all this, " I had undertaken the duty of choregus," belongs to the first part, beginning with " but my footsteps . . ." There are countless examples of this kind of construction in Demosthenes, particularly in the speeches against Philip; or rather,

---

[1] ἦ φιλοτμίαν Usener: ἡ φιλοτιμία codd.
[2] ἅπασι Vliet: ἅπαν codd.

συμβουλευτικοῖς τὰ⟩ [1] μὴ οὕτως ἔχοντα πλὴν ἑνὸς λόγου τοῦ περὶ Ἁλοννήσου, πολλὰ δὲ καὶ ἐν τοῖς δικανικοῖς ἀγῶσι τοῖς γε οὖν δημοσίοις. καὶ σχεδὸν ἔν τε τούτοις καὶ ταῖς δημηγορίαις, ᾧπερ ἔφην, ἂν διαγνοίης σημείῳ προχειροτάτῳ τὸν Δημοσθένους χαρακτῆρα. τῷ δὲ ἧττον ἢ μᾶλλον αὐτοῖς κεχρῆσθαι τὸν ἄνδρα πρὸς τὰς φύσεις ἀποβλέποντα τῶν ὑποθέσεων καὶ τὰς ἀξιώσεις τῶν προσώπων πλανηθήσεταί τις· ὅπερ ἴσως οὐκ ἄλογον.

10 φέρε δὴ καὶ τίνι διαλλάττει τῆς Θουκυδίδου λέξεως ἡ Δημοσθένους ἡ παρὰ τὸν αὐτὸν κατεσκευασμένη χαρακτῆρα, εἴπωμεν· ἀπαιτεῖ γὰρ ὁ λόγος. οὐχὶ τῷ ποιῷ μὰ Δία· τοῦτο μὲν γὰρ ὁμοίως ἐπιτηδεύουσιν ἀμφότεροι, λέγω δὲ τὸ ἐξαλλάττειν ἐκ τοῦ συνήθους καὶ μὴ τὸ κοινὸν ἀλλὰ τὸ περιττὸν διώκειν· τῷ δὲ ποσῷ καὶ ἔτι μᾶλλον τοῖς καιροῖς. ὃ μὲν γὰρ ἀταμιεύτως τῇ κατασκευῇ κέχρηται καὶ ἄγεται μᾶλλον ὑπ' αὐτῆς ἢ ⟨αὐτὸς⟩ [2] ἄγει καὶ οὐδὲ τὸν καιρὸν αὐτῆς ἐπίσταται λαβεῖν δεξιῶς, ἀλλὰ καὶ παρὰ τοῦτον πολλάκις ἁμαρτάνει. καθ' ὃ ἡ μὲν ἀμετρία τῆς ἐξαλλαγῆς ἀσαφῆ ποιεῖ τὴν λέξιν αὐτοῦ, τὸ δὲ μὴ κρατεῖν τῶν καιρῶν ἀηδῆ.[3] ὁ δὲ ῥήτωρ τοῦ τε [4] ἀρκοῦντος στοχάζεται καὶ τοὺς καιροὺς συμμετρεῖται οὐκ εἰς ἀνάθημα καὶ κτῆμα κα⟨τασκευάζων⟩ [5]

[1] lacunam indicavit Sylburg: ὀλίγα μὲν ἐν τοῖς συμβουλευτικοῖς τὰ supplevi.

[2] αὐτὸς inseruit Sylburg.

[3] ἀηδῆ Sylburg: ἀμηδῆ BP.

[4] τε Sylburg: δὲ codd.

there are few political speeches in which examples will not be found, the speech *On Halonnesus* being the solitary exception.[1] It is also found extensively in those of his speeches that were delivered in public actions. Broadly speaking, these and his political speeches provide the readiest illustration, in the manner I have described, of the style that is characteristically Demosthenic. But anyone who thinks that he adapted it, giving prominence to some aspects and suppressing others according to the nature of the subject and the requirements of the characters involved, will be in error; which is perhaps not unreasonable.

Now let me describe, as my thesis demands, in what 10
respects the style of Demosthenes, which has the same basic character as that of Thucydides, differs from it. The difference is not, of course, one of quality: both men cultivate the same manner of expression—I mean the pursuit of unusual and striking instead of common language. It is a matter of degree, and, even more, of choice of circumstances. Thucydides's use of this style is unrestrained: instead of controlling it he is carried away by it. He is not adept at seizing on the right occasion for its use, but often misses it. Thus his excessive use of far-fetched words results in obscurity, while his failure to choose opportune times for their use has a disagreeable effect. But the orator's aim is to satisfy the special needs of his case, and he makes his style conform to this practical requirement, not solely to that of per-

[1] An interesting observation since the genuineness of this speech has been often questioned.

[5] lacunam supplevit Sylburg.

τὴν λέξιν μόνον ὥσπερ ὁ συγγραφεύς, ἀλλὰ καὶ εἰς χρῆσιν. ὥστε οὔτε τὸ σαφὲς ἐκβέβηκεν, οὗ πρώτου τοῖς ἐναγωνίοις λόγοις δεῖ, τό τε δεινὸς εἶναι δοκεῖν, ἐφ' ᾧ μάλιστα φαίνεται σπουδάζων, προσείληφε. τοιαῦτα μὲν δή τινά ἐστιν, ἃ παρὰ τὸν ὑψηλὸν καὶ ἐγκατάσκευον καὶ ἐξηλλαγμένον τοῦ συνήθους χαρακτῆρα,[1] οὗ τὸ κράτος ἅπαν ἦν ἐν τῇ δεινότητι, καὶ Θουκυδίδην τὸν ἐν αὐτῷ πρωτεύσαντα[2] μιμούμενος ὁ Δημοσθένης κατεσκεύακεν.

11 ἃ δὲ παρὰ τὸν ἰσχνόν[3] τε καὶ ἀκριβῆ καὶ καθαρὸν [καὶ ζηλωτὸν][4] . . . ⟨ὃς⟩[5] ἀπὸ τοῦ διαλάμψαντος ἐν αὐτῷ Λυσιακὸς ἂν[6] εἰκότως λέγοιτο, τοιαῦτα. κωλύσει δ' οὐθέν, ἴσως δὲ καὶ χαριεστέραν ποιήσει τὴν θεωρίαν τεθεῖσα πρῶτον ἡ Λυσίου λέξις, ᾗ τὴν Δημοσθένους ἐοικέναι πείθομαι, διήγησίν τινα περιέχουσα ὑβριστικήν· "Ἄρχιππος γὰρ οὑτοσί, ὦ ἄνδρες Ἀθηναῖοι, ἀπεδύσατο μὲν εἰς τὴν αὐτὴν παλαίστραν, οὗπερ καὶ Τῖσις ὁ φεύγων τὴν δίκην. ὀργῆς δὲ γενομένης ἐς σκώμματά τε αὐτοῖς καὶ ἀντιλογίαν καὶ ἔχθραν καὶ λοιδορίαν κατέστησαν. ἔστιν οὖν Πυθέας ἐραστὴς μὲν τοῦ μειρακίου (πάντα γὰρ εἰρήσεται τἀληθῆ πρὸς ὑμᾶς), ἐπίτροπος δὲ ὑπὸ τοῦ πατρὸς καταλελειμμένος. οὗτος, ἐπειδὴ Τῖσις πρὸς αὐτὸν ἐν τῇ παλαίστρᾳ λοιδορίαν διηγήσατο, βουλόμενος χαρίζεσθαι καὶ δοκεῖν δεινὸς καὶ ἐπίβουλος εἶναι, ἐκέλευσεν αὐτόν, ὡς ἡμεῖς ἔκ τε

[1] χαρακτῆρα Sylburg: χαρακτῆρος codd.
[2] πρωτεύσαντα Reiske: πείσαντα codd.
[3] ἰσχνόν Kiessling: ἰσχυρόν M.

manent literary value, which the historian had in mind.[1] Accordingly he never abandons clarity, which is the first requisite of forensic oratory;[2] while in addition he earns a reputation for eloquence, which is clearly his primary object. These are some of the ways in which Demosthenes fashioned his language differently from the grand, artificial and unfamiliar style, whose power lies entirely in its rhetorical brilliance, and from his model Thucydides, its foremost exponent.

11 The qualities of this may be thus described, and contrasted with the plainness, precision and purity which should be imitated in that style which might be called "Lysianic" after its most distinguished exemplar. There will be no objection—rather it will probably enhance the reader's pleasure—if I first quote a passage of Lysias which I think resembles Demosthenes in its style. It comprises a narrative concerning a case of assault.[3]

"My client Archippus, Athenians, went to take exercise in the same gymnasium as Tisis, the defendant in this case. They had a quarrel, which led to mutual abuse and argument and ended in hostility and recrimination. Now Pytheas is in love with the lad (you will be told the whole truth), and had been appointed his guardian by his father. When Tisis told him about the exchange of insults in the gymnasium, Pytheas, wishing to please him and to appear a clever and conspiratorial fellow, advised him, as we

[1] Thucydides, i. 22. 4.
[2] Cf. Aristotle, *Rhetoric* iii. 2. 1.
[3] Frag. 232 Scheibe.

[4] καὶ ζηλωτὸν delevi. [5] ὃς supplevit Martin.
[6] δ'ἂν MBPv: om. δ' Martin.

τῶν πεπραγμένων ᾐσθήμεθα καὶ τῶν εὖ εἰδότων ἐπυθόμεθα, ἐν μὲν τῷ παρόντι διαλλαγῆναι, σκοπεῖν δέ, ὅπως αὐτὸν μόνον που λήψεται. πεισθεὶς δὲ ταῦτα καὶ διαλλαγεὶς [1] καὶ χρώμενος καὶ προσποιούμενος ἐπιτήδειος εἶναι εἰς τοῦτο μανίας τηλικοῦτος ὢν ἀφίστατο, ⟨ὥσθ' ὁπό⟩τ' [2] ἐτύγχανε μὲν οὖσα ἱπποδρομία Ἀνακείων ⟨κατέλαβε⟩ [3] δ' αὐτὸν μετ' ἐμοῦ παρὰ τὴν θύραν παριόντα· ⟨γείτονες γὰρ⟩ [4] ἀλλήλων τυγχάνουσιν ὄντες· τὸ μὲν πρῶτον ⟨συνδειπνεῖν⟩ [5] ἐκέλευεν, ἐπειδὴ δὲ οὐκ ἠθέλησεν ⟨ἐδεήθη ἥκειν αὐτὸν⟩ [6] ἐπὶ κῶμον, λέγων ὅτι μεθ' αὐτοῦ καὶ τὸ . . . . [7] δειπνήσαντες οὖν ἤδη συσκοτάζοντος ἐλθόντες κόπτομεν τὴν θύραν. οἳ δ' ἡμᾶς ἐκέλευον εἰσιέναι ἐπειδὴ δὲ ἔνδον ἐγενόμεθα, ἐμὲ μὲν ἐκβάλλουσιν ἐκ τῆς οἰκίας, τουτονὶ δὲ συναρπάσαντες ἔδησαν πρὸς τὸν κίονα, καὶ λαβὼν μάστιγα Τῖσις, ἐντείνας πολλὰς πληγάς, εἰς οἴκημα αὐτὸν καθεῖρξε. καὶ οὐκ ἐξήρκεσεν αὐτῷ ταῦτα μόνον ἐξαμαρτεῖν, ἀλλ' ἐζηλωκὼς μὲν τῶν νέων τοὺς πονηροτάτους ἐν τῇ πόλει, νεωστὶ δὲ τὰ πατρῷα παρειληφὼς καὶ προσποιούμενος νέος καὶ πλούσιος εἶναι, πάλιν τοὺς οἰκέτας ἐκέλευσεν ἡμέρας ἤδη γενομένης πρὸς τὸν κίονα αὐτὸν δήσαντας μαστιγοῦν. οὕτω δὲ τοῦ σώματος ἤδη πονήρως διακειμένου Ἀντίμαχον μεταπεμψάμενος τῶν μὲν γεγενημένων οὐθὲν εἶπεν, ἔλεγε δ' ὡς αὐτὸς μὲν δειπνῶν τύχοι, οὗτος δὲ μεθύων ἔλθοι, ἐκκόψας δὲ τὴν θύραν καὶ

[1] διαλλαγεὶς Scheibe: ἀπαλλαγεὶς codd.
[2] ὥσθ' ὁπό lacunam supplevit Radermacher.
[3] κατέλαβε lacunam supplevit Radermacher.

have ascertained from the events and learned from well-informed people, to make up their quarrel for the time being, but to look out for an opportunity of catching him somewhere on his own. Tisis was persuaded to do this. The quarrel was patched up, and he treated Archippus as a friend and pretended to be devoted to him. Then, for a man of his age, he took leave of his senses to an incredible degree. On the day of the horse-races at the festival of Anakeia, he met Archippus and me as we were passing his front door (they happen to be neighbours). He first invited him to dinner, and when he declined, asked him to come to a party instead, saying that he would be ⟨there with a few friends⟩. On the evening of the party we had our dinner, and it was already getting dark when we knocked at his door, and were told to come in. When we were inside, they threw me out of the house, seized him and tied him to a pillar. Then Tisis took a whip and flogged him severely, and locked him up in a room. And he was not satisfied merely with this assault, but tried to rival the city's worst young bravos. Also, he had recently inherited his father's estate, and was playing the part of the wealthy young heir. So, when day had dawned, he again ordered his servants to tie him to the pillar and flog him. While he was in this sorry physical state, Tisis sent for Antimachus. He told him nothing of what had happened, but said that he was having dinner when Archippus arrived drunk, broke the door

---

[4] γείτονες γὰρ lacunam supplevit Johannes.
[5] συνδειπνεῖν lacunam supplevit Johannes.
[6] lacunam supplevit Johannes.
[7] lacuna MB.

εἰσελθὼν κακῶς λέγοι αὐτὸν καὶ τὸν Ἀντίμαχον καὶ τὰς γυναῖκας αὐτῶν. Ἀντίμαχος δὲ ὠργίζετο μὲν αὐτοῖς ὡς μεγάλα ἡμαρτηκόσιν, ὅμως δὲ μάρτυρας παρακαλέσας ἠρώτα αὐτόν, πῶς εἰσέλθοι. ὃ δὲ κελεύσαντος Τίσιδος καὶ τῶν οἰκείων[1] ἔφασκε. συμβουλευόντων δὲ τῶν εἰσελθόντων ὡς τάχιστα λῦσαι καὶ τὰ γεγενημένα δεινὰ νομιζόντων εἶναι ἀπέδοσαν αὐτὸν τοῖς ἀδελφοῖς. οὐ δυναμένου δὲ βαδίζειν, ἐκόμισαν αὐτὸν εἰς τὸ Δεῖγμα ἐν κλίνῃ καὶ ἐπέδειξαν πολλοῖς μὲν Ἀθηναίων πολλοῖς δὲ καὶ τῶν ἄλλων ξένων οὕτως διακείμενον, ὥστε τοὺς ἰδόντας μὴ μόνον τοῖς ποιήσασιν ὀργίζεσθαι ἀλλὰ καὶ τῆς πόλεως κατηγορεῖν, ὅτι οὐ δημοσίᾳ οὐδὲ παραχρῆμα τοὺς τὰ τοιαῦτα ἐξαμαρτάνοντας τιμωρεῖται."

12 αὕτη μὲν ἡ Λυσίου διήγησις ἐκ τοῦ κατὰ Τίσιδος λόγου. ἣν δὲ νῦν μέλλω λέγειν, Δημοσθένους ἐκ τοῦ κατὰ Κόνωνος, ἧς τὴν πραγματικὴν ὁμοιότητα ἐάσαντες . . . .[2] τὴν ἐν τῇ λέξει σκοπῶμεν· "Ἐξήλθομεν ἔτος τουτὶ τρίτον εἰς Πάνακτον φρουρᾶς ἡμῖν προγραφείσης. ἐσκήνωσαν οὖν οἱ υἱεῖς οἱ Κόνωνος τουτουὶ ἐγγὺς ἡμῶν, ὡς οὐκ ἂν ἐβουλόμην. ἡ γὰρ ἐξ ἀρχῆς ἔχθρα καὶ τὰ προσκρούματα ἐκεῖθεν ἡμῖν συνέβη· ἑξῆς δὲ ἀκούσεσθε. ἔπινον ἑκάστοτε οὗτοι τὴν ἡμέραν ὅλην, ἐπειδὴ τάχιστα ἀριστήσειαν, καὶ τοῦθ', ἕωσπερ ἦμεν ἐν τῇ φρουρᾷ, διετέλουν ποιοῦντες· ἡμεῖς δ', ὥσπερ ἐνθάδε εἰώθειμεν, οὕτω διήγομεν καὶ ἔξω. καὶ ἣν

[1] οἰκείων Usener: οἰκέτων MBP.
[2] lacuna MBP.

open, came in and insulted himself, Antimachus and their womenfolk. Antimachus was incensed by their grossly criminal action, but still called for witnesses and asked Archippus how he had gained entry. He replied that he was invited in by Tisis and his friends. Some persons who had entered the house after the assault took a serious view of what had happened and advised Tisis and his friend to release Archippus as soon as possible, so they handed him over to his brothers. As he was unable to walk, they carried him to the Market [1] on a stretcher. There the many citizens and foreigners who were shown how he had been treated were not only angry with the perpetrators, but also blamed the state for not exacting immediate and public penalties from criminals of this sort."

That is the narrative from Lysias's speech *Against* 12
Tisis. The one I am about to quote is from Demosthenes's speech *Against Conon*, which is similar in its subject-matter. . . . But let us leave that and examine the stylistic (similarity): [2]

"Two years ago we were assigned to garrison duty at Panactum, and went there. The sons of Conon here pitched their tents near ours, and I wish they had not, for it was from that time that our enmity and quarrelling began, as you will now hear. These men spent the whole of every day in drinking, starting straight after breakfast. They did this all the time we were serving there; while we followed the same regimen there as at home. And they would be far gone in their cups even at the time when others were

[1] The *Deigma* was a market in the modern sense, where merchants displayed their wares.

[2] *Against Conon*, 3–9.

δειπνοποιεῖσθαι τοῖς ἄλλοις ὥραν συμβαίνοι, ταύτην ἂν οὗτοι ἐπαρῴνουν ἤδη, τὰ μὲν πολλὰ εἰς τοὺς παῖδας τοὺς ἀκολούθους ἡμῶν, τελευτῶντες δὲ καὶ εἰς ἡμᾶς αὐτούς. φήσαντες γὰρ καπνίζειν αὐτοὺς ὀψοποιουμένους τοὺς παῖδας ἢ κακῶς λέγειν, ὅ τι τύχοιεν, ἔτυπτον καὶ τὰς ἀμίδας κατεσκεδάννυσαν καὶ προσεούρουν καὶ ἀσελγείας καὶ ὕβρεως οὐδ' ὁτιοῦν ἀπέλειπον. ὁρῶντες δὲ ἡμεῖς ταῦτα καὶ λυπούμενοι τὸ μὲν πρῶτον ἀπεπεμψάμεθα· ὡς δ' ἐχλεύαζον ἡμᾶς καὶ οὐκ ἐπαύοντο, τῷ στρατηγῷ τὸ πρᾶγμα εἴπομεν κοινῇ πάντες οἱ σύσσιτοι προσελθόντες, οὐδὲν ἐγὼ τῶν ἄλλων ἔξω. λοιδορηθέντος δὲ αὐτοῖς ἐκείνου καὶ κακίσαντος αὐτούς, οὐ μόνον περὶ ὧν εἰς ἡμᾶς ἠσέλγαινον ἀλλὰ καὶ περὶ ὧν ἐποίουν ὅλως ἐν τῷ στρατοπέδῳ, τοσούτου ἐδέησαν παύσασθαι ἢ αἰσχυνθῆναι, ὥστε, ἐπειδὴ θᾶττον συνεσκότασεν, εὐθὺς ὡς ἡμᾶς εἰσεπήδησαν ταύτῃ τῇ ἑσπέρᾳ. καὶ τὸ μὲν πρῶτον κακῶς ἔλεγον, ἔπειτα δὲ καὶ πληγὰς ἐνέτειναν ἐμοὶ καὶ τοσαύτην κραυγὴν καὶ θόρυβον περὶ τὴν σκηνὴν ἐποίησαν, ὥστε καὶ τὸν στρατηγὸν καὶ τοὺς ταξιάρχους ἐλθεῖν καὶ τῶν ἄλλων τινὰς στρατιωτῶν, οἳ διεκώλυσαν μηδὲν ἡμᾶς ἀνήκεστον παθεῖν μηδ' αὐτοὺς ποιῆσαι παροινουμένους ὑπὸ τούτων. τοῦ δὲ πράγματος εἰς τοῦτο παρελθόντος, ὡς δεῦρο ἀνήλθομεν, ἦν ἡμῖν, οἷον εἰκός, ἐκ τούτων ὀργὴ καὶ ἔχθρα πρὸς ἀλλήλους. οὐ μὴν ἔγωγε ᾤμην δεῖν οὔτε δίκην λαχεῖν αὐτοῖς οὔτε λόγον ποιεῖσθαι τῶν συμβάντων. ἀλλ' ἐκεῖν' ἁπλῶς ἐγνώκειν τὸ λοιπὸν εὐλαβεῖσθαι καὶ φυλάττεσθαι μὴ πλησιάζειν ὡς τοὺς τοιούτους. πρῶτον μὲν οὖν, ὧν εἴρηκα,

having their dinner, and mostly inflicted their drunken behaviour upon the servants who attended us, but finally ended up by insulting us directly. After accusing our servants of annoying them with smoke when they cooked, or being insolent to them, and making any other allegation that occurred to them, they assaulted them, emptied the chamber-pots over them and urinated over them, and left no act of wanton violence undone. On seeing this we were vexed, but at first we dismissed it; but when they continued to insult us and would not stop, we formed a deputation and reported the matter to the general—not myself alone, but all messmates together. He rebuked them severely, not only for their outrageous treatment of ourselves, but also for their general conduct in the camp. But far from stopping or being ashamed of their actions, no sooner was it dusk on the very same evening than they assaulted us, beginning with insults, but then resorting to blows against me, in the course of which they raised such a din and a noise around the tent that the general and the captains and some of the other soldiers came, and prevented our receiving irreparable injury, or indeed meting it out, to our drunken assailants.

The matter having reached such a point, it was natural that, when we returned home, there should, as a result of these quarrels, be a feeling of anger and hostility between us. Yet I most certainly did not think it necessary to file a suit against them or take any account of what had occurred: I simply made up my mind to take good care and precaution to avoid the society of these men and their evil ways. Now I wish firstly to furnish witnesses to what I have said,

τούτων βούλομαι τὰς μαρτυρίας παρασχόμενος μετὰ ταῦτα, ὅσα ὑπὸ τούτου πέπονθα, ἐπιδεῖξαι, ἵνα εἰσῆτε, ὅτι ⟨ᾧ⟩ προσῆκε τοῖς τὸ πρῶτον ἁμαρτηθεῖσιν ἐπιτιμᾶν, οὗτος αὐτὸς πρὸς τούτοις πολλῷ δεινότερα διαπέπρακται.—Μάρτυρες.—Ὧν μὲν τοίνυν οὐδένα ᾤμην δεῖν λόγον ποιεῖσθαι, ταῦτά ἐστι. χρόνῳ δ' ὕστερον οὐ πολλῷ περιπατοῦντος ὥσπερ εἰώθειν ⟨ἑσπέρας⟩ ἐν ἀγορᾷ μου μετὰ Φανοστράτου τοῦ Κηφισέως τῶν ἡλικιωτῶν τινος παρέρχεται Κτησίας, ὁ υἱὸς ⟨ὁ⟩ τούτου μεθύων κατὰ τὸ Λεωκόριον ἐγγὺς ἰὼν Πυθοδώρου. κατιδὼν δὲ ἡμᾶς καὶ κραυγάσας καὶ διαλεχθείς τι πρὸς αὑτὸν οὕτως, ὡς ἂν μεθύων, ὥστε μὴ μαθεῖν, ὅ τι λέγει, παρῆλθε πρὸς Μελίτην ἄνω. ἔπινον δ' ἄρα ἐνταῦθα παρὰ Παμφίλῳ τῷ γναφεῖ Κόνων οὑτοσὶ Θεόδωρός τις Ἀλκιβιάδης Σπίνθαρος ὁ Εὐβούλου Θεογένης ὁ Ἀνδρομένους πολλοί τινες, οὓς ἐξαναστήσας ὁ Κτησίας ἐπορεύετο εἰς τὴν ἀγοράν. καὶ ἡμῖν συμβαίνει ἀναστρέφουσιν ἐκ τοῦ Φερρεφαττίου καὶ περιπατοῦσι πάλιν κατ' αὐτό πως τὸ Λεωκόριον εἶναι, καὶ τούτοις περιτυγχάνομεν. ὡς δ' ἀνεμίχθημεν, εἷς μὲν αὐτῶν ἀγνώς τις τῷ Φανοστράτῳ προσπίπτει καὶ κατεῖχεν ἐκεῖνον. Κόνων δὲ οὑτοσὶ καὶ ὁ υἱὸς αὐτοῦ καὶ ὁ Ἀνδρομένους υἱὸς ἐμοὶ περιπεσόντες τὸ μὲν πρῶτον ἐξέδυον, εἶτα ὑποσκελίσαντες καὶ ῥάξαντες εἰς τὸν βόρβορον οὕτω διέθηκαν ἐναλλόμενοι καὶ ὑβρίζοντες, ὥστε τὸ μὲν χεῖλος διακόψαι τοὺς δ' ὀφθαλμοὺς συγκλεῖσαι. οὕτω δὲ κακῶς ἔχοντα κατέλιπον, ὥστε μήτε ἀναστῆναι μήτε φθέγξασθαι δύνασθαι. κείμενος δ' αὐτῶν ἤκουον

after which I shall show what injuries I have suffered at this man's hands, so that you may know that the very man who ought to have disapproved of the original crimes has himself capped them with deeds that are far more outrageous.

WITNESSES

Those, then, are the deeds of which I did not think it necessary to take any account. A short time later, I was taking my usual evening walk in the market-place with a friend of my own age, Phanostratus of the deme Cephisia, when Ctesias, the defendant's son came by drunk, by the Leocorium, and passed near the house of Pythodorus. Seeing us, he raised a shout, carried on a private conversation with himself as drunken men do, which we could not understand, and went on up to Melite. Now Conon here, a certain Theodorus, Alcibiades, Spintharus the son of Eubulus, Theogenes the son of Andromenes and a number of others were having a drinking-party in the house of Pamphilus the fuller. Ctesias roused them and set off for the market-place, and we met up with them just as we happened to be returning from the temple of Persephone and were walking back somewhere near the Leocorium. When we closed, one of them, whom I failed to identify, fell on Phanostratus and pinned him. Conon here, his son and the son of Andromenes set about me, first stripping me, then tripping me up and throwing me in the mud, jumped on me and caused me such injuries that my lip was split open and my eyes were closed up. They left me in such a sorry state that I was unable to stand up or to speak. As I lay there I heard them say many

πολλὰ καὶ δεινὰ λεγόντων. καὶ τὰ μὲν ἄλλα βλασφημίας ἔχει τινάς, ἃς κἂν ὀνομάζειν ὀκνήσαιμι, ὃ δὲ τῆς ὕβρεώς ἐστι τῆς τούτου σημεῖον καὶ τεκμήριον, ὡς πᾶν τὸ πρᾶγμα ὑπὸ τούτου γενόμενον, τοῦθ' ὑμῖν ἐρῶ· ᾔδεν γὰρ τοὺς ἀλεκτρυόνας μιμούμενος τοὺς νενικηκότας, οἱ δὲ κροτεῖν αὐτὸν ἠξίουν τοῖς ἀγκῶσιν ἀντὶ πτερύγων τὰς πλευράς."

13 ταῦτ' οὐ καθαρὰ καὶ ἀκριβῆ καὶ σαφῆ καὶ διὰ τῶν κυρίων τε καὶ κοινῶν ὀνομάτων κατεσκευασμένα ὥσπερ τὰ Λυσίου; ἐμοὶ μὲν γὰρ ὑπάρχειν δοκεῖ. τί δέ; οὐχὶ σύντομα καὶ στρογγύλα καὶ ἀληθείας μεστὰ καὶ τὴν ἀφελῆ καὶ ἀκατάσκευον ἐπιφαίνοντα φύσιν, καθάπερ ἐκεῖνα; πάντων μὲν οὖν μάλιστα. οὐχὶ δὲ καὶ πιθανὰ καὶ ἐν ἤθει λεγόμενά τινι καὶ τὸ πρέπον τοῖς ὑποκειμένοις προσώποις τε καὶ πράγμασι φυλάττοντα; ἡδονῆς δὲ ἄρα καὶ πειθοῦς καὶ χαρίτων καιροῦ τε καὶ τῆς ἄλλης ἁπάσης τῆς τοῖς Λυσιακοῖς ἐπανθούσης ἀρετῆς οὐχὶ πολλὴ μοῖρα; οὐκ ἔνεστ' ἄλλως εἰπεῖν. εἰ γοῦν μὴ διὰ τῆς ἐπιγραφῆς, οὗ τινός ἐστιν, ἑκάτερος τῶν λόγων γνώριμος ἦν, ἀλλ' ἀνεπιγράφοις περιετύχομεν αὐτοῖς, οὐ πολλοὺς ἂν ἡμῶν οἴομαι διαγνῶναι ῥᾳδίως, πότερος Δημοσθένους ἐστὶν ἢ Λυσίου· τοσαύτην οἱ χαρακτῆρες ὁμοιότητα πρὸς ἀλλήλους ἔχουσι. τοιοῦτός ἐστι καὶ ὁ πρὸς Ἀπολλόδωρον ὑπὲρ Φορμίωνος καὶ ὁ κατ' Ὀλυμπιοδώρου [τῆς][1] βλάβης καὶ ὁ πρὸς Βοιωτὸν ὑπὲρ τοῦ ὀνόματος ἥ τε πρὸς Εὐβουλίδην ἔφεσις καὶ ἡ πρὸς Μακάρτατον διαδικασία καὶ οἱ

[1] τῆς delevit Krüger.

shocking things, much of which contained some element of impropriety which I would be reluctant to repeat in your presence; but as to what constitutes evidence and proof of his outrage, and for the fact he was the one who did it all, I shall tell you this: he began to crow, imitating the fighting cocks who have won a victory, while his companions told him to flap his arms against his sides like wings."

Is this not pure, precise and lucid, and composed in 13
standard, ordinary words like the language of Lysias? I take these qualities for granted: but is it not also concise, terse and full of realism, while displaying the same simplicity and absence of artifice as the other? It seems to me to have these qualities above all. And is it not also persuasive? Does it not convey a certain moral tone, and carefully preserve an atmosphere suitable to the persons and the events which it describes? And again, does it not contain in large measure the charm, the persuasiveness, the elegance, the taste and all the other qualities which adorn the eloquence of Lysias? Undeniably it does! Indeed, if we did not know from their titles who their authors were, but they had come down to us anonymously, I doubt whether many of us could easily decide which of the two was by Demosthenes and which by Lysias, so closely similar are their styles. So, too, is the speech in the action for Phormio against Apollodorus,[1] the speech in an action for damages against Olympiodorus,[2] that against Boeotus in defence of a name,[3] the appeal against Eubulides,[4] the speech in the dispute with Macartatus[5] and all the other private

[1] The speech *For Phormio* (Or. 36).
[2] Or. 48.
[3] Or. 40.
[4] Or. 57.
[5] Or. 43.

ἄλλοι πάντες οἱ ἰδιωτικοὶ λόγοι οὐ πολλῷ πλείους τῶν εἴκοσιν ὄντες. οἷς γε δὴ κατὰ τὸ παρὸν ἐντετυχηκὼς γνώσῃ, ὁποῖα λέγω. καὶ τῶν δημοσίων δὲ ἀγώνων πολλὰ μέρη τούτῳ κατεσκεύασται τῷ χαρακτῆρι. ἔφερον δ' ἂν ἐξ ἑκάστου τὰ παραδείγματα, εἰ μὴ πλείων ἔμελλε τοῦ μετρίου γενήσεσθαι ὁ λόγος. ἐν οἷς δῆλός ἐστι περὶ καλλιλογίαν καὶ σεμνότητα καὶ πάσας τὰς ἐπιθέτους κατασκευὰς ⟨οὐ⟩ [1] μᾶλλον ἐσπουδακὼς ἢ περὶ τὴν ἀκρίβειαν. ὁ δὲ πρὸς τὴν ἐπιστολὴν καὶ τοὺς πρέσβεις τοὺς παρὰ Φιλίππου ῥηθεὶς λόγος, ὃν ἐπιγράφει Καλλίμαχος ὑπὲρ Ἁλοννήσου, ὁ τὴν ἀρχὴν τήνδε ἔχων· "Ὦ ἄνδρες Ἀθηναῖοι, οὐκ ἔστιν, ὅπως αἱ αἰτίαι, ἃς Φίλιππος αἰτιᾶται" ὅλος ἐστὶν ἀκριβὴς καὶ λεπτὸς καὶ τὸν Λυσιακὸν χαρακτῆρα ἐκμέμακται εἰς ὄνυχα, ἐξαλλαγῆς δὲ ἢ σεμνολογίας ἢ δεινότητος ἢ τῶν ἄλλων τινός, ἃ τῇ Δημοσθένους δυνάμει παρακολουθεῖν πέφυκεν, ὀλίγην ἐπίδειξιν ἔχει. τίς οὖν ἐστι κἂν τούτοις ἡ διαφορά; καὶ πῶς ἂν διαγνοίη τις, ὅταν εἰς τὸν ἀναγκαῖον καταβῇ χαρακτῆρα ὁ Δημοσθένης, πῇ κρείττων ἐστὶ Λυσίου καὶ κατὰ τὴν λέξιν; ἀξιοῖς γὰρ δὴ καὶ τοῦτο μαθεῖν. φυσική τις ἐπιτρέχει τοῖς Λυσίου λόγοις εὐστομία καὶ χάρις, ὥσπερ ἔφην καὶ πρότερον, ᾗ προὔχει πλὴν Δημοσθένους τῶν ἄλλων ῥητόρων. αὕτη μέντοι, καθάπερ νότιός τις αὖρα, μέχρι προοιμίου καὶ διηγήσεως αὐτὸν ἄγει, ὅταν δ' εἰς τοὺς ἀποδεικτικοὺς ἔλθῃ λόγους, ἀμυδρά τις γίνεται καὶ ἀσθενής, ἐν δὲ δὴ τοῖς παθητικοῖς εἰς τέλος ἀποσβέννυται· τόνος γὰρ οὐ

[1] οὐ inseruit Vliet.

speeches, of which there are not many more than twenty. You will know which ones I mean, having encountered them already. Many sections of his political speeches are also written in this style, and I would give examples from each of these, but for the fact that this would protract my discourse unduly. In these sections he is clearly more concerned with precision than with fine language, dignity and all the other extra refinements. The speech in which he opposed Philip's letter and his ambassadors, which Callimachus [1] calls *For Halonnesus*, and which begins with the words: [2] "Athenians, it is not possible that the charges which Philip makes . . ." is precise and detailed throughout and is fashioned to the nail in the Lysianic mould. There is little effort to make a show of strange or dignified language, or of rhetorical brilliance, or of any of the qualities associated with the art of Demosthenes. What, then, is the difference between them? And how can one judge, when Demosthenes has recourse to this economical style, in what ways he expresses himself more effectively than Lysias? This, too, you will want to know. As I said before, a certain natural euphony and charm flows over the speeches of Lysias, and in this quality he is superior to all other orators except Demosthenes. Now this carries him like a southerly breeze through introduction and narrative, but when it comes to the proof section it becomes fitful and feeble, and when it comes to the final arousing of emotions, it dies away altogether, for it has little reserve of energy or power. But Demosthenes's style has great energy and no

[1] See note 1, p. 185.

[2] Or. 7. 1. This and Or. 40, 43 and 48 are now regarded by many as spurious.

πολὺς αὐτῇ πρόσεστιν οὐδ' ἰσχύς. παρὰ δὲ τῷ Δημοσθένει πολὺς μὲν ὁ τόνος, αὐτάρκης δ' ἡ χάρις, ὥστε κἂν ταύτῃ τῷ διαρκεῖ καὶ μετρίῳ νικᾶν κἂν ἐκείνῳ τῷ παντὶ προέχειν. τοῦτο παρατήρημα δεύτερον, ᾧ διαγνοίη τις ἂν τὴν Δημοσθένους διάλεκτον, ὅταν εἰς ταῦτα τἀναγκαῖα συνάγηται. οὐ γὰρ ὥσπερ τὴν ἐξαλλαγὴν καὶ περιττολογίαν καὶ πάντας τοὺς ἐπιθέτους ἐκδύεται κόσμους, οὕτως καὶ τὸ μέγεθος καὶ τὸν τόνον, ἀλλ' ἔστιν αὐτῆς ἀναφαίρετος οὗτος εἴτ' ἄρα συγγενὴς εἴτε ἀσκήσει παρὼν εἰς ῥῆσιν. ἐπιτάσεις μέντοι καὶ ἀνέσεις λαμβάνει τινὰς ἀναλόγους. καὶ ταῦτ' ἤδη γνώριμα οἷς λέγω, καὶ οὐθὲν δεόμεθα παραδειγμάτων.

14 ὥστε περὶ μὲν τοῦ χαρακτῆρος . . .[1] τοῦ δὲ ῥητορικοῦ γένους τοῦ μεταξὺ τῶν ἄκρων ἑκατέρων, ὃ ἀτελὲς[2] παραλαβὼν ὁ Δημοσθένης παρ' Ἰσοκράτους τε καὶ ἔτι προτέρου Θρασυμάχου καὶ τελευταίου Πλάτωνος ἐτελείωσεν ὅσον ἦν ἀνθρωπίνῃ φύσει δυνατόν, πολλὰ μὲν ἄν τις ἐκ τῶν κατὰ Φιλίππου δημηγοριῶν πολλὰ δ' ἐκ τῶν ⟨ἄλλων⟩[3] δημοσίων λόγων παραδείγματα λάβοι, πλεῖστα δὲ καὶ κάλλιστα ἐκ τῆς ὑπὲρ Κτησιφῶντος ἀπολογίας· οὗτος γὰρ δή μοι δοκεῖ καλλίστῃ καὶ μετριωτάτῃ κατασκευῇ λέξεως κεχρῆσθαι ὁ λόγος. εἰ μὲν οὖν χρόνον ἀρκοῦντα εἶχον, καὶ τὰς λέξεις αὐτὰς ἂν παρετίθην. πολλῶν δέ μοι καὶ ἀναγκαίων ἔτι καταλειπομένων, τοῦτο μὲν ἐάσω, δείγμασι δὲ

lack of charm; so that while in the latter he succeeds by having it in a sufficient and moderate degree, in the former he is quite unrivalled. This is a second criterion which enables us to distinguish the style of Demosthenes, when it is reduced to these essentials: he does not divest himself of his grandeur and his energy as he does of his strange and elaborate diction and all other forms of extra ornamentation, but this quality is inseparable from his style and is inherent in his diction, whether it is natural to him or he has cultivated it. It does, however, admit of some relative heightening or relaxation. As this is already known to my readers, I need not quote examples.

⟨Sufficient has been said⟩ about ⟨this⟩ style. The 14
style or oratory between these two extremes, which Demosthenes inherited in an imperfect form from Isocrates, from Thrasymachus before him, and ultimately from Plato, was developed by him to the highest degree of perfection that is humanly possible. Many examples of it may be found in the *Philippic* speeches and in the other public orations, but the greatest number and the finest are in his *Defence of Ctesiphon*. This speech, in fact, seems to me to contain the adornments of style in their finest form and their most balanced measure. If I had sufficient time I should quote the actual passages, but since I still have much essential ground to cover, I shall pass over this subject and refer for the present to some

---

[1] lacunam fort. *τούτου ἅλις,* implendam esse censuit Radermacher.

[2] *ὃ ἀτελὲς* Sadée: *ὂν ατελῆ* codd.

[3] *ἄλλων* inseruit Radermacher.

μόνον ἐν τῷ παρόντι χρήσομαι βραχυτάτοις ὡς ἐν εἰδόσι λέγων. ἔστι δὴ τὰ τοιαῦτα τοῦ μέσου χαρακτῆρος παραδείγματα ἐκ μὲν τῆς Αἰσχίνου κατηγορίας· "Ἀεὶ μὲν γάρ, ὦ ἄνδρες Ἀθηναῖοι, προσήκει μισεῖν καὶ κολάζειν τοὺς προδότας καὶ δωροδόκους, μάλιστα δὲ νῦν ἐπὶ τοῦ καιροῦ τούτου γένοιτ' ἂν καὶ πάντας ὠφελήσειεν ἀνθρώπους κοινῇ. νόσημα γάρ, ὦ ἄνδρες Ἀθηναῖοι, δεινὸν ἐμπέπτωκεν εἰς τὴν Ἑλλάδα καὶ χαλεπόν, ὃ πολλῆς τινος εὐτυχίας καὶ παρ' ὑμῶν ἐπιμελείας δεόμενον" καὶ ⟨τὰ⟩ [1] ἑπόμενα τούτοις. ἐκ δὲ τῆς Ἀριστοκράτους κατηγορίας. "Πολλὰ μὲν δὴ παρ' ἡμῖν ἐστι τοιαῦτα, οἷα οὐχ ἑτέρωθι, ἓν δ' οὖν ἰδιώτατον πάντων καὶ σεμνότατον τὸ ἐν Ἀρείῳ πάγῳ δικαστήριον, περὶ οὗ τοσαῦτά ἐστι καλὰ παραδεδομένα καὶ μυθώδη καὶ ὧν αὐτοὶ μάρτυρες ἐσμέν, ὅσα περὶ οὐδενὸς ἄλλου δικαστηρίου" καὶ τὰ ἑξῆς. ἐκ δὲ τοῦ περὶ τῶν ἀτελειῶν λόγου· "Πρῶτον μὲν τοίνυν Κόνωνα σκοπεῖτε, εἰ ἄρα ἄξιον καταμεμψαμένους ἢ τὸν ἄνδρα ἢ τὰ πεπραγμένα ἄκυρόν τι ποιῆσαι τῶν ἐκείνῳ δοθέντων. οὗτος γάρ, ὡς ὑμῶν τινῶν ἔστιν ἀκοῦσαι τῶν κατὰ τὴν αὐτὴν ἡλικίαν ὄντων, μετὰ τὴν τοῦ δήμου κάθοδον τὴν ἐκ Πειραιέως ἀσθενοῦς ἡμῶν τῆς πόλεως οὔσης" καὶ τὰ ἀκόλουθα. ἐκ δὲ τῆς ὑπὲρ Κτησιφῶντος ἀπολογίας· "Ἃ μὲν οὖν πρὸ τοῦ πολιτεύεσθαι ⟨καὶ⟩ δημηγορεῖν ἐμὲ προὔλαβε καὶ κατέσχε Φίλιππος, ἐάσω· οὐδὲν γὰρ ἡγοῦμαι τούτων εἶναι πρὸς ἐμέ· ἃ δὲ ἀφ' ἧς ἡμέρας ἐπὶ ταῦτα ἐπέστην ἐγώ, διεκώλυον λαβεῖν, ταῦτα

[1] τὰ inseruit Sylburg.

very short examples, assuming that my readers are well-informed. The following are instances of the middle style, the first being from the *Prosecution of Aeschines*:[1]

"Athenians, it is always proper to abhor and to punish treachery and corruption, but now at this moment such treatment would be especially appropriate and in the common interest of all mankind. For a dread and cruel malady has befallen Greece, gentlemen, which it will require a large measure of good fortune and care on your part to avoid."

And so forth. And in the *Prosecution of Aristocrates*, where he says:[2]

"We have many institutions that are unlike any elsewhere, but the most peculiar and venerable of all is the Court of the Areopagus. There are more fine traditions connected with it, some legendary, others to which we can ourselves testify, than there are about any other court."

And so on. And from the speech *On Tax Evasion*:[3]

"First, then, consider the case of Conon. Would it have been right to condemn the man or his actions and cancel any of the privileges that had been granted to him? Some of you will have heard from men living at the time, after the return of the democratic party from the Piraeus, in the days when our city was weak . . ."

And so forth. And from the *Defence of Ctesiphon*:[4]

"I shall pass over the conquests which Philip made and held before I began my political career, for I do not consider any of these to be my concern. But I shall draw to your attention those in which I frus-

[1] Or. 19. 258.
[2] Or. 23. 65.
[3] Or. 20. 68.
[4] Or. 18. 60.

ἀναμνήσω καὶ περὶ τούτων ὑφέξω λόγον, τοσοῦτον ὑπειπών· πλεονέκτημα, ὦ ἄνδρες Ἀθηναῖοι, μέγα ὑπῆρξε Φιλίππῳ. παρὰ γὰρ τοῖς Ἕλλησιν οὐ τισὶν ἀλλὰ πᾶσιν ὁμοίως φορὰ προδοτῶν καὶ δωροδόκων καὶ θεοῖς ἐχθρῶν ἀνθρώπων συνέβη, ὅσην οὐδεὶς τὸ πρότερον μέμνηται γεγονυῖαν" καὶ τὰ συναπτόμενα τούτοις.

τοῦτον ἔγωγε τὸν χαρακτῆρα . . .[1] εἴ τις μὴ μάλιστα ἀποδέχοιτο τὴν αἰτίαν, δι' ἣν οὔτε τὰ Θουκυδίδεια ἐκεῖνα περιττὰ καὶ ἐξηλλαγμένα τοῦ συνήθους κράτιστα ἡγοῦμαι οὔτ' ἐν [2] τοῖς Λυσιακοῖς τοῖς ἰσχνοῖς καὶ συνεσπασμένοις τὴν τελείαν τῆς λέξεως ἀρετὴν τίθεμαι, τοῦτ' ἂν εἴποιμι πρὸς αὐτόν· οἱ συνιόντες εἰς τὰς ἐκκλησίας καὶ τὰ δικαστήρια καὶ τοὺς ἄλλους συλλόγους, ἔνθα πολιτικῶν δεῖ λόγων, οὔτε δεινοὶ καὶ περιττοὶ πάντες εἰσὶ καὶ τὸν Θουκυδίδου νοῦν ἔχοντες οὔθ' ἅπαντες ἰδιῶται καὶ κατασκευῆς λόγων γενναίων ἄπειροι, ἀλλ' οἳ μὲν ἀπὸ γεωργίας οἳ δ' ἀπὸ θαλαττουργίας οἳ δ' ἀπὸ τῶν βαναύσων τεχνῶν συνερρυηκότες, οἷς ἁπλούστερον καὶ κοινότερον διαλεγόμενος μᾶλλον ἄν τις ἀρέσαι. τὸ γὰρ ἀκριβὲς καὶ περιττὸν καὶ ξένον καὶ πᾶν, ὅ τι μὴ σύνηθες αὐτοῖς ἀκούειν τε καὶ λέγειν, ὀχληρῶς διατίθησιν αὐτούς, καὶ ὥσπέρ τι τῶν πάνυ ἀνιαρῶν ἐδεσμάτων ἢ ποτῶν ἀποστρέφει τοὺς στομάχους, οὕτως ἐκεῖνα ὀχληρῶς διατίθησι τὰς ἀκοάς. οἱ δὲ πολιτικοί τε καὶ ἀπ' ἀγορᾶς καὶ διὰ τῆς ἐγκυκλίου παιδείας ἐληλυθότες, οἷς οὐκ ἔνι τὸν αὐτὸν ὅνπερ ἐκείνοις διαλέγεσθαι τρόπον,

[1] lacunam indicavit Radermacher.

trated him from the very day of my entry into politics, and will accept responsibility for their consequences, but with this proviso only: Philip had a great advantage from the start, men of Athens, for it happened that among the Greeks—not some, but all alike—there sprang up a crop of traitors, and corrupt, god-forsaken men, such as no one can remember existing before."

And the sequel to this.

This style I consider ⟨to be the ideal mixture of 15
grandeur and simplicity⟩; and if anyone should fail to accept wholeheartedly my reason for not regarding the exaggerated artificiality and remoteness from normality of Thucydides's style as the most effective style, or for not finding perfection in the spare, condensed style of Lysias, I should say this to him: those who attend the public assemblies, the law-courts and other meetings where civic speeches have to be made, are neither all outstanding intellectual geniuses like Thucydides, nor all simpletons with no experience of how a good speech is composed. They are a collection of men who work on the land and the sea, and common tradesmen, whose sympathies are most readily won with a comparatively straightforward and ordinary style of oratory. A finicky, exaggerated or exotic style, or any manner of speaking that they are not themselves accustomed to use or to hear merely renders them hostile: just as any food or drink that is altogether unpalatable upsets the stomach, so this style offends the ear. This artificial, exaggerated and exotic style should be addressed to seasoned politicians, men experienced in public life and with a

---

[2] ἐν Sadée: ἐπὶ codd.

ἀλλὰ δεῖ τὴν ἐγκατάσκευον καὶ περιττὴν καὶ ξένην διάλεκτον τούτοις προσφέρειν. εἰσὶ μὲν οὖν ἴσως ἐλάττους οἱ τοιοῦτοι τῶν ἑτέρων, μᾶλλον δὲ πολλοστὸν ἐκείνων μέρος, καὶ τοῦτο οὐθεὶς ἀγνοεῖ· οὐ μὴν καταφρονεῖσθαί γε διὰ ταῦτα ἄξιοι.[1] ὁ μὲν οὖν τῶν ὀλίγων καὶ εὐπαιδεύτων στοχαζόμενος λόγος οὐκ ἔσται τῷ φαύλῳ καὶ ἀμαθεῖ πλήθει πιθανός, ὁ δὲ τοῖς πολλοῖς καὶ ἰδιώταις ἀρέσκειν ἀξιῶν καταφρονηθήσεται πρὸς τῶν χαριεστέρων, ὁ δ' ἀμφότερα τἀκροατήρια[2] πείθειν ζητῶν ἧττον ἀποτεύξεται τοῦ τέλους. ἔστι δὲ οὗτος ὁ μεμιγμένος ἐξ ἀμφοτέρων τῶν χαρακτήρων. διὰ ταῦτα ἐγὼ τὴν οὕτως κατεσκευασμένην λέξιν μετριωτάτην εἶναι τῶν ἄλλων νενόμικα καὶ τῶν λόγων τούτους μάλιστα ἀποδέχομαι τοὺς πεφευγότας ἑκατέρου τῶν χαρακτήρων τὰς ὑπερβολάς.

16 εἰρηκὼς δὲ κατ' ἀρχάς, ὅτι μοι δοκοῦσιν Ἰσοκράτης τε καὶ Πλάτων κράτιστα τῶν ἄλλων ἐπιτετηδευκέναι τοῦτο τὸ γένος τοῦ χαρακτῆρος καὶ προαγαγεῖν μὲν αὐτὸ ἐπὶ μήκιστον, οὐ μὴν καὶ τελειῶσαι, ὅσα δ' ἐνέλιπεν ἐκείνων ἑκάτερος, ταῦτα Δημοσθένην ἐξειργασμένον ἐπιδείξειν ὑποσχόμενος, ἐπὶ τοῦτ' ἤδη πορεύσομαι, τὰς ἄριστα δοκούσας ἔχειν παρ' ἑκατέρῳ[3] τῶν ἀνδρῶν λέξεις προχειρισάμενος καὶ ἀντιπαραθεὶς αὐταῖς τὰς Δημοσθένους, ὅσαι περὶ[4] τὰς αὐτὰς συνετάχθησαν ὑποθέσεις, ἵνα μᾶλλον αἱ τῶν ἀνδρῶν προαιρέσεις τε καὶ δυνάμεις γένωνται καταφανεῖς τὴν ἀκριβεστάτην βάσανον ἐπὶ τῶν ὁμοίων ἔργων λαβοῦσαι.

[1] ἄξιοι Sylburg: ἀξιοῖ codd.
[2] τἀκροατήρια Reiske: τὰ κριτήρια codd.

broad education, who cannot be talked to in the same way as ordinary people. These connoisseurs are perhaps a minority: indeed, everyone knows that they are a very small minority; but they do not deserve to be despised for that reason.

Thus a speech that is intended for the well-educated few will not appeal to the vulgar and ignorant masses, while a speech which is intended to please the majority of ordinary men will be despised by men of refinement. But the speech which aims to persuade both these extreme classes of audience is less likely to fail in its objective. Such a speech would be a blend of the two types of style. That is why I have come to regard this style of composition as the most effective medium, and the oratory of which I most approve is that which avoids the excesses of the plain and the grand style.

I said at the beginning [1] that I consider Isocrates 16
and Plato the most accomplished practitioners of this kind of style, carrying its possibilities to greater lengths than anyone else, but falling short of perfection. I promised to show how Demosthenes overcame the faults which neither of them was able to avoid, and will now proceed to fulfil this promise, selecting passages from both which seem to represent their best writing and comparing them with passages of Demosthenes on the same subjects. The policies of the men and their rhetorical powers will be seen more clearly when examined minutely in the context of similar events.

[1] *i.e.* at the beginning of his discussion of the middle style, ch. 3.

---

[3] ἑκατέρῳ Sylburg: ἑκατέρων codd.
[4] περὶ Krüger: παρὰ codd.

17 εἰσαγέσθω δὲ πρῶτος Ἰσοκράτης, καὶ τούτου λαμβανέσθω λέξις ἐκ τοῦ περὶ τῆς εἰρήνης λόγου χαριέστατα δοκοῦσα ἔχειν, ἣν αὐτὸς ἐν τῷ περὶ τῆς ἀντιδόσεως λόγῳ προφέρεται μέγα ἐπ' αὐτῇ φρονῶν, δι' ἧς συγκρίνει τὴν ἐπὶ τῶν προγόνων πολιτείαν τῇ τότε καθεστώσῃ καὶ τὰς πράξεις τὰς παλαιὰς ἀντιπαρατίθησι ταῖς νέαις, τὰς μὲν ἀρχαίας ἐπαινῶν τὰς δ' ἐν τῷ καθ' ἑαυτὸν χρόνῳ μεμφόμενος, τῆς τε μεταβολῆς τῆς ἐπὶ τὰ χείρω τοὺς δημαγωγοὺς ἀποφαίνων αἰτίους ὡς οὐ τὰ κράτιστα εἰσηγουμένους ἀλλὰ τὰ πρὸς ἡδονὴν τῷ πλήθει δημηγοροῦντας. μακροτέρας δ' οὔσης τῆς συγκρίσεως αὐτὰ τὰ κυριώτατα ὑπ' ἐμοῦ παρείληπται. ἔστι δὲ ταυτί· "Τίς γὰρ ἂν ἄλλοθεν ἐπελθὼν καὶ μὴ συνδιεφθαρμένος ἡμῖν, ἀλλ' ἐξαίφνης ἐπιστὰς τοῖς γιγνομένοις οὐκ ἂν μαίνεσθαι καὶ παραφρονεῖν ἡμᾶς νομίσειεν, οἳ φιλοτιμούμεθα μὲν ἐπὶ τοῖς τῶν προγόνων ἔργοις καὶ τὴν πόλιν ἐκ τῶν τότε πραχθέντων ἐγκωμιάζειν ἀξιοῦμεν, οὐδὲν δὲ τῶν αὐτῶν ἐκείνοις πράττομεν ἀλλὰ πᾶν τοὐναντίον; οἳ μὲν γὰρ ὑπὲρ τῶν Ἑλλήνων τοῖς βαρβάροις πολεμοῦντες διετέλεσαν, ἡμεῖς δὲ τοὺς ἐκ τῆς Ἀσίας τὸν βίον ποριζομένους ἐκεῖθεν ἀναστήσαντες ἐπὶ τοὺς Ἕλληνας ἠγάγομεν. κἀκεῖνοι μὲν ἐλευθεροῦντες τὰς πόλεις τὰς Ἑλληνίδας καὶ βοηθοῦντες αὐταῖς τῆς ἡγεμονίας ἠξιώθησαν, ἡμεῖς δὲ καταδουλούμενοι καὶ τἀναντία τοῖς τότε πράττοντες ἀγανακτοῦμεν, εἰ μὴ τὴν αὐτὴν τιμὴν ἐκείνοις ἕξομεν. οἳ τοσοῦτον ἀπολελείμμεθα καὶ τοῖς ἔργοις καὶ ταῖς διανοίαις τῶν κατ' ἐκεῖνον τὸν

Let us first introduce Isocrates, and let us choose from his works a passage which is considered the most elegant in his speech *On the Peace*, and which he esteemed so highly that he included it in his speech *On the Exchange*. In it he compares the constitution in the days of his forefathers with that of his own day, and contrasts the achievements of ancient with those of modern times, praising the old and criticising those of his contemporaries, and showing the demagogues to be responsible for the deterioration because, instead of recommending the best policies they made speeches to gratify the masses. The comparison proceeds at considerable length, and I have reproduced only the most relevant part of it:[1] 17

" Now what if a stranger from abroad were to come and suddenly find himself embroiled in our affairs, before having the time to become corrupted by our depravity: would he not think us insane and beside ourselves, when we glory in the deeds of our ancestors, and think it right to sing the city's praises by recounting the achievements of their day, and yet act in no way like them but do exactly the opposite? For whereas they waged ceaseless war on behalf of the Greeks against the barbarians, we expelled from their homes those who derive their livelihood from Asia and led them against the Greeks; and whereas they liberated the cities of Greece and came to their aid, and so earned the right to be their leaders, we try to enslave them and then feel aggrieved when we are not honoured as they were. We fall so far short of the men of those times in both our deeds and our aspirations that, whereas they had the courage to

[1] 41–50.

χρόνον γενομένων, ὅσον οἱ μὲν ὑπὲρ τῆς τῶν Ἑλλήνων σωτηρίας τήν τε πατρίδα τὴν ἑαυτῶν ἐκλιπεῖν ἐτόλμησαν καὶ μαχόμενοι καὶ ναυμαχοῦντες τοὺς βαρβάρους ἐνίκησαν, ἡμεῖς δ' οὐδ' ὑπὲρ τῆς ἡμετέρας πλεονεξίας κινδυνεύειν ἀξιοῦμεν, ἀλλ' ἄρχειν μὲν ἁπάντων ζητοῦμεν στρατεύειν δ' οὐκ ἐθέλομεν, καὶ πόλεμον μὲν μικροῦ δεῖν πρὸς πάντας ἀνθρώπους ἀναιρούμεθα, πρὸς δὲ τοῦτον οὐχ ἡμᾶς αὐτοὺς ἀσκοῦμεν ἀλλ' ἀνθρώπους τοὺς μὲν ἀπόλιδας τοὺς δ' αὐτομόλους τοὺς δ' ἐκ τῶν ἄλλων κακουργιῶν συνερρυηκότας, οἷς ὁπόταν τινὲς διδῶσι πλείω μισθόν, μετ' ἐκείνων ἐφ' ἡμᾶς ἀκολουθήσουσιν ἀλλ' ὅμως οὕτως αὐτοὺς ἀγαπῶμεν, ὥσθ' ὑπὲρ μὲν τῶν παίδων τῶν ἡμετέρων, εἴπερ τινὲς ἐξαμαρτάνοιεν, οὐκ ἂν ἐθελήσαιμεν δίκας ὑποσχεῖν, ὑπὲρ δὲ τῆς ἐκείνων ἁρπαγῆς καὶ βίας καὶ παρανομίας μελλόντων τῶν ἐγκλημάτων ἐφ' ἡμᾶς ἥκειν οὐχ ὅπως ἀγανακτοῦμεν ἀλλὰ καὶ χαίρομεν, ὅταν ἀκούσωμεν αὐτοὺς τοιοῦτόν τι διαπεπραγμένους. εἰς τοῦτο δὲ μωρίας ἐληλύθαμεν, ὥστ' αὐτοὶ μὲν ἐνδεεῖς ἐσμεν τῶν καθ' ἡμέραν, ξενοτροφεῖν δὲ ἐπικεχειρήκαμεν καὶ τοὺς συμμάχους τοὺς ἡμετέρους αὐτῶν ἰδίᾳ λυμαινόμεθα καὶ δασμολογοῦμεν, ἵνα τοῖς ἁπάντων κοινοῖς ἀνθρώπων ἐχθροῖς τὸν μισθὸν ἐκπορίζωμεν. τοσούτῳ δὲ [καὶ] χείρους ἐσμὲν τῶν προγόνων, οὐ μόνον τῶν εὐδοκιμησάντων ἀλλὰ καὶ τῶν μισηθέντων, ὅσον ἐκεῖνοι μὲν εἰ πολεμεῖν πρός τινας ψηφίσαιντο, μεστῆς οὔσης ἀργυρίου καὶ χρυσίου τῆς ἀκροπόλεως ὅμως ὑπὲρ τῶν δοξάντων τοῖς αὑτῶν σώμασιν ᾤοντο δεῖν κινδυνεύειν, ἡμεῖς δ' εἰς τοσαύτην

leave their country in order to save Greece, and fought and conquered the barbarians on both land and sea, we do not see fit to run any risk, even for our own gain, but seek to rule over all mankind, though we are unwilling to take the field ourselves, and undertake to wage war upon almost the whole world, and yet do not train ourselves for this but employ instead stateless men, deserters and fugitives who have come together as the result of other crimes and who, whenever others offer them higher pay, will follow their leadership against us. And yet we are so keen on these mercenaries that while we would willingly accept responsibility for the acts of our own children if they offended against anyone, yet for the brigandage, the violence and the lawlessness of these men, the blame for which will be laid at our door, we not only feel no grievance, but actually rejoice when we hear that they have done some such crime. And we have reached such a state of stupidity that, although we ourselves are short of daily necessities, we have undertaken to support a mercenary army and we maltreat our own allies and extort money from them in order to provide pay for the common enemies of all mankind. And so far are we inferior to our ancestors, both those who enjoyed the esteem of the Greeks and those who were hated by them, that whereas they, when they decided to wage war against any state, regarded it as their duty, even though the Acropolis was full of silver and gold, to face danger in their own persons in support of their resolutions, we, by contrast, in spite of extreme poverty and our

ἀπορίαν ἐληλυθότες καὶ τοσοῦτοι τὸ πλῆθος ὄντες, ὥσπερ βασιλεὺς ὁ μέγας μισθωτοῖς χρώμεθα τοῖς στρατοπέδοις. καὶ τότε μέν, εἰ τριήρεις ἐπληροῦμεν, τοὺς μὲν ξένους καὶ τοὺς δούλους ναύτας ἐνεβιβάζομεν τοὺς δὲ πολίτας μεθ' ὅπλων ἐξεπέμπομεν, νῦν δὲ τοῖς μὲν ξένοις ὁπλίταις χρώμεθα τοὺς δὲ πολίτας ἐλαύνειν ἀναγκάζομεν, ὥσθ', ὁπόταν ἀποβαίνωσιν εἰς τὴν τῶν πολεμίων, οἱ μὲν ἄρχειν τῶν Ἑλλήνων ἀξιοῦντες ὑπηρέσιον ἔχοντες ἐκβαίνουσιν, οἱ δὲ τοιοῦτοι τὰς φύσεις ὄντες, οἵους ὀλίγῳ πρότερον διῆλθον, μεθ' ὅπλων κινδυνεύουσιν. ἀλλὰ γὰρ καὶ τὰ κατὰ τὴν πόλιν ἰδὼν ἄν τις καλῶς διοικούμενα καὶ περὶ τῶν ἄλλων θαρσήσειεν; ἀλλ' οὐκ ἂν ἐπ' αὐτοῖς τούτοις μάλιστ' ἀγανακτήσειεν; οἵτινες αὐτόχθονες μὲν εἶναι φαμὲν καὶ τὴν πόλιν ταύτην προτέραν οἰκισθῆναι τῶν ἄλλων, προσῆκον δ' ἡμᾶς ἅπασιν εἶναι παράδειγμα τοῦ καλῶς τε καὶ τεταγμένως πολιτεύεσθαι χεῖρον καὶ ταραχωδέστερον τὴν ἡμετέραν αὐτῶν διοικοῦμεν τῶν ἄρτι τὰς πόλεις οἰκιζόντων. καὶ σεμνυνόμεθα μὲν καὶ μεγαλοφρονοῦμεν ἐπὶ τῷ βέλτιον τῶν ἄλλων γεγονέναι, ῥᾷον δὲ μεταδίδομεν τοῖς βουλομένοις ταύτης τῆς εὐγενείας ἢ Τριβαλλοί τε καὶ Λευκανοὶ τῆς δυσγενείας."

18 ἡ μὲν οὖν Ἰσοκράτους λέξις ἡ κάλλιστα τῶν ἄλλων δοκοῦσα ἔχειν τοιαύτη τίς ἐστι, πολλῶν μὲν ἕνεκα θαυμάζειν ἀξία· καθαρεύει τε γὰρ εἴ τις ἄλλη τοῖς ὀνόμασι [1] καὶ τὴν διάλεκτόν ἐστιν ἀκριβής, φανερά τ' ἐστὶ καὶ κοινὴ καὶ τὰς ἄλλας ἀρετὰς ἁπάσας περιείληφεν, ἐξ ὧν ἂν μάλιστα

large numbers, employ mercenary armies, like the Great King. In those days, when they manned their triremes, they put on board crews of foreigners and slaves, but sent out the citizens to fight under arms. But now we use mercenaries as our fighting troops and make our citizens row, with the result that when they land on enemy territory the would-be rulers of Greece disembark each carrying his rowing-cushion, while the men who are of the character I have just described, face the risks under arms. However, if one could see that our domestic policy was well-managed, could not one be optimistic about the rest? But is it not this that gives cause for most exasperation? For we assert that we are original inhabitants of this land, and that our city was founded before all others: but although we ought thus to be an example to all the world of good and orderly government, we manage our state in a worse and more disorderly manner than those who are just founding their cities. And we glory and pride ourselves in being of better birth than the rest, but we are readier to share this noble birthright with any who desire it than are the Triballians or the Lucanians to share their ignoble origin."

Such is the style of Isocrates, which is reputed to be 18
the finest of all;[1] and it deserves our admiration for many reasons. No style is purer in its vocabulary or more precise in its idiom. It is clear and employs ordinary words, and has all the other virtues that are conducive to a lucid style. It also has many of the

[1] Perhaps Dionysius is here referring specifically to beauty of sound and artistic construction, since in *Isaeus*, 20 Demosthenes is said to be universally judged the greatest orator.

---

[1] ὀνόμασι Krüger: νοήμασι codd.

γένοιτο διάλεκτος σαφής. πολλοὺς δὲ καὶ τῶν ἐπιθέτων κόσμων ἔχει· καὶ γὰρ ὑψηλὴ καὶ σεμνὴ καὶ ἀξιωματικὴ καλλιρρήμων τε καὶ ἡδεῖα καὶ εὔμορφος ἀποχρώντως ἐστίν, οὐ μὴν τελεία γε κατὰ τοῦτο τὸ μέρος, ἀλλ' ἔστιν ὧν ἄν τις αὐτὴν ὡς ἐλλειπόντων μέμψαιτο καὶ οὐ μὰ Δία τῶν φαυλοτάτων. πρῶτον μὲν τῆς συντομίας· στοχαζομένη γὰρ τοῦ σαφοῦς ὀλιγωρεῖ πολλάκις τοῦ μετρίου. ἐχρῆν δὲ ὁμοίως προνοεῖν ἀμφοτέρων. μετὰ τοῦτο τῆς συστροφῆς· ὑπτία γάρ ἐστι καὶ ὑπαγωγικὴ καὶ περιρρέουσα τοῖς νοήμασιν, ὥσπερ εἰσὶν αἱ τῶν ἱστορικῶν, ἡ δ' ἐναγώνιος στρογγύλη τε εἶναι βούλεται καὶ συγκεκροτημένη καὶ μηδὲν ἔχουσα κολπῶδες. ἔτι πρὸς τούτοις κἀκεῖνα πρόσεστι τῷ ἀνδρί. ἄτολμός ἐστι περὶ τὰς τροπικὰς κατασκευὰς καὶ ψοφοδεὴς καὶ οὐκ εἰσφέρεται τόνους κραταιούς. καίτοι γε τοῖς ἀθληταῖς τῆς ἀληθινῆς λέξεως ἰσχυρὰς τὰς ἁφὰς προσεῖναι δεῖ καὶ ἀφύκτους τὰς λαβάς. παθαίνειν τε οὐ δύναται τοὺς ἀκροωμένους, ὁπόσα βούλεται, τὰ πολλὰ δὲ οὐδὲ βούλεται, πείθεται δὲ ἀποχρῆν τῷ πολιτικῷ διάνοιαν ἀποδείξασθαι σπουδαίαν καὶ ἦθος ἐπιεικές. καὶ τυγχάνει μέντοι γε τούτων ἑκατέρου· δεῖ γὰρ τἀληθῆ μαρτυρεῖν. ἦν δὲ ἄρα πάντων ἰσχυρότατον τῷ μέλλοντι πείθειν δῆμον ἢ δικαστήριον, ἐπὶ τὰ πάθη τοὺς ἀκροατὰς ἀγαγεῖν. οὐδὲ δὴ τοῦ πρέποντος ἐν ἅπασιν ἐπιτυγχάνει, ἀνθηρὰν δὲ καὶ θεατρικὴν ἐκ παντὸς ἀξιῶν εἶναι τὴν διάλεκτον, ὡς τῆς ἡδονῆς ἅπαν ἐχούσης ἐν λόγοις τὸ κράτος, ἀπολείπεταί ποτε τοῦ πρέποντος. οὐχ ἅπαντα δέ γε τὰ πράγματα τὴν

additional ornaments, being lofty, stately and dignified, composed in elegant language, agreeable and shapely in its structure to a sufficient degree. But it is not perfect in this respect, and certain by no means unimportant deficiencies call for criticism. First there is the question of conciseness: in its quest for clarity it often neglects moderation, whereas it should have taken thought for both. Next, compactness: it is sprawling and sluggish, and carries more thought than it can hold, like the style of an historian,[1] whereas practical oratory wants to be welded into a round mass with no concavities. And Isocrates has still other faults. He is timid in his use of metaphor and afraid of harsh sound, and never introduces an emphatic note. Yet contestants in real oratorical combat need to have a firm grip and an ineluctable hold. Again, he cannot stir his audience's emotions as much as he wishes, and for the most part he does not even wish to do so. He believes that it is enough for a politician to manifest good intentions and a respectable character, and it must be confessed that he does succeed in these objectives. But, after all, the most potent weapon for a political speaker or a forensic pleader is to draw his audience into an emotional state of mind. Again, Isocrates does not always strike the right note for the occasion. This is because he insists on making his language colourful and showy at all costs, believing that in literature pleasure should reign supreme. Consequently he sometimes fails to achieve the required effect, since not all subjects demand the same manner of ex-

[1] Cf. *De Compositione Verborum*, 4; Cicero, *De Oratore*, ii. 15. 62: *verborum autem ratio et genus orationis fusum atque tractum.*

αὐτὴν ἀπαιτεῖ διάλεκτον, ἀλλ' ἔστιν ὥσπερ σώμασι πρέπουσά τις ἐσθής, οὕτως καὶ νοήμασιν ἁρμόττουσά τις ὀνομασία.[1] τὸ δ' ἐκ παντὸς ἡδύνειν τὰς ἀκοὰς εὐφώνων τε καὶ μαλακῶν[2] ὀνομάτων ἐκλογῇ καὶ πάντα ἀξιοῦν εἰς εὐρύθμους κατακλείειν περιόδων ἁρμονίας καὶ διὰ τῶν θεατρικῶν σχημάτων καλλωπίζειν τὸν λόγον οὐκ ἦν πανταχῇ χρήσιμον. ἀλλὰ τοῦτό γε διδάσκουσιν ἡμᾶς καὶ οἱ τὰ ἔπη καὶ οἱ τὰς τραγῳδίας καὶ οἱ τὰ μέλη τὰ σπουδαῖα γράψαντες, οὐ τοσαύτην ποιούμενοι τῆς ἡδονῆς δόσιν, ὅσην τῆς ἀληθείας.

19 εἰ δὲ ὀρθῶς ἐπιλογίζομαι ταῦτ' ἐγὼ καὶ ἔστιν ἐν ταύταις ταῖς ἀρεταῖς ἐνδεέστερος ὁ ἀνήρ, πάρεστι τῷ βουλομένῳ σκοπεῖν ἐπὶ τῆς ἀρτίως παρατεθείσης λέξεως ποιουμένῳ τὴν ἐξέτασιν. εὐθέως γοῦν τὴν πρώτην διάνοιαν ὀλίγοις ὀνόμασιν ἐξενεχθῆναι δυναμένην μακρὰν ποιεῖ κυκλογραφῶν καὶ δὶς ἢ τρὶς τὰ αὐτὰ λέγων. ἐνῆν μὲν οὖν ἐν τῷ πρώτῳ κώλῳ τῷ "τίς γὰρ ἂν ἄλλοθεν ἐπελθὼν" τὸ "καὶ μὴ συνδιεφθαρμένος ἡμῖν, ἀλλ' ἐξαίφνης ἐπιστὰς τοῖς γινομένοις·" δυνάμει γὰρ ἄμφω ταὐτά. καὶ ἐν τῷ "οἳ φιλοτιμούμεθα μὲν ἐπὶ τοῖς τῶν προγόνων ἔργοις" τὸ "καὶ τὴν πόλιν ἐκ τῶν τότε πραχθέντων ἐγκωμιάζειν ἀξιοῦμεν·" τὸ γὰρ αὐτὸ φιλοτιμεῖσθαί τε καὶ ἐπαινεῖν. καὶ ἐν τῷ "οὐδὲν δὲ τῶν αὐτῶν ἐκείνοις πράττομεν" τὸ "ἀλλὰ πᾶν τοὐναντίον·" ἤρκει γὰρ αὐτῶν εἰρῆσθαι θάτερον. ἐξῆν δέ γε[3] μίαν ἐκ τοῖν δυοῖν ποιῆσαι περίοδον καὶ συντομωτέραν καὶ χαριεστέραν· "τίς γὰρ ἂν ἄλλοθεν ἐπελθὼν οὐκ ἂν μαίνεσθαι νομίσειεν ἡμᾶς, οἳ

pression: just as certain clothes suit certain bodies, so certain language fits certain thought. To please the ear by every means, selecting fair- and soft-sounding words, to insist on wrapping up everything in rhythmically constructed periods, and bedecking a speech with showy figures is not, as we have seen, always advantageous. But that is a lesson which we learn from the writers of epic, tragic and serious lyric poetry, who laid less stress on the demands of pleasure than on those of truth.

Any reader can judge for himself whether my argu- 19
ment is sound and Isocrates is inferior in these qualities by examining the passage which I have just quoted. The very first idea could have been expressed in a few words, but he spins it out by circumlocution and by saying the same thing two or three times. Thus in the first sentence, beginning " Now what if a stranger from abroad " we have ". . . and suddenly find himself embroiled in our affairs, before having the time to become corrupted by our depravity ": both clauses expressing the same idea. And the clause " When we glory in the deeds of our ancestors " is followed by " and think it right to sing the city's praises ": " glory " and " praise " mean the same thing. The clause ". . . and yet act in no way like them " is followed by " but do the exact opposite ": only one of these was necessary. It would have been possible to make one period out of two, and a more elegant one at that, in the following way: " What stranger from abroad would not think us insane, when we glory in the deeds of our ancestors,

---

[1] τις ὀνομασία Sylburg: τοῖς ὀνόμασι codd.
[2] μαλακῶν Sadée: ἐκλεκτῶν codd.
[3] δέ γε Sadée: τε γὰρ codd.

φιλοτιμούμεθα μὲν ἐπὶ τοῖς τῶν προγόνων ἔργοις, οὐδὲν δὲ τῶν αὐτῶν ἐκείνοις πράττομεν;" πολλὰ τοιαῦτά ἐστι παραπληρώματα καθ' ἑκάστην ὀλίγου δεῖν περίοδον οὐκ ἀναγκαίαν ἔχοντα χώραν, ἃ ποιεῖ τὴν ἑρμηνείαν ἀμετροτέραν, τὴν δὲ περίοδον κομψοτέραν. μακρὰ μὲν οὖν ἡ λέξις οὕτως ἐστὶν αὐτῷ, πλατεῖα δὲ καὶ ἀσυγκρότητος πῶς; "κἀκεῖνοι μὲν ἐλευθεροῦντες τὰς πόλεις τὰς Ἑλληνίδας καὶ βοηθοῦντες αὐταῖς τῆς ἡγεμονίας ἠξιώθησαν, ἡμεῖς δὲ καταδουλούμενοι καὶ τἀναντία τοῖς τότε πράττοντες ἀγανακτοῦμεν, εἰ μὴ τὴν αὐτὴν τιμὴν ἐκείνοις ἕξομεν." ταῦτα κεκολπωμένα σφίγξαι μᾶλλον ἐνῆν καὶ στρογγυλώτερα ὧδέ πως ποιῆσαι· "κἀκεῖνοι μὲν ἐλευθεροῦντες τὴν Ἑλλάδα καὶ σῴζοντες ἐπὶ τὴν ἡγεμονίαν προῆλθον, ἡμεῖς δὲ καταδουλούμενοι καὶ διολλύντες ἀγανακτοῦμεν, εἰ μὴ τῶν ἴσων τευξόμεθα." καὶ ἡ μετὰ ταῦτα διάνοια πλατέως τε εἴρηται καὶ ἀσυγκρότητός ἐστιν· "οἳ τοσοῦτον ἀπολελείμμεθα καὶ τοῖς ἔργοις καὶ ταῖς διανοίαις τῶν κατ' ἐκεῖνον τὸν χρόνον γενομένων, ὅσον οἳ μὲν ὑπὲρ τῆς τῶν Ἑλλήνων ἐλευθερίας τήν τε πατρίδα τὴν ἑαυτῶν ἐκλιπεῖν ἐτόλμησαν καὶ μαχόμενοι καὶ ναυμαχοῦντες τοὺς βαρβάρους ἐνίκησαν." ἐξῆν δέ γε αὐτῆς ἐπιστρέψαι τὸ πλάτος οὕτως ἐξενέγκαντα· "οἳ τοσούτῳ χείρους ἐσμὲν τῶν προγόνων, ὅσον οἳ μὲν ὑπὲρ τοῦ σῶσαι τοὺς Ἕλληνας τήν τε πατρίδα τὴν ἑαυτῶν ἐξέλιπον καὶ μαχόμενοι πρὸς τοὺς βαρβάρους ἐνίκησαν." μυρία καὶ ταύτης ἐστὶ λαβεῖν τῆς ἀσθενείας δείγματα. ἔξω γὰρ ὀλίγων τινῶν, οἷς οὐκ ἐκ προνοίας μᾶλλον ἢ κατ' αὐτοματι-

but act in no way like them?" There are many such examples of padding in almost every period; its presence is unnecessary, merely making the expression more inflated and the period more ornate. This is what makes the passage long-winded. What makes it flat and disjointed? Consider: "and whereas they liberated the cities of Greece and came to their aid, and so earned the right to be their leaders, we try to enslave them and then feel aggrieved when we are not honoured to be as they were." This meandering sentence could have been compressed and rounded off more effectively in this way: "They attained to the leadership of Greece by freeing her and saving her, while we, who are trying to enslave and destroy her, are aggrieved that we are not to be accorded equal honour." And the following idea is flatly expressed and incoherent: "We fall so far short of the men of those times in both our deeds and our aspirations that, whereas they had the courage to leave their country in order to save Greece, and fought and conquered the barbarians on both land and sea. . . ." It would certainly have been possible to correct this flatness by expressing it like this: "We who are so much worse than our ancestors, in as much as they, in order to save the Greeks, abandoned their city, fought the barbarians and defeated them." One could find countless examples of this ineffective style also: indeed, this flatness is general throughout his writings apart from

σμὸν συμβέβηκε τὸ συνεστράφθαι, τἆλλα ἐν πλάτει λέγεται.

20 ἄτονος δὲ δὴ καὶ λαβὰς οὐ κραταιὰς ἔχουσα πῶς ἐστιν ἡ λέξις; τῷ [1] ἐπιφέρειν τινὰ τοῖς εἰρημένοις διάνοιαν τοιαύτην [2] "τοσοῦτον δὲ χείρους ἐσμὲν τῶν προγόνων οὐ μόνον τῶν εὐδοκιμησάντων ἀλλὰ καὶ τῶν μισηθέντων, ὅσον ἐκεῖνοι μὲν εἰ πολεμεῖν πρός τινα ψηφίσαιντο, μεστῆς οὔσης ἀργυρίου καὶ χρυσίου τῆς ἀκροπόλεως ὅμως ὑπὲρ τῶν δοξάντων τοῖς ἑαυτῶν σώμασιν ᾤοντο δεῖν κινδυνεύειν, ἡμεῖς δ' εἰς τοσαύτην ἀπορίαν ἐληλυθότες καὶ τοσοῦτοι τὸ πλῆθος ὄντες, ὥσπερ βασιλεὺς ὁ μέγας μισθωτοῖς χρώμεθα τοῖς στρατοπέδοις." φέρε δὲ πῶς ἐνῆν αὐτὴν εἰπεῖν στρογγυλωτέραν; "ἀλλὰ ταῦτα μὲν ἴσως χείρους ἐσμὲν τῶν προγόνων, τὰ δ' ἄλλα βελτίους, οὐ λέγω τῶν εὐδοκιμησάντων, πόθεν γάρ; ἀλλὰ τῶν μισηθέντων. καὶ τίς οὐκ οἶδεν, ὅτι ἐκεῖνοι μὲν πλείστων ποτὲ πληρώσαντες χρημάτων τὴν ἀκρόπολιν οὐ κατεμισθοφόρουν τὸν κοινὸν πλοῦτον εἰς τοὺς πολεμίους, ἀλλὰ ἀπὸ τῶν ἰδίων εἰσφέροντες ἔστιν ὅτε καὶ τοῖς ἑαυτῶν σώμασι κινδυνεύειν ἠξίουν; ἡμεῖς δὲ οὕτως ὄντες ἄποροι καὶ τοσοῦτοι τὸ πλῆθος μισθοφόροις τοῖς στρατεύμασι πολεμοῦμεν ὥσπερ καὶ βασιλεὺς ὁ μέγας." ἀλλὰ μὴν ὅτι γε ἄψυχός ἐστιν ἡ διάλεκτος αὐτοῦ καὶ οὐ παθητικὴ πνεύματός τε, οὗ μάλιστα δεῖ τοῖς ἐναγωνίοις λόγοις, ἐλαχίστην ἔχουσα μοῖραν, οἴομαι μὲν ἔγωγε καὶ χωρὶς ὑπομνήσεως ἅπασιν εἶναι φανερόν.

[1] ἔχουσα πῶς ἐστιν ἡ λέξις; τῷ Sylburg: ἔχουσά πως ἐστὶν ἡ λέξις τῷ MBP.

a few instances of concise expression which arise as much by chance as by design.

Why is it that this style lacks intensity and the 20
power to hold the reader fast? Because it adds to the passage I have quoted a sentence like this:[1] "And so far are we inferior to our ancestors, both those who enjoyed the esteem of the Greeks and those who were hated by them, that whereas they, when they decided to wage war against any state, regarded it as their duty, even though the Acropolis was full of silver and gold, to face danger in their own persons in support of their resolutions, we, by contrast, in spite of extreme poverty and our large numbers, employ mercenary armies, like the Great King." Now see how this could have been rendered more concisely: "But perhaps we are worse in this respect than our ancestors, but better in other respects—I do not mean those of good repute, for how could I? but those who were hated. Who does not know that they filled the Acropolis with money over the years, but did not squander this public wealth on the enemy by hiring mercenaries to fight them, but often both paid extra taxes out of their own pockets and risked their lives by fighting? But we are both poor and numerous, and yet hire men to fight for us just like the Great King." Well, as to the lack of life and feeling in his style, and the virtual absence of spirit, an essential quality in practical oratory, I personally think these faults are plain to everyone, even without my reminding them. Still, if examples of this also are required,

[1] 47.

[2] τοιαύτην Krüger: ταύτην codd.

εἰ δὲ ἄρα καὶ παραδειγμάτων δεῖ, πολλῶν ὄντων, ἅ τις ἂν εἰπεῖν ἔχοι, μιᾷ διανοίᾳ χρησάμενος ἀρκεσθήσομαι. διαδέχεται δὴ τὴν ὀλίγῳ πρότερον ἐξετασθεῖσαν ἀντίθεσιν ἑτέρα τοιαύτη τις ἀντίθεσις· "καὶ τότε μέν, εἰ τριήρεις ἐπληροῦμεν, τοὺς μὲν ξένους καὶ δούλους ναύτας ἐνεβιβάζομεν τοὺς δὲ πολίτας μεθ' ὅπλων ἐξεπέμπομεν, νῦν δὲ τοῖς μὲν ξένοις ὁπλίταις χρώμεθα τοὺς δὲ πολίτας ἐλαύνειν ἀναγκάζομεν, ὥσθ' ὁπόταν ἀποβαίνωσιν εἰς τὴν τῶν πολεμίων, οἱ μὲν ἄρχειν τῶν Ἑλλήνων ἀξιοῦντες ὑπηρέσιον ἔχοντες ἐκβαίνουσιν, οἱ δὲ τοιοῦτοι τὰς φύσεις ὄντες, οἵους ὀλίγῳ πρότερον εἶπον, μεθ' ὅπλων κινδυνεύουσιν." ἐν τούτοις οὐ μέμφομαι τὸν ἄνδρα τοῦ λήματος [1] (γενναία γὰρ ἡ διάνοια καὶ δυναμένη κινῆσαι πάθος), τὸ δὲ τῆς λέξεως λεῖον καὶ μαλακὸν αἰτιῶμαι. τραχεῖαν γὰρ ἔδει καὶ πικρὰν εἶναι καὶ πληγῇ τι παραπλήσιον ποιεῖν· ἡ δ' ἔστιν ὑγρὰ καὶ ὁμαλὴ καὶ ὥσπερ ἔλαιον ἀψοφητὶ διὰ τῆς ἀκοῆς ῥέουσα, θέλγειν γέ τοι καὶ ἡδύνειν ζητοῦσα τὴν ἀκοήν. ἀλλ' εὖ τοῖς σχήμασιν ἔχει πρὸς ἀγῶνας πολλοῖς οὖσι καὶ ποικίλοις καὶ διὰ τούτων παθαίνει τοὺς ἀκούοντας; πολλοῦ γε καὶ δεῖ. τὰ γὰρ ἐκλύοντα μάλιστα τὴν δύναμιν αὐτῆς καὶ ἀποστρέφοντα τὴν ἀκοὴν ταῦτ' [2] ἔστι τὰ μειρακιώδη πάρισα καὶ τὰ ψυχρὰ ἀντίθετα καὶ τὰ παραπλήσια τούτοις. αὐτίκα ἐν αὐτῇ ταύτῃ τῇ λέξει, περὶ ἧς ὁ λόγος, τό τε πρᾶγμα ὅλον ἐστὶν ἀντίθεσις καὶ τὰ κατὰ μέρος αὐτοῦ νοήματα ἓν πρὸς ἓν ἀντίκειται καὶ τῶν περιόδων ἑκάστη δι' ἀντιθέτων κατεσκεύασται, ὥστ'

[1] λήματος Sylburg: λήμματος codd.

although there are plenty that could be adduced, I shall content myself with one idea. The antithesis which we have just examined is picked up by another, which runs as follows: "In those days, when we manned our triremes, we put on board crews of foreigners and slaves, but sent out the citizens to fight under arms. But now we use mercenaries as our fighting troops and make our citizens row, with the result that whenever they land on enemy territory the would-be rulers of Greece disembark each carrying his rowing-cushion, while the men who are of the character I have just described, face the risks under arms." I do not criticise the temper of the orator here, for the idea is noble and capable of stirring emotion, but I disapprove of the smoothness and softness [1] of the language. It ought to be rough and harsh, and have almost the effect of a blow, but in fact it is languid, flowing evenly and soundlessly through the ear like oil, all because it is seeking to soothe and gratify it. But is he well-equipped for debate by virtue of the number and variety of his figures, with which he arouses his readers' emotions? Far from it! It is just these juvenile parallelisms, frigid antitheses and similar devices that are chiefly responsible for weakening his style and merely diverting the ear. For example, in the actual passage we are discussing, the whole subject is an antithesis, in which the constituent ideas are set out in contrasting pairs, and each period is constructed in an antithetical framework to a degree

[1] μαλακὸς is also used in musical writing to describe low pitch.

---

[2] ταῦτ' Krüger: τοῦτ' codd.

ἀποκναίειν τοὺς ἀκούοντας ἀηδίᾳ καὶ κόρῳ. ὃ δὲ λέγω, τοιοῦτόν ἐστι. πάσης διανοίας καὶ περιόδου καὶ λήμματος αἵ τε ἀρχαὶ καὶ αἱ ἐπιφοραὶ τοιαῦταί εἰσιν· οἱ[1] μὲν γὰρ ἡμεῖς δέ, ⟨καί·⟩[2] κἀκεῖνοι μὲν ἡμεῖς δέ, καί· τότε μὲν νῦν δέ, καί· ὅσον οἳ μὲν ἡμεῖς δέ, καί· τοῦτο μὲν τοῦτο δέ. ταῦτ' ἀπὸ τῆς ἀρχῆς ἕως τελευτῆς κεκύκλωκε. τροπαὶ δὲ καὶ μεταβολαὶ καὶ ποικιλίαι σχημάτων, ἃ πέφυκε λύειν τὸν τῆς διανοίας κόπον,[3] οὐδαμοῦ. πολλὰ ἄν τις ἔχοι τοιαῦτα ἐπιτιμᾶν Ἰσοκράτει τῶν περὶ τὴν διάλεκτον ἐλλειμμάτων, ἀλλὰ καὶ ταῦθ' ἱκανά.

21 εἰσαγέσθω δὴ μετὰ τοῦτον ὁ Δημοσθένης, καὶ λαμβανέσθω κἀκείνου λέξις ἐκ μιᾶς τῶν κατὰ Φιλίππου δημηγορίας, δι' ἧς καὶ αὐτὸς συγκρίνει τὰ καθ' ἑαυτὸν ἔργα τοῖς ἐπὶ τῶν προγόνων καὶ τοὺς νέους δημαγωγοὺς τοῖς παλαιοῖς, οὐ καθ' ἓν ἔργον ἕκαστον ἀρχαῖον ἔργῳ καινῷ παρατιθεὶς οὐδὲ πάντα μικρολογῶν συγκρίσει, ἀλλὰ ὅλῃ ⟨τῇ θέσει⟩[4] ποιούμενος ὅλην τὴν ἀντίθεσιν διεξοδικὴν οὕτως· "Καίτοι σκέψασθε, ὦ ἄνδρες Ἀθηναῖοι, ἅ τις ἂν κεφάλαια εἰπεῖν ἔχοι τῶν τε ἐπὶ τῶν προγόνων ἔργων καὶ τῶν ἐφ' ὑμῶν. ἔσται δὲ βραχὺς καὶ γνώριμος ὑμῖν ὁ λόγος. οὐ γὰρ ἀλλοτρίοις χρωμένοις ὑμῖν παραδείγμασιν ἀλλ' οἰκείοις, ὦ ἄνδρες Ἀθηναῖοι, εὐδαίμοσιν ἔξεστι γίγνεσθαι. ἐκεῖνοι τοίνυν, οἷς οὐκ ἐχαρίζοντο οἱ λέγοντες, οὐδ' ἐφίλουν αὐτούς, ὥσπερ ὑμᾶς οὗτοι

[1] οἱ Sadée: ἐκεῖνος MB.
[2] καί inseruit Sadée.
[3] κόπον Reiske: σκόπον codd.
[4] τῇ θέσει inseruit Reiske.

which exhausts the hearer with a feeling of distaste and surfeit. This is what I mean: the first and second member of every idea and period and every argument are contrasted like this: "They in their day . . . we now," "those men . . . we . . . ," "in those times . . . today," "inasmuch as they . . . we," "on the one hand . . . on the other." This construction recurs constantly from beginning to end. Transposition, alteration or variation of figures, which are natural means of relieving the monotony of the thought, are nowhere to be found. One could find many such passages in which Isocrates deserves criticism for deficiencies in his manner of expression; but these will suffice.

After Isocrates, let us introduce Demosthenes, and 21
take a passage from one of his harangues against Philip in which he, like Isocrates, compares the behaviour of his contemporaries with that of his ancestors, and modern politicians with those of former times. He does not set out each separate pair of actions in finicky detail, old and new, and compare them, but carries the whole antithesis through the whole theme by arranging the items in two contrasting groups, thus:[1]

"Yet observe, Athenians, what a summary contrast may be drawn between the state's achievements in the time of your ancestors and in your own day. The tale will be brief and familiar to all; for you need not look abroad for examples that provide the key to your future prosperity, but at home, Athenians. Our forefathers, whose speakers did not humour or caress them, as those of today do you, for forty-five years

[1] *Olynth.* iii. 23–32.

νῦν, πέντε μὲν καὶ τετταράκοντα ἔτη τῶν Ἑλλήνων ἑκόντων· πλείω δ' ἢ μύρια τάλαντα εἰς τὴν ἀκρόπολιν συνήγαγον· ὑπήκουε δὲ ὁ ταύτην τὴν χώραν ἔχων αὐτοῖς βασιλεύς, ὥσπερ ἐστὶ προσῆκον βάρβαρον Ἕλλησι· πολλὰ δὲ καὶ καλὰ καὶ πεζῇ καὶ ναυμαχοῦντες ἔστησαν τρόπαια αὐτοὶ στρατευόμενοι· μόνοι δ' ἀνθρώπων κρείττω τὴν ἐπὶ τοῖς ἔργοις δόξαν τῶν φθονούντων κατέλιπον. ἐπὶ μὲν δὴ τῶν Ἑλληνικῶν ἦσαν τοιοῦτοι, ἐν δὲ τοῖς κατὰ τὴν πόλιν αὐτὴν θεάσασθε ὁποῖοι ἔν ⟨τε⟩ τοῖς κοινοῖς καὶ ἐν τοῖς ἰδίοις. δημόσια μὲν τοίνυν οἰκοδομήματα καὶ κάλλη τοσαῦτα καὶ τοιαῦτα κατεσκεύασαν ἡμῖν ἱερῶν καὶ τῶν ἐν τούτοις ἀναθημάτων, ὥστε μηδενὶ τῶν ἐπιγιγνομένων ὑπερβολὴν λειφθῆναι. ἰδίᾳ δὲ οὕτω σώφρονες ἦσαν καὶ σφόδρα ἐν τῷ τῆς πολιτείας ἤθει μένοντες, ὥστε τὴν Ἀριστείδου καὶ Μιλτιάδου καὶ τῶν τότε λαμπρῶν οἰκίαν εἴ τις ἄρ' οἶδεν ὑμῶν ὁποία ποτ' ἐστίν, ὁρᾷ τῆς τοῦ γείτονος οὐδὲν σεμνοτέραν οὖσαν. οὐ γὰρ εἰς περιουσίαν αὐτοῖς ἐπράττετο τὰ τῆς πόλεως, ἀλλὰ τὸ κοινὸν ἕκαστος αὔξειν ᾤετο δεῖν. ἐκ δὲ τοῦ τὰ μὲν Ἑλληνικὰ πιστῶς, τὰ δὲ πρὸς τοὺς θεοὺς εὐσεβῶς, τὰ δ' ἐν αὐτοῖς ἴσως διοικεῖν μεγάλην εἰκότως ἐκέκτηντο εὐδαιμονίαν. τότε μὲν δὴ τοῦτον τὸν τρόπον εἶχε τὰ πράγματα ἐκείνοις χρωμένοις, οἷς εἶπον, προστάταις. νυνὶ δὲ πῶς ἡμῖν ὑπὸ τῶν χρηστῶν τῶν νῦν τὰ πράγματα ἔξει; ἆρά γε ὁμοίως καὶ παραπλησίως; καὶ τὰ μὲν ἄλλα σιωπῶ πολλὰ ἔχων εἰπεῖν· ἀλλ' ὅσης πάντες ὁρᾶτε ἐρημίας ἐπειλημμένοι καὶ Λακεδαιμονίων

ruled the Greeks with their consent; they accumulated more than ten thousand talents in their treasury; the king of that land submitted to them, as a barbarian should to Greeks; they set up many glorious monuments to commemorate victories won by their own fighting on land and sea; and they alone among mankind have left behind them a reputation which envy cannot erase. Such were their achievements in Hellenic affairs: now see what they were like in their domestic affairs, both as citizens and as men. In public they erected for our benefit such a wealth of beautiful buildings and other objects, such as temples and the dedicated objects in them, that posterity has been left no chance to surpass them. In their private life they were so moderate, and adhered so steadfastly to the national tradition, that anyone who knows the style of house which Aristides had, or Miltiades, or other famous men of that day, is aware that it was no grander than his neighbour's. They did not engage in politics for personal profit, but each felt it his duty to enrich the commonwealth. By conduct honourable towards the other Greeks, reverence towards the gods and fair dealing in domestic matters, they deservedly achieved great prosperity.

"That is how the state fared in the old days under the statesmen I have mentioned. How is it faring now under the worthies of the present day? Is there any similarity or resemblance? I pass over many topics on which I could wax eloquent; but with the dearth of competition which you all observe, the Spartans being in eclipse, the Thebans being fully

μὲν ἀπολωλότων, Θηβαίων δ' ἀσχόλων ὄντων, τῶν δ' ἄλλων οὐδενὸς ὄντος ἀξιόχρεω περὶ τῶν πρωτείων ὑμῖν ἀνταῖραι, ἐξὸν ἡμῖν καὶ τὰ ἡμέτερα αὐτῶν ἀσφαλῶς ἔχειν καὶ τὰ τῶν ἄλλων δίκαια βραβεύειν, ἀπεστερήμεθα μὲν χώρας οἰκείας, πλείω δ' ἢ χίλια καὶ πεντακόσια τάλαντα ἀνηλώκαμεν εἰς οὐδὲν δέον, οὓς δὲ ἐν τῷ πολέμῳ συμμάχους ἐκτησάμεθα, εἰρήνης οὔσης ἀπολωλέκασιν οὗτοι, ἐχθρὸν δ' ἐφ' ἡμᾶς αὐτοὺς τηλικοῦτον ἠσκήκαμεν. ἢ φρασάτω τις ἐμοὶ παρελθών, πόθεν ἄλλοθεν ἰσχυρὸς γέγονεν ἢ παρ' ἡμῶν αὐτῶν ὁ Φίλιππος; ἀλλ' ὦ τᾶν εἰ ταῦτα φαύλως, τά γε ἐν αὐτῇ τῇ πόλει νῦν ἄμεινον ἔχει. καὶ τί ἂν εἰπεῖν τις ἔχοι; τὰς ἐπάλξεις, ἃς κονιῶμεν, καὶ τὰς ὁδούς, ἃς ἐπισκευάζομεν, καὶ κρήνας καὶ λήρους; ἀποβλέψατε δὴ πρὸς τοὺς ταῦτα πολιτευομένους, ὧν οἳ μὲν ἐκ πτωχῶν πλούσιοι γεγόνασιν, οἳ δ' ἐξ ἀδόξων ἔντιμοι, ἔνιοι δὲ τὰς ἰδίας οἰκίας τῶν δημοσίων οἰκοδομημάτων σεμνοτέρας εἰσὶ κατεσκευασμένοι, ὅσῳ δὲ τὰ τῆς πόλεως ἐλάττω γέγονε, τοσούτῳ τὰ τούτων ηὔξηται. τί δὴ τὸ πάντων αἴτιον τούτων; καὶ τί δή ποτ' εἶχεν ἅπαντα καλῶς τότε καὶ νῦν οὐκ ὀρθῶς; ὅτι τὸ μὲν πρῶτον καὶ στρατεύεσθαι τολμῶν αὐτὸς ὁ δῆμος δεσπότης τῶν πολιτευομένων ἦν καὶ κύριος αὐτὸς ἁπάντων τῶν ἀγαθῶν, καὶ ἀγαπητὸν ἦν παρὰ τοῦ δήμου τῶν ἄλλων ἑκάστῳ καὶ τιμῆς καὶ ἀρχῆς καὶ ἀγαθοῦ τινος μεταλαβεῖν. νῦν δὲ τοὐναντίον κύριοι μὲν τῶν ἀγαθῶν οἱ πολιτευόμενοι καὶ διὰ τούτων ἅπαντα πράττεται, ὑμεῖς δὲ ὁ δῆμος ἐκνενευρισμέ-

occupied and none of the rest capable of challenging us for supremacy, it should be possible for us to hold our own securely and arbitrate the claims of others. Yet we have been deprived of territory which belongs to us, and have spent more than one thousand five hundred talents to no purpose; these politicians have lost in peace time those allies which we gained in war, and we have trained up a formidable enemy to fight against us. Or let anyone come forward and tell me from where else Philip obtained his power, if not from us. Well, my dear sir, you might say, if our foreign affairs are in a bad way, at any rate things at home are better now. What possible proof is there of this? The parapets which we whitewash? The roads which we repair? The fountains and the other nonsense? Look at the statesmen who are responsible for these: some have risen from beggary to opulence, or from obscurity to honour; some have made their private houses more splendid than public buildings, and their wealth has increased at the same pace as the fortunes of the state have declined.

"What is the cause of all this? Why on earth did everything go well then and go badly now? In the first place, because in those days the people themselves had the courage to be soldiers, and hence were masters of the politicians and had direct control over everything worth having; and every official was glad to receive from the people his share of honour, his post or any other good things. But now, on the contrary, the politicians have control of the prizes and conduct all the business, while you, the people, ener-

νοι καὶ περιῃρημένοι χρήματα, συμμάχους, ἐν ὑπηρέτου καὶ προσθήκης μέρει γεγένησθε, ἀγαπῶντες, ἂν μεταδῶσι θεωρικὸν ὑμῖν ἢ βοηδρόμια πέμψωσιν οὗτοι. καὶ τὸ πάντων ἀνανδρότατον· τῶν ὑμετέρων αὐτῶν χάριν προσοφείλετε. οἳ δ' ἐν αὐτῇ τῇ πόλει καθείρξαντες ὑμᾶς ἐπάγουσιν ἐπὶ ταῦτα καὶ τιθασεύουσι, χειροήθεις αὑτοῖς ποιοῦντες. ἔστι δ' οὐδέποτ', οἶμαι, μέγα καὶ νεανικὸν φρόνημα λαβεῖν μικρὰ καὶ φαῦλα πράττοντας. ὁποῖ' ἄττα γὰρ ἂν τὰ ἐπιτηδεύματα τῶν ἀνθρώπων ᾖ, τοιοῦτον ἀνάγκη καὶ τὸ φρόνημα ἔχειν. ταῦτα μὰ τὴν Δήμητρα οὐκ ἂν θαυμάσαιμι εἰ μείζων εἰπόντι μοι γένοιτο παρ' ὑμῶν βλάβη ἢ τῶν πεποιηκότων αὐτὰ ἑκάστῳ. οὐδὲ γὰρ παρρησία περὶ πάντων ἀεὶ παρ' ὑμῖν ἐστιν, ἀλλ' ἔγωγ' ὅτι καὶ νῦν γέγονε, θαυμάζω." ταύτην τὴν διάλεξιν τίς οὐκ ἂν ὁμολογήσειε καὶ κατὰ τἆλλα μὲν πάντα διαφέρειν τῆς Ἰσοκράτους; καὶ γὰρ εὐγενέστερον ἐκείνης καὶ μεγαλοπρεπέστερον ἡρμήνευκε τὰ πράγματα καὶ ⟨εὐπρεπεστέροις⟩ [1] περιείληφεν ὀνόμασι συγκεκρότηταί τε καὶ συνέσπασται καὶ περιτετόρευται τοῖς νοήμασιν ἄμεινον ἰσχύϊ τε πλείονι κέχρηται καὶ τόνοις ἐμβριθεστέροις καὶ πέφευγε τὰ ψυχρὰ καὶ μειρακιώδη σχήματα, οἷς ἐκείνη καλλωπίζεται πέρα τοῦ μετρίου· μάλιστα δὲ κατὰ τὸ δραστήριον καὶ ἐναγώνιον καὶ ἐμπαθὲς ὅλῳ καὶ τῷ παντὶ κρεῖττον ἔχει ἐκείνης. ἐγὼ γοῦν, ὃ πρὸς ἀμφοτέρας πάσχω τὰς λέξεις, ἐρῶ· οἴομαι δὲ κοινόν τι πάθος ἁπάντων ἐρεῖν καὶ οὐκ ἐμὸν ἴδιον μόνου.

vated, stripped of your wealth and your allies, have become like underlings and mere accessories, content if these men dole you out tickets for the theatre or regale you with festival processions; and, the unmanliest part of all, you are grateful to receive what is actually yours. They coop you up in the city itself, then lead you to these diversions and make you tame and submissive to their hands. It is impossible, I believe, ever to conceive great and noble aspirations when you are engaged in petty and mean employment: men's thoughts will necessarily be on the same level as the occupation they pursue. Upon my word, I should not be surprised if I were punished more severely by you for mentioning these things than the men who severally brought them about: for one cannot always even speak freely to you on all subjects, and I am surprised that I have been allowed to do so now."

Who would not agree that this passage is in a general way superior to that of Isocrates? And in particular he has expressed the subject-matter in a nobler and more dignified way than Isocrates; he has clothed it in ⟨more seemly⟩ words, and unified, compressed and shaped it better to the thought. He has deployed more force and more powerful emphasis, and avoided the frigid and juvenile figures which adorn the other's style to excess. But above all, the whole of it, in its energy, vehemence and feeling, is wholly and entirely superior to the style of Isocrates. At any rate I propose to describe my feelings when I read both orators, feelings which, I think, are not uniquely mine but are experienced by everyone.

[1] lacunam indicavit Radermacher: *εὐπρεπεστέροις* conieci.

22 ὅταν μέν τινα τῶν Ἰσοκράτους ἀναγινώσκω λόγων, εἴτε τῶν πρὸς τὰ δικαστήρια καὶ τὰς ἐκκλησίας γεγραμμένων ἢ τῶν . . .[1] ἐν ἤθει σπουδαῖος γίνομαι καὶ πολὺ τὸ εὐσταθὲς ἔχω τῆς γνώμης, ὥσπερ οἱ τῶν σπονδείων αὐλημάτων ἢ τῶν Δωρίων τε κἀναρμονίων μελῶν ἀκροώμενοι. ὅταν δὲ ⟨τῶν⟩[2] Δημοσθένους τινὰ λάβω λόγων, ἐνθουσιῶ τε καὶ δεῦρο κἀκεῖσε ἄγομαι, πάθος ἕτερον ἐξ ἑτέρου μεταλαμβάνων, ἀπιστῶν, ἀγωνιῶν, δεδιώς, καταφρονῶν, μισῶν, ἐλεῶν, εὐνοῶν, ὀργιζόμενος, φθονῶν, ἅπαντα τὰ πάθη μεταλαμβάνων, ὅσα κρατεῖν πέφυκεν ἀνθρωπίνης γνώμης· διαφέρειν τε οὐδὲν ἐμαυτῷ δοκῶ τῶν τὰ μητρῷα καὶ τὰ κορυβαντικὰ καὶ ὅσα τούτοις παραπλήσιά ἐστι, τελουμένων, εἴτε ὀσμαῖς ἐκεῖνοί γε ⟨εἴτ ὄψεσιν⟩[3] εἴτε ἤχοις εἴτε τῶν δαιμόνων πνεύματι αὐτῶν κινούμενοι τὰς πολλὰς καὶ ποικίλας ἐκεῖνοι λαμβάνουσι φαντασίας. καὶ δή ποτε καὶ ἐνεθυμήθην, τί ποτε τοὺς τότε ἀνθρώπους ἀκούοντας αὐτοῦ λέγοντος ταῦτα πάσχειν εἰκὸς ἦν. ὅπου γὰρ ἡμεῖς οἱ τοσοῦτον ἀπηρτημένοι τοῖς χρόνοις καὶ οὐθὲν πρὸς τὰ πράγματα πεπονθότες οὕτως ὑπαγόμεθα καὶ κρατούμεθα καί, ὅποι ποτ' ἂν ἡμᾶς ὁ λόγος ἄγῃ, πορευόμεθα, πῶς τότε Ἀθηναῖοί τε καὶ οἱ ἄλλοι Ἕλληνες ἤγοντο ὑπὸ τοῦ ἀνδρὸς ἐπὶ τῶν ἀληθινῶν τε καὶ ἰδίων ἀγώνων, αὐτοῦ λέγοντος ἐκείνου τὰ ἑαυτοῦ μετὰ τῆς ἀξιώσεως, ἧς εἶχε, τὴν αὐτοπάθειαν καὶ τὸ

[1] lacunam indicavit Sylburg.
[2] τῶν inseruit Krüger.
[3] lacunam supplevit Radermacher.

Whenever I read a speech of Isocrates, whether it 22
be forensic, political (or epideictic), I become serious and feel a great tranquillity of mind, like those listening to libation-music played on reed-pipes or to Dorian or enharmonic melodies.[1] But when I pick up one of Demosthenes's speeches, I am transported: I am led hither and thither, feeling one emotion after another—disbelief, anguish, terror, contempt, hatred, pity, goodwill, anger, envy—every emotion in turn that can sway the human mind. I feel exactly the same as those who take part in the Corybantic dances and the rites of Cybele the Mother-Goddess,[2] and other similar ceremonies, whether it is because these celebrants are inspired by the scents, ⟨sights⟩, or sound or by the influence of the deities themselves, that they experience many and various sensations. And I have often wondered what on earth those men who actually heard him make these speeches could have felt. For if we, who are so far removed in time and unaffected by the events, are so carried away and overpowered that we follow wherever the speech leads us, how must the Athenians and the rest of the Greeks have been excited at the time by the orator addressing them on live and personal issues, using all

[1] The character of both types of music being that of slow-moving dignity, in "spondaic" rhythm (— —). "Enharmonic" refers to one of the species of the tetrachord scale (e.g. E to A) in which intervals of quarter-tones were used. The context suggests that such melodies were felt to be capable of inducing intensified, lofty emotions in their audiences, and it is of some interest to find quarter-tones used by certain modern composers, e.g. Ernest Bloch, with a similar purpose.

[2] The rites of Cybele, originally a Lydian deity, lasted some twelve days in March, and culminated in joyful banqueting and the ceremonial bathing of the statue of the goddess.

παράστημα τῆς ψυχῆς ἀποδεικνυμένου, κοσμοῦντος ἅπαντα καὶ χρωματίζοντος τῇ πρεπούσῃ ὑποκρίσει, ἧς δεινότατος ἀσκητὴς ἐγένετο, ὡς ἅπαντές τε ὁμολογοῦσι καὶ ἐξ αὐτῶν ἰδεῖν ἔστι τῶν λόγων, ὧν ἄρτι προηνεγκάμην, οὓς οὐκ ἔνι τῷ βουλομένῳ ἐν ἡδονῇ ὡς ἀνάγνωσμα διελθεῖν, ἀλλ' αὐτοὶ διδάσκουσι, πῶς αὐτοὺς ὑποκρίνεσθαι δεῖ, νῦν μὲν εἰρωνευόμενον, νῦν δὲ ἀγανακτοῦντα, νῦν δὲ νεμεσῶντα, δεδιττόμενόν τε αὖ καὶ θεραπεύοντα καὶ νουθετοῦντα καὶ παρορμῶντα καὶ πάνθ', ἃ βούλεται ποιεῖν ἡ λέξις, ἀποδεικνύμενον ἐπὶ τῆς προφορᾶς. εἰ δὴ τὸ διὰ τοσούτων ⟨ἐτῶν⟩[1] ἐγκαταμισγόμενον[2] τοῖς βυβλίοις πνεῦμα τοσαύτην ἰσχὺν ἔχει καὶ οὕτως ἀγωγόν ἐστι τῶν ἀνθρώπων, ἦ που τότε ὑπερφυές τι καὶ δεινὸν χρῆμα ἦν ἐπὶ τῶν ἐκείνου λόγων.

23 ἀλλὰ γάρ, ἵνα μὴ περὶ ταῦτα διατρίβων ἀναγκασθῶ παραλιπεῖν τι τῶν περιλειπομένων, Ἰσοκράτην μὲν καὶ τὸν χαρακτῆρα τῆς ἀγωγῆς ἐκείνης ἐάσω, περὶ δὲ Πλάτωνος ἤδη διαλέξομαι τά γ' ἐμοὶ δοκοῦντα μετὰ παρρησίας, οὐθὲν οὔτε τῇ δόξῃ τἀνδρὸς προστιθεὶς οὔτε τῆς ἀληθείας ἀφαιρούμενος, καὶ μάλιστα ἐπεί τινες ἀξιοῦσι πάντων αὐτὸν ἀποφαίνειν φιλοσόφων τε καὶ ῥητόρων ἑρμηνεῦσαι τὰ πράγματα δαιμονιώτατον παρακελεύονταί τε ἡμῖν ὅρῳ καὶ κανόνι χρῆσθαι καθαρῶν ἅμα καὶ ἰσχυρῶν λόγων[3] τούτῳ τῷ ἀνδρί. ἤδη δέ τινων ἤκουσα ἐγὼ λεγόντων, ὡς, εἰ καὶ παρὰ θεοῖς διάλεκτός ἐστιν, ᾗ τὸ τῶν ἀνθρώπων κέχρηται γένος, οὐκ ἄλλως ὁ βασιλεὺς ὧν αὐτῶν διαλέγεται

[1] ἐτῶν inseruit Cobet.

his prestige to display his own feelings and to bare his soul, and adding beauty and colour to every word with the appropriate delivery, of which art he was, as everyone agrees, the most brilliant exponent.[1] This faculty can be seen in the actual passage I have just quoted. No one can pick it up and read it at will and for diversion, since the words themselves tell what actions must accompany their readings: the reciter must feign now irony, now indignation, now rage, now fear, now solicitude, now admonition, now exhortation; everything, in fact, which the words require, he must portray in his delivery. If, then, the spirit with which Demosthenes's pages are still imbued after so many years possesses so much power and moves his readers in this way, surely to hear him delivering his speeches at the time must have been an extraordinary and overwhelming experience.

However, if I were to spend too much time on these 23
matters I might be forced to leave the rest of my discussion incomplete. I shall therefore pass on from Isocrates and the characteristics of his style to Plato. I shall speak freely, making no concessions to the man's reputation or being less than truthful. This impartial treatment is especially necessary because some claim that he is the supreme literary genius among philosophers and orators, and urge us to regard him as the definitive norm for both plain and forceful writing. I have even heard it said, that if the gods speak in the same language as men, the king of the gods can only speak in the language of Plato. In

[1] See esp. [Plutarch], *Lives of the Ten Orators*, 845B.

---

[2] ἐγκαταμισγόμενον Sylburg: ἐγκαταμιγόμενον MBP.
[3] λόγων Sylburg: ὁ λόγος.

θεὸς ἢ ὡς Πλάτων. πρὸς δὴ τοιαύτας ὑπολήψεις καὶ τερατείας ἀνθρώπων ἡμιτελῶν περὶ λόγους, οἳ τὴν εὐγενῆ κατασκευὴν οὐκ ἴσασιν ἥ τίς ποτ' ἐστὶν οὐδὲ δύνανται, πᾶσαν εἰρωνείαν ἀφείς, ὡς πέφυκα, διαλέξομαι. ὃν δὲ ἀξιῶ τρόπον ποιήσασθαι τὴν ἐξέτασιν αὐτοῦ, βούλομαι προειπεῖν. ἐγὼ τὴν μὲν ἐν τοῖς διαλόγοις δεινότητα τοῦ ἀνδρὸς καὶ μάλιστα ἐν οἷς ἂν φυλάττῃ τὸν Σωκρατικὸν χαρακτῆρα, ὥσπερ ἐν τῷ Φιλήβῳ, πάνυ ἄγαμαί τε καὶ τεθαύμακα, τῆς δ' ἀπειροκαλίας αὐτὸν οὐδεπώποτ' ἐζήλωσα τῆς ἐν ταῖς ἐπιθέτοις κατασκευαῖς, ὥσπερ ἔφην καὶ πρότερον, καὶ πάντων ἥκιστα ἐν οἷς ἂν εἰς πολιτικὰς ὑποθέσεις συγκαθεὶς [1] ἐγκώμια καὶ ψόγους κατηγορίας τε καὶ ἀπολογίας ἐπιχειρῇ γράφειν. ἕτερος γάρ τις αὐτοῦ γίνεται τότε καὶ καταισχύνει τὴν φιλόσοφον ἀξίωσιν. κἀμοί γε πολλάκις ἐπῆλθεν εἰπεῖν ἐπὶ τῶν τοιούτων αὐτοῦ λόγων, ὃ πεποίηται παρ' Ὁμήρῳ πρὸς τὴν Ἀφροδίτην ὁ Ζεὺς λέγων·

Οὔ τοι, τέκνον ἐμόν, δέδοται πολεμήια ἔργα,
ἀλλὰ σύ γ' ἱμερόεντα μετέρχεο ἔργα γάμοιο

Σωκρατικῶν διαλόγων, ταῦτα δὲ πολιτικοῖς καὶ ῥήτορσιν ἀνδράσι μελήσει. ποιοῦμαι δὲ τῆς ἐμαυτοῦ δόξης κοινοὺς κριτὰς τοὺς φιλολόγους ἅπαντας, ὑπεξαιρούμενος, εἴ τινές εἰσι φιλότιμοι καὶ πρὸς τὰς δόξας ἀλλὰ μὴ πρὸς τὴν ἀλήθειαν κρίνοντες τὰ πράγματα. τὸ μὲν οὖν ἐκλέγειν ἐξ ἁπάντων αὐτοῦ τῶν λόγων, εἴ τι κάκιστον εἴρηται, ὃ ποιοῦσιν ἕτεροί τινες, κἄπειτα τούτοις ἀντιπαρατιθέναι τὴν κράτιστα ἔχουσαν Δημοσθένους λέξιν

dealing with these extravagant flights of fancy of men who are only half-educated in rhetoric, and who do not and cannot know what noble style is like, I shall speak, setting aside all dissimulation, as is my way. But first I wish to explain how I propose to conduct my examination of him. I feel nothing but wonder and delight at Plato's skill in the dialogues, especially those in which he preserves the Socratic character, like the *Philebus*; but, as I said earlier, I have never admired his tasteless use of the secondary devices of style, especially in those dialogues in which he introduces themes of praise and blame into political discussions and tries to make them into speeches for the prosecution and the defence. In these cases he writes in a manner foreign to his nature and dishonours his profession as a philosopher. It has often occurred to me to describe his essays in this vein in the words with which Homer makes Zeus address Aphrodite:[1]

Fell deeds of war are not for thee, my child:
  Go now, *your* work is wedded love's delights.

"Socratic dialogues are your métier, Plato: let orators and politicians concern themselves with this kind of writing.[2] I invite all lovers of literature to examine the validity of my opinion, except those who are ambitious, and make their judgments with an eye to their own reputations rather than the truth. I did not approve of certain other critics' method of selecting the worst passage from all his writings, and then comparing this with one of Demosthenes's finest

[1] *Iliad*, v. 428–429. [2] *id.* 430.

---

[1] συγκαθεὶς Reiske: συγκραθεὶς codd.

οὐκ ἐδοκίμαζον, τὸ δ᾽ ἐκ τῶν ἀμφοτέρων μάλιστα εὐδοκιμούντων, ταῦτα παρ᾽ ἄλληλα θεὶς ἐξετάζειν τὰ κρείττω τοῦτ᾽ ἔδοξ᾽ [1] εἶναι δίκαιον, καὶ ἐπ᾽ αὐτὸ τοδὶ τρέψομαι τὸ μέρος. δικανικὸς μὲν οὖν λόγος εἷς ἐστι Πλάτωνι, Σωκράτους ἀπολογία, δικαστηρίου μὲν ἢ ἀγορᾶς οὐδὲ θύρας ἰδών, κατ᾽ ἄλλην δέ τινα βούλησιν γεγραμμένος, οὔτ᾽ ἐν λόγοις τόπον ἔχων οὔτ᾽ ἐν διαλόγοις. τοῦτον [2] μὲν οὖν ἐῶ. δημηγορία δὲ οὐδεμία, πλὴν εἴ τις ἄρα τὰς ἐπιστολὰς βούλεται δημηγορίας καλεῖν. ἀφείσθωσαν δὴ καὶ αὗται.[3] ἐγκώμια δ᾽ ἐν τῷ συμποσίῳ πολλὰ μὲν ἔρωτος, ὧν ἔνια οὐκ ἄξια σπουδῆς, ἓν δὲ Σωκράτους ὁποῖον δή ποτε· οὐθὲν γὰρ δέομαι νῦν γε [4] περὶ τούτου λέγειν. κράτιστος δὴ πάντων τῶν πολιτικῶν λόγων ὁ Μενέξενος, ἐν ᾧ τὸν ἐπιτάφιον διεξέρχεται λόγον, ὡς μὲν ἐμοὶ δοκεῖ, Θουκυδίδην παραμιμούμενος, ὡς δὲ αὐτός φησιν, Ἀρχῖνον καὶ Δίωνα. τοῦτον δὴ παραλήψομαι τὸν λόγον καὶ παρ᾽ αὐτὸν ἐξετάσω Δημοσθένους λέξεις τινάς, οὐκ ἐκ τοῦ ⟨ἐπιταφίου⟩· τοῦτον [5] μὲν γὰρ οὐχ ἡγοῦμαι ὑπ᾽ ἐκείνου τοῦ ἀνδρὸς γεγράφθαι· ἀλλ᾽ ἐκ τῶν ἄλλων αὐτοῦ λόγων, ὅσοι περί τε τοῦ καλοῦ καὶ τῆς ἀρετῆς εἴρηνται, μᾶλλον δ᾽ ἐξ ἑνὸς ἀγῶνος· οὐ γὰρ ἔχω καιρὸν ὅσοις βούλομαι παραδείγμασι χρήσα-

[1] ἔδοξα Krüger: ἔδοξεν codd.
[2] τοῦτον Reiske: τοῦτο codd.
[3] αὗται Krüger: αὐταὶ codd.
[4] γε Sadée: δὲ codd.
[5] τοῦ ἐπιταφίου· τοῦτον Cobet: τούτου· τὸν codd.

[1] It seems not to have occurred to Dionysius that Plato may

passages. To me the fair course seemed to be to set side by side passages from the most renowned works of each and to decide which was the best; and this is the procedure I propose to adopt. There is one forensic speech by Plato, the *Apology of Socrates*; but this never saw even the threshold of a law-court or an open assembly, but was written for another purpose and belongs to the category neither of oratory nor of dialogue. I therefore pass it over. He also wrote no public speech, unless we are to call his letters public speeches. Let us therefore leave these out of consideration also. There is a considerable amount of laudatory writing on the subject of love in the *Symposium*, but some of it is not worth serious attention; and there is an encomium of a sort spoken by Socrates which I need not discuss here. The most important of all his political discourses is the *Menexenus*,[1] in which he gives a complete funeral speech, taking Thucydides as his model in my opinion, but according to himself Archinus and Dio.[2] I shall take this speech and compare it with certain passages of Demosthenes, choosing these not from the *Epitaphios*, as I do not think that speech was written by him, but from other speeches of his in which honour and valour are discussed, and more particularly from one speech, since I have not the time to provide as many examples as I should like, though nothing would please me more

have composed the *Menexenus* as a parodic pastiche of existing *epitaphioi*, or that in any case Plato was not a serious competitor in the field of oratory. His attitude to Plato is hopelessly partisan, and reflects the acerbity of the controversy. Dionysius finds it necessary to defend his position in the *Letter to Pompeius*.

[2] *Menexenus*, 234B.

σθαι, πάντων μάλιστα βουληθεὶς ἄν. τοιοῦτος μὲν δή τις ὁ τρόπος ἔσται μοι τῆς συγκρίσεως.

24 λαμβανέσθω δὲ πρότερος Πλάτων, καὶ ἐπειδὴ μέγα φρονεῖν ἔοικεν ἐπί τε ἀκριβείᾳ καὶ σεμνότητι ὀνομάτων, ταῦτα ἐπὶ τῶν αὐτοῦ βασανίσω, ἀρξάμενος, ὅθεν περ κἀκεῖνος, τοῦ λόγου· "Ἔργῳ μὲν ἡμῖν οἵδε ἔχουσι τὰ προσήκοντα σφίσιν αὐτοῖς, ὧν τυχόντες πορεύονται τὴν εἱμαρμένην πορείαν." ἡ μὲν εἰσβολὴ θαυμαστὴ καὶ πρέπουσα τοῖς ὑποκειμένοις πράγμασι κάλλους τε ὀνομάτων ἕνεκα καὶ σεμνότητος καὶ ἁρμονίας, τὰ δ' ἐπιλεγόμενα οὐκέθ' ὅμοια τοῖς πρώτοις, αὐτίκα ⟨τό⟩·[1] "προπεμφθέντες κοινῇ μὲν ὑπὸ τῆς πόλεως, ἰδίᾳ δὲ ὑπὸ τῶν οἰκείων." ἐν γὰρ τῷ πάντα τὰ προσήκοντα σφίσιν αὐτοῖς ἔχειν τοὺς θαπτομένους ἐνῆν καὶ τὸ προπεμφθῆναι τὰ σώματ' αὐτῶν ἐπὶ τὰς ταφὰς δημοσίᾳ τε καὶ ἰδίᾳ. ὥστε ⟨οὐκ⟩[2] ἀναγκαῖον ἦν πάλιν ταὐτὸ λέγειν· εἰ μὴ κράτιστον ⟨ἁπάντων⟩[3] τῶν περὶ τὰς ταφὰς νομίμων τοῦτο ὑπελάμβανεν ὁ ἀνὴρ εἶναι, λέγω δὴ τὸ παρεῖναι πολλοὺς ταῖς ἐκκομιδαῖς, καὶ οὐθὲν ἄτοπον ἐδόκει ποιεῖν συμπεριλαβών τε αὐτὸ τοῖς ἄλλοις καὶ χωρὶς ὑπὲρ αὐτοῦ μόνου λέγων. ἠλίθιος ἄρα τις ἦν, εἰ τοῦτον ἐδόκει τοῖς τελευτήσασι λαμπρότατον εἶναι τῶν κόσμων,[4] οἷς ἡ πόλις αὐτοὺς ἐκόσμει. ἵνα γὰρ ἀφῶ πάντα τὰ ἄλλα, τὸ δημοσίᾳ γηροτροφεῖσθαι τοὺς πατέρας αὐτῶν ἄχρι θανάτου καὶ παιδεύεσθαι τοὺς υἱεῖς ἕως ἥβης πόσῳ κρεῖττον

[1] τό addidit Usener.
[2] οὐκ lacunam supplevit Sylburg.
[3] ἁπάντων lacunam supplevit Vliet.

than to do so. This, then, will be my method of comparison.

Let us take Plato first; and since he appears to 24
take pride in the precision and dignity of his language, we shall examine his performance in this respect, beginning where he himself begins the speech:[1]

"These men already have from us their due in deed; and having received it they are going their appointed way . . ."

This beginning is admirable and appropriate to the subject in the beauty of the words, their dignity and melody. But the immediate sequel does not match these opening words: ". . . escorted publicly by the state and privately by their relations."

The idea that the bodies of those who were being buried had been escorted to the burial-ground both publicly and privately was implicit in the statement that they had received all that was due to them, so that it was unnecessary to say the same thing again, unless the speaker thought this to be the most important of the customs relating to state funerals, that the procession should be attended by a large crowd, and saw nothing incongruous in singling it out for reference after including it among the other details. Certainly anyone who thought that the procession was the most splendid distinction which the state bestowed upon its dead would be silly: for, to pass over everything else, what of the provision that their fathers should be maintained for the rest of their lives and that their children should be educated until adult-

[1] *Menexenus*, 236D.

[4] τῶν κόσμων Sylburg: τὸν κόσμον codd.

ἦν τοῦ προπέμπεσθαι τὰ σώματα δημοσίᾳ; ἐμοὶ μὲν δοκεῖ μακρῷ. οὐκοῦν οὐκ ἀναγκαία, Πλάτων,[1] ἥδε ἡ προσθήκη. ἀλλ' ἄρα γε εἰ μὴ τοῦ ἀναγκαίου, κάλλους γε ἢ τῶν ἄλλων τινὸς τῶν ἐπιθέτων ἕνεκα κόσμων παρείληπται τὸ κῶλον αὐτῷ τουτί; πολλοῦ γε καὶ δεῖ· πρὸς γὰρ τῷ μηδὲν ἔχειν σπουδῆς ἄξιον ⟨μήτε κατὰ τὴν ἐκλογὴν τῶν ὀνομάτων⟩ [2] μήτε κατὰ τὴν σύνθεσιν προσδιαφθείρει καὶ τὴν πρὸ αὐτοῦ [3] περίοδον, λυμαίνεται γοῦν τήν τε συμμετρίαν αὐτῆς καὶ τὴν εὐφωνίαν. νῦν μὲν γὰρ δυσὶ περιλαμβανομένη κώλοις σύμμετρός ἐστι καὶ ἐναρμόνιος καὶ στρογγύλη καὶ βάσιν εἴληφεν ἀσφαλῆ· ἐὰν δὲ προσλάβῃ τουτὶ τὸ κῶλον, ἅπαντα ταῦτα ἀπεκρίθησαν, καὶ μεταλήψεται τὸν ἱστορικὸν ἀντὶ τοῦ λογικοῦ τύπον. εἰ δὲ χωρίσαντες τοῦτο τὸ κῶλον ἀπὸ τῶν προηγουμένων αὐτὸ καθ' αὐτὸ ἐξοίσομεν, οὔτε [4] περίοδος ἡμῖν γενήσεται καθ' ἑαυτὸ γενόμενον οὔτε ἦθος ἢ πάθος ἕξει μὰ Δία οὔτε ἄλλην πειθὼ καὶ χάριν οὐδεμίαν. εἰ δὴ μήτε τοῦ ἀναγκαίου χάριν ἡ προσθήκη παρείληπται μήτε τοῦ περιττοῦ (περὶ ταῦτα δὲ καὶ ἐν τούτοις ἡ τῆς λέξεως κατασκευή), τίς ἂν τοῦτο ἔτι ἕτερον ὀνομάσειεν εἰ μὴ τοῦθ' ὅπερ ἐστὶν ἀληθῶς,[5] ἀκαιρίαν; τούτοις ἐκεῖνα ἐπιτίθησιν ὁ ἀνήρ· "Λόγῳ δὲ δὴ τὸν λειπόμενον κόσμον ὅ τε νόμος προστάττει τούτοις ἀποδοῦναι τοῖς ἀνδράσι καὶ χρή." τὸ καὶ χρὴ πάλιν ⟨ἐνταῦθα⟩ [6] κείμενον

[1] Πλάτων Usener: Πλάτωνι BP.
[2] μήτε κατὰ τὴν ἐκλογὴν τῶν ὀνομάτων inseruit Sadée.
[3] αὐτοῦ Sylburg: αὐτῆς MP.

hood at public expense? How much more important is this than the public funeral procession? Much more, I think! So this addition, Plato, was unnecessary. But I suppose you might argue that, although unnecessary, this clause was included in order to add beauty or some other ancillary quality. But this is far from being its effect: for in addition to contributing nothing worthwhile either in the choice of words or their composition, it also destroys the period which precedes it, or at least impairs both its balance and musical quality. In its simple form it comprises two balanced clauses: it is melodious and rounded, and proceeds with a firm tread. But if this clause is added to it, all these qualities are at once dispelled, and the style will become historical rather than rhetorical. If, however, we separate this from the preceding clauses and deliver it by itself, it will not give us a period on its own, nor indeed will it have any moral or emotional content, nor any other power to persuade or charm us. Hence, if the addition was made neither for reasons of necessity nor for the sake of emphasis (the two factors with which stylistic artifice is concerned), what else can it be called except what it actually is, bad taste? After this our author writes:[1]

"It remains to pay tribute to these heroes in words, as the law ordains, and as we are bound to do."

Here again, what is the purpose of adding "as we

[1] *Menexenus*, 236D.

---

[4] οὔτε Sadée: οὐ codd.
[5] ἀληθῶς Sylburg: ἀληθὲς ὡς codd.
[6] ἐνταῦθα lacunam supplevit Sylburg.

ἐπὶ τελευτῆς τίνος ἕνεκα παρείληπται καὶ διὰ τί; πότερα σαφεστέραν ποιῆσαι τὴν λέξιν; ἀλλὰ καὶ χωρὶς τῆς προσθέσεως ταύτης ἐστὶ σαφής. εἴ γε οὖν οὕτως εἶχε· "Λόγῳ δὲ δὴ τὸν λειπόμενον κόσμον ὁ νόμος ἀποδοῦναι προστάττει τοῖς ἀνδράσι," τίς ἂν ταύτην ἐμέμψατο ὡς οὐ σαφῆ; ἀλλὰ τοῦτο ἥδιον ἀκουσθῆναι καὶ μεγαλοπρεπέστερον; πᾶν μὲν οὖν τοὐναντίον ἠφάνικεν αὐτῆς τὸ σεμνὸν καὶ λελύμανται. καὶ τοῦτο οὐ λόγῳ δεῖ μαθεῖν ἕκαστον, ἀλλ᾽ ἐκ τῶν ἑαυτοῦ γνῶναι παθῶν. ταῖς γὰρ ἀλόγοις αἰσθήσεσιν ἅπαντα τὰ ὀχληρὰ καὶ ἡδέα κρίνεται, καὶ οὐθὲν δεῖ ταύταις οὔτε διδαχῆς οὔτε παραμυθίας.

25 συκοφαντεῖς τὸ πρᾶγμα, τάχ᾽ ἂν εἴποι τις, εὐέπειαν ἀπαιτῶν καὶ καλλιλογίαν παρὰ ἀνδρὸς οὐ ταῦτα σοφοῦ. τὰς νοήσεις ἐξέταζε, εἰ καλαὶ καὶ μεγαλοπρεπεῖς εἰσι καὶ παρ᾽ οὐθενὶ [1] τῶν ἄλλων κείμεναι. περὶ ταύτας ἐκεῖνος ἐσπούδαζεν, ἐν ταύταις δεινὸς ἦν. τούτων εὐθύνας παρ᾽ αὐτοῦ λάμβανε, τὸν δὲ τρόπον τῆς λέξεως ἔα. καὶ πῶς ἔνι ταῦτ᾽ εἰπεῖν; τοὐναντίον γὰρ ἅπαντες ἴσασιν, ὅτι πλείονι κέχρηται φιλοτιμίᾳ περὶ τὴν ἑρμηνείαν ὁ φιλόσοφος ἢ περὶ τὰ πράγματα. μυρία τούτου τεκμήρια φέρειν ἔχοι τις ἄν, ἀλλ᾽ ἀπόχρη λόγος εἷς οὗτος ἐπιδείξασθαι τὴν κενοσπουδίαν τοῦ ἀνδρός, ᾗ κέχρηται περὶ τὸν περιττὸν καλλωπισμὸν τῆς ἀπαγγελίας. αὐτίκα γε οὖν τοῖς προειρημένοις ἐπιτιθεὶς διάνοιάν τινα οὔτε περιττὴν οὔτε θαυμαστὴν ἀλλ᾽ ὑπὸ πολλῶν εἰρημένην καὶ πολλάκις (ὅτι γὰρ ὁ τῶν καλῶν ἔργων ἔπαινος ἀθανάτους

are bound to do" at the end? Does it make the meaning clearer? It is clear without this addition. If it were written as follows:

"It remains to pay tribute to these heroes in words, as the law ordains."

Who would have criticised it for obscurity? But perhaps the form that we have sounds better and is more impressive? Quite the contrary: its dignity has been removed and destroyed. It needs no word of mine to show this: every reader is aware of it through his own feelings, for it is the senses, untutored by reason, that decide in all cases what is distasteful and what is pleasant, and they need neither instruction nor persuasion in these matters.

25 But perhaps someone will say: "You are misrepresenting the matter, demanding beauty of language and elegance of style from an author who is not expert in these matters. Examine his ideas, and see whether they possess nobility and grandeur, and are uniquely his. Ideas were his concern, and it was in these that his genius lay. Call him to account for these, and leave his style alone." How can one say this? Everyone knows the reverse to have been the case, that the philosopher prided himself more on his powers of expression than upon his subject-matter. One could produce countless passages to prove this point, but the following single example is sufficient to show the misdirected zeal which he exerts in the excessive ornamentation of his speech. Immediately after the above passage he adds a sentiment that is neither extraordinary nor remarkable, but has often been expressed by many (for the view that the praise

---

[1] οὐθενὶ Usener: οὐδὲν PBv.

τὰς τιμὰς καὶ τὰς μνήμας δύναται ποιεῖν τοῖς ἀγαθοῖς, μυρίοις τῶν ἔμπροσθεν εἴρηται), συνιδὼν οὐθὲν οὔτε σοφὸν οὔτε περιττὸν τὴν γνώμην ἔχουσαν, ὅπερ οἶμαι λοιπὸν ἦν, ⟨τῷ κάλλει⟩ [1] τῆς ἑρμηνείας αὐτὴν ἡδύνειν βούλεται. ἔπειθ' ὥσπερ τὰ μειράκια καταβὰς ἀπὸ τῶν γενναίων καὶ μεγαλοπρεπῶν ὀνομάτων τε καὶ σχημάτων ἐπὶ τὰ θεατρικὰ τὰ Γοργίεια [2] ταυτὶ παραγίνεται, τὰς ἀντιθέσεις καὶ τὰς παρισώσεις λέγω, καὶ διὰ τῶν λήρων τούτων κοσμεῖ τὴν φράσιν.

26 ἀκούσωμεν δὲ αὐτοῦ, πῶς λέγει· "Ἔργων γὰρ εὖ πραχθέντων λόγῳ καλῶς ῥηθέντι μνήμη καὶ κόσμος τοῖς πράξασι γίνεται παρὰ τῶν ἀκουσάντων." ἐνταῦθα τοῖς μὲν ἔργοις ὁ λόγος ἀντίκειται, τῷ δὲ πραχθῆναι τὸ ῥηθῆναι, μετωνόμασται δὲ ἀντὶ τοῦ εὖ τὸ καλῶς, παρισοῦται [3] δὲ τὰ τρία μόρια τοῦ λόγου τοῖς τρισί. τοῦ δὲ ἀσφαλῶς βῆναι τὴν περίοδον ἕνεκα καὶ οὐθενὸς ἀναγκαίου, τέλος ἤδη τῆς διανοίας ἐχούσης, προσείληπται τὸ παρὰ τῶν ἀκουσάντων. ἆρά γε ὁμοίως ἡρμήνευται ὁ αὐτὸς νοῦς οὑτοσὶ τοῖς ποιηταῖς, οὓς περιφρονεῖ καὶ ἀπελαύνει τῆς πολιτείας ὁ φιλόσοφος, ἢ κάλλιον καὶ γενναιότερον; "Πρέπει δ' ἐσλοῖσιν [4] ὑμνεῖσθαι καλλίσταις ἀοιδαῖς. τοῦτο γὰρ ἀθανάτοις τιμαῖσι ποτιψαύει μόνον· ῥηθὲν . . . [5] θνᾴσκει δὲ σιγαθὲν [6] καλὸν ἔργον." Πίνδαρος τοῦτο

[1] τῷ κάλλει lacunam supplevit Sadée.
[2] Γοργίεια Reiske: γόργεια codd.
[3] παρισοῦται Sadée: παρισοῦνται MB.
[4] δ' ἐσλοῖσιν Sylburg: δὲ ὅλοισιν codd.
[5] lacuna post ῥηθὲν verbis huiusmodi supplenda: *μὲν καὶ φαῦλον ἐσαεὶ μένει.*

of noble deeds can immortalise the honour and the memory of brave men has been stated by countless numbers of writers before). Realising that this idea contained nothing clever or unusual, he seeks to do the one thing left to him, to make it attractive by the beauty of its expression. Then, with youthful rashness, he descends from his noble and impressive language and figures of speech and has recourse to the familiar histrionics of Gorgias—I mean antithesis and balanced clauses,[1] and uses these trashy devices to adorn his style.

Let us hear how he speaks:[2] 26

" For by words finely spoken fame and honour for deeds nobly done are given to the doers by the hearers."

In this " words " are contrasted with " deeds," and speech with action, " nobly " is changed to " finely " and the sentence is arranged in two corresponding tricola. The phrase " by the hearers " is added in order to ensure the balanced movement of the period, being otherwise unnecessary since the thought is already complete. How is the same idea expressed by the poets, whom our philosopher despises and wishes to expel from his city-state? Equally well, or more beautifully and more nobly?

" It is right that the good be lauded with the finest songs, for this is the only tribute which approaches that accorded the immortals. For when spoken of, ⟨a deed, even when small, lives for ever⟩, but even a noble deed perishes if condemned to silence."

[1] See note 1, p. 137.
[2] *Menexenus*, 236E.

---

[6] δὲ σιγαθὲν Barnes: δ' ἐπιταθὲν codd.

πεποίηκεν εἰς Ἀλέξανδρον τὸν Μακεδόνα, περὶ τὰ μέλη καὶ τοὺς ῥυθμοὺς μᾶλλον ἢ περὶ τὴν λέξιν ἐσπουδακώς. Πλάτων δέ, ὃς ἐπαγγέλλεται σοφίαν, τρυφεροῖς καλλωπίζει καὶ περιέργοις σχήμασι τὴν φράσιν. καὶ οὔπω τοῦθ' ἱκανόν, ἀλλὰ καὶ ἐν τῇ μετ' αὐτὴν περιόδῳ τὰ αὐτὰ ποιῶν φανήσεται. φησὶ γάρ· "Δεῖ δὴ τοιούτου τινὸς λόγου, ὅστις τοὺς μὲν τετελευτηκότας ἱκανῶς ἐπαινέσει, τοῖς δὲ ζῶσιν εὐμενῶς παραινέσει." οὐκοῦν ἐπίρρημα ἐπιρρήματι ἀντιπαράκειται καὶ ῥήματι ῥῆμα, τὸ μὲν ἱκανῶς τῷ εὐμενῶς, τῷ δ' ἐπαινέσει τὸ παραινέσει, καὶ ταῦτα πάρισα· οὐ Λικύμνιοι ταῦτ' εἰσὶν οὐδ' Ἀγάθωνες οἱ λέγοντες "ὕβριν ἢ ⟨κύ⟩πριν [1] μισθῷ ποθὲν ἢ μόχθον πατρίδων," ἀλλ' ὁ δαιμόνιος ἑρμηνεῦσαι Πλάτων. καὶ οὐ τοῖς σχήμασιν ἐπιτιμῶ· φέρει γάρ ποτε καὶ ταῦτα τοῖς λόγοις ὥραν. οὐ χάρι⟨ν οὐ ψέγω⟩ [2] οὐδ' αὐτὴν τὴν ἐπιτήδευσιν αὐτῶν καὶ τὴν ἀκαιρίαν ⟨μόνην μέμφο⟩μαι [3]καὶ μάλιστα ὅταν ὑπὸ τοιούτου γίνηται ἀνδρός, ᾧ κανόνι ὀρθοεπείας χρήσασθαι ἀξιοῦμεν. ἐν γὰρ δὴ τῷ αὐτῷ λόγῳ τούτῳ κἀκεῖνά ἐστιν· "Ὧν δ' οὔτε ποιητής πω δόξαν ἀξίαν ἐπ' ἀξίοις λαβὼν ἔχει," καὶ αὖθις· "Τειχισαμένη καὶ ναυπηγησαμένη, ἐκδεξαμένη τὸν πόλεμον," καὶ ἔτι. "Ὧν

[1] κύπριν Schmidt: πρὶν MBP.
[2] lacunam supplevit Radermacher.
[3] lacunam supplevit Radermacher.

Pindar[1] wrote these verses for Alexander of Macedon,[2] and he was more concerned with the music and rhythm of the words than with what they said. But Plato, who professes wisdom, dresses up his language with affected and exaggerated figures of speech. And even this is not enough: we shall find him doing the same thing again in the following period. He says:[3]

"A discourse is needed which will duly extol the dead and gently exhort the living."

Here adverb is contrasted with adverb ("duly" with "gently") and verb with verb ("extol" with "exhort"), and the clauses are equal in length. The author is not one of those Lycymniuses or Agathons who write lines like "Lust and love levied, or labour for our lands,"[4] but that brilliant stylist Plato. I do not criticise these figures in themselves, for even they can sometimes add beauty to a passage. Therefore it is not their use in principle that I condemn, only their use at the wrong time, especially when the author responsible is one whom we expect to use as our standard of correct style. We have the following examples in the same speech:

". . . deeds of which no poet yet has won fame worthy of their worth"[5]

and again:

". . . building fortifications and making naval preparations after entering the war"[6]

[1] Frag. 121 Bergk.
[2] Alexander I (*c.* 495–450 B.C.).
[3] *Menexenus*, 236E.
[4] Perhaps not a *verbatim* quotation.
[5] *Menexenus*, 239C.
[6] *Menexenus*, 245B.

ἕνεκα καὶ πρῶτον καὶ ὕστατον καὶ διὰ παντὸς πᾶσαν πάντως προθυμίαν πειρᾶσθε ἔχειν," καὶ πάλιν· "Φέροντες μὲν τὰς συμφορὰς ἀνδρείως δόξουσι τῷ ὄντι ἀνδρείων παίδων πατέρες εἶναι," κἀκεῖνά γε ἔτι·[1] "Τοὺς μὲν παιδεύοντες κοσμίως, τοὺς δὲ γηροτροφοῦντες ἀξίως," καὶ πάλιν που· "Καὶ αὐτὸς δέομαι ὑπὲρ ἐκείνων, τῶν μὲν μιμεῖσθαι τοὺς ἑαυτῶν, τῶν δὲ καρτερεῖν ὑπὲρ ἑαυτῶν," καὶ ταυτί· "Πολιτεία γὰρ ἀνθρώπων τροφή ἐστι καὶ ἡ μὲν ἀγαθὴ ἀγαθῶν, μὴ καλὴ δὲ κακῶν." κἀκεῖνα δ' ἔτι· "Νικήσαντες μὲν τοὺς πολεμίους, λυσάμενοι δὲ τοὺς φιλίους, ἀναξίου τύχης τυχόντες." πολύς ἐστι τῶν τοιούτων σχημάτων ὄχλος δι' ὅλου τοῦ ἐπιταφίου. ἀλλ' ἐάσας τὸ περὶ τούτων ἀκριβολογεῖν ἐπ' ἐκεῖνά τ' ἐλεύσομαι[2] καί μοι πάνυ μὲν αἰδουμένῳ καὶ ὀκνοῦντι εἰπεῖν, ὅμως δ' εἰρήσεται, ὅτι παχύτητος καὶ ἀδυνασίας ἔδοξεν εἶναι μηνύματ' αὐτά.

27 προειπὼν γὰρ ὁ ἀνήρ, ποῖόν τι σχῆμα λαβεῖν

[1] ἔτι Sylburg: ὅτι codd.
[2] τ' ἐλεύσομαι Sylburg: τελεύσομαι BP.

---

[1] *Menexenus*, 247A.
[2] *Menexenus*, 247D.
[3] *Menexenus*, 248D.
[4] *Menexenus*, 248E.
[5] *Menexenus*, 238C.
[6] *Menexenus*, 243C.
[7] *Menexenus*, 237B.

and further:

". . . therefore make this your first and last and abiding and all-absorbing aim "[1]

and again:

". . . and if they bear their losses bravely, they will be deemed in truth brave fathers of brave sons "[2]

then there is this:

". . . bringing up our sons respectably and caring for our parents worthily "[3]

and again somewhere:

". . . On their behalf I appeal personally to the children to imitate the example of their parents, and to the parents to bear their own lot with patience "[4]

and this:

" The nurture of men's minds is government:
Good makes them good, but evil makes them bad "[5]

and then there is this:

". . . Conquering their enemies and delivering their friends, they yet suffered an unworthy fate."[6]

There is a large mass of such figures throughout the whole of this funeral speech. I shall not examine them in detail, however, but shall pass on to another point which I feel most ashamed and reluctant to make, but which must be made: that these figures are evidence of clumsiness and incapacity.

Having begun by saying what form would be ap- 27
propriate for his speech, the author writes:[7]

ἁρμόττει τὸν λόγον ἐπιτίθησι ταυτί· "Ἐπὶ τούτοις τὴν τῶν ἔργων πρᾶξιν ἐπιδείξωμεν, ὡς καλὴν καὶ ἀξίαν τούτων ἀπεφήναντο." ἔργων πρᾶξιν ἀξίαν ἀποφηναμένους οὐκ οἶδα εἴ τις ἂν ἠξίωσεν εἰπεῖν τῶν τὴν λεπτὴν καὶ ἀκριβῆ καὶ καθαρὰν διάλεκτον ἐπιτηδευόντων. πράττεται μὲν γὰρ τὰ πράγματα ἐργάζεται δὲ τὰ ἔργα ἀποφάνσεως [1] δὲ ἀξιοῦται τὰ λεκτά.[2] τουτὶ μὲν δὴ παχὺ εἴρηται τὸ ⟨δ' ἐπὶ⟩ [3] τούτῳ λεγόμενον ἐνθύμημα ἀσθενέστερον· διὰ μακροῦ τε γὰρ καὶ ἀκατάλληλον καὶ οὔτε δεινότητα ἔχον οὔτε σύνταξιν· "Τῆς δ' εὐγενείας πρῶτον ὑπῆρξε τοῖσδε ἡ τῶν προγόνων γένεσις, οὐκ ἔπηλυς οὖσα οὐδὲ τοὺς ἐκγόνους τούτους ἀποφηναμένη μετοικοῦντας ἐν τῇ χώρᾳ ἄλλοθεν σφῶν ἡκόντων, ἀλλ' αὐτόχθονας καὶ τῷ ὄντι πατρίδα οἰκοῦντας καὶ ζῶντας καὶ τρεφομένους οὐχ ὑπὸ μητρυιᾶς ὡς οἱ ἄλλοι, ἀλλ' ὑπὸ μητρὸς τῆς χώρας, ἐν ᾗ ᾤκουν, καὶ νῦν κεῖσθαι τελευτήσαντας ἐν οἰκείοις τόποις τῆς τεκούσης τε καὶ θρεψάσης καὶ ὑποδεξαμένης." ποῖον ἔθνος ἀνθρώπων καθαρᾷ διαλέκτῳ χρώμενον ἐρεῖ γένεσιν τὴν μὲν αὐτόχθονα τὴν δὲ ἐπήλυδα; ἡμῖν γὰρ δή τι συμβεβηκός ἐστι τὸ εἶναι αὐτόχθοσιν ἢ μὴ ἐπιχωρίοις, οὐχὶ τῇ γενέσει. δύναται γοῦν τις ἀλλαχῇ γενόμενος ἀνὴρ ἑτέρωσε μετοικῆσαι ἡ δὲ γένεσις αὐτὴ τοῦτο παθεῖν οὐ δύναται. τίς δ' ἂν ἀξιώσειε τῶν εὖ διαλέγεσθαι σπουδαζόντων εἰπεῖν, ὅτι ἡ γένεσις ἡ τῶν προγόνων τοὺς ὕστερον γενησομένους ἀπεφήνατο αὐτόχθονας καὶ

[1] ἀποφάνσεως Krüger: ἀποφάσεως codd.

"Then let us describe the performance of their deeds, how noble and worthy of their birth and upbringing they revealed it to be."

I doubt whether anyone claiming to write in a refined, precise and pure style would have thought fit to speak of people "revealing the performance of deeds." Actions are performed, deeds are done; but revealing refers properly to what is spoken. This sentence is clumsily expressed, and the argument which follows it is distinctly weak: it is prolonged and irregular, and has neither rhetorical power nor coherence:[1]

"The first factor of their good birth was their ancestral stock. This was not foreign, nor did it reveal these its descendants as immigrants to the land, their parents having come from abroad, but as children of the soil, truly dwelling and living in their own land; nurtured, not like other men, by a stepmother but by their own motherland, in which they dwelt, and now lie after death in their resting-places in the mother who bore and reared and has now received them."

What kind of men who practise clarity of expression will talk of "children of the soil" and "foreign"? Being "born of the soil" or "not native" is an attribute of ourselves, not of our birth. A man can, of course, be born in one place and go to live in another, but this cannot happen to birth itself. What serious student of discourse would see fit to say that the circumstances of their ancestors' birth "revealed" that their descendants would be native

[1] *Menexenus*, 237B.

---

[2] λεκτά Sylburg: ἄληπτα codd.
[3] lacunam supplevit Sylburg.

μὴ μετοίκους εἶναι τῆς χώρας, ἐν ᾗ ἐγένοντο; οὔτε γὰρ ἡ γένεσις αὐτή τι ἀποφαίνεσθαι φύσιν ἔχει, οὔτε μετοικεῖν τις, ἐν ᾗ ἂν γένηται· ἀλλ' ἀποφαινόμεθα μὲν ἡμεῖς τὰ λεκτά, μετοικοῦσι δ' οἱ ἐξ ἄλλης ἀφικόμενοι χώρας ἐν τῇ ὑποδεξαμένῃ. τίς δὲ βουλόμενος σῴζειν τὴν ἀκολουθίαν, εἰπὼν τὴν γένεσιν καὶ περὶ ταύτης τὸν λόγον ἀποδιδοὺς ἐπιζεύξειεν ἂν τὸ ἄλλοθεν σφῶν ἡκόντων, τὸ ἀρρενικὸν τῷ θηλυκῷ καὶ τῷ ἑνικῷ τὸ πληθυντικόν;[1] ἦν γὰρ δή που κατάλληλος ὁ λόγος, εἰ πρὸς τὴν γένεσιν ἀναφέρων, ὑπὲρ ἧς ὁ λόγος ἦν, ἐπέθηκεν· "ἄλλοθεν αὐτῆς ἡκούσης." ἐπὶ δὲ τῶν ἀνδρῶν μέλλων ποιεῖσθαι τὸν λόγον ἐξ ἀρχῆς οὕτως ἂν κατεστήσατο τὴν φράσιν· "τῆς δ' εὐγενείας πρῶτον ὑπῆρξαν τοῖσδε οἱ πρόγονοι, οὐχὶ ἐπήλυδες ὄντες οὐδὲ τοὺς ἐκγόνους τούτους ἀποφήναντες μετοικοῦντας ἐν τῇ χώρᾳ, ἄλλοθεν σφῶν ἡκόντων, ἀλλ' αὐτόχθονας."

28 ἄξιον δέ, ὃ καὶ περὶ τῆς εὐγενείας τῶν ἀνδρῶν εἴρηκε, τὴν χώραν πρῶτον ἐπαινῶν, ἐξ ἧς ἐγένοντο, μὴ παρέργως ἰδεῖν. φησὶ δὴ θεοφιλῆ αὐτὴν εἶναι καὶ παρέχεται τούτου μάρτυρας τοὺς ἀμφισβητήσαντας περὶ αὐτῆς θεούς, κοινόν τι πρᾶγμα καὶ ὑπὸ πάντων σχεδὸν τῶν ἐπαινεσάντων τὴν πόλιν εἰρημένον. καὶ οὐ τοῦτο συκοφαντεῖν ἄξιον, ἀλλά, πῶς ἡρμήνευκεν αὐτά,[2] καταμαθεῖν· "Μαρτυρεῖ δ' ἡμῖν τῷ λόγῳ ἡ τῶν ἀμφισβητησάντων περὶ αὐτῆς θεῶν ἔρις τε καὶ κρίσις. ἣν δὲ θεοὶ ἐπῄνεσαν,

[1] τῷ ἑνικῷ τὸ πληθυντικὸν Reiske: τὸ ἑνικὸν τῷ πληθυντικῷ codd.

[2] αὐτά Krüger: αὐτήν codd.

and not immigrants into the land in which they were born? For it is not in the nature of birth, in itself, to be able to reveal anything, nor can any person be termed an " immigrant " in relation to the place in which he was born. It is we who " reveal " a statement, and men are said to be " immigrants " into the land which receives them on their arrival from elsewhere. And what writer who was concerned with preserving the grammatical sequence would first speak of " birth," and then, while developing his account of this, tack on to it " their parents having come from abroad," linking masculine to feminine, plural to singular? The sentence would have had some coherence if he had referred back to " birth," which is the subject, and added " it having come from abroad." Or if he was intending to make " men " the subject he might have made the sentence regular from the outset like this:

" The first factor of their noble birth was provided by their ancestors: for they were not foreigners, revealing their offspring as immigrants because of their own foreign birth, but natives."

And his reference to the noble birth of the men, 28
which begins with an encomium of the land whence they came, deserves more than a cursory glance. He says that the gods love it, and provides testimony to this claim in their quarrels for possession of it. This is a commonplace used by almost all those who have praised the city. We should not quibble about this, but we should notice how he expresses this sentiment:[1]

" My statement is proved by the strife and solution that occurred between the gods concerning her.

[1] *Menexenus*, 237C.

πῶς οὐχ ὑπ᾽ ἀνθρώπων γε συμπάντων δικαία ἐπαινεῖσθαι;" ταπεινή μοι δοκεῖ καὶ ἄζηλος ἡ λέξις καὶ οὐδὲν ἔχουσα τῆς περιμαχήτου πόλεως ἄξιον, ὡς ἐμοὶ δοκεῖ. ποῖος γὰρ ἐνθάδε πλοῦτος ὀνομάτων; ποία σεμνότης; ποῖον ὕψος; τί οὐ μαλακώτερον τῆς ἀξίας; τί δ᾽ οὐκ ἐνδεέστερον τῆς ἀληθείας; οὕτως ἐχρῆν ὑπὸ Πλάτωνος εἰρῆσθαι τὴν [1] Ἀθηνᾶς καὶ Ποσειδῶνος ὑπὲρ τῆς Ἀττικῆς στάσιν ἔριν τε καὶ κρίσιν; οὕτως τὸν ἔρωτα, ὃν ἔσχον οἱ θεοὶ τῶν ἐν αὐτῇ τιμῶν, εἰς φαῦλόν τι καὶ μέτριον ῥῆμα ἀγαγεῖν "ἣν δὲ θεοὶ ἐπῄνεσαν" εἰπόντα; ἀλλὰ [2] γὰρ ἃ μετὰ ταῦτα ἐπιτίθησιν εἰς ἔπαινον τῆς γῆς, ὅτι γένος τε τὸ ἀνθρώπων πρώτη ἐγεννήσατο καὶ καρποὺς ἡμέρους αὐτῷ [3] συνεξήνεγκεν, ἄξιον ἰδεῖν· "Ἐξελέξατο δὲ τῶν ζῴων καὶ ἐγέννησεν ἄνθρωπον, ὃ συνέσει τε ὑπερέχει τῶν ἄλλων καὶ δίκην καὶ θεοὺς μόνον νομίζει." οὐκ οἶδα, εἴ τι [4] λαμπρότατον ἄλλο πρᾶγμα τούτου εὐτελέστερον εἴρηται Πλάτωνι καὶ ἰδιωτικώτερον. δῶμεν αὐτῷ τὸ τοῦ ἀνθρώπου ἐγκώμιον οὕτως εἰπεῖν ὀλιγώρως καὶ ἀσθενῶς· ἀλλὰ περί γε τῆς τροφῆς αὐτοῦ γενναίᾳ χρήσεται φράσει· "Μόνη γὰρ ἐν τῷ τότε καὶ πρώτη τροφὴν ἀνθρωπείαν ἤνεγκεν τὸν τῶν πυρῶν καὶ κριθῶν καρπόν." ὦ θεοὶ καὶ δαίμονες, ποῦ τὸ Πλατωνικὸν νᾶμα τὸ πλούσιον καὶ τὰς μεγάλας κατασκευὰς καχλάζον; οὕτως μικρολογεῖ καὶ κατὰ στράγγα ῥεῖ τὸ δωδεκάκρουνον ἐκεῖνο στόμα

[1] τὴν Krüger: τῆς codd.
[2] εἰπόντα; ἀλλὰ Reiske: εἰπὼν τὰ ἄλλα codd.
[3] αὐτῷ Capperonnier: αὐτῶν MBP.
[4] εἴ τι Sadée: εἰ ἐπὶ codd.

And ought not the land which the gods praised to be praised also by all mankind?"

This seems to me a mean passage, and one not to be imitated, for I think it contains nothing worthy of the city which the gods fought over. Does it contain any rich language? Any dignity? Any sublimity? Is it not all pitched in a lower key than it should be? Is it not all smaller than life-size? Is this the way in which Plato should have described the quarrel and the dispute between Athene and Poseidon and its solution? By reducing the desire which the gods felt for honour at her shrines to the common, ordinary phrase "which the gods praised?" But we should look at what he adds after this in praise of the land, saying that it was the first to give birth to the human race and provide them with cultivated fruits from its soil. I do not know whether Plato has described any other subject of such extreme importance more economically and in such commonplace language:[1]

"She chose man from all the beasts and brought him forth, man who is superior to the rest in intelligence, and alone recognises justice and religion."

Let us allow that man should be praised so belittlingly and so lamely. But he will use noble language to describe his sustenance:[2]

"In those days she alone and first of all brought forth wheat and barley as food for men."

Heavens above! Where is that rich fountain of Platonic eloquence that bubbles out his elaborate sentences in profusion? Does the wise man's mouth with its twelve springs[3] issue such trifles, its flow

[1] *Menexenus*, 237D. [2] *Menexenus*, 238A.
[3] Cratinus Frag. 7 Meineke.

[5] χρήσεται Krüger: χρήσει καὶ MBP.

τοῦ σοφοῦ; ἐταμιεύσατο νὴ Δία καὶ ὑφῆκε τῆς κατασκευῆς ἑκών, ἴσως τις ἐρεῖ. καὶ πῶς; ὃς οὐκ οἴεται τὸ γάλα σεμνὸν εἶναι ὄνομα, ἀλλὰ πηγὴν τροφῆς αὐτὸ μετονομάζει διὰ τῶν ἑξῆς.

29 ἐῶμεν καὶ τοῦτο, πῶς δὲ τῆς δωρεᾶς αὐτῆς εἶπε τὸ μέγεθος, ἐξετάσωμεν· "Ὧι κάλλιστα καὶ ἄριστα τρέφεται τὸ ἀνθρώπειον γένος." εἰ τῶν ἐπιγείων τις ἡμῶν καὶ χαμαὶ ἐρχομένων "κάλλιστα καὶ ἄριστα" εἶπεν, ὅσον ἂν ἐκίνησε γέλωτα· πλὴν ἀφείσθω καὶ τοῦτο. "Τούτου δὲ τοῦ καρποῦ οὐκ ἐφθόνησεν, ἀλλ' ἔνειμε καὶ τοῖς ἄλλοις." εἴ τις βουλήσεται παράδειγμα λαβεῖν ⟨ψυχρῶς ἐσχηματισ⟩μένης[1] λέξεως, ἡ τοῦ καρποῦ μὴ φθονήσασα γῆ οὐχὶ πρώτη παρακείσεται; ἐμοὶ μὲν γὰρ δοκεῖ. ἡ δὲ μεταδοῦσα τῶν ἑαυτῆς ἀγαθῶν ἅπασιν ἀνθρώποις καὶ τηλικούτῳ κατασπείρασα πλούτῳ βάρβαρόν τε καὶ Ἑλλάδα γῆν τούτοις ἀξία κοσμεῖσθαι τοῖς ῥήμασιν, ὅτι οὐκ ἐφθόνησε τῶν σπερμάτων καὶ ὅτι ἔνειμεν αὐτὰ τοῖς ἄλλοις; οὐ τοῦ μὲν "μὴ φθονῆσαι τοῖς πέλας" οὐδὲ μεμνῆσθαι [τοῖς πέλας] παντάπασιν ἐχρῆν, τὸ δὲ[2] "νεῖμαι τοῦ καρποῦ" σεμνοτέρῳ ὀνόματι δωρεᾶς ἢ χάριτος ἢ ἄλλου τινὸς τῶν τοιούτων περιλαβεῖν; ἐῶ ταῦτα. τὴν δὲ τῆς Ἀθηνᾶς δωρεὰν οὕτως εἴρηκεν· "Μετὰ δὲ ταῦτα ἐλαίου γένεσιν, πόνων ἀρωγήν, ἀνῆκε τοῖς ἐκγόνοις." περιφράσεις πάλιν ἐνταῦθα καὶ διθύραμβοι.

[1] ψυχρῶς ἐσχηματισ lacunam supplevit Radermacher.

[2] παντάπασιν ἐχρῆν, τὸ δὲ Reiske: παντάπασι κέχρηντα MBP.

reduced to a trickle? Perhaps someone will say that he restrained his use of embellishment and restricted it deliberately. How can this be? He is the same author who, in an adjacent passage,[1] does not think "milk" is a grand enough word, but substitutes "fount of nourishment" for it.

Let us pass over this too, and examine how he has 29
described the magnitude of the gift itself: ". . . which is the best and noblest food for men."[2] If any one of us earthly groundlings had said "best and noblest," how much ridicule would he have provoked! But let us leave that question too. Consider: "And she did not grudge this fruit but imparted this to the rest also."[3] If anyone wants an example of the ⟨frigidly contrived⟩ style, would not "the earth who grudges not her fruit" provide him with a first-class one? I think it would. Does the power that shared her bounties among all men, spreading such great riches over the Greek and the barbarian world alike, deserve to be honoured in such words as these, that "she did not grudge her seed and she spread it among others?" Was it not completely unnecessary even to mention her not grudging it to her neighbours, and should not the sharing of her fruit have been rendered by a more dignified word such as "bounty" or "benison" or the like? I let all that go.

This is how he described the gifts of Athene:

"After these she gave the production of the olive to her children, as succour to their toils."[4]

Here once more we have circumlocutions and in-

[1] *Menexenus*, 237E.
[2] *Menexenus*, 238A.
[3] *Menexenus*, 238A.
[4] *Menexenus*, 238A.

καὶ τί δεῖ τὰ πλείω λέγειν; δι᾿ ὅλου γὰρ ἄν τις εὕροι τοῦ λόγου πορευόμενος τὰ μὲν οὐκ ἀκριβῶς οὐδὲ λεπτῶς εἰρημένα, τὰ δὲ μειρακιωδῶς καὶ ψυχρῶς, τὰ δὲ οὐκ ἔχοντα ἰσχὺν καὶ τόνον, τὰ δὲ ἡδονῆς ἐνδεᾶ καὶ χαρίτων, τὰ δὲ διθυραμβώδη καὶ φορτικά. ἐγὼ δ᾿ ἠξίουν πάντα γενναῖα εἶναι καὶ σπουδῆς ἄξια. Πλάτων γάρ ἐστιν ὁ ταῦτα γράφων, ὃς εἰ μὴ καὶ τὰ πρωτεῖα οἴσεται τῆς λέξεως, περί γε τῶν δευτερείων πολὺν ἀγῶνα παρέξει τοῖς διαμιλλησομένοις. ἀλλὰ περὶ μὲν τούτων ἅλις.

30 ἃ δὲ δὴ κράτιστα εἰρῆσθαι τῷ ἀνδρὶ δοκοῦσί τινες ἐπὶ τῇ τελευτῇ τοῦ λόγου, κἀγὼ σύμφημι, ταῦτα παραθεὶς ἐπὶ τὸν Δημοσθένην τρέψομαι. ὁ δὴ τὸν ἔπαινον αὐτῶν διεξιὼν φησὶν ἐπισκῆψαι τοῖς παροῦσιν ἐν τῷ πολέμῳ τοὺς μέλλοντας τελευτᾶν, ἃ χρὴ πρὸς τοὺς ἑαυτῶν παῖδάς τε καὶ πατέρας ἀπαγγέλλειν, εἴ τι παθεῖν αὐτοὺς συμβαίη κατὰ τὴν μάχην. ἔστι δὲ τάδε· “Φράσω δὲ ὑμῖν, ἅ τε ἤκουσα αὐτῶν ἐκείνων καὶ οἷα νῦν ἡδέως ἂν εἴποιεν ὑμῖν ἀναλαβόντες δύναμιν, τεκμαιρόμενος ἐξ ὧν τότ᾿ ἔλεγον. ἀλλὰ χρὴ νομίζειν ἀκούειν αὐτῶν ἐκείνων, ἃ ἂν ἀπαγγέλλω. ἔστι δὲ τάδε· ὦ παῖδες, ὅτι μέν ἐστε πατέρων ἀγαθῶν, αὐτὸ μηνύει τὸ νῦν παρόν. ἡμῖν γὰρ ἐξὸν ζῆν μὴ καλῶς, καλῶς αἱρούμεθα μᾶλλον τελευτᾶν, πρὶν ὑμᾶς τε καὶ τοὺς ἔπειτα εἰς ὀνείδη καταστῆσαι καὶ πρὶν τοὺς ἡμετέρους πατέρας καὶ πᾶν τὸ πρόσθεν γένος αἰσχῦναι, ἡγούμενοι τῷ τοὺς αὑτοῦ αἰσχύνοντι ἀβίωτον εἶναι καὶ τῷ τοιούτῳ οὔτε τινὰ ἀνθρώπων οὔτε

flated language. What further illustration is needed? If we were to go through the whole speech we should find many examples of inaccurate and unrefined expression, some of them juvenile and frigid, others lacking in force and vigour, others deficient in grace and charm and others bombastic and vulgar. Yet I should have expected everything to be noble and worthy of our esteem. After all, the author of this speech is Plato, and if he is not the champion stylist, at least he will provide stiff opposition to any future contestants for second place. But that is enough on this subject.

Some consider that the concluding pages of the 30
author contain the best writing in the speech. I agree, and will turn to them for purposes of comparison with Demosthenes. He makes his eulogy of the dead, saying that, when about to die, they had left instructions to their companions in the war as to what they should tell their sons and their fathers if anything should happen to them in the battle. These are his words:[1]

"I shall tell you what I hear from their very lips, and what they would gladly say to you now if their power of speech were restored, judging from what they said then. But you must imagine that you hear them saying what I now repeat to you:

"Sons, the present event proves that you are sons of brave fathers; for we could have lived dishonourably, but we have preferred to die honourably rather than bring you and your children into disgrace, and rather than dishonour our own fathers and forefathers; since we consider that life is not life to one who is a dishonour to his race, and that to such a one neither

[1] *Menexenus*, 246C–248E.

θεῶν φίλον εἶναι, οὔτ᾿ ἐπὶ γῆς οὔθ᾿ ὕστερον τελευτήσαντι. χρὴ οὖν μεμνημένους τῶν ἡμετέρων λόγων, ἤν τι καὶ ἄλλο ἀσκῆτε, ἀσκεῖν μετ᾿ ἀρετῆς, εἰδότας ὅτι τούτου λειπόμενα πάντα καὶ κτήματα καὶ ἐπιτηδεύματα αἰσχρὰ καὶ κακά. οὔτε γὰρ πλοῦτος κάλλος φέρει τῷ κεκτημένῳ ἀνανδρίαν (ἄλλοις γὰρ ὁ τοιοῦτος πλουτήσει καὶ οὐχὶ ἑαυτῷ), οὔτε κάλλος σώματος οὔτ᾿ ἰσχὺς δειλῷ καὶ κακῷ συνοικοῦντα πρέποντα φαίνεται, ἀλλ᾿ ἀπρεπῆ καὶ ἐπιφανεστέραν ἔχοντα τὴν δειλίαν, πᾶσά τε ἐπιστήμη χωριζομένη δικαιοσύνης καὶ τῆς ἄλλης ἀρετῆς πανουργία, ἀλλ᾿ οὐ σοφία φαίνεται. ὧν ἕνεκα καὶ πρῶτον καὶ ὕστατον καὶ διὰ παντὸς πᾶσαν πάντως προθυμίαν πειρᾶσθε ἔχειν, ὅπως μάλιστα μὲν ὑπερβαλεῖσθε καὶ ἡμᾶς καὶ τοὺς πρόσθεν εὐκλείᾳ, εἰ δὲ μή, ἴστε, ὡς ἡμῖν, ἂν μὲν νικῶμεν ὑμᾶς ἀρετῇ, ἡ νίκη αἰσχύνην φέρει, ἡ δὲ ἧττα, ἐὰν ἡττώμεθα, εὐδαιμονίαν. μᾶλλον δ᾿ ἂν νικῴμεθα καὶ ὑμεῖς νικῴητε, εἰ παρασκευάσαισθε τῇ τῶν προγόνων δόξῃ μὴ καταχρησόμενοι μηδ᾿ ἀναλώσοντες ταύτην, γνόντες ὅτι ἀνδρὶ οἰομένῳ τι εἶναι οὐκ ἔστιν αἴσχιον οὐδὲν ἢ παρέχειν ἑαυτὸν τιμώμενον μὴ δι᾿ αὑτόν, ἀλλὰ διὰ δόξαν προγόνων. εἶναι μὲν γὰρ τιμὰς γονέων ἐκγόνοις καλὸς θησαυρὸς καὶ μεγαλοπρεπής, καταχρήσασθαι δὲ χρημάτων καὶ τιμῶν θησαυρῷ καὶ μὴ τοῖς ἐκγόνοις παραδιδόναι αἰσχρὸν καὶ ἄνανδρον ἀπορίᾳ ἰδίων αὐτοῦ κτημάτων τε καὶ εὐδοξιῶν. καὶ ἢν μὲν ταῦτα ἐπιτηδεύσητε, φίλοι παρὰ φίλους ἡμᾶς ἀφίξεσθε, ὅταν ὑμᾶς ἡ προσήκουσα μοῖρα κομίσῃ, ἀμελήσαντας

men nor gods are friendly, either while he is on the earth or later after he has passed away. Remember our words, then, and whatever pursuit you follow, let virtue be the condition of its attainment, and know that without this all possessions and professions are dishonourable and evil. For neither does wealth bring honour to its possessor, if he be a coward (such a man will be wealthy to the benefit of others, not of himself). Nor does beauty and strength of body, when dwelling in a base and cowardly man, appear comely, but the reverse of comely, rendering his cowardice more conspicuous. And all knowledge, when divorced from justice and virtue, is seen to be cunning and not wisdom. Therefore make this your first and last and constant and all-absorbing aim, to exceed, if you can, not only us but all your ancestors in glory. If you fail, be sure that if we defeat you in virtue, our victory brings us shame, but if we are beaten, defeat brings happiness. And we shall most likely be defeated, and you will most likely be the victors in the contest, if you learn so to order your lives as not to abuse or waste the reputation of your ancestors, knowing that to a man who has self-respect nothing is more dishonourable than to be honoured, not for his own sake, but on account of the reputation of his ancestors. The honour of parents is a fair and noble treasure to their posterity, but to have the use of a treasure of wealth and honour, and to leave none to your successors, because you have neither money nor reputation of your own, is both base and dishonourable. And if you follow our precepts you will be received by us as friends, when the hour of destiny brings you here; but if you neglect our words and are disgraced, no one will welcome you in a friendly spirit.

δὲ ὑμᾶς καὶ κακισθέντας οὐδεὶς εὐμενῶς ὑποδέξεται. τοῖς μὲν οὖν παισὶ ταῦτ᾿ εἰρήσθω. πατέρας δὲ ἡμῶν, οἷς εἰσι, καὶ μητέρας ἀεὶ χρὴ παραμυθεῖσθαι ὡς ῥᾷστα φέρειν τὴν συμφοράν, ἣν ἄρα συμβῇ γενέσθαι, καὶ μὴ συνοδύρεσθαι. οὐ γὰρ τοῦ λυπήσοντος προσδεήσονται· ἱκανὴ γὰρ ἔσται καὶ ἡ γενομένη τύχη τοῦτο πορίζειν. ἀλλ᾿ ἰωμένους καὶ πραΰνοντας ἀναμιμνήσκειν αὐτούς, ὅτι, ὧν εὔχοντο, τὰ μέγιστα αὐτοῖς οἱ θεοὶ ἐπήκοοι γεγόνασιν. οὐ γὰρ ἀθανάτους σφίσι τοὺς παῖδας εὔχοντο γενέσθαι, ἀλλ᾿ ἀγαθοὺς καὶ εὐκλεεῖς, ὧν ἔτυχον μεγίστων ἀγαθῶν ὄντων. πάντα δ᾿ οὐ ῥᾴδιον θνητῷ ἀνδρὶ κατὰ νοῦν ἐν τῷ σφετέρῳ βίῳ ἐκβαίνειν. καὶ φέροντες μὲν τὰς συμφορὰς ἀνδρείως δόξουσι τῷ ὄντι ἀνδρείων παίδων πατέρες εἶναι καὶ αὐτοὶ τοιοῦτοι, ὑπείκοντες δ᾿ ὑποψίαν παρέξουσιν ἢ μὴ ἡμέτεροι εἶναι ἢ ἡμῶν τοὺς ἐπαινοῦντας καταψεύδεσθαι. χρὴ δὲ οὐδέτερα τούτων, ἀλλ᾿ ἐκείνους μάλιστα ἐπαινέτας ἡμῶν εἶναι ἔργῳ, παρέχοντας αὑτοὺς φαινομένους τῷ ὄντι πατέρας ὄντας ἄνδρας ἀνδρῶν. πάλαι γὰρ τὸ μηδὲν ἄγαν λεγόμενον καλῶς δοκεῖ λέγεσθαι· τῷ ὄντι γὰρ εὖ λέγεται. ὅτῳ γὰρ ἀνδρὶ εἰς ἑαυτὸν ἀνήρτηται πάντα τὰ πρὸς εὐδαιμονίαν φέροντα ἢ ἐγγὺς τούτου, καὶ μὴ ἐν ἄλλοις ἀνθρώποις αἰωρεῖται, ἐξ ὧν ἢ εὖ ἢ κακῶς πραξάντων πλανᾶσθαι ἠναγκάσθη καὶ τὰ ἐκείνου, τούτῳ ἄριστα παρεσκεύασται ζῆν, οὗτός ἐστιν ὁ σώφρων καὶ οὗτος ἀνδρεῖος καὶ φρόνιμος, οὗτος γιγνομένων παίδων καὶ χρημάτων καὶ διαφθειρομένων καὶ μάλιστα πείθεται τῇ παροιμίᾳ· οὔτε γὰρ χαίρων

This is the message that is to be delivered to our children.

"Some of us have fathers and mothers still living, and you should keep urging them to bear the calamity as lightly as possible, if indeed it should befall them; do not commiserate with them, for they will have sorrows enough, provided by what has already happened, and will not need anyone to stir them up. We wish you to soothe them and heal their wounds, reminding them that the gods have granted the most important requests they have made to them: for they prayed, not that their children might live for ever, but that they should be brave and esteemed; and this, which is the greatest good, they have attained. A mortal man cannot expect to have everything turning out in his own life according to his will, and they, if they bear their misfortunes bravely, will really be deemed the brave fathers of brave sons; whereas if they yield to their sorrows, either they will be suspected of not being our parents, or we of not being the men which our panegyrists declare us to be. Neither of these things ought to happen, but rather they should be our chief and genuine panegyrists, who show in their own lives that they are true men, and the fathers of men. The old saying "Nothing in excess" is thought to be sound counsel; and in fact it is. When all, or nearly all, that is required for a man's happiness rests with himself, and he is not hanging in suspense on other men, varying perforce between good and evil fortune according to theirs, he has his life ordered for the best. Such is the temperate, valiant and wise man, such is the man who, when children and wealth are given to him, and when they are taken away, is most obedient to the proverb:

οὔτε λυπούμενος ἄγαν φανήσεται διὰ τὸ αὑτῷ πεποιθέναι. τοιούτους δὴ ἡμεῖς ἀξιοῦμεν καὶ τοὺς ἡμετέρους εἶναι καὶ βουλόμεθα καὶ φαμέν. καὶ ἡμᾶς αὐτοὺς νῦν παρέχομεν τοιούτους, οὐκ ἀγανακτοῦντας οὐδὲ φοβουμένους ἄγαν, εἰ δεῖ τελευτᾶν ἐν τῷ παρόντι. δεόμεθα δὲ καὶ πατέρων καὶ μητέρων, τῇ αὐτῇ ταύτῃ διανοίᾳ χρωμένους τὸν ἐπίλοιπον βίον διάγειν καὶ εἰδέναι, ὅτι οὐ θρηνοῦντες οὐδ' ὀλοφυρόμενοι ἡμᾶς ἡμῖν μάλιστα χαριοῦνται. ἀλλ' εἴ τίς ἐστι τοῖς τετελευτηκόσιν αἴσθησις τῶν ζώντων, οὕτως ἀχάριστοι εἶεν ἂν μάλιστα, ἑαυτούς τε κακοῦντες καὶ βαρέως φέροντες τὰς συμφοράς, κούφως δὲ καὶ μετρίως μάλιστ' ἂν χαρίζοιντο. τὰ μὲν γὰρ ἡμέτερα τελευτὴν ἤδη ἕξει, ἥπερ καλλίστη γίγνεται ἀνθρώποις· ὥστε πρέπει αὐτὰ μᾶλλον κοσμεῖν ἢ θρηνεῖν. γυναικῶν δὲ τῶν ἡμετέρων καὶ παίδων ἐπιμελούμενοι καὶ τρέφοντες καὶ ἐνταῦθα τὸν νοῦν τρέποντες τῆς τε τύχης μάλιστ' ἂν εἶεν ἐν λήθῃ καὶ ζῷεν κάλλιον καὶ ὀρθότερον καὶ ἡμῖν προσφιλέστερον. ταῦτα δὴ ἱκανὰ τοῖς ἡμετέροις παρ' ἡμῶν ἀπαγγέλλειν. τῇ δὲ πόλει παρακελευόμεθα, ὅπως ἡμῖν καὶ πατέρων καὶ υἱῶν ἐπιμελήσονται, τοὺς μὲν παιδεύοντες κοσμίως, τοὺς δὲ γηροτροφοῦντες ἀξίως. νῦν δ' ἴσμεν, ὅτι, κἂν μὴ ἡμεῖς παρακελευώμεθα, ἱκανῶς ἐπιμελήσεται. ταῦτ' οὖν, ὦ γονεῖς καὶ παῖδες τῶν τελευτησάντων, ἐκεῖνοί τ' ἐπέσκηπτον ὑμῖν ἀπαγγέλλειν κἀγὼ ὡς δύναμαι προθυμότατα ἀπαγγέλλω." αὕτη δοκεῖ κάλλιστα ἔχειν, Πλάτων, ἡ λέξις ἐν τούτῳ τῷ λόγῳ. ἔχει μέντοι τὰ πλείω

" Neither rejoice nor grieve too much "; for it will be clear that he relies upon himself. This is how we think our parents should be: we wish and claim them to be so. And with this in mind we present ourselves now, neither resenting it too much, nor fearing too much, if we are to die at this time. And we beg our fathers and mothers to retain these feelings for the rest of their lives, and to be assured that not to sorrow and lament over us will be the best way to please us. But, if the dead have any perception of the living, they will displease us most by making themselves miserable and by taking their misfortunes too much to heart, and please us best if they bear their loss lightly and with moderation. Soon our life will have the noblest end attainable by man, and this should be glorified rather than lamented. And if they will direct their minds to the care and nurture of our wives and children, they will thereby most readily forget their misfortunes, and live in a better and nobler way, and one more acceptable to us.

" This is all we need to say to our families. But to the state we say: take care of our parents and of our sons, bringing up our sons to be responsible citizens and tending for our parents in their old age. But we now know that she will of her own accord do this satisfactorily, without prompting from us."

" These, then, parents and children of the dead, is the message which they bade us deliver to you, and which I report to you with all the conviction at my command."

This seems to me to be the finest passage, Plato, that you have written in this speech. Certainly most

καλῶς (οὐ γὰρ δοκεῖ ψεύδεσθαι), πλὴν ὅτι πολιτικόν γε τὸ σχῆμα αὐτῆς ἐστιν, οὐκ ἐναγώνιον.

31 ἀντιπαρεξετάσωμεν οὖν ταύτῃ Δημοσθένους λαβόντες λέξιν ἐκ τοῦ ὑπὲρ Κτησιφῶντος λόγου. ἔστι δ' οὐ παράκλησις Ἀθηναίων ἐπὶ τὸ καλὸν καὶ τὴν ἀρετήν, ὥσπερ παρὰ τῷ Πλάτωνι, ἀλλ' ἐγκώμιον τῆς πόλεως, ὅτι πάντα ἡγεῖται τἆλλα ἐλάττω τιμῆς καὶ δόξης, ἧς φέρουσι καλαὶ πράξεις, κἂν εἰ μή τις αὐτὰς μέλλοι κατορθοῦν. ἔστι δ' ἡ λέξις ἥδε· " Ἐπειδὴ δὲ πολὺς τοῖς συμβεβηκόσιν ἔγκειται, βούλομαί τι καὶ παράδοξον εἰπεῖν, καί μου, πρὸς Διὸς καὶ θεῶν, μηδεὶς τὴν ὑπερβολὴν θαυμάσῃ, ἀλλὰ μετ' εὐνοίας ἃ λέγω θεωρησάτω. εἰ γὰρ ἦν ἅπασι πρόδηλα τὰ μέλλοντα γενήσεσθαι καὶ προῄδεσαν ἅπαντες καὶ σὺ προὔλεγες καὶ διεμαρτύρου βοῶν καὶ κεκραγώς ὃς οὐδ' ἐφθέγξω, οὐδ' οὕτως ἀποστατέον τῇ πόλει τούτων ἦν εἴπερ δόξης ἢ προγόνων ἢ τοῦ μέλλοντος αἰῶνος εἶχε λόγον. νῦν μέν γε ἀποτυχεῖν δοκεῖ τῶν πραγμάτων ὃ πᾶσι κοινόν ἐστιν ἀνθρώποις ὅταν τῷ θεῷ ταῦτα δοκῇ· τότε δ' ἀξιοῦσα προεστάναι τῶν Ἑλλήνων εἶτα ἀποστᾶσα τούτου Φιλίππῳ προδεδωκέναι πάντας ἂν ἔσχεν αἰτίαν. εἰ γὰρ ταῦτα προεῖτο ἀκονιτί περὶ ὧν οὐδένα κίνδυνον ὅντινοῦν οὐχ ὑπέμειναν οἱ πρόγονοι τίς οὐχὶ κατέπτυσεν ἄν σου; μὴ γὰρ τῆς πόλεώς γε μηδ' ἐμοῦ. τίσι δ' ὀφθαλμοῖς, πρὸς Διός, ἑωρῶμεν ἂν τοὺς εἰς τὴν πόλιν ἀνθρώπους ἀφικνουμένους εἰ τὰ μὲν

of it is good (I do not feel justified in concealing the truth), except that its form is that of a political set-piece rather than a live speech.

Let us now set beside this a passage of Demosthenes, taken from his *Defence of Ctesiphon*. This is not an oration urging the Athenians on to virtue and courage, like Plato's speech, but an encomium of the city for her subordination of all things to honour and her good name, which noble actions bring, and will bring, even if they might not be successful. The passage is as follows: [1] 31

"But since he insists so strongly on the outcome, I will even assert something of a paradox; and, by heaven, no one must marvel at its boldness, but should consider what I have to say with good will. If then the results had been foreseen by all, and you had foretold them, Aeschines, and protested with clamour and outcry—you who never opened your mouth—not even then should the city have abandoned her position, if she had any regard for her glory, her ancestors or posterity. As it is, she seems to have failed in her affairs, which is the common experience of mankind when Heaven so decrees; but in those days, when she claimed to be the first city in Greece, if she had then abandoned this claim, she would have incurred the charge of betraying all to Philip. Why, if we had resigned without a struggle what our ancestors had undergone every possible danger to win, who would not have utterly despised you? Let me not say, despised the city and myself! With what eyes, by Heaven, could we have looked upon strangers visiting the city, if matters had come

[1] *De Corona*, 199–209. The comparison could not be more unfair.

πράγματα εἰς ὅπερ νυνὶ περιέστη, ἡγεμὼν δὲ καὶ κύριος ᾑρέθη Φίλιππος ἁπάντων, τὸν δ' ὑπὲρ τοῦ μὴ γενέσθαι ταῦτα ἀγῶνα ἕτεροί τινες χωρὶς ἡμῶν ἦσαν πεποιημένοι, καὶ ταῦτα μηδεπώποτε τῆς πόλεως ἐν τοῖς πρόσθε χρόνοις ἀσφάλειαν ἄδοξον μᾶλλον ἢ τὸν ὑπὲρ τῶν καλῶν κίνδυνον ᾑρημένης; τίς γὰρ οὐκ οἶδεν Ἑλλήνων, τίς δὲ βαρβάρων ὅτι καὶ παρὰ ⟨Θηβαίων καὶ παρὰ⟩ τῶν τούτων ἔτι πρότερον ἰσχυρῶν γενομένων Λακεδαιμονίων καὶ παρὰ τοῦ Περσῶν βασιλέως μετὰ πολλῆς χάριτος τοῦτ' ἂν ἀσμένως ἐδόθη τῇ πόλει, ὅ τι βούλεται, λαβούσῃ καὶ τὰ ἑαυτῆς ἐχούσῃ τὸ κελευόμενον ποιεῖν καὶ ἐᾶν ἕτερον τῶν Ἑλλήνων προεστάναι; ἀλλ' οὐκ ἦν, ὡς ἔοικε, ταῦτα τοῖς τότε Ἀθηναίοις πάτρια οὐδ' ἀνεκτὰ οὐδ' ἔμφυτα, οὐδ' ἐδυνήθη πώποτε τὴν πόλιν οὐδεὶς ἐκ παντὸς τοῦ χρόνου πεῖσαι τοῖς ἰσχύουσι μὲν μὴ δίκαια δὲ πράττουσι προστιθεμένην ἀσφαλῶς δουλεύειν. ἀλλ' ἀγωνιζομένη περὶ πρωτείων καὶ τιμῆς καὶ δόξης κινδυνεύουσα πάντα τὸν αἰῶνα διετέλεσε. καὶ ταῦθ' οὕτως σεμνὰ καὶ καλὰ καὶ προσήκοντα τοῖς ὑμετέροις ἤθεσιν ὑμεῖς ὑπολαμβάνετε εἶναι ὥστε καὶ τῶν προγόνων τοὺς ταῦτα πράξαντας μάλιστα ἐπαινεῖτε, εἰκότως. τίς γὰρ οὐκ ἂν ἀγάσαιτο τῶν ἀνδρῶν ἐκείνων τῆς ἀρετῆς, οἳ καὶ τὴν χώραν καὶ τὴν πόλιν ἐκλιπεῖν ὑπέμειναν, εἰς τὰς τριήρεις ἐμβάντες, ὑπὲρ τοῦ μὴ τὸ κελευόμενον ποιῆσαι, τὸν μὲν ταῦτα συμβουλεύσαντα Θεμιστοκλέα στρατηγὸν ἑλόμενοι, τὸν δ' ὑπακούειν ἀποφηνάμενον τοῖς ἐπιταττομένοις Κυρσίλον καταλιθώσαντες οὐ μόνον αὐτόν,

to their present state, and Philip had been chosen leader and lord over all, but other people without us had made the struggle to prevent it; especially when in former times our country had never preferred an ignominious security to the battle for honour? For what Greek or what barbarian is ignorant that by the Thebans, or by the Lacedaemonians who were strong before them, or by the Persian king, permission would thankfully and gladly have been given to our city to take what she pleased and hold what she had, provided that she would accept foreign law and let another power hold sway over Greece? But, as it seems, to the Athenians of that day, such conduct would not have been traditional, or endurable, or natural: no one could at any time have persuaded the city to attach herself in secure subjection to the powerful and the unjust. Through every age she persevered in the perilous struggle for supremacy, honour and glory. And this you suppose to be so noble and congenial to your principles, that you accord the greatest praise to those of your ancestors who acted in such a spirit, and rightly so. For who would not admire the virtue of those men, who resolutely embarked in their triremes and left country and home, rather than admit foreign dominion, choosing as their general Themistocles, the man who advocated this course, and stoning to death Cyrsilus who advised submission to the terms imposed—not him only, but

ἀλλὰ καὶ αἱ γυναῖκες αἱ ὑμέτεραι τὴν γυναῖκα αὐτοῦ; οὐ γὰρ ἐζήτουν οἱ τότε Ἀθηναῖοι οὔτε ῥήτορα οὔτε στρατηγὸν δι' ὅτου δουλεύσουσιν εὐτυχῶς, ἀλλ' οὐδὲ ζῆν ἠξίουν, εἰ μὴ μετ' ἐλευθερίας ἐξέσται τοῦτο ποιεῖν. ἡγεῖτο γὰρ αὐτῶν ἕκαστος οὐχὶ τῷ πατρὶ καὶ τῇ μητρὶ μόνον γεγενῆσθαι, ἀλλὰ καὶ τῇ πατρίδι. διαφέρει δὲ τί; ὅτι ὁ μὲν τοῖς γονεῦσι μόνον γεγενῆσθαι νομίζων τὸν τῆς εἱμαρμένης καὶ τὸν αὐτόματον θάνατον περιμένει, ὁ δὲ καὶ τῇ πατρίδι, ὑπὲρ τοῦ μὴ ταύτην ἐπιδεῖν δουλεύουσαν ἀποθνῄσκειν ἐθελήσει καὶ φοβερωτέρας ἡγήσεται τοῦ θανάτου τὰς ὕβρεις καὶ τὰς ἀτιμίας, ἃς ἐν δουλευούσῃ τῇ πόλει φέρειν ἀνάγκη. εἰ μὲν τοίνυν τοῦτ' ἐπεχείρησα νῦν λέγειν ὡς ἐγὼ προήγαγον ὑμᾶς ἄξια τῶν προγόνων φρονεῖν, τίς οὐκ ἂν εἰκότως ἐπετίμησέ μοι; νῦν δ' ἐγὼ μὲν ὑμετέρας τὰς τοιαύτας προαιρέσεις ἀποφαίνω καὶ δείκνυμι, ὅτι καὶ πρὸ ἐμοῦ τοῦτ' εἶχε τὸ φρόνημα ἡ πόλις. τῆς μέντοι διακονίας τῆς ἐφ' ἑκάστοις τῶν πεπραγμένων καὶ ἐμαυτῷ μετεῖναί φημι. οὗτος δὲ ὁ τῶν ὅλων κατηγορῶν καὶ κελεύων ὑμᾶς ἐμοὶ πικρῶς ἔχειν ὡς φόβων καὶ κινδύνων αἰτίῳ τῇ πόλει τῆς μὲν εἰς τὸ παρὸν τιμῆς ἐμὲ ἀποστερῆσαι γλίχεται, τὰ δ' εἰς ἅπαντα τὸν χρόνον ἐγκώμια ὑμῶν ἀφαιρεῖται. εἰ γὰρ ὡς οὐ τὰ βέλτιστα ἐμοῦ πολιτευσαμένου καταψηφιεῖσθε, διημαρτηκέναι δόξετε, οὐ τῇ τῆς τύχης ἀγνωμοσύνῃ τὰ συμβάντα παθεῖν. ἀλλ' οὐκ ἔστιν, ὅπως ἡμάρτετε, ἄνδρες Ἀθηναῖοι, τὸν ὑπὲρ τῆς ἁπάντων ἐλευθερίας καὶ σωτηρίας κίνδυνον ἀράμενοι οὐ μὰ τοὺς ἐν Μαραθῶνι

your wives stoning his wife? Yes; in those days the Athenians did not look for an orator or a general who would help them to a pleasant servitude: they scorned to live, if it could not be with freedom. Each of them considered that he was born not to his mother and father alone, but also to his country. What is the difference? The man who thinks himself born to his parents only waits for his appointed and natural end: the man who thinks himself born for his country also will sooner perish than see her in slavery, and will regard the insults and indignities which must be tolerated in a city enslaved, as more to be feared than death.

"If I had tried to say that I attempted to imbue you with sentiments worthy of your ancestors, there is not a man who would not justly have rebuked me. What I declare is, that such attitudes are your own; and I assert that this was the spirit of the city even before my time, though certainly in the execution of individual measures I claim a share also for myself. But my opponent, in arraigning the whole issue, and urging you to be hostile towards me as the cause of your alarms and dangers, shows his eagerness to deprive me of an honour of the moment, but in doing so is robbing you of praises that should endure for ever. For if, believing that I did not advocate the best policies, you should cast your votes against us, you will appear to have done wrong not to have suffered the consequences of the callousness of fortune. But never, never, can you have done wrong, Athenians, in undertaking the battle for freedom and the salvation of all. I swear it by your forefathers—those that met the peril

προκινδυνεύσαντας τῶν προγόνων καὶ τοὺς ἐν Πλαταιαῖς παραταξαμένους καὶ τοὺς ἐν Σαλαμῖνι ναυμαχήσαντας καὶ τοὺς ἐπ' Ἀρτεμισίῳ καὶ πολλοὺς ἑτέρους τοὺς ἐν τοῖς δημοσίοις μνήμασι κειμένους ἀγαθοὺς ἄνδρας, οὓς ἅπαντας ὁμοίως ἡ πόλις τῆς αὐτῆς ἀξιώσασα τιμῆς ἔθαψεν, Αἰσχίνη, οὐχὶ τοὺς κρατήσαντας αὐτῶν οὐδὲ τοὺς κατορθώσαντας μόνους, δικαίως. ὃ μὲν γὰρ ἦν ἀγαθῶν ἀνδρῶν ἔργον, ἅπασι πέπρακται, τῇ τύχῃ δέ, ἣν ὁ δαίμων ἔνειμεν ἑκάστοις, ταύτῃ κέχρηνται."

32 οὐθείς ἐστιν, ὃς οὐχ ὁμολογήσειεν, εἰ μόνον ἔχοι μετρίαν αἴσθησιν περὶ λόγους [1] καὶ μήτε βάσκανος εἴη [2] μήτε δύσερίς τις, τοσούτῳ διαφέρειν τὴν ἀρτίως παρατεθεῖσαν λέξιν τῆς προτέρας, ὅσῳ διαλλάττει πολεμιστήρια μὲν ὅπλα πομπευτηρίων, ἀληθιναὶ δὲ ὄψεις [3] εἰδώλων, ἐν ἡλίῳ δὲ καὶ πόνοις τεθραμμένα σώματα τῶν σκιὰς καὶ ῥᾳστώνας διωκόντων. ἣ μὲν γὰρ οὐδὲν ἔξω τῆς εὐμορφίας ἐπιτηδεύει καὶ παρὰ τοῦτ' ἔστιν αὐτῆς τὸ καλὸν [4] ἐν ἀναληθέσιν,[5] ἣ δὲ οὐδέν, ὅ τι οὐκ ἐπὶ τὸ χρήσιμον καὶ ἀληθινὸν ἄγει. καί μοι δοκεῖ τις οὐκ ἂν ἁμαρτεῖν τὴν μὲν Πλάτωνος λέξιν εἰκάσας ἀνθηρῷ χωρίῳ καταγωγὰς ἡδείας ἔχοντι καὶ τέρψεις ἐφημέρους, τὴν δὲ Δημοσθένους διάλεκτον εὐκάρπῳ καὶ παμφόρῳ γῇ καὶ οὔτε τῶν ἀναγκαίων εἰς βίον οὔτε τῶν περιττῶν εἰς τέρψιν σπανιζούσῃ.[6] δυνάμενος δ' ἄν, εἰ βουλοί-

[1] λόγους Sylburg: λόγου codd.
[2] εἴη Krüger: ᾖ codd.
[3] ὄψεις Sylburg: ὄψις codd.

at Marathon, those who fought shoulder to shoulder at Plataea, those who fought in the ships at Salamis and Artemisium, and many other brave men who lie at rest in the public tombs, all of whom the city thought worthy of the same funeral honour, Aeschines, not only the successful or victorious; and justly so! For all of them have done the duty of brave men: their fortune has been such as Heaven has assigned to each."

Every reader, even one with only a moderate 32
appreciation of oratory, unless he be malicious and of a contentious disposition, would admit that the passage which I have just quoted is as different from the preceding one as are the weapons of war from those used in ceremonial processions, real things from images, and bodies developed by hard work in the sunlight from those that pursue a life of ease in the shade. The former aims at nothing beyond formal beauty, and is consequently at its best when describing unreal situations; the latter concerns itself with nothing which does not lead to a useful and practical end. I think one would not be far wrong to compare the style of Plato to a country spot full of flowers, which affords a congenial resting-place and passing delectation to the traveller;[1] whereas that of Demosthenes is like a field of rich and fertile land, which yields freely both the necessities of life and the extra luxuries that men enjoy. I could, if I so

[1] Cf. Plato, *Phaedrus*, 239C.

---

[4] *καλὸν* Toup: *κακὸν* codd.
[5] *ἀναληθέσι* Toup: *ἀληθέσιν* MB.
[6] *σπανιζούσῃ* Sylburg: *σπανίζουσαν* codd.

μην, καὶ τὰ κατὰ μέρος ἑκατέρας [1] κατορθώματα ἐξετάζειν καὶ δεικνύειν, ὅσῳ κρείττων ἐστὶν ἡ Δημοσθένους λέξις τῆς Πλατωνικῆς οὐ μόνον κατὰ τὸ ἀληθινὸν καὶ πρὸς ἀγῶνας ἐπιτήδειον (τοῦτο γὰρ ὡς πρὸς εἰδότας [2] ὁμοίως ἅπαντας οὐδὲ λόγου δεῖν οἶμαι), ἀλλὰ καὶ κατὰ τὸ τροπικόν, περὶ ὃ μάλιστα δεινὸς ὁ Πλάτων εἶναι δοκεῖ, καὶ πολλὰς ἔχων ἀφορμὰς λόγων ταύτην μὲν εἰς ἕτερον καιρὸν ἀναβάλλομαι τὴν θεωρίαν, εἴπερ περιέσται μοι χρόνος· ἰδίαν γὰρ οὐκ ὀκνήσω περὶ αὐτῆς ἐξενέγκαι πραγματείαν. νυνὶ δέ, ὅσα ἐν τῷ παρόντι ἥρμοττεν, εἴρηται. ἐπειδὴ δὲ παρελθεῖν ἡμῖν οὐκ ἐνῆν Πλάτωνα, ᾧ τὰ πρωτεῖά τινες ἀπονέμουσι, κατατρῖψαι δὲ τὸν χρόνον [3] περὶ μίαν ταύτην ⟨τὴν⟩ [4] θεωρίαν ἐπιλελησμένου τῆς ὑποθέσεως ἦν, τῇδέ μοι περιγεγράφθω. βούλομαι δὲ δὴ καὶ συλλογίσασθαι τὰ εἰρημένα ἐξ ἀρχῆς καὶ δεῖξαι πάνθ', ὅσα ὑπεσχόμην ἀρχόμενος τῆς θεωρίας τοῦ λεκτικοῦ τόπου, πεποιηκότα ἐμαυτόν.

33 ἡ πρόθεσις ἦν μοι καὶ τὸ ἐπάγγελμα τοῦ λόγου, κρατίστῃ λέξει καὶ πρὸς ἅπασαν ἀνθρώπου φύσιν ἡρμοσμένῃ μετριώτατα Δημοσθένη κεχρημένον ἐπιδεῖξαι, καὶ τοῦτό γε συνάγειν ἐπειρώμην οὐκ ἐξ αὐτῆς ἐκείνης μόνης τὰς πίστεις διδούς (ᾔδειν γὰρ ὅτι οὐδὲν αὔταρκές ἐστιν ἐφ' ἑαυτοῦ θεωρούμενον, οἷόν ἐστιν, ὀφθῆναι καὶ καθαρῶς), ἀλλ' ἀντιπαρατιθεὶς αὐτῇ τὰς τῶν ἄλλων ῥητόρων τε καὶ φιλοσόφων λέξεις τὰς κράτιστα δοκούσας

[1] ἑκατέρας Reiske: ἑκάτερα codd.
[2] πρὸς εἰδότας Sylburg: προειδότας codd.

desired, examine and demonstrate the individual felicities of each style, which would establish the superiority of Demosthenes's to that of Plato not only as an instrument of practical oratory in actual contests (I assume that all my readers are equally aware of this and do not need to be told), but also in its use of figurative language, which is considered to be Plato's great strength. There are many ways in which I could begin a discussion of this subject, but I am postponing this examination until another occasion, if time permits. I shall not hesitate to publish a separate treatise on it; but for the present I have said all that was required. It was not possible for me to pass Plato by, as some award him the palm for eloquence: while to devote all my time to this one study would have suggested that I had forgotten my main subject; so I must set my limit here. I wish to recapitulate my argument from the beginning, and show that I have done all that I promised to do at the start of my examination of the subject of style.

My purpose, and the avowed object of my treatise, 33
was to show that Demosthenes uses most judiciously the best style, and the one which is most perfectly adapted to all aspects of human nature. I tried to prove this not purely from internal evidence (for I knew that it was not possible to see clearly what anything is really like by observing it on its own, independently of other things), but by comparing examples of his style with what are considered to be the best passages of other authors, both orators and

---

[3] χρόνον Krüger: λόγον codd.
[4] τὴν inseruit Sadée.

ἔχειν καὶ τῇ δι' ἀλλήλων βασάνῳ φανερὰν ποιῶν τὴν ἀμείνω. ἵν' οὖν[1] τὴν φυσικὴν ὁδὸν ὁ λόγος μοι λάβῃ, τοὺς χαρακτῆρας τῶν διαλέκτων τοὺς ἀξιολογωτάτους κατηριθμησάμην καὶ τοὺς πρωτεύσαντας[2] ἐν αὐτοῖς ἄνδρας ἐπῆλθον, ἔπειτα δείξας ἀτελεῖς ἅπαντας ἐκείνους καὶ καθ' ὃ μάλιστα ἀστοχεῖν ἕκαστον ὑπελάμβανον τοῦ τέλους ἐκλογισάμενος διὰ βραχέων, ἦλθον ἐπὶ τὸν Δημοσθένη. τοῦτον δὲ ἑνὸς μὲν οὐδενὸς ἀποφηνάμενος οὔτε χαρακτῆρος οὔτ' ἀνδρὸς ζηλωτὴν γενέσθαι, ἐξ ἁπάντων δὲ τὰ κράτιστα ἐκλεξάμενον κοινὴν καὶ φιλάνθρωπον τὴν ἑρμηνείαν κατεσκευακέναι καὶ κατὰ τοῦτο μάλιστα διαφέρειν τῶν ἄλλων, πίστεις ὑπὲρ τοῦδε παρειχόμην, διελόμενος μὲν τὴν λέξιν εἰς τρεῖς χαρακτῆρας τοὺς γενικωτάτους τόν τε ἰσχνὸν καὶ τὸν ὑψηλὸν καὶ τὸν μεταξὺ τούτων, ἀποδεικνὺς δ' αὐτὸν ἐν τοῖς τρισὶ γένεσι κατορθοῦντα τῶν ἄλλων μάλιστα, λέξεις τινὰςαὐ τοῦ λαμβάνων, αἷς ἀντιπαρεξήταζον ἑτέρας ὁμοειδεῖς λόγου μὲν ἀξίας, οὐ μὴν ἀνεπιλήπτους γε τελέως οὐδ', ὥσπερ ἐκείνη, πάσας τὰς ἀρετὰς ἐχούσας. καὶ γὰρ ἥ τε Ἰσοκράτους καὶ Πλάτωνος καίτοι[3] θαυμασιωτάτων ἀνδρῶν μνήμη καὶ σύγκρισις οὐκ ἔξω τοῦ εἰκότος ἐγίγνετό μοι, ἀλλ', ἐπεὶ τοῦ μέσου καὶ κρατίστου χαρακτῆρος οὗτοι ζηλωταὶ γενόμενοι μεγίστης δόξης ἔτυχον, ἵνα δείξαιμι, κἂν εἰ τῶν ἄλλων ἀμείνους εἰσί, Δημοσθένει γε οὐκ ἀξίους ὄντας ἁμιλλᾶσθαι περὶ τῶν ἀριστείων.

ὀλίγα τούτοις ἔτι προσθεὶς περὶ τῆς λέξεως, ἐπὶ τὸ καταλειπόμενον τῆς προκειμένης[4] θεωρίας

[1] ἵν' οὖν Reiske: ἵνα codd.

philosophers, and showing by comparative examination which was the better in each case. To enable my argument to take its natural course, I enumerated the most important characteristics of style and considered the orators who excelled in each. Then, after showing all these to be imperfect and indicating briefly in what respects I thought each fell short of perfection, I came to Demosthenes. I showed that he pretended to no single style and imitated no single orator, but by selecting the best qualities from all of them developed a style with a universal appeal, which is what chiefly distinguishes him from all other writers. I proved this by dividing style into three basic types, plain, grand and intermediate. I showed that he was the most successful of them all in these three types of style, by taking passages from him and comparing them with others which were similar in form and quite estimable, but not entirely above criticism, nor, like the specimen from Demosthenes, replete with all the virtues. It did not seem to me unreasonable to recall Isocrates and Plato, for all their wonderful accomplishment, and to compare them with Demosthenes: since both had acquired the highest reputation as exponents of the middle style, which is also the best, I could thereby show that, though they might be superior to all others, they were not worthy to compete for the palm with Demosthenes.

I shall make a few more observations concerning 34
his style before proceeding to the rest of my ⟨pro-

[2] πρωτεύσαντας Kiessling: πρώτους ὄντας codd.
[3] καίτοι Kiessling: καὶ τῶν codd.
[4] προκειμένης lacunam supplevit Usener.

34 μέρος μεταβήσομαι, ταῦτα δὲ ἔστιν, ἃ τοῖς τρισὶ πλάσμασιν ὁμοίως παρέπεται καὶ ἔστι παντὸς λόγου Δημοσθενικοῦ μηνύματα χαρακτηριστικὰ καὶ ἀνυφαίρετα. ὑπομνήσω δὲ πρῶτον μέν, ἃ τοῖς ἄλλοις πλάσμασιν ἔφην τὰ δοκοῦντά μοι ὡς [1] ἰδίας ἀρετὰς συμβεβηκέναι τοῖς Δημοσθένους, ἵν' εὐσύνοπτος μᾶλλον γένηταί μοι ὁ λόγος. δοκεῖ δή μοι τῶν μὲν ὑψηλῇ καὶ περιττῇ καὶ ἐξηλλαγμένῃ λέξει κεχρημένων κατὰ τὸ σαφέστερον καὶ κοινότερον τῇ ἑρμηνείᾳ κεχρῆσθαι προὔχειν ὁ Δημοσθένης. τούτων γὰρ ἐν πάσῃ κατασκευῇ στοχάζεται μέγεθος ἐχούσῃ καὶ ταύταις κέχρηται χαρακτηρικωτάταις ἀρεταῖς ἐπὶ τῆς ὑψηλῆς καὶ ξενοπρεποῦς ὀνομασίας ὥς γε μάλιστα. τῶν δὲ τὴν λιτὴν καὶ ἰσχνὴν καὶ ἀπέριττον ἐπιτηδευόντων φράσιν τῷ τόνῳ τῆς λέξεως ἐδόκει μοι διαλλάττειν καὶ τῷ βάρει καὶ τῇ στριφνότητι καὶ τῷ πικραίνειν ὡς ἐπὶ τὸ πολύ· ταῦτα γὰρ ἐστιν ἐκείνου χαρακτηρικὰ τοῦ πλάσματος παρ' αὐτῷ καὶ τὰ παραπλήσια τούτοις. τῶν δὲ τὴν μέσην διάλεκτον ἠσκηκότων, ἣν δὴ κρατίστην ἀποφαίνομαι, κατὰ ταυτὶ διαφέρειν αὐτὸν ὑπελάμβανον· κατὰ τὴν ποικιλίαν, κατὰ τὴν συμμετρίαν, κατὰ τὴν εὐκαιρίαν, ἔτι πρὸς τούτοις κατὰ τὸ παθητικόν τε καὶ ἐναγώνιον καὶ δραστήριον καὶ τελευταῖον τὸ πρέπον, ὃ τῶν ἄστρων ψαύει παρὰ Δημοσθένει. ταῦτα μὲν οὖν χωρὶς ἑκάστῳ τῶν τριῶν πλασμάτων παρακολουθεῖν ἔφην καὶ ἐκ τούτων ἠξίουν τὴν Δημοσθένους δύναμιν ⟨εὑρεῖν τε καὶ τὸν ἴδιον αὐτοῦ χαρακτῆρα⟩ [2] πεφυκότα μὲν καὶ τοῖς ἄλλοις παρακολουθεῖν πλάσμασι, κρατίστην δὲ ὄψιν ἔχοντα

posed⟩ examination. They are equally associated with all three forms and are characteristics which place an individual and indelible stamp on every speech of Demosthenes. To enable the reader to comprehend my argument more easily, I shall begin by reminding him, as I did in earlier discussions of other individual styles, of the qualities ⟨which I considered to be⟩ the special attributes of Demosthenes's oratory. Now I consider Demosthenes superior to those who use the grand, striking, extraordinary expressions in that he employs clearer and more ordinary language. He aims to achieve clarity and to use ordinary language in every important passage, and employs them as his most characteristic qualities especially in passages which also contain elevated and exotic words. He seemed to me superior to the exponents of the plain, simple and unemphatic manner of expression by the intensity, gravity and close texture of his style and his general pungency of expression. These and related qualities are characteristic of his writing in this form. As to the middle style, which I declare to be the best, I considered that he was superior to the others who practised it in the following respects: in variety, balance and timing, and furthermore in arousing emotion, vividness and energy and finally in propriety, which reaches its acme in Demosthenes. I proposed to pursue each of these three forms of style individually, and expected ⟨to discover from⟩ this examination the genius of Demosthenes ⟨and his peculiar character⟩, which, though conforming by nature with these types

[1] τὰ δοκοῦντά μοι ὡς supplevi lacunam a Radermachero indicatam.

[2] lacunam supplevi sensum secutus.

καὶ ἐκπρεπεστάτην ἐν τούτοις τοῖς χωρίοις. εἰ δέ τις ἀξιώσει συκοφαντεῖν τὴν διαίρεσιν, ἐπειδὴ τὰς κοινῇ παρακολουθούσας πᾶσι τοῖς πλάσμασιν ἀρετὰς τρίχα διανείμασα τὸ ἴδιον ἑκάσταις ἀποδίδωσιν, ἐκεῖνα ἂν εἴποιμι πρὸς αὐτόν, ὅτι καθ' ὃ μάλιστα χωρίον ἑκάστη τῶν ἀρετῶν ὄψιν τε ἡδίστην ἔχει καὶ χρῆσιν ὠφελιμωτάτην, κατὰ τοῦτο τάττειν αὐτὴν ἀξιῶ, ἐπεὶ καὶ τῆς σαφηνείας καὶ τῆς συντομίας καὶ τοῦ πιθανοῦ χωρίον ἀποφαίνουσιν οἱ τεχνογράφοι τὴν διήγησιν ⟨οὐχ⟩ [1] ὡς οὐκ ἀλλαχοῦ οὐδαμοῦ δέον ἐξετάζεσθαι τὰς ἀρετὰς ταύτας (πάνυ γὰρ ἄτοπον), ἀλλ' ὡς [2] ἐν τῇ διηγήσει δέον [3] μάλιστα.

35 φέρε δὴ τούτων εἰρημένων ἡμῖν λέγωμεν ἤδη καὶ ⟨περὶ τῆς συνθέσεως⟩ [4] τῶν ὀνομάτων ᾗ κέχρηται ὁ ἀνήρ. ὅτι μὲν οὖν περιττή τίς ἐστιν ἡ τῆς λέξεως τῆς Δημοσθένους ἁρμονία καὶ μακρῷ δή τινι διαλλάττουσα τὰς τῶν ἄλλων ῥητόρων, οὐκ ἐμὸς ὁ μῦθος. ἅπαντες γὰρ εὖ οἶδ' ὅτι ταύτην αὐτῷ τὴν ἀρετὴν ἂν μαρτυρήσειαν, ὅσοι μὴ παντάπασι πολιτικῶν εἰσιν ἄπειροι λόγων, ὅπου γε καὶ οἱ κατὰ τὴν αὐτὴν ἡλικίαν ἀκμάσαντες ἐκείνῳ θαυμάζοντές τε [5] δῆλοί εἰσιν αὐτὸν καὶ

[1] οὐχ inseruit Reiske.
[2] ἀλλ' ὡς Reiske: ἄλλως codd.
[3] δέον Reiske: δὲ codd.
[4] περὶ τῆς συνθέσεως inseruit Reiske.
[5] θαυμάζοντές τε Reiske: θαυμάζοντες δὲ codd.

---

[1] This very difficult chapter owes some of its obscurity to the lacuna after δύναμιν, which renders the meaning of χωρίοις uncertain. "Passages" is scarcely satisfactory, since λέξεις has been used to render this sense in **33**. It may conceivably refer

severally, was most conspicuous and outstanding in those sections.[1] But if anyone sees fit to criticise this separate treatment on the ground that it assigns to the three styles individually qualities which belong to all three in common, and a single individual style to each, I might answer him as follows: my method is to place each quality in the section where it looks happiest and serves the most useful purpose. In the same way the rhetoricians declare that the narrative is the section for clarity, conciseness and persuasiveness, not because these virtues should not be studied anywhere else (for that would be quite absurd), but because they are most necessary in the narrative.

Now that this has been said, let us next consider 35
how the orator constructs his words into sentences. The view that his arrangement of words is extraordinarily artistic and far superior to that of all other orators "is not my invention."[2] I am sure that all those who have the slightest knowledge of political oratory would confirm that he possesses this quality, since all who reached their prime with him clearly

to the conventional divisions of the speech in view of the analogy which Dionysius makes with them at the end of the chapter. Dionysius is defending his method of dividing his examination of Demosthenes's style into separate studies of his performance in the three types (πλάσματα) of style by arguing that by using this method he is able to show that Demosthenes contributed new, but related qualities to each style, and thus established his superiority over the leading exponents, Thucydides, Isocrates and Plato, and Lysias.

[2] It was evidently a subject of controversy, however. Among early critics of Demosthenes, in addition to his political opponents Aeschines and Demades, were Pytheas, Theophrastus and Demetrius of Phalerum. In more recent times the Romans had generally accorded Demosthenes less praise than Dionysius would have liked.

ζηλοῦντες[1] ταύτης μάλιστα τῆς εὐτεχνίας, καίτοι τινὲς οὐδ᾿ οἰκείως διακείμενοι πρὸς αὐτόν, ὥστε κολακείας ἐξενέγκασθαι δόξαν, ἀλλ᾿ ἔνιοί γε καὶ σφόδρα ἀπεχθεῖς καὶ ἀδιαλλάκτους ἐπανῃρημένοι πολέμους. ὧν ἦν Αἰσχίνης ὁ ῥήτωρ, ἀνὴρ λαμπροτάτῃ φύσει περὶ λόγους χρησάμενος, ὃς οὐ πολὺ ἂν ἀπέχειν δοκεῖ τῶν ἄλλων ῥητόρων καὶ μετὰ Δημοσθένην μηδενὸς δεύτερος ἀριθμεῖσθαι. οὗτος μὲν δὴ τῆς ἄλλης δεινότητος, ἣ περὶ τὸν ἄνδρα τοῦτον ἐγένετο κατὰ τὸ λεκτικόν ἔστιν ἃ[2] διακνίζει καὶ συκοφαντεῖ, πρᾶγμα ἐχθροῦ ποιῶν. καὶ γὰρ καινότητα ὀνομάτων καὶ ἀηδίαν καὶ περιεργίαν καὶ τὸ σκοτεινὸν δὴ τοῦτο καὶ πικρὸν καὶ ἄλλα πολλὰ τοιαῦτα προστρίβεται αὐτῷ, βασκαίνων μέν, ὥσπερ ἔφην, καὶ ταῦτα, ὅμως δ᾿ οὖν ἀφορμάς γέ τινας τοῦ συκοφαντεῖν εὐλόγους λαμβάνων. περὶ δὲ τῆς συνθέσεως τῶν ὀνομάτων οὐδὲν οὔτε μεῖζον ⟨οὔτ᾿ ἔλαττον δύναται κατηγορεῖν, ἢ ἔγκλημα⟩[3] ἢ καταγέλωτα φέρον. καὶ[4] οὐχὶ τοῦτό πω θαυμάζειν ἄξιον, ἀλλ᾿ ὅτι καὶ μαρτυρῶν πολλαχῇ τὴν ἀρετὴν τῷ ῥήτορι κατάδηλός ἐστι καὶ ζηλῶν. φανερὸν δὲ τοῦτο γένοιτ᾿ ἂν ἐξ ὧν αὐτὸς εἴρηκε, τότε μὲν οὕτω πως γράφων· "Ὅταν δὲ ἄνθρωπος ἐξ ὀνομάτων συγκείμενος καὶ τούτων πικρῶν καὶ περιέργων" (ἐν γὰρ δὴ τούτοις οὐ τὴν ἐκλογὴν ἐπαινεῖ τῶν ὀνομάτων αὐτοῦ μὰ Δία· τίς γὰρ ἂν γένοιτο πικρᾶς καὶ περιέργου ζῆλος ὀνομασίας;), ἐν ἑτέρῳ δὲ τόπῳ

[1] καὶ ζηλοῦντες Reiske: καλοῦντες codd.
[2] ἔστιν ἃ Reiske: ἔτι codd.
[3] οὔτ᾿ ἔλαττον δύναται κατηγορεῖν, ἢ ἔγκλημα supplevi.

admired and tried to imitate him particularly in this accomplishment. And yet some of these were not his friends, and therefore cannot be accused of flattery; while others were extremely hostile and waged war against him irreconcilably. One of these was the orator Aeschines, a man with a brilliant natural talent for speaking, who, it is thought, would probably have been comparable in ability with the other orators, and second to none after Demosthenes. This orator shows his hostility by disparaging and criticising certain aspects of Demosthenes's stylistic brilliance. He taxes him with his use of neologism,[1] his bluntness, his over-elaboration,[2] his well-known obscurity,[3] his pungency and many other faults of that sort. His criticisms are made in a carping spirit, as I have said, yet are not entirely without reasonable grounds. But regarding his composition Aeschines is unable to bring any charges, great or small, or any that might expose Demosthenes to censure or to ridicule. Even this is not altogether surprising; what is remarkable is that in many passages he plainly acknowledges Demosthenes's ability in this respect and tries to imitate him. This would appear evident from his own statements. On one occasion he says this: " but when a man is made up of words, and harsh, laboured words at that "[4] (where, of course, he is certainly not praising his choice of words, for surely nobody would want to imitate harsh and laboured words?). In another place [5] he says this:

[1] ii. 40.
[2] iii. 229.
[3] ii. 34.
[4] iii. 229.
[5] iii. 143.

---

[4] καὶ Reiske: ἢ codd.

οὑτωσὶ λέγων· "Ὡς ὑμᾶς ὀρρωδῶ κακῶς πάσχοντας τὴν σύνθεσιν τῶν Δημοσθένους ὀνομάτων ἀγαπήσαντας." καὶ γὰρ ἐνταῦθα πάλιν οὐ δέδοικε, μὴ τὸ κάλλος καὶ τὴν μεγαλοπρέπειαν αὐτοῦ τῶν ὀνομάτων ἀγαπήσωσιν Ἀθηναῖοι, ἀλλὰ μὴ λάθωσιν ὑπὸ [1] τῆς συνθέσεως γοητευθέντες, ὥστε καὶ τῶν φανερῶν αὐτὸν ἀδικημάτων ἀφεῖναι διὰ τὰς σειρῆνας τὰς ἐπὶ τῆς ἁρμονίας. ἐκ δὲ τούτων οὐ χαλεπὸν ἰδεῖν, ὅτι δεινότητα μὲν αὐτῷ, ὅσην οὐχ ἑτέρῳ, μαρτυρῶν καὶ ταῖς σειρῆσιν ἀπεικάζων αὐτοῦ τὴν μουσικήν, ἀγάμενος δὲ οὐ τῆς ἐκλογῆς τῶν ὀνομάτων αὐτόν, ἀλλὰ τῆς συνθέσεως, ἀναμφιλόγως αὐτῷ ταύτην παρακεχώρηκε τὴν ἀρετήν.

36 τουτὶ μὲν οὖν τὸ μέρος, ὡς οὐ πολλοῦ λόγου δεόμενον, λέγω δὴ τὸ περιττὸν εἶναι συνθέτην ὀνομάτων τὸν Δημοσθένην, μαρτυρίαις τε ἀξιοχρέοις καὶ τῷ μηδένα τἀναντία ἔχειν εἰπεῖν βεβαιούμενον ἐάσω. τίς δὲ ὁ τῆς ἁρμονίας αὐτοῦ χαρακτὴρ καὶ ἀπὸ ποίας γέγονεν ἐπιτηδεύσεως τοιοῦτος καὶ πῶς ἂν τις αὐτὸν διαγνοίη παρεξετάζων ἑτέροις, ταυτὶ [2] πειράσομαι λέγειν, ἐκεῖνα προειπών. πολλή τις ἐγένετο ἐν τοῖς ἀρχαίοις ἐπιθυμία καὶ πρόνοια τοῦ καλῶς ἁρμόττειν τὰ ὀνόματα ἔν τε μέτροις καὶ δίχα μέτρων, καὶ πάντες, ὅσοι [3] σπουδαίας ἐβουλήθησαν ἐξενεγκεῖν γραφάς, οὐ μόνον ἐζήτησαν ὀνομάσαι τὰ νοήματα καλῶς, ἀλλὰ καὶ αὐτὰ ⟨τὰ ὀνόματα⟩ εὐκόσμῳ συνθέσει περιλαβεῖν· πλὴν οὐ τὴν αὐτήν γε πάντες ἐπετήδευσαν ἁρμονίαν, ὥστ᾽ οὐδὲ κατὰ τὰς αὐτὰς

[1] ὑπὸ Sylburg: ἀπὸ codd.

" I shudder to think that you are suffering the consequences of enjoying Demosthenes's fine phrases." Here again he is not afraid that the beauty and eloquence of Demosthenes's words may give pleasure to the Athenians, but that his skill in putting them together may cast a spell over them without their realising it, and the Siren-music effected by his melodious composition should lull them into forgiving his crimes. It is not difficult to see from this that Aeschines is acknowledging his unique brilliance and, in comparing him to the Sirens, the musical quality of his composition. It is not his choice of words that he admires, but the way he puts them together: this latter quality he concedes to him without question.

I shall leave the subject of Demosthenes's extra- 36
ordinary ability at composition: there is plenty of sound evidence to confirm it and nobody to contradict, and therefore it requires no lengthy argument. But what is the distinctive quality of his melodious composition and what technique has he practised to attain it? And by what criteria can we compare it with others and distinguish it from them? I shall try to answer these questions, but first let me say this. Much energy and thought was spent by ancient writers on the beautiful arrangement of words, both in verse and in prose; and all those who wanted to produce serious works of literature sought not only to express their ideas beautifully as regards individual words, but also to put the words themselves together in a beautiful and orderly combination. They did not, however, all follow the same

---

[2] ταυτὶ Sadée: ταύτῃ codd.
[3] ὅσοι Krüger: οἱ BP.

ἦλθον ἅπαντες ὁδούς. τούτου δ' αἰτίας οἴομαι γενέσθαι πολλάς. πρώτην[1] μὲν τὴν ἑκάστου φύσιν, ᾗ ἄλλοι πρὸς ἄλλα πεφύκαμεν εὖ, δευτέραν δὲ τὴν ἐκ λόγου καὶ προαιρέσεως ἐμφυομένην δόξαν, δι' ἣν τὰ μὲν ἀσπαζόμεθα, τοῖς δ' ἐπαχθόμεθα,[2] τρίτην δὲ τὴν ἐκ συνηθείας χρονίου κατασκευαζομένην ὑπόληψιν ὡς σπουδῆς ἀξίων, ὧν ἂν τοὺς ἐθισμοὺς λάβωμεν, τετάρτην ἔτι[3] τὴν πρὸς οὓς ἂν φιλοτιμούμενοι τυγχάνωμεν,[4] ὁποῖ' ἅττα[5] ἂν ἐκεῖνοι ζηλῶσιν, ἀναφοράν τε καὶ μίμησιν· ἔχοι δ' ἄν τις καὶ ἄλλα λέγειν, ἀλλὰ ἐγὼ τὰ φανερώτατα εἰπὼν ἐῶ τὰ λοιπά. ὅθεν οἱ μὲν τὴν εὐσταθῆ καὶ βαρεῖαν καὶ αὐστηρὰν καὶ φιλάρχαιον καὶ σεμνὴν καὶ φεύγουσαν ἅπαν τὸ κομψὸν ἐπιτηδεύουσιν ἁρμονίαν, οἱ δὲ τὴν γλαφυρὰν καὶ λιγυρὰν καὶ θεατρικὴν καὶ πολὺ τὸ κομψὸν καὶ μαλακὸν[6] ἐπιφαίνουσαν, ᾗ πανηγύρεις τε κηλοῦνται καὶ ὁ συμφορητὸς ὄχλος, οἱ δὲ συνθέντες ἀφ' ἑκατέρας τὰ χρησιμώτατα τὴν[7] μικτὴν καὶ μέσην ἐζήλωσαν ἀγωγήν.

37 τρεῖς γὰρ δὴ συνθέσεως σπουδαίας χαρακτῆρες οὗτοι οἱ γενικώτατοι, οἱ δ' ἄλλοι παρὰ τούτους τε καὶ ἀπὸ τούτων εἰσὶ κατεσκευασμένοι, πολλοὶ σφόδρα ὄντες, ἐπιτάσει τε καὶ ἀνέσει διαφέροντες ἀλλήλων. εἰλικρινὴς μὲν οὖν ἁρμονία καὶ ἀκραιφ-

[1] πρώτην Krüger: πρῶτον codd.
[2] ἐπαχθόμεθα Vliet: ἀπεχθόμεθα codd.
[3] ἔτι Sylburg: ἐπὶ codd.
[4] τυγχάνωμεν Krüger: τυγχάνομεν codd.
[5] ἅττα Sylburg: αὐτὰ codd.
[6] μαλακὸν Sylburg: μάλα codd.
[7] τὰ χρησιμώτατα τὴν Krüger: χρησιμωτάτην codd.

principles of arrangement, and hence did not all proceed along the same lines. I think there were many reasons for this. First there is individual nature, which endows us with different talents. Secondly there is the prejudice which reason and inclination have implanted in us, causing us to be attracted to some subjects and repelled by others. Thirdly there is the assumption induced by long familiarity that what we have become accustomed to is admirable. And fourthly there is the tendency to make whatever standard our rivals seek to attain our own point of reference and object of imitation. One could adduce many other reasons, but these are the most obvious, so I leave the rest unsaid. Hence some writers cultivate the firm, grave, austere style of composition with its old-fashioned dignity and avoidance of all frills, while others use the polished, articulate, spectacular style, full of ornament and delicate touches, the style with which festival audiences and cosmopolitan crowds are lulled into silence; and other, combining the best elements of each, have made the mean between these two, which is a mixture of both, their objective.

Now there are three basic types of literary com- 37
position.[1] All others are modifications or developments of these, and there are many kinds, differing from one another in the strength or weakness of the degree to which each is present. A style that is pure

[1] The following chapters (37–41) contain substantially the same material as *De Compositione Verborum*, 22–24. The main difference is the synthetic and mimetic approach here, whereas in the *De Compositione Verborum* he concentrates on analysis. In the present treatise he is a teacher, in the other a literary critic.

νὴς χαρακτὴρ κατὰ πᾶν οὐκ ἂν εὑρεθείη παρ' οὐδενὶ οὔτε ἐμμέτρων οὔτε πεζῶν ποιητῇ λόγων, οὐδὲ χρὴ μαρτύρια τοιαῦτα παρ' οὐδενὸς ἀπαιτεῖν. ὅπου γὰρ οὐδὲ τῶν στοιχείων τῶν πρώτων, ἐξ ὧν ἡ τοῦ παντὸς συνέστη φύσις, γῆς τε καὶ ὕδατος καὶ ἀέρος καὶ πυρός, οὐδὲν εἰλικρινές ἐστιν, ἀλλὰ πάντα μετέχει πάντων, ὠνόμασται δ' ἕκαστον αὐτῶν κατὰ τὸ πλεονάζον, τί θαυμαστόν, εἰ αἱ τῆς λέξεως ἁρμονίαι τρεῖς οὖσαι τὸν ἀριθμὸν οὐκ ἔχουσιν εἰλικρινῆ τὴν φύσιν οὐδ' ἀνεπίμικτον, ἀλλ' ἐκ τῶν ὡς ἐπὶ τὸ πολὺ συμβεβηκότων αὐτοῖς ὀνόματός τε ἠξίωνται καὶ χαρακτῆρος ἰδίου; ὥσθ', ὅταν παρέχωμαι δείγματα ἑκάστης καὶ μαρτύρια φέρω, λέξεις τινὰς παρατιθεὶς τῶν χρησαμένων αὐταῖς ποιητῶν τε καὶ συγγραφέων, μηδεὶς συκοφαντείτω τὰς ἐπιπλοκὰς καὶ τὰς κατὰ μόρια ποιότητας αὐτῶν, ἀλλὰ κατὰ τὸ πλεονάζον ἕκαστον τῶν παραλαμβανομένων σκοπείτω, τεκμαιρόμενος, εἰ πολλαχῇ τοιοῦτόν ἐστι τὸ δεικνύμενον, οὐκ εἰ ἁπανταχῇ.

38 τῆς μὲν οὖν αὐστηρᾶς καὶ φιλαρχαίου καὶ μὴ τὸ κομψὸν ἀλλὰ τὸ σεμνὸν ἐπιτηδευούσης ἁρμονίας τοιόσδε ὁ χαρακτήρ· ὀνόμασι χρῆσθαι φιλεῖ μεγάλοις καὶ μακροσυλλάβοις καὶ ταῖς ἕδραις αὐτῶν εἶναι πλατέως [1] πάνυ βεβηκυίαις, χρόνων τε ἀξιολόγων ἐμπεριλήψει διορίζεσθαι θάτερα ἀπὸ τῶν ἑτέρων. τοῦτο τὸ σχῆμα [ἀπὸ] [2] τῆς ἁρμονίας ποιοῦσιν αἱ τῶν φωνηέντων γραμμάτων παραθέσεις, ὅταν ἥ τε προηγουμένη λέξις εἰς ἓν τούτων λήγῃ καὶ ἡ συνάπτουσα ταύτῃ τὴν ἀρχὴν ἀπὸ τούτων τινὸς λαμβάνῃ. ἀναγκαῖον γὰρ ἦν [3] χρόνον τινὰ

and completely uncontaminated with others is impossible to find in any author, whether of poetry or of prose, and we should not expect any of them to furnish evidence of such a kind. For since none of the original elements of which the natural world is composed (earth, water, air and fire) is to be found in its pure form, but each substance contains a portion of all four and is named according to that element in it which is dominant, what wonder is it that the three methods of composition have no individual existence independently of one another, but are identified in accordance with their prevalent qualities? Thus, when I give examples and illustrations of each, and append passages from those poets and prose writers who use them, let nobody object that their styles are complex and differ in matters of detail, but let him judge each example by its predominant feature, and decide whether this feature is generally, not whether it is universally present.

The following are the characteristics of the austere, 38
old-fashioned style of composition, which aims at dignity rather than elegance. Long words with long syllables are favoured, each with a broad, firm foundation,[1] and each separated from its neighbour by a considerable interval of time. This form of composition is achieved by the following: the juxtaposition of vowels when the first of two words ends with a vowel and the following word begins with one. This makes an appreciable pause necessary between

[1] The metaphor from building is expanded in *De Compositione Verborum*, 22.

---

[1] πλατέως Sylburg: πλουσίως codd.
[2] ἀπὸ delevit Sylburg.
[3] ἦν Usener: εἶναι codd.

μέσον ἀμφοῖν ἀξιόλογον ἀπολαμβάνεσθαι. καὶ μηδεὶς εἴπῃ· "τί δὲ τοῦτό ἐστιν, ἢ πῶς ἄν τις γένοιτο χρόνος ⟨οἷός τε συναφῇ ὀνόματα⟩ [1] ἀπ' ἀλλήλων διεστάναι κατὰ τὰς τῶν φωνηέντων συμβολάς;" δείκνυται γὰρ ὑπό τε μουσικῶν καὶ μετρικῶν ὁ διὰ μέσου τῶν φωνηέντων χρόνος ἑτέρων παρεμβολῇ γραμμάτων ἡμιφώνων ἀναπληροῦσθαι δυνάμενος. τοῦτο δ' οὐκ ἂν ἐγίγνετο μὴ σιωπῆς τινος ἀξιολόγου διειργούσης τὰ φωνήεντα ἀπ' ἀλλήλων. πρῶτον μὲν δὴ τοῦτο τῆς ἁρμονίας ταύτης ἐστὶν ἰδίωμα ὡς ἐπὶ τὸ πολύ. ἕτερον δὲ τοιοῦτον· ἀνακοπὰς καὶ ἀντιστηριγμοὺς λαμβάνειν καὶ τραχύτητας ἐν ταῖς συμπλοκαῖς τῶν ὀνομάτων ἐπιστυφούσας τὴν ἀκοὴν ἡσυχῇ βούλεται. ἐνταῦθα πάλιν ἡ τῶν ἀφώνων τε καὶ ἡμιφώνων [2] γραμμάτων δύναμις αἰτία, ὁπότ' ἂν τὰ λήγοντα τῶν ἡγουμένων μόρια ἢ [3] γράμματα τοῖς ἡγουμένοις μηδὲν τῶν ἐπιφερομένων μήτε συναλείφεσθαι μήτε συγχεῖσθαι φύσιν ἔχῃ. πολὺ γὰρ δὴ τὸ ἀντίτυπον ἐν ταῖς τούτων συμβολαῖς γίνεται, ὥσπερ γε καὶ ἐν αὐτοῖς τοῖς ὀνόμασιν, ὅταν ἐκ τῶν τραχυνόντων τὴν φωνὴν γραμμάτων αἱ καλούμεναι συλλαβαὶ συντεθῶσι. πολλῆς δέ τινος ἐνταῦθα δεῖ τῆς τεχνήσεως, ἵνα μὴ κακόφωνοι μηδὲ ἀηδεῖς μηδὲ ἄλλην τινὰ ὄχλησιν ἐπενεγκάμεναι ταῖς ἀκοαῖς λάθωσιν αἱ τοιαῦται συζυγίαι, ἀλλ' ἐπανθῇ τις αὐταῖς χνοῦς ἀρχαιοπινὴς καὶ χάρις ἀβίαστος. ἀρκεῖ γάρ, ὡς ἐν εἰδόσι λέγοντας, ὅτι φύσιν ἔχει μηδὲν τῶν σπουδαίων ῥημάτων ἄμοιρον ὥρας εἶναι καὶ χάριτος ἰδίας, τοσοῦτον μόνον εἰπεῖν.

the two words. And nobody should ask: "What does this mean? How can any pause arise to cause a hiatus between consecutive words through the clashing of vowels?" The existence of such a pause is shown by the practice of musical and metrical writers of inserting semivowels between them, which has the effect of filling it in.[1] This would not happen unless an appreciable interval of silence separated the vowels from one another. This is the first general peculiarity of this style. Another is the following: it tends to employ clashes and collisions and harsh combinations, which cause us to prick up our ears slightly. Again it is the effect of certain consonants and semivowels that is responsible for this, whenever the final syllables or letters of leading words cannot in any natural way combine with the leading letters of the following words or fuse with them. Such clashes have a very jarring effect, as they do within words themselves when their syllables are composed of letters which roughen the sound. Great skill is thus needed here to ensure that such combinations do not find their way in unnoticed to produce ugly or unpleasant sounds, or otherwise offend the ear. Rather they should confer a delicate bloom of antiquity upon the passage, and an unforced charm. It is enough to point out to well-informed readers that no serious literature is naturally devoid of beauty and individual charm.

[1] The ν *ephelkustikon.*

---

[1] *οἷός τε συναφῇ ὀνόματα* hiatum implevit Usener et emendavit lectionem corruptam.
[2] *ἡμιφώνων* Sylburg: *ἐμφώνων* MBv.
[3] *μόρια ᾖ* substitui: *μορίων ᾖ* codd.

39 ἐν μὲν δὴ τοῖς ἐλαχίστοις τε καὶ στοιχειώδεσι μορίοις τῆς λέξεως ταῦτα χαρακτηρικὰ τῆς πρώτης ἐστὶν ἁρμονίας, ἐν δὲ τοῖς καλουμένοις κώλοις, ἃ συντίθεται [1] μὲν ἐκ τῶν ὀνομάτων, συμπληροῖ δὲ τὰς περιόδους, οὐ μόνον ταῦτα, ἀλλὰ καὶ ⟨τὸ⟩ [2] τοὺς ῥυθμοὺς τοὺς καταμετροῦντας αὐτὰ μὴ ταπεινοὺς μηδὲ μαλθακοὺς μηδ᾽ ἀγεννεῖς εἶναι, ὑψηλοὺς δὲ καὶ ἀνδρώδεις καὶ μεγαλοπρεπεῖς. οὐ γὰρ δὴ φαῦλόν τι πρᾶγμα ῥυθμὸς ἐν λόγοις οὐδὲ προσθήκης τινὸς μοῖραν ἔχον οὐκ ἀναγκαίας, ἀλλ᾽ εἰ δεῖ τἀληθές, ὡς ἐμὴ δόξα, εἰπεῖν, ἁπάντων κυριώτατον τῶν γοητεύειν δυναμένων καὶ κηλεῖν τὰς ἀκοάς. πρὸς δὲ τοῖς ῥυθμοῖς καὶ τὸ τοὺς σχηματισμοὺς [τῶν ἐννοιῶν] [3] γενναίους εἶναι καὶ ἀξιωματικοὺς οὐ μόνον τοὺς κατὰ τὰς νοήσεις ἀλλὰ καὶ κατ᾽ αὐτὴν τὴν λέξιν συνισταμένους. ἐξαριθμεῖσθαι δὲ νῦν, ὅσα γένη σχηματισμῶν ἐστι τῶν τε κατωνομασμένων καὶ τῶν ἀκατονομάστων, καὶ τίσιν αὐτῶν ἡ τοιαύτη μάλιστα πέφυκεν ἁρμονία χαίρειν, οὐκ ἔχω καιρόν. ἔτι τῆς ἁρμονίας ταύτης οἰκεῖόν ἐστι καὶ τὸ τὰς περιόδους αὐτουργούς τινας εἶναι καὶ ἀφελεῖς καὶ μήτε συναπαρτιζούσας [4] ἑαυταῖς τὸν νοῦν μήτε συμμεμετρημένας τῷ πνεύματι τοῦ λέγοντος μηδέ γε παραπληρώμασι τῶν ὀνομάτων οὐκ ἀναγκαίοις ὡς πρὸς τὴν ὑποκειμένην διάνοιαν χρωμένας μηδ᾽ εἰς θεατρικούς τινας καὶ γλαφυροὺς καταληγούσας ῥυθμούς. καθόλου δέ γε οὐδὲ ἀσπάζεται τὸ ἐμπερίοδον ἥδε ἡ σύνθεσις ὡς τὰ πολλά, ἀποιήτως δέ πως καὶ ἀφελῶς καὶ τὰ πλείω κομματικῶς κατεσκευάσθαι βούλεται, παράδειγμα

Such, then, are the characteristics of the first kind 39
of composition, reduced to its smallest and most elementary terms. When it comes to the formation of what are called clauses, which are composed of words and which combine to form periods, we find not only the above elements but also rhythmic schemes. These must not be mean, effete or ignoble, but elevated, virile and impressive. Rhythm is a not unimportant factor in prose: it is not to be classed as an inessential adjunct, but to tell the truth, I consider it the most potent device of all for bewitching and beguiling the ear. The figures of speech also, like the rhythms, should be noble and dignified, the figures of language no less than the figures of thought. I have not time here to give a classified list of figures of speech, both named hitherto and unnamed, and which of them are appropriate to this kind of composition. Another peculiarity of this style is that the periods are independent and simple, neither coming to an end simultaneously with the sense, nor calculated to suit the breathing of the speaker. Again, they do not use as padding words which are not needed to bring out the underlying sense, nor do they have any sort of spectacular or polished rhythmical endings. In fact, this type of composition does not favour the use of periods for the most part, but prefers a certain unaffected simplicity of construction, with mostly short phrases, imitating the artlessness of

---

1 *συντίθεται* Sylburg: *συντίθενται* codd.
2 *τὸ* inseruit Reiske.
3 *τῶν ἐννοίων* delevit Krüger.
4 *συναπαρτιζούσας* Dindorf: *συναρπαζούσας* codd.

ποιουμένη τὴν ἀκατάσκευον φύσιν. εἰ δέ ποτε ἀκολουθήσειεν τοῖς ἀνεπιτηδεύτως συντιθεμένοις κώλοις ἢ περιόδοις ἢ βάσεσιν εὔρυθμος,[1] τὸ συμβὰν ἐκ τῆς αὐτομάτου τύχης οὐκ ἀπωθεῖται. καὶ ταῦτα δ' ἔτι τῆς ἀρχαίας καὶ αὐστηρᾶς ἁρμονίας ἐστὶ χαρακτηρικά· τὸ μήτε συνδέσμοις χρῆσθαι πολλοῖς μήτ' ἄρθροις συνεχέσιν ἀλλ' ἔστιν ὅτε καὶ τῶν ἀναγκαίων ἐλάττοσιν, τὸ [2] μὴ χρονίζειν ἐπὶ τῶν αὐτῶν πτώσεων τὸν λόγον ἀλλὰ θαμινὰ μεταπίπτειν,[3] τὸ [4] τῆς ἀκολουθίας τῶν προεξενεχθέντων ὑπεροπτικῶς ἔχειν τὴν φράσιν μηδὲ κατ' ἄλληλα, τὸ [5] περιττῶς καὶ ἰδίως καὶ μὴ κατὰ τὴν ὑπόληψιν ἢ βούλησιν τῶν πολλῶν συζεύγνυσθαι τὰ μόρια. καὶ παραδείγματα δὲ αὐτῆς ποιητῶν μὲν καὶ μελοποιῶν ἥ τ' Αἰσχύλου λέξις ὀλίγου δεῖν πᾶσα καὶ ἡ Πινδάρου, χωρὶς ὅτι μὴ τὰ Παρθένεια καὶ εἴ τινα [6] τούτοις ὁμοίας ἀπαιτεῖ κατασκευάς· διαφαίνεται δέ τις ὁμοία κἀν τούτοις εὐγένεια καὶ σεμνότης ἁρμονίας τὸν ἀρχαῖον φυλάττουσα πίνον. συγγραφέων δὲ λαμπρότατός τε καὶ μάλιστα τῶν ἄλλων κατορθῶν περὶ ταύτην τὴν ἰδέαν Θουκυδίδης. εἰ δέ τῳ δοκεῖ μαρτυρίων ἔτι δεῖν τῷ λόγῳ, παρελθὼν τοὺς ποιητὰς ἐκ τῆς Θουκυδίδου λέξεως ταυτὶ ⟨λαμβάνω⟩.[7] "Τούτου δὲ τοῦ πολέμου μῆκός τε μέγα προὔβη, παθήματά τε ξυνέβη γενέσθαι τῇ Ἑλλάδι πολλὰ οἷα οὐχ ἕτερα ἐν ἴσῳ χρόνῳ. οὔτε γὰρ πόλεις τοσαίδε ληφθεῖσαι ἠρημώθησαν αἳ

[1] εὔρυθμος Reiske: εὐρύθμοις codd.
[2] τὸ Sylburg: τοῦ codd.
[3] μεταπίπτειν Sylburg: μεταπέμπειν codd.

nature herself. But if pleasing rhythm should sometimes result from the unstudied composition of these clauses, periods or *clausulae*, the spontaneous gift of fortune is not rejected. The old-fashioned, austere style has the following features also: it does not use connective words much, and the article is not consistently employed, but actually less on occasion than is necessary. The constructions do not continue for long in the same cases, but frequently change. The expression pays little attention to agreement with what has gone before or to self-consistency. The members are combined in an unusual and individual way, and not as most people would expect or require. There are examples of this, in poetry spoken or sung, in nearly all the verse of Aeschylus and Pindar, except that Pindar's *Partheneia* and other poems of that kind require a different style, though even in these a certain stately nobility is still apparent, preserving the patina of antiquity. The most brilliant and successful exponent of this style among the historians is Thucydides; so if anyone thinks that my account requires further illustration of the characteristics I have described, let me pass over the poets and take this passage from him:[1]

"Now this war lasted for a long time, and Greece underwent many sufferings in the course of it such as had never been experienced before in an equal time: for never before were so many cities taken and laid

[1] i. 23. 1–4.

---

[4] τὸ Sylburg: τῷ codd.
[5] τὸ Sylburg: τῷ codd.
[6] τινα Sylburg: τινας codd.
[7] λαμβάνω lacunam a Reiske indicatam supplevi.

μὲν ὑπὸ βαρβάρων, αἳ δὲ ὑπὸ σφῶν αὐτῶν ἀντιπολεμούντων, εἰσὶ δὲ αἳ καὶ οἰκήτορας μετέβαλον ἁλισκόμεναι, οὔτε φυγαὶ τοσαίδε ἀνθρώπων καὶ φόνος ὃ μὲν κατ᾽ αὐτὸν τὸν πόλεμον, ὃ δὲ διὰ τὸ στασιάζειν. τά τε πρότερον ἀκοῇ μὲν λεγόμενα, ἔργῳ δὲ σπανιώτερον βεβαιούμενα οὐκ ἄπιστα κατέστη σεισμῶν τε πέρι, οἳ ἐπὶ πλεῖστον ἅμα μέρος γῆς καὶ ἰσχυρότατοι οἱ αὐτοὶ ἐπέσχον, ἡλίου τ᾽ ἐκλείψεις, αἳ πυκνότεραι παρὰ τὰ ἐκ τοῦ πρὶν χρόνου μνημονευόμενα συνέβησαν, αὐχμοί τ᾽ ἔστιν παρ᾽ οἷς μεγάλοι καὶ ἀπ᾽ αὐτῶν καὶ λιμοὶ καὶ ἡ οὐχ ἥκιστα βλάψασα καὶ μέρος τι φθείρασα ἡ λοιμώδης νόσος." ἡ μὲν δὴ πρώτη τῶν ἁρμονιῶν ἡ γεννικὴ καὶ αὐστηρὰ καὶ μεγαλόφρων καὶ τὸ ἀρχαιοπρεπὲς διώκουσα τοιάδε τίς ἐστι κατὰ τὸν χαρακτῆρα.

40 ἡ δὲ μετὰ ταύτην ⟨ἡ⟩ [1] γλαφυρὰ καὶ θεατρικὴ καὶ τὸ κομψὸν αἱρουμένη πρὸ τοῦ σεμνοῦ τοιαύτη· ὀνομάτων αἰεὶ βούλεται λαμβάνειν τὰ λειότατα καὶ μαλακώτατα, τὴν εὐφωνίαν θηρωμένη καὶ τὴν εὐμέλειαν,[2] ἐξ αὐτῶν δὲ τὸ ἡδύ. ἔπειτα οὐχ ὡς ἔτυχεν ἀξιοῖ ταῦτα τιθέναι οὐδὲ ἀπερισκέπτως συναρμόττειν θάτερα τοῖς ἑτέροις, ἀλλὰ διακρίνουσα τὰ ποῖα τοῖς ποίοις [καὶ] παρατιθέμενα [3] μουσικωτέρους [4] ποιεῖν δυνήσεται τοὺς ἤχους, καὶ σκοποῦσα κατὰ ποῖον σχῆμα ληφθέντα χαριεστέρας ἀποτελέσει τὰς συζυγίας, οὕτως συναρμόττειν ἕκαστα πειρᾶται, πολλὴν σφόδρα ποιουμένη φροντίδα τοῦ συνεξέσθαι καὶ συνηλεῖ-

[1] ἡ inseruit Krüger.
[2] εὐμέλειαν Sylburg: ἐκμέλειαν P ἐμμέλειαν MB.

waste, some by the barbarians and some as the result of internecine strife, and in yet others the inhabitants changed after their capture. Nor was there before so much banishment of men and bloodshed, both resulting from the war itself and from sedition. And things which previously were spoken of from hearsay, but rarely confirmed by fact, were rendered not incredible, both regarding earthquakes, which at once extended over a very large part of the world, and were at the same time the most violent, and eclipses of the sun, which occurred more frequently than had ever been recorded in previous history; and in some places there were great droughts, with famines resulting from them, and finally that most disastrous visitation, which destroyed a portion of mankind, the plague."

Such are the distinctive features of the first kind of style, which is noble, austere and grand in conception, and has an old-fashioned flavour.

The next kind of composition, the polished, spec- 40
tacular kind, chooses to be decorative rather than dignified. It always prefers the smoothest and blandest words because its object is euphony and musical effect, and the pleasure they produce. Then it does not see fit to place these words casually or to fit them together carelessly, but decides what combinations will be able to make these sounds more musical and arranges them in parallel clauses. Attention is also paid to finding what arrangement will produce the more attractive combination of words, and this arrangement is adopted where possible; and very great care is taken to ensure that the

---

[3] τὰ ποῖα τοῖς ποίοις παρατιθέμενα Sylburg: τὰ ποιὰ τοῖς ἀποίοις καὶ παρατιθεμένη codd.

[4] μουσικωτέρους Usener: μουσικωτάτους MBP.

φθαι [1] καὶ προπετεῖς ἁπάντων αὐτῶν εἶναι τὰς ἁρμονίας. καὶ διὰ τοῦτο φεύγει μὲν ἁπάσῃ σπουδῇ τὰς τῶν φωνηέτων συμβολὰς ὡς τὴν λειότητα καὶ τὴν εὐέπειαν διασπώσας, φεύγει δέ, ὅση δύναμις αὐτῇ, τῶν ἡμιφώνων τε καὶ ἀφώνων γραμμάτων τὰς συζυγίας, ὅσαι τραχύνουσι τοὺς ἤχους καὶ ταράττειν δύνανται τὰς ἀκοάς. ἐπειδὴ γὰρ οὐκ ἐνδέχεται πᾶσαν σημαίνουσαν σῶμα ἢ πρᾶγμα λέξιν ἐξ εὐφώνων συγκεῖσθαι γραμμάτων καὶ μαλακῶν, ἀλλ' ἐνίοτε συγκεῖσθαι τὰς αὐτὰς καὶ κακῶς ἐνδέχεται, ὃ μὴ [2] δίδωσιν ἡ φύσις, τοῦτο πειρᾶται λαμβάνειν ταῖς συζυγίαις αὐταῖς καὶ ⟨οὕτω τὰς φωνὰς⟩ [3] ποιεῖν ἡδίους καὶ μαλακωτέρας. καὶ δῆτα καὶ παρεμβάλλειν αὖ ταῖς ⟨ἀναγκαίαις⟩ [3] τινὰς ἑτέρας λέξεις ὑπομένει πρὸς τὸν ὑποκείμενον νοῦν οὔτ' ἀναγκαίας οὔτ' ἴσως χρησίμας, δεσμοῦ δέ τινος ἢ κόλλης τάξιν ταῖς πρὸ αὐτῶν καὶ μετ' αὐτὰς [4] κειμέναις ὀνομασίαις παρεξομένας, ἵνα μὴ συναπτόμεναι πρὸς ἀλλήλας αἵ καταλήγουσαί τε εἰς τραχὺ γράμμα καὶ αἱ τὴν ἀρχὴν ἀπό τινος τοιούτου λαμβάνουσαι σπαδονισμοὺς τῶν ἤχων ποιῶσι καὶ ἀντιτυπίας, τῇ δὲ παρεμπιπτούσῃ λέξει προσαναπαυόμεναι μαλακοὺς φαίνεσθαι ποιῶσι τοὺς ἤχους καὶ συνεχεῖς. τὸ γὰρ ὅλον ἐστὶν αὐτῆς βούλημα καὶ ἡ πολλὴ πραγματεία περὶ τὸ συσπασθῆναί τε καὶ συνυφάνθαι πάντα τὰ μόρια τῆς περιόδου, μιᾶς λέξεως ἀποτελοῦντα φαντασίαν, καὶ ἔτι πρὸς τούτῳ περὶ τὸ πᾶσαν εἶναι τὴν λέξιν, ὥσπερ ἐν ταῖς μουσικαῖς συμφωνίαις, ἡδεῖαν καὶ λιγυράν. τούτων δὲ τὸ μὲν αἱ τῶν

order in which they are all arranged produces a polished sentence that flows smoothly and swiftly. For this reason every effort is made to avoid the clashing of vowels, as this breaks up the smoothness and the euphony. Avoided, too, as far as possible, are the combinations of semivowels and consonants which roughen the sound and can offend the ear by their harshness. Since it is impossible to describe every animate or inanimate thing in letters which sound pleasing and soft, but the arrangement of these same letters can also be bad on occasion, it is this arrangement of the words themselves with a view to a pleasanter and gentler effect, which nature does not itself supply, that is the concern of the smooth style. Indeed, it is quite prepared to allow unnecessary words to be added to the necessary which contribute nothing to the underlying sense, and perhaps have no useful purpose, but are intended to serve as a sort of connection or bonding between what precedes and what follows, so that words ending and words beginning with rough letters may not clash, choking the sound and producing dissonance. The intervening phrase provides a rest and makes the sound appear soft and unbroken. The whole intention and special concern of this kind of composition is to draw and weave together all the members of the period, achieving the impression of one continuous passage, and furthermore to impart a sweet and clear-sounding quality to the whole utterance, as to a musical performance. The first of these is achieved by fitting

---

[1] *συνηλεῖφθαι* Reiske: *συνειλῆφθαι* codd.
[2] *μὴ* Krüger: *δὴ* codd.
[3] lacunas supplevit Radermacher.
[4] *μετ' αὐτὰς* Reiske: *μετὰ ταύτας* codd.

ἁρμονιῶν ἀκρίβειαι ποιοῦσι, τὸ δ' αἱ τῶν γραμμάτων [1] δυνάμεις οἰκείως ἐχόντων πρὸς ἄλληλα ταῖς κατὰ τοὺς νόμους συμπαθείαις, ὑπὲρ ὧν ἑτέρας ἐπιστήμης ⟨ἡ⟩ [2] θεωρία. ἐπιτρόχαλος δή τις γίνεται καὶ καταφερὴς ἡ ῥύσις τῆς λέξεως, ὥσπερ κατὰ πρανοῦς φερόμενα χωρίου νάματα [3] μηδενὸς αὐτοῖς ἀντικρούοντος,[4] καὶ διαρρεῖ διὰ τῆς ἀκοῆς ἡδέως πως καὶ ἀσπαστῶς οὐδὲν ἧττον ἢ τὰ δι' ᾠδῆς καὶ ὀργάνου μουσωθέντα κρούματα καὶ μέλη. ἔτι τῆς συνθέσεως ταύτης ἐστὶ καὶ τὰ κῶλα δεινῶς ποιήμασιν ἐμφερῆ, μαλακόφωνα καὶ λεῖα, πολὺ τὸ κωτίλον ἔχοντα κατά τινα φιλότητα φυσικὴν συζευγνύμενα ἀλλήλοις. ἐξ ὧν ἡ περίοδος συνέστηκεν· οὐδὲν γὰρ ἔξω περιόδου συντίθησιν. ἔτι τῶν ῥυθμῶν, εἰς ἃς διαστέλλεται περιόδους, οὐ τοὺς ἀξιωματικοὺς βούλεται λαμβάνειν ἀλλὰ τοὺς χαριεστάτους. εὐκόρυφοι δὴ φαίνονται καὶ εὔγραμμοι διὰ τοῦτο καὶ εἰς ἕδραν ἀσφαλῆ τελευτῶσι. τῶν δὲ σχημάτων διώκει [5] τὰ κινητικώτατα τῶν ὄχλων· καλλωπίζεται γὰρ καὶ τέθηλε τούτοις, ἂν ἄχρι τοῦ μὴ λυπῆσαι τὰς ἀκοὰς προβαίνοι, ὧν [6] εἰσὶν αἵ τε παρισώσεις καὶ παρομοιώσεις καὶ ἀντιθέσεις καὶ τὰ παρωνομασμένα τά τε ἀντιστρέφοντα καὶ τὰ ἐπαναφερόμενα καὶ ἄλλα πολλὰ τοιαῦτα ποιητικῆς καὶ μελικῆς λέξεως ὄργανα. τοιαῦτά τινά μοι καὶ ταύτης εἶναι φαίνεται χαρακτηριστικὰ τῆς ἁρμονίας. παραδείγματα δ' αὐτῆς ποιοῦμαι ποιητῶν μὲν Ἡσίοδόν τε καὶ Σαπφὼ καὶ Ἀνακρέοντα,

[1] γραμμάτων Krüger: πραγμάτων codd.
[2] ἡ inseruit Krüger.

the letters together with precision, the second by establishing the proper relation of the different letters through the affinities arising from the laws of melody; which is another subject of study. The flow of the words becomes lively and rapid, like streams running down a hillside when their course is unimpeded, and ear is affected with the same welcome and gentle sensation as with the sound of music played on instruments and sung by voices. Again, the clauses that make up this type of composition are remarkably like the verses of poetry, soft in sound and smooth, full of beguiling words and joined to one another by a certain natural affinity. It is of these that the period is composed; and the structure is exclusively periodic. The rhythms preferred for the *clausulae* of these periods are not the most dignified but the most elegant; for it is these which give them their well-rounded and well-defined appearance and enable them to end on a firm note. The figures of speech favoured are those which most excite the emotions of mass audiences. These add an exuberant beauty when used in moderation that does not offend the ear. I am here referring to the figures of parallelism in length and sound, to antithesis, paronomasia, antistrophe, anaphora and many of the other devices of this kind used in poetry, spoken or sung.

Such are the features which seem to me to characterise this style. I consider its exemplars among the poets to be Hesiod, Sappho and Anacreon, and

[3] *νάματα* Kiessling: *σώματα* codd.
[4] *ἀντικρούοντος* Sylburg: *ἀνακρούοντος* codd.
[5] *διώκει* Sylburg: *δεῖ διώκειν* M.
[6] *ὧν* Holwell: *ὡς* codd.

τῶν δὲ πεζῇ λέξει χρησαμένων Ἰσοκράτην τε τὸν Ἀθηναῖον καὶ τοὺς ἐκείνῳ πλησιάσαντας. εἴρηνται μὲν οὖν καὶ πρότερον ἤδη λέξεις τινές, ἐν αἷς τὸν ὅλον χαρακτῆρα αὐτοῦ τῆς λέξεως ὑπέγραφον, ἐξ ὧν καὶ τὰ περὶ τὴν σύνθεσιν, εἰ τοιαῦτά ἐστιν οἷα λέγομεν ἡμεῖς, οὐ χαλεπῶς ἄν τις ἴδοι. ἵνα δὲ μὴ δόξωμεν διαρτᾶν τὰς ἀκολουθίας, τοὺς ἀναγινώσκοντας ἐπὶ τὰ ἐν ἀρχαῖς ῥηθέντα παραδείγματα κελεύοντες ἀναστρέφειν, λαμβανέσθω κἀνταῦθα ἐκ τῶν Πανηγυρικῶν αὐτοῦ λόγων λέξις οὐ πολλὴν διατριβὴν παρέξουσα τοῖς ἀναγνωσομένοις, ἐν ᾗ διεξέρχεται τὰ πραχθέντα Ἀθηναίοις περὶ τὴν ἐν Σαλαμῖνι ναυμαχίαν. ἔστι δὲ ἥδε·

"Ἐπειδὴ γὰρ οὐχ οἷοί τε ἦσαν πρὸς ἀμφοτέρας ἅμα παρατάξασθαι τὰς δυνάμεις, παραλαβόντες ἅπαντα τὸν ὄχλον ἐκ τῆς πόλεως εἰς τὴν ἐχομένην νῆσον ἐξέπλευσαν, ἵν' ἐν μέρει καὶ μὴ πρὸς ἑκάτερα κινδυνεύωσι. καίτοι πῶς ἂν ἐκείνων ἄνδρες ἀμείνους ἢ μᾶλλον φιλέλληνες ὄντες ἐπιδειχθεῖεν, οἵτινες ἔτλησαν ἐπιδεῖν, ὥστε μὴ τοῖς πολλοῖς αἴτιοι γενέσθαι τῆς δουλείας, ἐρήμην μὲν τὴν πόλιν γιγνομένην, τὴν δὲ χώραν πορθουμένην, ἱερὰ δὲ συλώμενα καὶ νεὼς ἐμπιμπραμένους, ἅπαντα δὲ τὸν πόλεμον περὶ τὴν πατρίδα τὴν αὑτῶν γενόμενον; καὶ μὴν οὐδὲ[1] ταῦτ' ἀπέχρησεν αὐτοῖς, ἀλλὰ πρὸς διακοσίας καὶ χιλίας τριήρεις μόνοι διαναυμαχεῖν οὐκ ἐμέλλησαν, οὐ μὴν εἰάθησάν γε. καταισχυνθέντες τε γὰρ Πελοποννήσιοι τὴν ἀρετὴν αὐτῶν καὶ νομίσαντες προδιαφθαρέντων μὲν τῶν ἡμετέρων οὐδ' αὐτοὶ

[1] καὶ μὴν οὐδὲ Ritschl: καὶ μηδὲ MBP.

among prose writers Isocrates the Athenian and his followers. I have already quoted some passages to illustrate the general character of his style, and these could also be used to check the truth of my statements concerning his composition. In order to avoid seeming to interrupt the sequence of my argument by asking my readers to turn back to examples given at the beginning, let me introduce here too a passage from his *Panegyricus* which will not take up much of the reader's time. It is the one in which he describes the actions of the Athenians in the Salamis sea- 480 B.C. campaign:[1]

". . . For when they were not able to draw themselves up against both the land and the sea forces at once, they took with them the entire population, abandoned the city, and sailed to the neighbouring island, in order that they might face the threat from each of the two forces in turn and not from both at once. And yet how could men be shown to be braver or more fervent lovers of Greece than our ancestors who, to avoid bringing slavery upon the rest of Greece, endured seeing their city made desolate, their land plundered, their sanctuaries rifled, their temples burned, and the whole weight of the war pressing upon their country? And indeed even this was not enough for them, but they were ready to give battle on the sea on their own against twelve hundred triremes. They were not in fact allowed to fight alone; for the Peloponnesians, put to shame by their courage, and thinking, moreover, that if the Athenians should be first destroyed, they could

[1] *Panegyricus*, 96–99.

σωθήσεσθαι, κατορθωσάντων δ' εἰς ἀτιμίαν τὰς αὑτῶν πόλεις καταστήσειν, ἠναγκάσθησαν μετασχεῖν τῶν κινδύνων. καὶ τοὺς μὲν θορύβους τοὺς ἐν τῷ πράγματι γιγνομένους καὶ τὰς κραυγὰς καὶ τὰς παρακελεύσεις, ἃ κοινὰ πάντων ἐστὶ τῶν ναυμαχούντων, οὐκ οἶδ' ὅ τι δεῖ λέγοντας διατρίβειν. ἃ δ' ἔστιν ἴδια καὶ τῆς ἡγεμονίας ἄξια καὶ τοῖς προειρημένοις ὁμολογούμενα, ταῦτα δ' ἐμὸν ἔργον ἐστὶν εἰπεῖν. τοσοῦτον γὰρ ἡ πόλις ἡμῶν διέφερεν, ὅτε ἦν ἀκέραιος, ὥστε ἀνάστατος γενομένη πλείους μὲν συνεβάλετο τριήρεις εἰς τὸν κίνδυνον τὸν ὑπὲρ τῆς Ἑλλάδος ἢ σύμπαντες οἱ ναυμαχήσαντες, [δυναμένας δὲ πρὸς δὶς τοσαύτας κινδυνεύειν].[1] οὐδεὶς γ' οὖν πρὸς ἡμᾶς οὕτως ἔχει δυσμενῶς, ὅστις οὐκ ἂν ὁμολογήσειε διὰ μὲν τὴν ναυμαχίαν ἡμᾶς τῷ πολέμῳ κρατῆσαι, ταύτης δὲ τὴν πόλιν αἰτίαν γεγενῆσθαι. καίτοι μελλούσης στρατείας ἐπὶ τοὺς βαρβάρους ἔσεσθαι τίνας χρὴ τὴν ἡγεμονίαν ἔχειν; οὐ τοὺς ἐν τῷ προτέρῳ πολέμῳ μάλιστα εὐδοκιμήσαντας καὶ πολλάκις μὲν ἰδίᾳ προκινδυνεύσαντας, ἐν δὲ τοῖς κοινοῖς τῶν ἀγώνων ἀριστείων ἀξιωθέντας; οὐ τοὺς τὴν αὑτῶν καταλιπόντας περὶ τῆς τῶν ἄλλων σωτηρίας καὶ τό γε παλαιὸν οἰκιστὰς πλείστων πόλεων γενομένους καὶ πάλιν αὐτὰς ἐκ τῶν μεγίστων συμφορῶν διασώσαντας; πῶς δ' οὐκ ἂν δεινὰ πάθοιμεν, εἰ τῶν κακῶν πλεῖστον μέρος μετασχόντες ἔλαττον ταῖς τιμαῖς ἔχειν ἀξιωθείημεν καὶ τότε προταχθέντες πρὸ[2] τῶν ἄλλων νῦν ἑτέροις ἀκολουθεῖν ἀναγκασθείημεν;"

[1] δυναμένας δὲ πρὸς δὶς τοσαύτας κινδυνεύειν seclusi ab Isocrate omissa. [2] πρὸ Sylburg: πρὸς MBP.

not themselves be saved from destruction, and that if the Athenians should succeed, their own cities would be brought into ill-repute, were forced to share the danger. Now as to the din that arose during the action, and the shoutings and the cheers—things which are common to all sea battles, I see no reason to waste time in describing these. My task is to speak on those matters which are distinctive and confirm our claims to leadership, and which corroborate the arguments already advanced. Thus I say that our city was so far superior while she stood unharmed that even after she had been laid waste she contributed more ships to the battle for Greece than all the other states put together who fought in the battle; and nobody is so prejudiced against us that he would not acknowledge that it was by winning the sea-battle that we prevailed in the war, and the credit for this is due to Athens.

" Who then should have the leadership of the proposed campaign against the barbarians? Should it not be those who distinguished themselves above all others in the war that preceded it? Should it not be those who many times bore, alone, the brunt of the battle, and in the common struggles of the Greeks were awarded the prize of valour? Should it not be those who abandoned their own country to save the rest of Greece, who in early times founded very many Greek cities, and who later delivered them from the greatest disasters? How could it not be an outrage upon us if, having taken a very large share of the evils of war, we should be thought to deserve a lesser share of its honours, and if, having at that time been in the front rank in the battle for all Greece, we should now be forced to follow the lead of others."

41 τῆς δὲ τρίτης ἁρμονίας, ἣν ἔφην μικτὴν ἐξ ἀμφοῖν εἶναι τὰ χρησιμώτατα ἐκλέγουσαν ἀφ' ἑκατέρας, οὐδείς ἐστι χαρακτὴρ ἴδιος, ἀλλ' ὡς ἂν οἱ μετιόντες αὐτὴν[1] προαιρέσεως ἔχωσιν ἢ δυνάμεως τὰ μὲν φυγεῖν, τὰ δὲ λαβεῖν, οὕτως κίρνανται καθάπερ ἐν τῇ ζωγραφίᾳ τὰ μίγματα. ταύτης τῆς ἁρμονίας κράτιστος μὲν ἐγένετο κανὼν ὁ ποιητὴς Ὅμηρος, καὶ οὐκ ἄν τις εἴποι λέξιν ἄμεινον ἡρμοσμένην τῆς ἐκείνου πρὸς ἄμφω ταῦτα, λέγω δὲ τήν τε ἡδονὴν καὶ τὸ σεμνόν. ἐζήλωσαν δὲ αὐτὸν ἐπῶν τε πολλοὶ ποιηταὶ καὶ μελῶν, ἔτι δὲ τραγῳδίας τε καὶ κωμῳδίας, συγγραφεῖς τε ἀρχαῖοι καὶ φιλόσοφοι καὶ ῥήτορες. ὧν ἁπάντων μεμνῆσθαι πολὺ ἂν ἔργον εἴη, ἀρκέσει δὲ τῶν ἐν λόγοις δυναστευσάντων, οὓς ἐγὼ κρατίστους εἶναι πείθομαι, δύο παρασχέσθαι μόνους, συγγραφέων μὲν Ἡρόδοτον, φιλοσόφων δὲ Πλάτωνα· καὶ γὰρ καὶ ἀξίωμα καὶ χάρις αὐτῶν ἐπιτρέχει ταῖς ἁρμονίαις. εἰ δὲ ὀρθὰ ἐγὼ καὶ εἰκότα ἔγνωκα περὶ αὐτῶν, ἐξετάσαι τῷ βουλομένῳ σκοπεῖν ἔστιν. φέρε δὴ τίς οὐκ ἂν ὁμολογήσειεν τῆς τε αὐστηρᾶς καὶ τῆς ἡδείας ἁρμονίας μέσην εἶναι τήνδε τὴν λέξιν καὶ τὰ κράτιστα εἰληφέναι παρ' ἑκατέρας, ᾗ κέχρηται Ἡρόδοτος Ξέρξῃ περιθεὶς τὸν λόγον, ὅτ' ἐβουλεύετο περὶ τῆς πρὸς τοὺς Ἕλληνας στρατείας; μετακεκόμισται δ' εἰς τὴν Ἀτθίδα διάλεκτον ἡ λέξις· "ἄνδρες Πέρσαι, οὔτ' αὐτὸς καθηγήσομαι

[1] αὐτὴν Sylburg: αὐτῷ codd.

[1] vii. 8. Herodotus was something of an embarrassment to Dionysius, since he was both a fellow citizen of Halicarnassus

As to the third kind of composition, which I described as a mixture obtained by selecting the best qualities of the other two, it has no quality peculiar to itself but, like the mixture of colours on the artist's palette, varies according to the purpose and the selective ability of the person trying to use it. The standard of excellence in this style was set by Homer, and there is no style that could be said to combine the two qualities of charm and dignity more effectively. Many epic and lyric poets sought to rival him; so, too, did many comic and tragic poets, and the older historians, philosophers and orators. It would be a laborious task to name all these: I shall therefore confine myself to the prominent writers of prose, from which I select only two that I consider the finest—Herodotus of the historians and Plato of the philosophers, whose styles are irradiated with both dignity and grace. Anyone who likes to consider it can test whether this judgment of mine is fair and reasonable. But come now, who would not agree that the following passage is half-way between the austere and the agreeable style, and draws on the best elements of each? It contains the words which Herodotus puts into the mouth of Xerxes when he was considering whether to march against the Greeks. I have converted the original passage into the Attic dialect:[1] 41

"Men of Persia, I shall not be the first to introduce

and a writer whom he genuinely admired as a master of style, but could never be a satisfactory model because he wrote in the Ionic dialect and could not, even by Dionysius, be subjected to rules of purity and propriety which could have had no meaning for him. Hence the vague terms in which the comparison between Herodotus and Thucydides in the *Letter to Pompeius* (3) is made.

νόμον τόνδ' ἐν ὑμῖν τιθεὶς παραδεξάμενός τε αὐτῷ χρήσομαι. ὡς ἐγὼ πυνθάνομαι τῶν πρεσβυτέρων, οὐδένα χρόνον ἠτρεμήσαμεν, ἐξ οὗ παρελάβομεν τὴν ἡγεμονίαν τήνδε παρὰ Μήδων, Κύρου καθελόντος Ἀστυάγην· ἀλλὰ θεός τε οὕτως ἐνάγει καὶ αὐτοῖς ἡμῖν πολλὰ ἐπιοῦσι συμφέρεται ἐπὶ τὸ ἄμεινον. ἃ μὲν δὴ Κῦρός τε καὶ Καμβύσης πατήρ τε ὁ ἐμὸς Δαρεῖος κατειργάσαντο ⟨καὶ προσεκτήσαντο⟩ ἔθνη, ἐπισταμένοις οὐκ ἄν τις λέγοι. ἐγὼ δ', ἐπειδὴ παρέλαβον τὸν θρόνον τοῦτον, ἐφρόντιζον, ὅπως μὴ λείψομαι τῶν πρότερον γενομένων ἐν τῇ τιμῇ τῇδε μηδ' ἐλάσσω προσκτήσομαι δύναμιν Πέρσαις. φροντίζων δὲ εὑρίσκω ἅμα μὲν κῦδος ἡμῖν προσγινόμενον χώραν τε ἧς νῦν κεκτήμεθα οὐκ ἐλάσσονα οὐδὲ φλαυροτέραν παμφορωτέραν τε, ἅμα δὲ τιμωρίαν καὶ τίσιν γινομένην. διὰ δὴ ταῦτα νῦν ὑμᾶς ἐγὼ συνέλεξα, ἵνα, ἃ διανοοῦμαι πράττειν, ὑποθῶ ὑμῖν· μέλλω ζεύξας τὸν Ἑλλήσποντον ἐλαύνειν στρατὸν διὰ τῆς Εὐρώπης ἐπὶ τὴν Ἑλλάδα, ἵνα Ἀθηναίους τιμωρήσωμαι, ὅσα δὴ πεποιήκασι Πέρσας τε καὶ πατέρα τὸν ἐμόν. ὁρᾶτε μὲν δὴ καὶ Δαρεῖον προθυμούμενον στρατεύεσθαι ἐπὶ τοὺς ἄνδρας τούτους, ἀλλ' ὁ μὲν τετελεύτηκε, καὶ οὐκ ἐξεγένετ' αὐτῷ τιμωρήσασθαι, ἐγὼ δ' ὑπέρ τ' ἐκείνου καὶ τῶν ἄλλων Περσῶν οὐ πρότερον παύσομαι, πρὶν ἕλω τε καὶ πυρώσω τὰς Ἀθήνας. οἵ γε ἐμέ τε καὶ πατέρα τὸν ἐμὸν ὑπῆρξαν ἄδικα ποιοῦντες· πρῶτα μὲν εἰς Σάρδεις ἐλθόντες ἅμα Ἀρισταγόρᾳ τῷ Μιλησίῳ, δούλῳ δὲ ἡμετέρῳ, ἐνέπρησαν τά τε ἄλση καὶ τὰ ἱερά. δεύτερα δὲ

this custom among you, but shall use it, having received it from my forefathers. Our elders tell me
that we have never remained inactive since we took
over the hegemony from the Medes when Cyrus over- 550 B.C.
threw Astyages: but that is how the god leads the
way, and we who follow him receive many benefits as
a result. As to the achievements of Cyrus, Cambyses 528–522 B.C.
and my father Darius, and the nations they annexed, 522–485 B.C.
no one need tell you about them since you know them
already. But I, since I have succeeded to this throne,
have been considering by what means I may not fall
short of my predecessors in this honour, nor make a
smaller addition to Persian power. And on consideration I find that we may at the same time increase our renown and add to our possession a territory no smaller or more trifling compared with that
which we now possess but even more productive,
while at the same time exacting punishment and
requital. It is for these reasons that I have called
you together now, in order to put to you what I propose to do. I intend to bridge the Hellespont and
march an army through Europe against Greece, in
order to punish the Athenians for what they did to the
Persians and to my father. Now of course you have
seen Darius eagerly preparing to march against 485 B.C.
these men; but he died, and hence was not able to
avenge his own wrongs. But I, acting on his behalf
and on behalf of Persia as a whole, shall not rest until
I have captured and burnt Athens, for they were the
first to do wrong by injuring me and my father. First
they came to Sardis with Aristagoras of Miletus, our 497 B.C.
servant, and burnt down the groves and the temples.

ἡμᾶς οἷα ἔδρασαν εἰς τὴν γῆν τὴν σφετέραν ἀποβάντας, ὅτε Δᾶτίς τε καὶ Ἀρταφέρνης ἐστρατήγουν, ἐπίστασθέ που πάντες. τούτων μέντοι ἕνεκα ἀνώρμημαι ἐπ' αὐτοὺς στρατεύεσθαι, ἀγαθὰ δ' ἐν αὐτοῖς τοσάδε ἀνευρίσκω λογιζόμενος· εἰ τούτους τε καὶ τοὺς τούτοις πλησιοχώρους καταστρεψόμεθα, οἳ Πέλοπος τοῦ Φρυγὸς νέμονται χώραν, γῆν [τε] τὴν Περσίδα ἀποδείξομεν τῷ Διὸς αἰθέρι ὅμορον οὖσαν. οὐ γὰρ δὴ χώραν γε οὐδεμίαν κατόψεται ὁ ἥλιος ὅμορον οὖσαν τῇ ἡμετέρᾳ, ἀλλ' αὐτὰς ἁπάσας ἐγὼ ἅμα ὑμῖν μίαν χώραν θήσω, διὰ πάσης ἐξελθὼν τῆς Εὐρώπης. πυνθάνομαι γὰρ ὧδε ἔχειν· οὔτε τινὰ πόλιν αὐτῶν οὐδεμίαν οὔτε ἔθνος ἀνθρώπων οὐδὲν ὑπολείπεσθαι ἡμῖν, ὃ οἷόν τε ἔσται ἐλθεῖν εἰς μάχην, τούτων, ὧν ἔλεξα, ὑπεξῃρημένων. οὕτως οἵ τε ἡμῖν αἴτιοι ἕξουσι δούλιον ζυγὸν οἵ τε ἀναίτιοι. ὑμεῖς δ' ἂν μοι τάδε ποιοῦντες χαρίζοισθε· ἐπειδὰν ὑμῖν[1] σημήνω τὸν χρόνον, εἰς ὃν ἡμῖν ἥκειν δοκεῖ, προθύμως ἅπαντας δεῖ παρεῖναι. ὃς δ' ἂν ἔλθῃ ἔχων κατεσκευασμένον στρατὸν κάλλιστα, δώσω αὐτῷ δωρεάν, ἣ δὴ τιμιωτάτη[2] νομίζεται ἐν ἡμετέρου. ποιητέα μὲν δὴ ταῦτ' ἐστὶν οὕτω. ἵνα δὲ μὴ ἰδιοβουλεύειν ὑμῖν δοκῶ, τίθημι τὸ πρᾶγμα ἐς μέσον, γνώμην κελεύων ὑμῶν τὸν βουλόμενον ἀποφαίνεσθαι."

42 ἐβουλόμην ἔτι πλείω παρασχέσθαι παραδείγματα τῆς τοῦ συγγραφέως ἀγωγῆς· ἰσχυροτέρα γὰρ ἡ πίστις οὕτως ἂν ἐγένετο. νῦν δ' ἐξείργομαι, σπεύδων ἐπὶ τὰ προκείμενα καὶ ἅμα δόξαν

[1] ὑμῖν Sylburg: ἡμῖν MBP.

Secondly, how they treated us when we landed on their territory, when Datis and Artaphernes led our 490 B.C. forces, I suppose you all know. These are the reasons which have made me eager to march against them; and on reflection I find the following advantages in this course: if we subdue these men and their neighbours, who inhabit the country of Pelops the Phrygian, we shall make Persian territory conterminous with the air of Heaven itself; for the sun will not look down upon any land bordering on ours, but I, with your help, will make all these lands into one by marching through the whole of Europe. For I am informed that such is the case, and that no city and no nation will be left to face us in battle when the states I have mentioned have been removed. Thus both those who are guilty and those who are innocent will have to bear the yoke of slavery. But you, by doing what I require, will please me: all of you must come promptly when I give you the signal to come to me; and the one who comes with the best-equipped army shall receive a present of what is regarded as most valuable in our land. That is what you must do; but in order that I should not seem to you to be following my own counsel, I lay the matter open for discussion, and invite whoever wishes to do so to state his opinion."

I should have liked to give more examples of the 42
historian's manner, because that would have made my argument more convincing; but I am prevented from doing so by my desire to proceed with the subject in hand, and also by my concern to avoid the charge of

---

[2] ἡ δὴ τιμιωτάτη Reiske: ἤδη τιμιωτάτην ἡ MBP.

ὑφορώμενος ἀκαιρίας. συγγνώσεται δή μοι καὶ Πλάτων ὁ θαυμάσιος, εἰ μὴ παραθήσομαι κἀκείνου λέξεις. ἡ γὰρ ὑπόμνησις ὡς ἐν εἰδόσιν ἱκανή. ταῦτα δὲ δὴ βουλόμενος τάς τε διαφορὰς τῶν ἁρμονιῶν καὶ τοὺς χαρακτῆρας αὐτῶν καὶ τοὺς πρωτεύσαντας ἐν αὐτοῖς διῆλθον, ἵν', ἐπειδὰν ἀποφαίνωμαι γνώμην ὅτι τὴν μέσην τε καὶ μικτὴν ἁρμονίαν ἐπετήδευσεν ὁ Δημοσθένης, μηδεὶς ὑποτυγχάνῃ μοι ταῦτα λέγων· "αἱ γὰρ ἄκραι τίνες εἰσὶν ἁρμονίαι; καὶ τίς αὐτῶν ἑκατέρας ⟨ἡ⟩ φύσις καὶ τίς ἡ μῖξις ἣ ἡ κρᾶσις αὕτη;[1] οὐδὲν γὰρ δεῖ τῶν ἄκρων." τούτου μὲν δὴ πρώτου χάριν, ὥσπερ ἔφην, ἐκεῖνα ἠναγκάσθην προειπεῖν, ἔπειτα, ἵνα μοι μὴ μονόκωλος ᾖ μηδὲ αὐστηρὸς ὁ λόγος, ἀλλ' ἔχῃ τινὰς εὐπαιδεύτους διαγωγάς. οὔτε γὰρ πιστοῦν[2] τὰς τοιαύτας προσθήκας οὔτε ἀπαιτοῦντος τοῦ λόγου παραλιπεῖν καλῶς ἂν ἔχοι.

43 δεδειγμένης δή μοι τῆς αἱρέσεως τοῦ ῥήτορος ταύτης ἤδη τις παρ' ἑαυτῷ σκοπείτω τὰ λεχθέντα, ὅτι τοιαῦτ' ἐστίν, ἐνθυμούμενος μὲν ὅσα σεμνῶς κατεσκεύασται τῷ ἀνδρὶ καὶ αὐστηρῶς καὶ ἀξιωματικῶς, ἐνθυμούμενος δὲ ὅσα τερπνῶς καὶ ἡδέως. εἰ δὲ κἀνταῦθα δόξει τι δεῖν [ἡ πίστις][3] ἀποδείξεως, ὅντινα βούλεται τῶν λόγων αὐτοῦ προχειρισάμενος καὶ ἀφ' οὗ βούλεται μέρους ἀρξάμενος καταβαινέτω τε καὶ σκοπείτω τῶν λεγομένων ἕκαστον, εἰ τὰ μὲν ἀναβεβλημένας ἔχει τὰς ἁρμονίας καὶ διεστώσας, τὰ δὲ προσκολλώσας καὶ συμπεπυκνωμένας, καὶ τὰ μὲν ἀποτραχύνει

[1] αὕτη Sylburg: αὐτὴ codd.
[2] πιστοῦν Sylburg: πιστεύειν codd.

lacking a sense of proportion. Now I am sure that the admirable Plato will forgive me if I do not quote specimens from his writings too, for passing reference is enough for those who are familiar with them. My purpose in describing the differences between these modes of composition and their distinguishing features, and the leading exponents of each, was to ensure that, when I stated it as my opinion that Demosthenes employed the intermediate, mixed form of composition, nobody would interrupt and say "What are the extreme forms of composition, and what is the nature of each by itself and what is this mixture and blend? For extremes serve no purpose." This was the initial reason why, as I said, I was forced to deal with these questions first: the second reason was that I did not wish my treatise to be too one-sided and rigorous, only that it should contain some erudite diversions; for just as it would not be fair to insist on such additions, so it would be wrong to omit them when the argument demands them.

Now that I have shown the qualities of Demos- 43
thenes's chosen style, the reader may examine his speeches for himself. He will observe that they are composed as I have described, now serious, austere and dignified, now pleasant and agreeable. And if he still feels in need of illustration, let him take in his hand any of the speeches, beginning at any point he wishes, and read on, analysing every sentence and seeing whether the structure is sometimes halting and broken up, sometimes coherent and compact; sometimes harshly grating on the ear, sometimes

---

[3] ἡ πίστις seclusit Radermacher

τε καὶ πικραίνει τὴν ἀκοήν, τὰ δὲ πραΰνει καὶ λεαίνει, καὶ τὰ μὲν εἰς πάθος ἐκτρέπει τοὺς ἀκούοντας, τὰ δ' εἰς ἦθος ὑπάγεται, τὰ δ' ἄλλας τινὰς ἐργάζεται καὶ πολλὰς διαφορὰς παρ' αὐτὴν τὴν σύνθεσιν. οἷά ἐστι ταυτί (χρήσομαι δὲ παραδείγμασιν οὐκ ἐξ ἐπιτηδεύσεως, ἀλλ' οἷς ἐνέτυχον, ἐξ ἑνὸς τῶν Φιλιππικῶν λαβών)· "Εἰ δέ τις ὑμῶν, ὦ ἄνδρες Ἀθηναῖοι, τὸν Φίλιππον εὐτυχοῦντα ὁρῶν ταύτῃ φοβερὸν προσπολεμῆσαι νομίζει, σώφρονος μὲν ἀνθρώπου προνοίᾳ χρῆται· μεγάλη γὰρ ῥοπή, μᾶλλον δὲ ὅλον ἡ τύχη παρὰ πάντ' ἐστὶ τὰ τῶν ἀνθρώπων πράγματα. οὐ μὴν ἀλλ' ἔγωγε, εἴ τις αἵρεσίν μοι δοίη, τὴν τῆς ἡμετέρας πόλεως τύχην ἂν ἑλοίμην ἐθελόντων, ἃ προσήκει, ποιεῖν ὑμῶν καὶ κατὰ μικρόν, ἢ τὴν ἐκείνου." ἐν ταῖς τρισὶ περιόδοις ταύταις τὰ μὲν ἄλλα ὀνόματα πάντα εὐφώνως τε σύγκειται καὶ ἡδέως τῷ συνεχεῖς σφόδρα καὶ μαλακὰς αὐτῶν εἶναι τὰς ἁρμονίας. ὀλίγα δ' ἐστὶ παντάπασιν, ἃ διΐστησι τὰς ἁρμονίας καὶ τραχείας φαίνεσθαι ποιεῖ αὐτάς, ἐν μὲν τῇ πρώτῃ περιόδῳ κατὰ δύο τόπους [1] τὰ φωνήεντα συγκρουόμενα ἔν τε τῷ "ὦ ἄνδρες Ἀθηναῖοι" καὶ ἐν τῷ "εὐτυχοῦντα ὁρῶν," ἃ διΐστησι τὸ συναφές. καὶ κατ' ἄλλους δύο τόπους [2] ἢ τρεῖς τὰ ἡμίφωνα ⟨καὶ ἄφωνα⟩ [3] παραπίπτοντα ἀλλήλοις τὰ φύσιν οὐκ ἔχοντα συναλείφεσθαι ἔν τε τῷ "τὸν Φίλιππον" καὶ ἐν τῷ "ταύτῃ φοβερὸν προσπολεμῆσαι" ταράττει τοὺς ἤχους μετρίως καὶ οὐκ ἐᾷ φαίνεσθαι μαλακούς. ἐν δὲ τῇ δευτέρᾳ περιόδῳ τραχύνεται μὲν ἡ σύνθεσις ἐν τῷ "μεγάλη γὰρ ῥοπή," διὰ τὸ

gently soothing; sometimes impelling hearers to emotion, sometimes leading gently on to moral seriousness; and producing many different effects in the actual composition. Here is an example (I shall use illustrations chosen not deliberately but at random, from one of the speeches against Philip):[1]

"If any of you, Athenians, regards Philip as a formidable opponent because you see him enjoying good fortune, that is sound reasoning. Fortune is of great importance—or rather, she is all-important—in all human affairs. But that is not to say that, given the choice, I should not prefer our city's fortune to Philip's, if only you would do your duty even to a slight degree."

In these three periods the arrangement of the words is in general harmonious and pleasing, because of the very smooth and even composition. There is indeed little in the whole passage that tends to disrupt this smooth arrangement and make it appear rough: in the first period two examples of hiatus, *ὦ ἄνδρες Ἀθηναῖοι* and *εὐτυχοῦντα ὁρᾶν*, which arrest the continuity; and in two or three places semivowels and consonants which do not naturally combine are found side by side, *τὸν Φίλιππον* and in the phrase *ταύτῃ φοβερὸν προσπολεμῆσαι*. These cause a slight conflict of sounds and prevent them from seeming even. In the second period there is roughness in the phrase *μεγάλη γὰρ ῥοπή* because the two *ρ*s do not

[1] *Olynth.* ii. 22.

---

[1] *τόπους* Kiessling: *τρόπους* codd.
[2] *τόπους* Kiessling: *τρόπους* codd.
[3] *καὶ ἄφωνα* inseruit Radermacher.

μὴ συναλείφεσθαι τὰ δύο ρ ρ καὶ ἐν τῷ "ἀνθρώπων πράγματα" διὰ τὸ μὴ συλλεαίνεσθαι ⟨τὸ ν⟩[1] τῷ ἑξῆς. διασπᾶται δ' ἐν τῷ "μᾶλλον δὲ ὅλον ἡ τύχη," βραχέων φωνηέντων πολὺν[2] τὸν μεταξὺ χρόνον περιλαμβανόντων. ἐν δὲ τῇ τρίτῃ περιόδῳ τὰ φωνήεντα μέν, εἴ τις αὐτὰ βούλοιτο συναλείψας ἐκθλίβειν ὥσπερ τὸ οἴομαι καὶ δέον, οὐκ ἂν εὕροι[3] συμπλεκόμενα[4] ἀλλήλοις τῶν δὲ συμφωνουμένων δυσὶν ἢ τρισὶν χωρίοις τὴν λειότητα μὴ φυλάττουσαι σὺν τοῖς παρακειμένοις εὑρεθήσονται ἐν τῷ "αἵρεσίν μοι δοίη" καὶ ἐν τῷ "τὴν τῆς ἡμετέρας πόλεως." μέχρι μὲν δὴ τῶνδε ἡ δευτέρα τὰ πρωτεῖα ἁρμονία φέρει, ἐν δὲ τοῖς ἑξῆς ἡ προτέρα (διέσπασται ⟨γὰρ⟩[5] μᾶλλον τῆς ἑτέρας)· "Πολὺ γὰρ πλείους ἀφορμὰς εἰς τὸ τὴν παρὰ τῶν θεῶν εὔνοιαν ἔχειν ὁρῶ ὑμῖν ἐνούσας ἢ ἐκείνῳ. ἀλλ', οἴομαι, καθήμεθα οὐδὲν ποιοῦντες· οὐκ ἔνι δ' αὐτὸν ἀργοῦντα οὐδὲ φίλοις ἐπιτάττειν, μή τί γε θεοῖς." ἐν τούτοις γὰρ δὴ τά τε φωνήεντα πολλαχῇ συγκρουόμενα δῆλά ἐστι καὶ τὰ ἡμίφωνα καὶ ἄφωνα, ἐξ ὧν στηριγμούς τε καὶ ἐγκαθισμοὺς αἱ ἁρμονίαι λαμβάνουσι καὶ τραχύτητας αἱ φωναὶ συχνάς. ἔπειθ' αἱ ταύταις ἐπιβάλλουσαι περίοδοι διαστάσεις μὲν οὐ λαμβάνουσι φωνηέντων, καὶ παρὰ τοῦτο ἐπιτρόχαλος αὐτῶν ἐστιν ἡ σύνθεσις, ἀφώνων δὲ καὶ ἡμιφώνων συμβολαῖς διαχαραττόμεναι τραχύνουσι τὴν φωνὴν συμμέτρως. καὶ τἆλλα δὲ τὸν αὐτὸν ἅπαντα κατεσκεύασται τρόπον. τί γὰρ δεῖ τὰ πλείω

[1] τὸ ν inseruit Radermacher.
[2] πολὺν Sylburg: πολὺ codd.

coalesce, and in *ἀνθρώπων πράγματα* because the *ν* does not combine smoothly with what follows; and the sentence is dislocated by *μᾶλλον δὲ ὅλον ἡ τύχη* in which short vowels involve the phrase in a long time-interval. In the third period, if one wished to blend the vowels and press them into union, as is done with *οἴομαι* and *δέον*, no case of consecutive vowels could be found. In two or three places the periods will be found not preserving smoothness between adjacent words, as in *αἵρεσίν μοι δοίη* and *τὴν τῆς ἡμετέρας πόλεως*. Up to this point the second mode of composition predominates. In the following passage it is the first, since it is more disjointed than the other:[1]

"For I see that you have many more claims to divine favour than he has. But we sit, I presume, doing nothing; and a man who is himself idle cannot require even his friends to help him, much less the gods."

Here are several obvious cases of hiatus and of the clashing of semi-vowels and consonants, which cause syllables to be sustained and prolonged and the sound to be frequently roughened. Then the periods that follow contain no clashing of vowels, so that from this point of view the sentences run swiftly; but there is a corresponding jarring of consonants and semi-vowels which roughens the sound. The rest, too, is all composed in a similar manner. Need I prolong the dis-

[1] *Olynth.* ii. 22–23.

---

[3] εὖροι Reiske: εὔροις codd.
[4] συμπλεκόμενα Sadée: συντυπαιμένοισ Pv.
[5] γὰρ inseruit Reiske.

λέγοντα μηκύνειν; οὐ μόνον δὲ αἱ τῶν ὀνομάτων συζυγίαι τὴν μικτὴν ἁρμονίαν λαμβάνουσι παρ' αὐτῷ καὶ μέσην, ἀλλὰ καὶ αἱ τῶν κώλων κατασκευαί τε καὶ συνθέσεις καὶ τὰ τῶν περιόδων μήκη τε καὶ σχήματα καὶ οἱ περιλαμβάνοντες αὐτάς τε καὶ τὰ κῶλα ῥυθμοί. καὶ γὰρ καὶ κατὰ κόμματα πολλὰ εἴρηται τῷ ἀνδρὶ, καὶ τὰ ⟨ἐν τοῖς συμβουλευτικοῖς λόγοις⟩ [1] πλεῖστά γε οὕτως κατεσκεύασται, καὶ ἐν περιόδοις οὐκ ὀλίγα. τῶν δὲ περιόδων αἳ μέν εἰσιν εὐκόρυφοι καὶ στρογγύλαι ὥσπερ ἀπὸ τόρνου, αἳ δὲ ὕπτιαί τε καὶ κεχυμέναι καὶ οὐκ ἔχουσαι τὰς βάσεις περιττάς. μήκει τε αἳ μὲν ἐλάττους,[2] ὥστε συμμετρηθῆναι πρὸς ἀνδρὸς πνεῦμα, αἳ δὲ πολλῷ μείζους, οἷαι καὶ μέχρι τῆς τετάρτης ἀναπαύσεως προελθοῦσαι τότε λήγειν εἰς πέρας. τῶν τε σχημάτων ἔνθα μὲν ἄν τις εὕροι τὰ σεμνὰ καὶ αὐστηρὰ καὶ ἀρχαῖα πλεονάζοντα, ἔνθα δὲ τὰ λιγυρὰ καὶ γλαφυρὰ καὶ θεατρικά. καὶ τῶν ῥυθμῶν πολλαχῇ μὲν τοὺς ἀνδρώδεις καὶ ἀξιωματικοὺς καὶ εὐγενεῖς, σπανίως δέ που τοὺς ὑπορχηματικούς τε καὶ Ἰωνικῶς [3] διακλωμένους. ὑπὲρ ὧν ὀλίγον ὕστερον ἐροῦμεν· ἕτερος γὰρ ἐπιτηδειότερος αὐτοῖς ἔσται τόπος. νυνὶ δέ, ὃ προσαπαιτεῖν ἔοικεν ὁ λόγος, ἔτι προσθείς, ἐπὶ τὰ λοιπὰ τῶν προκειμένων μεταβήσομαι.

44 τί δὲ τοῦτ' ἔστιν; ἐπειδὴ κρατίστην μὲν ἔφην εἶναι τὴν μικτὴν σύνθεσιν, ταύτῃ δὲ κεχρῆσθαί φημι τὸν Δημοσθένην ἁπάντων μετριώτατα τῶν ἄλλων, ἐπιτάσεις δὲ καὶ ἀνέσεις ἀξιολόγους ἐν αὐτῇ ποιεῖσθαι, τοτὲ μὲν ἀξιωματικωτέραν, τοτὲ

cussion? His use of the mixed, middle style is seen not only in his word-order, but also in the structure and arrangement of his clauses, the length and formation of his periods, and the rhythms which round both these off. Indeed, much of what the orator writes is in short phrases, and a very high proportion of the sentences (in his deliberative speeches) are composed in this way, while not a few are composed in periods. Some of these periods are well-turned and roundly finished, as if on a lathe, others are flat and diffuse, and lack a strongly rhythmical *clausula.* As to length, some are relatively short, so as to correspond to a man's single breath, while others are much longer, not reaching their conclusion until the speaker has paused four times for breath. As to figures of speech, one might find in one passage the serious, austere and old-fashioned figures predominating, in another the articulate, polished and spectacular ones. The most frequent rhythms will be the manly, dignified and noble ones, rarely the loose rhythms of the Ionian choral dance. I shall say more of these a little later at a more appropriate place, but shall now deal with a further point which seems to me to be demanded by the present discussion, before passing on to the rest of my subject.

What is this matter? I pronounced the mixed 44
style to be the best, and I claim that Demosthenes uses it with a finer sense of proportion than any other writer, intensifying and relaxing it substantially, im-

---

[1] *ἐν τοῖς συμβουλευτικοῖς λόγοις* supplevi lacunam a Reiske indicatam.

[2] *ἐλάττους* Sadée: *θάττους* codd.

[3] *Ἰωνικῶς* Cobet: *ἰωνικοὺς καὶ* codd.

δ' εὐπρεπεστέραν ποιοῦντα τὴν ἀγωγήν, τί δή ποτε βουλόμενος οὐ πορεύεται μίαν αἰεὶ καὶ τὴν αὐτὴν ὁδόν; καὶ τὸ ἐν τῷδε ἢ τῷδε πλεονάζειν χαρακτῆρι ποίοις τισὶν ὁρίζει κανόσι; δοκεῖ δή μοι φύσει τε καὶ πείρᾳ διδαχθεὶς ὁ ἀνὴρ πρῶτον μὲν ἐκεῖνο καταμαθεῖν, ὅτι οὐχ ὁμοίας ἀπαιτοῦσι κατασκευὰς λέξεως οἱ πρὸς τὰς πανηγύρεις καὶ σχολὰς συρρέοντες ὄχλοι τοῖς εἰς τὰ δικαστήρια καὶ τὰς ἐκκλησίας ἀπαντῶσιν, ἀλλ' οἱ μὲν ἀπάτης ὀρέγονται καὶ ψυχαγωγίας, οἳ δὲ διδαχῆς, ὧν ἐπιζητοῦσι, καὶ ὠφελείας. οὔτε δὴ τὸν ἐν δικαστηρίοις λόγον ᾤετο δεῖν κωτίλλειν καὶ λιγαίνειν, οὔτε τὸν ἐπιδεικτικὸν αὐχμοῦ μεστὸν εἶναι καὶ πίνου. πανηγυρικοὺς μὲν οὖν λόγους οὐκ ἔχομεν αὐτοῦ παρασχέσθαι· πάντας γὰρ ἔγωγε τοὺς ἀναφερομένους εἰς αὐτὸν ἀλλοτρίους εἶναι πείθομαι καὶ οὐδὲ κατὰ μικρὸν ἔχοντας τὸν ἐκείνου χαρακτῆρα οὔτ' ἐν τοῖς νοήμασιν ⟨οὔτ' ἐν τοῖς ὀνόμασι⟩,[1] τῆς δὲ συνθέσεως ὅλῳ καὶ τῷ παντὶ λειπομένους. ὧν ἐστιν ὅ τε φορτικὸς καὶ κενὸς καὶ παιδαριώδης ἐπιτάφιος καὶ τὸ τοῦ σοφιστικοῦ λήρου μεστὸν ἐγκώμιον εἰς Παυσανίαν. τὰς δὲ περὶ τούτων ἀποδείξεις οὐχ οὗτος ὁ καιρὸς λέγειν.
45 ἐκ δὲ τῶν ἐναγωνίων αὐτοῦ λόγων, ὁπόσοι πρὸς δικαστήρια γεγόνασιν ἢ πρὸς ἐκκλησίας, τεκμαίρομαι, ὅτι ταύτην τὴν γνώμην ὁ ἀνὴρ εἶχεν. ὁρῶ γὰρ αὐτόν, εἴ ποτε λάβοι πράγματα χαριεστέρας δεόμενα κατασκευῆς, πανηγυρικὴν αὐτοῖς ἀποδιδόντα τῆς λέξεως ἁρμονίαν, ὡς ἐν τῷ κατὰ Ἀριστοκράτους πεποίηκε λόγῳ πολλαχῇ μὲν καὶ

[1] οὔτ' ἐν τοῖς ὀνόμασι addidit Reiske.

parting now a more dignified, now a more engaging manner. What is his purpose in not always following one and the same path? On what principles does he determine his use of one style rather than the other? I think that our orator initially learnt by natural taste and experience that crowds which flock to festivals and schools require different forms of address from those who attend the political assemblies and the law-courts. The former wish to be diverted and entertained, the latter to be given information and assistance in the matters with which they are concerned.[1] He did not think either that the forensic speech should employ hypnotic or striking phonetic effects, or that the ceremonial speech should be full of a dry and musty antiquity. We have no festival speeches of his to provide us with illustration, as I am convinced that all those ascribed to him are by other authors, since they are completely uncharacteristic of him in both language and thought, and their composition is altogether inferior in every way. One of these is the *Funeral Oration*,[2] a vulgar, empty, puerile work; another is the *Encomium to Pausanias*,[3] which is full of the humbug of the sophists. But this is not the occasion to demonstrate the spuriousness of these works. For my proof that he held the above opinion I turn to the speeches he composed for actual contests, whether in the law-courts or in the assembly. I notice how, when he is dealing with a subject which requires a more attractive presentation, he composes it in the style of a festival speech. He does this in several passages in the speech *Against Aristocrates*,

[1] Aristotle, *Rhetoric* i. 3. 1–2.
[2] Or. 60.
[3] Not extant.

ἄλλῃ, μάλιστα δ᾿ ἐν οἷς τὸν περὶ τῶν νόμων ἀποδίδωσι λόγον καὶ τὸν περὶ τῶν φονικῶν δικαστηρίων, ἐφ᾿ ἧς χρείας ἕκαστον αὐτῶν τέτακται· κἀν [1] τῷ κατὰ Λεπτίνου περὶ τῆς ἀτελείας κατὰ πολλὰ μέρη, μάλιστα δ᾿ ἐν τοῖς ἐγκωμίοις τῶν εὐεργετῶν τῆς πόλεως Χαβρίου τε καὶ Κόνωνος καί τινων ἑτέρων, κἀν τῷ περὶ τοῦ στεφάνου καὶ ἐν ἄλλοις συχνοῖς. τοῦτο δὲ δή μοι πρῶτον ἐνθυμηθεὶς δοκεῖ συμμεθαρμόζεσθαι ταῖς ὑποθέσεσι τὸν χαρακτῆρα τῆς συνθέσεως καὶ ἔτι μετὰ τοῦτο τὰς ἰδέας τοῦ λόγου καταμαθών, ὅτι οὐχ ἅπασαι τὸν αὐτὸν ἀπαιτοῦσιν οὔτε ἐκλογῆς ὀνομάτων κόσμον οὔτε συνθέσεως, ἀλλ᾿ αἳ μὲν τὸν γλαφυρώτερον [2] αἳ δὲ τὸν αὐστηρότερον, καὶ τῇ τούτων ἀκολουθήσας χρείᾳ τὰ μὲν προοίμια καὶ τὰς διηγήσεις ποιεῖν [τὸ] [3] πλεῖον ἐχούσας τοῦ σεμνοῦ τὸ ἡδύ, τὰς δὲ πίστεις καὶ τοὺς ἐπιλόγους τῆς μὲν ἡδείας συνθέσεως ἐλάττω μοῖραν ἐχούσας, τῆς δὲ αὐστηρᾶς καὶ πεπινωμένης πλείω. ἐν αἷς μὲν γὰρ δεῖ κολακευθῆναι τὸν ἀκροατὴν καὶ παρακολουθῆσαι τοῖς πράγμασι κακῶν ἀλλοτρίων διηγήσεις αὐχμηρὰς ἐνίοτε καὶ ἀηδεῖς ἀκούοντα, ἔνθα εἰ μὴ τὸ παρηδῦνον ἡ σύνθεσις ἐπενέγκοι ἢ παραμυθήσαιτο τὸν τῆς διανοίας κόπον,[4] οὐχ ἕξουσιν αἱ πίστεις βάσιν ἀσφαλῆ· ἐν οἷς δὲ τὰ πρὸς τὴν ἀλήθειαν καὶ τὸ συμφέρον συντείνοντα λέγεσθαι· ταῦτα δὲ ἁπλοϊκῶς πως καὶ γενναίως καὶ μετὰ σεμνότητος αὐστηρᾶς ἀπαιτοῦσιν οἱ πολλοὶ μανθάνειν, τὸ δὲ κωτίλον ἐν τούτοις καὶ

[1] κἀν Sylburg: καὶ codd.
[2] γλαφυρώτερον Sylburg: γλαφυρώτατον codd.

and particularly when he is giving an account of the laws and the constitution of the homicide courts, and describes the function of each. He writes in a similar style in the speech *Against Leptines On Tax-Evasion* in many places, and in particular in the speeches in which he praises the city's benefactors Chabrias, Conon and certain other citizens. There are similar passages in the speech *On the Crown* and many others. It is clear, I think, that it was in recognition of this principle that Demosthenes first adapted the style of his composition to his themes, and further, after this, when he had fully grasped that the different genres do not all require the same choice of words and composition, but that some call for a more polished, others a more austere style, following these requirements he invested his introductions and his narratives with more charm than dignity, and his proofs and perorations with a smaller measure of charm and a thicker incrustation of old-fashioned austerity. In the narrative the audience must be coaxed along as they follow the course of events: for accounts of other men's misfortunes can sometimes make dry and unedifying listening, in which case, unless the narrative is composed in such a way as to introduce the required element of diversion to relieve their jaded minds,[1] the proof will have no firm foundations. In the proofs and perorations topics relating to truth and advantage must be introduced. People expect to be informed of these with a certain noble simplicity

[1] Cf. *Ad Herennium* i. 13; iii. 14.

---

[3] τὸ delevit Sadée.
[4] κόπον Reiske: σκοπὸν codd.

ἀπατηλὸν ὥραν οὐκ ἔχει ἐπὶ τῶν ἐναγωνίων λόγων. οὐ τὴν αὐτὴν οὖν ἐπιστάμενος ἁπάντων φύσιν οὐδὲ τοὺς αὐτοὺς ᾤετο δεῖν πᾶσι προσήκειν κόσμους, ἀλλὰ τοῖς μὲν δημηγορικοῖς τὸ ἀξίωμα καὶ τὴν μεγαληγορίαν μᾶλλον ἁρμόττειν, τοῖς δὲ δικανικοῖς, ἔνθα τῶν ἀλλοτρίων ἀκουστὴς γίνεται κακῶν ὁ δικαστής, ψυχῆς τε καὶ τῶν ἄλλων, ὅσα τιμιώτατά ἐστιν ἀνθρώποις, ἀγών,[1] τὴν χάριν καὶ τὴν ἡδονὴν καὶ τὴν ἀπάτην καὶ τὰ παραπλήσια τούτοις. διὰ τοῦτο ἐν μὲν ταῖς συμβουλαῖς καὶ μάλιστα ταῖς κατὰ Φιλίππου κατακορεστέραις κέχρηται ταῖς αὐστηραῖς[2] ἁρμονίαις, ἐν δὲ τοῖς πρὸς τὰ δικαστήρια συνταχθεῖσι ταῖς γλαφυραῖς. καὶ αὐτῶν δὲ τῶν δικανικῶν πάλιν ἐν μὲν τοῖς δημοσίοις, ἔνθα τὸ ἀξίωμα ἔδει τῆς πόλεως φυλάξαι, ταῖς μεγαλοπρεπεστέραις πλείοσιν, ἐν
46 δὲ τοῖς ἰδιωτικοῖς ἐλάττοσι. συνελόντι δ' εἰπεῖν, οὐ μόνον παρὰ τὰς ἰδιότητας τῶν λόγων καὶ τὰς παραλλαγὰς τῶν ὑποθέσεων διαφόρους ᾤετο δεῖν ποιεῖσθαι τὰς κράσεις τῶν ἐν τῇ συνθέσει χαρακτήρων, ἀλλὰ καὶ παρ' αὐτὰ τὰ γένη τῶν ἐπιχειρημάτων τὰ συμπληρωτικὰ μέρη διαφόρους ἔχοντα τὰς φύσεις ὁρῶν διαλλαττούσαις κατασκευαῖς τῆς[3] ἁρμονίας ἐπειρᾶτο κοσμεῖν, ἄλλως μὲν τὰς γνωμολογίας συντιθείς, ἄλλως δὲ τὰ ἐνθυμήματα, διαφόρως δὲ τὰ παραδείγματα. πολὺς ἂν εἴη λόγος, εἰ τὰς διαφορὰς ἁπάσας βουλοίμην λέγειν, ὅσας ἐκεῖνος ὁ δαιμόνιος ἀνὴρ ὁρῶν καὶ πρὸς

[1] ἀγών Reiske: ἀχρείων codd.
[2] αὐστηραῖς Reiske: τοιαύταις codd.

and in a serious, austere style: cajoling guile has no place in these sections in practical oratory.

Thus Demosthenes, realising that not all kinds of oratory have the same nature, thought that similarly they did not all require the same sort of ornamentation, but that dignity and magniloquence are more suited to political oratory, while in forensic oratory, in which the juryman hears of other men's misfortunes, when life and everything else which men hold dearest are at stake, charm, and devices which please and beguile, and similar qualities must be used. Consequently his deliberative speeches, especially those against Philip, are more saturated with the austere style, those composed for the law-courts with the polished style. And again, of the forensic speeches themselves, those which are concerned with public cases, in which the protection of the state's dignity was involved, contain a larger measure of the grand style, while private speeches contain a smaller measure.

To summarise: he not only considered it necessary 46
to vary the mixture of styles of composition according to the individual requirements of his speeches and their different subject-matter, but also saw that the constituent parts of the various forms of argument were of a different nature from one another, and tried to invest them with different styles, couching his aphoristic utterances in one kind of language, his arguments in another and his examples in a different form again. I should have to write at length to describe all the different forms of composition envisaged by this inspired orator, and to show how, by

---

[3] τῆς Usener: τὰς codd.

χρῶμα ἕκαστον αἰεὶ σχηματίζων τὸν λόγον, ἀνέσει τε καὶ ἐπιτάσει ταμιευόμενος τῶν ἁρμονιῶν ἑκατέραν, τοὺς καλοὺς ἐκείνους λόγους ἀνέπλασεν. παραδειγμάτων δ' οὐκ οἴομαι δεῖν ἐνταῦθα, ἵνα μοι μείζονα πίστιν ὁ λόγος λάβῃ τῶν ἔργων τοῦ ῥήτορος ἐξεταζομένων, εἰ τοιαῦτά ἐστιν, οἷα λέγω. πολὺ γὰρ ⟨ἂν⟩ ἡ σύνταξις τὸ μῆκος λάβοι, καὶ δέος, μή ποτε εἰς τοὺς σχολικοὺς ἐκβῇ χαρακτῆρας ἐκ τῶν ὑπομνηματικῶν. ὀλίγα δὲ ληφθέντα τῶν πολλῶν ἱκανὰ τεκμήρια, καὶ ἅμα πρὸς ἐπισταμένους (οὐ γὰρ δή γε τοῖς ἀπείροις τοῦ ἀνδρὸς τάδε γράφω) τὸ δεῖξαι τὰ πράγματα συμβολικῶς ἀπόχρη. ἐπάνειμι δ' οὖν ἐπὶ τὰ λοιπά, ὧν ἐν ἀρχῇ προὐθέμην ἐρεῖν.

47 δεύτερον δὴ κεφάλαιον ἦν ἐπιδεῖξαι, τίσι θεωρήμασι χρώμενος καὶ διὰ ποίας ἀσκήσεως προελθὼν τὸ κράτιστον μέρος ἔλαβε τῆς ⟨μικτῆς καὶ μέσης⟩ [1] ἁρμονίας. ἐρῶ δὴ καὶ περὶ τούτων, ὡς ἔχω δόξης. δυεῖν ὄντων τελῶν περὶ πᾶν ἔργον, ὡς εἰπεῖν, ὧν τε φύσις δημιουργὸς καὶ ὧν αἱ τέχναι μητέρες, τοῦ καλοῦ καὶ τῆς ἡδονῆς, εἶδεν, ὅτι κἂν τοῖς λόγοις τοῖς τε ἐμμέτροις καὶ τοῖς ἔξω τοῦ μέτρου κατασκευαζομένοις . . .[2] ἔμελλεν ἀποχρώντως ἕξειν ἀμφοτέρων τούτων. χωρισθὲν γὰρ ἑκάτερον αὐτῶν θατέρου πρὸς τῷ μὴ τέλειον εἶναι καὶ τὴν ἰδίαν ἀρετὴν ἀμαυροτέραν ἴσχει. ταῦτα δὴ συνιδὼν καὶ τῆς μὲν αὐστηρᾶς τὸ

adjusting his language to every shade of emphasis required, regulating each of the two styles by relaxation and intensification, he fashioned these noble orations of his. I do not think I need to support my thesis here by examining specimen passages from his speeches to see whether they are as I say: for this would make my treatise much longer, and it would be in danger of assuming the character of a text-book instead of an essay. A small selection from the many examples available is enough to prove my point; and besides, for those who know the orator's work (and this treatise is not intended for those who do not), a token proof is quite sufficient. I shall therefore return to the remainder of my original programme.

The second topic to deal with was: What principles 47
did he follow and what practical means did he employ to master the most important aspects of the mixed, intermediate style? I shall say what I think on these matters also. Virtually every work, whether it is created by nature or mothered by the arts, has two objectives, pleasure and beauty.[1] Demosthenes knew that nobody can achieve anything worthwhile either as a poet or as a prose author without a sufficient measure of both. Each, when separated from the other, in addition to being incomplete, maintains its own qualities only in an attenuated form. Realising this, and understanding beauty to be the object of the

[1] A statement suggesting perhaps Epicurean affinities, but possibly derived from Dionysius's reading of Plato: perhaps the *Philebus*, which he mentions in 23 as a dialogue which he admires. Cf. Plato, *Protagoras*, 351B.

---

[1] μικτῆς καὶ μέσης supplevit lacunam Sadée.
[2] lacunam indicavit Radermacher, coniecit οὐδεὶς ἀξιόλογος ἐγένετο, εἰ μή.

καλὸν ὑπολαβὼν εἶναι τέλος, τῆς δὲ γλαφυρᾶς τὸ ἡδύ, ἐζήτει, τίνα ποιητικὰ τοῦ κάλλους ἐστὶ καὶ τίνα τῆς ἡδονῆς. εὕρισκε δὴ τὰ μὲν αὐτὰ ἀμφοτέρων ὄντα αἴτια, τὰ μέλη καὶ τοὺς ῥυθμοὺς καὶ τὰς μεταβολὰς καὶ τὸ παρακολουθοῦν ἅπασιν αὐτοῖς πρέπον,[1] οὐ μὴν κατὰ τὸν αὐτὸν τρόπον ἑκάτερα σχηματιζόμενα. ὃν δὲ λόγον ἔχει τούτων ἕκαστον, ἐγὼ πειράσομαι διδάσκειν.

48 τοῖς πρώτοις μορίοις τῆς λέξεως, ἃ δὴ στοιχεῖα ὑπό τινων καλεῖται, εἴτε τρία ταῦτ᾽ ἐστίν, ὡς Θεοδέκτῃ τε καὶ Ἀριστοτέλει δοκεῖ, ὀνόματα καὶ ῥήματα καὶ σύνδεσμοι, εἴτε τέτταρα, ὡς τοῖς περὶ Ζήνωνα τὸν Στωικόν, εἴτε πλείω, δύο ταῦτα ἀκολουθεῖ μέλος καὶ χρόνος ἴσα. κατὰ μὲν δὴ τὰς ὀξύτητάς τε καὶ βαρύτητας αὐτῶν τάττεται τὸ μέλος, κατὰ δὲ τὰ μήκη καὶ τὰς βραχύτητας ὁ χρόνος. οὗτος δὲ γίγνεται ῥυθμός, εἴτε ἀπὸ δυεῖν ἀρξάμενος συνίστασθαι βραχειῶν, ὥσπερ οἴονταί τινες καὶ καλοῦσι τὸν οὕτως κατασκευασθέντα ῥυθμὸν ἡγεμόνα, πρῶτον ἔχοντα λόγον τῶν ἴσων ἄρσει τε καὶ θέσει χρόνων, εἴτε ἀπὸ τριῶν βραχειῶν, ὡς τοῖς περὶ Ἀριστόξενον ἔδοξεν, ὃς ἐν τῷ διπλασίῳ κατεσκεύασται λόγῳ πρῶτον. τοῖς δ᾽ ἐκ τῶν πρώτων μορίων τῆς λέξεως συντιθεμένοις τό τε μέλος εἰς αὔξησιν ἤδη συμπροάγει καὶ οἱ ῥυθμοὶ προβαίνουσιν εἰς τὰ καλούμενα μέτρα. ὅταν δὲ μέλλῃ τούτων ἑκάτερον ὑπεραίρειν τὸ μέτριον, ἡ μεταβολὴ τότε εἰσελθοῦσα ταμιεύεται τὸ οἰκεῖον αὐτῶν ἀγαθὸν ἑκατέρου. ἐπειδὰν δὲ τὴν ἁρμόττουσαν ταῦτα χώραν λάβῃ,

[1] πρέπον Radermacher: παραίτιον MBP.

severe style and charm that of the polished style, he tried to discover what constitutes beauty and what charm. And he discovered that both had the same elements, tone, rhythm, variation and propriety of use, which accompanies all these; but that the relationship of one to the others was not always the same. I shall try to explain the meaning of each of these terms.

The primary parts of speech, which some call the 48
elements, whether they be three, as Theodectes [1] and Aristotle believe—nouns, verbs and conjunctions—or four, as Zeno and the Stoic School say,[2] or more, are always accompanied by two phenomena of equal importance, tone and time. Tone is distinguished in them in accordance with their high and low pitch, and time by length and shortness. Time develops into rhythm. This is first constituted either from two short syllables, according to some, who call the rhythm thus produced the " leading " rhythm, because it has the first ratio of times that is equal in rise and fall; or from three shorts, as Aristoxenus [3] and his school held, which is the first rhythm composed in the ratio of two to one. When the primary parts of speech are put together, the tone at once contributes towards heightening their effect, and the rhythms develop into what is called metre. And whenever either of these threatens to overstep the bounds of moderation, then variation steps in and safeguards the individual

[1] See note 4, p. 227.

[2] The division of opinion is not so clear-cut as Dionysius suggests: Aristotle may have recognised four parts of speech (*Poetics*, 20).

[3] Born *c.* 375 B.C. The leading ancient writer on musical theory. A pupil of Aristotle, he also wrote biographical and historical miscellanea as part of a huge literary output.

τότε ἀποδίδωσιν αὐτοῖς τὴν προσήκουσαν ὥραν τὸ πρέπον. καὶ τοῦτο οὐ χαλεπὸν ἐπὶ τῶν τῆς μουσικῆς ἔργων καταμαθεῖν. φέρε γάρ, εἴ τις ᾠδαῖς ἢ κρούμασιν ὀργάνων τὸ κάλλιστον ἐντείνας μέλος ῥυθμοῦ μηδένα ποιοῖτο [1] λόγον, ἔσθ' ὅπως ἄν τις ἀνάσχοιτο τῆς τοιαύτης μουσικῆς; τί δέ; εἰ τούτων μὲν ἀμφοτέρων προνοηθείη μετρίως, μένοι δ' ἐπὶ τῆς αὐτῆς μελῳδίας καὶ τῶν αὐτῶν ῥυθμῶν, οὐδὲν ἐξαλλάττων οὐδὲ ποικίλλων, ἆρ' οὐχ ὅλον ἂν διαφθείροι [2] τὸ ἀγαθόν; εἰ δὲ καὶ τούτου στοχάσαιτο, μηδεμίαν δὲ πρόνοιαν ἔχων φαίνοιτο τοῦ πρέποντος τοῖς ὑποκειμένοις, οὐκ ἀνόνητος αὐτῷ πᾶς ὁ περὶ ἐκεῖνα ἔσται πόνος; ἐμοί γ' οὖν δοκεῖ. ταῦτα δὴ καταμαθὼν ὁ Δημοσθένης τά τε μέλη τῶν ὀνομάτων καὶ κώλων καὶ τοὺς χρόνους αὐτῶν ἐπιλογιζόμενος οὕτω συναρμόττειν αὐτὰ [3] ἐπειρᾶτο, ὥστ' ἐμμελῆ φαίνεσθαι καὶ εὔρυθμα,[4] ἐξαλλάττειν τε καὶ ποικίλλειν ἑκάτερον αὐτῶν ἐπειρᾶτο μυρίοις ὅσοις σχήμασι καὶ τρόποις καὶ τοῦ πρέποντος ὅσην οὐδεὶς τῶν περὶ λόγους σπουδαζόντων ἐποιεῖτο δόσιν. ἐνθυμηθεὶς δέ, ὥσπερ ἔφην, ὡς διὰ τῶν αὐτῶν τούτων θεωρημάτων ὅ τε ἡδὺς γίνεται λόγος καὶ ὁ καλός, ἐσκόπει πάλιν, τί ποτε ἦν τὸ αἴτιον, ὅτι τὰ αὐτὰ οὐ τῶν αὐτῶν ἦν ποιητικά. εὕρισκε δὴ τῶν τε μελῶν οὔσας διαφοράς, αἳ ποιοῦσιν ἃ μὲν ἀξιωματικὰ φαίνεσθαι αὐτῶν ἃ δὲ γλαφυρά, ὥσπερ ἐν τοῖς μουσικοῖς ἔχει πρὸς τὴν ἁρμονίαν τὸ χρῶμα, κἀν τοῖς ῥυθμοῖς δὲ τὸ

[1] ποιοῖτο Krüger: ποιῆται codd.
[2] διαφθείροι Sylburg: διαφθείρῃ codd.

quality of each; and when these have assumed their proper place in the ordered scheme, then propriety supplies them with the beauty that is their due. This procedure can easily be seen to obtain in performance music. Consider: if in composing the most beautiful melody for vocal or instrumental performance one paid no attention to rhythm, could the resulting music possibly be endurable? And what if the performer paid due attention to both of these, but persisted in the same melody and rhythm without any change or even decoration, would he not destroy the whole merit of the piece? Again, if he aimed at variation too, but clearly took no thought for propriety in relation to his subjects, would not all his efforts in the other parts be fruitless? Certainly *I* think so! Well, Demosthenes realised this, and, taking into account the tones and the quantities of his words and clauses, tried to arrange them in such a way that they should appear melodious and rhythmical. He tried to alternate and decorate each of these with countless figures and tropes, and conferred upon his speeches a degree of appropriateness to their subject unmatched by any other serious writer of prose. Observing, as I have said, that attractiveness and beauty in writing are achieved by means of these same phenomena, he considered again why the same means did not produce the same results. He discovered that there were differences between tones which make some of them seem dignified and others polished, in the same way as in music the mode governs the nature of the melody. He found that

[3] *αὐτὰ* Sylburg: *αὐτὰς* codd.
[4] *εὔρυθμα* Sylburg: *εὔρυθμον* codd.

παραπλήσιον γινόμενον, ὥστε τοὺς μὲν ἀξιωματικοὺς αὐτῶν φαίνεσθαι καὶ μεγαλοπρεπεῖς, τοὺς δὲ τρυφεροὺς καὶ μαλακούς. ἔν τε ταῖς μεταβολαῖς τοτὲ μὲν τὸ ἀρχαιοπρεπὲς καὶ αὐστηρόν, τοτὲ δὲ τὸ μελιχρὸν [1] καὶ φιλόκαινον ἐμφαινόμενον, τό τε δὴ πρέπον ἁπάντων μάλιστα μεγάλην παρέχον εἰς ἑκάτερον αὐτῶν ῥοπήν.[2] συνιδὼν δὴ ταῦτα, ὁπότε μὲν τοῦ καλοῦ πλείονος δεῖν αὐτῷ τῇ κατασκευῇ ὑπολάβοι, τάς τε ἐμμελείας ἐποίει μεγαλοπρεπεῖς καὶ τοὺς ῥυθμοὺς ἀξιωματικοὺς καὶ τὰς μεταβολὰς γενναίας. ὁπότε δὲ τῆς ἑτέρας αὐτῷ φανείη δεῖσθαι συνθέσεως ἡ λέξις, πάντα ταῦτα κατεβίβαζεν ἐπὶ τὸ μουσικώτερον. καὶ μηδεὶς ὑπολάβῃ θαυμαστὸν εἶναι τὸν λόγον, εἰ καὶ τῇ πεζῇ λέξει φημί δεῖν ἐμμελείας καὶ εὐρυθμίας καὶ μεταβολῶν, ὥσπερ ταῖς ᾠδαῖς καὶ τοῖς ὀργάνοις, εἰ μηδενὸς τούτων ἀντιλαμβάνεται τῆς Δημοσθένους ἀκούων λέξεως, μηδὲ κακουργεῖν με ὑπολάβῃ τὰ ⟨μὴ⟩ [3] προσόντα τῇ ψιλῇ λέξει προσμαρτυροῦντα. ἔχει γὰρ ταῦτα ἡ καλῶς κατεσκευασμένη λέξις καὶ μάλιστά γε ἡ τοῦδε τοῦ ῥήτορος. τῇ δ' εὐκαιρίᾳ καὶ τῇ ποσότητι τὴν αἴσθησιν διαλανθάνει· τὰ μὲν γὰρ συγκέχυται, τὰ δὲ συνέφθαρται, τὰ δ' ἄλλῳ τινὶ τρόπῳ τὴν ἀκρίβειαν ἐκβέβηκεν τῆς κατασκευῆς, ὥστε αὐτὴν ἐξηλλάχθαι δοκεῖν τῷ παντὶ καὶ κατὰ μηδὲν ἐοικέναι τοῖς ποιήμασιν.

49 ἆρά γε ἀπαιτήσει μέ τις ἐνταυθοῖ λόγον μελῶν τε καὶ ῥυθμῶν καὶ τῶν ἐν ταῖς μεταβολαῖς

[1] τοτὲ δὲ τὸ μελιχρὸν Usener: τὸ δὲ λεγόμενον ἐχθρὸν codd.
[2] ῥοπὴν Sylburg: τρόπον codd.

much the same happens in the case of rhythms also, so that some appear dignified and impressive, others delicate and soft;[1] while variation gives us old-fashioned severity at one point, and sweetness and novelty at another. And it is appropriateness that has the greatest power of all to sway the effect in either direction. Having grasped these facts, whenever he thought his style needed more beauty, he made his modulations stately, his rhythms dignified and his variations noble; and whenever the passage seemed to him to require the other kind of composition he reverted to the more harmonious use of all these elements. Now nobody should be surprised to hear me say that prose should have good melody, rhythm and variation like vocal and instrumental music, if he cannot pick out any of these qualities when he listens to a passage of Demosthenes; nor should he think me dishonest in attributing to mere prose qualities which do not belong to it, for well-composed prose can contain these qualities, and especially the prose of this orator. Used at the right time and in the right proportion, they go unnoticed by our senses: some are fused together, and others have passed into one another, and others have departed in some other way from the precision of their arrangement, so that it seems to be totally changed and to bear no resemblance at all to poetry.

Perhaps someone will ask me at this point to 49
describe tones, rhythm and the figures used in varia-

[1] For the effects of the various metres, see *De Compositione Verborum*, 18.

---

[3] μὴ inseruit Sylburg.

σχημάτων καὶ τοῦ ἐν ἑκάστῳ πρέποντος,[1] ἀξιῶν ἀκοῦσαι, τίνα τε αὐτῶν ἐστιν, οἷς ἡ φιλάρχαιος ἁρμονία κοσμεῖται, καὶ τίνα τῆς κωτίλης γένοιτ' ἂν ἁρμονίας; ἢ οἰκειοτέραν τὴν ἐκ παιδὸς ἐπιφερόμενος εὐμουσίαν, ἣν ἔκ τε μουσικῆς καὶ γραμματικῆς ἔσχηκεν, αἳ ταῦτ' ἔχουσι τὰ θεωρήματα, ἐπιλαβόντα τὸ χρονίζειν ἐν τοῖς κοινοῖς καὶ γνωρίμοις τὸν λόγον οὐ συκοφαντήσει, ἄλλως τε καὶ τοῦ καιροῦ τὰ μέτρα ὁρῶν; οἴομαι μὲν οὖν, ὡς καὶ δόξαν ἐπιεικῆ περὶ τῶν ἄλλων ἔχω, ἀρξάμενος ἀπὸ σοῦ, φίλτατε Ἀμμαῖε, καὶ ἐκ τῆς εὐμουσίας τῆς σῆς λαμβάνων. εἰ δέ τις ἀπαιτήσει καὶ ταῦτ' ἔτι μαθεῖν ὅπῃ ποτ' ἔχει, τοὺς ὑπομνηματισμοὺς ἡμῶν λαβών, οὓς περὶ τῆς συνθέσεως τῶν ὀνομάτων πεπραγματεύμεθα, πάντα ὅσα ποθεῖ τῶν ἐνθάδε παραλειπομένων εἴσεται. ἐγὼ δὲ τῇδέ πῃ περιγράψας τὸν ὑπὲρ τούτων λόγον ἐπὶ τὸ περιλειπόμενον[2] ἐλεύσομαι μέρος.

50 ὑπεσχόμην γὰρ καὶ τοῦτο δείξειν ἔτι, πῶς ἄν τις διαγνοίη τὸν χαρακτῆρα τῆς Δημοσθένους συνθέσεως καὶ ποίοις χρώμενος σημείοις ἀπὸ τῶν ἄλλων διορίσειεν. ἓν μὲν οὖν οὐδέν ἐστι παράσημον αὐτῆς ἐκφανὲς οὕτως, ὥστε μόνῃ ταύτῃ καὶ μηδεμιᾷ τῶν ἄλλων παρακολουθεῖν, ἡ δὲ συνδρομή τε καὶ πλεονασμός, οἷς ἐλέγχεσθαι πέφυκε παντὸς πράγματος καὶ σώματος γνῶσις, ἴδιος αὐτῆς γίνεται χαρακτήρ. χρήσομαι δ' εἰκόνι φανερᾷ τῆς σαφηνείας ἕνεκα τοῖς σώμασι τῶν

[1] τοῦ πρέποντος Reiske: τοὺς πρέποντας codd.
[2] περιλειπόμενον Radermacher: περιλειπομένων Sylburg: παραλειπομένων codd.

tion, and what constitutes propriety in the case of each, expecting to hear which of them goes to form the old-fashioned style, and which produces the ingratiating style. Or will he think it more appropriate to apply the artistic sense which he has acquired from childhood in his education in grammar and music, which cover these subjects, and refrain from criticising a treatise in which the time to be spent on common and familiar subjects is restricted; especially when he sees that the proper limits of relevance are being observed. I think he will and I am optimistic that others will too, taking you and your artistic sense as my starting-point, my dear Ammaeus. But anyone who still demands to learn how these things are can take my treatise *On Literary Composition*,[1] where he will discover all that he wants to know of the subjects omitted from the present treatise. For my part, having outlined the subject in this way, I shall pass on to the remainder of my study.

Now I promised to show further how one can recog- 50
nise the characteristics of Demosthenes's style of composition, and what indications one can use to distinguish it from those of other authors. There is in fact no single clear distinguishing mark which one should rely on to the exclusion of others, but the concentration and amplification which he brings to his examination of every subject and every person amount to a special characteristic of his style. To illustrate my point, I shall draw an obvious comparison from the human body. Every man has

[1] See Introduction, pp. xxiii–xxiv.

ἀνθρώπων. ἅπασι δή που συμβέβηκε μέγεθός τε καὶ χρῶμα καὶ σχῆμα καὶ μέλη καὶ ῥυθμός τις τῶν μελῶν καὶ τὰ παραπλήσια τούτοις. εἰ δή τις ἀφ' ἑνὸς τούτων ἀξιώσει τὸν χαρακτῆρα σκοπεῖν, οὐδὲν ἀκριβὲς εἴσεται. ἐν πολλαῖς γὰρ ἂν εὕροι μορφαῖς τοιοῦτόν τι ἕτερον, οἷον ἔθετο τῆς μιᾶς μορφῆς σύμβολον. ἐὰν δὲ πάντα συνθῇ τὰ [1] συμβεβηκότα τῇ μορφῇ ἢ τὰ πλεῖστα ἢ τὰ κυριώτατα, ταχεῖάν τε πάνυ τὴν γνῶσιν λήψεται καὶ οὐκ ἐπιστήσεται [2] ταῖς ὁμοιότησι. τοῦτο δὴ ποιεῖν ἀξιώσαιμ' ἂν καὶ τοὺς βουλομένους τὴν σύνθεσιν ἀκριβῶς εἰδέναι τὴν Δημοσθένους, ἐκ πολλῶν αὐτὴν δοκιμάζειν ἰδιωμάτων, λέγω δὴ τῶν κρατίστων τε καὶ κυριωτάτων· πρῶτον ἐκ τῆς ἐμμελείας, ἧς κριτήριον ἄριστον ἡ ἄλογος αἴσθησις. δεῖ δὲ αὐτῇ τριβῆς πολλῆς καὶ κατηχήσεως χρονίου· οὐ γὰρ δὴ πλάσται μὲν καὶ ζωγράφων παῖδες, εἰ μὴ πολλὴν ἐμπειρίαν λάβοιεν, χρόνῳ τρίψαντες τὰς ὁράσεις μακρῷ περὶ τὰς τῶν ἀρχαίων δημιουργῶν τέχνας, οὐκ ἂν εὐπετῶς αὐτὰς διαγνοῖεν καὶ οὐκ ἂν ἔχοιεν εἰπεῖν βεβαίως, ὅτι [τῇ φήμῃ παραλαβόντες] [3] τουτὶ μέν ἐστι Πολυκλείτου τὸ ἔργον, τουτὶ δὲ Φειδίου, τουτὶ δὲ Ἀλκαμένους, καὶ τῶν γραφῶν Πολυγνώτου μὲν αὕτη, Τιμάνθους δὲ ἐκείνη, αὕτη δὲ Παρρασίου. λόγων δὲ ἆρα τινὲς ἀκριβῶς ἐξ ὀλίγων παραγγελμάτων καὶ προσκαίρου κατηχήσεως ἐμμελοῦς ἁρμονίας εἴσονται φύσιν; πολλοῦ γε καὶ δεῖ.

[1] συνθῇ τὰ Reiske: τὰ συνήθη codd.
[2] ἐπιστήσεται conieci: ἐπίσεται P ἐπι . . . σεται M.
[3] τῇ φήμῃ παραλαβόντες delevit Radermacher.

stature, colour, shape, limbs and a certain rhythm to his limbs and other qualities of this kind. Now if anyone expects to detect the general character of the whole from one of these, he will not obtain accurate knowledge; for he might find in many other physical forms another instance of what he took to be a token of the one form. But if he puts together all, or the majority, or the most important of the attributes of this form, he will quickly come to understand its nature completely, and not stop short in his examination of similarities. I should recommend all those who wish to understand the style of Demosthenes to do this: to form their judgment from several of its properties, that is to say the most important and significant of them. He should first consider its melody, of which the most reliable test is the instinctive feeling; but this requires much practice and prolonged instruction. Sculptors and painters without long experience in training the eye by studying the works of the old masters would not be able to identify them readily, and would not be able to say with confidence that this piece of sculpture is by Polyclitus,[1] this by Phidias,[2] this by Alcamenes;[3] and that this painting is by Polygnotus,[4] this by Timanthes[5] and this by Parrhasius.[6] So with literature: is anyone going to understand in detail the nature of melodious composition after learning a few rules of thumb and attending a brief intensive course? Impossible!

[1] See note 2, p. 112. [2] See note 3, p. 113.

[3] Perhaps a pupil of Phidias (*c.* 460–400 B.C.).

[4] The first great classical Athenian painter (fl. *c.* 475–447 B.C.).

[5] Fifth-century painter from Cynthus who settled at Sicyon.

[6] Athenian painter, contemporary of Timanthes, famed for his ability at portraying detail and for subtlety of outline.

τοῦτο μὲν δὴ πρῶτον οἴομαι δεῖν σκοπεῖν ἐπιστήμῃ γε καὶ ἔθει, μετὰ δὲ τοῦτο τὴν εὐρυθμίαν. οὐ γὰρ ἔστι λέξις οὐδεμία Δημοσθένους, ἥτις οὐκ ἐμπεριείληφε ῥυθμοὺς καὶ μέτρα τὰ μὲν ἀπηρτισμένα καὶ τέλεια, τὰ δ' ἀτελῆ, τοιαύτην ἐπιπλοκὴν ἔχοντα ἐν ἀλλήλοις καὶ οὕτως συνηρμοσμένα, ὥστε μὴ δῆλον εἶναι, ὅτι ἐστὶ μέτρα. οὐ γὰρ ἂν ἄλλως γένοιτο πολιτικὴ λέξις παρ' αὐτὴν τὴν σύνθεσιν ἐμφερὴς ποιήμασιν, ἂν μὴ περιέχῃ μέτρα καὶ ῥυθμούς τινας ἐγκατακεχωρισμένους ἀδήλως. οὐ μέντοι γε προσήκει αὐτὴν ἔμμετρον οὐδ' ἔρρυθμον εἶναι δοκεῖν, ἵνα μὴ γένηται ποίημα ἢ μέλος, ἐκβᾶσα τὸν αὐτῆς χαρακτῆρα, ἀλλ' εὔρυθμον αὐτὴν ἀπόχρη φαίνεσθαι καὶ εὔμετρον. οὕτω γὰρ ἂν εἴη ποιητικὴ μέν, οὐ μὴν ποίημά γε, καὶ μελίζουσα μέν, οὐ μὴν μέλος. τίνα δ' ἔχει ταῦτα διαφοράν, οὐ χαλεπὸν ἰδεῖν. ἡ μὲν ὅμοια παραλαμβάνουσα μέτρα καὶ ῥυθμοὺς τεταγμένους εἴτε κατὰ στίχον εἴτε κατὰ περίοδον, ἣν καλοῦσιν ⟨οἱ⟩ [1] μουσικοὶ στροφήν, κἄπειτα πάλιν τοῖς αὐτοῖς ῥυθμοῖς καὶ μέτροις ἐπὶ τῶν αὐτῶν στίχων ἢ περιόδων, ἃς ἀντιστρόφους ὀνομάζουσι, χρωμένη καὶ τῷ σχήματι τούτῳ τῆς κατασκευῆς ἀπὸ τῆς ἀρχῆς μέχρι τοῦ τέλους προβαίνουσα ἔμμετρός τ' ἐστὶ καὶ ἔρρυθμος, καὶ ὀνόματα κεῖται τῇ τοιαύτῃ λέξει μέτρον καὶ μέλος, ἡ δὲ περιπεπλανημένα μέτρα καὶ ῥυθμοὺς ἀτάκτους ἐμπεριλαμβάνουσα καὶ μήτε ἀκολουθίαν αὐτῶν φυλάττουσα μήτε ὁμοζυγίαν μήτ' ἄλλην ὁμοιότητα τεταγμένην μηδεμίαν εὔρυθμος μέν ἐστι καὶ εὔμετρος, ἐπειδὴ διαπεποίκιλται μέτροις τε καὶ ῥυθμοῖς τισιν, οὐ

This, then, is the first subject that I think they should study, learning about it and becoming familiar with it; and after it the right use of rhythm. For there is no passage in Demosthenes that does not contain rhythms and metre, some perfect and complete, some incomplete, wrought in such complex relationship to one another and so dovetailed together that their metrical character is not obvious to us. It would not otherwise be possible to create a political speech whose actual composition resembled that of poetry if the metres and rhythms it contained were not unobtrusively introduced. But it should certainly not appear to have a regular metre or rhythm, for fear that it may become a poem or a song, losing its proper character. It is sufficient for it to give the impression of containing pleasing rhythm and metre: for in this way it would have a poetical quality, but would not be a poem, and a singing quality without being song. It is not difficult to see the difference: the one adopts similar metres and rhythms arranged either in lines or in a stanza (which the writers on music call a *strophe*), followed by the same rhythms and metres correspondingly used in lines or stanzas, which they call *antistrophes.* This form of arrangement is adopted throughout and results in a regular scheme of metre and rhythm. Such writing has the terms *metre* and *melody* applied to it. But writing which contains haphazard metres and irregular rhythms, and which observes in their use neither sequence nor correspondence nor any other form of organised uniformity is rhythmical and metrical, since

---

[1] *οἱ* inseruit Sylburg.

μὴν ἔρρυθμός γε οὐδὲ ἔμμετρος, ἐπειδὴ οὐχὶ τοῖς αὐτοῖς οὐδὲ κατὰ ταὐτὰ ἔχουσι. τοιαύτην δή [1] φημι πᾶσαν εἶναι λέξιν πολιτικήν, ἐν ᾗ τὸ ποιητικὸν ἐμφαίνεται κάλλος. ᾗ καὶ τὸν Δημοσθένη κεχρημένον ὁρῶ. τὰς δὲ περὶ τούτου τοῦ μέρους πίστεις ἐν τοῖς περὶ τῆς συνθέσεως γραφεῖσιν ἀποδεδωκὼς οὐκ ἀναγκαῖον ἡγοῦμαι κἀνταῦθα λέγειν. τρίτον ἔτι καὶ τέταρτον ἰδίωμα τῆς συνθέσεως τοῦ ῥήτορος ἦν τό τε ἐξαλλάττειν παντοδαπῶς καὶ τὸ σχηματίζειν ποικίλως τὰ κῶλα καὶ τὰς περιόδους. οὐδὲ γὰρ ἔστιν οὐδεὶς ἁπλῶς τόπος, ὃς [2] οὐχὶ διαπεποίκιλται ταῖς τε ἐξαλλαγαῖς καὶ τοῖς σχηματισμοῖς, ὡς ἅπαντες ἴσασι, καί μοι δοκεῖ ταῦτα μὴ λόγων δεῖσθαι γνώριμα καὶ τοῖς φαυλοτάτοις ὄντα.

51 ταυτί μοι δοκεῖ μηνύματα τῆς συνθέσεως εἶναι τῆς Δημοσθένους ⟨ἀνυφαίρετα⟩ [3] καὶ χαρακτηρικά, ἐξ ὧν ἄν τις αὐτὴν διαγνοίη πᾶσαν, ἐξετάζειν βουληθείς. εἰ δέ τις ὑποτεύξεται πρὸς ταῦτα θαυμάζειν λέγων, εἰ καὶ κακοδαίμων οὕτως ἦν ὁ τηλικοῦτος ἀνήρ, ὥσθ', ὅτε γράφοι τοὺς λόγους, ἄνω καὶ κάτω στρέφειν τὰ μόρια τῆς λέξεως καὶ τὰ ἐκ τούτων συντιθέμενα κῶλα, ἐμμελείας τε καὶ ῥυθμοὺς καὶ μέτρα, μουσικῆς οἰκεῖα θεωρίας πράγματα καὶ ποιητικῆς, εἰς τὴν πολιτικὴν ἐναρμόττων φράσιν, ᾗ τούτων οὐδενὸς μέτεστιν, πρῶτον μὲν ἐκεῖνο ἐνθυμηθήτω, ὅτι ὁ τοσαύτης δόξης ἠξιωμένος ἀνὴρ ἐπὶ λόγοις, ὅσης οὐδεὶς τῶν πρότερον, αἰώνια συνταττόμενος ἔργα καὶ τῷ πάντα βασανίζοντι χρόνῳ παραδιδούς, οὐδὲν ἐκ

[1] δή Radermacher: δὲ codd.

it is variegated by certain metres and rhythms, but it is not *in* rhythm nor *in* metre because they lack consistency and uniform frequency. I consider that all political oratory which shows the beauty of poetry is like this; and I see Demosthenes as one of its exponents. I have presented my arguments on this subject in my treatise *On Literary Composition*, and do not think it necessary to repeat them here. The third and fourth characteristics of Demosthenes's style are, as we saw, his use of all forms of clause and period and of figures of speech to give them variety; and indeed there is not a single passage that is not diversified by clausal variation and figures of speech. This is common knowledge, and I think that what is familiar even to the most ignorant requires no illustration.

These I regard as the essential and characteristic 51
features of Demosthenes's style of composition, which should enable the student who wishes to examine it to recognise it in all its forms. If anyone should reply to this, saying that he is surprised that so great a man should be such a victim of misfortune that whenever he writes speeches he turns his words upside down, and also the clauses formed from them, trying to introduce into the language of political oratory melody, rhythm and metre, the ingredients of music and poetry, which are entirely foreign media—if he should say this, let him first consider that the man who enjoyed an unparalleled reputation as an orator and composed speeches that were to be immortal, and handed them down to Posterity, the

[2] ὃς Sylburg: οἷος M.
[3] ἀνυφαίρετα inseruit Radermacher.

τοῦ ἐπιτυχόντος ἔγραφεν. ἀλλ᾽ ὥσπερ τῆς ἐν τοῖς νοήμασιν οἰκονομίας πολλὴν ἐποιεῖτο δόσιν, οὕτω καὶ τῆς [1] ἐν τοῖς ὀνόμασιν ἁρμονίας, ὁρῶν γε δὴ τούτους τοὺς θαυμαζομένους ἐπὶ σοφίᾳ καὶ κρατίστων λόγων ποιητὰς νομιζομένους Ἰσοκράτην καὶ Πλάτωνα γλυπτοῖς καὶ τορευτοῖς ἐοικότας ἐκφέροντας λόγους, ἐνθυμούμενος δ᾽, ὅτι τοῦ λέγειν εὖ διττὴ ἡ διαίρεσίς ἐστιν, εἴς τε τὸν πραγματικὸν τόπον [2] καὶ εἰς τὸν λεκτικόν, καὶ τούτων πάλιν ἀμφοτέρων εἰς τὰς ἴσας διαιρεθέντων τομάς, τοῦ πραγματικοῦ μὲν εἴς τε τὴν παρασκευήν, ἣν οἱ παλαιοὶ καλοῦσιν εὕρεσιν, καὶ εἰς τὴν χρῆσιν τῶν παρεσκευασμένων,[3] ἣν προσαγορεύουσιν οἰκονομίαν, τοῦ λεκτικοῦ δὲ εἴς τε τὴν ἐκλογὴν τῶν ὀνομάτων καὶ εἰς τὴν σύνθεσιν τῶν ἐκλεγέντων, ἐν ἑκατέρῳ τούτων πλείω μοῖραν ἔχει τὰ δεύτερα τῶν προτέρων· τὸ μὲν οἰκονομικὸν ἐν τῷ πραγματικῷ, τὸ δὲ συνθετικὸν [4] ἐν τῷ λεκτικῷ. περὶ ὧν οὐ καιρὸς ἐν τῷ παρόντι μηκύνειν. ταῦτα γὰρ ἐννοηθείη ἄν, εἴ τις μὴ κομιδῇ σκαιὸς ἢ δύσερις, καὶ οὐκ ἂν θαυμάσειεν, εἰ φροντὶς ἐγένετο Δημοσθένει [ἔτι] [5] μελῶν καὶ ῥυθμῶν καὶ σχημάτων, καὶ τῶν ἄλλων πάντων, οἷς ἡδεῖα καὶ καλὴ γίνεται σύνθεσις. τοὐναντίον γὰρ μᾶλλον ὑπολάβοι τις ⟨ἂν⟩ [6] ἀνὴρ μήτε ὀλιγόπονος μήτε ἀψίκορος [7]

[1] τῆς ἁρμονίας Sylburg: τὴν ἁρμονίαν codd.
[2] τόπον Reiske: τρόπον codd.
[3] παρεσκευασμένων Sylburg: παρασκευασμένων codd.
[4] συνθετικὸν Krüger: συντιθέμενον codd.
[5] ἔτι delevit Reiske.
[6] ἂν inseruit Reiske.
[7] ἀψίκορος Casaubon: τερψίχορος MP.

Universal Scrutiniser, wrote nothing casually; but just as he laid great stress upon the arrangement of his ideas, so he showed the same concern for the melodious order of words. He observed that Isocrates and Plato were admired as philosophers and regarded as the finest of writers because their works seemed to have been composed in an exquisitely chiselled and turned style. He observed that good oratory depends on two factors, selection of subject-matter and style of delivery, and that these two are each divided into two equal sections, subject-matter into preparation, which the early rhetoricians call *invention*, and deployment of the prepared material, which they call *arrangement*; [1] and style into choice of words, and composition of the words chosen.[2] In both of these sections the second is the more important, arrangement in the case of subject-matter and composition in the case of style. But this is not the time to enlarge on these topics. These, then, are the points which our critic would consider, if he is not completely dense or contentious, and he would not be surprised to find Demosthenes concerning himself with music and rhythm, with figurative expression, and with all the other factors that contribute towards charm and beauty of composition. On the contrary, anyone who took some trouble, and did not treat the matter superficially, and had a modicum of

[1] Aristotle's *Rhetoric* is thus divided, the first two books being devoted to invention, and the third to style (chs. 1–12) and arrangement (τάξις) (chs. 13–19).

[2] See *Isocrates*, 3.

μήτε ἀκρόσοφος ἄπορον εἶναι καὶ ἀμήχανον, ἢ μηδεμίαν ἐπιμέλειαν πεποιῆσθαι τὸν ῥήτορα τῆς ἁρμονίας τῶν λόγων ἢ φαύλην τινά, βουλόμενον μνημεῖα τῆς ἑαυτοῦ διανοίας ἀθάνατα καταλιπεῖν. οὐ γὰρ δή τοι πλάσται μὲν καὶ γραφεῖς ἐν ὕλῃ φθαρτῇ χειρῶν εὐστοχίας ἐνδεικνύμενοι τοσούτους εἰσφέρονται πόνους, ὥστε καὶ φλέβια καὶ πτίλα καὶ χνοῦς καὶ τὰ τούτοις ὅμοια εἰς ἄκρον ἐξεργάζεσθαι καὶ κατατήκειν εἰς ταῦτα τὰς τέχνας, πολιτικὸς δ' ἄρα δημιουργός, πάντας ὑπεράρας τοὺς καθ' αὑτὸν φύσει τε καὶ πόνῳ, τῶν ἐλαχίστων τινὸς εἰς τὸ εὖ λέγειν, εἰ δὴ καὶ ταῦτα ἐλάχιστα, ὠλιγώρησε.

52 βουλοίμην δ' ἂν καὶ ταῦτα ἐνθυμηθῆναι [διότι] [1] τοὺς ἔτι δυσπείστως [2] ἔχοντας πρὸς τὰ εἰρημένα, ὅτι μειράκιον μὲν ἔτι ὄντα καὶ νεωστὶ τοῦ μαθήματος ἁπτόμενον αὐτὸν οὐκ ἄλογον ἦν καὶ ταῦτα καὶ τἆλλα πάντα διὰ πολλῆς ἐπιμελείας τε καὶ φροντίδος ἔχειν, ἐπειδὴ δ' ἡ χρόνιος ἄσκησις ἕξιν αὐτῷ ἐνεποίησε πολλὴν καὶ τύπους ἰσχυροὺς ἐνειργάσατο τῶν αἰεὶ μελετωμένων, τότε ἀπὸ τοῦ ῥᾴστου τε καὶ τῆς ἕξεως αὐτὸ ποιεῖν. οἷόν τι γίνεται καὶ περὶ τὰς ἄλλας τέχνας καὶ οὐχ ἥκιστα περὶ τὴν καλουμένην γραμματικήν. ἱκανὴ γὰρ αὕτη καὶ τὰς ἄλλας τεκμηριῶσαι, φανερωτάτη πασῶν οὖσα καὶ θαυμασιωτάτη. ταύτην γὰρ ὅταν ἐκμάθωμεν, πρῶτον μὲν τὰ ὀνόματα τῶν στοιχείων τῆς φωνῆς ἀναλαμβάνομεν, ἃ καλεῖται γράμματα. ἔπειτα ⟨τοὺς⟩ [3] τύπους τε αὐτῶν

[1] διότι delevit Sylburg.
[2] δυσπείστως Sylburg: δυσπίστως codd.

intelligence, would find it impossible and impracticable for the orator to have completely neglected melodious composition in his speeches, or to have considered it but little, if he wished to leave them as an undying monument to his genius. For surely, if sculptors and painters demonstrate their manual skills upon perishable materials, yet apply themselves with such industry that they depict with the highest perfection even small veins, young plumage, the first beard's down and the like, and exhaust their art upon such details, would a professional politician, who had raised himself above all his contemporaries through natural ability and hard work, have neglected the smallest means, if smallest they be, of making himself a good orator?

I should like those who are still unconvinced by my 52
arguments to consider that it would not have been unreasonable to expect him, while still a young man and new to his studies, to have examined these and all other aspects of the subject with great care; but that after long training had imbued him with great empirical skill, and left in his mind a firm impression of whatever he had been studying, he then wrote with the utmost facility, drawing on his experience. The same sort of thing happens in other arts, not least in that which is called *grammar*. Our findings concerning grammar can be applied to other arts, since it is the best-known of all and the most remarkable. When we learn grammar properly, we begin by learning by heart the names of the elements of sound, which we call *letters*.[1] Then we learn how they are

[1] Cf. Plato, *Protagoras*, 325E.

[3] τοὺς inseruit Sauppe.

καὶ δυνάμεις. ὅταν δὲ ταῦτα μάθωμεν, τότε τὰς συλλαβὰς αὐτῶν καὶ τὰ περὶ ταύτας[1] πάθη. κρατήσαντες δὲ τούτων τὰ τοῦ λόγου μόρια, ὀνόματα λέγω καὶ ῥήματα καὶ συνδέσμους, καὶ τὰ συμβεβηκότα τούτοις, συστολάς, ἐκτάσεις, ὀξύτητας, βαρύτητας, γένη, πτώσεις, ἀριθμούς, ἐγκλίσεις, τὰ ἄλλα παραπλήσια τούτοις μυρία ὄντα.[2] ὅταν δὲ τὴν τούτων ἁπάντων ἐπιστήμην περιλάβωμεν, τότε ἀρχόμεθα γράφειν τε καὶ ἀναγινώσκειν, κατὰ συλλαβὴν μὲν καὶ βραδέως τὸ πρῶτον, ἅτε νεαρᾶς οὔσης ἔτι τῆς ἕξεως, προβαίνοντος δὲ τοῦ χρόνου καὶ τὸν νοῦν ἰσχυρὸν τῇ ψυχῇ περιτιθέντος ἐκ τῆς συνεχοῦς μελέτης, τότ' ἀπταίστως τε καὶ κατὰ πολλὴν εὐπέτειαν, καὶ πᾶν ὅ τι ἂν ἐπιδῷ τις βυβλίον οὐδὲν ἐκείνων ἔτι τῶν πολλῶν θεωρημάτων ἀναπολοῦντες ἅμα νοήσει[3] διερχόμεθα. τοιοῦτον δή τι καὶ περὶ ταύτην ὑποληπτέον γενέσθαι τὴν τέχνην, ἐκ τῶν μικρῶν καὶ γλίσχρων θεωρημάτων αὐξομένην τὴν ἕξιν σὺν χρόνῳ ῥᾳδίως αὐτῶν κρατεῖν, ὥστε ἅμα νοήσει κεκριμένον τε καὶ ἄπταιστον αὐτῆς εἶναι τὸ ἔργον. εἰ δέ τῳ δοκεῖ ταῦτα καὶ πόνου πολλοῦ καὶ πραγματείας μεγάλης ἔργα εἶναι, καὶ μάλα ὀρθῶς δοκεῖ κατὰ τὸν Δημοσθένη· οὐδὲν γὰρ τῶν μεγάλων μικρῶν ἐστι πόνων ὤνιον. ἀλλ' ἐὰν ἐπιλογίσηται τοὺς ἀκολουθοῦντας αὐτοῖς καρπούς, μᾶλλον δ' ἐὰν ἕνα μόνον τὸν ἔπαινον, ὃν ἀποδίδωσιν ὁ χρόνος καὶ ζῶσι καὶ μετὰ τὴν τελευτήν, πᾶσαν ἡγήσεται τήν (τε) πραγματείαν ἐλάττω τῆς προσηκούσης.

[1] ταύτας Sylburg: ταῦτα MBP.

written and what they sound like. When we have discovered this, we learn how they combine to form syllables, and how these behave. Having mastered this, we learn about the parts of speech—I mean nouns, verbs and conjunctions and their properties, the shortening and lengthening of syllables and the high and low pitch of accents; genders, cases, numbers, moods and countless other related things. When we have acquired knowledge of all these things, we then begin to write and to read, slowly at first and syllable by syllable, because our skill is as yet undeveloped. But as time goes on and endows the mind, through constant practice, with a sound understanding, we proceed unfalteringly and with great ease, and read through any book we are given at sight, without thumbing through our text-books for all those rules. The same sort of process must be assumed in the case of rhetoric: skill in it grows, beginning with the learning of small and petty rules, which are easily mastered with time, until we choose our words instantaneously and practise the art with unfaltering assurance. If anyone thinks that this level of proficiency requires much toil and great application, he is quite right in Demosthenes's view, for, as he says, nothing great can be bought with little exertion.[1] But if he calculates the benefits that accrue from these studies, or rather if he considers only one—the praise that time repays both in life and after death, he will consider all the labour involved disproportionately small.

[1] *On the Chersonese*, 48.

---

[2] *ὄντα* Krüger: *ὀνόματα* codd.
[3] *νοήσει* Sylburg: *νοήσεις* BP.

53 εἷς ἔτι μοι καταλείπεται λόγος ὁ περὶ τῆς ὑποκρίσεως, ὡς κεκόσμηκε τὴν λέξιν ἁνήρ, ἀναγκαίας ἀρετῆς οὔσης περὶ λόγους καὶ μάλιστα τοὺς πολιτικούς. ἧς παρούσης μὲν καὶ ταῖς ἄλλαις ἀρεταῖς γίνεται χώρα καὶ τόπος,[1] ἀπούσης δὲ οὐδὲ ὁτιοῦν ὄφελος οὐδ' ἐκείνων οὐδεμιᾶς. τεκμήραιτο δ' ἄν τις, ἡλίκην ἰσχὺν τοῦτο τὸ στοιχεῖον ἔχει, καταμαθών, ὅσον ἀλλήλων ἀλλάττουσιν οἱ τραγῳδίας τε καὶ κωμῳδίας ὑποκρινόμενοι. τὰ γὰρ αὐτὰ ποιήματα λέγοντες οὐχ ὡσαύτως ἡμᾶς κηλοῦσιν ἅπαντες, ἀλλ' ἐνίοις ἐπαχθόμεθα καὶ ὥσπερ ἀδικούμενοί τι καθυποκρινομένοις καὶ διαφθείρουσι τὰς βουλήσεις τῶν ποιημάτων χαλεπαίνομεν. ταύτης δή φημι τῆς ἀρετῆς πάνυ δεῖν τοῖς ἐναγωνίοις λόγοις, εἰ μέλλουσιν ἕξειν πολὺ τὸ ἀληθινὸν καὶ ἔμψυχον. ἧς πλείστην ὥσπερ καὶ τῶν ἄλλων πρόνοιαν ἔσχεν οὗτος ὁ ἀνήρ. διττὴν δὲ τὴν φύσιν αὐτῆς οὖσαν ὁρῶν, περὶ ἄμφω τὰ μέρη σφόδρα ἐσπούδασε. καὶ γὰρ τὰ πάθη τὰ τῆς φωνῆς καὶ τὰ σχήματα τοῦ σώματος, ὡς κράτιστα ἕξειν ἔμελλεν, οὐ μικρῷ πόνῳ κατειργάσατο, καίτοι φύσει πρὸς ταῦτα οὐ πάνυ εὐτυχεῖ χρησάμενος, ὡς Δημήτριός τε ὁ Φαληρεύς φησι καὶ οἱ ἄλλοι πάντες οἱ τὸν βίον αὐτοῦ συγγράψαντες. τί δὴ ταῦτα πρὸς τὴν λέξιν αὐτοῦ συντείνει; φαίη τις ἄν. ἡ λέξις μὲν οὖν, εἴποιμ' ἄν, οἰκείως κατεσκεύασται πρὸς ταῦτα, μεστὴ πολλῶν οὖσα ἠθῶν καὶ παθῶν καὶ διδάσκουσα, οἵας ὑποκρίσεως αὐτῇ δεῖ. ὥστε τοὺς ἀναγινώσκοντας τὸν ῥήτορα τοῦτον ἐπιμελῶς χρὴ παρατηρεῖν, ἵνα τοῦτον ἕκαστα λέγηται τὸν

There remains one further topic to discuss, the 53
manner in which he embellished his speeches in delivery. This is an essential feature of oratory, especially political oratory. When it is present the other qualities find place and scope, but when it is absent none of these is of any use at all. One may judge the importance of this element by observing how different the performances of individual tragic and comic actors are. They do not all charm us equally when they recite the same lines, but some annoy us and make us feel angry with them as if we felt injured at their ruining the sense of the lines by their bad acting. Now I maintain that this faculty is most necessary in practical oratory, if it is to be really convincing and animated. Demosthenes took the same special care over it as over other aspects of technique. He saw that its nature was twofold, and studied both parts thoroughly. He worked hard on both, the modulation of the voice and the movements of the body, and cultivated both to the best possible effect in spite of a constitution which, according to Demetrius of Phaleron and all his other biographers, was ill-suited to such exertions.[1] Now, what has this to do with his literary style? someone might ask: to which I should reply, that his style is designed to accommodate it, being full of moral and emotional overtones, and thus dictating the form of the delivery. Accordingly, whoever recites his speeches should take special care to deliver every sentence in the manner

[1] Plutarch, *Demosthenes*, 8; [Plutarch], *Lives of the Ten Orators*, 844E, F.

---

[1] τόπος Kiessling: τότε codd.

τρόπον, ᾗ ἐκεῖνος ἐβούλετο. αὐτὴ γὰρ ἡ λέξις διδάσκει τοὺς ἔχοντας ψυχὴν εὐκίνητον, μεθ' οἵας αὐτὴν ὑποκρίσεως ἐκφέρεσθαι δεήσει. ὃ δὴ ἐγὼ σαφὲς [1] ἐπὶ τῶν παραδειγμάτων [2] ποιήσω.

54 φέρε γὰρ ἐπιχειρείτω τις προφέρεσθαι τούσδε τοὺς ἀριθμούς· "Ὄλυνθον μὲν δὴ καὶ Μεθώνην καὶ Ἀπολλωνίαν καὶ δύο καὶ τριάκοντα πόλεις ἐπὶ Θρᾴκης ἐῶ, ἃς ἁπάσας οὕτως ὠμῶς ἀνῄρηκεν, ὥστε μηδ', εἰ πώποτε ᾠκίσθησαν, ῥᾴδιον ἦν προσελθόντας εἰπεῖν. καὶ τὸ Φωκέων τοσοῦτον ἔθνος ἀνῃρημένον σιωπῶ." ἐνταῦθα ἡ λέξις αὐτὴ διδάσκει, τίνος ὑποκρίσεως δεῖ αὐτῇ. διῃρηκὼς γὰρ τὸ πλῆθος τῶν ἀνῃρημένων ὑπὸ Φιλίππου πόλεων ἐπὶ Θρᾴκης οὔ φησιν ἐρεῖν. οὐχὶ ταῦτ' οὖν εἰρωνευόμενον δεῖ λέγειν καὶ ἅμα ὑπαγανακτοῦντα καὶ παρεντείνοντα τὸν ἦχον; εἶτ' εἰ καὶ φησὶν οὐκ ἔχειν ἐρεῖν ταῦθ' ὥσπερ δεινὰ καὶ πέρα δεινῶν, ὅμως ὀδύρεται πόλεων κατάλογον καὶ τελείαν [3] ἀναίρεσιν [4] διέξεισιν, ὡς οὐδ' ἴχνος ἔτι λοιπὸν ἐχουσῶν τῆς παλαιᾶς οἰκήσεως. οὐ δι' ὀργῆς τ' οὖν ταῦτα ὑπερβαλλούσης καὶ οἴκτου λέγεσθαι προσήκει; τίνες οὖν εἰσιν ὀργῆς καὶ ὀλοφυρμοῦ τόνοι καὶ ἐγκλίσεις καὶ σχηματισμοὶ προσώπου καὶ φοραὶ χειρῶν; ἃς οἱ κατ' ἀλήθειαν ταῦτα πεπονθότες ἐπιτελοῦσι. πάνυ γὰρ εὔηθες ἄλλο τι ζητεῖν ὑποκρίσεως διδασκαλεῖον,[5] ἀφέντας τὴν ἀλήθειαν. καὶ αὖθις ἐπιφέρει ὁ ἀνήρ· " ἀλλὰ

[1] σαφὲς Sylburg: σαφῶς codd.
[2] παραδειγμάτων Krüger: πραγμάτων codd.
[3] τελείαν Usener: ταχεῖαν codd.
[4] ἀναίρεσιν Sylburg: αἵρεσιν MB αἷρεσιν P.
[5] διδασκαλεῖον Reiske: διδασκαλιον codd.

intended by the orator; for the style itself prescribes to the susceptible reader the kind of delivery that will be required. I shall elucidate this point with examples.

Now suppose someone tries to deliver the following catalogue:[1] 54

"Olynthus and Methone and Apollonia, and thirty-two cities on the borders of Thrace I pass over, all of which he so cruelly destroyed that a visitor could hardly tell even whether they were ever inhabited; and of the extermination of a great people like the Phocians, I say nothing."

Here the words themselves show what kind of delivery is needed for them. Having specified the numbers of cities in Thrace destroyed by Philip he says he will not give them. Surely this requires an ironic tone of delivery, with an undertone of indignation and with heightened intensity of utterance. Then, although he says he cannot recite the list because of their terrible, or worse than terrible fate, he nevertheless goes on to give a pathetic list of the cities and describes their complete destruction, implying that not a vestige was left of their former habitation. Surely this demands an overwhelmingly angry and tragic manner of delivery? What, then, are the tones and accents of voice, the facial expressions and manual gestures that portray anger and grief? Those which men actually experiencing these emotions employ; for it would be silly to reject real life, and look for another school to teach us delivery. Then the orator inveighs as follows:[2]

"But what is the condition of Thessaly? Has he

[1] *Phil.* iii. 26.
[2] *Phil.* iii. 26.

Θετταλία πῶς ἔχει; οὐχὶ τὰς πολιτείας αὐτῶν ἀφῄρηται καὶ τετραρχίας καθέστακεν, ἵνα μὴ μόνον κατὰ πόλεις, ἀλλὰ καὶ κατὰ ἔθνη δουλεύωσιν; αἱ δ' ἐν Εὐβοίᾳ πόλεις οὐκ ἤδη τυραννοῦνται, καὶ ταῦτα ἐν νήσῳ ⟨πλησίον⟩ [1] Θηβῶν καὶ Ἀθηνῶν;" ταῦτα πάλιν ἑτέραν ὑπόκρισιν ἀπαιτεῖ. πυνθάνεται γάρ, εἶτ' ἀνθυποφέρει καὶ παρ' ἕκαστον ἀγανακτεῖ καὶ τὸ δεινὸν αὔξει. ἴδιον δὲ δή που σχῆμα πεύσεως, ἴδιον δ' ἀνθυποφορᾶς, ἴδιον δ' αὐξήσεως· οὐ δύναται ταῦτα ἑνὶ τόνῳ καὶ μιᾷ μορφῇ φωνῆς λέγεσθαι. τούτοις ἐκεῖνα ἕπεται· "καὶ οὐ γράφει μὲν ταῦτα, τοῖς δ' ἔργοις οὐ ποιεῖ, ἀλλ' ἐφ' Ἑλλήσποντον οἴχεται, πρότερον ἧκεν ἐπ' Ἀμβρακίαν, Ἦλιν ἔχει τηλικαύτην πόλιν ἐν Πελοποννήσῳ, Μεγάροις ἐπεβούλευσεν· οὔθ' ἡ Ἑλλὰς οὔθ' ἡ βάρβαρος χωρεῖ τὴν πλεονεξίαν τοῦ ἀνθρώπου." ταῦτα ἔνεστι προφέρεσθαι ἡδονῇ ἐν παρῳδικοῖς [2] μέλεσιν ὥσπερ ἱστορίαν; οὐκ αὐτὰ βοᾷ [3] καὶ διδάσκει, πῶς αὐτὰ δεῖ λέγεσθαι, μόνον οὐ φωνὴν ἀφιέντα· "ἐνταῦθα ἀστεῖον ἦχον, ταῦτα ἐσπευσμένως εἰπέ, ταῦτ' ἀναβεβλημένως, δευρὶ δ' ἀπόλιπε τὸ συνεχές, ἐνταυθοῖ σύναψον τὰ ἑξῆς, τούτοις συνάλγησον, τούτων καταφρόνησον, ταῦτα ἐκδειματώθητι, ταῦτα διάσυρον, ταῦτα αὔξησον;" ἐμοὶ μὲν δοκεῖ. οὐκοῦν ἔστιν ἀλόγου ζῴου ψυχὴν ἔχοντα, μᾶλλον δὲ λίθου φύσιν νωθράν, ἀναίσθητον, ἀκίνητον, ἀπαθῆ, τὴν Δημοσθένους προφέρεσθαι λέξιν; πολλοῦ γε καὶ δεῖ, ἐπεὶ τὸ κάλλιστον

[1] πλησίον ex Demosthene addidit v.
[2] παροδικοῖς Usener: παρωδικοῖς codd.
[3] οὐκ αὐτὰ βοᾷ Dobree: οὐ καταβοᾷ MP.

not deprived her of her constitutions and has he not established tetrarchies, to parcel her out for slavery not only by cities, but even by provinces? And are not the cities of Euboea now governed by despots, and that although they are on an island close to Thebes and Athens?"

This requires another form of delivery again. He asks a question, then supplies the answer, and at every step expresses anger and heightens the sense of indignation. Now question, answer and exaggeration each has its own appropriate delivery, so that they cannot be delivered in the same pitch and tone of voice. Next follow these words:[1]

"Nor does he write like this, and fail to follow up his words with deeds; but he has gone to the Hellespont, and earlier marched to Ambracia; he holds Elis, that great city in the Peloponnese; he has plotted to seize Megara: neither Greece nor barbarian lands can contain the man's ambition."

Could these words be uttered for entertainment in the tones of a burlesque as if it were history? Do they not themselves cry aloud and tell us how they should be delivered, almost saying in so many words, "Here the tone should be urbane, here you should speak urgently, here in a relaxed manner; at this point you should break the continuity, at that maintain the sequence; here show sympathy, there contempt; be terrified at this, ridicule this, and exaggerate that?" It seems so to me. Is it possible, then, for a man with the mind of an unreasoning animal, or rather the inert nature of a stone, without sensitivity, susceptibility or feeling, to deliver the speeches of Demosthenes? Far from it! Such a

[1] *Phil.* iii. 27.

αὐτῆς ἀγαθὸν ἀπολεῖται, τὸ πνεῦμα, καὶ οὐδὲν διοίσει σώματος καλοῦ μέν, ἀκινήτου δὲ καὶ νεκροῦ. πόλλ' ἂν τις εἰς τοῦτο τὸ μέρος εἰπεῖν ἔχοι,[1] τοῦ δὲ συντάγματος ἱκανὸν εἰληφότος ἤδη μῆκος αὐτοῦ που καταπαῦσαι χρὴ τὸν λόγον, ἐκεῖνο ἔτι νὴ Δία τοῖς εἰρημένοις προσαποδόντας, ὅτι πάσας ἔχουσα τὰς ἀρετὰς ἡ Δημοσθένους λέξις λείπεται εὐτραπελίας,[2] ἣν οἱ πολλοὶ καλοῦσι χάριν. πλεῖστον γὰρ αὐτῆς μετέχει μέρος . . .

Οὐ γάρ πως ἅμα πάντα θεοὶ δόσαν ἀνθρώποισιν,

ὧς[3] καὶ τοὺς ἀστεϊσμοὺς ἅμα ἐν τοῖς Δημοσθένους λόγοις. οὐδὲν γάρ, ὧν ἑτέροις τισὶν ἔδωκεν ἀγαθῶν ὁ δαίμων, ἐκείνῳ ἐφθόνησεν.

55 ἃ δέ γε Αἰσχίνης περὶ αὐτοῦ γράφει συκοφαντῶν, ὥσπερ ἔφην, τοτὲ μὲν ὡς πικροῖς καὶ περιέργοις ὀνόμασι χρωμένου, τοτὲ δ' ὡς ἀηδέσι καὶ φορτικοῖς, ῥᾳδίας ἔχει τὰς ἀπολογίας. εἴ γέ τοι βουληθείη τις χωρὶς ἕκαστον τῶν ἐγκλημάτων σκοπεῖν, τὰ μὲν ἐπαίνου μᾶλλον ἢ κατηγορίας ἄξια εὑρήσει, τὰ δ' οὐκ ἀληθῶς εἰρημένα ὑπ' αὐτοῦ. τὸ μὲν γὰρ πικραίνειν τὴν διάλεκτον, ὅταν ἀπαιτῶσιν οἱ καιροί (πολλάκις δὲ ἀπαιτοῦσι καὶ μάλιστα ἐν τοῖς παθητικοῖς τῶν ἐπιχειρημάτων), ἐγκώμιόν ἐστι τοῦ ῥήτορος, εἴ γε[4] δὴ τὸ ποιεῖν τὸν ἀκροατὴν αὐστηρὸν τῶν νόμων φύλακα καὶ πικρὸν ἐξεταστὴν τῶν ἀδικημάτων καὶ τιμωρὸν

[1] ἔχοι Reiske: ἔχει codd.
[2] εὐτραπελίας Sylburg: εὐτραπελείας codd.
[3] ὧς scripsi: ὡς codd.
[4] εἴ γε Sylburg: εἴτε codd.

speaker would destroy their noblest quality, animation, rendering them like a body that is beautiful, but is dead and cannot move. One could say much more on this subject, but as this treatise is already long enough I suppose I must conclude my discussion soon. However, I should certainly not end without adding one further comment, that with all its virtues, the style of Demosthenes is lacking in the ready wit which most people call "charm," a quality found in abundance. . . .

But, just as Homer says[1] that "the gods by no means bestow all their gifts at once on men," so it is with instances of urbanity in the speeches of Demosthenes. But fate did not begrudge him any of the other gifts which they bestowed on some of his rivals.

As I said, the criticisms which Aeschines maliciously 55
makes of him, on one occasion noting that he uses "harsh and laboured words,"[2] and on another that he uses "disgusting and vulgar words,"[3] can be easily rebutted. Anyone who considers these charges separately will find that the former quality deserves praise rather than blame, and that the latter is a false charge. For to say that his language is harsh, when the occasion demands harshness (and such occasions often arise, especially in arguments charged with emotion), is to praise the orator, particularly if we regard it either as the exclusive or as the primary function of rhetoric to make its hearers strict in main-

[1] *Iliad* iii. 320.
[2] 3. 229.
[3] 3. 166.

ἀπαραίτητον τῶν παρανομούντων παρὰ τῆς ῥητορικῆς δυνάμεως ἢ μόνον ἢ μάλιστα τῶν ἄλλων ἀπαιτοῦμεν.[1] ἀμήχανον δὲ τρυφεροῖς ὀνόμασι καλλωπίζοντα τὴν διάλεκτον ὀργὴν ἢ μῖσος ἢ τῶν παραπλησίων τι κινῆσαι παθῶν, ἀλλ' ἀνάγκη καὶ νοήματ' ἐξευρεῖν, ἃ δὴ τῶν τοιούτων ἔσται παθῶν ἀγωγά, καὶ ὀνόμασι τοιούτοις αὐτὰ περιλαβεῖν, οἷς πέφυκεν ἀκοὴ πικραίνεσθαι. εἰ μὲν οὖν μὴ κατὰ τὸν οἰκεῖον καιρὸν τῇ πικραινούσῃ διαλέκτῳ χρώμενον ἀπεδείκνυεν αὐτὸν ἢ πλεονάζοντα ἐν αὐτῇ καὶ τῆς ποσότητος ἀστοχοῦντα, εἰκότως ἂν ὡς ἁμαρτάνοντα διέβαλλεν. ὁ δὲ τούτων μὲν οὐδέτερον ἔχει δεικνύναι, κοινῶς δὲ διαβάλλει τὴν παθητικὴν διάλεκτον, οὖσαν ἐπιτηδειοτάτην εἰς πολιτικοὺς παραλαμβάνεσθαι λόγους, λεληθότα ἐγκώμια μεταφέρων εἰς τὰς κατηγορίας, ὥσπερ ἔφην.

56 τὰ δ' αὐτὰ καὶ περὶ τῆς περιέργου λέξεως ἔχοι τις ἂν εἰπεῖν πρὸς τὸν Αἰσχίνην, ἐπειδὴ καὶ ταύτην αὐτοῦ χλευάζει τὴν ἀρετήν. δεχέσθω δέ τις τὴν περιεργίαν τῶν ὀνομάτων ὑπ' αὐτοῦ ⟨λεγομένην⟩[2] λέγεσθαι νυνὶ περιττὴν ἐργασίαν καὶ ἐξηλλαγμένην τῶν ἐν ἔθει. οὐ γὰρ δή γε εἰ ὁ καθ' ἡμᾶς βίος πολλὰ καὶ ἄλλα εἰκῇ τιθεὶς ἐπὶ τοῖς πράγμασιν ὀνόματα καὶ ταύτην ἀδιαφόρως κυκλεῖ τὴν λέξιν ἐπὶ τῆς πολυπραγμοσύνης, οὕτω καὶ τοὺς ἀρχαίους εἰκὸς αὐτῇ κεχρῆσθαι. εἰ μὲν οὖν τὴν ἀκαιρίαν ἢ τὸν πλεονασμὸν τῆς ἐξηλλαγμένης ἑρμηνείας διασύρων καὶ ταῦτα εἴρηκεν, ὡς τοῦ Δημοσθένους περὶ ἑκάτερον αὐτῶν ἁμαρτάνοντος, ψεύδεται περιφανῶς. ὁ γὰρ ἀνὴρ ἐν μὲν

taining the law, severe in investigating crime and inexorable in punishing wrongdoers.[1] It is impossible to excite anger, hatred or similar emotions by using delicate and decorative language: sentiments must be found to induce such emotions, and these must be expressed in words which naturally offend the ear. Of course, if Aeschines had been able to show that Demosthenes chose the wrong time to use his harsh language, or to have misjudged the amount required and used it to excess, he could reasonably have censured him for his error. But he can prove neither of these things, and in making a general criticism of emotional language, which is in fact very suitable for political oratory, he is unconsciously praising Demosthenes in the act of censure, as I have said.

One could make the same reply to Aeschines's 56
charge of using laboured language, the other quality of Demosthenes's style which he ridicules. Let us assume that what he calls the laboured use of words is what we now call the richly-wrought, strange manner of composition: because the fact that our age, while attaching many other names to things at random, also gives indiscriminate currency to this expression in the sense of "over-activity," does not make it at all likely that the older writers also used it in this way. Therefore, if Aeschines actually made this remark in scoffing at Demosthenes's lack of taste or excessive recourse to strange expression, implying that he was at fault in both respects, he was clearly wrong. Demosthenes, on the frequent occasions

[1] Cf. *Antiquitates Romanae*, ii. 67.

---

[1] ἀπαιτοῦμεν Reiske: ἐπαινοῦμεν codd.
[2] λεγομένην inseruit Radermacher.

ταῖς δημηγορίαις καὶ τοῖς δημοσίοις ἀγῶσι πρὸς τὸ μέγεθος καὶ τὸ ἀξίωμα τῶν ὑποθέσεων ἀποβλέπων κέχρηται τῇ τοιαύτῃ κατασκευῇ πολλάκις, ἐν δὲ τοῖς ἰδιωτικοῖς λόγοις, οὓς περὶ μικρῶν συμβολαίων ἰδιώταις ἀνθρώποις γέγραφε, τὴν κοινὴν καὶ συνήθη λέξιν ἐπιτηδεύει, σπανίως δέ ποτε τὴν περιττὴν καὶ οὐδὲ ταύτην ἐπ' αὐτοφώρῳ, ἀλλ' ὥστε λαθεῖν. εἰ δὲ κἀνταῦθα τῷ γένει τῆς ἐξαλλαγῆς ὅλῳ πολεμῶν ταῦτ' εἴρηκεν Αἰσχίνης, ἄτοπόν τι ποιεῖ πρᾶγμα, ταύτην διασύρων τὴν δεινότητα, ἧς πλείστης τῷ ῥήτορι δεῖ. τὸ γὰρ μὴ τοῖς πολλοῖς ὁμοίως ἐκφέρειν τὰς νοήσεις, ἀλλ' ἐπὶ τὸ σεμνότερον καὶ ποιητικώτερον ἐκβιβάζειν τὴν ὀνομασίαν παρὰ τῆς πολιτικῆς δυνάμεως μάλιστα ἀπαιτοῦμεν.[1] ταῦτα μὲν οὖν ἐγκώμια τῆς Δημοσθένους δεινότητος ὄντα ὡς ἁμαρτήματα φέρων Αἰσχίνης οὐκ ἀληθῶς μέν, εὐλόγως δ' ἴσως, ἐχθρὸς ὢν καὶ οὐδὲν ἄλλο[2] διαβάλλειν δυνάμενος, ἀπερισκέπτως, ὡς ἐγὼ κρίνω, συκοφαντεῖ.

57 τὸ δὲ φάσκειν φορτικοῖς καὶ ἀηδέσι τοῖς ὀνόμασιν αὐτὸν κεχρῆσθαι πόθεν ἐπῆλθεν αὐτῷ λέγειν ὑπὲρ πάντα ἔγωγε τεθαύμακα. οὐδὲν γὰρ εὑρίσκω τούτων παρὰ Δημοσθένει κείμενον, ὧν εἰρηκέναι φησὶν αὐτὸν Αἰσχίνης, οἷον ὅτι "οὐ δεῖ τῆς φιλίας ἀπορρῆξαι τὴν συμμαχίαν" καὶ ὅτι "ἀμπελουργοῦσί τινες τὴν πόλιν" καὶ "ὑποτέτμηται τὰ νεῦρα τοῦ δήμου" καὶ "φορμορραφούμεθα" καὶ "ἐπὶ τὰ στενά τινες ὥσπερ τὰς βελόνας διείρουσιν," οἷς αὐτὸς ἐπιτίθησι διακωμῳδῶν· "ταῦτα δέ, ὦ κίναδος, τί ἐστι; ῥήματα ἢ

when he uses this style in speeches in debates and public lawsuits is paying due regard to the importance and the dignity of his subjects; but in the speeches he wrote for private clients in minor lawsuits, he uses ordinary, normal language, rarely any striking words, and even these not manifestly but inconspicuously. Here again, if Aeschines is quarrelling with the whole principle of employing unusual words, his attitude is extraordinary, since he is disparaging that aspect of an orator's brilliance that is his most necessary quality; for the ability to express his thoughts differently from the mass of the people, to extend his vocabulary to include more dignified and poetical language, is the faculty we most require in a politician. Thus Aeschines, falsely though perhaps plausibly, imputes as faults what are really tributes to Demosthenes's genius. In my judgment, his criticisms are the indiscriminate carpings of an enemy who can find no other ammunition for slander. As to his allegation that Demosthenes uses vulgar and disgusting words, how it occurred to him to make this charge I find the most baffling question of all; for I cannot find in his speeches any of the expressions which Aeschines ascribes to him, like "we must not *tear away* the alliance from our friendship,"[1] "certain men are *pruning* the city" and "the *sinews* of the state have been cut" and "we are being *sewn up like a mat*," and "certain men are *drawing us like needles* into tight places," to which he adds his own jesting question: "What are these, you rogue, phrases or

[1] iii. 72.

---

[1] ἀπαιτοῦμεν Reiske: ἀπαιτοῦντες MP.
[2] ἄλλο Reiske: μᾶλλον codd.

θαύματα;" οὐδέ γε ἄλλα τινὰ φορτικὰ καὶ ἀηδῆ ὀνόματα ἐν οὐδενὶ τῶν Δημοσθένους λόγων εὑρεῖν δεδύνημαι καὶ ταῦτα πέντε ἢ ἓξ μυριάδας στίχων ἐκείνου τοῦ ἀνδρὸς καταλελοιπότος. εἰ μέντοι τινὲς ἐν τοῖς ψευδεπιγράφοις εἰσὶ λόγοις ἀηδεῖς καὶ φορτικαὶ καὶ ἄγροικοι κατασκευαί, ὡς ἐν τοῖς [1] κατ' Ἀριστογείτονος β' καὶ ἐν τῇ ἀπολογίᾳ τῶν δώρων καὶ ἐν τῷ ⟨περὶ τοῦ⟩ [2] μὴ ἐκδοῦναι Ἅρπαλον καὶ ἐν τῷ κατὰ Νεαίρας καὶ ἐν τῷ περὶ τῶν πρὸς Ἀλέξανδρον συνθηκῶν ἐν ἄλλοις τε συχνοῖς, οὓς ὁ Δημοσθένης οὐκ ἔγραψεν, ἐν ἑτέρᾳ δηλοῦταί μοι πραγματείᾳ τὰ περὶ Δημοσθένη. καὶ περὶ μὲν ὧν Αἰσχίνης ἐπιτετίμηκεν αὐτῷ, ταῦτα ἱκανά.

58 ἤδη δέ που κἀκεῖνό τινες οἱ μὲν ὡς χαρακτηρικὸν οἱ δ' ὡς ἁμάρτημα τοῦ ῥήτορος ἐσημειώσαντο, λέγω δὲ τὸ πολλοῖς ὀνόμασι τὸ αὐτὸ πρᾶγμα δηλοῦν ἐνίοτε δή, οἷά ἐστι ταυτί· "Φιλίππῳ δ' ἐξέσται καὶ πράττειν καὶ ποιεῖν, ὅ τι βούλεται" καὶ "τὸν Μειδίαν τοῦτον οὐκ εἰδώς, ὅστις ποτ' ἐστίν, οὐδὲ γιγνώσκων" καὶ "τῆς ἀδελφῆς ἐναντίον κόρης ἔτι καὶ παιδὸς οὔσης" καὶ πάντα τὰ τοιαῦτα. ὅσοι μὲν οὖν ἰδίωμα τοῦ χαρακτῆρος αὐτὸ ἀποφαίνουσι τοῦ Δημοσθένους, ὀρθῶς λέγουσι· κέχρηται γὰρ αὐτῷ χρησίμως ὁ ἀνήρ, ὥσπερ καὶ τῇ τμητικῇ καὶ τῇ βραχυλογίᾳ πάντων γε μᾶλλον καὶ εὐκαιρότερον. ὅσοι δ' ἐν ἁμαρτήματος αὐτὸ μοίρᾳ φέρουσι, τὰς αἰτίας οὐκ ἐξητακότες,

[1] τοῖς Blass: τῇ codd.
[2] περὶ τοῦ inseruit Radermacher.

freaks?"[1] Nor have I been able to find any other vulgar or disgusting words in any of Demosthenes's speeches in spite of the fact that fifty or sixty thousand lines of the orator's speeches survive. If, however, there are some disgusting, vulgar and crude passages in the speeches that have been falsely ascribed to him, like the second speech *Against Aristogeiton*, the *Defence on the Bribery Charge*, the speech *On the Sheltering of Harpalus*, *Against Neaira*, *On the Treaty with Alexander* or in many others which Demosthenes did not write, that is another matter: the facts about Demosthenes are set out in another treatise of mine. That is enough concerning Aeschines's criticisms.

There is a further quality which some have noticed 58
as an idiosyncrasy, and others have imputed as a fault. I refer to his occasional use of several words to describe a single thing, like "Philip will be able to behave and do as he wishes"[2] and "not knowing or recognising who this man Midias was,"[3] and "in front of his sister who was still a girl and a child,"[4] and all other such cases. Those who say that this is an idiosyncrasy of Demosthenes are correct, for the orator makes effective use of it, just as he uses the clipped, brief style more often and with surer taste than any other orator. But those who class this use of pleonasm as a fault without examining the purpose behind his

[1] iii. 166.
[2] *Phil.* iii. 3.
[3] *Against Midias*, 78.
[4] *Against Midias*, 79.

δι᾽ ἃς εἰώθει πλεονάζειν ἐνίοτε ἐν τοῖς ὀνόμασιν, οὐ δεόντως αὐτοῦ κατηγοροῦσιν, ἀλλ᾽ ἐοίκασιν οἱ τοῦτο συκοφαντοῦντες τὴν βραχυλογίαν ἐκ παντὸς ἀπαιτεῖν, ἥν, ὅπερ εἶπον, παντὸς μᾶλλον καὶ εὐκαιρότερον παρέχεται, τῶν δὲ ἄλλων ἀρετῶν οὐδεμίαν, οὐκέτι συνορῶντες ὅτι καὶ τῆς σαφηνείας δεῖ στοχάζεσθαι τὸν ῥήτορα καὶ τῆς ἐναργείας καὶ τῆς αὐξήσεως καὶ τῆς περὶ τὴν σύνθεσιν τῶν ὀνομάτων εὐρυθμίας, ὑπὲρ ἅπαντα δὲ ταῦτα τοῦ παθητικήν τε καὶ ἠθικὴν καὶ ἐναγώνιον ποιεῖν τὴν λέξιν, ἐν οἷς ἐστιν ἡ πλείστη τοῦ πιθανοῦ μοῖρα. τούτων δὲ τῶν ἀρετῶν ἑκάστην οὐχ ἡ βραχυλογία κράτιστα δύναται ποιεῖν, ἀλλὰ καὶ ὁ πλεονασμὸς ἐνίων ὀνομάτων, ᾧ καὶ ὁ Δημοσθένης κέχρηται. ἔφερον δ᾽ ἄν σοι παραδείγματα τῶν εἰρημένων, εἰ μὴ κοπώδης ἔμελλον φανήσεσθαι πρὸς σὲ δῆτα λέγων. ταῦτα, ὦ κράτιστε Ἀμμαῖε, γράφειν εἴχομέν σοι περὶ τῆς Δημοσθένους λέξεως. ἐὰν δὲ σῴζῃ τὸ δαιμόνιον ἡμᾶς, καὶ περὶ τῆς πραγματικῆς αὐτοῦ δεινότητος, ἔτι μείζονος ἢ τοῦδε καὶ θαυμαστοτέρου θεωρήματος, ἐν τοῖς ἑξῆς γραφησομένοις ἀποδώσομέν σοι τὸν λόγον.

occasional use of it in his writing accuse him unjustly, and leave themselves open to the charge of always demanding brevity; which, as I have said, Demosthenes uses more frequently and with surer taste than anyone else. Such men require no other virtue, losing sight of the fact that, while the orator ought admittedly to aim at clarity, vividness, amplification and good rhythmical composition, he should aim above all at making his style capable of arousing emotion and evoking moral tone and assuming the force of live debate, because the art of persuasion depends most of all on these. The best means of achieving each of these qualities is not brevity, but the pleonastic use of certain words; which is what Demosthenes actually employs. I would have given you examples of what I have said but for the risk of becoming a bore, especially as it is you that I am addressing. That is all I have to say about the style of Demosthenes, my dear Ammaeus. If god preserves me, I shall present you in a subsequent treatise with an even longer and more remarkable account than this of his genius in the treatment of subject-matter.

THUCYDIDES

INTRODUCTION

Dionysius shared his profession with the subject of this essay. He is a historian criticising another historian for the benefit of a third,[1] and he does so with a practical attention to the tools of their common trade which earns our admiration for its thoroughness and evident appreciation of the difficulties of the task of writing history. No historian was more aware of these difficulties than Thucydides. He knew that the initial collection of reliable material was a formidable task,[2] that the temptation to court popularity by dramatising and romanticising the facts was great [3] and that there was more than one way of arranging historical material.[4] Dionysius is unequivocal in his praise of Thucydides's passion for truth, and for his judgment of motives and of individual character. He is less happy about Thucydides' seasonal arrangement of events, and shows by means of an analysis of book III how this arrangement destroys the continuity. He also points to contradictions, inconsistencies, obscurities and instances of false emphasis

[1] Q. Aelius Tubero. See G. W. Bowersock, *Augustus and the Greek World*. (Oxford) 1965 p. 129.

[2] i. 20.

[3] i. 22. 4.

[4] v. 20. 2–3.

in book I. One curious effect of these criticisms is that Dionysius and Thucydides appear to have exchanged their former roles: Dionysius has become the conscientious historian and Thucydides the rhetorician. Annalistic treatment enables Thucydides, with maximum dramatic effect, to juxtapose the Funeral Speech, with its lofty praise of Athens, and the Plague; and his dramatisation of the Melian affair, which Dionysius finds to be full of distasteful un-Athenian sentiments, serves to show the Athenian temper before the Sicilian Expedition. In some cases, on the other hand, Dionysius, writing after the composition of many highly emotionalised Hellenistic accounts of the capture and sacking of cities, finds Thucydides too cold and detached. Regarding the arrangement of book I, Dionysius's criticisms fail to take into account the fact that both the *Archaeologia* and the *Pentecontaetia* are, in their different ways, historical digests included to illustrate particular arguments which the historian has made concerning this war and wars in general. In any case, Dionysius's suggestion that book I would be improved by the removal of ch. 2–20 seems drastic, not to say arrogant. On the other hand, he has nothing but praise for Thucydides's celebrated narrative of the battle in the Great Harbour of Syracuse.[1] Although Dionysius is here discussing style, not subject-matter, Thucydides's treatment of this climactic event in the Sicilian Expedition satisfies the requirements of the right degree of emphasis for different historical episodes, which he has laid down in chs. 13–18.

The examination of Thucydides's style begins in ch. 22, and is wide-ranging. It begins with vocabu-

[1] ch. 27.

lary and word-order. Thucydides emerges as a true pioneer, not in the sense that the individual elements of his style were entirely new, but that he was the first historian to combine them. The elements are mostly those of the Grand Style, of which Thucydides has been named as a leading exponent in the *Demosthenes*.[1] But Dionysius also refers to his penchant for forming new substantives and for seeking variation, and to his use of Gorgianic figures.[2] After this excellent description of Thucydides's style a quotation from the opening chapters of the *History* is followed by a lacuna of some length, and when we return Dionysius is quoting a passage from book 4 (ch. 34). He criticises its tortuous structure and offers a clearer version of Thucydides's narrative. Then, after quoting with admiration the narrative of the battle in the Great Harbour of Syracuse, he turns to the famous excursus on revolution in book III 81ff., criticises it for its circuitous structure and obscure language and once more offers a clearer alternative. Some modern students might prefer Dionysius's version, but if they were to do so they would be seen to share his incomplete understanding of Thucydides's view of history. He betrays it when he describes this and similar passages as "narratives" (διηγήματα):[3] they are concerned not with action but with the study of human psychology, a subject which was central to Thucydides's conception of history. He appreciated its complexities and considered that it required an elevated, allusive style which was entirely different from that used in the narration of events.

[1] ch. 39.
[2] ch. 24.
[3] ch. 33.

When he comes to consider Thucydides's speeches in ch. 34, subject-matter precedes style once more. Since speeches are the products of the historian's invention to a greater extent than narrative, the question of the appropriateness of the words to the occasion, to the speaker and to the audience is important. Once again Dionysius contrasts good with bad. Firstly, two dialogues: he praises the dialogue between the Plataeans and the Spartans in book 2. 71–75 for its purity, lucidity and brevity, Lysianic qualities appropriate to a quasi-forensic setting. The Melian Dialogue, on the other hand, he finds offensive on grounds of both style and argument. The latter in particular offends his sense of propriety: the sentiments expressed are both unworthy of Athens and inappropriate to the situation. Dionysius's historical sense has deserted him, and the hidebound rhetorician has taken over: consequently it has not occurred to him that one of the purposes of the Melian dialogue was to dramatise the consummation of a process of change from imperial idealism, such as is portrayed in the Funeral Speech of Pericles, to the mentality of stark power politics which increasingly dominated the actions of his successors to the leadership of Athens. After these dialogues Dionysius continues to balance criticism with praise, and gives a catalogue of speeches which he admires, followed by one of those of which he does not approve. From the latter he selects two for more detailed criticism. Once more the rhetorical criterion of appropriateness dominates the discussion, but some of his stylistic criticisms are reasonable, and consistent with his judgments elsewhere. Nevertheless it is a pity that Dionysius did not approach Thucydides in this essay

with a more open mind and more of the adventurous spirit of *νεωτεροποιΐα* (innovation) and *τὸ τολμηρόν* (enterprise) which the Spartans had found in the Athenians,[1] and which Dionysius himself had previously found in Thucydides.[2] After all, Thucydides regarded his style as a challenge to his readers, not as mere entertainment, and there is no reason to believe that he would have seen any sense in attempts to compare his speeches with those delivered in the law-courts and assemblies of his day. Again, Dionysius surely exaggerates the difficulties which his style presented to his contemporaries in Augustan Rome. There interest in Thucydides arose out of Atticism,[3] and Cicero attempted to check this,[4] but his opposition stimulated men who found his own style uncongenial to turn to the historian whose style he had criticised. Among these was Sallust, and there may have been others, including no doubt many writers of lesser talent who responded superficially to the more obvious Thucydidean traits.[5]

Finally we return to Dionysius's hero Demosthenes, who finds a place in the essay as Thucydides's most distinguished imitator. The pupil is persuaded that this is Thucydides's greatest literary achievement. In spite of this, however, Dionysius has succeeded in this essay in showing how Thucydides stood out in relation to his predecessors and contemporaries in the field of historiography. He has also made many valid criticisms of his style. Partisanship does not appear

[1] Thucydides i. 102. 3.
[2] *Demosthenes*, 2.
[3] See R. Syme, *Sallust* (Cambridge, 1964) p. 52.
[4] *Brutus*, 95. 325.
[5] Syme, *loc. cit.*

until the final chapters, and by then we have a sound idea of the critic's own limitations. Altogether, the *Thucydides* is the most thorough and balanced of his critical essays on individual authors.

ΔΙΟΝΥΣΙΟΥ ΑΛΙΚΑΡΝΑΣΕΩΣ
ΠΕΡΙ ΘΟΥΚΥΔΙΔΟΥ

1 Ἐν τοῖς προεκδοθεῖσι περὶ τῆς μιμήσεως ὑπομνηματισμοῖς ἐπεληλυθὼς οὓς ὑπελάμβανον ἐπιφανεστάτους εἶναι ποιητάς τε καὶ συγγραφεῖς, ὦ Κόιντε Αἴλιε Τουβέρων, καὶ δεδηλωκὼς ἐν ὀλίγοις, τίνας [1] ἕκαστος αὐτῶν εἰσφέρεται πραγματικάς τε καὶ λεκτικὰς ἀρετάς, καὶ πῇ μάλιστα χείρων ἑαυτοῦ γίνεται κατὰ τὰς ἀποτυχίας, εἴ τε τῆς προαιρέσεως οὐχ ἅπαντα κατὰ τὸν ἀκριβέστατον λογισμὸν ὁρώσης εἴ τε τῆς δυνάμεως οὐκ ἐν ἅπασι τοῖς ἔργοις κατορθούσης, ἵνα τοῖς προαιρουμένοις γράφειν τε καὶ λέγειν εὖ καλοὶ καὶ δεδοκιμασμένοι κανόνες ὦσιν, ἐφ᾿ ὧν ποιήσονται τὰς κατὰ μέρος γυμνασίας μὴ πάντα μιμούμενοι τὰ παρ᾿ ἐκείνοις κείμενα τοῖς ἀνδράσιν, ἀλλὰ τὰς μὲν ἀρετὰς αὐτῶν λαμβάνοντες, τὰς δ᾿ ἀποτυχίας φυλαττόμενοι· ἁψάμενός τε τῶν συγγραφέων ἐδήλωσα καὶ περὶ Θουκυδίδου τὰ δοκοῦντά μοι, συντόμῳ τε καὶ κεφαλαιώδει γραφῇ περιλαβών, οὐ δι᾿ ὀλιγωρίαν καὶ ῥᾳστώνην οὐδὲ διὰ σπάνιν τῶν δυνησομένων βεβαιῶσαι τὰς προθέσεις, ἀλλὰ τῆς εὐκαιρίας τῶν γραφομένων στοχαζόμενος, ὡς

[1] τίνας Krüger: τινὰς ἃς MP.

ON THUCYDIDES

In the treatise *On Imitation* [1] which I published earlier, Quintus Aelius Tubero,[2] I discussed those poets and prose authors whom I considered to be outstanding. I indicated briefly the good qualities of content and style contributed by each, and where his failings caused him to fall furthest below his own standards, either because his purpose did not enable him to grasp the scope of his subject in the fullest detail, or because his literary powers did not measure up to it throughout the whole of his work. I did this in order that those who intend to become good writers and speakers should have sound and approved standards by which to carry out their individual exercises, not imitating all the qualities of these authors, but adopting their good qualities and guarding against their failings. When I came to deal with the historians, I gave my opinion of Thucydides, but expressed it in a brief and summary manner. This I did not because I thought little of him or because I was lazy, nor because I was short of arguments to support my statements: I was brief because I was concerned with presenting my material on a scale appropriate to the work in hand; and I treated the 1

[1] An earlier work consisting of three essays: (1) *On the Nature of Imitation*; (2) *Authors to be imitated*; (3) *Technique of Imitation*. See *Letter to Pompeius*, 3.

[2] See note 1, p. 456.

καὶ περὶ τῶν ἄλλων ἐποίησα. οὐ γὰρ ἦν ἀκριβῆ καὶ διεξοδικὴν δήλωσιν ὑπὲρ ἑκάστου τῶν ἀνδρῶν ποιεῖσθαι, προελόμενον εἰς ἐλάχιστον ὄγκον συναγαγεῖν τὴν πραγματείαν. σοῦ δὲ βουληθέντος ἰδίαν συντάξασθαί με περὶ Θουκυδίδου γραφὴν ἅπαντα περιειληφυῖαν τὰ δεόμενα λόγων, ἀναβαλόμενος τὴν περὶ Δημοσθένους πραγματείαν, ἣν εἶχον ἐν χερσίν, ὑπεσχόμην τε ποιήσειν, ὡς προῃροῦ, καὶ τελέσας τὴν ὑπόσχεσιν ἀποδίδωμι.

2 Μέλλων δὲ τῶν κατὰ μέρος ἅπτεσθαι λόγων, ὀλίγα περὶ ἐμαυτοῦ τε καὶ τοῦ γένους τῆς πραγματείας βούλομαι προειπεῖν· οὐ σοῦ μὰ Δία καὶ τῶν σοὶ παραπλησίων ἕνεκα, τῶν ἀπὸ παντὸς τοῦ βελτίστου κρινόντων τὰ πράγματα καὶ μηδὲν ἡγουμένων χρῆμα τιμιώτερον τῆς ἀληθείας· ἀλλὰ τῶν ἄλλων, ὅσοις πολὺ τὸ [1] φιλαίτιον ἔνεστιν ⟨εἴτε κατὰ τὸν ζῆλον⟩ [2] τῶν ἀρχαίων γινόμενον [3] εἴτε κατὰ τὴν ὑπεροψίαν τῶν ἐπὶ τῆς αὐτῆς ἡλικίας εἴτε κατ᾽ ἀμφότερα ταῦτα τὰ πάθη κοινὰ τῆς ἀνθρωπίνης ὄντα φύσεως. ὑποπτεύω γὰρ ἔσεσθαί τινας τῶν ἀναγνωσομένων τὴν γραφὴν τοὺς ἐπιτιμήσοντας ἡμῖν, ὅτι τολμῶμεν ἀποφαίνειν Θουκυδίδην τὸν ἁπάντων κράτιστον τῶν ἱστοριογράφων καὶ κατὰ τὴν προαίρεσίν ποτε τῶν λόγων ἁμαρτάνοντα καὶ κατὰ τὴν δύναμιν ἐξασθενοῦντα, καὶ διὰ τοῦθ᾽ οὗτος ἡμᾶς ὁ λογισμὸς εἰσῆλθεν, ὅτι παράδοξα καινοτομεῖν πράγματα πρῶτοι καὶ μόνοι δόξομεν, εἴ τι τῶν ὑπὸ Θουκυδίδου γραφέντων συκοφαντεῖν ἐπιβαλοίμεθα, οὐ ταῖς κοιναῖς μόνον [4] ἐναντιούμενοι δόξαις, ἃς

[1] ὅσοις πολὺ τὸ Radermacher: ὅσοις τὸ αὐτὸ MP.

other authors in the same way. It was not possible to give a detailed and thorough critique of each author's work when I had chosen to reduce my material to the smallest possible quantity. But when you expressed the desire that I should write a separate essay on Thucydides, including everything that required comment, I promised to set aside the work on Demosthenes that I had in hand, and do as you preferred.[1] Here is the essay, in fulfilment of my promise.

Since I intend to deal with my subject in detail, I 2
wish to begin with a few words about my own attitude and about this form of treatment. I do this not with you in mind and those like you, who are completely honest in your judgments and value nothing more highly than the truth, but on account of all those others who take great delight in finding fault, whether because they envy the writers of old or because they despise their own contemporaries, or for both these reasons, which are common human failings. I suspect that some readers of this treatise will censure me for daring to express the view that Thucydides, the greatest of the historians, is occasionally at fault in his choice of subject-matter and very weak in his powers of expression. Consequently, the thought has occurred to me that I shall seem like a lone pioneer breaking new and unexpected ground if I take it upon myself to discredit any part of Thucydides's work: for I should not only be going against a

[1] See Introduction, p. xxiv.

---

[2] hiatum supplevit Kiessling.
[3] γινόμενον Mestwerdt: γινομένων MP.
[4] μόνον Kiessling: μόναις MP.

ἅπαντες ἐκ τοῦ μακροῦ χρόνου παραλαβόντες ἀναφαιρέτους ἔχουσιν, ἀλλὰ καὶ ταῖς ἰδίαις τῶν ἐπιφανεστάτων φιλοσόφων τε καὶ ῥητόρων μαρτυρίαις ἀπιστοῦντες, οἳ κανόνα τῆς ἱστορικῆς πραγματείας ἐκεῖνον ὑποτίθενται τὸν ἄνδρα καὶ τῆς περὶ τοὺς πολιτικοὺς λόγους δεινότητος ὅρον· ὧν οὔτε προαιρέσεις ἰσχυρᾶς . . .[1] ταύτας δὴ τὰς ἐπιτιμήσεις ἀπολύσασθαι βουλόμενος ἐχούσας τι θεατρικὸν καὶ τῶν πολλῶν ἀγωγόν, περὶ μὲν ἐμαυτοῦ τοσοῦτον ἀρκεσθήσομαι μόνον εἰπών, ὅτι τὸ φιλόνεικον τοῦτο καὶ δύσερι καὶ προσυλακτοῦν εἰκῇ πᾶσιν ἐν παντὶ πεφυλαγμένος τῷ βίῳ μέχρι τοῦ παρόντος καὶ οὐδεμίαν ἐκδεδωκὼς γραφήν, ἐν ᾗ κατηγορῶ τινος, ἔξω μιᾶς πραγματείας, ἣν συνεταξάμην ὑπὲρ τῆς πολιτικῆς φιλοσοφίας πρὸς τοὺς κατατρέχοντας αὐτῆς ἀδίκως, οὐκ ἂν ἐπεχείρησα νῦν πρῶτον εἰς τὸν ἐπιφανέστατον τῶν συγγραφέων τὴν οὔτ' ἐλευθέροις ἤθεσι πρέπουσαν οὔτ' ἐμαυτῷ συνήθη κακοήθειαν ἐναποδείκνυσθαι. περὶ δὲ τοῦ γένους τῆς γραφῆς πλείονα μὲν εἶχον λέγειν, ἀρκεσθήσομαι δὲ ὀλίγοις. εἰ δὲ ἀληθεῖς καὶ προσήκοντας ἐμαυτῷ προῄρημαι λόγους, σύ τε κρινεῖς καὶ τῶν ἄλλων φιλολόγων ἕκαστος.

3 Ἔστι δὴ τὸ βούλημά μου τῆς πραγματείας οὐ καταδρομὴ τῆς Θουκυδίδου προαιρέσεώς τε καὶ δυνάμεως, οὐδ' ἐκλογισμὸς τῶν ἁμαρτημάτων οὐδ' ἐξευτελισμὸς οὐδ' ἄλλο τι τοιοῦτον ἔργον οὐδέν, ἐν ᾧ τὰ μὲν κατορθώματα καὶ τὰς ἀρετὰς οὐδενὸς ἠξίωκα λόγου, τοῖς δὲ μὴ κατὰ τὸ κράτιστον εἰρημένοις ἐπιφύομαι· ἐκλογισμὸς δέ

[1] lacunam indicavit Reiske.

prevalent opinion established through a long tradition and firmly entrenched in all men's minds, but should also be making light of the personal testimony of the most distinguished philosophers and rhetoricians, who regard that author as a model historian and the standard of excellence in deliberative oratory. And yet the principles on which his methods were based are not irrefragable. . . . Although I wish to clear myself of these counter-criticisms, which have a certain specious attractiveness for the majority, I shall be content to say no more on my own account than this: that throughout my life hitherto I have avoided this quarrelsome, contentious and indiscriminately carping spirit; I have never published anything censorious, except one treatise which I wrote in defence of political philosophy,[1] in which I attacked its unfair detractors; and I should never have attempted, now for the first time, to display against the most distinguished of the historians a malice which is neither fitting for a man of a generous disposition, nor in keeping with my nature. I could have said more about the form of this treatise, but will be content with a few words. You and other scholars must each judge for himself the truth and fairness of the arguments on which I have relied.

The purpose of this treatise is certainly not to dis- 3
parage Thucydides's chosen subject or his ability to treat it, or to pick out his faults and belittle him, or to make any criticism which discounts his successes and his virtues and concentrates upon his less effective utterances. My examination will consider the

[1] This work has not survived. See Introd. pp. xvi, xxvi.

τις τοῦ χαρακτῆρος τῶν λόγων, ἅπαντα περιειληφώς, ὅσα συμβέβηκεν αὐτῷ κοινά τε πρὸς ἑτέρους καὶ διαφέροντα παρὰ τοὺς ἄλλους. ἐν οἷς ἀναγκαῖον ἦν μὴ τὰς ἀρετὰς λέγεσθαι μόνον, ἀλλὰ καὶ τὰς γειτνιώσας αὐταῖς κακίας. οὐδεμία γὰρ αὐτάρκης ἀνθρώπου φύσις οὔτ' ἐν λόγοις οὔτ' ἐν ἔργοις ἀναμάρτητος εἶναι, κρατίστη δὲ ἡ πλεῖστα μὲν ἐπιτυγχάνουσα, ἐλάχιστα δὲ ἀστοχοῦσα. ἐπὶ ταύτην δὴ τὴν ὑπόθεσιν ἀναφέρων ἕκαστος τὰ ῥηθησόμενα μὴ τῆς προαιρέσεώς μου γενέσθω κατήγορος, ἀλλὰ τῶν ἰδίων τοῦ χαρακτῆρος ἔργων ἐξεταστὴς δίκαιος. ὅτι δ' οὐκ ἐγὼ τοῦτο πρῶτος ἐπικεχείρηκα ποιεῖν, ἀλλὰ πολλοὶ καὶ πάλαι καὶ καθ' ἡμᾶς, οὐ φιλαπεχθήμονας προελόμενοι γραφὰς ἀλλὰ θεωρητικὰς τῆς ἀληθείας, μυρίους παρασχέσθαι δυνάμενος μάρτυρας, δυεῖν ἀνδράσιν ἀρκεσθήσομαι μόνοις, Ἀριστοτέλει καὶ Πλάτωνι. Ἀριστοτέλης τε γὰρ οὐχ ἅπαντα κατὰ τὸ κράτιστον εἰρῆσθαι πείθεται τῷ καθηγητῇ Πλάτωνι· ὧν ἐστι τὰ περὶ τῆς ἰδέας καὶ τὰ περὶ τἀγαθοῦ καὶ τὰ περὶ τῆς πολιτείας· αὐτός τε ὁ Πλάτων Παρμενίδην καὶ Πρωταγόραν καὶ Ζήνωνα καὶ τῶν ἄλλων φυσιολόγων οὐκ ὀλίγους ἡμαρτηκότας ἀποδεικνύναι βούλεται· καὶ οὐδεὶς αὐτῷ κατ' αὐτό γε τοῦτο ἐπιτιμᾷ, ἐνθυμούμενος ὅτι τῆς φιλοσόφου θεωρίας σκοπός ἐστιν ἡ τῆς ἀληθείας γνῶσις, ἀφ' ἧς καὶ τὸ τοῦ βίου τέλος γίνεται φανερόν. ὅπου δὴ τοὺς περὶ δογμάτων διαφερομένους οὐδεὶς μέμφεται τῆς προαιρέσεως, εἰ μὴ πάντα τὰ τῶν πρεσβυτέρων ἐπαινοῦσιν, ἦ που τούς γε προελομένους χαρακτήρων ἰδιότητα δηλῶσαι

character of his style in all its aspects, and will distinguish which qualities he has in common with others and which are peculiar to him alone. This makes it necessary for me to mention not only his virtues, but also the vices which are associated with them. No complete human being has the self-sufficiency to be infallible in either word or deed: the best is the man who hits the mark most often, and misses it least. Every reader should apply this assumption to what I am about to say, and not criticise my choice of subject, but examine fairly the peculiar effects of Thucydides's style. I am not the first to attempt such a task: many ancient and modern writers have tried to do the same, writing not in a contentious spirit but in order to discover the truth. I can produce innumerable witnesses to this statement, but I shall be content with two, Plato and Aristotle. Aristotle does not believe that his master Plato said the last word on all subjects, including his account of the Forms, the Good and the Ideal State; and Plato himself tries to show that Parmenides, Protagoras, Zeno [1] and several other of the natural philosophers were wrong. Nobody criticises him merely for this, for it is recognised that the goal of philosophical studies is the discovery of the truth, by which the purpose of life itself is revealed. Therefore, since nobody questions the purpose of those who argue about philosophical doctrines if they do not approve of all their predecessors' conclusions, why should literary critics who have chosen to describe an author's individual style be censured when they do not ascribe to it all the quali-

[1] Zeno of Elea, the 5th-century philosopher.

μέμψαιτ' ἄν τις, εἰ μὴ πάσας μαρτυροῦσι τοῖς πρὸ αὐτῶν καὶ τὰς μὴ προσούσας ἀρετάς;

4 Ἓν ἔτι λείπεταί μοι μέρος ἀπολογίας δεόμενον, ἐπίφθονον μέν τι κατηγόρημα καὶ τοῖς πολλοῖς κεχαρισμένον, ῥᾳδίως δ' ἐξελεγχθῆναι δυνησόμενον, ὡς οὐκ ἔστιν ὑγιές. οὐ γὰρ εἰ τῇ δυνάμει λειπόμεθα Θουκυδίδου τε καὶ τῶν ἄλλων ἀνδρῶν, καὶ τὸ θεωρητικὸν αὐτῶν ἀπολωλέκαμεν. οὐδὲ γὰρ τὰς Ἀπελλοῦ[1] καὶ Ζεύξιδος καὶ Πρωτογένους καὶ τῶν ἄλλων γραφέων τῶν διωνομασμένων τέχνας οἱ μὴ τὰς αὐτὰς ἔχοντες ἐκείνοις ἀρετὰς κρίνειν κεκώλυνται, οὐδὲ τὰ Φειδίου καὶ Πολυκλείτου καὶ Μύρωνος ἔργα οἱ μὴ τηλικοῦτοι δημιουργοί. ἐῶ γὰρ λέγειν, ὅτι πολλῶν ἔργων οὐχ ἧττων τοῦ τεχνίτου κριτὴς ὁ ἰδιώτης, τῶν τε δι' αἰσθήσεως ἀλόγου καὶ τοῖς πάθεσι καταλαμβανομένων, καὶ ὅτι πᾶσα τέχνη τούτων στοχάζεται τῶν κριτηρίων καὶ ἀπὸ τούτων λαμβάνει τὴν ἀρχήν. ἅλις ἔστω μοι προοιμίων, ἵνα μὴ λάθω περὶ ταῦτα κατατρίψας τὸν λόγον.

5 Μέλλων δὲ ἄρχεσθαι τῆς περὶ Θουκυδίδου γραφῆς ὀλίγα βούλομαι περὶ τῶν ἄλλων συγγραφέων εἰπεῖν, τῶν τε πρεσβυτέρων καὶ τῶν κατὰ τοὺς αὐτοὺς ἀκμασάντων ἐκείνῳ χρόνους, ἐξ ὧν ἔσται καταφανὴς ἥ τε προαίρεσις τοῦ ἀνδρός, ᾗ χρησάμενος διήλλαξε τοὺς πρὸ αὐτοῦ, καὶ ἡ δύναμις. ἀρχαῖοι μὲν οὖν συγγραφεῖς πολλοὶ καὶ κατὰ πολλοὺς τόπους ἐγένοντο πρὸ τοῦ

[1] Ἀπελλοῦ Krüger: ἀπέλλου codd.

---

[1] The most important of the logographers listed here and below are Hecataeus, whose *Periegesis* was probably one of

ties allowed to it by earlier critics, when these include some which it does not possess?

4 One further question remains to be answered; it is an odious charge and is in favour in popular quarters, but it can easily be shown to be unsound. The fact that I fall short of Thucydides and other authors in ability does not mean that I have forfeited the right to examine their style. Men who do not possess the same artistic powers as Apelles, Zeuxis, Protogenes and the other famous painters have not been barred from passing judgment on their work; and the same is true of the lesser craftsmen who have appraised the sculpture of Phidias, Polyclitus and Myron. I need not say that the layman is as competent a judge of many things as the expert—those things which are apprehended by the irrational senses and the feelings—and that these are the faculties which all forms of art aim to stimulate and are the reason for its creation. That much must suffice for my introduction, so that I may not waste words on this subject however unconsciously.

5 Before I begin to write about Thucydides I propose to say a little about the other historians, both his predecessors and those who flourished during his lifetime. This will show both his purpose, in which he surpassed his predecessors, and his special talents. There were many early historians in many places before the Peloponnesian War,[1] including Eugeon of

Herodotus's chief literary sources; Charon, a contemporary of Herodotus who wrote on the Persian Wars; Xanthus, whose strange tales had an Eastern flavour; and Hellanicus, an older contemporary of Thucydides who recorded many important facts of Athenian local history. See Pearson, *The Early Ionian Historians*; Usher, *The Historians of Greece and Rome*, pp. 2–3, 25–26.

Πελοποννησιακοῦ πολέμου· ἐν οἷς ἐστιν Εὐγέων τε ὁ Σάμιος καὶ Δηίοχος ὁ Προκοννήσιος καὶ Εὔδημος ὁ Πάριος καὶ Δημοκλῆς ὁ Φυγελεὺς καὶ Ἑκαταῖος ὁ Μιλήσιος, ὅ τε Ἀργεῖος Ἀκουσίλαος καὶ ὁ Λαμψακηνὸς Χάρων καὶ ὁ Καλχηδόνιος Μελησαγόρας,[1] ὀλίγῳ δὲ πρεσβύτεροι τῶν Πελοποννησιακῶν καὶ μέχρι τῆς Θουκυδίδου παρεκτείναντες ἡλικίας Ἑλλάνικός τε ὁ Λέσβιος καὶ Δαμάστης ὁ Σιγειεὺς [2] καὶ Ξενομήδης ὁ Χῖος καὶ Ξάνθος ὁ Λυδὸς καὶ ἄλλοι συχνοί. οὗτοι προαιρέσει τε ὁμοίᾳ ἐχρήσαντο περὶ τὴν ἐκλογὴν τῶν ὑποθέσεων καὶ δυνάμεις οὐ πολύ τι διαφερούσας ἔσχον ἀλλήλων, οἱ μὲν τὰς Ἑλληνικὰς ἀναγράφοντες ἱστορίας, οἱ δὲ τὰς βαρβαρικάς, [καὶ] [3] αὐτάς τε ταύτας οὐ συνάπτοντες ἀλλήλαις, ἀλλὰ κατ' ἔθνη καὶ κατὰ πόλεις διαιροῦντες καὶ χωρὶς ἀλλήλων ἐκφέροντες, ἕνα καὶ τὸν αὐτὸν φυλάττοντες σκοπόν, ὅσαι διεσῴζοντο παρὰ τοῖς ἐπιχωρίοις μνῆμαι κατὰ ἔθνη τε καὶ κατὰ πόλεις, εἴ τ' ἐν ἱεροῖς εἴ τ' ἐν βεβήλοις ἀποκείμεναι γραφαί, ταύτας εἰς τὴν κοινὴν ἁπάντων γνῶσιν ἐξενεγκεῖν, οἵας παρέλαβον, μήτε προστιθέντες αὐταῖς τι μήτε ἀφαιροῦντες· ἐν αἷς καὶ μῦθοί τινες ἐνῆσαν ἀπὸ τοῦ πολλοῦ πεπιστευμένοι χρόνου καὶ θεατρικαί τινες περιπέτειαι πολὺ τὸ ἠλίθιον ἔχειν τοῖς νῦν δοκοῦσαι· λέξιν τε ὡς ἐπὶ τὸ πολὺ τὴν αὐτὴν ἅπαντες ἐπιτηδεύσαντες, ὅσοι τοὺς αὐτοὺς προείλοντο τῶν διαλέκτων χαρακτῆρας, τὴν σαφῆ καὶ κοινὴν καὶ καθαρὰν καὶ σύντομον καὶ τοῖς πράγμασι προσφυῆ καὶ μηδεμίαν σκευωρίαν ἐπιφαίνουσαν τεχνικήν· ἐπιτρέχει μέντοι τις ὥρα τοῖς ἔργοις

Samos, Deiochus of Proconnesus, Eudemus of Paros, Democles of Phygele, Hecataeus of Miletus, Acusilaus of Argos, Charon of Lampsacus and Melesagoras of Calchedon. Among those who were born not long before the Peloponnesian War and survived into Thucydides's own lifetime were Hellanicus of Lesbos, Damastes of Sigeum, Xenomedes of Chios, Xanthus of Lydia and many others. These men chose their subjects on similar principles and did not differ greatly in ability. Some wrote Greek history, others that of foreign lands, without any connection but divided up by single tribes and cities and published separately. They all had the same aim: to make generally known the traditions of the past as they found them preserved in local monuments and religious and secular records in the various tribal and urban centres, without adding to or subtracting from them. These accounts contained some stories which had been believed from remote antiquity, and many dramatic tales of changing fortunes which men of today would think quite silly. Those who wrote in the same dialect also tended to employ the same sort of diction—clear, ordinary, pure, concise, suited to the events and exhibiting no artificial trappings. And

[1] *Χαλκηδόνιος* codd. Μεληαγόρας Dudith: ἀμεληαγόρας codd.

[2] Σιγειεὺς Krüger: *ὁ σιγεὺς* M.

[3] *καὶ* delevit Radermacher.

αὐτῶν καὶ χάρις, τοῖς μὲν πλείων, τοῖς δ' ἐλάττων, δι' ἣν ἔτι μένουσιν αὐτῶν αἱ γραφαί. ὁ δ' Ἁλικαρνασεὺς Ἡρόδοτος, γενόμενος ὀλίγῳ πρότερον τῶν Περσικῶν, παρεκτείνας δὲ μέχρι τῶν Πελοποννησιακῶν, τήν τε πραγματικὴν προαίρεσιν ἐπὶ τὸ μεῖζον ἐξήνεγκε καὶ λαμπρότερον, οὔτε πόλεως μιᾶς οὔτ' ἔθνους ἑνὸς ἱστορίαν προελόμενος ἀναγράψαι, πολλὰς δὲ καὶ διαφόρους πράξεις ἔκ τε τῆς Εὐρώπης ἔκ τε τῆς Ἀσίας εἰς μιᾶς[1] περιγραφὴν πραγματείας συναγαγεῖν[2] (ἀρξάμενος γοῦν ἀπὸ τῆς τῶν Λυδῶν δυναστείας μέχρι τοῦ Περσικοῦ πολέμου κατεβίβασε τὴν ἱστορίαν, πάσας τὰς ἐν τοῖς κʹ καὶ διακοσίοις ἔτεσι γενομένας πράξεις ἐπιφανεῖς Ἑλλήνων τε καὶ βαρβάρων μιᾷ συντάξει περιλαβών), καὶ τῇ λέξει προσαπέδωκε τὰς παραλειφθείσας ὑπὸ τῶν πρὸ αὐτοῦ συγγραφέων ἀρετάς.

6 Τούτοις ἐπιγενόμενος Θουκυδίδης οὔτ' ἐφ' ἑνὸς ἐβουλήθη τόπου καθιδρῦσαι τὴν ἱστορίαν, ὡς οἱ περὶ τὸν Ἑλλάνικον ἐποίησαν, οὔτε τὰς ἐξ ἁπάσης χώρας Ἕλλησιν ἢ βαρβάροις ἐπιτελεσθείσας πράξεις εἰς μίαν ἱστορίαν συναγαγεῖν, μιμησάμενος Ἡρόδοτον· τῆς μὲν προτέρας ὑπεριδὼν ὡς εὐτελοῦς καὶ ταπεινῆς καὶ πολλὰ οὐ δυνησομένης τοὺς ἀναγινώσκοντας ὠφελῆσαι· τῆς δ' ὑστέρας ὡς μείζονος ἢ δυνατῆς πεσεῖν εἰς σύνοψιν ἀνθρωπίνου λογισμοῦ κατὰ τὸν ἀκριβέστατον τῶν τρόπων· ἕνα δὲ προχειρισάμενος πόλεμον, ὃν ἐπολέμησαν Ἀθηναῖοι καὶ Πελοποννήσιοι πρὸς ἀλλήλους, τοῦτον ἐσπούδασεν ἀναγράψαι· ἐρρωμένος τε τὸ

[1] μιᾶς Krüger: μίαν codd.

yet their writings are tinged with a certain freshness and charm, some more than others, and this has ensured their survival. But Herodotus of Halicarnassus, who was born shortly before the Persian War[1] and survived into the Peloponnesian War, enlarged the scope and added to the splendour of the subject. He chose not to record the history of one city or of a single nation, but to gather together accounts of many different events which occurred in Europe and Asia, and assemble them in a single comprehensive work. He made the Lydian Empire his starting-point, and brought his account down to the Persian War, including in a single narrative all the important events which occurred in the Greek and barbarian world during this period of two hundred and twenty years; furthermore, he invested his style with all the virtues which previous historians had neglected.

Thucydides came after these historians, but he did 6
not wish to confine his history to a single locality, as Hellanicus and his imitators had done, nor to follow Herodotus and bring together into a single history the deeds accomplished by Greeks and barbarians all over the world. The first he considered a paltry and unambitious subject, and one not likely to give its readers much edification; the second he thought too large a subject for the human mind to study in the closest detail. He therefore took one war, that in which the Athenians and the Peloponnesians fought against one another, and applied himself exclusively to the task of plotting its course. He retained his

[1] *i.e.* The Expedition of Xerxes, 480–479 B.C.

---

[2] συναγαγεῖν Sadée: ἀγαγεῖν codd.

σῶμα καὶ τὴν διάνοιαν ὑγιαίνων καὶ μέχρι παντὸς αὐτοῦ βιώσας, καὶ οὐκ ἐκ τῶν ἐπιτυχόντων ἀκουσμάτων τὰς πράξεις συντιθείς, ἀλλ' οἷς μὲν αὐτὸς παρῆν, ἐξ ἐμπειρίας, ὧν δ' ἀπελείφθη διὰ τὴν φυγήν, παρὰ τῶν ἄριστα γινωσκόντων πυνθανόμενος. πρῶτον μὲν δὴ κατὰ τοῦτο διήλλαξε τῶν πρὸ αὐτοῦ συγγραφέων, λέγω δὲ κατὰ τὸ λαβεῖν ὑπόθεσιν μήτε μονόκωλον παντάπασι μήτ' εἰς πολλὰ μεμερισμένην καὶ ἀσυνάρτητα κεφάλαια· ἔπειτα κατὰ τὸ μηδὲν αὐτῇ μυθῶδες προσάψαι, μηδ' εἰς ἀπάτην καὶ γοητείαν τῶν πολλῶν ἐκτρέψαι τὴν γραφήν, ὡς οἱ πρὸ αὐτοῦ πάντες ἐποίησαν, Λαμίας τινὰς ἱστοροῦντες ἐν ὕλαις καὶ νάπαις ἐκ γῆς ἀνιεμένας, καὶ Ναΐδας ἀμφιβίους ἐκ Ταρτάρων ἐξιούσας καὶ διὰ πελάγους νηχομένας καὶ μιξόθηρας, καὶ ταύτας εἰς ὁμιλίαν ἀνθρώποις συνερχομένας, καὶ ἐκ θνητῶν καὶ θείων συνουσιῶν γονὰς ἡμιθέους, καὶ ἄλλας τινὰς ἀπίστους τῷ καθ' ἡμᾶς βίῳ καὶ πολὺ τὸ ἀνόητον ἔχειν δοκούσας ἱστορίας.

7 Ταῦτα δ' εἰπεῖν προήχθην οὐκ ἐπιτιμῶν ἐκείνοις τοῖς ἀνδράσιν, ἀλλὰ καὶ πολλὴν ἔχων συγγνώμην, εἰ καὶ τῶν μυθικῶν ἥψαντο πλασμάτων, ἐθνικὰς καὶ τοπικὰς ἐκφέροντες ἱστορίας· ἐν ἅπασι γὰρ ἀνθρώποις καὶ κοινῇ κατὰ τόπους καὶ κατὰ πόλεις ἰδίᾳ μνῆμαί τινες ἐσῴζοντο καὶ τῶν τοιούτων ἀκουσμάτων, ὥσπερ ἔφην, ἃς διαδεχόμενοι παῖδες παρὰ πατέρων ἐπιμελὲς ἐποιοῦντο παρα-

---

[1] Eugeon (Euagon?) of Samos is the probable source of this story.

physical health and soundness of mind, and survived to see the end of the war. He did not piece together his account of actions from casual report, but was able to write as a participant in some, while others which he was prevented by his exile from witnessing he learned by questioning the most reliable informants. Thus he differed from the earlier historians firstly in the choice of his subject, which was neither completely monothematic nor divided up into a number of disconnected topics, and secondly by his exclusion of all legendary material and his refusal to make his history an instrument for deceiving and captivating the common people, as all his predecessors had done when they wrote stories like those of female monsters at Lamia rising up out of the earth in the woods and glades, and amphibious Naiads issuing forth from Tartarus, half-human and half-animal, swimming across the ocean and joining the society of men, and producing from this union of mortals and divine beings a race of demigods;[1] and other stories which seem incredible and largely ridiculous to us in these days.

I have been led to speak in such terms about these 7
men not because I think they deserve criticism: on the contrary, I can fully understand how writers of tribal and local history should have encountered stories of a fictional nature; for, as I have said, in all human societies records were preserved, by common tradition in rural areas and in single repositaries in cities. These records contained legends such as I have described; and children, inheriting them from their parents took care to hand them on to the next

διδόναι τοῖς ἐκγόνοις καὶ τοὺς βουλομένους αὐτὰς εἰς τὸ κοινὸν ἐκφέρειν οὕτως ἠξίουν συγγράφειν, ὡς παρὰ τῶν ἀρχαίων ἐδέξαντο. ἐκείνοις μὲν οὖν τοῖς ἀνδράσιν ἀναγκαῖον ἦν ποικίλλειν τοῖς μυθώδεσιν ἐπεισοδίοις τὰς τοπικὰς ἀναγραφάς. Θουκυδίδῃ δὲ τῷ προελομένῳ μίαν ὑπόθεσιν, ᾗ παρεγίνετο αὐτός, οὐχ ἥρμοττεν ἐγκαταμίσγειν [1] τῇ διηγήσει τὰς θεατρικὰς γοητείας οὐδὲ πρὸς τὴν ἀπάτην ἁρμόττεσθαι τῶν ἀναγνωσομένων, ἣν ἐκεῖναι πεφύκασι φέρειν αἱ συντάξεις, ἀλλὰ πρὸς τὴν ὠφέλειαν, ὡς αὐτὸς ἐν τῷ προοιμίῳ τῆς ἱστορίας δεδήλωκε κατὰ λέξιν οὕτως γράφων· "καὶ ἐς μὲν ἀκρόασιν τὸ μὴ μυθῶδες αὐτῶν ἀτερπέστερον φαίνεται· ὅσοι δὲ βουλήσονται τῶν τε γεγονότων τὸ σαφὲς σκοπεῖν, καὶ τῶν μελλόντων ποτὲ κατὰ τὸ ἀνθρώπειον τοιούτων καὶ παραπλησίων ἔσεσθαι, ὠφέλιμα κρίνειν αὐτὰ ἀρκούντως ἕξει· κτῆμά τε ἐς ἀεὶ μᾶλλον ἢ ἀγώνισμα ἐς τὸ παραχρῆμα ἀκούειν ξύγκειται."

8 Μαρτυρεῖται δὲ τῷ ἀνδρὶ τάχα μὲν ὑπὸ πάντων φιλοσόφων τε καὶ ῥητόρων, εἰ δὲ μή, τῶν γε πλείστων, ὅτι καὶ τῆς ἀληθείας, ἧς ἱέρειαν [2] εἶναι τὴν ἱστορίαν βουλόμεθα, πλείστην ἐποιήσατο πρόνοιαν, οὔτε προστιθεὶς τοῖς πράγμασιν οὐδὲν ὃ μὴ δίκαιον οὔτε ἀφαιρῶν, οὐδὲ ἐνεξουσιάζων τῇ γραφῇ, ἀνέγκλητον δὲ καὶ καθαρὰν τὴν προαίρεσιν ἀπὸ παντὸς φθόνου καὶ πάσης κολακείας φυλάττων, μάλιστα δ' ἐν ταῖς περὶ τῶν ἀγαθῶν

[1] ἐγκαταμίσγειν Kiessling: ἐγκαταμίγειν MP.
[2] ἱέρειαν Reiske, correctorem codicis Bodleiani sequens: ἱερὰν codd.

generation, and expected those wishing to publish them to write them down in the form in which they had received them from antiquity. Thus these local historians were obliged to embellish their accounts with mythological digressions. Thucydides, however, chose a single episode in which he personally participated: it was therefore inappropriate for him to adulterate his narrative with entertaining fantasies or to arrange it in a way which would confuse his readers, as his predecessors' compositions would naturally do. His purpose was to benefit his readers, as he himself has made clear in the introduction of his history, in a passage in which the actual words are as follows:[1]

"The absence of legend from my history seems less attractive to a listener; but if it should be judged useful by those who wish to have a clear view of the past from which to interpret the future, which in the nature of human affairs will follow a similar if not identical pattern, I shall be satisfied. My work is composed to be a possession for ever, not an occasional piece for a single hearing."

All, or at least the majority, of philosophers and 8
rhetoricians support the historian's claim. History is the High Priestess of Truth in our view, and Thucydides concerned himself above all with recording the truth, neither adding to nor subtracting from the facts unjustifiably, nor allowing himself any literary licence, but blamelessly and single-mindedly maintaining the principle of avoiding all malice and flattery, especially when passing judgment on great

[1] i. 22.

ἀνδρῶν γνώμαις. καὶ γὰρ Θεμιστοκλέους ἐν τῇ πρώτῃ βύβλῳ μνησθεὶς τὰς ὑπαρχούσας αὐτῷ ἀρετὰς ἀφθόνως ἐπελήλυθε, καὶ τῶν Περικλέους πολιτευμάτων ἁψάμενος ἐν τῇ δευτέρᾳ βύβλῳ τῆς διαβεβοημένης περὶ αὐτοῦ δόξης ἄξιον εἴρηκεν ἐγκώμιον· περί τε Δημοσθένους τοῦ στρατηγοῦ καὶ Νικίου τοῦ Νικηράτου καὶ Ἀλκιβιάδου τοῦ Κλεινίου καὶ ἄλλων στρατηγῶν τε καὶ ῥητόρων ἀναγκασθεὶς λέγειν, ὅσα προσήκοντα ἦν ἑκάστῳ, δεδήλωκε. παραδείγματα δὲ περὶ αὐτῶν φέρειν οὐ δέομαι τοῖς διεληλυθόσιν αὐτοῦ τὰς ἱστορίας. ταῦτα μὲν οὖν ἂν ἔχοι τις εἰπεῖν, ἃ περὶ τὸν πραγματικὸν τόπον ὁ συγγραφεὺς κατορθοῖ, καλὰ καὶ μιμήσεως ἄξια. [κράτιστον δὲ πάντων τὸ μηδὲν ἑκουσίως ψεύδεσθαι μηδὲ μιαίνειν τὴν αὑτοῦ [1] συνείδησιν.] [2]

9 ἃ δ' ἐλλιπέστερον κατεσκεύασε καὶ ἐφ' οἷς ἐγκαλοῦσιν αὐτῷ τινες, περὶ τὸ τεχνικώτερον μέρος ἐστὶ τοῦ πραγματικοῦ, τὸ λεγόμενον μὲν οἰκονομικόν, ἐν ἁπάσαις δὲ γραφαῖς ἐπιζητούμενον, ἐάν τε φιλοσόφους προέληταί τις ὑποθέσεις ἐάν τε ῥητορικάς. ταῦτα δέ ἐστι τὰ περὶ τὴν διαίρεσιν καὶ τὰ περὶ τὴν τάξιν καὶ τὰ περὶ τὰς ἐξεργασίας. ἄρξομαι δ' ἀπὸ τῆς διαιρέσεως, προειπὼν ὅτι τῶν πρὸ αὐτοῦ γενομένων συγγραφέων ἢ κατὰ τόπους μεριζόντων τὰς ἀναγραφὰς ἢ κατὰ χρόνους εὐπαρακολουθήτους ἐκεῖνος οὐδετέραν τούτων τῶν διαιρέσεων ἐδοκίμασεν. οὔτε γὰρ τοῖς τόποις, ἐν οἷς αἱ πράξεις ἐπετελέσθησαν, ἀκολουθῶν ἐμέρισε

[1] αὑτοῦ Krüger: αὐτοῦ codd.
[2] κράτιστον . . . συνείδησιν delevit Sadée.

men. For example, in his reference to Themistocles in the first book, he generously lists all his virtues,[1] and when, in the second book, he considers the political achievements of Pericles, he writes an encomium worthy of the great man's far-famed reputation.[2] Again, when he has to write about Demosthenes the general,[3] Nicias the son of Niceratus,[4] Alcibiades the son of Cleinias [5] and other generals and politicians, he makes clear all that was due to each of them. It is unnecessary for me to quote examples to those who have read the whole history. These are the aspects of subject-matter in which Thucydides may be said to be successful. They are admirable and worthy of imitation. [The most important thing of all is never to lie willingly or to defile one's own conscience.]

One aspect of his composition is less satisfactory, 9
and has given rise to some criticism. It concerns the more artistic side of the presentation of subject-matter, that which is called *arrangement*,[6] which is required in every kind of writing, whether one selects philosophical or rhetorical themes. It consists of division, order and method of development.[7] I shall begin with division. My first observation is that, whereas earlier historians divided their accounts either topographically or by means of a simple chronological framework, Thucydides adopted neither of these methods of division. He took neither the places in which events occurred as his basis of division,

[1] i. 138. 3–6.
[2] ii. 65.
[3] Dionysius has suffered a slip of memory: no such passage exists.
[4] vii. 86. 5.
[5] vi. 15. 2–4.
[6] Aristotle's word for this is ταξις (*Rhetoric*, iii. 12. 6), but [Longinus] 1. 4 and Quintilian (iii. 3. 9) use οἰκονομία. Cf. *De Compositione Verborum*, 18.
[7] A new method of division. See Grube, *The Greek and Roman Critics*, p. 226.

τὰς διηγήσεις, ὡς Ἡρόδοτός τε καὶ Ἑλλάνικος καὶ ἄλλοι τινὲς τῶν πρὸ αὐτοῦ συγγραφέων ἐποίησαν· οὔτε τοῖς χρόνοις, ὡς οἱ τὴν τοπικὴν ἐκδόντες ἱστορίαν προείλοντο, ἤτοι ταῖς διαδοχαῖς τῶν βασιλέων μερίζοντες τὰς ἀναγραφὰς ἢ ταῖς τῶν ἱερέων ἢ ταῖς περιόδοις τῶν ὀλυμπιάδων ἢ τοῖς ἀποδεικνυμένοις ἄρχουσιν ἐπὶ τὰς ἐνιαυσίους ἀρχάς. καινὴν δέ τινα καὶ ἀτριβῆ τοῖς ἄλλοις πορευθῆναι βουληθεὶς ὁδὸν θερείαις καὶ χειμερίοις ⟨ὥραις ἀκολουθῶν⟩ [1] ἐμέρισε τὴν ἱστορίαν. ἐκ δὲ τούτου συμβέβηκεν αὐτῷ τοὐναντίον ἢ προσεδόκησεν. οὐ γὰρ σαφεστέρα γέγονεν ἡ διαίρεσις τῶν χρόνων ἀλλὰ δυσπαρακολουθητοτέρα κατὰ τὰς ὥρας ἐφ' ᾧ θαυμάζειν ἄξιον, πῶς αὐτὸν ἔλαθεν, ὅτι πολλῶν ἅμα πραγμάτων κατὰ πολλοὺς τόπους γινομένων εἰς μικρὰς κατακερματιζομένη τομὰς ἡ διήγησις οὐκ ἀπολήψεται τὸ "τηλαυγὲς φῶς" ἐκεῖνο "καὶ καθαρόν," ὡς ἐξ αὐτῶν γίνεται τῶν πραγμάτων φανερόν. ἐν γοῦν τῇ τρίτῃ βύβλῳ (ταύτῃ γὰρ ἀρκεσθήσομαι μόνῃ) τὰ περὶ Μυτιληναίους ἀρξάμενος γράφειν, πρὶν ὅλην ἐκπληρῶσαι τὴν διήγησιν, ἐπὶ τὰ Λακεδαιμονίων ἄπεισιν ἔργα· καὶ οὐδὲ ταῦτα συγκορυφώσας τῆς Πλαταιέων μέμνηται πολιορκίας· ἀφεὶς δὲ καὶ ταύτην ἀτελῆ τοῦ Μυτιληναϊκοῦ μέμνηται πολέμου· εἶτ' ἐκεῖθεν ἄγει τὴν διήγησιν ἐπὶ τὰ περὶ Κέρκυραν, ὡς ἐστασίασαν οἱ μὲν Λακεδαιμονίους, οἱ δ' Ἀθηναίους ἐπαγόμενοι· ἀφεὶς δὲ καὶ ταῦτα ἡμιτελῆ περὶ τῆς

[1] lacunam supplevit Schoell.

---

[1] As did Philochorus of Athens.

[2] The method first used by Timaeus of Tauromenium.

as Herodotus, Hellanicus and some of his other predecessors had done; nor time, which the local historians had preferred, dividing their records according to the accession of kings or priests,[1] or by the periods of the Olympiads,[2] or by the appointment of civil magistrates to annual office. He wished to follow a new path, untrodden by others, and so divided his history by summers and winters. The result of this was contrary to his expectations: the seasonal division of time led not to greater clarity but to greater obscurity. It is surprising how he failed to see that a narrative which is broken up into small sections describing the many actions which took place in many different places will not catch "the pure light shining from afar"; [3] as is clearly shown by what happens in practice. Thus in the third book (I shall confine myself to this single example) he begins his account of the Mytilenean episode,[4] but before completing this he turns to the activities of the Lacedaemonians; [5] and he does not even round these off before describing the siege of Plataea.[6] This in turn he leaves unfinished and recounts the Mytilenean War;[7] then from there he transfers his narrative to Corcyra [8] and describes the revolution in which one side brought in the Lacedaemonians and the other the Athenians. He then leaves this account, too, half-finished, and says a few words about the first

[3] Cf. Pindar, *Pythian Odes*, iii. 75.

[4] iii. 2.

[5] Not an adequate description of the contents of 7–19.

[6] 20–26, but not a complete account of their contents.

[7] 27–50.

[8] Dionysius omits ch. 51 and the conclusion of the Plataean episode (52–68); chs. 69–85 deal with the Corcyrean revolution.

εἰς Σικελίαν στρατείας τῆς προτέρας Ἀθηναίων ὀλίγα λέγει. εἶτα Ἀθηναίων ἔκπλουν ἐπὶ Πελοπόννησον ἀρξάμενος λέγειν καὶ Λακεδαιμονίων τὴν ἐπὶ Δωριεῖς στρατείαν τὰ περὶ Λευκάδα πραχθέντα ὑπὸ Δημοσθένους τοῦ στρατηγοῦ καὶ τὸν πρὸς Αἰτωλοὺς πόλεμον ἐπιπορεύεται· ἐκεῖθεν δὲ ἄπεισιν ἐπὶ Ναύπακτον. ἀτελεῖς δὲ καὶ τοὺς ἠπειρωτικοὺς πολέμους καταλιπὼν Σικελίας ἅπτεται πάλιν, καὶ μετὰ τοῦτο Δῆλον καθαίρει καὶ τὸ Ἀμφιλοχικὸν Ἄργος πολεμούμενον ὑπὸ Ἀμπρακιωτῶν καταλήγει.[1] καὶ τί δεῖ πλείω λέγειν; ὅλη γὰρ ἡ βύβλος οὕτω συγκέκοπται καὶ τὸ διηνεκὲς τῆς ἀπαγγελίας ἀπολώλεκε. πλανώμεθα δή, καθάπερ εἰκός, καὶ δυσκόλως τοῖς δηλουμένοις παρακολουθοῦμεν, ταραττομένης ἐν τῷ διασπᾶσθαι τὰ πράγματα τῆς διανοίας καὶ τὰς ἡμιτελεῖς τῶν ἀκουσθέντων μνήμας οὐ ῥᾳδίως οὐδ' ἀκριβῶς ἀναφερούσης. χρὴ δὲ τὴν ἱστορικὴν πραγματείαν εἰρομένην εἶναι καὶ ἀπερίσπαστον, ἄλλως τε ἐπειδὰν περὶ πολλῶν γίνηται πραγμάτων καὶ δυσκαταμαθήτων. ὅτι δὲ οὐκ ὀρθὸς ὁ κανὼν οὗτος οὐδ' οἰκεῖος ἱστορίᾳ, δῆλον. οὐδεὶς γὰρ τῶν μεταγενεστέρων συγγραφέων θερείαις καὶ χειμῶσι διεῖλε τὴν ἱστορίαν, ἀλλὰ πάντες τὰς τετριμμένας ⟨ὁδοὺς καὶ δυναμένας⟩[2] ἄγειν ἐπὶ τὴν σαφήνειαν μετῆλθον.

10 Αἰτιῶνται δὲ καὶ τὴν τάξιν αὐτοῦ τινες, ὡς οὔτε ἀρχὴν τῆς ἱστορίας εἰληφότος ἣν ἐχρῆν οὔτε τέλος ἐφηρμοκότος αὐτῇ τὸ πρέπον, οὐκ ἐλάχιστον μέρος εἶναι λέγοντες οἰκονομίας ἀγαθῆς ἀρχήν τε λαβεῖν, ἧς οὐκ ἂν εἴη τι πρότερον, καὶ τέλει

[1] καταλήγει conieci: καταλείπει codd. [2] addidit Usener.

Athenian expedition to Sicily.[1] He then begins his narrative of an Athenian naval raid on the Peloponnese and the Spartan land expedition against Doris,[2] and proceeds to the exploits of the general Demosthenes around Leucas and the war against the Aetolians.[3] Then he goes off to Naupactus and,[4] leaving these wars on the mainland also unfinished he touches on Sicily again,[5] and after this purifies Delos [6] and brings to its conclusion the war that is being waged by the Ambraciots against Amphilochian Argos.[7] What need I say further? The whole of the book is broken up in this way, and the continuity of the narrative is destroyed. Predictably, we wander here and there, and have difficulty in following the sequence of the events described, because our mind is confused by their separation and cannot easily or accurately recall the half-completed references which it has heard. But history should be presented as an uninterrupted sequence of events, particularly when it is concerned with a large number of them which are difficult to comprehend. It is clear that Thucydides's principle is wrong and ill-suited to history: for no subsequent historian divided up his narrative by summers and winters,[8] but all followed the well-worn roads which lead to clarity.

Some critics also find fault with the order of his 10
history, complaining that he neither chose the right beginning for it nor a fitting place to end it. They say that by no means the least important aspect of good arrangement is that a work should begin where

[1] 86–88. [2] 89–93. [3] 94–99. [4] 100–102.
[5] 103. [6] 104. [7] 105–114.

[8] Xenophon continued Thucydides's narrative in his *Hellenica,* using his seasonal division, but abandoned it before reaching the end of the war.

περιλαβεῖν τὴν πραγματείαν, ᾧ δόξει μηδὲν ἐνδεῖν· ὧν οὐδετέρου πρόνοιαν αὐτὸν πεποιῆσθαι τὴν προσήκουσαν. τὴν δὲ ἀφορμὴν ⟨αὐτὸς⟩ [1] αὐτοῖς τῆς κατηγορίας ταύτης ὁ συγγραφεὺς παρέσχηται· προειπὼν γάρ, ὡς μέγιστος ἐγένετο τῶν πρὸ αὐτοῦ πολέμων ὁ Πελοποννησιακὸς χρόνου τε μήκει καὶ παθημάτων πολλῶν συντυχίαις, τελευτῶν τοῦ προοιμίου τὰς αἰτίας βούλεται πρῶτον εἰπεῖν, ἀφ' ὧν τὴν ἀρχὴν ἔλαβε. διττὰς δὲ ταύτας ὑποθέμενος, τήν τε ἀληθῆ μέν, οὐκ εἰς ἅπαντας δὲ λεγομένην, τὴν αὔξησιν τῆς Ἀθηναίων πόλεως, καὶ τὴν οὐκ ἀληθῆ μέν, ὑπὸ δὲ Λακεδαιμονίων πλαττομένην, τὴν Ἀθήνηθεν ἀποσταλεῖσαν Κερκυραίοις κατὰ Κορινθίων συμμαχίαν, οὐκ ἀπὸ τῆς ἀληθοῦς καὶ αὐτῷ δοκούσης τὴν ἀρχὴν πεποίηται τῆς διηγήσεως, ἀλλ' ἀπὸ τῆς ἑτέρας, κατὰ λέξιν οὕτως γράφων· "ἤρξαντο δὲ Ἀθηναῖοι αὐτοῦ καὶ Πελοποννήσιοι, λύσαντες τὰς τριακοντούτεις σπονδάς, αἳ αὐτοῖς ἐγένοντο μετὰ Εὐβοίας ἅλωσιν. διότι δὲ ἔλυσαν, τὰς αἰτίας προέγραψα πρῶτον καὶ τὰς διαφορὰς τοῦ μή τινας ζητῆσαί ποτε, ἐξ ὅτου τοσοῦτος πόλεμος τοῖς Ἕλλησι κατέστη. τὴν μὲν γὰρ ἀληθεστάτην πρόφασιν, ἀφανεστάτην δὲ λόγῳ, τοὺς Ἀθηναίους ἡγοῦμαι μεγάλους γιγνομένους καὶ φόβον παρέχοντας τοῖς Λακεδαιμονίοις ἀναγκάσαι ἐς τὸ πολεμεῖν. αἱ δὲ ἐς τὸ φανερὸν λεγόμεναι αἰτίαι αἵδε ἦσαν. Ἐπίδαμνός ἐστι πόλις εἰς δεξιὰ ἐσπλέοντι τὸν Ἰόνιον κόλπον.

[1] αὐτὸς supplevit Usener.

---

[1] i. 1. 2, 21. 2.

nothing can be imagined as preceding it, and end where nothing further is felt to be required; and they claim that Thucydides has not paid due attention to either of these considerations. The historian himself has provided them with the ground for this charge. After saying at the start that the Peloponnesian War was far greater than any before, in regard both to length and to the amount of suffering involved,[1] at the end of his introduction he wants to preface his narrative with a statement of the reasons for the beginning of hostilities.[2] He gives two, the real cause, which is not generally publicised—the growth of Athenian power—and the false cause, which was fabricated by the Lacedaemonians—the sending of an allied force from Athens to help the Corcyreans against the Corinthians. However, he does not begin his narrative from the true cause, in which he himself believes, but from the other point. The passage runs in the following words:[3]

"The Athenians and the Peloponnesians began the war, dissolving the Thirty Years' Peace made after the conquest of Euboea. In answer to the question why they broke the treaty I have given first the grievances and points of dispute, in order that no one may ever need to ask how the Greeks came to start so great a war among themselves. The real cause I consider to have been that which was given least publicity, the growth of Athenian power, which made the Lacedaemonians afraid and forced them to make war. But the advertised causes were as follows.

"There is a city called Epidamnus on the right as one sails into the entrance to the Ionian Gulf. The

[2] i. 23. 4–6.
[3] i. 23. 4–24. 1.

προσοικοῦσιν δ' αὐτὴν Ταυλάντιοι βάρβαροι, Ἰλλυρικὸν ἔθνος." καὶ μετὰ τοῦτο διεξέρχεται τὰ περὶ Ἐπίδαμνον καὶ τὰ περὶ Κέρκυραν καὶ τὰ περὶ Ποτίδαιαν καὶ τὴν Πελοποννησίων σύνοδον εἰς Σπάρτην καὶ τοὺς ῥηθέντας ἐκεῖ κατὰ τῆς Ἀθηναίων πόλεως λόγους. ταῦτα δὲ μέχρι δισχιλίων ἐκμηκύνας στίχων, τότε περὶ τῆς ἑτέρας αἰτίας τὸν λόγον ἀποδίδωσι τῆς ἀληθοῦς τε καὶ αὐτῷ δοκούσης, ἐνθένδε ἀρξάμενος· "ἐψηφίσαντο δὲ οἱ Λακεδαιμόνιοι τὰς σπονδὰς λελύσθαι καὶ πολεμεῖν Ἀθηναίοις οὐ τοσοῦτον τῶν συμμάχων πεισθέντες τοῖς λόγοις, ὅσον φοβούμενοι τοὺς Ἀθηναίους, μὴ ἐπὶ μεῖζον δυνηθῶσιν, ὁρῶντες αὐτοῖς τὰ πολλὰ τῆς Ἑλλάδος ὑποχείρια ἤδη ὄντα. οἱ γὰρ Ἀθηναῖοι τρόπῳ τοιούτῳ ἦλθον ἐπὶ τὰ πράγματα, ἐν οἷς ηὐξήθησαν." οἷς ἐπιτίθησι τὰ ἔργα τῆς πόλεως, ὅσα μετὰ τὸν Περσικὸν πόλεμον ἕως τοῦ Πελοποννησιακοῦ διεπράξαντο, κεφαλαιωδῶς καὶ ἐπιτροχάδην ἐν ἐλάττοσιν ἢ πεντακοσίοις στίχοις. ἀναμνησθεὶς δ' ὅτι πρότερα τῶν Κερκυραϊκῶν ἦν καὶ οὐκ ἀπ' ἐκείνων ἔλαβε τὴν ἀρχὴν ὁ πόλεμος ἀλλ' ἀπὸ τούτων, ταῦτα πάλιν κατὰ λέξιν γράφει· "μετὰ ταῦτα δὲ ἤδη γίγνεται οὐ πολλοῖς ἔτεσιν ὕστερον τὰ προειρημένα, τά τε Κερκυραϊκὰ καὶ τὰ Ποτιδαιατικὰ καὶ ὅσα πρόφασις τοῦδε τοῦ πολέμου κατέστη. ταῦτα δὲ πάντα ὅσα ἔπραξαν οἱ Ἕλληνες πρός τε ἀλλήλους καὶ πρὸς τὸν βάρβαρον, ἐγένοντο ἐν ἔτεσι πεντήκοντα μάλιστα μεταξὺ τῆς τε Ξέρξου ἀναχωρήσεως καὶ τῆς ἀρχῆς τοῦδε τοῦ πολέμου· ἐν οἷς οἱ

neighbourhood is inhabited by the barbarian Taulantians, an Illyrian people. . . ."

After this he describes the operations at Epidamnus, Corcyra and Potidaea, the assembly of the Peloponnesians at Sparta, and the speeches made there against the Athenians. He allows his account of these events to extend to some two thousand lines, and only then deals with the true cause in which he himself believes. He begins thus:[1]

"The Lacedaemonians decided that the treaty had been broken and that war must be declared, not so much because they were persuaded by the arguments of their allies as because they feared that Athenian power would increase, seeing most of Greece already under their sway. The expansion of the Athenian empire took place through the following course of events. . . ."

He then describes all the activities of the city in the years between the Persian and the Peloponnesian War, skimming over them summarily in the space of fewer than five hundred lines. Then, after noting that these events preceded the Corcyrean episode, and that the war had its origins not in the latter but in the former, he goes on to write the following passage:[2]

"Not many years afterwards occurred the affairs of Corcyra and Potidaea already narrated, and the other events that were a pretext for this war. Approximately fifty years elapsed between the retreat of Xerxes and the beginning of the war: all these operations of the Greeks against one another and against the barbarian took place during those

[1] i. 88–89.1.
[2] i. 118. 1–2.

Ἀθηναῖοι τήν τε ἀρχὴν ἐγκρατεστέραν κατεστήσαντο καὶ αὐτοὶ ἐπὶ μέγα ἐχώρησαν δυνάμεως, οἱ δὲ Λακεδαιμόνιοι αἰσθόμενοι οὔτε ἐκώλυον, εἰ μὴ ἐπὶ βραχύ, ἡσύχαζόν τε τὸ πλέον τοῦ χρόνου, ὄντες μὲν καὶ πρὸ τοῦ μὴ ταχεῖς ἐς τοὺς πολέμους ἢν μὴ ἀναγκάζωνται, τότε δέ τι καὶ πολέμοις οἰκείοις ἐξειργόμενοι· πλὴν ἡ δύναμις τῶν Ἀθηναίων σαφῶς ᾔρετο καὶ τῆς συμμαχίας αὐτῶν ἥπτετο· τότε δὲ οὐκέτι ἐποιοῦντο ἀνασχετόν, ἀλλ' ἐπιχειρητέα ἐδόκει εἶναι πάσῃ προθυμίᾳ, καὶ καθαιρετέα ἡ ἰσχύς, ἢν δύνωνται, ἀραμένοις τόνδε
11 τὸν πόλεμον." ἐχρῆν δὲ αὐτὸν ἀρξάμενον τὰς αἰτίας τοῦ πολέμου ζητεῖν πρῶτον ἀποδοῦναι τὴν ἀληθῆ καὶ ἑαυτῷ δοκοῦσαν. ἥ τε γὰρ φύσις ἀπῄτει τὰ πρότερα τῶν ὑστέρων ἄρχειν καὶ τἀληθῆ πρὸ τῶν ψευδῶν λέγεσθαι, ἥ τε τῆς διηγήσεως εἰσβολὴ κρείττων ἂν ἐγίνετο μακρῷ, τοιαύτης οἰκονομίας τυχοῦσα. οὐδὲ γὰρ ἐκεῖνό τις ἂν εἰπεῖν ἔχοι τῶν ἀπολογεῖσθαι περὶ αὐτοῦ βουλομένων, ὅτι μικρὰ καὶ οὐκ ἄξια λόγου τὰ πράγματα ἦν ἢ κοινὰ καὶ κατημαξευμένα τοῖς πρὸ αὐτοῦ, ὥστε μὴ δεῖν ἀπὸ τούτων ἀρχὴν ποιεῖσθαι. αὐτὸς γὰρ ὡς ἐκλειφθέντα τὸν τόπον τοῦτον ὑπὸ τῶν ἀρχαίων ἄξιον ἱστορίας ὑπείληφεν, αὐταῖς λέξεσιν οὕτως γράφων· " ἔγραψα δὲ αὐτὰ καὶ τὴν ἐκβολὴν τοῦ λόγου ἐποιησάμην, διότι τοῖς πρὸ ἐμοῦ ἅπασιν ἐκλιπὲς τὸ χωρίον τοῦτο ἦν· καὶ ἢ τὰ πρὸ τῶν Μηδικῶν Ἑλληνικὰ ξυνετίθεσαν, ἢ αὐτὰ τὰ Μηδικά. τούτων δὲ ὧνπερ καὶ ἥψατο ἐν

[1] i. 97. 2.

years, and in that period the Athenians acquired a firmer hold on their empire and at home advanced to the height of their power. The Lacedaemonians saw what was happening, but for most of the time remained inactive and hardly attempted to interfere. They had never made war readily before this time unless compelled to do so, and were now somewhat embarrassed by wars near home. But the power of the Athenians was manifestly increasing and was threatening Sparta's allies. They now felt that the situation could no longer be endured, but that they must make a wholehearted effort to overthrow Athenian power, if they could, by starting this war."

But he ought to have stated at the beginning of his 11
enquiry into the true causes of the war the cause which he considered to be the true one: for not only was it a natural requirement that prior events should have precedence over later ones, and true causes be stated before false ones, but the start of his narrative would have been far more powerful if he had adopted this arrangement. It would not even be possible for anyone wishing to defend his methods to argue that these events were minor and insignificant, or that they were well-known and had become hackneyed by previous reference, so that it was unnecessary to start with them. He himself considered that it was because this period had been neglected by earlier writers that it merited historical enquiry; and he says so in an actual passage:[1]

"I have gone out of my way to write about this period because the writers who have preceded me have neglected it, treating either of Greek affairs before the Persian Wars, or of the Wars themselves. The only author to deal with the intervening period is

τῇ Ἀττικῇ συγγραφῇ Ἑλλάνικος, βραχέως τε καὶ τοῖς χρόνοις οὐκ ἀκριβῶς ἐπεμνήσθη· ἅμα δὲ καὶ τῆς ἀρχῆς ἀπόδειξιν ἔχει τῆς τῶν Ἀθηναίων, ἐν
12 οἵῳ τρόπῳ κατέστη." ἱκανὸν μὲν οὖν καὶ τοῦτο τεκμήριον ἦν τοῦ μὴ κατὰ τὸν ἄριστον τρόπον ᾠκονομῆσθαι τὴν διήγησιν ὑπ' αὐτοῦ, λέγω δὴ τὸ μὴ τὴν κατὰ φύσιν ἔχειν ἀρχήν. πρόσεστι δὲ τούτῳ καὶ τὸ μὴ εἰς ἃ ἔδει [1] κεφάλαια τετελευτηκέναι τὴν ἱστορίαν. ἔτη γὰρ ἑπτὰ καὶ εἴκοσιν περιειληφότος τοῦ πολέμου, πάντα τὸν χρόνον τοῦτον ἕως τῆς καταλύσεως αὐτοῦ βιώσας, μέχρι τοῦ δευτέρου καὶ εἰκοστοῦ κατεβίβασεν ἔτους τὴν ἱστορίαν, τῇ περὶ Κυνὸς σῆμα ναυμαχίᾳ τὴν ὀγδόην βύβλον παρεκτείνας, καὶ ταῦτα προειρηκὼς ἐν τῷ προοιμίῳ πάντα περιλήψεσθαι τὰ πραχθέντα κατὰ τόνδε τὸν πόλεμον· καὶ ἐν τῇ πέμπτῃ βύβλῳ πάλιν συνκεφαλαιοῦται τοὺς χρόνους, ἀφ' οὗ τε ἤρξατο καὶ μέχρι οὗ προελθὼν κατελύθη, ταῦτα κατὰ λέξιν γεγραφώς· "καὶ τοῖς ἀπὸ χρησμῶν τι ἰσχυρισαμένοις μόνον δὴ τοῦτο ὀχυρῶς ξυμβάν. ἀεὶ γὰρ ἔγωγε μέμνημαι καὶ ἀρχομένου τοῦ πολέμου καὶ μέχρι οὗ ἐτελεύτησε προφερόμενον ὑπὸ πολλῶν, ὅτι τρὶς ἐννέα ἔτη δέοι γενέσθαι αὐτόν. ἐπεβίων δὲ διὰ παντὸς αὐτοῦ, αἰσθανόμενός τε τῇ ἡλικίᾳ καὶ προσέχων τὴν γνώμην, ὅπως ἀκριβῶς τι εἴσομαι· καὶ ξυνέβη μοι φεύγειν τὴν ἐμαυτοῦ ἔτη εἴκοσι μετὰ τὴν εἰς Ἀμφίπολιν στρατηγίαν, καὶ γενομένῳ παρ' ἀμφοτέροις τοῖς πράγμασι καὶ οὐχ ἧσσον τοῖς Πελοποννησίοις διὰ τὴν φυγὴν καθ' ἡσυχίαν τι αὐτῶν μᾶλλον αἰσθέσθαι. τὴν

[1] ἔδει Krüger: δεῖ codd.

Hellanicus, in his Attic History; but his treatment is brief and chronologically inaccurate. My digression also serves to explain how the Athenian empire was established."

This, then, would have been sufficient in itself to 12
prove that his own narrative is not organised in the best possible way, by which I mean that it does not begin at the natural starting-point; and there is a further impression that his history does not end at an appropriate finishing-point. For although the war lasted twenty-seven years and he lived to see its conclusion, he brought his narrative down only to the twenty-second year by concluding the eighth book with the Battle of Cynossema, in spite of having expressed the intention in his introduction to include all the events of the war.[1] And again in the fifth book he reckons up the date at which it began and that which it had reached when it came to an end, in these words:[2]

"And those who put their faith in oracles were justified by the event in this one instance: for I well remember how, from the beginning to the end of the war, there was a current saying that it was to last thrice nine years. I lived through the whole of it, was of an age to follow it intelligently and took pains to discover the exact truth. It happened that I was banished from my country for twenty years after my command at Amphipolis. I was a witness of events on both sides, the Peloponnesian quite as much as the Athenian, because of my exile, and hence was better able to observe some of them at leisure. I shall

[1] Thucydides does not imply this purpose until v. 26.
[2] v. 26. 3–6.

οὖν μετὰ τὰ δέκα ἔτη διαφοράν τε καὶ ξύγχυσιν τῶν σπονδῶν καὶ τὰ ἔπειτα, ὡς ἐπολεμήθη, ἐξηγήσομαι."

13 Ὅτι δὲ καὶ περὶ τὰς ἐξεργασίας τῶν κεφαλαίων ἧττον ἐπιμελής ἐστιν, ἢ πλείονας τοῦ δέοντος λόγους ἀποδιδοὺς τοῖς ἐλαττόνων δεομένοις ἢ ῥᾳθυμότερον ἐπιτρέχων τὰ δεόμενα πλείονος ἐξεργασίας, πολλοῖς τεκμηρίοις βεβαιῶσαι δυνάμενος ὀλίγοις χρήσομαι· τὰς μὲν πρώτας Ἀθηναίων καὶ Πελοποννησίων ναυμαχίας ἀμφοτέρας περὶ τὴν τελευτὴν τῆς δευτέρας βύβλου γράφειν ἀρξάμενος, ἐν αἷς πρὸς ἑπτὰ καὶ τεσσαράκοντα ναῦς Πελοποννησίων εἴκοσι ναυσὶν Ἀθηναῖοι μόνοι * * * * πρὸς πολλαπλασίους τῶν βαρβάρων ναυμαχήσαντες ἃς μὲν διέφθειρον, ἃς δ' αὐτάνδρους ἔλαβον οὐκ ἐλάττους ἢ ὅσας ἔστειλαν ἐπὶ τὸν πόλεμον. θήσω δὲ καὶ τὴν λέξιν αὐτοῦ. "Ἐγένετο μετὰ ταῦτα καὶ ἐπ' Εὐρυμέδοντι ποταμῷ ἐν Παμφυλίᾳ πεζομαχία καὶ ναυμαχία Ἀθηναίων καὶ τῶν ξυμμάχων πρὸς Μήδους, καὶ ἐνίκων τῇ αὐτῇ ἡμέρᾳ ἀμφότερα Ἀθηναῖοι Κίμωνος τοῦ Μιλτιάδου στρατηγοῦντος, καὶ εἷλον τριήρεις Φοινίκων καὶ διέφθειρον τὰς πάσας διακοσίας." ὅμοια δ' ἐστὶ παρ' αὐτῷ καὶ τὰ κατὰ τὰς πεζικὰς μάχας ἢ μηκυνόμενα πέρα τοῦ δέοντος ἢ συναγόμενα εἰς ἔλαττον τοῦ μετρίου. τὰ μέν γε περὶ Πύλον Ἀθηναίοις πραχθέντα καὶ τὰ περὶ τὴν Σφακτηρίαν καλουμένην νῆσον, ἐν ᾗ Λακεδαιμονίους κατακλείσαντες ἐξεπολιόρκησαν, ἀρξάμενος ἐν τῇ τετάρτῃ

---

[1] ii. 83. [2] i. 100. 1.

therefore now narrate the quarrels which broke the treaty after the Ten Years' War, and the events of the war which followed."

I shall next show that he is not careful enough in 13
the development of certain episodes, either according too much space to unimportant matters, or skimming too nonchalantly over those requiring more thorough treatment. I could support this statement with many examples, but will use only a few. After beginning, towards the end of the second book,[1] to describe the 429 B.C.
first two sea-battles between the Athenians and the Peloponnesians, in which the Athenians on their own engaged forty-seven Peloponnesian ships with twenty of their own. . . .

(*Lacuna*)

. . . fought against far larger numbers of barbarians and destroyed some of their ships, while those which were captured with their crews were no fewer in number than those which the Greeks had commissioned for the war. I shall quote his account of this battle:[2]

"After this the Athenians and their allies fought a 468 B.C.
land and a sea battle against the Persians at the Eurymedon river in Pamphylia, and were victorious in both on the same day under Cimon the son of Miltiades; and they captured and destroyed Phoenician vessels numbering two hundred in all."

His treatment of land-battles is similar, being either unnecessarily extended or excessively condensed. His narrative of Athenian operations at Pylos and the island called Sphacteria, where they blockaded the 425 B.C.
Lacedaemonians and carried their position by siege,

βύβλῳ διηγεῖσθαι καὶ μεταξὺ τοῦ πολέμου τοῦδε πράξεις τινὰς ἑτέρας παραδιηγησάμενος, εἶτ' αὖθις ἐπιστρέψας ἐπὶ τὴν ἀπόδοσιν τῶν ἑξῆς, ἅπαντα τὰ γεγενημένα κατὰ τὰς μάχας ὑπ' ἀμφοτέρων διελήλυθεν ἀκριβῶς καὶ δυνατῶς, πλείους ἢ τριακοσίους στίχους αὐτὸς ἀποδεδωκὼς ταῖς μάχαις, καὶ ταῦτα οὐ πολλῶν ὄντων οὔτε τῶν ἀπολομένων οὔτε τῶν παραδόντων τὰ ὅπλα. αὐτός γέ τοι συγκεφαλαιούμενος τὰ περὶ τὴν μάχην κατὰ λέξιν οὕτως γράφει· "ἀπέθανον δὲ ἐν τῇ νήσῳ καὶ ζῶντες ἐλήφθησαν τοσοίδε· εἴκοσι μὲν ὁπλῖται διέβησαν καὶ τετρακόσιοι οἱ πάντες· τούτων ζῶντες ἐκομίσθησαν ὀκτὼ ἀποδέοντες τριακόσιοι, οἱ δ' ἄλλοι ἀπέθανον. καὶ Σπαρτιᾶται τούτων ἦσαν εἴκοσι καὶ ἑκατὸν τῶν ζώντων, Ἀθηναίων δὲ οὐ πολλοὶ διεφθάρησαν."

14 Τῆς δὲ Νικίου στρατηγίας μνησθείς, ὅτε ναῦς ἑξήκοντα καὶ δισχιλίους ⟨ὁπλίτας⟩ Ἀθηναίων ἐπαγόμενος ἐπὶ Πελοπόννησον ἔπλευσε, κατακλείσας δὲ Λακεδαιμονίους εἰς τὰ φρούρια, τοὺς ἐν Κυθήροις ⟨καὶ τοὺς ἐν Θυρέᾳ⟩ κατοικοῦντας Αἰγινήτας ἐξεπολιόρκησε καὶ τῆς ἄλλης Πελοποννήσου πολλὴν ἐδῄωσεν, ἐξ ἧς αἰχμαλώτων πλῆθος ἐπαγόμενος ἀπέπλευσεν εἰς τὰς Ἀθήνας, οὕτως εἴρηκεν ἐπιτροχάδην, περὶ μὲν τῶν ἐν Κυθήροις πραγμάτων· "καὶ μάχης γενομένης ὀλίγον μέν τινα χρόνον ὑπέστησαν οἱ Κυθήριοι· ἔπειτα τραπόμενοι κατέφυγον εἰς τὴν ἄνω πόλιν καὶ

is an example. He begins his account in the fourth book, and digresses to narrate certain other events which took place while this campaign was in progress. Then returning to his account of the succeeding actions, he describes with accuracy and force all that both sides did in the fighting, deliberately devoting more than three hundred lines to these battles, although the numbers who died or who laid down their arms were not great. In fact he himself concludes his narrative of the battle with these words:[1]

"The numbers of those who were killed or taken alive were as follows: Of the four hundred and twenty hoplites in all who made the crossing over to the island, two hundred and ninety-two were brought back alive to Athens; the rest perished. Of the survivors one hundred and twenty were full Spartan citizens. A small number of Athenians only were killed."

Alluding to the campaign conducted by Nicias,[2] 14
when he sailed against the Peloponnese with sixty ships and two thousand Athenian hoplites on board, shut the Lacedaemonians up in their guard-posts, reduced to surrender the Aeginetan colonists on the 424 B.C.
island of Cythera and in Thyrea, and ravaged wide areas of the Peloponnese as well, and after taking large numbers of prisoners sailed back to Athens, Thucydides rapidly sketches the operations in Cythera with these words:[3]

"A battle was fought, in which the Cytherians held their ground for a short time, then turned and fled to the upper city. Later they came to terms with

[1] iv. 38. 5.
[2] iv. 53–57.
[3] iv. 54. 2.

ὕστερον συνέβησαν πρὸς Νικίαν καὶ τοὺς ξυνάρχοντας, Ἀθηναίοις ἐπιτρέψαι περὶ σφῶν αὐτῶν πλὴν θανάτου." περὶ δὲ τῆς Αἰγινητῶν ἁλώσεως τῶν ἐν Θυρέᾳ· "ἐν τούτῳ δ' οἱ Ἀθηναῖοι κατασχόντες καὶ χωρήσαντες εὐθὺς πάσῃ τῇ στρατιᾷ αἱροῦσι τὴν Θυρέαν, καὶ τήν τε πόλιν κατέκαυσαν καὶ τὰ ἐνόντα ἐξεπόρθησαν, τούς τε Αἰγινήτας, ὅσοι μὴ ἐν χερσὶ διεφθάρησαν, ἄγοντες ἀφίκοντο εἰς τὰς Ἀθήνας." γενομένων δὲ περὶ τὰς πόλεις ἀμφοτέρας εὐθὺς ἐν ἀρχῇ τοῦ πολέμου μεγάλων συμφορῶν, δι' ἃς ἐπεθύμησαν ἀμφότεραι τῆς εἰρήνης, περὶ μὲν τῆς προτέρας, ὅτε Ἀθηναῖοι τετμημένης μὲν αὐτοῖς τῆς χώρας, οἰκοφθορημένης δὲ τῆς πόλεως ὑπὸ λοιμοῦ, πᾶσαν ἀπογνόντες βοήθειαν ἄλλην, ἀπέστειλαν πρεσβείαν εἰς Σπάρτην εἰρήνης τυχεῖν δεόμενοι, οὔτε τοὺς ἀποσταλέντας ἄνδρας εἴρηκεν οὔτε τοὺς ῥηθέντας ἐκεῖ λόγους ὑπ' αὐτῶν οὔτε τοὺς ἐναντιωθέντας, ὑφ' ὧν πεισθέντες Λακεδαιμόνιοι τὰς διαλλαγὰς ἀπεψηφίσαντο· φαύλως δέ πως καὶ ῥᾳθύμως ὡς περὶ μικρῶν καὶ ἀδόξων πραγμάτων ταῦτα εἴρηκε· "μετὰ δὲ τὴν δευτέραν εἰσβολὴν τῶν Πελοποννησίων οἱ Ἀθηναῖοι, ὡς ἥ τε γῆ αὐτῶν ἐτέτμητο τὸ δεύτερον καὶ ἡ νόσος ἐπέκειτο ἅμα καὶ ὁ πόλεμος, ἠλλοίωντο τὰς γνώμας, καὶ τὸν Περικλέα ἐν αἰτίᾳ εἶχον ὡς πείσαντα σφᾶς πολεμεῖν καὶ δι' ἐκεῖνον ταῖς ξυμφοραῖς περιπεπτωκότες· πρὸς δὲ τοὺς Λακεδαιμονίους ὥρμηντο συγχωρεῖν, καὶ πρέσβεις τινὰς πέμψαντες πρὸς αὐτοὺς ἄπρακτοι ἐγένοντο."

---

[1] iv. 57. 3.

Nicias and his colleagues, agreeing to place themselves in the Athenians' power on condition that their lives were spared."

And concerning the capture of the Aeginetans at Thyrea, he says:[1]

"Meanwhile the Athenians put in to land and immediately marched on Thyrea with their whole force, and captured it. They burnt the city and ravaged its contents, and carried away with them to Athens all the Aeginetans who had not fallen in the battle."

And when both cities, at the very outset of the war, had suffered major disasters which caused them to desire peace, with regard to the former one, when the Athenians, whose land had been ravaged and their city depopulated by the plague, despairing of every other remedy sent an embassy to Sparta to sue for 430 B.C.
peace, Thucydides does not give the names of the ambassadors or record the speeches they made there, nor the names of the opposing speakers whose arguments persuaded the Lacedaemonians to reject an armistice. His narrative is a rather jejune and careless affair, as if the episode were a minor one of no importance:[2]

"After the second Peloponnesian invasion, when their land had been ravaged once more, and the plague and the war together lay heavily upon the Athenians, a change came over their spirit. They blamed Pericles because he had persuaded them to go to war, and they felt that he was the cause of their falling into such misfortunes; and they were anxious to come to terms with the Lacedaemonians. They therefore sent envoys to them, but these met with no success."

[2] ii. 59. 1–2.

περὶ δὲ τῆς ὑστέρας, ὅτε Λακεδαιμόνιοι τοὺς περὶ Πύλον ἁλόντας τριακοσίους κομίσασθαι προθέμενοι πρεσβείαν [1] ἀπέστειλαν εἰς τὰς Ἀθήνας, καὶ τοὺς λόγους εἴρηκε τοὺς ὑπὸ τοῦ Λακεδαιμονίου ῥηθέντας τότε καὶ τὰς αἰτίας ἐπελήλυθε, δι' ἃς οὐκ ἐπετελέσθησαν αἱ σπονδαί. εἰ μὲν οὖν [2] ἐπὶ τῆς Ἀθηναίων πρεσβείας ⟨ἡ⟩ τὰ κεφάλαια τῶν γινομένων περιειληφυῖα δήλωσις ἤρκει, λόγων δὲ καὶ παρακλήσεων, αἷς ἐχρήσαντο οἱ πρέσβεις, οὐδὲν ἔδει, μήτε πεισθέντων μήτε δεξαμένων τὰς σπονδὰς Λακεδαιμονίων, τί δή ποτε οὐ τὴν αὐτὴν προαίρεσιν ἐφύλαξε καὶ ἐπὶ τῶν ἐκ τῆς Σπάρτης ἀφικομένων εἰς τὰς Ἀθήνας; οὐδὲ γὰρ ἐκεῖνοι διαπραξάμενοι τὴν εἰρήνην ἀπῆλθον. εἰ δ' ἀκριβῶς ἔδει [3] ταῦτα εἰρῆσθαι, διὰ τί παρέλιπε ῥᾳθύμως ἐκεῖνα; οὐ γὰρ δή γε ἀσθενείᾳ δυνάμεως ἐξείργετο περὶ ἀμφοτέρων τοὺς ἐνόντας εὑρεῖν τε καὶ ἐξειπεῖν λόγους. εἰ δὲ δὴ κατὰ λογισμόν τινα τὴν ἑτέραν προείλετο πρεσβείαν ἐξεργάσασθαι, οὐκ ἔχω συμβαλεῖν, κατὰ τί τὴν Λακωνικὴν προέκρινε τῆς Ἀττικῆς μᾶλλον, τὴν ὑστέραν τοῖς χρόνοις ἀντὶ τῆς προτέρας καὶ τὴν ἀλλοτρίαν ἀντὶ τῆς ἰδίας καὶ τὴν ἐπ' ἐλάττοσι κακοῖς γενομένην ἀντὶ τῆς ἐπὶ μείζοσι.

Πόλεών τε ἁλώσεις καὶ κατασκαφὰς καὶ ἀνδραποδισμοὺς καὶ ἄλλας τοιαύτας συμφορὰς πολλάκις ἀναγκασθεὶς γράφειν ποτὲ μὲν οὕτως ὠμὰ καὶ δεινὰ καὶ οἴκτων ἄξια φαίνεσθαι ποιεῖ τὰ πάθη, ὥστε μηδεμίαν ὑπερβολὴν μήτε ἱστοριογράφοις

[1] ἁλόντας—πρεσβείαν Krüger: ἀλλόντας—πρεσβείας codd.
[2] ἡ transposuit Krüger: οὖν ἡ codd.

But when he comes to describe the later occasion, when the Lacedaemonians sent an embassy to Athens to try to recover the three hundred men captured at 425 B.C.
Pylos, he both records the speech delivered by the Lacedaemonian envoy on that occasion and gives all the reasons why a treaty was not concluded.

If, therefore, in the case of the Athenian embassy 15
reference to the main points in the negotiations was all that was necessary, omitting the arguments and appeals used by the envoys because these failed to persuade the Lacedaemonians to agree to an armistice, why ever did Thucydides not follow the same procedure in the case of the embassy which came from Sparta to Athens, since those envoys, too, returned empty-handed from their peace mission? Or, if it was necessary to render an accurate account of the latter, why did he neglect the former so carelessly? He certainly did not lack the ability to discover and express the arguments inherent in the two situations. There may have been some reason for giving more thorough treatment to one embassy than to the other, but I cannot imagine why he attached more importance to the Spartan than to the Athenian—more to the later than to the earlier, to the enemy's rather than his own city's, to the one made under the lighter rather than the one made under the greater weight of misfortune.

Thucydides often has to describe the capture and destruction of cities, the enslavement of their inhabitants and other similar disasters. Sometimes he is so successful in portraying the cruelty, the horror and the pitiable nature of the sufferings involved, that

---

[3] ἔδει Krüger: δεῖ codd.

μήτε ποιηταῖς καταλιπεῖν· ποτὲ δὲ οὕτως ταπεινὰ καὶ μικρά, ὥστε μηδ' εἰς αἴσθησιν δεινῶν τι πεσεῖν γνώρισμα τοῖς ἀναγινώσκουσι τὸν ἄνδρα. λέγων τε ἃ περὶ τῆς Πλαταιέων πόλεως εἴρηκε καὶ περὶ τῆς Μυτιληναίων καὶ περὶ τῆς Μηλίων, οὐδὲν δέομαι τὰς λέξεις ἐκείνας φέρειν, ἐν αἷς ἀπὸ τῆς ἄκρας δυνάμεως ἐξείργασται τὰς συμφορὰς αὐτῶν. ἐν αἷς δ' ἐπιτρέχει καὶ μικρὰ ποιεῖ τὰ πάθη αὐτῇ ⟨τῇ βραχυλογίᾳ χρώμενος⟩ [1] κατὰ πολλοὺς τόπους τῆς ἱστορίας, τούτων μνησθήσομαι· "Περὶ δὲ τοὺς αὐτοὺς χρόνους τούτους Σκιωναίους [2] Ἀθηναῖοι ἐκπολιορκήσαντες ἀπέκτειναν τοὺς ἡβῶντας, παῖδας δὲ καὶ γυναῖκας ἠνδραπόδισαν καὶ τὴν γῆν Πλαταιεῦσιν ἔδωκαν νέμεσθαι." "Καὶ Ἀθηναῖοι πάλιν ἐς Εὔβοιαν διαβάντες Περικλέους στρατηγοῦντος κατεστρέψαντο πᾶσαν· καὶ τὴν ἄλλην ὁμολογίᾳ κατέστησαν, Ἑστιαιεῖς δ' ἐξοικίσαντες αὐτοὶ τὴν γῆν ἔσχον." "Ἀνέστησαν δὲ Αἰγινήτας τῷ αὐτῷ χρόνῳ τούτῳ ἐξ Αἰγίνης Ἀθηναῖοι αὐτούς τε καὶ γυναῖκας καὶ παῖδας, ἐπικαλέσαντες οὐχ ἥκιστα τοῦ πολέμου σφίσιν αἰτίους εἶναι· καὶ τὴν Αἴγιναν ἀσφαλέστερον ἐφαίνετο τῇ Πελοποννησίων ἐπικειμένην αὐτῶν πέμψαντες ἐποίκους ἔχειν."

16 Πολλὰ καὶ ἄλλα τις ἂν εὕροι δι' ὅλης τῆς ἱστορίας ἢ τῆς ἄκρας ἐξεργασίας τετυχηκότα καὶ

[1] τῇ βραχυλογίᾳ χρώμενος lacunam supplendam esse putat Usener.

[2] Σκιωναίους Sylburg: σικυωνίους MP.

---

[1] iii. 52–68.

he leaves other historians and poets no scope to improve on his work. But on other occasions he makes them seem so trivial and petty that he lets fall no hint to help his readers to appreciate the horrors. I need only refer to his narrative of the Plataean episode[1] 429 B.C.
and of the affairs of Mytilene[2] and Melos[3] without 428, 416 B.C.
quoting the passages themselves, in which the sufferings of the inhabitants are described with the utmost power. But I shall quote several passages in his history in which he touches lightly on human sufferings and, by sheer brevity, reduces them to insignificance:

"About the same time as this, the Athenians took Scione by siege, killed all the adult males and enslaved the women and children, and gave the land to the Plataeans to live in."[4] 421 B.C.

"The Athenians under the command of Pericles crossed over again to Euboea and reduced the whole island. They then settled it all by agreement except for Histiaea, which they occupied themselves after ejecting the inhabitants."[5] 447-446 B.C.

"At the same time the Athenians expelled the Aeginetans from Aegina, together with their women- 431 B.C.
folk and their children accusing them of being the main cause of the war. The island lies close to the Peloponnese, and they thought they would have more reliable neighbours if they sent out their own citizens to colonise it."[6]

One could find many other episodes throughout the 16
history as a whole that have been treated with

[2] iii. 27–50.
[3] v. 84–116.
[4] v. 32. 1.
[5] i. 114. 3.
[6] ii. 27. 1.

μήτε πρόσθεσιν δεχόμενα μήτ᾿ ἀφαίρεσιν, ἢ ῥᾳθύμως ἐπιτετροχασμένα καὶ οὐδὲ τὴν ἐλαχίστην ἔμφασιν ἔχοντα τῆς δεινότητος ἐκείνης, μάλιστα δ᾿ ἐν ταῖς δημηγορίαις καὶ ἐν τοῖς διαλόγοις καὶ ἐν ταῖς ἄλλαις ῥητορείαις. ὧν προνοούμενος ἔοικεν ἀτελῆ τὴν ἱστορίαν καταλιπεῖν, ὡς καὶ Κράτιππος ὁ συνακμάσας αὐτῷ καὶ τὰ παραλειφθέντα ὑπ᾿ αὐτοῦ συναγαγὼν γέγραφεν, οὐ μόνον ταῖς πράξεσιν αὐτὰς [1] ἐμποδὼν γεγενῆσθαι λέγων, ἀλλὰ καὶ τοῖς ἀκούουσιν ὀχληρὰς εἶναι. τοῦτό γέ τοι συνέντα αὐτὸν ἐν τοῖς τελευταίοις τῆς ἱστορίας φησὶ μηδεμίαν τάξαι ῥητορείαν, πολλῶν μὲν κατὰ τὴν Ἰωνίαν γενομένων, πολλῶν δ᾿ ἐν ταῖς Ἀθήναις, ὅσα διὰ λόγων καὶ δημηγοριῶν ἐπράχθη. εἴ γέ τοι τὴν πρώτην καὶ τὴν ὀγδόην βύβλον ἀντιπαρεξετάζοι τις ἀλλήλαις, οὔτε τῆς αὐτῆς ἂν προαιρέσεως δόξειεν ἀμφοτέρας ὑπάρχειν οὔτε τῆς αὐτῆς δυνάμεως· ἡ μὲν γὰρ ὀλίγα πράγματα καὶ μικρὰ περιέχουσα πληθύει τῶν ῥητορειῶν, ἡ δὲ περὶ πολλὰς καὶ μεγάλας συνταχθεῖσα πράξεις δημηγορικῶν σπανίζει λόγων.

17 Ἤδη δὲ ἔγωγε καὶ ἐν αὐταῖς ἔδοξα ταῖς ῥητορείαις τοῦτο συμβεβηκέναι τῷ ἀνδρὶ τὸ

[1] *αὐτὰς* Reiske: *αὐταῖς* codd.

---

[1] Probably the most distinguished of Thucydides's continuators, and possibly the author of the *Hellenica Oxyrhynchia*. See Bury, *The Ancient Greek Historians*, pp. 155–156; Bruce, *The Hellenica Oxyrhynchia*, pp. 25–26.

[2] The eighth book has long been thought to contain signs of haste and hence of incompleteness, and it is possible that

supreme craftsmanship, to which nothing could be added and from which nothing could be taken away, while others are treated with careless superficiality, bearing not the slightest sign of his genius. This inconsistency is to be found especially in the speeches, the dialogues and the other rhetorical passages. It was probably while attending to these inconsistencies that he left the work unfinished. Cratippus,[1] his contemporary and the editor of the history as he left it, has recorded this view, and said further that they not only impede the action but also cause annoyance to the audience. It was in realisation of this, he says, that Thucydides included no rhetorical passages in the last parts of his history, although many events took place in Ionia and many at Athens which were the results of public debates and discussions. A comparative examination of the first and eighth books would suggest that they had not been composed according to the same plan or with the same literary power: for the first book contains few actions, and those trivial, and yet abounds in rhetorical passages; whereas the other is concerned with many important events, but is devoid of political speeches.[2]

I myself had already formed the opinion that even 17
in the rhetorical passages our author evinces the same

Thucydides had intended to add speeches, but was prevented from doing so by death or other circumstances. But there are good literary reasons why the first book should contain a high proportion of speeches, since it is the book in which reasons, arguments and decisions are more important than actions, and this is a proper order of priorities at the beginning of a great war. Again, the considerable amount of reported speech in the eighth book might be thought to suggest that Thucydides did not intend to compose full speeches for inclusion in this book.

πάθος, ὥστε περὶ τὴν αὐτὴν ὑπόθεσιν καὶ ἐν τῷ αὐτῷ καιρῷ τιθέναι μὲν ἃς οὐκ ἔδει, παραλιπεῖν δὲ ἃς ἔδει λέγεσθαι. οἷόν τι καὶ περὶ τῆς Μυτιληναίων πόλεως ἐν τῇ τρίτῃ βύβλῳ πεποίηκε· μετὰ γὰρ τὴν ἅλωσιν αὐτῆς καὶ τὴν τῶν αἰχμαλώτων ἄφιξιν, οὓς ἀπέστειλεν ὁ στρατηγὸς Πάχης, διττῶν ἐκκλησιῶν γενομένων ἐν ταῖς Ἀθήναις τοὺς μὲν ἐν τῇ προτέρᾳ ῥηθέντας ὑπὸ τῶν δημαγωγῶν λόγους παρέλιπεν ὡς οὐκ ἀναγκαίους, ἐν ᾗ τούς τε αἰχμαλώτους ἀποκτεῖναι ὁ δῆμος ἐψηφίσατο καὶ τοὺς ἄλλους Μυτιληναίους ἡβηδόν, γυναῖκας δὲ καὶ παῖδας ἀνδραποδίσαι· τοὺς δ' ἐν τῇ ὑστεραίᾳ πάλιν ὑπὸ τῶν αὐτῶν ῥηθέντας, ἐν ᾗ μετάνοιά τις ὑπεισῆλθε τοὺς πολλούς, περὶ τὴν αὐτὴν συνταχθέντας ὑπόθεσιν παρέλαβεν ὡς ἀναγκαίους.

18 Ὁ δὲ δὴ περιβόητος ἐπιτάφιος, ὃν ἐν τῇ δευτέρᾳ βύβλῳ διελήλυθε, κατὰ τίνα δή ποτε λογισμὸν ἐν τούτῳ κεῖται τῷ τόπῳ μᾶλλον ἢ οὐκ ἐν ἑτέρῳ; εἴ τε γὰρ ἐν ταῖς μεγάλαις συμφοραῖς τῆς πόλεως, ἐν αἷς Ἀθηναίων πολλοὶ καὶ ἀγαθοὶ μαχόμενοι διεφθάρησαν, τοὺς εἰωθότας ὀλοφυρμοὺς ἐπ' αὐτοῖς ἐχρῆν λέγεσθαι, εἴ τ' ἐπὶ ταῖς μεγάλαις εὐπραγίαις, ἐξ ὧν δόξα τις ἐπιφανὴς ἢ δύναμις ἐγένετο τῇ πόλει, τιμᾶσθαι τοῖς ἐπιταφίοις ἐπαίνοις τοὺς ἀποθανόντας, ἐν ᾗ βούλεταί τις μᾶλλον βύβλῳ ἢ ἐν ταύτῃ τὸν ἐπιτάφιον ἥρμοττεν εἰρῆσθαι· ἐν ταύτῃ μὲν γὰρ οἱ κατὰ τὴν πρώτην τῶν Πελοποννησίων εἰσβολὴν πεσόντες Ἀθηναῖοι κομιδῇ τινες ἦσαν ὀλίγοι, καὶ οὐδ' οὗτοι λαμπρόν τι πράξαντες ἔργον, ὡς αὐτὸς ὁ Θουκυδίδης

weakness, namely that when dealing with the same subject on the same occasion he includes inessential and omits essential material. For example, in his account of the Mytilenean affair in the third book, after the capture of the town and the arrival of the prisoners sent by the general Paches, two meetings were held at Athens.[1] He omits as unnecessary the speeches made by the demagogues in the first meeting, in which the people voted to execute the prisoners and all the other adult young Mytilenean males, and to enslave the women and children; but he finds it necessary to include the speeches made by the same men at the second meeting, in which a change of heart gradually came over the majority, though the subject for which they were composed is the same as in the former debate.[2]

Then there is the renowned *Funeral Speech*, which 18
he gives in full in the second book:[3] what possible 431 B.C.
reason can he have had for including it at this point rather than at another? If he felt it desirable to record the lamentations customarily made over the many brave Athenians who died in the fighting in their city's great disasters; or again if he wished to praise those who fell in the act of winning the great victories which brought her signal glory or power, any book rather than this would have afforded a suitable place to record a funeral speech. The Athenian dead in this case are those who fell in the first Peloponnesian invasion; but they were quite few in number, and these few had done nothing distinguished, as Thucydides himself admits. Writing at

1 iii. 36.
2 iii. 36–49.
3 ii. 35–46.

γράφει· προειπὼν γὰρ περὶ τοῦ Περικλέους, ὅτι "τὴν πόλιν ἐφύλασσε καὶ δι᾽ ἡσυχίας μάλιστα ὅσον ἐδύνατο εἶχεν· ἱππέας μέντοι τινὰς ἐξέπεμπεν ἀεὶ τοῦ μὴ προδρόμους ἀπὸ τῆς στρατιᾶς ἐσπίπτοντας εἰς τοὺς ἀγροὺς τοὺς ἐγγὺς τῆς πόλεως κακουργεῖν," καὶ ἱππομαχίαν φησὶ γενέσθαι βραχεῖαν "ἐν Φρυγίοις τῶν τε Ἀθηναίων τέλει ἑνὶ τῶν ἱππέων καὶ Θεσσαλοῖς μετ᾽ αὐτῶν πρὸς τοὺς Βοιωτῶν ἱππέας· ἐν ᾗ οὐκ ἔλαττον ἔσχον οἱ Θεσσαλοὶ καὶ Ἀθηναῖοι, μέχρι οὗ προσβοηθησάντων τοῖς Βοιωτοῖς τῶν ὁπλιτῶν τροπὴ ἐγένετο αὐτῶν, καὶ ἀπέθανον τῶν Θεσσαλῶν καὶ Ἀθηναίων οὐ πολλοί· ἀνείλοντο μέντοι αὐτοὺς αὐθημερὸν ἀσπόνδους· καὶ οἱ Πελοποννήσιοι τρόπαιον τῇ ὑστεραίᾳ ἔστησαν." ἐν δὲ τῇ τετάρτῃ βύβλῳ οἱ μετὰ Δημοσθένους περὶ Πύλον ἀγωνισάμενοι πρὸς Λακεδαιμονίων δύναμιν καὶ ἐκ γῆς καὶ ἐκ θαλάττης καὶ νικήσαντες ἐν ἀμφοτέραις ταῖς μάχαις, δι᾽ οὓς ἡ πόλις αὐχήματος ἐπληρώθη, πολλῷ πλείους τε καὶ κρείττους ἦσαν ἐκείνων. τί δή ποτε οὖν ἐπὶ μὲν τοῖς ὀλίγοις ἱππεῦσι καὶ οὐδεμίαν οὔτε δόξαν οὔτε δύναμιν τῇ πόλει κτησαμένοις τάς τε ταφὰς ἀνοίγει τὰς δημοσίας ὁ συγγραφεὺς καὶ τὸν ἐπιφανέστατον τῶν δημαγωγῶν Περικλέα τὴν ὑψηλὴν τραγῳδίαν ἐκείνην εἰσάγει διατιθέμενον· ἐπὶ δὲ τοῖς πλείοσι καὶ κρείττοσι, δι᾽ οὓς ὑπέπεσον Ἀθηναίοις οἱ τὸν πόλεμον ἐξενέγκαντες κατ᾽ αὐτῶν, ἐπιτηδειοτέροις οὖσι ταύτης τῆς τιμῆς τυγχάνειν οὐκ ἐποίησε τὸν ἐπιτάφιον; ἵνα δὲ πάσας ἀφῶ τὰς ἄλλας μάχας τάς τε κατὰ γῆν καὶ κατὰ θάλατταν, ἐν αἷς πολλοὶ διεφθάρησαν, οὓς

the outset about Pericles,[1] that ". . . He watched over the city and kept it as calm as he could. However, he sent out cavalry from time to time to prevent patrols from the enemy army from making sudden raids on the farm-lands near the city and doing mischief," he goes on to say that a brief cavalry battle took place ". . . in Phrygian territory between a single detachment of Athenian cavalry with their Thessalian allies and the Boeotian cavalry, in which the Thessalians and Athenians were at least a match for their opponents, until the Boeotian infantry came to assist the horse, and they were compelled to retreat. The Athenians and the Thessalians lost a few men, but recovered their bodies on the same day without a truce. The next day the Peloponnesians set up a trophy." But those who, in the fourth book,[2] fought with Demosthenes against a force of the Lacedaemonians at Pylos on land and sea, and were 425 B.C.
victorious in both battles, filled their city with a new confidence; and they were more numerous and better troops than the others. Why ever, then, does the historian lay open the public tombs for a few cavalrymen who earned no glory and no power for the city, and introduce the most illustrious public orator, Pericles, to enact his performance of high tragedy, while he wrote no funeral speech for their better and more numerous fellow-countrymen, through whose actions the invaders of Athenian soil were humbled, and who therefore were more deserving of this honour? Leaving aside all the other land- and sea-battles in which many men died who deserved funeral

[1] ii. 22. 1–2.
[2] iv. 9–23; 26–40.

πολὺ δικαιότερον ἦν κοσμεῖσθαι τοῖς ἐπιταφίοις ἐπαίνοις ἢ τοὺς περιπόλους [1] τῆς Ἀττικῆς, ἱππεῖς δέκα ἢ πεντεκαίδεκα ὄντας, οἱ ἐν Σικελίᾳ μετὰ Νικίου καὶ Δημοσθένους ἀποθανόντες Ἀθηναίων καὶ τῶν συμμάχων ἔν τε ταῖς ναυμαχίαις ἔν τε τοῖς κατὰ γῆν ἀγῶσι καὶ τὸ τελευταῖον ἐν τῇ δυστήνῳ φυγῇ τετρακισμυρίων οὐκ ἐλάττους ὄντες καὶ οὐδὲ ταφῆς δυνηθέντες τυχεῖν τῆς νομίμου πόσῳ μᾶλλον ἦσαν ἐπιτηδειότεροι τυγχάνειν οἴκτων τε καὶ κόσμων ἐπιταφίων; ὁ δ᾽ οὕτως ἠμέληκε τῶν ἀνδρῶν, ὥστε μηδὲ τοῦτο αὐτὸ εἰπεῖν, ὅτι πένθος δημοσίᾳ προὔθετο ἡ πόλις καὶ τοὺς εἰωθότας ἐναγισμοὺς τοῖς ἐπὶ ξένης ἀποθανοῦσιν ἐπετέλεσεν καὶ τὸν ἐροῦντα ἐπ᾽ αὐτοῖς ἀπέδειξεν, ὃς τῶν τότε ῥητόρων λέγειν ἦν ἱκανώτατος. οὐ γὰρ δὴ εἰκὸς ἦν Ἀθηναίους ἐπὶ μὲν τοῖς πεντεκαίδεκα ἱππεῦσιν δημοσίᾳ πενθεῖν, τοὺς δ᾽ ἐν Σικελίᾳ πεσόντας, ἐν οἷς . . .[2] τῶν δ᾽ ἐκ καταλόγου πλείους οἱ διαφθαρέντες ἢ πεντακισχίλιοι, μηδεμιᾶς ἀξιῶσαι τιμῆς. ἀλλ᾽ ἔοικεν ὁ συγγραφεὺς (εἰρήσεται γὰρ ἃ φρονῶ) τῷ Περικλέους προσώπῳ βουλόμενος ἀποχρήσασθαι καὶ τὸν ἐπιτάφιον ἔπαινον ὡς ὑπ᾽ ἐκείνου ῥηθέντα συνθεῖναι, ἐπειδὴ [3] κατὰ τὸ δεύτερον ἔτος ἐτελεύτησεν ἀνὴρ τοῦδε τοῦ πολέμου καὶ οὐδεμιᾷ τῶν μετὰ ταῦτα γενομένων τῇ πόλει συμφορῶν παρεγένετο, εἰς ἐκεῖνο τὸ μικρὸν καὶ οὐκ ἄξιον σπουδῆς ἔργον τὸν ὑπὲρ τὴν ἀξίαν τοῦ πράγματος ἔπαινον ἀποθέσθαι.

19 Ἔτι δὲ μᾶλλον ἴδοι τις ἂν τὸ περὶ τὰς ἐξεργασίας

[1] περιπόλους Dudith: πολλοὺς codd.
[2] lacunam indicavit Usener.

tributes much more than the ten or fifteen cavalrymen of the Attic militia, what of those Athenians and
their allies who died in Sicily with Nicias and Demos- 414–413
thenes in the sea-battles, the land engagements and B.C.
finally in the lamentable retreat? There were no
fewer than forty thousand of them, and they could
not be given the customary burial-rites: how much
more did these men deserve to be mourned and
honoured with funeral speeches? But the historian
has ignored these men even to the extent of omitting
to say that the city decreed that they should be publicly mourned, and performed the ceremonies that
were customary for those who died abroad, and
appointed to speak over them the ablest orator of the
day. It certainly seems unlikely that the Athenians
would have conducted a state ceremony to mourn the
fifteen cavalrymen, and then regarded as unworthy
of any honour those who died in Sicily, whose deaths
included [1] . . . and more than five thousand from the
citizen levy. But it seems likely (and I shall speak
my mind), that the historian composed this funeral
eulogy and assigned it to Pericles because he wished
to make full use of his character; and since that
statesman died during the second year of the war and 429 B.C.
did not witness any of the misfortunes that befell the
city after that time, he reserves this minor and un-
inspiring event for him to adorn with exaggerated
praise.

One can see even better the unevenness of the 19

[1] In view of the δὲ, a parallel clause with μὲν may have dropped out, perhaps referring to the distinguished generals Lamachus, Nicias and Demosthenes, who died in Sicily.

[3] ἐπειδὴ Krüger: ἐπεὶ δὲ codd.

τοῦ συγγραφέως ἀνώμαλον ἐπιλογισάμενος, ὅτι πολλὰ καὶ μεγάλα πράγματα παραλιπὼν ⟨τὸ⟩ προοίμιον τῆς ἱστορίας μέχρι πεντακοσίων ἐκμηκύνει στίχων, τὰ πρὸ τοῦδε τοῦ πολέμου πραχθέντα τοῖς Ἕλλησι μικρὰ βουλόμενος ἀποδεῖξαι καὶ οὐκ ἄξια τῷδε παραβάλλεσθαι. οὔτε γὰρ τἀληθὲς οὕτως εἶχεν, ὡς ἐκ πολλῶν ἔστι παραδεῖξαι πραγμάτων, οὔτε ὁ τῆς τέχνης ὑπαγορεύει λόγος οὕτω μεθοδεύειν τὰς αὐξήσεις (οὐ γὰρ εἴ τι τῶν μικρῶν μεῖζόν ἐστι, διὰ τοῦτ᾽ ἐστὶν ἤδη μέγα, ἀλλ᾽ εἴ τι τῶν μεγάλων ὑπερέχει)· γέγονέ τε αὐτῷ τὸ προοίμιον, τοσαύτας εἰληφὸς ἀποδεικτικὰς τῆς προθέσεως ἐξεργασίας, ἱστορία τις αὐτὴ καθ᾽ αὑτήν. οἱ δὲ τὰς ῥητορικὰς συνταξάμενοι τέχνας παραγγέλλουσι δείγματα τῶν λόγων τὰ προοίμια ποιεῖν αὐτὰ τὰ κεφάλαια τῶν μελλόντων δηλοῦσθαι προλαμβάνοντας.[1] ὃ δὴ καὶ πεποίηκεν ὁ ἀνὴρ ἐπὶ τῷ τέλει τοῦ προοιμίου, μέλλων ἄρχεσθαι τῆς διηγήσεως, ἐν ἐλάττοσιν ἢ πεντήκοντα στίχοις· ὥστε τὰ πολλὰ ἐκεῖνα καὶ καταβλητικὰ τοῦ μεγέθους τῆς Ἑλλάδος οὐκ ἀναγκαίως αὐτῷ παρέλκεσθαι, ὅτι κατὰ τὸν Τρωικὸν πόλεμον οὔπω σύμπασα ἐκαλεῖτο ἑνὶ ὀνόματι ἡ Ἑλλάς, καὶ ὅτι περαιοῦσθαι ναυσὶν ἐπ᾽ ἀλλήλους οἱ τροφῆς ἀπορούμενοι ἤρξαντο καὶ προσπίπτοντες πόλεσιν ἀτειχίστοις καὶ κατὰ κώμας οἰκουμέναις ἥρπαζον καὶ τὸ πλεῖστον τοῦ βίου ἐντεῦθεν ἐποιοῦντο. τί δ᾽ ἦν ἀναγκαῖον περὶ τῆς Ἀθηναίων τρυφῆς, ᾗ τὸ παλαιὸν ἐχρῶντο, λέγειν, ὅτι κρωβύλους τε ἀνεπλέκοντο καὶ χρυσοῦς τέττιγας εἶχον ἐπὶ ταῖς

[1] προλαμβάνοντας Reiske: προσλαμβάνοντας codd.

historian's treatment if one considers that, while omitting many important events, he nevertheless makes his introduction some five hundred lines long as he attempts to prove that prior to this war the Greeks achieved little, and nothing worthy to be compared with it. The actual facts were not like this, as many historical events show, nor do artistic principles dictate this degree of exaggeration (for the fact that it is larger than small objects does not automatically make a thing large: this is so only when it surpasses something large). Again, the introduction contains so many elaborate arguments to prove his proposition, that it has become a sort of history on its own. The writers of the rhetorical handbooks prescribe that the introduction should adumbrate the arguments that are to be used by providing actual summaries of what is to be revealed later.[1] Thucydides has actually done this at the close of his introduction, dealing with it in fewer than fifty lines before he begins his narrative.[2] And this makes it unnecessary for him to drag in that lengthy disparagement of the greatness of Greece: that at the time of the Trojan War the whole of Greece was not yet called by that single name,[3] and that it was through shortage of food that they had begun to cross by sea into one another's territory, and attacked cities that were unwalled and inhabited in small settlements, and made most of their livelihood by this means.[4] Why was it necessary to mention the luxury enjoyed by Athenians in early times: how they plaited up their hair into top-knots and wore gold cicadas on their heads?[5] Or that the Lacedae-

[1] *Rhetorica ad Alexandrum*, 29.
[2] i. 23.
[3] i. 3.
[4] i. 5.
[5] i. 6. 3.

κεφαλαῖς; καὶ ὅτι Λακεδαιμόνιοι "ἐγυμνώθησάν τε πρῶτοι καὶ εἰς τὸ φανερὸν ἀποδύντες λίπα μετὰ τοῦ γυμνάζεσθαι ἠλείψαντο"; ὁ δὲ δὴ ναυπηγὸς ὁ Κορίνθιος Ἀμεινοκλῆς ὁ κατασκευάσας Σαμίοις πρῶτος τέτταρας τριήρεις, καὶ ὁ Σάμου τύραννος Πολυκράτης ὁ Ῥήνειαν ἑλὼν καὶ ἀναθεὶς τῷ Ἀπόλλωνι τῷ Δηλίῳ, καὶ οἱ Φωκαεῖς οἱ Μασσαλίαν οἰκίσαντες ὅτι ναυμαχίᾳ Καρχηδονίους ἐνίκων, καὶ τὰ ἄλλα ὅσα τούτοις ἐστὶν ὅμοια, τίνα καιρὸν εἶχε πρὸ τῆς διηγήσεως λέγεσθαι;

20 εἰ δ' ἔστιν ὅσιόν μοι καὶ θεμιτὸν εἰπεῖν ἃ φρονῶ, δοκεῖ μοι κράτιστον ἂν γενέσθαι ⟨τὸ⟩ προοίμιον, εἰ τὸ τελευταῖον αὐτοῦ μέρος τῇ προθέσει προσήρμοσε πάντα τὰ ἐν μέσῳ παραλιπὼν καὶ τοῦτον τὸν τρόπον αὐτὸ κατεσκεύασε· "Θουκυδίδης Ἀθηναῖος συνέγραψε τὸν πόλεμον τῶν Πελοποννησίων καὶ Ἀθηναίων, ὡς ἐπολέμησαν πρὸς ἀλλήλους, ἀρξάμενος εὐθὺς καθισταμένου καὶ ἐλπίσας μέγαν τε ἔσεσθαι καὶ ἀξιολογώτατον τῶν προγεγενημένων· τεκμαιρόμενος, ὅτι ἀκμάζοντές τε ἦσαν ἐς αὐτὸν ἀμφότεροι παρασκευῇ τῇ πάσῃ, καὶ τὸ ἄλλο Ἑλληνικὸν ὁρῶν ξυνιστάμενον πρὸς ἑκατέρους, τὸ μὲν εὐθύς, τὸ δὲ καὶ διανοούμενον. κίνησις γὰρ αὕτη δὴ μεγίστη τοῖς Ἕλλησιν ἐγένετο καὶ μέρει τινὶ τῶν βαρβάρων, ὡς δ' εἰπεῖν καὶ ἐπὶ πλεῖστον ἀνθρώπων. τὰ γὰρ πρὸ αὐτῶν καὶ ἔτι παλαιότερα σαφῶς μὲν εὑρεῖν διὰ χρόνου πλῆθος ἀδύνατον ἦν· ἐκ δὲ τεκμηρίων,

---

[1] i. 6. 5.
[2] i. 13. 3.
[3] i. 13. 6.
[4] i. 13. 6.
[5] i. 1.

monians ". . . were the first to exercise naked, stripping in public and rubbing themselves over with oil after their exercise?"[1] And what of the references to Ameinocles the Corinthian shipbuilder, who built the first triremes, four in number, for the
Samians;[2] to Polycrates the tyrant of Samos, who 545–523
captured Rheneia and dedicated it to Delian Apollo;[3] B.C. 535 B.C.
and to the Phocaeans, who colonised Massilia and defeated the Carthaginians in a sea-battle:[4] what occasion did he have to introduce these events and others like them before the narrative proper?

If I may be allowed to state my opinion without 20
giving offence to gods or men, I think that the introduction would have been most effective if he had made the concluding section follow directly upon the introductory section, omitting the whole of the middle section. The whole passage would then run as follows:[5]

"Thucydides, an Athenian, wrote the history of the war between the Peloponnesians and the Athenians, describing its course, beginning at the moment it broke out, and believing that it would be a great war and more worthy to be recorded than any of its predecessors. This I conclude from the fact that both sides were in every way at the height of preparedness for it, and because I saw that the rest of Greece was taking one side or the other, some immediately, and some intending to do so. Indeed, this was the greatest upheaval yet known in history, not only that of the Greeks, but including a part of the barbarian world, and extending, one might say, over most of the world. For although the events that preceded this, and those of even remoter antiquity could not, through the length of time, be ascertained clearly, yet

ὧν ἐπὶ μακρότατον σκοποῦντι πιστεύειν ξυμβαίνει, οὐ μεγάλα νομίζω γενέσθαι οὔτε κατὰ τοὺς πολέμους οὔτε ἐς τὰ ἄλλα· οὔτε ὡς ποιηταὶ ὑμνήκασι περὶ αὐτῶν ἐπὶ τὸ μεῖζον κοσμοῦντες, μᾶλλον πιστεύων, οὔτε ὡς λογογράφοι συνέθεσαν ἐπὶ τὸ προσαγωγότερον τῇ ἀκροάσει ἢ ἀληθέστερον, ὄντα ἀνεξέλεγκτα καὶ τὰ πολλὰ ὑπὸ χρόνου αὐτῶν ἀπίστως ἐπὶ τὸ μυθῶδες ἐκνενικηκότα· εὑρῆσθαι δὲ ἡγησάμενος ἐκ τῶν ἐπιφανεστάτων ὡς παλαιὰ εἶναι ἀποχρώντως. καὶ ὁ πόλεμος οὗτος, καίπερ τῶν ἀνθρώπων, ἐν ᾧ μὲν ἂν πολεμῶσι, τὸν παρόντα ἀεὶ μέγιστον κρινόντων, παυσαμένων δὲ τἀρχαῖα μᾶλλον θαυμαζόντων, ἀπ' αὐτῶν τῶν ἔργων σκοποῦσι δηλώσει ὅμως μείζων γεγενημένος αὐτῶν. καὶ ὅσα μὲν λόγῳ εἶπον ἕκαστοι ἢ μέλλοντες πολεμήσειν ἢ ἐν αὐτῷ ἤδη ὄντες, χαλεπὸν τὴν ἀκρίβειαν αὐτὴν τῶν λεχθέντων διαμνημονεῦσαι ἦν ἐμοί τε ὧν αὐτὸς ἤκουσα καὶ τοῖς ἄλλοθέν ποθεν ἐμοὶ ἀπαγγέλλουσιν· ὡς δ' ἂν ἐδόκουν μοι ἕκαστοι περὶ τῶν ἀεὶ παρόντων τὰ δέοντα μάλιστα εἰπεῖν, ἐχομένῳ ὅ τι ἐγγύτατα τῆς ξυμπάσης γνώμης τῶν ἀληθῶς λεχθέντων, οὕτως εἴρηται. τὰ δὲ ἔργα τῶν πραχθέντων ἐν τῷ πολέμῳ οὐκ ἐκ τοῦ παρατυχόντος ἠξίωσα γράφειν οὐδ' ὡς ἐμοὶ δοκεῖ, ἀλλ' οἷς τε αὐτὸς παρῆν καὶ παρὰ τῶν ἄλλων ὅσον δυνατὸν ἀκριβείᾳ περὶ ἑκάστου ἐπεξελθών. ἐπιπόνως δὲ εὑρίσκετο, διότι οἱ παρόντες τοῖς ἔργοις οὐ τὰ

---

[1] Dionysius now moves on to i. 21–23.

from such evidence as I am disposed, through research which has followed events as far back as possible, to trust, I believe that they were not great either with regard to wars or anything else. I have preferred not to place my trust in what the poets say about them,[1] embroidering them in exaggerated terms, or by the compositions of the chroniclers, which are designed to attract the ear rather than tell the truth, and whose subjects cannot be proved and have mostly, through the passage of time, come to be regarded as incredible fables. But I consider that I have established the facts satisfactorily from the clearest indications possible in matters of such antiquity. As to this war, although men always think that the war in which they are participating is the greatest while it is going on, but when it is over they revert to admiring wars of old more, yet an examination of the facts will show that it was much greater than any of the wars which preceded it. With reference to the speeches made by politicians on both sides either before or after the beginning of hostilities, it was difficult for me to obtain an exact record of what was said, either when I heard it myself or when it was reported to me by various informants; but I have made the speakers say what was in my opinion demanded of them by the various occasions, while adhering as closely as possible to the general sense of what was actually said. And with reference to the narrative of events, I did not allow myself to obtain it from the first source that came to hand, and did not trust even my own recollections, but followed up with the greatest possible accuracy both those at which I was myself present and those I heard about from others. This research involved hard work, because different eye-witnesses did

αὐτὰ περὶ τῶν αὐτῶν ἔλεγον, ἀλλ' ὡς ἑκατέρων τις εὐνοίας ἢ μνήμης ἔχοι. καὶ ἐς μὲν ἀκρόασιν ἴσως τὸ μὴ μυθῶδες αὐτῶν ἀτερπέστερον φανεῖται· ὅσοι δὲ βουλήσονται τῶν γεγονότων τὸ σαφὲς σκοπεῖν καὶ τῶν μελλόντων ποτὲ αὖθις κατὰ τὸ ἀνθρώπινον τοιούτων καὶ παραπλησίων ἔσεσθαι, ὠφέλιμα κρίνειν αὐτά, ἀρκούντως ἕξει· κτῆμά τε ἐς ἀεὶ μᾶλλον ἢ ἀγώνισμα εἰς τὸ παραχρῆμα ἀκούειν ξύγκειται. τῶν δὲ πρότερον ἔργων μέγιστον ἐπράχθη τὸ Μηδικόν· καὶ τοῦτο ὅμως δυεῖν ναυμαχίαιν καὶ πεζομαχίαιν τὴν κρίσιν ἔσχεν· τούτου δὲ τοῦ πολέμου μῆκός τε μέγα προὔβη παθήματά τε ξυνηνέχθη γενέσθαι ἐν αὐτῷ τῇ Ἑλλάδι οἷα οὐχ ἕτερα ἐν ἴσῳ χρόνῳ. οὔτε γὰρ πόλεις τοσαίδε ληφθεῖσαι ἠρημώθησαν αἳ μὲν ὑπὸ βαρβάρων, αἳ δ' ὑπὸ σφῶν αὐτῶν ἀντιπολεμούντων, εἰσὶ δὲ αἳ καὶ οἰκήτορας μετέβαλον ἁλισκόμεναι· οὔτε φυγαὶ τοσαίδε ἀνθρώπων καὶ φόνος ὃ μὲν κατ' αὐτὸν τὸν πόλεμον, ὃ δὲ διὰ τὸ στασιάζειν. τά τε πρότερον ἀκοῇ μὲν λεγόμενα, ἔργῳ δὲ σπανιώτερον βεβαιούμενα οὐκ ἄπιστα κατέστη σεισμῶν τε πέρι, οἳ ἐπὶ πλεῖστον ἅμα μέρος γῆς καὶ ἰσχυρότατοι οἱ αὐτοὶ ἐπέσχον, ἡλίου τε ἐκλείψεις, αἳ πυκνότεραι παρὰ τὰς ἐκ τοῦ πρὶν χρόνου μνημονευομένας ξυνέβησαν, αὐχμοί τε ἔστι παρ' οἷς μεγάλοι, καὶ ἀπ' αὐτῶν καὶ λιμοί· καὶ ἡ οὐχ ἥκιστα βλάψασα καὶ μέρος τι φθείρασα, ἡ λοιμώδης νόσος· ταῦτα γὰρ πάντα μετὰ τοῦδε τοῦ πολέμου ἅμα ξυνεπέθετο. ἤρξαντο δὲ αὐτοῦ Ἀθηναῖοι καὶ Πελοποννήσιοι λύσαντες τὰς τριακοντούτεις σπονδάς, αἳ αὐτοῖς ἐγένοντο μετ'

not give the same accounts of the same events, but each was influenced by partiality or by his memory. The absence of legend will perhaps detract from the listener's enjoyment; but if it should be judged useful by those who wish to have a clear view of the past from which to interpret the future, which in the nature of human affairs will follow a similar if not identical pattern, I shall be satisfied. My work is composed to be a possession for ever, not an occasional piece for a single hearing.

"Now of earlier achievements, the greatest was the Median War: yet even this was concluded in two sea-battles and two land-battles; whereas the present war was prolonged to a great length, and yet was short for the unparalleled amount of suffering it brought upon Greece in its time. Never had so many cities been taken and depopulated, here by the barbarians, here by the inhabitants engaged in civil strife (the old inhabitants sometimes being expelled and replaced by their conquerors). Never was there so much banishment and bloodshed, the result both of the war itself and of internecine strife. Earlier tales of earthquakes and eclipses of the sun, reported from hearsay and lacking concrete evidence to confirm them, were now made to seem credible, for the former occurred over the greater part of the world and were at the same time most violent, and the latter were more frequently recorded than in earlier accounts. Some districts experienced droughts also, and resultant famines; and last but not least damaging, the plague, which destroyed a portion of mankind. All these things befell the world during this war. It was started by the Athenians and the Peloponnesians, who dissolved the Thirty Years' Peace, which was

480–479 B.C.

Εὐβοίας ἅλωσιν. διότι δὲ ἔλυσαν, τὰς αἰτίας προέγραψα πρῶτον καὶ τὰς διαφορὰς τοῦ μή τινα ζητῆσαί ποτε, ἐξ ὅτου τοσοῦτος πόλεμος τοῖς Ἕλλησι κατέστη." Τὰ μὲν δὴ περὶ τὸ πραγματικὸν μέρος ἁμαρτήματά τε καὶ κατορθώματα τοῦ συγγραφέως ταῦτά ἐστι.

21 Τὰ δὲ περὶ τὸ λεκτικόν, ἐν ᾧ μάλιστα ὁ χαρακτὴρ αὐτοῦ διάδηλός ἐστι, μέλλω νυνὶ λέγειν. ἀνάγκη δὲ ἴσως καὶ περὶ ταύτης τῆς ἰδέας προειπεῖν, εἰς πόσα τε μέρη διαιρεῖσθαι πέφυκεν ἡ λέξις καὶ τίνας περιείληφεν ἀρετάς· ἔπειτα δηλῶσαι, πῶς ἔχουσαν αὐτὴν ὁ Θουκυδίδης παρὰ τῶν πρὸ αὐτοῦ γενομένων συγγραφέων παρέλαβε, καὶ τίνα μέρη πρῶτος ἁπάντων ἐκαίνωσεν, εἴ τ' ἐπὶ τὸ κρεῖττον εἴ τ' ἐπὶ τὸ χεῖρον, μηδὲν ἀποκρυψάμενον.[1]

22 Ὅτι μὲν οὖν ἅπασα λέξις εἰς δύο μέρη διαιρεῖται τὰ πρῶτα, εἴς τε τὴν ἐκλογὴν τῶν ὀνομάτων, ὑφ' ὧν δηλοῦται τὰ πράγματα, καὶ εἰς τὴν σύνθεσιν τῶν ἐλαττόνων τε καὶ μειζόνων μορίων, καὶ ὅτι τούτων αὖθις ἑκάτερον εἰς ἕτερα μόρια διαιρεῖται, ἡ μὲν ἐκλογὴ τῶν στοιχειωδῶν μορίων (ὀνοματικῶν λέγω καὶ ῥηματικῶν καὶ συνδετικῶν) εἴς τε τὴν κυρίαν φράσιν καὶ εἰς τὴν τροπικήν, ἡ δὲ σύνθεσις εἴς τε τὰ κόμματα καὶ τὰ κῶλα καὶ τὰς περιόδους, καὶ ὅτι τούτοις ἀμφοτέροις συμβέβηκε (λέγω δὴ τοῖς τε ἁπλοῖς καὶ ἀτόμοις ὀνόμασι καὶ τοῖς ἐκ τούτων συνθέτοις) τὰ καλούμενα σχήματα, καὶ ὅτι τῶν καλουμένων ἀρετῶν αἳ μέν εἰσιν ἀναγκαῖαι καὶ ἐν ἅπασιν ὀφείλουσι παρεῖναι τοῖς

[1] ἀποκρυψάμενον Reiske: ἀποκρυψάμενος codd.

made between them after the capture of Euboea. As 446 B.C.
to their reason for breaking the peace, I have first given their grounds of complaint and their differences, so that no one will ever need to ask the cause of such a great war among the Greeks."

These, then, are examples of the historian's failings and successes with regard to subject-matter.

I now propose to discuss his style, which more than 21
anything else reveals his individuality. But perhaps I should begin my discussion of this subject of style by defining its natural divisions and the qualities inherent in it, and then show the state in which Thucydides inherited the genre from his predecessors, and in what aspects of it he was the first of all to introduce innovations. I shall conceal neither the improvements he made nor his shortcomings.

It has been said many times that style in general is 22
divided in[1] the first instance into two parts—the choice of words, whereby the subject is described, and the combination of the lesser and the more important elements; and that each of these is further divided, the choice of the elementary parts of speech (namely, nouns, verbs and conjunctions)[2] being divided into direct and metaphorical expression, and combination into clauses, sentences and periods. Both of these (that is to say, simple, individual words and composite expressions), are subject to what is called figurative usage. Some of the 'virtues' ascribed to style are *essential*, and should be present in all writing, while

[1] Cf. *De Compositione Verborum*, 1, 3, 18, 20. Theophrastus designated three, adding the use of figures of speech. See *Isocrates*, 3.

[2] These three parts of speech were recognised by the earliest grammarians.

λόγοις, αἳ δ' ἐπίθετοι καὶ ὅταν ὑποστῶσιν αἱ πρῶται, τότε τὴν ἑαυτῶν ἰσχὺν λαμβάνουσιν, εἴρηται πολλοῖς πρότερον. ὥστε οὐδὲν δεῖ περὶ αὐτῶν ἐμὲ νυνὶ λέγειν οὐδ' ἐξ ὧν θεωρημάτων τε καὶ παραγγελμάτων τούτων τῶν ἀρετῶν ἑκάστη γίνεται, πολλῶν ὄντων· καὶ γὰρ ταῦτα τῆς ἀκριβεστάτης τέτευχεν ἐξεργασίας.

23 Τίσι δὲ αὐτῶν ἐχρήσαντο πάντες οἱ πρὸ Θουκυδίδου γενόμενοι συγγραφεῖς καὶ τίνων ἐπὶ μικρὸν ἥψαντο, ἐξ ἀρχῆς ἀναλαβών, ὥσπερ ὑπεσχόμην, κεφαλαιωδῶς διέξειμι· ἀκριβέστερον γὰρ οὕτως γνώσεταί τις τὸν ἴδιον τοῦ ἀνδρὸς χαρακτῆρα. οἱ μὲν οὖν ἀρχαῖοι πάνυ καὶ ἀπ' αὐτῶν μόνον γινωσκόμενοι τῶν ὀνομάτων ποίαν τινὰ λέξιν ἐπετήδευσαν, οὐκ ἔχω συμβαλεῖν, πότερα τὴν λιτὴν καὶ ἀκόσμητον καὶ μηδὲν ἔχουσαν περιττόν, ἀλλ' αὐτὰ τὰ χρήσιμα καὶ ἀναγκαῖα, ἢ τὴν πομπικὴν καὶ ἀξιωματικὴν καὶ ἐγκατάσκευον καὶ τοὺς ἐπιθέτους προσειληφυῖαν κόσμους. οὔτε γὰρ διασῴζονται τῶν πλειόνων αἱ γραφαὶ μέχρι τῶν καθ' ἡμᾶς χρόνων, οὔθ' αἱ διασῳζόμεναι παρὰ πᾶσιν ὡς ἐκείνων οὖσαι τῶν ἀνδρῶν πιστεύονται· ἐν αἷς εἰσιν αἵ τε Κάδμου τοῦ Μιλησίου καὶ Ἀρισταίου τοῦ Προκοννησίου καὶ τῶν παραπλησίων τούτοις. οἱ δὲ πρὸ τοῦ Πελοποννησιακοῦ γενόμενοι πολέμου καὶ μέχρι τῆς Θουκυδίδου παρεκτείναντες ἡλικίας ὁμοίας ἔσχον ἅπαντες ὡς ἐπὶ τὸ πολὺ προαιρέσεις, οἵ τε τὴν Ἰάδα προελόμενοι διάλεκτον τὴν ἐν τοῖς τότε χρόνοις μάλιστα

---

[1] The origin of this division of virtues is obscure.

others are *ancillary*,[1] and depend for their effect upon the presence of the essential virtues. All this has often been said before,[2] so that it is unnecessary for me to speak of them now, or to discuss the many principles and rules on which these virtues are each founded; for these matters also have been the subject of precise and elaborate theorisation.

I shall briefly outline which of these qualities were 23
exhibited by all the historians before Thucydides, and which were only imperfectly realised, beginning, as I have promised, from the earliest of them. This procedure will help the reader to distinguish the individual features of the author's style more precisely. As to the very first historians, who are known to us by their names alone, I cannot imagine what kind of style they employed, whether it was plain and unadorned, without any superfluous characteristics and meeting purely functional needs, or stately, dignified and elaborate, with the ancillary devices of ornamentation. The writings of most of them are not extant today, nor are the works which have survived, including those attributed to Cadmus of Miletus,[3] Aristaeus of Proconnesus [4] and other historians like them, universally accepted as genuine. The historians belonging to the generation preceding the Peloponnesian War, who survived into Thucydides's lifetime, in general had the same literary aims, whether they chose the Ionian dialect, which was at

[2] This is the first extant explicit reference to the system, though there are indirect references to it in Cicero, *De Partitione*, 31, *Brutus*, 261, *De Oratore*, iii. 52.

[3] Reputedly the first author of a history of a single city.

[4] Or Aristeas. A semi-legendary figure associated with the cult of Apollo. See Bolton, *Aristeas of Proconnesus*.

ἀνθοῦσαν καὶ οἱ τὴν ἀρχαίαν Ἀτθίδα μικράς τινας ἔχουσαν διαφορὰς παρὰ τὴν Ἰάδα. πάντες γὰρ οὗτοι, καθάπερ ἔφην, περὶ τὴν κυρίαν λέξιν μᾶλλον ἐσπούδασαν ἢ περὶ τὴν τροπικήν, ταύτην δὲ ὥσπερ ἥδυσμα παρελάμβανον, σύνθεσίν τε ὀνομάτων ὁμοίαν ἅπαντες ἐπετήδευσαν τὴν ἀφελῆ καὶ ἀνεπιτήδευτον, καὶ οὐδ' ἐν τῷ σχηματίζειν τὰς λέξεις ⟨καὶ⟩ [1] τὰς νοήσεις ἐξέβησαν ἐπὶ πολὺ τῆς τετριμμένης καὶ κοινῆς καὶ συνήθους ἅπασι διαλέκτου. τὰς μὲν οὖν ἀναγκαίας ἀρετὰς ἡ λέξις αὐτῶν πάντων ἔχει (καὶ γὰρ καθαρὰ καὶ σαφὴς καὶ σύντομός ἐστιν ἀποχρώντως, σῴζουσα τὸν ἴδιον ἑκάστη τῆς διαλέκτου χαρακτῆρα)· τὰς δ' ἐπιθέτους, ἐξ ὧν μάλιστα διάδηλος ἡ τοῦ ῥήτορος γίνεται δύναμις, οὔτε ἁπάσας οὔτε εἰς ἄκρον ἡκούσας, ἀλλ' ὀλίγας καὶ ἐπὶ βραχύ, ὕψος λέγω καὶ καλλιρημοσύνην καὶ σεμνολογίαν καὶ μεγαλοπρέπειαν· οὐδὲ δὴ τόνον οὐδὲ βάρος οὐδὲ πάθος διεγεῖρον [2] τὸν νοῦν οὐδὲ τὸ ἐρρωμένον καὶ ἐναγώνιον πνεῦμα, ἐξ ὧν ἡ καλουμένη γίνεται δεινότης· πλὴν ἑνὸς Ἡροδότου. οὗτος δὲ κατά ⟨τε⟩ [3] τὴν ἐκλογὴν τῶν ὀνομάτων καὶ κατὰ τὴν σύνθεσιν καὶ κατὰ τὴν τῶν σχηματισμῶν ποικιλίαν μακρῷ δή τινι τοὺς ἄλλους ὑπερεβάλετο, καὶ παρεσκεύασε τῇ κρατίστῃ ποιήσει τὴν πεζὴν φράσιν ὁμοίαν γενέσθαι πειθοῦς τε καὶ χαρίτων καὶ τῆς εἰς ἄκρον ἡκούσης ἡδονῆς ἕνεκα· ἀρετάς τε τὰς μεγίστας καὶ λαμπροτάτας ἔξω τῶν ἐναγωνίων οὐδὲν ἐν ταύταις ἐνέλιπεν, εἴτε οὐκ εὖ πεφυκὼς πρὸς αὐτὰς εἴτε κατὰ λογισμόν τινα ἑκουσίως ὑπεριδὼν ὡς οὐχ ἁρμοττουσῶν ἱστο-

the height of its popularity at the time, or in Old Attic, which differed but slightly from Ionic. All these historians, as I have said, cultivated a direct rather than a figurative style of writing, though they occasionally used the latter to add seasoning, as it were. All constructed their sentences in a similar manner, simply and without artifice, and even when they used figurative language to express their ideas they did not deviate from the well-worn, universally familiar language of normal speech. Thus the style of each of them has all the essential virtues, being sufficiently pure, clear and concise, and preserving the own individual qualities of the dialect chosen. But the ancillary virtues, which reveal most clearly an orator's special ability, are neither all present nor fully developed individually, but are found sparsely and in diluted form—I am referring to sublimity, eloquence, dignity and grandeur. Nor is there any intensity, any gravity, or any emotion to arouse the mind, nor any robust, combative spirit, all of which are essential to what we call genius. The sole exception is Herodotus. This historian was far superior to the rest in his choice of words, his composition and his varied use of figures of speech; and he made his prose style resemble the finest poetry by its persuasiveness, its charm and its utterly delightful effect. He lacked none of the most important and distinctive qualities of any of the genres of verse and prose, except those of practical oratory, for which he either had no natural aptitude, or which he avoided as a matter of policy because he considered them unsuitable for history.

---

[1] καὶ inseruit Krüger.
[2] διεγεῖρον Reiske: διεγείροντα M.
[3] τε inseruit Sadée.

ρίαις. οὔτε γὰρ δημηγορίαις πολλαῖς ὁ ἀνὴρ οὐδ' ἐναγωνίοις κέχρηται λόγοις, οὔτ' ἐν τῷ παθαίνειν καὶ δεινοποιεῖν τὰ πράγματα τὴν ἀλκὴν ἔχει.

24 Τούτῳ τε δὴ τῷ ἀνδρὶ Θουκυδίδης ἐπιβαλὼν καὶ τοῖς ἄλλοις, ὧν πρότερον ἐμνήσθην, καὶ συνιδὼν ἃς ἕκαστος αὐτῶν ἔσχεν ἀρετάς, ἴδιόν τινα χαρακτῆρα καὶ παρεωραμένον ἅπασι πρῶτος εἰς τὴν ἱστορικὴν πραγματείαν ἐσπούδασεν ἀγαγεῖν· ἐπὶ μὲν τῆς ἐκλογῆς τῶν ὀνομάτων τὴν τροπικὴν καὶ γλωττηματικὴν καὶ ἀπηρχαιωμένην καὶ ξένην λέξιν προελόμενος ἀντὶ τῆς κοινῆς καὶ συνήθους τοῖς κατ' αὐτὸν ἀνθρώποις· ἐπὶ δὲ τῆς συνθέσεως τῶν τ' ἐλαττόνων καὶ τῶν μειζόνων μορίων τὴν ἀξιωματικὴν καὶ αὐστηρὰν καὶ στιβαρὰν καὶ βεβηκυῖαν καὶ τραχύνουσαν ταῖς τῶν γραμμάτων ἀντιτυπίαις τὰς ἀκοὰς ἀντὶ τῆς λιγυρᾶς καὶ μαλακῆς καὶ συνεξεσμένης καὶ μηδὲν ἐχούσης ἀντίτυπον· ἐπὶ δὲ τῶν σχηματισμῶν, ἐν οἷς μάλιστα ἐβουλήθη διενέγκαι τῶν πρὸ αὐτοῦ, πλείστην εἰσενεγκάμενος σπουδήν. διετέλεσέ γέ τοι τὸν ἑπτακαιεικοσαετῆ χρόνον τοῦ πολέμου ἀπὸ τῆς ἀρχῆς ἕως τῆς τελευτῆς τὰς ὀκτὼ βύβλους, ἃς μόνας κατέλιπεν, στρέφων ἄνω καὶ κάτω καὶ καθ' ἓν ἕκαστον τῶν τῆς φράσεως μορίων ῥινῶν καὶ τορεύων· καὶ τοτὲ μὲν λόγον ἐξ ὀνόματος ποιῶν, τοτὲ δ' εἰς ὄνομα συνάγων τὸν λόγον· καὶ νῦν μὲν τὸ ῥηματικὸν ὀνοματικῶς ἐκφέρων, αὖθις δὲ τοὔνομα ῥῆμα ποιῶν, καὶ αὐτῶν γε τούτων ἀναστρέφων τὰς χρήσεις, ἵνα τὸ μὲν ὀνοματικὸν προσηγορικὸν γένηται, τὸ δὲ προσηγο-

Herodotus does not use many speeches either in a political or in a forensic style, nor does his strength lie in his ability to invest events with pathos or horror.

Following after Herodotus and the others whom I 24
mentioned before him, and perceiving their several qualities, Thucydides resolved to introduce into the writing of history an individual style which had been overlooked by his predecessors. In his choice of words he preferred those which were metaphorical, obscure, archaic and outlandish to those which were common and familiar to his contemporaries. In the construction of both shorter and longer clauses he chose the arrangements which were dignified, severe, compact and firm-footed, and those which jarred the ear by the clashing of inconsonant letters rather than those which were melodious, smooth, polished and free from any conflict of sound. To figures of speech, in which he was especially eager to outstrip his predecessors, he devoted particular attention. From the beginning to the end of the war, which 431–404 B.C.
lasted twenty-seven years, he never stopped revising his eight books (which are all that he left), and polishing and rounding off the individual phrases. Sometimes he makes a nominal phrase from a noun, and sometimes he condenses a phrase into a noun. Sometimes he expresses a verbal idea in a nominal form, and sometimes he changes a noun into a verb; and of the nouns themselves he inverts their normal use,

ρικὸν ὀνοματικῶς λέγηται· καὶ τὰ μὲν παθητικὰ ῥήματα δραστήρια, τὰ δὲ δραστήρια παθητικά· πληθυντικῶν τε καὶ ἑνικῶν ἐναλλάττων τὰς φύσεις καὶ ἀντικατηγορῶν ταῦτα ἀλλήλων· θηλυκά τε ἀρρενικοῖς καὶ ἀρρενικὰ θηλυκοῖς καὶ οὐδέτερα τούτων τισὶ συνάπτων, ἐξ ὧν ἡ κατὰ φύσιν ἀκολουθία πλανᾶται· τὰς δὲ τῶν ὀνοματικῶν ἢ μετοχικῶν πτώσεις ποτὲ μὲν πρὸς τὸ σημαινόμενον ἀπὸ τοῦ σημαίνοντος ἀποστρέφων, ποτὲ δὲ πρὸς τὸ σημαῖνον ἀπὸ τοῦ σημαινομένου· ἐν δὲ τοῖς συνδετικοῖς καὶ τοῖς προθετικοῖς μορίοις καὶ ἔτι μᾶλλον ἐν τοῖς διαρθροῦσι τὰς τῶν ὀνομάτων δυνάμεις ποιητοῦ τρόπον ἐνεξουσιάζων. πλεῖστα δ᾿ ἄν τις ⟨εὕροι⟩ παρ᾿ αὐτῷ σχήματα προσώπων τε ἀποστροφαῖς καὶ χρόνων ἐναλλαγαῖς καὶ τροπικῶν [1] σημειώσεων μεταφοραῖς ἐξηλλαγμένα τῶν συνήθων καὶ σολοικισμῶν λαμβάνοντα φαντασίας· ὁπόσα τε γίγνεται πράγματα ἀντὶ σωμάτων ἢ σώματα ἀντὶ πραγμάτων· καὶ ἐφ᾿ ὧν ἐνθυμημάτων ⟨τε καὶ νοημάτων⟩ αἱ μεταξὺ παρεμπτώσεις πολλαὶ γινόμεναι διὰ πολλοῦ τὴν ἀκολουθίαν κομίζονται· τά τε σκολιὰ καὶ πολύπλοκα καὶ δυσεξέλικτα καὶ τὰ ἄλλα τὰ συγγενῆ τούτοις. εὕροι δ᾿ ἄν τις οὐκ ὀλίγα καὶ τῶν θεατρικῶν σχημάτων κείμενα παρ᾿ αὐτῷ, τὰς παρισώσεις λέγω ⟨καὶ παρομοιώσεις⟩ καὶ παρονομασίας καὶ ἀντιθέσεις, ἐν αἷς ἐπλεόνασε Γοργίας ὁ Λεοντῖνος καὶ οἱ περὶ Πῶλον καὶ Λικύμνιον καὶ πολλοὶ ἄλλοι τῶν κατ᾿ αὐτὸν ἀκμασάντων. ἐκδηλότατα δὲ αὐτοῦ καὶ χαρακτηρικώτατά ἐστι τό τε πειρᾶσθαι δι᾿ ἐλαχίστων ὀνομάτων πλεῖστα σημαί-

[1] τροπικῶν Krüger: τοπικῶν codd.

interchanging common with proper nouns, and active with passive verbs. He alters the natural uses of singular and plural, and substitutes the one for the other. He combines masculines with feminines, feminines with masculines, sometimes neuters with both, thereby violating the natural agreement of gender. He sometimes changes the case of nouns or participles from subject to object, and sometimes from object to subject. In the use of conjunctions and prepositions, and especially in his use of particles which serve to bring out the force of individual words, he allows himself full poetic licence. One can find in his work a great many constructions which, through changes of person and variation of tense,[1] and through the use of obscure, figurative expressions, acquire the appearance of solecisms. Again, he often substitutes things for persons and persons for things. In his arguments ⟨and his sentences⟩ there are often parentheses which delay the conclusion for a long time; and his style is generally tortuous, involved, difficult to unravel, and has other similar properties. The ostentatious figures of speech are also to be found in his work in no small number—I mean those parallelisms in length and sound, word-play and antithesis, which were excessively used by Gorgias of Leontini, by Polus and Lycymnius[2] and their followers, and by many of his other contemporaries. But the most obvious of his characteristics is the effort to express as much as possible in the fewest possible

[1] For an exhaustive modern treatment of this feature of Thucydides's style, see J. Ros, *Die μεταβολή als Stilprinzip des Thukydides*.

[2] See note 1, p. 137.

νειν πράγματα καὶ πολλὰ συντιθέναι νοήματα εἰς ἕν, καὶ ἔτι προσδεχόμενόν τι τὸν ἀκροατὴν ἀκούσεσθαι καταλείπειν·[1] ὑφʼ ὧν ἀσαφὲς γίνεται τὸ βραχύ. ἵνα δὲ συνελὼν εἴπω, τέτταρα μέν ἐστιν ὥσπερ ὄργανα τῆς Θουκυδίδου λέξεως· τὸ ποιητικὸν τῶν ὀνομάτων, τὸ πολυειδὲς τῶν σχημάτων, τὸ τραχὺ τῆς ἁρμονίας, τὸ τάχος τῶν σημασιῶν· χρώματα δὲ αὐτῆς τό τε στριφνὸν καὶ τὸ πυκνόν, καὶ τὸ πικρὸν καὶ τὸ αὐστηρόν, καὶ τὸ ἐμβριθὲς καὶ τὸ δεινὸν καὶ (τὸ) φοβερόν, ὑπὲρ ἅπαντα δὲ ταῦτα τὸ παθητικόν. τοιοῦτος μὲν δή τίς ἐστιν ὁ Θουκυδίδης κατὰ τὸν τῆς λέξεως χαρακτῆρα, ᾧ παρὰ τοὺς ἄλλους διήνεγκεν. ὅταν μὲν οὖν ἥ τε προαίρεσις αὐτοῦ καὶ ἡ δύναμις συνεκδράμῃ, τέλεια γίνεται κατορθώματα καὶ δαιμόνια· ὅταν δὲ ἐλλείπῃ τὸ τῆς δυνάμεως, οὐ παραμείναντος μέχρι πάντων τοῦ τόνου, διὰ τὸ τάχος τῆς ἀπαγγελίας ἀσαφής τε ἡ λέξις γίνεται καὶ ἄλλας τινὰς ἐπιφέρει κῆρας οὐκ εὐπρεπεῖς. τὸ γὰρ ἐν ᾧ δεῖ τρόπῳ τὰ ξένα καὶ πεποιημένα λέγεσθαι καὶ μέχρι πόσου προελθόντα πεπαῦσθαι, καλὰ καὶ ἀναγκαῖα θεωρήματα ἐν πᾶσιν ὄντα τοῖς ἔργοις, οὐ διὰ πάσης τῆς ἱστορίας φυλάττει.

25 Προειρημένων δὲ τούτων κεφαλαιωδῶς ἐπὶ τὰς ἀποδείξεις αὐτῶν ὥρα τρέπεσθαι. ποιήσομαι δὲ οὐ χωρὶς ὑπὲρ ἑκάστης ἰδέας τὸν λόγον, ὑποτάττων αὐταῖς τὴν Θουκυδίδου λέξιν, ἀλλὰ κατὰ περιοχάς τινας καὶ τόπους, μέρη λαμβάνων τῆς τε διηγήσεως καὶ τῶν ῥητορειῶν καὶ παρατιθεὶς τοῖς τε πραγματικοῖς καὶ τοῖς λεκτικοῖς κατορθώμασιν ἢ ἁμαρτήμασι τὰς αἰτίας, διʼ ἃς τοιαῦτά ἐστι· δεηθεὶς σοῦ

words, and to combine many ideas into one, and to leave the listener still expecting to hear something more. These help to make his brevity obscure. I may summarise the instruments, so to speak, of Thucydides's style as follows: there are four—artificiality of vocabulary, variety of figures, harshness of word-order, rapidity of signification. The special features of his style include compactness and solidity, pungency and severity, vehemence, the ability to disturb and terrify and above all emotional power. Such are the characteristics of style by which Thucydides is distinguished from all the rest. When his purpose coincides with his special talent, he is completely and marvellously successful; but when his power is not being employed to its full capacity and his energy flags before his goal is reached, the speed with which the ideas are presented renders the passage obscure, and brings in its train certain other unattractive faults. These include a failure to observe throughout the whole of his history in what way strange and artificial language should be used, and how far he should go before stopping, although these are worthy, indeed necessary subjects for all literary artists to study.

After those brief introductory remarks, it is time to 25
turn to detailed proof. I shall not deal with each aspect of his style separately, subjoining an illustrative passage from Thucydides, but shall treat the subject under general headings and topics, taking sections of narrative and rhetorical passages, and setting out the reasons for his success or failure in style or subject-matter. I once again beg you, and

[1] καταλείπειν Reiske: καταλιπεῖν codd.

πάλιν καὶ τῶν ἄλλων φιλολόγων τῶν ἐντευξομένων τῇ γραφῇ, τὸ βούλημά μου τῆς ὑποθέσεως ἧς προῄρημαι σκοπεῖν, ὅτι χαρακτῆρός ἐστι δήλωσις ἅπαντα περιειληφυῖα τὰ συμβεβηκότα αὐτῷ καὶ δεόμενα λόγου, σκοπὸν ἔχουσα τὴν ὠφέλειαν αὐτῶν τῶν βουλησομένων μιμεῖσθαι τὸν ἄνδρα.

Ἐν ἀρχῇ μὲν οὖν τοῦ προοιμίου προθέσει χρησάμενος, ὅτι μέγιστος ἐγένετο τῶν πρὸ αὐτοῦ πολέμων ὁ Πελοποννησιακός, κατὰ λέξιν οὕτω γράφει· "τὰ γὰρ πρὸ αὐτῶν καὶ τὰ ἔτι παλαιότερα σαφῶς μὲν εὑρεῖν διὰ χρόνου πλῆθος ἀδύνατον ἦν· ἐκ δὲ τεκμηρίων, ὧν ἐπὶ μακρότατον σκοποῦντί μοι ξυνέβη πιστεῦσαι, οὐ μεγάλα νομίζω γενέσθαι οὔτε κατὰ τοὺς πολέμους οὔτε εἰς τὰ ἄλλα. φαίνεται γὰρ ἡ νῦν Ἑλλὰς καλουμένη οὐ πάλαι βεβαίως οἰκουμένη, ἀλλὰ μεταναστάσεις τε οὖσαι τὰ πρότερα καὶ ῥᾳδίως ἕκαστοι τὴν ἑαυτῶν ἀπολείποντες, βιαζόμενοι ὑπό τινων αἰεὶ πλειόνων. τῆς γὰρ ἐμπορίας οὐκ οὔσης, οὐδ' ἐπιμιγνύντες ἀδεῶς ἀλλήλοις οὔτε κατὰ γῆν οὔτε διὰ θαλάσσης, νεμόμενοί τε τὰ αὐτῶν ἕκαστοι, ὅσον ἀποζῆν, καὶ περιουσίαν χρημάτων οὐκ ἔχοντες οὐδὲ γῆν φυ⟨τεύοντες⟩ . . . . . [1]

. . ⟨γνώ⟩μη δεδουλωμένοι ὡς ἐπὶ Λακεδαιμονίους. καταφρονήσαντες οὖν αὐτῶν καὶ ἐμβοήσαντες ἀθρόοι ὥρμησαν ἐπ' αὐτούς." ἤδ' ἡ περιοχὴ ὤφελε μὲν κατεσκευάσθαι μὴ τοῦτον ὑπ' αὐτοῦ τὸν τρόπον, ἀλλὰ κοινότερον μᾶλλον καὶ ὠφελιμώ-

[1] lacuna ex Thucydide explenda.

---

[1] i. 1. 3 ff.

any other scholar who should happen to read this treatise, to observe the purpose of the investigation I have chosen to carry out: it is to reveal his peculiar character, including all the noteworthy qualities that are to be found in his style. My aim in so doing is to assist those who may actually wish to imitate him.

He begins his introduction with the proposition that the Peloponnesian War was the greatest up to his time. His words are as follows:[1]

"Although the events that preceded this, and those of remoter antiquity could not, through the length of time, be ascertained clearly, yet from such evidence as I am disposed, through research which has followed events as far back as possible, to trust, I conclude that they were not great either with regard to wars or anything else. For instance, it is evident that the country which is now called Greece was not regularly settled in ancient times. The people were migratory in those days and readily left their dwelling-places whenever they were forced to by more numerous invaders. There was no commerce, and no safe communication between them by land or sea. The several tribes occupied their own territory, living at subsistence level, neither accumulating reserves of wealth nor cultivating the land. . . ."

(*a lacuna of some length*)

". . . intimidated at the prospect of facing the Lacedaemonians. Consequently they despised them, and with a shout rushed on them all at once."[2]

This group of events should not have been arranged thus, but in a more normal and helpful way, making

[2] iv. 34. 1.

τερον, τοῦ τελευταίου μορίου τῷ πρώτῳ προστεθέντος, τῶν δὲ διὰ μέσου τὴν μετὰ ταῦτα χώραν λαβόντων. ἀγκυλωτέρα μὲν οὖν ἡ φράσις οὕτω σχηματισθεῖσα γέγονε καὶ δεινοτέρα, σαφεστέρα δὲ καὶ ἡδίων ἐκείνως ἂν κατασκευασθεῖσα· "Τῶν δὲ Λακεδαιμονίων οὐκέτι ἐπεκθεῖν, ᾗ προσπίπτοιεν, δυναμένων, γνόντες αὐτοὺς οἱ ψιλοὶ βραδυτέρους ἤδη, συστραφέντες καὶ ἐμβοήσαντες, ὥρμησαν ἐπ' αὐτοὺς ἀθρόοι· ἔκ τε τῆς ὄψεως τὸ θαρρεῖν προσειληφότες, ὅτι πολλαπλάσιοι ἦσαν, καὶ ἐκ τοῦ μηκέτι δεινοὺς αὐτοὺς ὁμοίως σφίσι φαίνεσθαι καταφρονήσαντες, ἐπειδὴ οὐκ εὐθὺς ἄξια τῆς προσδοκίας ἐπεπόνθεσαν, ἣν ἔσχον ὑπόληψιν, ὅτε πρῶτον ἀπέβαινον τῇ γνώμῃ δεδουλωμένοι ὡς
26 ἐπὶ Λακεδαιμονίους." ὑπεξαιρουμένης δὲ τῆς περιγραφῆς πάσης, τἆλλα πάντα ὠνόμασταί τε τοῖς προσφυεστάτοις ὀνόμασι καὶ περιείληπται τοῖς ἐπιτηδειοτάτοις σχηματισμοῖς, ἀρετῆς τε οὐδεμιᾶς ὡς εἰπεῖν οὔτε λεκτικῆς οὔτε πραγματικῆς ἐνδεῶς ἔσχηκεν· ἃς οὐδὲν δέομαι πάλιν ἐξαριθμεῖσθαι.

Ἐν δὲ τῇ ἑβδόμῃ βύβλῳ τὴν ἐσχάτην ναυμαχίαν Ἀθηναίων καὶ Συρακοσίων ἀφηγούμενος οὕτως ὠνόμακέ τε καὶ ἐσχημάτικε τὰ πραχθέντα· "ὁ δὲ Δημοσθένης καὶ Μένανδρος καὶ Εὐθύδημος (οὗτοι γὰρ ἐπὶ τὰς ναῦς τῶν Ἀθηναίων στρατηγοὶ ἐπέβησαν) ἄραντες ἀπὸ τοῦ ἑαυτῶν στρατοπέδου εὐθὺς ἔπλεον πρὸς τὸ ζεῦγμα τοῦ λιμένος καὶ τὸν παραλειφθέντα διέκπλουν, βουλόμενοι βιάσασθαι ἐς τὸ ἔξω. προεξαναγόμενοι δὲ οἱ Συρακόσιοι καὶ οἱ ξύμμαχοι ναυσὶ παραπλησίαις τὸν ἀριθμὸν καὶ

the final part follow upon the first, with the intervening parts coming after these. Thucydides's arrangement has produced a more compact and striking sentence, but it would have been clearer and more pleasing if it had been arranged thus:

"When the Lacedaemonians were no longer able to rush out upon their assailants, the skirmishers, sensing that they were already slower in their movements, rallied and with a shout rushed upon them all at once. They had gained encouragement from seeing their own great superiority in numbers; and because the enemy no longer seemed so formidable, they came to despise them, because they had not at once sustained the losses they had expected, and which they had assumed they would suffer as they first disembarked, when they were intimidated at the prospect of facing the Lacedaemonians."

Thus all circuitous structure is entirely removed, and everything that is left is given its most natural name and is expressed in the most suitable figures. There is virtually no quality either of style or of content in which it is deficient; and there is no need for me to enumerate these again.

In his narrative of the final naval battle between the Athenians and the Syracusans in the seventh book, he 413 B.C.
combines plain and figurative language as he describes the action thus:[1]

"Demosthenes, Menander and Euthydemus, who took the command on board, put out from their own camp and sailed straight to the barrier across the mouth of the harbour and to the passage left open, to try to force their way out. But the Syracusans and their allies had already put out with about the same

[1] vii. 69. 4–72. 1.

πρότερον κατά τε τὸν ἔκπλουν μέρει αὐτῶν ἐφύλασσον καὶ κατὰ τὸν ἄλλον κύκλῳ λιμένα, ὅπως πανταχόθεν ἅμα προσπίπτοιεν τοῖς Ἀθηναίοις· καὶ ὁ πεζὸς αὐτοῖς ἅμα παρεβοήθει, ᾗπερ καὶ αἱ νῆες κατίσχυον. ἦρχον δὲ τοῦ ναυτικοῦ τοῖς Συρακοσίοις Σικανὸς μὲν καὶ Ἀγάθαρχος, κέρας ἑκάτερος τοῦ παντὸς ἔχων, Πυθὴν δὲ καὶ οἱ Κορίνθιοι τὸ μέσον. ἐπειδὴ δὲ καὶ οἱ ἄλλοι Ἀθηναῖοι προσέμισγον τῷ ζεύγματι, τῇ μὲν πρώτῃ ῥύμῃ ἐπιπλέοντες ἐκράτουν τῶν τεταγμένων νεῶν πρὸς αὐτῷ καὶ ἐπειρῶντο λύειν τὰς κλείσεις· μετὰ δὲ τοῦτο πανταχόθεν σφίσι τῶν Συρακοσίων καὶ τῶν συμμάχων ἐπιφερομένων οὐ μόνον πρὸς τῷ ζεύγματι ἡ ναυμαχία, ἀλλὰ καὶ κατὰ τὸν λιμένα ἐγίγνετο· καὶ ἦν καρτερὰ καὶ οἵα οὐχ ἑτέρα τῶν πρότερον. πολλὴ μὲν γὰρ ἑκατέροις προθυμία ἀπὸ τῶν ναυτῶν ἐς τὸ ἐπιπλεῖν, ὁπότε κελευσθείη, ἐγίγνετο, πολλὴ δ᾿ ἡ ἀντιτέχνησις τῶν κυβερνητῶν καὶ ἀγωνισμὸς πρὸς ἀλλήλους, οἵ τε ἐπιβάται ἐθεράπευον, ὅτε προσπέσοι ναῦς νηί, μὴ λείπεσθαι τὰ ἀπὸ τοῦ καταστρώματος τῆς ἄλλης τέχνης, πᾶς τέ τις ἐν ᾧ προσετέτακτο αὐτὸς ἕκαστος ἠπείγετο πρῶτος φαίνεσθαι. ξυμπεσουσῶν δ᾿ ἐν ὀλίγῳ πολλῶν νεῶν (πλεῖσται γὰρ δὴ αὗται ἐν ὀλίγῳ ἐναυμάχησαν· βραχὺ γὰρ ἀπέλιπον ξυναμφότεραι διακόσιαι γενέσθαι) αἱ μὲν ἐκβολαὶ διὰ τὸ μὴ εἶναι τὰς ἀνακρούσεις καὶ διέκπλους ὀλίγαι ἐγίγνοντο· αἱ δὲ προσβολαί, ὡς τύχοι ναῦς νηὶ προσπεσοῦσα ἢ διὰ τὸ φυγεῖν ἢ ἄλλῃ ἐπιπλέουσι, πυκνότεραι ἦσαν. καὶ ὅσον μὲν χρόνον προσφέροιτο ναῦς, οἱ ἀπὸ τῶν κατα-

number of ships as before, a part of which kept guard at the outlet, the remainder all round the rest of the harbour, in order to attack the Athenians on all sides at once; while the land forces held themselves in readiness at the points where the ships preponderated. The Syracusan fleet was commanded by Sicanus and Agatharchus, who each had a wing of the whole force, with Pythen and the Corinthians in the centre. When the rest of the Athenians came up to the barrier, with the first shock of their charge they overpowered the ships stationed there, and tried to undo the fastenings; after this, as the Syracusans and their allies bore down upon them from all quarters, the battle spread from the barrier over the whole harbour, and was more determinedly fought than any of the preceding ones.

" On either side the rowers showed great zeal in bringing up their vessels at the boatswain's orders, and the helmsmen showed great skill in countermanoeuvring, and great rivalry with one another; and when the ships were along side one another, the soldiers did their best not to let their performance on deck be outdone by the skill of the other service; in short, every man strove to prove himself the first in his particular department. And since many ships were engaged in a small compass (for these were the largest fleets engaging in the narrowest space ever known, being altogether little short of two hundred), the regular attacks with the beak were few, there being no opportunity of backing water or of breaking the line; while the collisions caused by one ship fouling upon another, in trying either to evade or to attack a third, were more frequent. So long as a vessel was coming up to the charge the men on the decks rained

στρωμάτων τοῖς ἀκοντίοις καὶ τοξεύμασι καὶ λίθοις ἀφθόνοις ἐπ' αὐτὴν ἐχρῶντο· ἐπειδὴ δὲ προσμίξειαν, οἱ ἐπιβάται εἰς χεῖρας ἰόντες ἐπειρῶντο ταῖς ἀλλήλων ναυσὶν ἐπιβαίνειν. συνετύγχανέ τε πολλαχοῦ διὰ τὴν στενοχωρίαν τὰ μὲν ἄλλοις ἐμβεβληκέναι, τὰ δὲ αὐτοὺς ἐμβεβλῆσθαι, δύο τε περὶ μίαν καὶ ἔστιν ᾗ καὶ πλείους ναῦς κατ' ἀνάγκην ξυνηρτῆσθαι· καὶ τοῖς κυβερνήταις τῶν μὲν φυλακήν, τῶν δ' ἐπιβουλὴν μὴ καθ' ἓν ἕκαστον, κατὰ πολλὰ δὲ πανταχόθεν περιεστάναι, καὶ τὸν κτύπον μέγαν ἀπὸ πολλῶν νεῶν συμπιπτουσῶν, ἔκπληξίν τε ἅμα καὶ ἀποστέρησιν τῆς ἀκοῆς ὧν οἱ κελευσταὶ ἐφθέγγοντο παρέχειν. πολλὴ γὰρ ἑτέρα ἡ παρακέλευσις καὶ ἡ βοὴ ἀφ' ἑκατέρων τοῖς κελευσταῖς κατά τε τὴν τέχνην καὶ πρὸς τὴν ναυτικὴν φιλονεικίαν ἐγίγνετο· τοῖς μὲν Ἀθηναίοις βιάζεσθαί τε τὸν ἔκπλουν ἐπιβοῶντες, καὶ περὶ τῆς ἐς τὴν πατρίδα σωτηρίας νῦν, εἴ ποτε, προθύμως ἀντιλαμβάνεσθαι· τοῖς δὲ Συρακοσίοις καὶ ξυμμάχοις καλὸν εἶναι κωλῦσαί τε αὐτοὺς διαφυγεῖν, καὶ τὴν οἰκείαν ἑκάστους πατρίδα νικήσαντας ἐπαυξῆσαι· καὶ οἱ στρατηγοὶ προσέτι ἑκατέρων, εἴ τινά που ὁρῷεν μὴ κατ' ἀνάγκην πρύμναν κρουόμενον ἀνακαλοῦντες ὀνομαστὶ τὸν τριήραρχον ἠρώτων, οἱ μὲν Ἀθηναῖοι, εἰ τὴν πολεμιωτάτην γῆν οἰκειοτέραν ἤδη τῆς οὐ δι' ὀλίγου πόνου ἐκτημένης θαλάσσης ἡγούμενοι ἀποχωροῦσιν· οἱ δὲ Συρακόσιοι, εἰ οὓς σαφῶς ἴσασι προθυμουμένους Ἀθηναίους παντὶ τρόπῳ διαφυγεῖν, τούτους αὐτοὶ φεύγοντας φεύγουσιν.

spears and arrows and stones upon her; but once along side, the heavy infantry tried to board each other's ships, fighting hand to hand. In many cases also it happened, because of the narrow space, that a ship was charging an enemy on one side and being charged herself on another, and that two and sometimes more ships had unavoidably become entangled around one, making the helmsman attend to defence here, offence there, not to one thing at a time, but to many on all sides; while the great din caused by the number of ships clashing together not only spread terror, but made the orders of the boatswains inaudible. The orders and appeals which the boatswains on either side shouted incessantly, in the discharge of their duty and in the heat of the naval conflict were different: the Athenians they urged to force the passage out, and now if ever to show their zeal and lay hold of a safe return to their country; to the Syracusans and their allies they cried that it would be glorious to prevent the escape of the enemy, and, conquering, to exalt the countries that were theirs. The generals, moreover, on either side, if they saw any in any part of the battle backing water without being forced to do so, called out to the trierarch by name and asked him, if they were Athenians, whether they were retreating because they thought the totally hostile shore more their own now than that sea which had cost them so much labour to win; and if they were Syracusans, whether they were flying from the flying Athenians, whom they well knew to be eager to escape in whatever way they could.

ὅ τ' ἐκ τῆς γῆς πεζὸς ἀμφοτέρων ἰσορρόπου τῆς ναυμαχίας καθεστηκυίας πολὺν τὸν ἀγῶνα καὶ ξύστασιν τῆς γνώμης εἶχε, φιλονεικῶν μὲν ὁ αὐτόθεν περὶ τοῦ πλείονος ἤδη καλοῦ, δεδιότες δὲ οἱ ἐπελθόντες, μὴ τῶν παρόντων ἔτι χείρω πράξωσι. πάντων γὰρ δὴ ἀνακειμένων τοῖς Ἀθηναίοις ἐς τὰς ναῦς ὅ τε φόβος ἦν ὑπὲρ τοῦ μέλλοντος οὐδενὶ ἐοικὼς καὶ διὰ τὸ ἀνώμαλον καὶ τὴν ἔποψιν τῆς ναυμαχίας ἐκ τῆς γῆς ἠναγκάζοντο ἔχειν· δι' ὀλίγου γὰρ οὔσης τῆς θέας καὶ οὐ πάντων ἅμα ἐς τὸ αὐτὸ σκοπούντων, εἰ μέν τινες ἴδοιέν πη τοὺς σφετέρους ἐπικρατοῦντας, ἀνεθάρσησάν τε ἂν καὶ πρὸς ἀνάκλησιν θεῶν μὴ στερῆσαι σφᾶς τῆς σωτηρίας ἐτρέποντο· οἳ δὲ ἐπὶ τὸ ἡσσώμενον βλέψαντες ὀλοφυρμῷ τε ἅμα μετὰ βοῆς ἐχρῶντο καὶ ἀπὸ τῶν δρωμένων τῆς ὄψεως καὶ τὴν γνώμην μᾶλλον τῶν ἐν τῷ ἔργῳ ἐδουλοῦντο· ἄλλοι δὲ καὶ πρὸς ἀντίπαλόν τι τῆς ναυμαχίας ἀπιδόντες διὰ τὸ ἀκρίτως ξυνεχὲς τῆς ἁμίλλης καὶ τοῖς σώμασιν αὐτοῖς ἴσα τῇ δόξῃ περιδεῶς ξυναπονεύοντες ἐν τοῖς χαλεπώτατα διῆγον· ἀεὶ γὰρ παρ' ὀλίγον ἢ διέφευγον ἢ ἀπώλλυντο. ἦν τε ἐν τῷ στρατεύματι τῶν Ἀθηναίων, ἕως ἀγχώμαλα ἐναυμάχουν, πάντα ὁμοῦ ἀκοῦσαι, ὀλοφυρμὸς βοή, νικῶντες κρατούμενοι, ἄλλα ὅσα ἐν μεγάλῳ κινδύνῳ μέγα στρατόπεδον πολυειδῆ ἀναγκάζοιτο φθέγγεσθαι. παραπλήσια δὲ καὶ οἱ ἐπὶ τῶν νεῶν αὐτοῖς ἔπασχον, πρίν γε δὴ οἱ Συρακόσιοι καὶ οἱ ξύμμαχοι, ἐπὶ πολὺ ἀντισχούσης τῆς ναυμαχίας, ἔτρεψάν τε τοὺς Ἀθηναίους καὶ ἐπικείμενοι λαμπρῶς, πολλῇ κραυγῇ καὶ διακελευσμῷ χρώμενοι, κατεδίωκον ἐς τὴν γῆν. τότε δὴ ὁ μὲν

" Meanwhile the two armies on shore, while victory hung in the balance, were a prey to the most agonising and conflicting emotions, the natives thirsting for more glory than they had already won, while the invaders feared to find themselves in an even worse plight than before. Since Athenian fortunes depended on their fleet, their fear for the outcome was like nothing they had ever felt; while their view from the land was necessarily as uneven as the battle itself. Close to the scene of the action and not all looking at the same point at once, some saw their friends victorious and took courage, and fell to calling upon heaven not to deprive them of salvation, while others who had their eyes turned upon the losers wailed and cried aloud, and as spectators of the action, were more overcome by emotion than the actual combatants. Others again were gazing at some spot where the battle was evenly disputed: as the strife was protracted without a decision, they suffered the worst agony of all as their bodies flinched in vicarious terror at what they saw, as safety and destruction were each a close matter. In short, in that one Athenian army, as long as the sea fight remained doubtful, there was every sound to be heard at once, shrieks, cries, " We win," " We lose," and all the other manifold exclamations that a great host would utter in a great peril.

" And with the men on the ships it was nearly the same, until at last the Syracusans and their allies, after the battle had lasted a long while, put the Athenians to flight, and with much shouting and cheering chased them in open rout to the shore. The

ναυτικὸς στρατὸς ἄλλος ἄλλῃ, ὅσοι μὴ μετέωροι ἑάλωσαν, κατενεχθέντες ἐξέπεσον ἐς τὸ στρατόπεδον. ὁ δὲ πεζὸς οὐκέτι διαφόρως, ἀλλ' ἀπὸ μιᾶς ὁρμῆς οἰμωγῇ τε καὶ στόνῳ πάντες δυσανασχετοῦντες τὰ γιγνόμενα, οἱ μὲν ἐπὶ τὰς ναῦς παρεβοήθουν, οἱ δὲ πρὸς τὸ λοιπὸν τοῦ τείχους ἐς φυλακήν· ἄλλοι δὲ καὶ οἱ πλεῖστοι ἤδη περὶ σφᾶς αὐτοὺς καὶ ὅπῃ σωθήσονται διεσκόπουν. ἦν τε ἐν τῷ παραυτίκα οὐδεμιᾶς δὴ τῶν ξυμπασῶν ἐλάσσων ἔκπληξις. παραπλήσιά τε ἐπεπόνθεσαν καὶ ἔδρασαν αὐτοὶ ἐν Πύλῳ· διαφθαρεισῶν γὰρ τῶν νεῶν τοῖς Λακεδαιμονίοις προσαπώλλυντο αὐτοῖς καὶ οἱ ἐν τῇ νήσῳ ἄνδρες διαβεβηκότες. καὶ τότε τοῖς Ἀθηναίοις ἀνέλπιστον ἦν τὸ κατὰ γῆν σωθήσεσθαι, ἢν μή τι παρὰ λόγον γίγνηται. γενομένης δ' ἰσχυρᾶς τῆς ναυμαχίας καὶ πολλῶν νεῶν ἀμφοτέροις καὶ ἀνδρῶν ἀπολομένων οἱ Συρακόσιοι καὶ οἱ ξύμμαχοι ἐπικρατήσαντες τά τε ναυάγια καὶ τοὺς νεκροὺς ἀνείλοντο καὶ ἀποπλεύσαντες πρὸς τὴν πόλιν τρόπαιον ἔστησαν."

27 Ἐμοὶ μὲν δὴ ταῦτα καὶ τὰ παραπλήσια τούτοις ἄξια ζήλου τε καὶ μιμήσεως ἐφάνη, τήν τε μεγαληγορίαν τοῦ ἀνδρὸς καὶ τὴν καλλιλογίαν καὶ τὴν δεινότητα καὶ τὰς ἄλλας ἀρετὰς ἐν τούτοις τοῖς ἔργοις ἐπείσθην τελειοτάτας εἶναι, τεκμαιρόμενος, ὅτι πᾶσα ψυχὴ τούτῳ τῷ γένει τῆς λέξεως ἄγεται, καὶ οὔτε τὸ ἄλογον τῆς διανοίας κριτήριον, ᾧ πεφύκαμεν ἀντιλαμβάνεσθαι τῶν ἡδέων ἢ ἀνιαρῶν, ἀλλοτριοῦται πρὸς αὐτὸ οὔτε τὸ λογικόν, ἐφ' οὗ διαγιγνώσκεται τὸ ἐν ἑκάστῃ τέχνῃ καλόν· οὐδ' ἂν ἔχοιεν οὔθ' οἱ μὴ πάνυ

naval force, one one way, one another, as many as were not taken afloat, now ran ashore and rushed from on board their ships to their camp; while the army, no more divided, but carried away by one impulse, all with shrieks and groans deplored the result, and ran down, some to help the ships, others to guard what was left of their wall, while the remaining and most numerous part already began to consider how they should save themselves. Indeed the panic of the present moment had never been surpassed. They now suffered very nearly what they had inflicted at 425 B.C.
Pylos, as then the Lacedaemonians with the loss of their fleet lost also the men who had crossed over to the island, so now the Athenians had no hope of escaping by land without the help of some extraordinary chance. The sea fight having been a severe one, and many ships and lives having been lost on both sides, the victorious Syracusans and their allies now recovered their wrecks and their dead, sailed off to the city and set up a trophy."

This and narratives like it seemed to me admirable 27
and worthy of imitation, and I was convinced that in such passages as these we have perfect examples of the historian's sublime eloquence, the beauty of his language, his rhetorical brilliance and his other virtues. I was led to this conclusion when I observed that this style of writing appeals to all minds alike, since it offends neither our irrational aesthetic faculty, which is our natural instrument for distinguishing the pleasant from the distasteful, nor our reason, which enables us to judge individual technical excellence. Nobody, even the most inexperienced student of political oratory, could find a single objectionable word or figure of speech, nor could the most expert

λόγων ἔμπειροι πολιτικῶν εἰπεῖν, ἐφ' ὅτῳ δυσχεραίνουσιν ὀνόματι ἢ σχήματι, οὔθ' οἱ πάνυ περιττοὶ καὶ τῆς τῶν πολλῶν ὑπερορῶντες ἀμαθίας μέμψασθαι τὴν κατασκευὴν ταύτης τῆς λέξεως, ἀλλὰ καὶ τὸ τῶν πολλῶν καὶ ⟨τὸ⟩ τῶν ὀλίγων τὴν αὐτὴν ὑπόληψιν ἕξει· ὁ μέν γε πολὺς ἐκεῖνος ἰδιώτης οὐ δυσχερανεῖ τὸ φορτικὸν τῆς λέξεως καὶ σκολιὸν καὶ δυσπαρακολούθητον· ὁ δὲ σπάνιος καὶ οὐδ' ἐκ τῆς ἐπιτυχούσης ἀγωγῆς γιγνόμενος τεχνίτης οὐ μέμψεται τὸ ἀγεννὲς καὶ χαμαιτυπὲς καὶ ἀκατάσκευον. ἀλλὰ συνῳδὸν ἔσται τό τε λογικὸν καὶ τὸ ἄλογον κριτήριον, ὑφ' ὧν ἀμφοτέρων ἀξιοῦμεν ἅπαντα κρίνεσθαι κατὰ τὰς τέχνας.

. . . .[1] ⟨ἐὰν δ'⟩[2] . . . .

. . . . ἐργάσηται θάτερον, οὐκέτι καλὸν οὐδὲ
28 τέλειον ἀποδίδωσι τὸ ἕτερον. ἐγὼ γοῦν οὐκ ἔχω, πῶς ἐκεῖνα ἐπαινέσω τὰ δοκοῦντα μεγάλα καὶ θαυμαστὰ εἶναί τισιν, ὅσα μηδὲ τὰς πρώτας ἀρετὰς ἔχει καὶ κοινοτάτας, ἀλλ' ἐκνενίκηται τῷ περιέργῳ καὶ περιττῷ μήτε ἡδέα εἶναι μήτε ὠφέλιμα· ὧν ὀλίγα παρέξομαι δείγματα παρατιθεὶς εὐθὺς ἑκάστοις τὰς αἰτίας, δι' ἃς περιέστηκεν εἰς τὰς ἐναντίας ταῖς ἀρεταῖς κακίας. ἐν μὲν οὖν τῇ τρίτῃ βύβλῳ τὰ περὶ Κέρκυραν ὠμὰ καὶ ἀνόσια ἔργα διὰ τὴν στάσιν εἰς τοὺς δυνατωτάτους ἐκ τοῦ δήμου γενόμενα διεξιών, ἕως μὲν ἐν τῷ κοινῷ καὶ συνήθει τῆς διαλέκτου τρόπῳ τὰ πραχθέντα δηλοῖ, σαφῶς τε καὶ συντόμως καὶ δυνατῶς ἅπαντα εἴρηκεν· ἀρξάμενος δὲ ἐπιτραγῳδεῖν τὰς κοινὰς τῶν Ἑλλήνων συμφορὰς καὶ τὴν διάνοιαν ἐξαλλάττειν ἐκ τῶν ἐν ἔθει μακρῷ τινι

critic with the utmost contempt for the ignorance of the masses find fault with the style of this passage: the taste of the untutored majority and that of the educated few will be in agreement, for surely those laymen, and there are many of them, will find nothing base, tortuous or obscure to offend them, while the rare expert with his specialised training will find nothing ill-bred, humble or uncultivated. But reason and instinct will combine in one voice; and these are the two faculties with which we properly judge all works of art.

(*Lacuna*)

. . . ⟨but if one quality is developed to excess⟩, it destroys the nobility and perfection of the other.

Indeed, I cannot bring myself to praise those pas- 28
sages which some people find great and admirable, when they do not have even the essential and ordinary virtues, but have been forced to become neither agreeable nor instructive through being laboured and inflated. I shall illustrate this with a few examples, setting out directly beside them the reasons why virtues have given way to corresponding vices. In the third book, when he is describing the Corcyrean revolution and the inhuman atrocities committed against the leading democrats, so long as he tells the story in normal, familiar language, he says everything clearly, concisely and forcefully. But when he begins to dramatise the sufferings of the Greeks in general, and to divert his thoughts from its

---

[1] lacunam indicavit Sylburg.
[2] ἐὰν δ' supplevi.

γίγνεται χείρων αὐτὸς ἑαυτοῦ. ἔστι δὲ τὰ μὲν πρῶτα, ὧν οὐδεὶς ἂν ὡς ἡμαρτημένων ἐπιλάβοιτο, ταῦτα· "Κερκυραῖοι δὲ αἰσθόμενοι τάς τε Ἀττικὰς ναῦς προσπλεούσας τάς τε τῶν πολεμίων οἰχομένας λαβόντες τοὺς Μεσσηνίους εἰς τὴν πόλιν ἤγαγον πρότερον ἔξω ὄντας, καὶ τὰς ναῦς περιπλεῦσαι κελεύσαντες, ἃς ἐπλήρωσαν, ἐς τὸν Ὑλαϊκὸν λιμένα, ἐν ὅσῳ περιεκομίζοντο, τῶν ἐχθρῶν εἴ τινα λάβοιεν ἀπέκτεινον, καὶ ἐκ τῶν νεῶν ὅσους ἔπεισαν εἰσβῆναι ἐκβιβάζοντες ἀνεχρῶντο· εἰς τὸ Ἥραιόν τε ἐλθόντες, τῶν ἱκετῶν ὡς πεντήκοντα ἄνδρας δίκην ὑποσχεῖν ἔπεισαν καὶ κατέγνωσαν ἁπάντων θάνατον· οἱ δὲ πολλοὶ τῶν ἱκετῶν, ὅσοι οὐκ ἐπείσθησαν, ὡς ἑώρων τὰ γιγνόμενα, διέφθειρον ἐν τῷ ἱερῷ ἀλλήλους, καὶ ἐκ τῶν δένδρων τινὲς ἀπήγχοντο, οἳ δ' ὡς ἕκαστοι ἐδύναντο ἀνηλοῦντο. ἡμέρας τε ἑπτά, ἃς ἀφικόμενος ὁ Εὐρυμέδων ταῖς ἑξήκοντα ναυσὶ παρέμεινε, Κερκυραῖοι σφῶν αὐτῶν τοὺς ἐχθροὺς δοκοῦντας εἶναι ἐφόνευον, τὴν μὲν αἰτίαν ἐπιφέροντες τοῖς τὸν δῆμον καταλύουσιν· ἀπέθανον δέ τινες καὶ ἰδίας ἔχθρας ἕνεκα, καὶ ἄλλοι χρημάτων σφίσιν ὀφειλομένων ὑπὸ τῶν λαβόντων. πᾶσά τε ἰδέα κατέστη θανάτου, καὶ οἷον φιλεῖ ἐν τῷ τοιούτῳ γίγνεσθαι, οὐδὲν ὅ τι οὐ ξυνέβη, καὶ ἔτι περαιτέρω· καὶ γὰρ πατὴρ παῖδα ἀπέκτεινε, καὶ ἀπὸ τῶν ἱερῶν ἀπεσπῶντο καὶ πρὸς αὐτοῖς ἐκτείνοντο, οἳ δέ τινες καὶ περιοικοδομηθέντες ἐν τοῦ Διονύσου τῷ ἱερῷ ἀπέθανον. οὕτως ὠμὴ στάσις προυχώρησε,

[1] iii. 81. 2–82. 1.

accustomed channels, he falls far below his own standards. The opening sentences, with which nobody would find fault, are as follows:[1]

"The Corcyreans, learning that the Athenian ships were approaching and those of the enemy had withdrawn, brought the Messenians from outside the walls into the town, and ordered the ships which they had manned to sail round into the Hyllaic harbour, and while it was doing so killed whatever enemies they had captured, despatching afterwards as they landed them those whom they had persuaded to go on board the ships. Next they went to the sanctuary of Hera and persuaded about fifty men to stand trial, and condemned them all to death. The majority of the suppliants who had refused to do so, on seeing what was happening, killed each other there in the consecrated ground, while some hanged themselves upon the trees, and others destroyed themselves as they were severally able. For the seven days that Eurymedon stayed with his sixty ships, the Corcyreans were engaged in butchering those of their fellow-citizens whom they regarded as their enemies; and although the crime of which they were accused was that of attempting to put down the democracy, some were slain also for private enmity, others by their debtors because of money owed to them. Thus death raged in every form; and, as usually happens at such times, there was no length to which violence did not go, and even further than this: sons were killed by their fathers, and suppliants dragged from the altar or slain upon it; while some were even immured in the temple of Dionysus and died there. Such was the cruelty with which the revolution followed its course, and it seemed the more cruel because

καὶ ἔδοξε μᾶλλον, διότι ἐν τοῖς πρώτη ἐγένετο· ἐπεὶ ὕστερόν γε καὶ πᾶν ὡς εἰπεῖν τὸ Ἑλληνικὸν ἐκινήθη, διαφορῶν ⟨οὐσῶν⟩ ἑκασταχοῦ τοῖς τε τῶν δήμων προστάταις τοὺς Ἀθηναίους ἐπάγεσθαι καὶ τοῖς ὀλίγοις τοὺς Λακεδαιμονίους."

29 ἃ δὲ τούτοις ἐπιφέρει, σκολιὰ καὶ δυσπαρακολούθητα καὶ τὰς τῶν σχηματισμῶν πλοκὰς σολοικοφανεῖς ἔχοντα καὶ οὔτε τοῖς κατ' ἐκεῖνον τὸν βίον γενομένοις ἐπιτηδευθέντα οὔτε τοῖς ὕστερον, ὅτε μάλιστα ἤκμασεν ἡ πολιτικὴ δύναμις· ἃ μέλλω νυνὶ λέγειν· "ἐστασίαζέν τε οὖν τὰ τῶν πόλεων, καὶ τὰ ἐφυστερίζοντά που ἐπιπύστει [1] τῶν προγενομένων πολὺ ἐπέφερε τὴν ὑπερβολὴν τοῦ καινοῦσθαι τὰς διανοίας τῶν τ' ἐπιχειρήσεων περιτεχνήσει καὶ τῶν τιμωριῶν ἀτοπίᾳ." ἐν τούτοις τὸ μὲν πρῶτον τῶν κώλων περιπέφρασται πρὸς οὐδὲν ἀναγκαῖον· "ἐστασίαζέ τε [2] οὖν τὰ τῶν πόλεων"· ὑγιέστερον γὰρ ἦν εἰπεῖν "ἐστασίαζον αἱ πόλεις." τὸ δ' ἐπὶ τούτῳ λεγόμενον· "καὶ τὰ ἐφυστερίζοντά που" δυσείκαστόν ἐστι· σαφέστερον δ' ἂν ἐγένετο ῥηθὲν οὕτως· "αἱ δ' ὑστεροῦσαι πόλεις." οἷς ἐπίκειται· "ἐπιπύστει τῶν προγεγενημένων πολὺ ἐπέφερε τὴν ὑπερβολὴν ἐς τὸ καινοῦσθαι τὰς διανοίας"· βούλεται μὲν γὰρ λέγειν· "οἱ δὲ ὑστερίζοντες ἐπιπυνθανόμενοι τὰ γεγενημένα παρ' ἑτέροις ἐλάμβανον ὑπερβολὴν ἐπὶ τὸ διανοεῖσθαί τι καινότερον"· χωρὶς δὲ τῆς πλοκῆς οὐδὲ οἱ τῶν ὀνομάτων σχηματισμοὶ ταῖς ἀκοαῖς εἰσιν ἡδεῖς. τούτοις ἐπιφέρει κεφάλαιον

[1] ἐπιπύστει Reiske: ἐπὶ πύστει MP: πύστει Thuc.
[2] ἐστασίαζέ τε Sylburg: ἐστασιάζετο codd.

it was the first to occur. Later on, one may say, the whole Greek world was thrown into turmoil, as the partisans of democracy in each contending state tried to bring in the Athenians, and those of oligarchy the Spartans."

What he goes on to write, however, is tortuous and 29
difficult to follow, containing combinations of figures that verge upon solecism. Such a style was not employed either by his own or by succeeding generations, who wrote when politicians were at the height of their professional influence. I shall now quote the passage:[1]

"Revolution thus ran its course throughout the states, and those which experienced it later anywhere, having heard what had been done before, carried to a still greater excess the invention of new ideas through the elaborate ingenuity of their enterprises and the atrocity of their reprisals."

In the first of these clauses, the phrase "Revolution thus ran its course throughout the states" is an unnecessary periphrasis: it would have been sounder to write "The cities were in a state of revolution." The next expression, "those which experienced it later anywhere" is difficult to make out: it would have been clearer expressed thus: "the cities later affected." After that he writes: "having heard what had been done before, carried to a still greater excess the invention of new ideas." What he means to say is: "Later revolutionaries, hearing what had happened in other cities went to extremes in trying to devise something still more novel." In addition to the unhappy combination of figures, the use of substantival construction is not pleasing to the ear. This

[1] iii. 82. 3.

ἄλλο ποιητικῆς, μᾶλλον δὲ διθυραμβικῆς σκευωρίας οἰκειότερον· "τῶν τ' ἐπιχειρήσεων ἐπιτεχνήσει καὶ τῶν τιμωριῶν ἀτοπίᾳ· καὶ τὴν εἰωθυῖαν τῶν ὀνομάτων ἀξίωσιν ἐς τὰ ἔργα ἀντήλλαξαν τῇ δικαιώσει." ὃ γὰρ βούλεται δηλοῦν ἐν τῇ δυσεξελίκτῳ πλοκῇ, τοιοῦτόν ἐστι· "πολλὴν τὴν ἐπίδοσιν ἐλάμβανον εἰς τὸ διανοεῖσθαί τι καινότερον περὶ τὰς τέχνας τῶν ἐγχειρημάτων καὶ περὶ τὰς ὑπερβολὰς τῶν τιμωριῶν· τά τε εἰωθότα ὀνόματα ἐπὶ τοῖς πράγμασι λέγεσθαι μετατιθέντες ἄλλως ἠξίουν αὐτὰ καλεῖν." ἡ δ' "ἐπιτέχνησις" καὶ ἡ "τῶν τιμωριῶν ἀτοπία" καὶ ἡ "εἰωθυῖα τῶν ὀνομάτων ἀξίωσις" καὶ ἡ "εἰς τὰ ἔργα ἀντηλλαγμένη δικαίωσις" περιφράσεως ποιητικῆς ἐστιν οἰκειοτέρα. οἷς ἐπιτίθησι τὰ θεατρικὰ σχήματα ταυτί· "τόλμα μὲν γὰρ ἀλόγιστος ἀνδρία φιλέταιρος ἐνομίσθη, μέλλησις δὲ προμηθὴς δειλία εὐπρεπής"· παρομοιώσεις γὰρ ἀμφότερα ταῦτα καὶ παρισώσεις περιέχει, καὶ τὰ ἐπιθετα καλλωπισμοῦ χάριν κεῖται· τὸ γὰρ οὔτε θεατρικὸν . .[1] ἀλλ' ἀναγκαῖον τῆς λέξεως σχῆμα τοιοῦτ' ἂν ἦν· "τὴν μὲν γὰρ τόλμαν ἀνδρίαν ἐκάλουν, τὴν δὲ μέλλησιν δειλίαν." ὅμοια δὲ τούτοις ἐστὶ καὶ τὰ συναπτόμενα· "τὸ δὲ σῶφρον τοῦ ἀνάνδρου πρόσχημα, καὶ τὸ πρὸς ἅπαν συνετὸν ἐπὶ πᾶν ἀργόν"· κυριώτερον δ' ἂν οὕτως ἐλέχθη· "οἱ δὲ σώφρονες ἄνανδροι, καὶ οἱ συνετοὶ πρὸς ἅπαντα ἐν ἅπασιν ἀργοί."

30 εἰ μέχρι τούτων προελθὼν ἐπαύσατο τὰ μὲν καλλωπίζων, τὰ δὲ σκληραγωγῶν τὴν λέξιν, ἧττον ἂν ὀχληρὸς ἦν. νῦν δ' ἐπιτίθησιν· "ἀσφά-

clause is followed by another phrase which would be more at home in a poetical, or rather dithyrambic setting: " through the elaborate ingenuity of their enterprises and the atrocity of their reprisals; and they changed the normal meaning of words, as they thought fit, to suit their actions." By this inextricable combination what he is trying to convey is: " Men became much more interested in inventing new enterprises and in devising atrocity of reprisals; and they saw fit to substitute new names for the normal ones for these activities." " Ingenuity " and " atrocity " and " normal meaning of words " and " to suit their actions as they thought fit " are more suited to the circumlocutions of poetry. These are followed by the following pretentious figures: " Reckless bravado came to be regarded as the courage of a loyal ally; provident hesitation as specious cowardice." Both of these involve parallelism in sound and length, and the adjectives are included purely for the sake of decoration. The unpretentious, . . . way of putting it, framing the expression in essential terms, would have been: " Men called bravado courage, and hesitation cowardice." The sequel is in a similar vein: " moderation was a cloak for unmanliness, ability to understand all disinclination to act in any." A more direct way of saying this would have been: " moderate men were considered unmanly, and those able to understand everything passive in everything."

If he had not gone beyond this point with this 30
mixture of ornate and harsh expression, he would not
have been so tiresome. But as it is he continues with

[1] lacunam indicavit Reiske.

λεια δὲ τὸ ἐπιβουλεύσασθαι, ἀποτροπῆς πρόφασις εὔλογος. καὶ ὁ μὲν χαλεπαίνων πιστὸς ἀεί, ὁ δ' ἀντιλέγων αὐτῷ ὕποπτος." καὶ γὰρ ἐν τούτοις πάλιν ἄδηλον μέν ἐστι, τίνα βούλεται δηλοῦν τὸν χαλεπαίνοντα καὶ περὶ τίνος, τίνα δὲ τὸν ἀντιλέγοντα καὶ ἐφ' ὅτῳ. "ἐπιβουλεύσας δέ τις" φησί "τυχών τε ξυνετός, καὶ ὑπονοήσας ἔτι δεινότερος· προβουλεύσας δὲ ὅπως μηδὲν αὐτῷ δεήσει, τῆς ἑταιρίας διαλυτὴς καὶ τοὺς ἐναντίους ἐκπεπληγμένος." οὔτε γὰρ ὁ "τυχών" ἐμφαίνει μᾶλλον, ὃ βούλεται δηλοῦν, οὔτε ὁ αὐτὸς τυχών τε καὶ ὑπονοήσας ἅμα νοεῖσθαι δύναται, εἴ γε ὁ μὲν τυχὼν ἐπὶ τοῦ κατορθώσαντος καὶ ἐπιτυχόντος ὃ ἤλπισε λέγεται, ὁ δὲ ὑπονοήσας ἐπὶ τοῦ προαισθομένου τὸ μήπω πραχθὲν ἀλλ' ἔτι μέλλον [1] κακόν. καθαρὸς δὲ καὶ τηλαυγὴς ὁ νοῦς οὕτως ἂν ἦν· "οἵ τ' ἐπιβουλεύοντες ἑτέροις εἰ κατορθώσειαν, δεινοί· καὶ οἱ τὰς ἐπιβουλὰς προϋπονοοῦντες [2] εἰ φυλάξαιντο, ἔτι δεινότεροι· ὁ δὲ προϊδόμενος, ὅπως μηδὲν αὐτῷ δεήσει μήτ' ἐπιβουλῆς μήτε φυλακῆς, τάς τε ἑταιρίας διαλύειν ἐδόκει καὶ τοὺς ἐναντίους ἐκπεπλῆχθαι."

31 μίαν δὲ τούτοις ἐπιθεὶς περίοδον ἀγκύλως εἰρημένην καὶ δυνατῶς μετὰ τοῦ σαφῶς· "ἁπλῶς δὲ ὁ φθάσας τὸν μέλλοντα κακόν τι δρᾶν ἐπῃνεῖτο καὶ ὁ ἐπικελεύσας τὸν μὴ διανοούμενον" ποιητικῇ

[1] μέλλον Reiske: μᾶλλον codd.
[2] προϋπονοοῦντες Reiske: προεπινοοῦντες M.

---

[2] iii. 82. 5.
[3] iii. 82. 5.

these words:[1] " Plotting became a means of self-preservation, and a reasoned excuse for withdrawal. The advocate of extreme policies was always trusted, and his opponent suspected." Here again the identity of the " advocate of extreme policies " and his motives are obscure, as are those of " his opponent." Then he says:[2] " The successful conspirator was deemed clever, the man who disclosed a plot even more brilliant; but the man who planned to avoid needing either was accused of destroying his party and being afraid of his opponents." The word " successful " does not make any clearer what he wants to express; nor can the same person be conceived of as both " successful " and " disclosing a plot," assuming that " successful " is used of one who has successfully attained the object for which he hoped, and " disclosing a plot " is used of one who has anticipated an evil act which has not yet been perpetrated, but is still in the future. The sense would have been conspicuously clear if it had been rendered thus:

" Those who conspired against others were considered clever if they succeeded, those who foresaw conspiracies and guarded against them even cleverer; while the man who tried to ensure that he needed neither conspiracy nor protection against it was accused of destroying his party and being afraid of his opponents."

After adding one well-rounded sentence, in which 31
power is combined with clarity:[3] " In short, both the man who anticipated another in some evil and the man who suggested a crime to one who had no such idea were equally praised "; he will revert to poetic

[1] iii. 82. 4.

πάλιν χρήσεται μεταλήψει· "καὶ μὴν καὶ τὸ συγγενὲς τοῦ ἑταιρικοῦ ἀλλοτριώτερον ἐγένετο διὰ τὸ ἑτοιμότερον εἶναι ἀπροφασίστως τολμᾶν." τὸ γὰρ "συγγενές" καὶ τὸ "ἑταιρικόν" ⟨ἀντὶ τῆς συγγενείας καὶ τῆς ἑταιρίας⟩ [1] κείμενον μετείληπται· τό τε "ἀπροφασίστως τολμᾶν" ἄδηλον, εἴ τε ἐπὶ τῶν φίλων κεῖται νῦν εἴ τε ἐπὶ τῶν συγγενῶν. αἰτίαν γὰρ ἀποδιδούς, δι' ἣν τοὺς συγγενεῖς ἀλλοτριωτέρους ἔκρινον τῶν φίλων, ἐπιτίθησιν, ὅτι τόλμαν ἀπροφάσιστον παρείχοντο. σαφὴς δ' ἂν ἦν ⟨ὁ⟩ [2] λόγος, εἰ τοῦτον ἐξήνεγκε τὸν τρόπον κατὰ τὴν ἑαυτοῦ βούλησιν σχηματίζων· "καὶ μὴν καὶ τὸ ἑταιρικὸν οἰκειότερον ἐγένετο τοῦ συγγενοῦς διὰ τὸ ἑτοιμότερον εἶναι ἀπροφασίστως τολμᾶν." περιπέφρασται δὲ καὶ τὰ ἐπὶ τούτοις, καὶ οὔτε ἰσχυρῶς οὔτε σαφῶς ἀπήγγελται· "οὐ γὰρ μετὰ τῶν κειμένων νόμων ὠφελείας αἱ τοιαῦται σύνοδοι, ἀλλὰ παρὰ τοὺς καθεστῶτας πλεονεξίᾳ." ὁ μὲν νοῦς ἐστὶ τοιόσδε· "οὐ γὰρ ἐπὶ ταῖς κατὰ νόμον ὠφελείαις αἱ τῶν ἑταιριῶν ἐγίνοντο σύνοδοι, ἀλλ' ἐπὶ τῷ παρὰ τοὺς νόμους τι πλεονεκτεῖν." "Καὶ ὅρκοι" φησίν "εἴ που ἄρα ἐγίγνοντο συναλλαγῆς, ἐν τῷ αὐτίκα πρὸς τὸ ἄπορον ⟨ἑκατέρῳ⟩[3] διδόμενοι ἴσχυον, οὐκ ἐχόντων ἄλλοθεν δύναμιν"· ἐν τούτοις ὑπέρβατόν τε καὶ περίφρασις· οἱ μὲν γὰρ "ὅρκοι τῆς συναλλαγῆς" τὸ σημαινόμενον ἔχουσι τοιοῦτον· "οἱ δὲ περὶ τῆς φιλίας ὅρκοι εἴ που ἄρα γένοιντο." τὸ δὲ "ἴσχυον" δι' ὑπερβατοῦ κείμενον τῷ "αὐτίκα"

[1] ἀντὶ τῆς συγγενείας καὶ τῆς ἑταιρίας supplevit Usener ex scholio. [2] ὁ inseruit Krüger.

artificiality: " Moreover, ties of kindred became less binding than partisan ties, because the latter induced a greater readiness for unstinted action." " Kindred " and " partisan " have been substituted for " kinship " and " party." It is uncertain whether the phrase " for unstinted action " is here applied to one's friends or to one's relatives; for to supply the reason why they thought their kinsmen were less closely attached to them than their friends, he adds " because they showed readiness for unstinted action." The argument would have been clear if he had expressed it in the following manner, using his chosen figure: " Again ' comradely ' became more intimate than ' kindred,' owing to a greater readiness for unstinted action." What follows is also expressed in a circuitous way, and the description lacks both force and clarity: " For such associations are created not to benefit from the support of established laws, but to defy them and so win greater advantages. The sense of this is: " Political clubs were created not for mutual aid according to the laws, but to win greater advantages in defiance of them." " And," he says,[1] " oaths of reconciliation, in the few cases they were exchanged, held good only while immediate difficulties obtained and no other source offered support." This contains hyperbaton and periphrasis. " Oaths of reconciliation " means something like " oaths of friendship, in the few cases they were exchanged "; " held good " belongs with " immediate," though it is separated from it, for he is

[1] iii. 82. 7.

---

[3] ἑκατέρῳ Thuc.

ἕπεται, βούλεται γὰρ δηλοῦν "ἐν τῷ παραυτίκα ἴσχυον"· τὸ δὲ "πρὸς τὸ ἄπορον ἑκατέρῳ διδόμενοι, οὐκ ἐχόντων ἄλλοθεν δύναμιν" σαφέστερον ἂν ἦν οὕτως ἐξενεχθέν· "διὰ τὸ μηδεμίαν ἄλλην ἔχειν δύναμιν κατὰ τὸ ἄπορον ἑκατέρῳ διδόμενοι." τὸ δὲ κατάλληλον τῆς διανοίας ἦν ἂν τοιοῦτο· "οἱ δὲ περὶ τῆς φιλίας ὅρκοι εἴ που ἄρα γένοιντο, ἀπορίᾳ πίστεως ἄλλης ἑκατέρῳ
32 διδόμενοι ἐν τῷ παραχρῆμα ἴσχυον." σκολιώτερα δὲ τούτων ἐστὶ καὶ ἃ μετὰ ταῦτα τίθησιν· "ἐν δὲ τῷ παρατυχόντι ὁ φθάσας θαρρῆσαι εἰ ἴδοι ἄφρακτον, ἥδιον διὰ τὴν πίστιν ἐτιμωρεῖτο ἢ ἀπὸ τοῦ προφανοῦς· καὶ τό τε ἀσφαλὲς ἐλογίζετο, καὶ ὅτι ἀπάτῃ περιγενόμενος συνέσεως ἀγώνισμα προσελάμβανε".[1] τὸ δὴ "παρατυχὸν" ἀντὶ τοῦ "παραχρῆμα" κεῖται, τό τε "ἄφρακτον" ἀντὶ τοῦ ἀφυλάκτου" καὶ τὸ "ἥδιον τιμωρεῖσθαι διὰ τὴν πίστιν μᾶλλον ἢ ἀπὸ τοῦ προφανοῦς" σκοτεινῶς περιπέφρασται, καὶ ἐλλείπει τι μόριον εἰς τὸ συμπληρωθῆναι τὴν νόησιν. εἰκάζειν δὲ ἔστιν, ὅτι τοῦτο βούλεται λέγειν· "εἰ δέ που παρατύχοι τινὶ καιρὸς καὶ μάθοι τὸν ἐχθρὸν ἀφύλακτον, ἥδιον ἐτιμωρεῖτο, ὅτι πιστεύσαντι ἐπέθετο μᾶλλον ἢ φυλαττομένῳ· καὶ συνέσεως δόξαν προσελάμβανε, τό τε ἀσφαλὲς λογιζόμενος καὶ ὅτι διὰ

---

[1] iii. 82. 7.

trying to indicate that " they had held good for the time being." The expression " were exchanged . . . while immediate difficulties obtained and no other source offered support " would have been clearer rendered in this way: " The offer had been made by each side because it had no other source available on account of its difficulties." The sequence of thought would then have been like this: " Oaths of friendship, in the few cases they were exchanged, held good only temporarily, since the offer had been made by both sides only because of the lack of any other reliable source."

What he writes next is even more tortuous than this:[1] 32

" But the man who dared to strike the first blow when opportunity offered and he saw his enemy unfortified, thought revenge thus gained to be sweeter than that won openly, because it involved betrayal of trust. He further considered both the safety of his action, and also that in overcoming his enemy by deceit he was gaining the additional prize of superior intelligence."

" Opportunity " is used instead of " right moment." " unfortified " instead of " unguarded "; and the phrase " sweeter to gain revenge by betrayal of trust than to win it openly " is an obscure circumlocution, needing a further part to complete its sense. We can guess that he wishes to say:

" If the right moment presented itself to anyone and he perceived that his enemy was off his guard, he took revenge with greater pleasure because the victim had trusted him than if he had been off his guard. He also earned the reputation of being intelligent, in that he had calculated the safety of his

τὴν ἀπάτην αὐτοῦ περιεγένετο." "ῥᾷον δ' οἱ πολλοὶ κακοῦργοι" φησὶν "ὄντες δεξιοὶ κέκληνται ἢ ἀμαθεῖς ἀγαθοί, καὶ τῷ μὲν αἰσχύνονται, ἐπὶ δὲ τῷ ἀγάλλονται"· ταῦτα γὰρ ἀγκύλως μὲν εἴρηται καὶ βραχέως, ἐν ἀφανεῖ δὲ κείμενον ἔχει τὸ σημαινόμενον. χαλεπὸν γὰρ μαθεῖν, τίνας δή ποτε νοεῖ τοὺς ἀμαθεῖς τε καὶ ἀγαθούς· εἴ τε γὰρ ἀντιδιαστέλλεται πρὸς τοὺς κακούργους, οὐκ ἂν εἴησαν ἀμαθεῖς οἱ μὴ κακοί· εἴ τ' ἐπὶ τῶν ἀνοήτων καὶ ἀφρόνων τίθησι τοὺς ἀμαθεῖς, κατὰ τί δή ποτε τούτους ἀγαθοὺς καλεῖ; "καὶ τῷ μὲν αἰσχύνονται" τίνες; ἄδηλον γὰρ πότερον ἀμφότεροι ἢ οἱ ἀμαθεῖς. "ἐπὶ δὲ τῷ ἀγάλλονται" κἀνταῦθα ἄδηλον, τίνες· εἰ μὲν γὰρ ἐπ' ἀμφοτέρων τίθησιν, οὐκ ἔχει νοῦν· οὔτε γὰρ ἐπὶ τοῖς κακούργοις οἱ ἀγαθοὶ ἀγάλλονται οὔτ' ἐπὶ τοῖς ἀμαθέσιν οἱ κακοῦργοι αἰσχύνονται.

33 Οὗτος ὁ χαρακτὴρ τῆς ἀσαφοῦς καὶ πεπλεγμένης λέξεως, ἐν ᾗ πλείων ἔνεστι τῆς θέλξεως ἡ σκοτίζουσα τὴν διάνοιαν ὄχλησις, ἕως ἑκατὸν ἐκμηκύνεται στίχων. θήσω δὲ[1] καὶ τὰ ἑξῆς οὐδεμίαν ἔτι λέξιν ἐμαυτοῦ προστιθείς· "πάντων δ' αὐτῶν αἴτιον ἀρχὴ ἡ διὰ πλεονεξίαν καὶ φιλοτιμίαν, ἐκ δ' αὐτῶν καὶ ἐς τὸ φιλονεικεῖν καθισταμένων τὸ πρόθυμον. οἱ γὰρ ἐν ταῖς πόλεσι προστάντες, μετὰ ὀνόματος ἑκάτεροι εὐπρεποῦς, πλήθους τε ἰσονομίας πολιτικῆς καὶ ἀριστοκρατίας σώφρονος

[1] δὲ Krüger: δὴ codd.

action, and because he had overcome his opponent by deceit."

Then he says:[1]

"And in most cases villains are more ready to be called adroit than are good men to be called stupid: in the latter case they are ashamed, but in the former they pride themselves."

This is compact and brief, but its meaning lies concealed: for it is difficult to understand who in the world are meant by the "stupid" and the "good" men. If he is contrasting them with the "villains," men who are not wicked cannot be simpletons; and if he applies the term "stupid" to the silly and the senseless, by what reasoning can he call such men "good"? And who are those "latter" who "are ashamed?" For it is not clear whether this refers to both classes of men or only the simple men. It is also not clear who "the former" who "pride themselves" are: if it is meant to apply to both, it does not make sense, since good men do not take pride in being villains, nor are villains ashamed of being stupid.

These are the characteristics of the obscure and in- 33
volved style, which contains less charm than confusion to cloud the mind; and this passage goes on for a hundred lines. I shall quote the rest without any further comment of my own:[2]

"Now the cause of all these evils was the pursuit of power for the gratification of greed and ambition, and from these arose the lust for party faction once these parties became engaged in contention. The leaders in the cities, each professing an attractive policy—like the political equality of the people or

[1] iii. 82. 7.
[2] iii. 82. 8–83. 3.

προτιμήσει, τὰ μὲν κοινὰ λόγῳ θεραπεύοντες ἆθλα ἐποιοῦντο· παντὶ δὲ τρόπῳ ἀγωνιζόμενοι ἀλλήλων περιγενέσθαι ἐτόλμησάν τε τὰ δεινότατα, ἐπεξῄεσάν τε τὰς τιμωρίας ἔτι μείζους, οὐ μέχρι τοῦ δικαίου καὶ τῇ πόλει ξυμφόρου προστιθέντες, ἐς δὲ τὸ ἑκατέροις που αἰεὶ ἡδονὴν ἔχον ὁρίζοντες· καὶ ἢ μετὰ ψήφου ἀδίκου καταγνώσεως ἢ χειρὶ κτώμενοι τὸ κρατεῖν ἕτοιμοι ἦσαν τὴν αὐτίκα φιλονεικίαν ἐκπιμπλάναι. ὥστ' εὐσεβείᾳ μὲν οὐδέτεροι ἐνόμιζον, εὐπρεπείᾳ δὲ λόγου, οἷς ξυμβαίη ἐπιφθόνως τι διαπράξασθαι, ἄμεινον ἤκουον· τὰ δὲ μέσα τῶν πολιτῶν ὑπ' ἀμφοτέρων, ἢ ὅτι οὐ συνηγωνίζοντο ἢ ὅτι φθόνῳ τοῦ περιεῖναι, διεφθείροντο. οὕτω πᾶσα ἰδέα κατέστη κακοτροπίας διὰ τὰς στάσεις τῷ Ἑλληνικῷ· καὶ τὸ εὔηθες, οὗ τὸ γενναῖον πλεῖστον μετέχει, καταγελασθὲν ἠφανίσθη· τὸ δὲ ἀντιτετάχθαι ἀλλήλοις τῇ γνώμῃ ἀπίστως ἐπὶ πολὺ διήνεγκεν. οὐ γὰρ ἦν ὁ διαλύσων οὔτε λόγος ἐχυρὸς οὔτε ὅρκος φοβερός. κρείττους δὲ ὄντες πάντες λογισμῷ ἐς τὸ ἀνέλπιστον τοῦ βεβαίου μὴ παθεῖν μᾶλλον προεσκόπουν ἢ πιστεῦσαι ἐδύναντο. καὶ οἱ φαυλότεροι γνώμην ὡς τὰ πλείω περιεγίγνοντο. τῷ γὰρ δεδιέναι τό τε αὐτῶν ἐνδεὲς καὶ τὸ τῶν ἐναντίων ξυνετόν, μὴ λόγοις τε ἥττους ὦσι καὶ ἐκ τοῦ πολυτρόπου αὐτῶν τῆς γνώμης φθάσωσι προεπιβουλευόμενοι, τολμηρῶς πρὸς τὰ ἔργα ἐχώρουν· οἱ δὲ καταφρονοῦντες

moderate aristocracy, sought prizes for themselves in those public interests which they pretended to cherish, used every available weapon in their struggle for supremacy over each other and dared to commit the most dreadful crimes, and carried their acts of vengeance to excess, not stopping at what justice and the good of the state demanded, but making the party caprice of the moment the only limit; and whether the victim had been secured by unjust condemnation or by main force, they were ready to glut the animosity they felt at the moment. Thus morality was in fashion with neither party; but the use of fair phrases earned a better reputation for those who had perpetrated some odious crime; and the citizens who stayed in the middle were destroyed by both sides, either because they did not join them in their struggle, or because of envy that they should survive.

"Thus every form of villainy arose in Greece from these revolutions. Simplicity, which is a very large part of the noble nature, was laughed down and disappeared; mutual antagonism gave rise to mistrust and divided most men from their neighbours. Neither was a man's word strong enough nor his oath, to be sufficiently respected to put an end to the dissension; but all parties' minds reckoned on the hopelessness of things rather than on their reliability, were more intent upon avoiding harm than capable of confidence. In this the inferior intellects had the advantage for the most part: apprehensive of their own deficiencies and of the cleverness of their opponents, they were afraid of being worsted in debate and of being anticipated in conspiracy by their more versatile antagonists, and hence resorted to bold action; while their adversaries, arrogantly thinking that they

κἂν προαισθέσθαι, καὶ ἔργῳ οὐδὲν σφᾶς δεῖν λαμβάνειν, ἃ γνώμῃ ἔξεστιν, ἄφρακτοι μᾶλλον διεφθείροντο." Ἐκ πολλῶν ἔτι δυνάμενος παραδειγμάτων ποιῆσαι φανερόν, ὅτι κρείττων ἐστὶν ἐν τοῖς διηγήμασιν, ὅταν ἐν τῷ συνήθει καὶ κοινῷ τῆς διαλέκτου χαρακτῆρι μένῃ, χείρων δέ, ὅταν ἐκτρέψῃ τὴν διάλεκτον ἐκ τῆς συνήθους ἐπὶ τὰ ξένα ὀνόματα καὶ βεβιασμένα σχήματα, ὧν ἔνια σολοικισμῶν παρέχεται δόξαν, ἀρκεσθήσομαι τούτοις, ἵνα μὴ περαιτέρω τοῦ δέοντος ἡ γραφή μοι προβῇ.

34 Ἐπεὶ δὲ καὶ περὶ τῶν δημηγοριῶν αὐτοῦ τὰ δοκοῦντά μοι φανερὰ ποιήσειν ὑπεσχόμην, ἐν αἷς οἴονταί τινες τὴν ἄκραν τοῦ συγγραφέως εἶναι δύναμιν, διελόμενος καὶ ταύτην διχῇ τὴν θεωρίαν εἴς τε τὸ πραγματικὸν μέρος καὶ εἰς τὸ λεκτικὸν χωρὶς ὑπὲρ ἑκατέρου ποιήσομαι τὸν λόγον, ἀρξάμενος ἀπὸ τοῦ πραγματικοῦ. ἐν ᾧ πρώτην μὲν ἔχει μοῖραν ἡ τῶν ἐνθυμημάτων τε καὶ νοημάτων εὕρεσις, δευτέραν δὲ ἡ τῶν εὑρεθέντων χρῆσις· ἐκείνη μὲν ⟨ἐν⟩ τῇ φύσει μᾶλλον ἔχουσα τὴν ἰσχύν, αὕτη δὲ ἐν τῇ τέχνῃ. τούτων ἣ μὲν πλέον ἔχουσα τοῦ τεχνικοῦ τὸ φυσικὸν καὶ διδαχῆς ἐλάττονος δεομένη θαυμαστή τίς ἐστι παρὰ τῷ συγγραφεῖ· φέρει γὰρ ὥσπερ ἐκ πηγῆς πλουσίας ἄπειρόν τι χρῆμα νοημάτων τε καὶ ἐνθυμημάτων περιττῶν καὶ ξένων καὶ παραδόξων. ἣ δὲ πλεῖον ἔχουσα τὸ τεχνικὸν καὶ λαμπροτέραν ποιοῦσα φαίνεσθαι τὴν ἑτέραν ἐνδεεστέρα τοῦ δέοντος ἐπὶ πολλῶν. ὅσοι μὲν οὖν ἐκτεθαυμάκασιν αὐτὸν ὑπὲρ τὸ μέτριον, ὡς μηδὲν τῶν θεοφορήτων

would foresee their intentions, and that it was unnecessary to secure by action what they could secure by thought, were more often destroyed through being off their guard."

I could supply many more examples to prove that his narratives are more effective when he adheres to the familiar and normal style of speech, and less effective when he forsakes this familiar style and uses strange words and forced figures of speech, some of which have the appearance of solecisms. But I shall content myself with the foregoing examples, for fear that my treatise should become unduly long.

Since I have also promised to disclose my views on 34
his speeches, which some people think exhibit the historian's powers at their highest, I shall divide my discussion as before into two parts, content and style, and treat each separately, beginning with content. In the treatment of this the first place is occupied by the invention of arguments and ideas, the second by the deployment of this material, the former depending more upon native talent, the latter more upon art. The first, the product of natural ability rather than acquired skill, and requiring less training, is present to a remarkable degree in the historian: it draws forth an endless flow of striking, strange and unexpected ideas and arguments, as from a copious fountain. The second part, which involves a greater element of art, and whose function is to add lustre to the natural part, frequently falls short of requirements. Those who have admired Thucydides immoderately, crediting him with nothing less than

διαφέρειν, διὰ τὸ πλῆθος ἐοίκασι τῶν ἐνθυμημάτων τοῦτ' ἐσχηκέναι τὸ πάθος. οὓς ἐὰν διδάσκῃ τις ἐφ' ἑκάστῳ πράγματι παρατιθεὶς [1] τὸν λόγον, ὅτι ταυτὶ μὲν οὐκ ἦν ἐπιτήδεια ἐν τούτῳ τῷ καιρῷ καὶ ὑπὸ τούτων τῶν προσώπων λέγεσθαι, ταυτὶ δ' οὐκ ἐπὶ τούτοις τοῖς πράγμασιν οὐδὲ μέχρι τούτου, δυσχεραίνουσιν, ὅμοιόν τι πάσχοντες τοῖς κεκρατημένοις ὑφ' οἵας δή τινος ὄψεως ἔρωτι μὴ πολὺ ἀπέχοντι μανίας. ἐκεῖνοί τε γὰρ πάσας τὰς ἀρετάς, ὁπόσαι γίνονται περὶ μορφὰς εὐπρεπεῖς, ταῖς καταδεδουλωμέναις αὐτοὺς [2] προσεῖναι νομίζουσι, καὶ τοὺς ἐξονειδίζειν ἐπιχειροῦντας, εἴ τι περὶ αὐτὰς ὑπάρχει σίνος, ὡς βασκάνους καὶ συκοφάντας προβέβληνται· οὗτοί τε ὑπὸ τῆς μιᾶς ταύτης ἀρετῆς κεκαρωμένοι τὴν διάνοιαν ἅπαντα καὶ τὰ μὴ προσόντα τῷ συγγραφεῖ μαρτυροῦσιν· ἃ γὰρ ἕκαστος εἶναι βούλεται περὶ τὸ φιλούμενόν τε καὶ θαυμαζόμενον ὑφ' ἑαυτοῦ, ταῦτα οἴεται. ὅσοι δ' ἀδέκαστον τὴν διάνοιαν φυλάσσουσι καὶ τὴν ἐξέτασιν τῶν λόγων ἐπὶ τοὺς ὀρθοὺς κανόνας ἀναφέρουσιν, εἴτε φυσικῆς τινος κρίσεως μετειληφότες εἴτε καὶ διὰ διδαχῆς ἰσχυρὰ τὰ κριτήρια κατασκευάσαντες, οὔτε ἅπαντα ἐπαινοῦσιν ἐπ' ἴσης οὔτε πρὸς ἅπαντα δυσχεραίνουσιν, ἀλλὰ τοῖς μὲν κατορθώμασι τὴν προσήκουσαν μαρτυρίαν ἀπονέμουσιν, εἰ δέ τι διημάρτηται μέρος ἐν αὐτοῖς, οὐκ ἐπαινοῦσιν. ὅ γοῦν ἐπὶ πάντων ἐγὼ τῶν ἐμαυτοῦ θεωρημάτων κανόνας ὑποτιθέμενος οὔτε πρότερον ὤκνησα τὰ δοκοῦντά μοι φέρειν ἐς μέσον οὔτε νῦν ἀποτρέψομαι. διδοὺς δὴ τὸ πρῶτον, ὥσπερ καὶ κατ' ἀρχὰς ἔφην, τὸ

divine inspiration, seem to have been affected in this way by the sheer multitude of his ideas. If you take a speech and relate it to the particular circumstances in which it was made, and point out that one argument was inappropriate for use by these persons on this occasion, and another was unsuited for use in those circumstances and at such a length, his admirers take offence. They are suffering from the same sort of infatuation as a man overcome with an almost frantic love of some face or other. He thinks that the face which has captivated him possesses all the charms that go with a comely form; and those who attempt to criticise any blemishes that it has he accuses of slander and backbiting. In the same way Thucydides's admirers, hypnotised by this single virtue, also claim for him all the qualities that he does not possess: each man thinks what he wants to think about the object of his love and admiration. But those who keep an impartial mind and examine literature in accordance with correct standards, whether they are endowed with some natural power of appreciation or have developed their critical faculties by the help of instruction, do not praise everything alike or find fault with everything, but give due recognition to correct usage and withhold praise from any part that is seriously at fault.

Now in all my studies I have laid down my prin- 35
ciples of criticism: I have never previously hesitated to disclose my opinion, and shall not shrink from doing so now. I begin by repeating my acknowledge-

---

[1] παρατιθεὶς Sylburg: περιτιθεὶς codd.
[2] αὑτοὺς Sadée: αὐτοὺς codd.

περὶ τὴν εὕρεσιν τοῦ συγγραφέως εὔστοχον, καὶ εἴ τις ἄλλως προὐπείληφεν[1] εἴτε διὰ φιλονεικίαν εἴ-τε δι' ἀναισθησίαν, ἁμαρτάνειν αὐτὸν οἰόμενος, θάτερον οὐκέτι δίδωμι, τὸ περὶ τὰς οἰκονομίας αὐτοῦ[2] τεχνικόν, πλὴν ἐπ' ὀλίγων πάνυ δημηγοριῶν. ὁρῶ δὲ καὶ ⟨τὰ⟩[3] περὶ τὴν λέξιν ἐλαττώματα, περὶ ὧν ἤδη προείρηκα, πλεῖστα καὶ μέγιστα ταύταις συμβεβηκότα ταῖς ἰδέαις· καὶ γὰρ αἱ γλωττηματικαὶ καὶ ξέναι καὶ πεποιημέναι λέξεις ἐν ταύταις μάλιστα ἐπιπολάζουσι, καὶ τὰ πολύπλοκα καὶ ἀγκύλα καὶ βεβιασμένα σχήματα πλεῖστα περὶ ταύτας[4] ἐστίν. εἰ δὲ τὰ εἰκότα ἔγνωκα, σύ τε κρινεῖς καὶ τῶν ἄλλων ἕκαστος ἐπὶ τὴν ἐξέτασιν ἀγόμενος τῶν ἔργων. ἔσται δὲ κατὰ ταὐτὰ[5] ἡ παράθεσις αὐτῶν, ἀντιπαρεξεταζομένων τοῖς ἄριστά μοι δοκοῦσιν ἔχειν τῶν οὔτε κατὰ τὰς οἰκονομίας κατορθουμένων οὔτε κατὰ τὴν φράσιν ἀνεγκλήτων.

36 Ἐν μὲν οὖν τῇ δευτέρᾳ βύβλῳ ⟨τὴν⟩[6] ἐπὶ Πλαταιὰς Λακεδαιμονίων τε καὶ τῶν συμμάχων ἔλασιν ἀρξάμενος γράφειν ὑποτίθεται, τοῦ βασιλέως τῶν Λακεδαιμονίων Ἀρχιδάμου μέλλοντος δῃώσειν τὴν γῆν, πρέσβεις παρὰ τῶν Πλαταιέων ἀφιγμένους πρὸς αὐτόν, καὶ λόγους ἀποδίδωσιν, οἵους εἰκὸς ἦν ὑπὸ ἀμφοτέρων εἰρῆσθαι, τοῖς ⟨τε⟩[7] προσώποις πρέποντας καὶ τοῖς πράγμασιν οἰκείους καὶ μήτ' ἐλλείποντας[8] τοῦ μετρίου μήτε ὑπεραί-

[1] προὐπείληφεν Krüger: προσυπείληφεν codd.
[2] αὐτοῦ Sadée: αὐτῷ codd.
[3] τὰ inseruit Sadée.
[4] ταύτας Reiske: ταῦτα codd.

ment of the historian's felicity of invention, which I made at the outset;[1] and if anyone has rashly assumed otherwise, either from contentiousness or from insensitivity, I think he is mistaken. But I do not go so far as to concede the other point, that he is as skilful in arrangement, except in a very small number of his speeches. I also note that the stylistic shortcomings to which I have already referred occur most frequently and prominently in this genre: recondite, strange and poetical expressions are very much in evidence in the speeches, and many complex, intricate and forced figures are to be found in them. It is for you, and for every other student who is prompted to examine his work, to decide whether my judgments are reasonable. The comparison will be conducted in the same way as before: those passages which I consider to be his best will be contrasted with those in which the arrangement is unsatisfactory and the style is open to criticism.

The episode which he describes at the beginning of 36
the second book is the attack upon Plataea by the 429 B.C.
Lacedaemonians and their allies. It starts at the point where the Lacedaemonian king Archidamus is about to ravage the land, and Plataean envoys have arrived at his camp. Thucydides assigns to both sides speeches such as each might naturally have made. They are suited to the characters of the speakers and relevant to the situation, and neither inadequate nor

[1] ch. 27.

---

[5] κατὰ ταὐτὰ Reiske: κατὰ ταῦτα codd.
[6] τὴν inseruit Reiske.
[7] τε inseruit Usener.
[8] μήτ' ἐλλείποντας Reiske: μήτε λείποντας codd.

ροντας, λέξει τε κεκόσμηκεν αὐτοὺς καθαρᾷ καὶ σαφεῖ καὶ συντόμῳ καὶ τὰς ἄλλας ἀρετὰς ἐχούσῃ· τήν τε ἁρμονίαν οὕτως ἔναυλον ἀποδέδωκεν ⟨ὥσθ'⟩ ἅμα ⟨λόγοις⟩[1] τοῖς ἡδίστοις παρεξετάζεσθαι· "Τοῦ δ' ἐπιγιγνομένου θέρους οἱ Πελοποννήσιοι καὶ οἱ ξύμμαχοι ἐς μὲν τὴν Ἀττικὴν οὐκ ἐσέβαλον, ἐστράτευσαν δ' ἐπὶ Πλάταιαν· ἡγεῖτο δ' Ἀρχίδαμος ὁ Ζευξιδάμου Λακεδαιμονίων βασιλεύς· καὶ καθίσας τὸν στρατὸν ἔμελλε δῃώσειν τὴν γῆν. οἱ δὲ Πλαταιεῖς εὐθὺς πρέσβεις πέμψαντες πρὸς αὐτὸν ἔλεγον τοιάδε· Ἀρχίδαμε καὶ Λακεδαιμόνιοι, οὐ δίκαια ποιεῖτε οὐδὲ ἄξια οὔθ' ὑμῶν οὔτε πατέρων ὧν ἐστε, ἐς γῆν τὴν Πλαταιέων στρατεύοντες. Παυσανίας γὰρ ὁ Κλεομβρότου Λακεδαιμόνιος ἐλευθερώσας τὴν Ἑλλάδα ἀπὸ τῶν Μήδων μετὰ Ἑλλήνων τῶν ἐθελησάντων συνάρασθαι τοῦ κινδύνου καὶ τῆς μάχης, ἣ παρ' ἡμῖν ἐγένετο, θύσας ἐν τῇ Πλαταιέων ἀγορᾷ ἱερὰ Διὶ ἐλευθερίῳ καὶ ξυγκαλέσας πάντας τοὺς συμμάχους, ἀπεδίδου Πλαταιεῦσι γῆν καὶ πόλιν τὴν σφετέραν ἔχοντας αὐτονόμους οἰκεῖν, στρατεῦσαί τε μηδένα ποτὲ ἀδίκως ἐπ' αὐτοὺς μηδ' ἐπὶ δουλείᾳ· εἰ δὲ μή, ἀμύνειν τοὺς παρόντας ξυμμάχους κατὰ δύναμιν. τάδε μὲν ἡμῖν πατέρες οἱ ὑμέτεροι ἔδοσαν ἀρετῆς ἕνεκα καὶ προθυμίας τῆς ἐν ἐκείνοις τοῖς κινδύνοις γενομένης. ὑμεῖς δὲ τἀναντία ἐκείνοις δρᾶτε· μετὰ γὰρ Θηβαίων τῶν ἡμῖν ἐχθίστων ἐπὶ δουλείᾳ τῇ ἡμετέρᾳ ἥκετε. μάρτυρας δὲ θεοὺς τούς τε ὁρκίους τότε γενομένους ποιούμενοι καὶ τοὺς

[1] ὥσθ' et λόγοις supplevi.

overdone. He has furnished them with language which is pure, clear and concise and possesses all the other virtues besides; and the arrangement is so melodious that it bears comparison with the most graceful ⟨writing⟩.[1]

"The following summer the Peloponnesians and their allies did not make an incursion into Attica, but marched against Plataea under the leadership of Archidamus the son of Zeuxidamus, king of the Lacedaemonians. He had encamped his army and was about to ravage the land, when the Plataeans forthwith sent out ambassadors to him, who spoke as follows:

"Archidamus and men of Lacedaemon, what you are doing is neither right nor worthy of yourselves or of your fathers, when you march against the territory of the Plataeans. For Pausanias the son of Cleombrotus, the Lacedaemonian, when he had liberated Greece from the Medes in company with those Greeks who had been willing to face with him the peril of the battle that was fought near our city, after 479 B.C. sacrificing in the market-place of Plataea to Zeus the Liberator, and assembling all the allies, granted to the Plataeans the right to live in independent possession of their land and city, and that no one should ever make war upon them unjustly or enslave them; otherwise the allies then present should assist them to the best of their ability. These rewards your fathers gave us for the valour and zeal which we displayed in the face of those dangers. But you are doing the very opposite: for you have joined with the Thebans, our bitterest enemies, and come to enslave us. Therefore we call the gods to witness, both those who

[1] ii. 71.

ὑμετέρους πατρῴους καὶ ἡμετέρους ἐγχωρίους λέγομεν ὑμῖν, γῆν τὴν Πλαταιίδα μὴ ἀδικεῖν μηδὲ παραβαίνειν τοὺς ὅρκους, ἐᾶν δὲ οἰκεῖν αὐτονόμους, ὥσπερ Παυσανίας ἐδικαίωσε." τοιαῦτα τῶν Πλαταιέων λεγόντων Ἀρχίδαμος ἀποκρίνεται τοιάδε· "Δίκαια λέγετε, ὦ ἄνδρες Πλαταιεῖς, ἢν ποιῆτε ὅμοια τοῖς λόγοις. καθάπερ γὰρ Παυσανίας ὑμῖν παρέδωκεν, αὐτοί τε αὐτονομεῖσθε καὶ τοὺς ἄλλους ξυνελευθεροῦτε, ὅσοι μετασχόντες τῶν τότε κινδύνων ὑμῖν τε ξυνώμοσαν καί εἰσι νῦν ὑπ' Ἀθηναίοις· παρασκευή τε τοσήδε καὶ πόλεμος γεγένηται αὐτῶν ἕνεκα καὶ τῶν ἄλλων ἐλευθερώσεως. ἧς μάλιστα μὲν μετασχόντες καὶ αὐτοὶ ἐμμείνατε τοῖς ὅρκοις. εἰ δὲ μή, ἅπερ καὶ πρότερον ἤδη προὐκαλεσάμεθα, ἡσυχίαν ἄγετε νεμόμενοι τὰ ὑμέτερα αὐτῶν· καὶ ἔστε μηδὲ μεθ' ἑτέρων, δέχεσθε δ' ἀμφοτέρους φίλους, ἐπὶ πολέμῳ δὲ μηδετέρους. καὶ τάδε ἡμῖν ἀρκέσει." ὁ μὲν Ἀρχίδαμος τοσαῦτα εἶπεν. οἱ δὲ Πλαταιῶν πρέσβεις ἀκούσαντες ταῦτα εἰσῆλθον εἰς τὴν πόλιν· καὶ τῷ πλήθει τὰ ῥηθέντα κοινώσαντες ἀπεκρίναντο αὐτῷ, ὅτι ἀδύνατα εἴη σφίσι ποιεῖν, ἃ προκαλεῖται, ἄνευ Ἀθηναίων· παῖδες γὰρ σφῶν καὶ γυναῖκες παρ' ἐκείνοις εἴησαν. δεδιέναι δὲ καὶ περὶ πάσῃ τῇ πόλει, μὴ 'κείνων ἀποχωρησάντων Ἀθηναῖοι ἐλθόντες σφίσιν οὐκ ἐπιτρέπωσιν ἢ Θηβαῖοι ὡς ἔνορκοι ὄντες κατὰ τὸ ἀμφοτέρους δέχεσθαι αὖθις σφῶν τὴν πόλιν πειράσωσι καταλαβεῖν. ὁ δὲ θαρσύνων αὐτοὺς πρὸς ταῦτα ἔφη·

at that time received the oaths, and those of your own fathers and of our country, and charge you not to injure Plataean territory, nor break the oaths, but to let us live independent, as Pausanias saw fit to allow us."

"When the Plataeans had made such a speech, Archidamus replied in this manner:[1]

"Your words are just, Plataeans, if you act in accordance with them. Enjoy the freedom which Pausanias granted you yourselves, and also help in setting the rest of Greece free, those men who shared the dangers of those days with you and are now under Athenian rule, for whose liberation all this preparation and war has been undertaken. Do you, then, abide by the oaths, preferably by taking part in this liberation; but if not, then, as we proposed before, remain at peace in the enjoyment of your own possessions, and do not join either side, but receive both as friends, and for warlike purposes neither the one nor the other. And this will satisfy us."

"Such were the words of Archidamus. Having heard them the Plataean envoys returned to the city, and after communicating to the whole people what had been said, replied to him that it was impossible for them to do what he proposed without consulting the Athenians; for their children and wives were at Athens; and that they also had fears for the whole city, lest when the Lacedaemonians had retired, the Athenians might come and not leave it in their hands; or the Thebans, as signatories to the agreement that they should "receive both parties," might in their turn try to seize their city. To encourage them on both these points Archidamus said:

[1] ii. 72–75.

"Ὑμεῖς δὲ πόλιν μὲν καὶ οἰκίας ἡμῖν παράδοτε τοῖς Λακεδαιμονίοις, καὶ γῆς ὅρους ἀποδείξατε, καὶ δένδρα τὰ ὑμέτερα καὶ εἴ τι ἄλλο δυνατὸν εἰς ἀριθμὸν ἐλθεῖν· αὐτοὶ δὲ μεταχωρήσατε ὅποι βούλεσθε, ἕως ἂν ὁ πόλεμος ᾖ· ἐπειδὰν δὲ παρέλθῃ, ἀποδώσομεν ὑμῖν, ἃ ἂν παραλάβωμεν· μέχρι δὲ τοῦδε ἕξομεν ὑμῖν παρακαταθήκην ἐργαζόμενοι καὶ ἀποφορὰν φέροντες, ἣ ἂν ὑμῖν ἱκανὴ μέλλῃ ἔσεσθαι." οἱ δὲ ἀκούσαντες αὖθις εἰσῆλθον εἰς τὴν πόλιν, καὶ βουλευσάμενοι μετὰ τοῦ πλήθους ἔλεξαν, ὅτι βούλονται Ἀθηναίοις κοινῶσαι πρῶτον ἃ προκαλεῖται, καὶ ἢν πείθωσιν αὐτούς, ποιεῖν ταῦτα. μέχρι δὲ τούτου σπείσασθαι σφίσιν ἐκέλευον καὶ τὴν γῆν μὴ δῃοῦν. ὁ δ' ἡμέρας τε ἐσπείσατο, ἐν αἷς εἰκὸς ἦν κομισθῆναι, καὶ τὴν γῆν οὐκ ἔτεμνεν. ἐλθόντες δὲ οἱ Πλαταιεῖς πρέσβεις ὡς τοὺς Ἀθηναίους καὶ βουλευσάμενοι μετ' αὐτῶν πάλιν ἦλθον ἀγγέλλοντες τοῖς ἐν τῇ πόλει τοιάδε· "Οὔτ' ἐν τῷ πρὸ τοῦ χρόνῳ, ἄνδρες Πλαταιεῖς, ἀφ' οὗ ξύμμαχοι ἐγενόμεθα, Ἀθηναῖοί φασιν ἐν οὐδενὶ ὑμᾶς προέσθαι ἀδικουμένους οὔτε νῦν περιόψεσθαι, βοηθήσειν δὲ κατὰ δύναμιν· ἐπισκήπτουσίν τε ὑμῖν πρὸς τῶν ὅρκων, οὓς οἱ πατέρες ὤμοσαν, μηδὲν νεωτερίζειν περὶ τὴν συμμαχίαν." τοιαῦτα τῶν πρέσβεων ἀπαγγειλάντων οἱ Πλαταιεῖς ἐβουλεύσαντο Ἀθηναίους μὴ προδιδόναι, ἀλλ' ἀνασχέσθαι καὶ γῆν τεμνομένην, εἰ δέοι, ὁρῶντας καὶ ἄλλο πάσχοντας, ὅ τι ἂν ξυμβαίνῃ· ἐξελθεῖν τε μηδένα ἔτι, ἀλλ' ἀπὸ τοῦ

" In that case give up your city and houses to us, the Lacedaemonians, and indicate the boundaries of your territories and your trees and anything else that can be counted; and yourselves move wherever you please for the duration of the war. When it is over, we will restore to you whatever we may have received. Till then we will hold it in trust, cultivating it, and bringing to you such produce as will meet your needs sufficiently."

" When they had heard his proposal, they went again into the city, and after consulting with the people, said that they wished first to communicate to the Athenians what he proposed, and if they gained their agreement, then to do so: but till that time they begged him to grant them a truce, and not to lay waste the land. So he granted them a truce for the number of days they might take until their return, and in the meantime did not begin to ravage the land. The Plataean envoys went to consult with the Athenians, and on their return delivered the following message to those in the city:

" Men of Plataea, the Athenians say that never in time past, since we became allies, have they on any occasion deserted us when injured; nor will they neglect us now, but will assist us to the best of their power. And they charge you by the oaths which your father swore, not to depart from the terms of the alliance."

" When the ambassadors had delivered this message, the Plataeans resolved not to play false to the Athenians, but to endure, if necessary, both to see their land ravaged, and to suffer whatever else might befall them. They resolved also that no one should go out again, but that they should make their reply

τείχους ἀποκρίνασθαι, ὅτι ἀδύνατά ἐστι σφίσι ποιεῖν ἃ Λακεδαιμόνιοι προκαλοῦνται. ὡς δ' ἀπεκρίναντο, ἐντεῦθεν δὴ πρῶτον μὲν ἐς ἐπιμαρτυρίαν καὶ θεῶν καὶ ἡρώων τῶν ἐγχωρίων Ἀρχίδαμος ὁ βασιλεὺς κατέστη λέγων ὧδε· "Θεοὶ ὅσοι γῆν τὴν Πλαταιίδα ἔχετε, καὶ ἥρωες, ξυνίστορες ἔστε, ὅτι οὔτε τὴν ἀρχὴν ἀδίκως, ἐκλιπόντων δὲ τῶνδε προτέρων τὸ ξυνώμοτον ἐπὶ γῆν τήνδε ἤλθομεν, ἐν ᾗ οἱ πατέρες ἡμῶν εὐξάμενοι ὑμῖν Μήδων ἐκράτησαν καὶ παρέσχετε αὐτὴν εὐμενῆ ἐναγωνίσασθαι τοῖς Ἕλλησιν, οὔτε νῦν ἤν τι ποιῶμεν, ἀδικήσομεν· προκαλεσάμενοι γὰρ πολλὰ καὶ εἰκότα οὐ τυγχάνομεν. ξυγγνώμονες δὲ ἔστε τῆς μὲν ἀδικίας κολάζεσθαι τοῖς ὑπάρχουσι προτέροις, τῆς δὲ τιμωρίας τυγχάνειν τοῖς ἐπιφέρουσι νομίμως." τοσαῦτα ἐπιθειάσας καθίστη εἰς πόλεμον τὸν στρατόν."

37 Ἐξετάσωμεν δὴ παρὰ τοῦτον τὸν διάλογον ⟨τὸν⟩ [1] οὕτω καλῶς καὶ περιττῶς ἔχοντα ἕτερον αὐτοῦ διάλογον, ὃν μάλιστα ἐπαινοῦσιν οἱ τοῦ χαρακτῆρος τούτου θαυμασταί. ὑποτίθεται δή, στρατιὰν ἀποστειλάντων Ἀθηναίων ἐπὶ Μηλίους Λακεδαιμονίων ἀποίκους, πρὶν ἄρξασθαι τοῦ πολέμου, τὸν στρατηγὸν τῶν Ἀθηναίων καὶ τοὺς προβούλους τῶν Μηλίων συνιόντας εἰς λόγους περὶ καταλύσεως τοῦ πολέμου· καὶ κατ' ἀρχὰς μὲν ἐκ τοῦ ἰδίου προσώπου δηλοῖ τὰ λεχθέντα ὑφ' ἑκατέρων, ἐπὶ μιᾶς δ' ἀποκρίσεως τοῦτο τὸ σχῆμα διατηρήσας, τὸ διηγηματικόν, προσωποποιεῖ τὸν μετὰ ταῦτα διάλογον καὶ δραματίζει.

[1] τὸν inseruit Usener.

from the wall, to the effect that it was impossible to do as the Lacedaemonians proposed. When they had given this answer, King Archidamus proceeded in the first place to call to witness the gods and heroes of the land, in these words:

"O gods and heroes who dwell in the land of Plataea, bear witness that it was neither unjustly in the first instance, but when these men had first broken the agreement they had sworn to, that we came against this land, in which our fathers prayed to you before they conquered the Medes, and which you made an auspicious land for Greeks to contend in. Nor shall we act unjustly now, whatever we may do; for although we have made many reasonable proposals, we are having no success. Grant then that those may be punished for the wrong who were the first to begin, and that those may obtain revenge who are lawfully trying to exact it."

"Having thus appealed to the gods, he committed his army to the war."

Let us compare this splendid and remarkable dia- 37
logue with another which is greatly praised by admirers of his style. The episode in question is that in which the Athenians have sent an expedition against the Melians, who were Spartan colonists; but 416 B.C.
before beginning hostilities the Athenian general and the Melian leaders meet to discuss possible terms of peace.[1] Thucydides begins by stating in his own person what each side said, but after maintaining this form of reported speech for only one exchange of argument, he dramatises the rest of the dialogue and makes the characters speak for themselves. The Athenian opens the dialogue with these words:[2]

[1] v. 84. [2] v. 85.

ἄρχει δ' ὁ Ἀθηναῖος τάδε λέγων· "Ἐπειδὴ οὐ πρὸς τὸ πλῆθος οἱ λόγοι γίγνονται, ὅπως δὴ μὴ συνεχεῖ ῥήσει οἱ λαοὶ ἐπαγωγὰ καὶ ἀνέλεγκτα ἐς ἅπαξ ἀκούσαντες ἡμῶν ἀπατηθῶσι (γιγνώσκομεν γὰρ ὅτι τοῦτο φρονεῖ ἡμῶν ἡ ἐς τοὺς ὀλίγους ἀγωγή), ὑμεῖς οἱ προκαθήμενοι ἔτι ἀσφαλέστερον ποιήσετε. καὶ μηδ' ὑμεῖς ἑνὶ λόγῳ ἀλλὰ πρὸς τὸ μὴ δοκοῦν ἐπιτηδείως λέγεσθαι εὐθὺς ὑπολαμβάνοντες κρίνετε· καὶ πρῶτον, εἰ ἀρέσκει ὡς λέγομεν, εἴπατε." οἱ δὲ τῶν Μηλίων σύνεδροι ἀπεκρίναντο· Ἡ μὲν ἐπιείκεια τοῦ διδάσκειν καθ' ἡσυχίαν ἀλλήλους οὐ ψέγεται· τὰ δὲ τοῦ πολέμου παρόντα ἤδη καὶ οὐ μέλλοντα διαφέροντα αὐτοῦ φαίνετε." τοῦτο τὸ τελευταῖον εἴ τις ἐν τοῖς σχήμασιν ἀξιώσει φέρειν, οὐκ ἂν φθάνοι πάντας τοὺς σολοικισμούς, ὅσοι γίγνονται παρὰ τοὺς ἀριθμοὺς καὶ παρὰ τὰς πτώσεις, σχήματα καλῶν; προθεὶς γὰρ "ἡ μὲν ἐπιείκεια τοῦ διδάσκειν καθ' ἡσυχίαν οὐ ψέγεται," ἔπειτα συνάψας τῷ ἑνικῷ καὶ κατὰ τὴν ὀρθὴν ἐξενηνεγμένῳ[1] πτῶσιν "τὰ δὲ τοῦ πολέμου παρόντα ἤδη καὶ οὐ μέλλοντα" ἐπιζεύγνυσι τούτοις ἑνικὸν καὶ κατὰ τὴν γενικὴν ἐσχηματισμένον πτῶσιν, εἴ τε ἄρθρον δεικτικὸν βούλεταί τις αὐτὸ καλεῖν εἴ τε ἀντονομασίαν, τὸ "αὐτοῦ"· τοῦτο δὲ οὔτε τῷ θηλυκῷ καὶ ἑνικῷ καὶ ὀνοματικῷ προσαρμοττόμενον σῴζει τὴν ἀκολουθίαν οὔτε τῷ πληθυντικῷ καὶ οὐδετέρῳ ⟨καὶ⟩[2] κατὰ τὴν αἰτιατικὴν ἐσχηματισμένῳ πτῶσιν. ἦν δ' ἂν ὁ λόγος κατάλληλος οὕτω σχηματισθείς·

[1] ἐξενηνεγμένῳ Sylburg: ἐξενηνεγμένα codd.
[2] καὶ inseruit Bücheler.

" Since the debate is not being held before the people, for fear, I suppose, that in listening to a single uninterrupted speech by us, they may be deceived by seductive arguments which they are unable to test at a single hearing (for we are perfectly aware that this is the purpose of our being brought before a select few), you who are their representatives will produce an even safer result. You too must not reply in a single long speech, but must decide immediately on each point of dispute as it arises. Now say first whether you like what we suggest." The Melian representatives replied:[1]

" The reasonableness of a quiet explanation of our respective positions meets with no criticism from us. But you indicate clearly a different intention from this by the preparations you are making for war now, and not in the future."

Surely anyone proposing to classify this last sentence as an example of figurative language would immediately have to give the same name to all the solecisms of number and case-usage? For he begins with " The reasonableness of a quiet explanation meets with no criticism," then he follows the nominative singular subject with the accusative " preparations for immediate, not future war," and " from this," in the genitive singular, which, whether we wish to call it a demonstrative article or a pronoun, corresponds neither to the nominative singular feminine nor to the accusative plural neuter, and therefore fails to preserve the agreement. The sentence would have been self-consistent if it had been constructed as follows:

[1] v. 86.

"ἡ μὲν ἐπιείκεια τοῦ διδάσκειν καθ' ἡσυχίαν ἀλλήλους οὐ ψέγεται, τὰ δὲ τοῦ πολέμου παρόντα ἤδη καὶ οὐ μέλλοντα διαφέροντα αὐτῆς φαίνεται." τούτοις ἐπιτίθησιν ἐνθύμημα νενοημένον μὲν οὐκ ἀτόπως, ἡρμηνευμένον δὲ οὐκ εὐπαρακολουθήτως· "Εἰ μὲν τοίνων ὑπονοίας τῶν μελλόντων λογιούμενοι ἢ ἄλλο τι ξυνήκετε, ἢ ἐκ τῶν παρόντων καὶ ὧν ὁρᾶτε περὶ σωτηρίας βουλεύσαντες τῇ πόλει,
38 παυόμεθα· εἰ δ' ἐπὶ τοῦτο, λέγοιμεν ἄν." καὶ μετὰ τοῦτο ἀποστρέψας τοῦ διηγήματος τὸν διάλογον ἐπὶ τὸ δραματικὸν ταῦτα τὸν Ἀθηναῖον ἀποκρινόμενον ποιεῖ· "Εἰκὸς μὲν καὶ ξυγγνώμη, ἐν τῷ τοιῷδε καθεστῶτας ἐπὶ πολλὰ καὶ λέγοντας καὶ δοκοῦντας τραπέσθαι." ἔπειτα εὐσχήμονα πρόθεσιν ὑποθέμενος "ἡ μέντοι ξύνοδος καὶ περὶ σωτηρίας ἤδη πάρεστι, καὶ ὁ λόγος, ᾧ προκαλεῖσθε τρόπῳ, εἰ δοκεῖ, γιγνέσθω" πρῶτον μὲν εὕρηκεν ἐνθύμημα οὔτε τῆς Ἀθηναίων πόλεως ἄξιον οὔτ' ἐπὶ τοιούτοις πράγμασιν ἁρμόττον λέγεσθαι "Ἡμεῖς τοίνυν οὔτε αὐτοὶ μετ' ὀνομάτων καλῶν, ὡς ἢ δικαίως τὸν Μῆδον καταλύσαντες ἄρχομεν, ἢ ἀδικούμενοι νῦν ἐπεξερχόμεθα, λόγων μῆκος ἄπιστον παρέξομεν·" τοῦτο δέ ἐστιν ὁμολογοῦντος τὴν ἐπὶ τοὺς μηδὲν ἀδικοῦντας στράτευσιν, ἐπειδὴ περὶ μηδετέρου τούτων βούλεται τὸν λόγον ὑπέχειν· οἷς ἐπιτίθησιν "οὔθ' ὑμᾶς ἀξιοῦμεν ἢ

---

1 v. 87.

2 v. 88. Thucydides actually assigns this to the Melian spokesmen.

3 v. 89.

" The reasonableness of a quiet explanation of our respective positions meets with no criticism from us, but the preparations which you are making for immediate, not future war are clearly contrary to reason."

After this he introduces an idea which is by no means ill-conceived, but which is expressed in a form that is difficult to understand:[1]

" If you have come merely to argue about what you suppose may happen, or for any other reason than to deliberate for the safety of your city in the situation in which you see it now, we have no more to say; but if the latter is your intention, we can talk."

After this he changes the style of the dialogue from 38
narrative to dramatic, and makes the Athenian answer:[2]

" It is a natural and excusable thing that men in your position should have much to say and should try many expedients in speech and thought."

Then, after introducing a noble sentiment:

" But this conference has met now to consider the question of our preservation, so let the argument proceed, if you please, in the manner you propose "—he first conjures up a sentiment which is both unworthy of the Athenians, and does not fit the situation:[3]

" Now we Athenians shall use no fine words or long and unconvincing arguments to try to prove that we have earned our empire by conquering the Persians, or that we are attacking you now because you are injuring us."

This is tantamount to an admission that the expedition is against innocent victims, in that he does not wish to support either of these statements with argument. He then continues:

ὅτι Λακεδαιμονίων ἄποικοι ὄντες οὐ ξυνεστρατεύσατε ἢ ὡς ἡμᾶς οὐδὲν ἠδικήκατε λέγοντας οἴεσθαι πείσειν, τὰ δυνατὰ δ' ἐξ ὧν ἑκάτεροι ἀληθῶς φρονοῦμεν διαπράσσεσθαι." τοῦτο δέ ἐστιν· "ὑμεῖς μὲν ἀληθῶς φρονοῦντες ὅτι ἀδικεῖσθε, τὴν ἀνάγκην φέρετε καὶ εἴκετε· ἡμεῖς δὲ οὐκ ἀγνοοῦντες, ὅτι ἀδικοῦμεν ὑμᾶς, τῆς ἀσθενείας ὑμῶν περιεσόμεθα τῇ βίᾳ· ταῦτα γὰρ ἑκατέροις δυνατά." ἔπειτα τὴν αἰτίαν ἀποδοῦναι τούτου βουληθεὶς ἐπιλέγει· "ὅτι δίκαια μὲν ἐν τῷ ἀνθρωπείῳ λόγῳ ἀπὸ τῆς ἴσης ἀνάγκης κρίνεται, δυνατὰ δὲ οἱ προὔχοντες πράσσουσι καὶ οἱ ἀσθενεῖς ξυγχω-
39 ροῦσι." βασιλεῦσι γὰρ βαρβάροις ταῦτα πρὸς Ἕλληνας ἥρμοττε λέγειν· Ἀθηναίοις δὲ πρὸς τοὺς Ἕλληνας, οὓς ἠλευθέρωσαν ἀπὸ τῶν Μήδων, οὐκ ἦν προσήκοντα εἰρῆσθαι, ὅτι τὰ δίκαια τοῖς ἴσοις ἐστὶ πρὸς ἀλλήλους, τὰ δὲ βίαια τοῖς ἰσχυροῖς πρὸς τοὺς ἀσθενεῖς. ὀλίγα δὲ πρὸς ταῦτα τῶν Μηλίων ἀποκριναμένων, ὅτι καλῶς ἂν ἔχοι τοῖς Ἀθηναίοις προνοεῖν τοῦ δικαίου, μὴ καὶ αὐτοί ποτε σφαλέντες ὑπ' ἄλλων ἐν ἐξουσίᾳ γένωνται καὶ τὰ αὐτὰ πάσχωσιν ὑπὸ τῶν ἰσχυροτέρων, ἀποκρινόμενον ποιεῖ τὸν Ἀθηναῖον "Ἡμεῖς δὲ τῆς ἡμετέρας ἀρχῆς, ἢν καὶ παυθῇ, οὐκ ἀθυμοῦμεν τὴν τελευτήν," τούτου δ' αἰτίαν ἀποδιδόντα, ὅτι κἂν καταλύσωσιν αὐτῶν Λακεδαιμόνιοι τὴν ἀρχήν, συγγνώμην ἕξουσι, καὶ αὐτοὶ

"Nor do we expect you to hope to convince us by arguing that, although a colony of the Lacedaemonians, you have not joined their expeditions, or that you have never done us any wrong. But we do expect you to try to achieve what is practicable, in view of what we both correctly have in mind.

This means: "You are correct in thinking that you are being wronged, but you must put up with it and yield. We are quite aware that we are treating you unjustly, but we shall overcome your weakness with our strength: such are our respective capabilities." Then, by way of explanation of this, he adds:

"We both know that the question of justice enters into human affairs only where the pressure of constraint is equal, and that the powerful exact what they can and the weak concede what they must."

These would have been suitable words for bar- 39
barian kings to address to Greeks, but no Athenian should have spoken thus to Greeks whom they had liberated from the Persians, saying that right is a matter of reciprocity between equals, whereas force is exerted by the strong against the weak. When the Melians have replied briefly to this, suggesting that the Athenians would do well to consider what is right in case they should themselves one day slip up and find themselves in the power of others, and suffer the same fate at the hands of stronger enemies, Thucydides makes the Athenian representative reply:[1]

"The possible fall of our empire is not an event to which we look forward with dismay."

And he gives as his reason for this statement that, even if the Lacedaemonians should destroy their empire, they would treat them with indulgence, since

[1] v. 91.

πολλὰ τοιαῦτα πράσσοντες. θήσω δὲ καὶ τὴν λέξιν αὐτοῦ· "οὐ γὰρ οἱ ἄρχοντες ἄλλων, ὥσπερ καὶ Λακεδαιμόνιοι, οὗτοι δεινοὶ τοῖς νικηθεῖσι." τοῦτο δὲ ὅμοιόν ἐστι τῷ λέγειν, ὅτι παρὰ τοῖς τυράννοις οὐ μισοῦνται τύραννοι. οἷς ἐπιτίθησιν "καὶ περὶ μὲν τούτου ἡμῖν ἀφείσθω κινδυνεύεσθαι," ὃ μόγις ἂν εἶπεν τῶν καταποντιστῶν τις ἢ λῃστῶν "οὐδὲν ἐπιστρέφομαι τῆς μετὰ ταῦτα τιμωρίας χαρισάμενος ἐπιθυμίαις ἐν τῷ παρόντι." ἔπειτ' ὀλίγων τῶν μεταξὺ γενομένων ἀμοιβαίων καὶ τῶν Μηλίων εἰς ἐπιεικῆ συγκαταβαινόντων αἵρεσιν "Ὥστε δὲ ἡσυχίαν ἄγοντας ἡμᾶς φίλους μὲν εἶναι ἀντὶ πολεμίων, ξυμμάχους δὲ μηδετέρων οὐκ ἂν δέξαισθε;" ἀποκρινόμενον ποιεῖ τὸν Ἀθηναῖον "Οὐ γὰρ τοσοῦτον ἡμᾶς βλάπτει ἡ ἔχθρα ὑμῶν, ὅσον ἡ φιλία μὲν ἀσθενείας, τὸ δὲ μῖσος δυνάμεως παράδειγμα τοῖς ἀρχομένοις δηλούμενον," ἐνθύμημα πονηρὸν καὶ σκολιῶς ἀπηγγελμένον· εἰ δὲ τὸ νόημα βούλεταί τις αὐτοῦ σκοπεῖν, τοιόνδε ἐστίν, ὅτι "φιλοῦντες μὲν ἡμᾶς ἀσθενεῖς φαίνεσθαι πρὸς τοὺς ἄλλους ποιήσετε, μισοῦντες δὲ ἰσχυρούς· οὐ γὰρ ζητοῦμεν εὐνοίᾳ τῶν ὑπηκόων ἄρχειν, ἀλλὰ φόβῳ." τούτοις ἕτερα προσθεὶς πάλιν ἀμοιβαῖα περίεργα καὶ πικρά, τοὺς Μηλίους ὑποτίθεται λέγοντας, ὅτι κοινὰς τὰς

---

[1] v. 94.
[2] v. 95.
[3] v. 102.

they often behave in the same way themselves. I shall quote his actual words:

" Ruling states, like that of the Lacedaemonians, are not as formidable as that to their conquered enemies."

This is equivalent to saying that tyrants are not hated among tyrants. He then continues:

" But this is a danger which you may leave to us."

Which is equivalent to saying " Once I have gratified my present desires I do not trouble about future retribution," a sentiment which would scarcely have been uttered by a pirate or a freebooter. Then, after a few further exchanges have taken place, and the Melians come to the point of suggesting a reasonable compromise:[1]

" Would you not accept as a solution our neutrality, whereby we should be inactive, regarding you as friends rather than as enemies, but neither side as our ally?"

He makes the Athenian reply:[2]

" No, for your enmity does us less harm than the realisation by our subjects that your friendship is evidence of our weakness and your hatred of our power."

A base sentiment, awkwardly expressed, the sense of which, if anyone wishes to examine it, is something like this: " If you show us friendship you will make us seem weak in the eyes of others, but if you hate us we shall be thought strong; for we seek to rule our subjects not by the help of their good will but through their fear."

After adding still further laboured and harsh 40
exchanges, he next makes the Melians say[3] that all who engage in war are subject to the same forces of

τύχας φέρουσιν οἱ πολέμιοι καὶ "τὸ μὲν εἶξαι εὐθὺς ἀνέλπιστον, μετὰ δὲ τοῦ δρωμένου ἔτι καὶ στῆναι ἐλπὶς ὀρθῶς." πρὸς ταῦτα ποιεῖ τὸν Ἀθηναῖον ἀποκρινόμενον λαβυρίνθων σκολιώτερα περὶ τῆς ἐλπίδος ἐπὶ κακῷ τοῖς ἀνθρώποις γινομένης, κατὰ λέξιν οὕτως γράφων· "Ἐλπὶς δὲ κινδύνου παραμύθιον οὖσα τοὺς μὲν ἀπὸ περιουσίας χρωμένους αὐτῇ κἂν βλάψῃ, οὐ καθεῖλεν· τοῖς δὲ ἐς πᾶν τὸ ὑπάρχον ἀναρριπτοῦσι (δάπανος γὰρ φύσει) ἅμα τε γιγνώσκεται σφαλέντων, καὶ ἐν ὅτῳ φυλάξεταί τις αὐτὴν γνωρισθεῖσαν, οὐκ ἐλλείπει. ὃ ὑμεῖς ἀσθενεῖς τε καὶ ἐπὶ ῥοπῆς μιᾶς ὄντες μὴ βούλεσθε παθεῖν μηδ᾽ ὁμοιωθῆναι τοῖς πολλοῖς, οἷς παρὸν ἀνθρωπείως ἔτι σῴζεσθαι, ἐπειδὰν πιεζομένους αὐτοὺς ἐπιλείπωσιν αἱ φανεραὶ ἐλπίδες, ἐπὶ τὰς ἀφανεῖς καθίστανται, μαντικήν τε καὶ χρησμοὺς καὶ ὅσα τοιαῦτα μετ᾽ ἐλπίδων λυμαίνεται." ταῦτ᾽ οὐκ οἶδα πῶς ἄν τις ἐπαινέσειεν ὡς προσήκοντα εἰρῆσθαι στρατηγοῖς Ἀθηναίων, ὅτι λυμαίνεται τοὺς ἀνθρώπους ἡ παρὰ τῶν θεῶν ἐλπὶς καὶ οὔτε χρησμῶν ὄφελος οὔτε μαντικῆς τοῖς εὐσεβῆ καὶ δίκαιον προῃρημένοις τὸν βίον. εἰ γάρ τι καὶ ἄλλο, τῆς Ἀθηναίων πόλεως καὶ τοῦτ᾽ ἐν τοῖς πρώτοις ἐστὶν ἐγκώμιον, τὸ περὶ παντὸς πράγματος καὶ ἐν παντὶ καιρῷ τοῖς θεοῖς ἕπεσθαι καὶ μηδὲν ἄνευ μαντικῆς καὶ χρησμῶν ἐπιτελεῖν. λεγόντων τε τῶν Μηλίων, ὅτι σὺν τῇ παρὰ τῶν θεῶν βοηθείᾳ καὶ Λακεδαιμονίοις πεποίθασιν, οὓς εἰ καὶ διὰ μηδὲν ἄλλο, διὰ γοῦν

[1] v. 103.

chance, and "to yield at once would be to abandon hope, but with the help of action there is still some hope that we shall remain unsubdued." He makes the Athenian reply to this with an argument which is more tortuous than a maze, on the subject of the hope which men feel when they are in danger. The passage runs as follows:[1]

"Hope is a comfort in the hour of danger, and when those who employ her have ample resources, though damaging, she is not disastrous; but those who go so far as to risk their all (for she is extravagant by nature) recognise her only in the hour of their fall, whereas so long as one will guard against her after she has been recognised, she does not fail him. You are weak, and a single turn of the scale may ruin you: do not choose to suffer, like most others who might yet be saved by human means but who, when they find themselves hard pressed and palpable grounds of confidence gone, have recourse to the invisible, to prophesies and oracles and the like, which ruin men by the hopes they inspire."

I do not know how these words can be considered appropriate in the mouths of Athenian generals. They imply that divinely-inspired hope is harmful to men, and that oracles and prophesy are of no use to those who have chosen a pious and just way of life. Now if one aspect of Athenian life is to be singled out for special praise it is that they followed divine guidance on every matter and in every crisis, and took no decisive action without consulting soothsayers and oracles. And when the Melians say that, in addition to divine aid, they have placed their trust in the Lacedaemonians, who would help them from a feeling of shame, if for no other reason, and would not stand

τὴν αἰσχύνην αὐτοῖς βοηθήσειν καὶ οὐ περιόψεσθαι συγγενεῖς ἀπολλυμένους, αὐθαδέστερον ἔτι τὸν Ἀθηναῖον ἀποκρινόμενον εἰσάγει· "Τῆς μὲν τοίνυν πρὸς τὸ θεῖον εὐμενείας οὐδ' ἡμεῖς οἰόμεθα λελείψεσθαι· οὐδὲν γὰρ ἔξω τῆς μὲν ἀνθρωπείας, τῆς δ' εἰς τὸ θεῖον νεμέσεως τῶν τ' εἰς σφᾶς αὐτοὺς βουλήσεων δικαιοῦμεν ἢ πράσσομεν. ἡγούμεθα γὰρ τό τε θεῖον δόξῃ τἀνθρώπειόν τε σαφῶς διὰ παντὸς ἀπὸ φύσεως ἀναγκαίως, οὗ ἂν κρατῇ, ἄρχειν·" τούτων ὁ νοῦς ἔστι μὲν δυσείκαστος καὶ τοῖς πάνυ δοκοῦσιν ἐμπείρως τοῦ ἀνδρὸς ἔχειν, κατακλείεται δ' εἰς τοιοῦτόν τι πέρας, ὅτι τὸ μὲν θεῖον δόξῃ γινώσκουσιν ἅπαντες, τὰ δὲ πρὸς ἀλλήλους δίκαια τῷ κοινῷ τῆς φύσεως κρίνουσι νόμῳ· οὗτος δ' ἔστιν ἄρχειν ὧν ἂν δύνηταί τις κρατεῖν. ἀκόλουθα καὶ ταῦτα τοῖς πρώτοις καὶ οὔτε Ἀθηναίοις οὔτε Ἕλλησι πρέποντα εἰρῆσθαι.

41 Πολλὰς δυνάμενος ἔτι διανοίας παρασχέσθαι τὸ συνετὸν ἐχούσας πονηρόν, ἵνα μὴ πλείων ὁ λόγος γένοιτό μοι τοῦ μετρίου, τὴν τελευταίαν ἔτι προσθήκην παραλήψομαι μόνην, ἣν ἀπαλλαττόμενος ἐκ τοῦ συλλόγου ὁ Ἀθηναῖος εἴρηκεν· "ἀλλ' ὑμῶν τὰ μὲν ἰσχυρὰ ὄντα ἐλπιζόμενα μέλλεται, τὰ δὲ παρόντα βραχέα πρὸς τὰ ἤδη ἀντιτεταγμένα περιγενέσθαι. πολλήν γε ἀλογίαν" φησί "τῆς διανοίας παρέχετε, εἰ μὴ μεταστησάμενοι ἡμᾶς ἄλλό τι τῶνδε σωφρονέστερον γνώσεσθε." οἷς ἐπιτίθησιν "οὐ γὰρ δὴ ἐπί γε τὴν ἐν τοῖς

---

[1] v. 105.

by and watch their kinsmen being destroyed, Thucydides makes the Athenian retort in an even more arrogant manner:[1]

"As for the favour of the gods, we expect to have quite as much as you: for we are not claiming or doing anything which goes beyond the accepted limits of men's personal desires or of what is allowed them in relation to other men or with regard to the gods. For of the gods we believe, and of men we know, that by a universal law of their nature they will rule whomever they can conquer."

The meaning of this is difficult to conjecture, even for those who think they are quite familiar with the author; and the argument ends in some such conclusion as this, that everyone thinks he knows what the will of the gods is, but decides his own rights in relation to his fellows according to a common law of human nature, that it is right to rule anyone whom you can conquer. This is consequent upon the first arguments, and should not be heard coming either from an Athenian or from any other Greek.

I could furnish many more examples of clever but 41
perverted thinking, but in order to avoid unduly prolonging my argument I shall quote only the parting words with which the Athenian representative breaks off the dialogue:[2]

"But your strongest arguments, being objects of hope, are still in the future, but your present power is small compared with what is now arrayed against you. You are showing a great want of reason," he says, "unless you come to a more sensible conclusion after letting us withdraw." He then adds: "For surely

[2] v. 111.

αἰσχροῖς καὶ προὔπτοις κινδύνοις πλεῖστα διαφθείρουσαν ἀνθρώπους αἰσχύνην τρέψεσθε. πολλοῖς γὰρ προορωμένοις ἔτι ἐς οἷα φέρονται τὸ αἰσχρὸν καλούμενον ὀνόματος ἐπαγωγοῦ δυνάμεις ἐπεσπάσατο ἡσσηθεῖσι τοῦ ῥήματος ἔργῳ συμφοραῖς ἀνηκέστοις ὁρῶντας περιπεσεῖν."

Τούτων τῶν λόγων ὅτι μὲν οὔτε αὐτὸς μετέσχεν ὁ συγγραφεὺς τῷ συλλόγῳ τότε παρατυχὼν οὔτε τῶν διαθεμένων αὐτοὺς Ἀθηναίων ἢ Μηλίων ἤκουσεν, ἐξ ὧν αὐτὸς ἐν τῇ πρὸ ταύτης [1] βύβλῳ περὶ αὑτοῦ [2] γράφει, μαθεῖν ῥᾴδιον, ὅτι μετὰ τὴν ἐν Ἀμφιπόλει στρατηγίαν ἐξελαθεὶς τῆς πατρίδος πάντα τὸν λοιπὸν τοῦ πολέμου χρόνον ἐν Θρᾴκῃ διέτριψε. λείπεται δὴ σκοπεῖν, εἰ τοῖς τε πράγμασι προσήκοντα καὶ τοῖς συνεληλυθόσιν εἰς τὸν σύλλογον προσώποις ἁρμόττοντα πέπλακε ⟨τὸν⟩ [3] διάλογον "ἐχόμενος ὡς ἔγγιστα τῆς συμπάσης γνώμης τῶν ἀληθῶς λεχθέντων," ὡς αὐτὸς ἐν τῷ προοιμίῳ τῆς ἱστορίας προείρηκεν. ἆρ' οὖν ὥσπερ τοῖς Μηλίοις οἰκεῖοι καὶ προσήκοντες ἦσαν οἱ περὶ τῆς ἐλευθερίας λόγοι παρακαλοῦντες τοὺς Ἀθηναίους μὴ καταδουλοῦσθαι πόλιν Ἑλληνίδα μηδὲν ἁμαρτάνουσαν εἰς αὐτούς, οὕτως καὶ τοῖς Ἀθηναίων στρατηγοῖς πρέποντες ἦσαν οἱ περὶ τῶν δικαίων μήτ' ἐξετάζειν ἐῶντες μήτε λέγειν, ἀλλὰ τὸν τῆς βίας καὶ πλεονεξίας νόμον εἰσάγοντες καὶ ταῦτ' εἶναι δίκαια τοῖς ἀσθενέσιν ἀποφαίνοντες, ὅσα τοῖς ἰσχυροτέροις δοκεῖ; ἐγὼ μὲν γὰρ οὐκ

[1] πρὸ ταύτης Krüger: πρὸ αὐτῆς codd.
[2] αὑτοῦ Krüger: αὐτοῦ codd.
[3] τὸν inseruit Sadée.

you are not going to turn to that false sense shame of which, when dangers threaten that are disgraceful because foreseen, has ruined men so often. Even when people can foresee the direction in which they are heading, the idea of shame often draws down upon them the powerful implications of a misleading name; so that, unable to resist a word, they fall in fact, with their eyes open, into irretrievable disaster."

From what the historian writes about himself in the previous book,[1] it is easy to deduce that he neither was present at this meeting nor took part personally in the discussion, nor received a report of it from any of the Athenian or Melian spokesmen, because he spent all the rest of the war, after his command at Amphipolis, in exile in Thrace.[2] It now remains to **424 B.C.**
consider whether he has composed the dialogue in such a way that it is consistent with the facts and fits the character of the delegates to the meeting, "adhering as closely as possible to the general sense of what was actually said," as he said he would do in his introduction.[3] Very well. The arguments about freedom, calling upon the Athenians not to enslave a Greek city that has done them no wrong, were fitting and appropriate for the Melians. But were the speeches of the Athenian generals equally appropriate, when they did not allow discussion or even mention of justice, but introduced the law of violence and greed and declared that for the weak justice is the will of the stronger? I do not think that such arguments

[1] cf. iv. 104–108; v. 26.5.

[2] Thucydides's Thracian connections are mentioned by his biographer Marcellinus, who also says that Thucydides died in Thrace (45, 55).

[3] i. 22.

οἴομαι τοῖς ἐκ τῆς εὐνομωτάτης πόλεως ἐπὶ τὰς ἔξω πόλεις ἀποστελλομένοις ἡγεμόσι ταῦτα προσήκειν λέγεσθαι, οὐδ' ἂν ἀξιώσαιμι τοὺς μὲν μικροπολίτας καὶ μηδὲν ἔργον ἐπιφανὲς ἀποδειξαμένους Μηλίους πλέονα τοῦ καλοῦ ποιεῖσθαι πρόνοιαν ἢ τοῦ ἀσφαλοῦς καὶ πάντα ἑτοίμους εἶναι τὰ δεινὰ ὑποφέρειν, ἵνα μηδὲν ἄσχημον ἀναγκασθῶσι πράττειν, τοὺς δὲ προελομένους τήν τε χώραν καὶ τὴν πόλιν ἐκλιπεῖν κατὰ τὸν Περσικὸν πόλεμον Ἀθηναίους, ἵνα μηδὲν αἰσχρὸν ὑπομείνωσιν ἐπίταγμα, τῶν ταὐτὰ [1] προαιρουμένων ὡς ἀνοήτων κατηγορεῖν. οἴομαι δ', ὅτι κἂν εἴ τινες ἄλλοι παρόντων Ἀθηναίων ταῦτα ἐπεχείρουν λέγειν, ἐπαχθῶς ἤνεγκαν ἂν οἱ τὸν κοινὸν βίον ἐξημερώσαντες. ἐγὼ μὲν δὴ διὰ ταύτας τὰς αἰτίας οὐκ ἐπαινῶ τὸν διάλογον τοῦτον ἀντιπαρεξετάζων τὸν ἕτερον. ἐν ἐκείνῳ μὲν γὰρ Ἀρχίδαμος ὁ Λακεδαιμόνιος δίκαιά τε προκαλεῖται τοὺς Πλαταιεῖς καὶ λέξει κέχρηται καθαρᾷ καὶ σαφεῖ καὶ οὐδὲν ἐχούσῃ σχῆμα βεβασανισμένον οὐδὲ ἀνακόλουθον· ἐν τούτῳ δὲ οἱ φρονιμώτατοι τῶν Ἑλλήνων αἴσχιστα μὲν ἐνθυμήματα φέρουσιν, ἀηδεστάτῃ δ' αὐτὰ περιλαμβάνουσι λέξει· εἰ μὴ ἄρα μνησικακῶν ὁ συγγραφεὺς τῇ πόλει διὰ τὴν καταδίκην ταῦτα τὰ ὀνείδη κατεσκέδασεν αὐτῆς, ἐξ ὧν ἅπαντες μισήσειν αὐτὴν ἔμελλον. ἃ γὰρ οἱ προεστηκότες τῶν πόλεων καὶ τηλικαύτας ἐξουσίας πιστευόμενοι φρονεῖν τε καὶ λέγειν ⟨ἐοίκασι⟩ [2] πρὸς τὰς πόλεις ὑπὲρ τῆς αὑτῶν πατρίδος, ταῦτα κοινὰ ὑπολαμβάνουσιν ἅπαντες εἶναι τῆς ἀποστελ-

[1] ταὐτὰ Sylburg: ταῦτα codd.

as these would be fittingly used by the leaders of the city with the best laws in the world when they are on missions abroad, nor should I expect the inhabitants of a tiny state like Melos, who never did anything to distinguish themselves, to prefer the nobler to the safer policy and to be prepared to undergo every kind of suffering in order to avoid the necessity of a discreditable course of action; while the Athenians, who during the Persian War chose to leave their land and their city rather than submit to any base imposition, accuse them of being senseless when they follow the same principles. I think that if anyone else had attempted to express these views in the presence of the Athenians, the latter, who had civilised the life of all mankind, would have been offended. For these reasons I find this dialogue inferior by comparison with the earlier one. In that former dialogue the demands which the Lacedaemonian Archidamus makes on the Plataeans are fair, and he speaks in pure, clear language without any tortured or disordered forms of expression; whereas in the Melian Dialogue the wisest of the Greeks adduce the most disgraceful arguments, and invest them with the most disagreeable language. Perhaps it was because the historian bore his city a grudge for the sentence passed on him that he has deluged her with these reproaches, which were calculated to make her universally hated: for when the leaders of a state, entrusted by her with great power and appointed to represent her on missions to other states, seem to express certain views, those views are assumed by all

---

[2] ἐοίκασι inseruit Usener.

λούσης πόλεως αὐτούς. καὶ περὶ μὲν τῶν διαλόγων ἅλις.

42 Τῶν δὲ δημηγορικῶν λόγων τεθαύμακα μὲν τὸν ἐν τῇ πρώτῃ βύβλῳ ῥηθέντα ἐν Ἀθήναις ὑπὸ Περικλέους περὶ τοῦ μὴ εἴκειν Λακεδαιμονίοις, τὸν ἔχοντα τήνδε τὴν ἀρχήν· "Τῆς μὲν γνώμης, ὦ ἄνδρες Ἀθηναῖοι, ἀεὶ τῆς αὐτῆς ἔχομαι, μὴ εἴκειν Πελοποννησίοις" ὡς καὶ τοῖς ἐνθυμήμασιν ἡρμηνευμένον δαιμονίως καὶ οὔτε κατὰ τὴν σύνθεσιν τῶν μορίων οὔτε κατὰ τὴν ἐξαλλαγὴν τῶν σχηματισμῶν τῶν ἀνακολούθων καὶ βεβιασμένων ἐνοχλοῦντα τὰς ἀκοάς, πάσας δὲ περιειληφότα τὰς ἀρετάς, ὁπόσαι γίγνονται περὶ δημηγορικοὺς ⟨λόγους⟩·[1] καὶ τοὺς ὑπὸ Νικίου τοῦ στρατηγοῦ ῥηθέντας ἐν Ἀθήναις ὑπὲρ τῆς εἰς Σικελίαν στρατείας· τήν τε πεμφθεῖσαν ὑπὸ αὐτοῦ τοῖς Ἀθηναίοις ἐπιστολήν, ἐν ᾗ χρῄζει συμμαχίας ἄλλης καὶ διαδόχου, κάμνων τὸ σῶμα ὑπὸ νόσου· καὶ τὴν παράκλησιν τῶν στρατιωτῶν, ἣν ἐποιήσατο πρὸ τῆς τελευταίας ναυμαχίας· καὶ τὸν παραμυθητικὸν λόγον, ὅτε πεζῇ τὴν στρατιὰν ἔμελλεν ἀπάγειν, ἀπολωλεκὼς τὰς τριήρεις ἁπάσας· καὶ εἴ τινές εἰσιν ἄλλαι τοιαῦται δημηγορίαι καθαραὶ καὶ σαφεῖς καὶ εἰς τοὺς ἀληθινοὺς ἀγῶνας ἐπιτήδειοι. ὑπὲρ ἁπάσας δὲ τὰς ἐν ταῖς ἑπτὰ βύβλοις φερομένας τὴν Πλαταιέων ἀπολογίαν τεθαύμακα παρ' οὐδὲν οὕτως ἕτερον ὡς τὸ μὴ βεβασανίσθαι μηδὲ κατεπιτετηδεῦσθαι, ἀληθεῖ δέ τινι καὶ φυσικῷ κεκοσμῆσθαι χρώματι. τά τε γὰρ ἐνθυμή-

[1] λόγους supplevit Krüger.

to be those of the state which sent them out. That is sufficient on the subject of the dialogues.

Among the political speeches, I admire the one in 42
the second book which Pericles made at Athens about not giving in to the Lacedaemonians. It begins with these words:[1]

"I hold firmly to the same opinion as ever, Athenians, that we should not yield to the Peloponnesians. . . ."

Its arguments are brilliantly conveyed, and it does not offend the ear either by the arrangement of its parts or by any perversity in the choice of figures that are obscure and forced, and it contains all the virtues of political oratory. I find the same qualities in the speeches made by the general Nicias at Athens on the subject of the Sicilian Expedition,[2] and in the letter sent by him to the Athenians, in which he asked for reinforcements and a successor in his command because he was exhausted as the result of ill-health;[3] and the speech in which he rallied his men before the final sea-battle;[4] and the consolatory speech which he made as he was about to withdraw his army by land after losing all the ships;[5] and all the other speeches in this style—pure, clear and suitable for the crises of real life. But most of all the speeches contained in the seven books I admire the defence of the Plataeans,[6] not so much for any other reason as because there is nothing tortured or contrived about it, but it is adorned with authentic natural colouring.

[1] i. 140–144.
[2] vi. 9–14; 20–23.
[3] vii. 11–15.
[4] vii. 61–64.
[5] vii. 77.
[6] iii. 53–59. See note 8, p. 483.

ματα πάθους ἐστὶ μεστὰ καὶ ἡ λέξις οὐκ ἀποστρέφουσα τὰς ἀκοάς· ἥ τε γὰρ σύνθεσις εὐεπὴς καὶ τὰ σχήματα τῶν πραγμάτων ἴδια. ταῦτα δὴ τὰ Θουκυδίδου ζηλωτὰ ἔργα, καὶ ἀπὸ τούτων τὰ μιμήματα τοῖς ἱστοριογραφοῦσιν ὑποτίθεμαι [1] λαμβάνειν.

43 Τὴν δ' ἐν τῇ δευτέρᾳ βύβλῳ Περικλέους ἀπολογίαν, ἣν ὑπὲρ αὑτοῦ διετίθετο τραχυνομένων Ἀθηναίων, ὅτι τὸν πόλεμον ἔπεισεν αὐτοὺς ἀναλαβεῖν, οὐχ ὅλην ἐπαινῶ· οὐδὲ τὰς περὶ τῆς Μυτιληναίων πόλεως δημηγορίας, ἃς διέθεντο Κλέων καὶ Διόδοτος, ⟨τὰς⟩ [2] ἐν τῇ τρίτῃ βύβλῳ· οὐδὲ τὴν Ἑρμοκράτους τοῦ Συρακοσίου πρὸς Καμαριναίους· οὐδὲ τὴν Εὐφήμου τοῦ πρεσβευτοῦ τῶν Ἀθηναίων τὴν ἐναντίαν ταύτης, οὐδὲ τὰς ὁμοίας ταύταις· οὐ γὰρ ἀνάγκη πάσας ἐξαριθμεῖσθαι τὰς εἰς τὸν αὐτὸν κατεσκευασμένας τῆς διαλέκτου χαρακτῆρα. ἵνα δὲ μὴ δόξῃ τις φάσεις ἀναποδείκτους με λέγειν, πολλὰς παρασχέσθαι πίστεις δυνάμενος δυσὶν ἀρκεσθήσομαι δημηγορίαις, ἵνα μὴ μακρὸς ὁ λόγος γένηται, τῇ Περικλέους ἀπολογίᾳ καὶ τῇ Ἑρμοκράτους πρὸς Καμαριναίους κατηγορίᾳ κατὰ τῆς Ἀθηναίων πόλεως.

44 Ὁ μὲν οὖν Περικλῆς ταῦτα λέγει· "Καὶ προσδεχομένῳ μοι τὰ τῆς ὀργῆς ὑμῶν εἰς ἐμὲ γεγένηται (αἰσθάνομαι γὰρ τὰς αἰτίας), καὶ ἐκκλησίαν τούτου ἕνεκα ξυνήγαγον, ὅπως ὑπομνήσω καὶ μέμψωμαι, εἴ τι μὴ ὀρθῶς ἢ ἐμοὶ χαλεπαίνετε ἢ ταῖς ξυμφοραῖς εἴκετε." ταῦτα Θουκυδίδῃ μὲν

[1] ὑποτίθεμαι Reiske: ὑποτίθεται codd.
[2] τὰς inseruit Usener.

The arguments are full of feeling, and the language does not distract the listener from them. The composition is euphonious and the figures of speech are suited to the subject. These are the speeches of Thucydides which should be emulated, and it is from these that I suggest writers of history should select their models for imitation.

43 I do not approve of the whole of Pericles's speech in the second book, the one which he composed in his own defence when the Athenians were angry with 430 B.C.
him for persuading them to embark upon the war; nor again of the debate between Cleon and Diodotus about Mytilene in the third book,[1] or the speech of 427 B.C.
Hermocrates the Syracusan to the men of Camarina,[2] or the reply to it by the Athenian envoy Euphemus,[3] 414 B.C.
or of others like these (I need not enumerate all that are composed in the same stylistic vein). But to prevent anyone from thinking that I am making statements which cannot be substantiated, I shall, in the interests of brevity, be content to furnish two from a large number of possible examples—Pericles's defence and Hermocrates's indictment of the Athenians before the men of Camarina.

44 These are Pericles's words:[4]

"Not only was I expecting this outburst of indignation against me (because I perceive the reasons for it), but I actually summoned a meeting of the assembly for the express purpose of reminding you of your decisions and of reproving you for your inconsiderate anger and your inconstancy in the face of misfortune."

[1] iii. 37–40.
[2] vi. 76–80.
[3] vi. 82–87.
[4] ii. 60.

γράφοντι περὶ τοῦ ἀνδρὸς ἐν ἱστορικῷ σχήματι προσήκοντα ἦν, Περικλεῖ δὲ ἀπολογουμένῳ πρὸς ἠρεθισμένον ὄχλον οὐκ ἦν ἐπιτήδεια εἰρῆσθαι, καὶ ταῦτα ἐν ἀρχαῖς τῆς ἀπολογίας, πρὶν ἑτέροις τισὶν ἀπομειλίξασθαι λόγοις τὰς ὀργὰς τῶν εἰκότως ἐπὶ ταῖς συμφοραῖς ἀχθομένων, τετμημένης μὲν ὑπὸ Λακεδαιμονίων τῆς κρατίστης γῆς, πολλοῦ δὲ κατὰ τὸν λοιμὸν ἀπολωλότος ὄχλου, τὴν δ' αἰτίαν τῶν κακῶν τούτων τοῦ πολέμου παρεσχηκότος, ὃν ὑπ' ἐκείνου πεισθέντες ἀνεδέξαντο. σχῆμά τε οὐ τοῦτο τῇ διανοίᾳ πρεπωδέστατον ἦν, τὸ ἐπιτιμητικόν, ἀλλὰ τὸ παραιτητικόν· οὐ γὰρ ἐρεθίζειν προσήκει [1] τὰς τῶν ὄχλων ὀργὰς τοὺς δημηγοροῦντας ἀλλὰ πραΰνειν. τούτοις ἐπιτίθησι διάνοιαν ἀληθῆ μὲν καὶ δεινῶς ἀπηγγελμένην, οὐ μέντοι γε τῷ παρόντι καιρῷ χρησίμην· "ἐγὼ γὰρ ἡγοῦμαι" φησί "πόλιν πλείω ξύμπασαν ὀρθουμένην ὠφελεῖν τοὺς ἰδιώτας ἢ καθ' ἕκαστον τῶν πολιτῶν εὐπραγοῦσαν, ἀθρόαν δὲ σφαλλομένην. καλῶς μὲν γὰρ φερόμενος ἀνὴρ τὸ καθ' ἑαυτὸν διαφθειρομένης τῆς πατρίδος οὐδὲν ἧσσον ξυναπόλλυται, κακοτυχῶν δὲ ἐν εὐτυχούσῃ πολλῷ μᾶλλον διασῴζεται." εἰ μὲν γὰρ ἰδίᾳ τινὲς ἐβλάπτοντο τῶν πολιτῶν, εὐτύχει δὲ τὸ κοινόν, καλῶς ⟨ἂν⟩ [2] ταῦτ' ἔλεγεν· ἐπεὶ δ' ἐν ταῖς ἐσχάταις συμφοραῖς ἦσαν ἅπαντες, οὐκετι καλῶς. οὐδὲ γὰρ ἡ περὶ τοῦ μέλλοντος ἐλπίς, ὅτι ταῦτα πρὸς ἀγαθοῦ τῇ πόλει γενήσεται τὰ δεινά, βέβαιον εἶχέν τι· ἀφανὲς γὰρ ἀνθρώπῳ τὸ μέλλον καὶ πρὸς τὰ

[1] προσήκει Reiske: προσῆκε codd.
[2] ἂν inseruit Sadée.

These would have been suitable words for Thucydides to use in a historical statement about Pericles, but they are not appropriate words to put in his mouth when he is defending himself before an incensed crowd, especially at the beginning of his speech, before he has said something else to appease their anger. For they have good reason to be vexed at their plight: their best land has been laid waste by the Lacedaemonians, and a large number of them have perished in the plague; and the cause of these disasters is the war which they undertook on his advice. The best manner of address for his purpose would have been, not this reproachful one, but rather a more conciliatory one: political speakers should soothe, not inflame the anger of crowds. He follows this with a statement which is true and strikingly expressed, but is certainly not applicable to the current situation:[1]

"I consider it better for private persons themselves that the state as a whole should flourish than fare well in its individuals but suffer as a whole; for if a private man's country is destroyed, however successful he may be in his own affairs, he nevertheless is destroyed with her; whereas an unfortunate citizen in a fortunate state has a far better chance of survival."

If the citizens were suffering private hardship, but the state enjoying good fortune, this would be an effective argument. But as all were in the direst straits, it loses its point. Nor did the future hold much assurance that these sufferings would be for the benefit of the city: for the future is unrevealed to

[1] ii. 60. 2.

παρόντα τὰς περὶ τῶν ἐσομένων γνώμας αἱ τύχαι τρέπουσι. Τούτοις ἐπιτίθησιν ἔτι φορτικωτέραν διάνοιαν καὶ ἥκιστα τῷ παρόντι καιρῷ πρέπουσαν· "καίτοι ἐμοὶ τοιούτῳ ἀνδρὶ ὀργίζεσθε, ὃς οὐδενὸς οἴομαι ἥσσων εἶναι γνῶναί τε τὰ δέοντα καὶ ἑρμηνεῦσαι ταῦτα, φιλόπολίς τε καὶ χρημάτων κρείσσων." θαυμαστὸν γάρ, εἰ Περικλῆς ὁ μέγιστος τῶν τότε ῥητόρων ἠγνόει τοῦτο, ὃ μηδεὶς ἂν τῶν ἐχόντων μέτριον νοῦν ἠγνόησεν, ὅτι πανταχῇ μὲν οἱ μὴ τεταμιευμένως ἐπαινοῦντες τὰς ἑαυτῶν ἀρετὰς ἐπαχθεῖς τοῖς ἀκούουσι φαίνονται, μάλιστα δ' ἐν τοῖς πρὸς τὰ δικαστήρια καὶ τὰς ἐκκλησίας ἀγῶσιν, ἐν οἷς γε δὴ μὴ περὶ τιμῶν αὐτοῖς ἐστιν ἀλλὰ περὶ τιμωριῶν ὁ κίνδυνος· τότε γὰρ οὐκ ἐπαχθεῖς μόνον εἰσὶν ἑτέροις, ἀλλὰ καὶ δυστυχεῖς ἑαυτοῖς ἐκκαλούμενοι τὸν παρὰ τῶν πολλῶν φθόνον· ὅταν δὲ τοὺς αὐτούς τις ἔχῃ δικαστάς τε καὶ κατηγόρους, μυρίων αὐτῷ δεῖ δακρύων τε καὶ οἴκτων εἰς αὐτὸ τοῦτο πρῶτον τὸ μετ' εὐνοίας ἀκουσθῆναι. ὁ δὲ δημαγωγὸς οὐκ ἀρκεῖται τούτοις ἀλλ' ἐπεξεργάζεταί τε τούτοις καὶ μεταφράζει τὰ ῥηθέντα· "ὅ τε γὰρ γνούς" φησί "καὶ μὴ σαφῶς διδάξας ἐν ἴσῳ καὶ εἰ μὴ ἐνεθυμήθη, ὅ τ' ἔχων ἀμφότερα, τῇ δὲ πόλει δύσνους οὐκ ἂν ὁμοίως τι οἰκείως φράζοι· προσόντος δὲ καὶ τοῦδε,

---

[1] ii. 60. 5.

man, and fortune makes us adapt our expectations of things to come to present realities.

He follows this with an even more banal statement 45
and one not at all appropriate to the crisis of the moment:[1]

"Yet I, the man with whom you are angry, am as capable, I believe, as any of devising and explaining a sound policy; and I am, moreover, patriotic and incorruptible."

It would be remarkable if Pericles, the greatest orator of his day, did not know what every man of average intelligence must have known, that while in all orations speakers who praise their own virtues without restraint invariably exasperate their audiences, this is especially so when they are on trial in the law-courts or in the assembly, where they face the prospect not of loss of prestige but of actual punishment. In such circumstances they not only annoy others but also bring misfortune upon themselves by evoking the hatred of the populace; but in cases where the jury and prosecution are one and the same, a defendant needs to arm himself with oceans of tears and pleas for pity in order to achieve this very objective of a favourable hearing from the start. But our popular leader is not satisfied with these words, but elaborates on them and puts what he has already said into different words:[2]

"Now a man who has formed a plan," he says "but has not expounded it clearly might as well have thought of no plan at all; or, if he possessed both ability and eloquence, but had not the city's good at heart, he could not express himself suitably; and if he had patriotism, too, but were not indifferent to

[2] ii. 60. 6.

χρήμασι δὲ νικωμένου, τὰ ξύμπαντα τούτου ἑνὸς ἂν πωλοῖτο." οὐκ οἶδ' ὅς τις ἂν ὁμολογήσειεν, ὥσπερ ἀληθῆ ταῦτα ἦν, οὕτως καὶ προσήκοντα εἶναι ὑπὸ Περικλέους ἐν Ἀθηναίοις ἠρεθισμένοις πρὸς αὐτοὺς λέγεσθαι. ἦν δέ γε οὐχ ἡ τῶν κρατίστων ἐνθυμημάτων τε καὶ νοημάτων εὕρεσις αὐτὴ καθ' ἑαυτὴν ἀξία σπουδῆς, εἰ μὴ καὶ τοῖς πράγμασιν εἴη προσήκοντα καὶ τοῖς προσώποις καὶ τοῖς καιροῖς καὶ τοῖς ἄλλοις ἅπασιν· ἀλλ' ὥσπερ [1] καὶ κατ' ἀρχὰς ἔφην, τὴν ἑαυτοῦ γνώμην ἀποδεικνύμενος ὁ συγγραφεύς, ἣν εἶχε περὶ τῆς Περικλέους ἀρετῆς, παρὰ τόπον ἔοικεν εἰρηκέναι ταῦτα. ἐχρῆν δέ γε αὐτὸν μὲν ὅ τι βούλεται περὶ τοῦ ἀνδρὸς ἀποφαίνεσθαι, τῷ δὲ κινδυνεύοντι τοὺς ταπεινοὺς καὶ παραιτητικοὺς τῆς ὀργῆς ἀποδοῦναι λόγους· τοῦτο γὰρ ἦν πρέπον τῷ μιμεῖσθαι βουλομένῳ συγγραφεῖ τὴν ἀλήθειαν.

46 Ὀχληρὰ δὲ κἀκεῖνα τὰ μειρακιώδη καλλωπίσματα τῆς λέξεως καὶ τὰ πολύπλοκα τῶν ἐνθυμημάτων σχήματα·[2] "ἰέναι δὲ τοῖς ἐχθροῖς ὁμόσε καὶ ἀμύνεσθαι μὴ φρονήματι μόνον, ἀλλὰ καὶ καταφρονήματι. φρόνημα μὲν γὰρ καὶ ὑπὸ ἀμαθίας εὐτυχοῦς καὶ δειλῷ τινι ἐγγίγνεται· καταφρόνησις δέ, ὃς ἂν καὶ γνώμῃ πιστεύῃ τῶν ἐναντίων προέχειν· ὃ ἡμῖν ὑπάρχει. καὶ τὴν τόλμαν ἀπὸ τῆς ὁμοίας τύχης ἡ σύνεσις ἐκ τοῦ ὑπέρφρονος ὀχυρωτέραν παρεχεται· ἐλπίδι τε ἧσσον πιστεύει, ἧς ἐν τῷ ἀπόρῳ ἡ ἰσχύς· γνώμῃ δὲ ἀπὸ τῶν ὑπαρχόντων, ἧς βεβαιοτέρα ἡ πρόνοια." τά τε γὰρ "φρονή-

[1] ὥσπερ Sadée: ὅπερ codd.
[2] σχήματα Krüger: ὀνόματα codd.

bribery, all his good qualities could be sold for money alone."

No one, I suppose, will deny the truth of this statement; but equally no one would suggest that it was a suitable one for Pericles, speaking before an angry audience of Athenians, to make to their faces. The invention of the most potent arguments is not to be admired for its own sake, unless they be appropriate to the characters, the situation, and all other relevant factors. But as I said at the beginning,[1] the historian seems to have used these words, in which he is expressing his own opinion regarding the ability of Pericles, in the wrong context. He was quite entitled to describe the statesman's qualities as he pleased, but as a defendant Pericles should have been made to speak humbly and in such a manner as to turn away the jury's anger. This would have been the proper procedure for a historian who sought to imitate real life.

46 Tiresome also are the juvenile embellishments of language and the intricately constructed arguments of this passage: [2]

"You must confront your enemies therefore not only with spirit but in a spirit of scorn. Spirit can even be the result of lucky folly, and occur in a coward; but rational scorn belongs only to the man who trusts his judgment that he is superior to his enemies; which is our position. When fortune is impartial, intelligence based on a spirit of superiority makes courage more unshakable: it relies not so much on hope, which is effective in extremity, as on judgment based upon fact, whose foresight is more dependable."

[1] ch. 44 *init.*

[2] ii. 62. 3.

ματα" ψυχρότερά ἐστι καὶ τῆς Γοργίου προαιρέσεως μᾶλλον οἰκειότερα, ἥ τε τῶν ὀνομάτων ἐξήγησις ἀμφότερον [1] σοφιστικὴ καὶ ἀπειρόκαλος· ἥ τε τόλμα ἣν "ἀπὸ τῆς ὁμοίας τύχης ἡ σύνεσις ἐκ τοῦ ὑπέρφρονος ὀχυρωτέραν παρέχεται" τῶν Ἡρακλειτείων σκοτεινῶν ἀσαφεστέραν ἔχει τὴν δήλωσιν, ἥ τε τῆς ἐλπίδος "ἐν τῷ ἀπόρῳ ἰσχύς" καὶ ἡ τῆς γνώμης "ἀπὸ τῶν ὑπαρχόντων βεβαιοτέρα πρόνοια" ποιητικώτερον περιπέφρασται· βούλεται γὰρ λέγειν, ὅτι δεῖ τῇ γνώμῃ πιστεύειν μᾶλλον, ἣν ἐκ τῶν παρόντων λαμβάνομεν, ἢ ταῖς
47 ἐλπίσιν, ὧν ἐν τῷ μέλλοντι [2] ἐστὶν ἡ ἰσχύς. ἤδη δ' ἔγωγε κἀκεῖνο ἐνεθυμήθην, ὅτι παραμυθούμενος τὴν ὀργὴν τὴν κατειληφυῖαν αὐτοὺς ἐπὶ ταῖς παρούσαις συμφοραῖς, ὧν αἱ πλείους παράλογοί τε συνέβησαν αὐτοῖς καὶ ἀπροσδόκητοι, καὶ παρακαλῶν τὰς συμφορὰς γενναίως ὑφίστασθαι μὴ ἀφανίζοντας τὴν τῆς πόλεως ἀξίωσιν, ἀπαλγήσαντας δὲ τὰ ἴδια τοῦ κοινοῦ τῆς σωτηρίας ἀντιλαμβάνεσθαι, καὶ μετὰ τοῦτο διεξελθών, ὅτι τὴν κατὰ θάλατταν ἀρχὴν βεβαίως ἔχοντες οὔτε ὑπὸ βασιλέως οὔτε ὑπὸ Λακεδαιμονίων οὔτε ὑπ' ἄλλου ἀνθρώπων ἔθνους οὐδενὸς καταλυθήσονται (ὧν ἡ πίστις οὐχ ἡ παροῦσα ἦν ἀλλ' ἡ μέλλουσα, οὐδ' ἐν τῇ προνοίᾳ τὸ βέβαιον ἔχουσα ἀλλ' ἐν ταῖς ἐλπίσιν), ἔπειτα τούτων ἐπιλαθόμενος ἀξιοῖ μὴ πιστεύειν τῇ ἐλπίδι, ἧς ἐν τῷ ἀπόρῳ ἡ ἰσχύς. ἐναντία γὰρ δὴ ταῦτα ἀλλήλοις, εἴ γε δὴ τὸ μὲν

[1] ἀμφότερον Reiske: ἀμφοτέρων codd.
[2] τῷ μέλλοντι Sadée: τῷ μέλλειν codd.

The word-play on " spirit " is rather frigid, and closer to the Gorgianic style, and the definitions of the nouns both sophistical and lacking in taste. " Courage," which " when fortune is impartial, is rendered more unshakable by an intelligence based on a spirit of superiority," is more puzzling to explain than the dark sayings of Heraclitus,[1] and the definition of " hope " as " effective in extremity " and of " judgment " as that whose " foresight is more dependable when based on fact," are circumlocutions of a rather poetical character. What he means to say is that one should put more trust in knowledge, which is based upon present circumstances, than upon hopes, whose power lies in the future.

It has also just occurred to me that after trying to 47
soothe the anger which has seized them on account of their present misfortunes, most of which had come upon them unforeseen and unexpected, and exhorting them to endure these misfortunes nobly, and not to efface the city's fame but to forget private sorrows and strive for the common safety; after this, when he has explained that if they maintain their maritime empire securely, neither the King of Persia nor the Lacedaemonians nor any other people in the world will overthrow them (the proof of which is not in the present but in the future, and depends not upon foresight but upon hopes), he forgets these arguments and says that they should not rely upon hope, which is effective in extremities. Of course, these sentiments are mutually contradictory, if in fact they were already experiencing the sufferings in question, whereas

[1] The famous Ephesian philosopher (fl. c. 500 B.C.), whose opinions are preserved in a large collection of aphoristic statements, many of them of doubtful interpretation.

λυποῦν τὴν αἴσθησιν εἶχεν ἤδη παροῦσαν, τῆς δ' ὠφελείας ἡ δήλωσις ἔτι ἀπῆν.

ἀλλ' ὥσπερ ταῦτα οὐκ ἐπαινῶ οὔτε κατὰ τὸ πραγματικὸν μέρος οὔτε κατὰ τὸ λεκτικόν, οὕτως ἐκεῖνα τεθαύμακα ὡς νενοημένα τε ἀκριβῶς καὶ ἡρμηνευμένα περιττῶς καὶ συγκείμενα ἡδέως· "καὶ γὰρ οἷς μὲν αἵρεσις γεγένηται τὰ ἄλλα εὐτυχοῦσι, πολλὴ ἄνοια πολεμῆσαι· εἰ δ' ἀναγκαῖον ἦν ἢ εἴξαντας εὐθὺς τοῖς πέλας ὑπακοῦσαι ἢ κινδυνεύσαντας περιγενέσθαι, ὁ φυγὼν τὸν κίνδυνον τοῦ ὑποστάντος μεμπτότερος· καὶ ἐγὼ μὲν ὁ αὐτός εἰμι καὶ οὐκ ἐξίσταμαι, ὑμεῖς δὲ μεταβάλλετε, ἐπειδὴ ξυνέβη ὑμῖν πεισθῆναι μὲν ἀκεραίοις, μεταμέλειν δὲ κακουμένοις." καὶ ἔτι ἐκεῖνα· "δουλοῖ γὰρ φρόνημα τὸ αἰφνίδιον καὶ τὸ ἀπροσδόκητον καὶ τὸ πλείστῳ παραλόγῳ ξυμβαῖνον· ⟨ὃ ὑμῖν πρὸς τοῖς ἄλλοις οὐχ ἥκιστα καὶ κατὰ τὴν νόσον γεγένηται⟩.[1] ὅμως δὲ πόλιν μεγάλην οἰκοῦντας καὶ ἐν ἤθεσιν ἀντιπάλοις αὐτῇ τεθραμμένους χρεὼν καὶ τὰς συμφορὰς ἐθέλειν ὑφίστασθαι καὶ τὴν ἀξίωσιν μὴ ἀφανίζειν· ἐν ἴσῳ γὰρ οἱ ἄνθρωποι δικαιοῦσι τῆς τε ὑπαρχούσης δόξης αἰτιᾶσθαι, ὅστις ἂν μαλακίᾳ ἐλλείπῃ, καὶ τῆς μὴ προσηκούσης μισεῖν τὸν θρασύτητι ὀρεγόμενον." καὶ ἔτι τὰ διεγείροντα τὰς ψυχὰς τῶν Ἀθηναίων ἐπὶ τὸ φρόνημα τὸ πάτριον ταυτί· "τῆς τε πόλεως ὑμᾶς εἰκὸς τῷ τιμωμένῳ ἀπὸ τοῦ ἄρχειν,

[1] ὃ—γεγένηται ex Thucydide inserui.

---

[1] ii. 61. 1.

there was as yet no clear indication that assistance was to come.

But just as in this passage I do not commend the subject-matter or the style, so I admire the earlier passage for the precision of its thought, the forcefulness of its expression, and the pleasing character of its composition:[1]

"For those who have the choice and are prosperous otherwise, it is very foolish to make war. But when they must either submit and be subject to their neighbour, or risk all for survival, then he who shuns, not he who meets the danger, is the more culpable. For myself, my position is the same and I do not move from it; but you are changing your ground: you were persuaded when you were unharmed, but change your minds under suffering."

I also admire:[2]

"Anything which is sudden and unexpected and completely incalculable subdues the spirit of man; and this has been your particular fate with regard to the plague. Nevertheless, being citizens of a great city and brought up under customs which match its greatness, you should be willing to endure calamities and not to efface her fame. For while it is felt to be justifiable to hate the presumption of those who claim a reputation to which they have no right, it is thought to be no less so to condemn the faint-heartedness of those who do not live up to their reputation."

And the following exhortation, designed to arouse the hearts of the Athenians to patriotic feelings:[3]

"Again, you should uphold the imperial dignity of

[2] ii. 61. 3.
[3] ii. 63.

ᾧ ὑπὲρ ἅπαντας ἀγάλλεσθε, βοηθεῖν καὶ μὴ φεύγειν τοὺς πόνους, ἢ μηδὲ τὰς τιμὰς διώκειν· μηδὲ νομίσαι περὶ ἑνὸς μόνου, δουλείας ἀντ' ἐλευθερίας, ἀγωνίζεσθαι, ἀλλὰ καὶ ἀρχῆς στερήσεως καὶ κινδύνου ὧν ἐν τῇ ἀρχῇ ἀπήχθεσθε. ἧς οὐδ' ἐκστῆναι ἔτι ὑμῖν ἔστιν, εἴ τις καὶ τόδε ἐν τῷ παρόντι δεδιὼς ἀπραγμοσύνῃ ἀνδραγαθίζεται. ὡς τυραννίδα γὰρ ἤδη ἔχετε αὐτήν, ἣν λαβεῖν μὲν ἄδικον δοκεῖ εἶναι, ἀφεῖναι δὲ ἐπικίνδυνον," καὶ τὰ τούτοις ὅμοια, ὅσα τάς τε ἐξαλλαγὰς τῶν ὀνομάτων καὶ τῶν σχημάτων μετρίας ἔχει καὶ οὔτε περιέργους οὔτε δυσπαρακολουθήτους.

48 'Εκ δὲ τῆς 'Ερμοκράτους δημηγορίας ἐπαινεῖν μὲν ἔχω ταῦτα τὰ κατορθώματα τοῦ συγγραφέως· " ἀλλ' οὐ γὰρ δὴ τὴν 'Αθηναίων εὐκατηγόρητον οὖσαν πόλιν νῦν ἥκομεν ἀποφανοῦντες ἐν εἰδόσιν, ὅσα ἀδικεῖ· πολὺ δὲ μᾶλλον ἡμᾶς αὐτοὺς αἰτιασόμενοι, ὅτι ἔχοντες παραδείγματα τῶν ἐκεῖ 'Ελλήνων, ὡς ἐδουλώθησαν οὐκ ἀμύνοντες σφίσιν αὐτοῖς, καὶ νῦν ἐφ' ἡμᾶς τὰ αὐτὰ παρόντα σοφίσματα, Λεοντίνων τε ξυγγενῶν κατοικίσεις καὶ Αἰγεσταίων ξυμμάχων ἐπικουρίας, οὐ ξυστραφέντες βουλόμεθα προθυμότερον δεῖξαι αὐτοῖς, ὅτι οὐκ Ἴωνες ταῦτά εἰσιν οὐδὲ 'Ελλησπόντιοι καὶ νησιῶται, οἳ δεσπότην ἢ Μῆδον ἢ ἕνα γέ τινα ἀεὶ μεταβάλλοντες δουλοῦνται, ἀλλὰ Δωριεῖς ἐλεύθεροι ἀπ' αὐτονόμου τῆς Πελοποννήσου τὴν Σικελίαν οἰκοῦντες. ἢ

[1] vi. 77.

your city, in which you take pride above all others, by not shunning hardships; otherwise you should not seek a share in her glory either. And do not imagine that you are fighting about a single issue, freedom or slavery: you have an empire to lose, and there is also the danger to which the hatred of your empire has exposed you. And it is no longer possible for you even to resign your power, in case anyone is persuaded by present fear to act the brave man's part—and do nothing. For by this time your empire has become like a tyranny, which men regard as wrong to seize, but dangerous to let go."

I admire these and similar passages, in which unusual words and figures of speech are used discreetly, without complication and without obscurity.

From the speech which the historian assigns to 48
Hermocrates I can commend the following effective passages:[1]

"But we have not now come to demonstrate that the Athenian state is open to accusation, before an audience which knows about its misdeeds. Our purpose is much more to blame ourselves: for though we have examples from among the Greeks in the East of states which have been enslaved because they did not stand by one another, and now see the same tricks being used against us, as we hear of the restoration of the Leontines, who are called "kinsmen," and of aid being brought to the Egestaeans, who are called "allies," yet we are not more ready to combine and show them that here are no Ionians, Hellespontines or Islanders, who live in permanent servitude to one master or another, whether he be a tyrant, or a Mede, or anyone else, but free Dorians from the independent land of the Peloponnese who

μένομεν, ἕως ἂν ἕκαστοι κατὰ πόλεις ληφθῶμεν, εἰδότες ὅτι ταύτῃ μόνον ἁλωτοί ἐσμεν;" ταῦτα γὰρ ἐν τῷ σαφεῖ καὶ καθαρῷ τῆς διαλέκτου τρόπῳ λεγόμενα προσείληφε καὶ τὸ τάχος καὶ τὸ κάλλος καὶ τὸν τόνον καὶ τὴν μεγαλοπρέπειαν καὶ τὴν δεινότητα, καὶ πάθους ἐστὶν ἐναγωνίου μεστά· οἷς ἂν καὶ ἐν δικαστηρίῳ χρήσαιτό τις καὶ ἐν ἐκκλησίαις, καὶ φίλοις διαλεγόμενος. καὶ ἔτι πρὸς τούτοις ἐκεῖνα· "εἴ τέ τις φθονεῖ μὲν ἢ καὶ φοβεῖται (ἀμφότερα γὰρ τάδε πάσχει τὰ μείζω), διὰ δ' αὐτὰ τὰς Συρακούσας κακωθῆναι μέν, ἵνα σωφρονισθῶμεν, βούλεται, περιγενέσθαι δὲ ἕνεκα τῆς ἑαυτοῦ ἀσφαλείας, οὐκ ἀνθρωπείας δυνάμεως βούλησιν ἐλπίζει. οὐ γὰρ οἷόν τε ἅμα τῆς τε ἐπιθυμίας καὶ τῆς τύχης τὸν αὐτὸν ὁμοίως ταμίαν γενέσθαι," καὶ τὰ ἐπὶ τελευτῇ κείμενα τοῦ λόγου· "δεόμεθα οὖν καὶ μαρτυρόμεθα, εἰ μὴ πείσομεν, ὅτι ἐπιβουλευόμεθα μὲν ὑπὸ Ἰώνων ἀεὶ πολεμίων, προδιδόμεθα δὲ ὑφ' ὑμῶν Δωριεῖς Δωριέων· καὶ εἰ καταστρέψονται ἡμᾶς Ἀθηναῖοι, ταῖς μὲν ὑμετέραις γνώμαις κρατήσουσι, τῷ δ' αὐτῶν ὀνόματι τιμηθήσονται, καὶ τῆς νίκης οὐκ ἄλλον τινὰ ἆθλον ἢ τὸν τὴν νίκην παρασχόντα λήψονται." ταῦτα μὲν δὴ καὶ τὰ παραπλήσια τούτοις καλὰ καὶ ζήλου ἄξια ἡγοῦμαι. ἐκεῖνα δ' οὐκ οἶδ' ὅπως ἂν ἐπαινέσαιμι· "νῦν γὰρ εἰς τὴν Σικελίαν προφάσει μέν, ᾗ πυνθάνεσθε, διανοίᾳ δέ, ἣν πάντες

[1] vi. 78. 2.

dwell in Sicily. Are we going to wait until our cities are taken one by one, when we know that this is the only way in which we can be conquered?"

In addition to being expressed in clear and pure language, this passage has rapid movement, beauty, intensity, impressiveness and rhetorical brilliance, and is full of vehement emotion: qualities which a speaker might employ in the law-courts, in public meetings and in conversations with his friends. Then there is the following passage:[1]

"And if anyone envies and even fears us (for superior power is exposed to both), and so wants Syracuse to be damaged so that we may be taught a lesson, but to survive for his own safety's sake, he is hoping for the fulfilment of a wish which human power cannot grant; for it is not possible for the same person at the same time to control similarly both his desire and his fortune."

And the concluding passage of the speech:[2]

"So we entreat you and, if we fail to persuade you, we call you to witness that, although the Ionians, our perpetual enemies, are conspiring against us, it is you, Dorians like ourselves, who are betraying us; and if the Athenians conquer us, your decision will have gained them the day, but the honour will be all their own, and the prize of their victory will be none other than the agents who made it possible."

This and similar passages I consider fine and worthy of imitation. But I cannot bring myself to praise this:[3]

"Now they have now come to Sicily on a pretext which you can all understand, but with an intention

[2] vi. 80. 3.
[3] vi. 76. 2.

ὑπονοοῦμεν. καί μοι δοκοῦσιν οὐ Λεοντίνους βούλεσθαι κατοικίσαι, ἀλλ' ἡμᾶς μᾶλλον ἐξοικίσαι." ψυχρὰ γὰρ ἡ παρονομασία καὶ οὐ προσβάλλουσα πάθος, ἀλλ' ἐπιτήδευσιν. καὶ ἔτι τὰ πεπλεγμένα καὶ πολλὰς τὰς ἕλικας ἔχοντα σχήματα ταυτί· "καὶ οὐ περὶ τῆς ἐλευθερίας ἄρα οὔτε οἵδε τῶν Ἑλλήνων οὔτε οἱ Ἕλληνες τῆς ἑαυτῶν τῷ Μήδῳ ἀντέστησαν, περὶ δὲ τοῦ, οἱ μὲν σφίσιν ἀλλὰ μὴ ἐκείνῳ καταδουλώσεως, οἱ δ' ἐπὶ δεσπότου μεταβολῇ οὐκ ἀξυνετωτέρου, κακοξυνετωτέρου δέ." καὶ ἔτι τὸ κατακορὲς τῆς μεταγωγῆς ⟨τῆς⟩[1] ἔκ τε τοῦ πληθυντικοῦ εἰς τὸ ἑνικὸν καὶ ἐκ τοῦ περὶ προσώπων λόγου εἰς τὸ τοῦ λέγοντος πρόσωπον· "καὶ εἴ τῳ ἄρα παρέστηκε τὸν μὲν Συρακόσιον, ἑαυτὸν δ' οὐ πολέμιον εἶναι τῷ Ἀθηναίῳ καὶ δεινὸν ἡγεῖται ὑπέρ γε τῆς ἐμῆς κινδυνεύειν, ἐνθυμηθήτω οὐ περὶ τῆς ἐμῆς μᾶλλον, ἐν ἴσῳ δὲ καὶ τῆς ἑαυτοῦ ἅμα ἐν τῇ ἐμῇ μαχόμενος, τοσούτῳ δὲ καὶ ἀσφαλέστερον, ὅσῳ οὐ προδιεφθαρμένου ἐμοῦ, ἔχων δὲ ξύμμαχον ἐμὲ καὶ οὐκ ἔρημος ἀγωνιεῖται· τόν τε Ἀθηναῖον μὴ τὴν τοῦ Συρακοσίου ἔχθραν κολάσασθαι, ⟨τῇ δ' ἐμῇ προφάσει τὴν ἐκείνου δουλείαν βεβαιώσασθαι βούλεσθαι⟩.[2] ταῦτα γὰρ καὶ μειρακιώδη καὶ περίεργα καὶ τῶν λεγομένων αἰνιγμάτων ἀσαφέστερα. καὶ ἐκεῖνα ἔτι πρὸς τούτοις· "καὶ εἰ γνώμῃ ἁμάρτοι, τοῖς αὐτοῦ κακοῖς ὀλοφυρθεὶς τάχ' ἂν ἴσως καὶ τοῖς ἐμοῖς ἀγαθοῖς ποτε βουληθείη αὖθις φθονῆσαι·

[1] τῆς inseruit Usener.

[2] τῇ δ' ἐμῇ προφάσει τὴν ἐκείνου δουλείαν βεβαιώσασθαι βούλεσθαι inserui ex Thucydide.

which we all suspect. In my view they want not to repopulate Leontini, but rather to depopulate Sicily."

The word-play is frigid, conveying not emotion but artificiality. The same applies to the following complicated structure with its many convolutions:[1]

"It was not for freedom that they opposed the Persian king, neither these for the freedom of Greece nor the Greeks for that of themselves, but the former with a view to enslavement, and the latter with a view to a change of master, not more imprudent but more impudent."

And again, the wearisome substitution of singular for plural and the change from other persons to the speaker's own person in the following:[2]

"If anyone has reflected that not he, but the Syracusan, is the enemy of the Athenian, and objects to risking his life for my country, let him consider that he will not really be fighting for my country any more than fighting in mine for his own, and with less danger, because I shall not have been destroyed already, but he will have me as an ally and will not be fighting alone; and that the Athenian intends not so much to punish the Syracusan's hostility ⟨as to use me as a pretext to secure the friendship of the Camarinians⟩."

This is juvenile and overdone, and is more obscure than what we call riddles. So too with this sentence:[3]

"And if he should make an error of judgment, after lamenting our own misfortunes he may perhaps wish that he may still have my prosperity to envy; but he

[1] vi. 76. 4.
[2] vi. 78. 1.
[3] vi. 78. 3.

ἀδύνατον δὲ προεμένῳ καὶ μὴ τοὺς αὐτοὺς κινδύνους οὐ περὶ τῶν ὀνομάτων, ἀλλὰ περὶ τῶν ἔργων ἐθελήσαντι προσλαβεῖν." οἷς ἐπιτίθησιν οὐδὲ μειρακίῳ προσῆκον ἐπιφώνημα· "λόγῳ μὲν γὰρ τὴν ἡμετέραν δύναμιν σῴζοι ἄν τις, ἔργῳ δὲ τὴν ἑαυτοῦ σωτηρίαν."

49 Ἔστι δὲ καὶ ἄλλα ἐν τῇ δημηγορίᾳ ταύτῃ μέμψεως ἄξια, περὶ ὧν οὐδὲν δέομαι τὰ πλείω λέγειν· ἱκανῶς δ' οἴομαι καὶ διὰ τούτων φανερὸν πεποιηκέναι τὸ προκείμενον, ὅτι τῆς Θουκυδίδου λέξεως κρατίστη μέν ἐστιν ἡ μετρίως ἐκβεβηκυῖα τὰ συνήθη καὶ τὰς πρώτας καὶ ἀναγκαίας ἀρετὰς φυλάσσουσα, χείρων δὲ ἡ λαμβάνουσα πολλὴν ἐκτροπὴν ἐκ τῶν κοινῶν ὀνομάτων τε καὶ σχημάτων εἰς τὰ ξένα καὶ βεβιασμένα καὶ ἀνακολούθητα, δι' ἣν οὐδὲ τῶν ἄλλων ἀρετῶν οὐδεμίαι τὴν ἑαυτῶν ἐπιδείκνυνται δύναμιν. οὔτε γὰρ ἐν ταῖς ἐκκλησίαις χρήσιμόν ἐστι τοῦτο τὸ γένος τῆς φράσεως, ἐν αἷς ὑπὲρ εἰρήνης καὶ πολέμου καὶ νόμων εἰσφορᾶς καὶ πολιτειῶν κόσμου καὶ τῶν ἄλλων τῶν κοινῶν καὶ μεγάλων αἱ πόλεις βουλευσόμεναι συνέρχονται, οὔτ' ἐν τοῖς δικαστηρίοις, ἔνθα περὶ θανάτου καὶ φυγῆς καὶ ἀτιμίας καὶ δεσμῶν καὶ χρημάτων ἀφαιρέσεως οἱ λόγοι πρὸς τοὺς ἀνειληφότας τὴν ὑπὲρ τούτων ἐξουσίαν λέγονται (⟨καὶ γὰρ αἱ τοιαῦται ῥητορεῖ⟩αι [1] λυποῦσι τὸν πολιτικὸν ὄχλον οὐκ ὄντα τῶν τοιούτων ἀκουσμάτων ἐν ἔθει), οὔτ' ἐν ταῖς ἰδιωτικαῖς ὁμιλίαις, ἐν αἷς περὶ τῶν βιωτικῶν διαλεγόμεθα πολίταις ἢ φίλοις ἢ συγγενέσιν διηγούμενοί τι τῶν συμβεβηκότων ἑαυτοῖς ἢ

cannot bring me back again once he has abandoned me and refused to accept his share of a common danger which, far from being imaginary, is only too real.''

And this is followed by an utterance which one would not expect even from a callow youth:

" For though in name you may be saving us, in reality you will be saving yourselves."

There are other things in this speech that deserve 49
censure, but there is no need for me to spend further words on them. I think that the above examples illustrate clearly enough my thesis, that Thucydides's style is at its best when it does not depart unduly from normality, and preserves the primary and essential virtues; but that it is less good when it admits much divergence from common vocabulary and figures to strange, forced and inconsequent ones, since this prevents any one of its other virtues from displaying its effect. It serves no useful purpose to employ this manner of address in public assemblies, where citizens come together to deliberate on questions of peace and war, on legislation and on the ordering of the constitution, and other important matters of common concern. Nor is it suited to the law-courts, where the issues include death, exile, disfranchisement, imprisonment, and confiscation of property, and the audience is a jury empowered to impose these penalties: ⟨for such displays of rhetoric⟩ antagonise the average citizen body, which is not accustomed to hear that sort of thing. And it is not suitable for private conversations, in which we discuss everyday matters with fellow-citizens, friends or relations,

[1] implevi lacunam Usenerum secutus.

συμβουλευόμενοι περί τινος τῶν ἀναγκαίων, ἢ νουθετοῦντες ἢ παρακαλοῦντες ἢ συνηδόμενοι τοῖς ἀγαθοῖς ἢ συναλγοῦντες τοῖς κακοῖς· ἐῶ γὰρ λέγειν, ὅτι τῶν οὕτως διαλεγομένων οὐδὲ αἱ μητέρες ἂν καὶ οἱ πατέρες ἀνάσχοιντο διὰ τὴν ἀηδίαν, ἀλλ' ὥσπερ ἀλλοεθνοῦς γλώσσης ἀκούοντες τῶν ἑρμηνευσόντων ἂν δεηθεῖεν. ταῦτα ἔστιν ἃ περὶ τοῦ συγγραφέως ἐπείσθην, μετὰ πάσης ἀληθείας εἰρημένα κατὰ τὴν ἐμὴν δύναμιν.

50 Ἀνάγκη δὲ καὶ τὰ λεγόμενα ὑπὲρ αὐτοῦ τισιν ἐξετάσαι δι' ὀλίγων,[1] ἵνα μηδὲν παρεικέναι δοκῶ. ὅτι μὲν οὖν οὔτ' εἰς τοὺς πολιτικοὺς ἀγῶνας ἐπιτήδειός ἐστιν οὔτ' εἰς τὰς ὁμιλίας τὰς ἰδιωτικὰς [2] οὗτος ὁ χαρακτήρ, ἅπαντες ὁμολογήσουσιν οἱ μὴ διεφθαρμένοι τὴν διάνοιαν ἀλλ' ἐν τῷ κατὰ φύσιν τὰς αἰσθήσεις ἔχοντες. ἐπιχειροῦσι δέ τινες οὐκ ἄδοξοι σοφισταὶ λέγειν, ὅτι τοῖς μὲν πρὸς τὰς ὀχλικὰς ἐντεύξεις παρεσκευασμένοις καὶ τὰ δίκαια λέγουσιν οὐκ ἔστιν ἐπιτήδειος οὗτος ὁ χαρακτήρ, τοῖς δὲ τὰς ἱστορικὰς πραγματείας ἐκφέρουσιν, αἷς μεγαλοπρεπείας τε δεῖ καὶ σεμνολογίας καὶ καταπλήξεως, παντὸς μάλιστα προσήκει ταύτην ἀσκεῖν τὴν φράσιν τὴν γλωττηματικήν τε καὶ ἀπηρχαιωμένην καὶ τροπικὴν καὶ ἐξηλλαγμένην τῶν ἐν ἔθει σχημάτων ἐπὶ τὸ ξένον καὶ περιττόν. οὐ γὰρ ἀγοραίοις ἀνθρώποις οὐδ' ἐπιδιφρίοις ἢ χειροτέχναις οὐδὲ τοῖς ἄλλοις οἳ μὴ μετέσχον ἀγωγῆς ἐλευθερίου ταύτας κατασκευάζεσθαι τὰς γραφάς, ἀλλ' ἀνδράσι διὰ τῶν ἐγκυκλίων μαθημάτων ἐπὶ ῥητορικήν τε ⟨καὶ⟩ φιλοσοφίαν ἐληλυθόσιν, οἷς οὐδὲν φανήσεται τούτων ξένον. ἤδη

describing some experience of ours, considering some urgent problem, giving advice or asking for help, and sharing other men's joys and sorrows. I shall pass over the fact that if people spoke like this, not even their fathers or mothers could bear the unpleasantness of listening to them: they would need an interpreter, as if they were listening to a foreign tongue. These are the convictions I have formed about the historian. I have stated them with complete candour, and to the best of my ability.

I must also briefly examine certain other views 50
about Thucydides, so that it may not be thought that I have omitted anything. That his style is not suitable for political debates or private conversations will be admitted by all men whose judgment is unimpaired and who have their natural powers of perception. But certain quite reputable critics try to argue that, although this style is not suitable for an orator intending to address a popular audience, or for a litigant, those who are producing a work of history, which requires an impressive, dignified and striking style, should find Thucydides's recondite, archaic, figurative language, which diverges from normality towards the novel and the extravagant, eminently appropriate to employ. They contend that the author was not composing these writings of his for the man in the street, the workman at the bench, the artisan or any other person who has not enjoyed a liberal education, but for those who have passed through the standard courses to the study of rhetoric and philosophy, to whom none of these usages will seem strange. And

---

[1] δι' ὀλίγων Reiske: διὰ λόγων codd.
[2] ἰδιωτικὰς Sadée: βιωτικὰς codd.

δέ τινες ἐπεχείρησαν λέγειν, ὡς οὐ τῶν μεθ' ἑαυτὸν ἐσομένων στοχαζόμενος ὁ συγγραφεὺς οὕτως ἔγραψε τὰς ἱστορίας, ἀλλὰ τῶν καθ' ἑαυτὸν ὄντων, οἷς ἦν ἡ διάλεκτος ⟨αὕτη συνήθης καὶ γνώριμος ἅπασιν⟩ . . .[1] χρήσιμος οὗτος ὁ χαρακτὴρ οὔτ' εἰς τοὺς συμβουλευτικοὺς ⟨οὔτ' εἰς τοὺς δικανικοὺς[2] ἀγῶνας, ἐν οἷς οἵ τ' ἐκκλησιάζοντες καὶ οἱ δικάζοντες, οὐχ οἵους ὁ Θουκυδίδης ὑπέθετο, συνέρχονται.

51 Πρὸς μὲν οὖν τοὺς οἰομένους μόνων εἶναι τῶν εὐπαιδεύτων ἀναγνῶναί τε καὶ συνεῖναι τὴν Θουκυδίδου διάλεκτον ταῦτα λέγειν ἔχω, ὅτι τὸ τοῦ πράγματος ἀναγκαῖόν τε καὶ χρήσιμον ἅπασιν (οὐδὲν γὰρ ⟨ἂν⟩[3] ἀναγκαιότερον γένοιτο οὐδὲ πολυωφελέστερον) ἀναιροῦσιν ἐκ τοῦ κοινοῦ βίου, ὀλίγων παντάπασιν ἀνθρώπων οὕτω ποιοῦντες, ὥσπερ ἐν ταῖς ὀλιγαρχουμέναις ἢ τυραννουμέναις πόλεσιν· εὐαρίθμητοι γάρ τινές εἰσιν οἷοι πάντα τὰ Θουκυδίδου συμβαλεῖν, καὶ οὐδ' οὗτοι χωρὶς ἐξηγήσεως γραμματικῆς ἔνια. πρὸς δὲ τοὺς ἐπὶ τὸν ἀρχαῖον βίον ἀναφέροντας τὴν Θουκυδίδου διάλεκτον ὡς δὴ τοῖς τότε ἀνθρώποις οὖσαν συνήθη, βραχὺς ἀπόχρη μοι λόγος καὶ σαφής, ὅτι πολλῶν γενομένων Ἀθήνησι κατὰ τὸν Πελοποννησιακὸν πόλεμον ῥητόρων τε καὶ φιλοσόφων οὐδεὶς αὐτῶν κέχρηται ταύτῃ τῇ διαλέκτῳ, οὔθ'[4] οἱ περὶ Ἀνδοκίδην καὶ Ἀντιφῶντα καὶ Λυσίαν ῥήτορες οὔθ' οἱ περὶ

[1] lacunam a Sylburgo indicatam post διάλεκτος partim explendam αὕτη συνήθης καὶ γνώριμος ἅπασιν . . . esse censeo.
[2] inseruit Sylburg. [3] ἂν inseruit Reiske.
[4] διαλέκτῳ, οὔθ' Krüger: διαλέκτω οὐδ' codd.

some have now tried to make out that the historian wrote in this way because he was aiming not at posterity but at his contemporaries, to all of whose ears his language ⟨was familiar and comprehensible⟩. . . . But this style is not suitable for deliberative or forensic oratory, in which the audiences who assemble for political meetings or to serve as jurymen are not such as Thucydides supposed them to be.

Now to those who think that Thucydides's language can be read with understanding only by the well-educated, I have this to say: that in confining it to an extremely small minority of readers, they are removing from ordinary men's lives a necessary and universally useful subject of study (for nothing could be more necessary or more widely beneficial). It becomes the property of a few, like government under an oligarchy or a tyrant; for the number of men who can understand the whole of Thucydides can easily be counted, and even these cannot understand certain passages without a linguistic commentary. But to those who refer Thucydides's language to its historical period and assert that it was familiar to the people of that time, I am content with a short and obvious reply: that none of the many orators and philosophers who lived at Athens during the Peloponnesian War used this style, neither Andocides,[1] Antiphon,[2] Lysias and their fellow orators, nor 51

[1] Athenian aristocrat, born *c.* 440 B.C. whose three surviving speeches, all written for his own use, show an imperfect but progressively improving knowledge of rhetorical theory. See MacDowell's edition of the *De Mysteriis*.

[2] See note 1, p. 228.

Κριτίαν καὶ Ἀντισθένη καὶ Ξενοφῶντα Σωκρατικοί. ἐκ δὴ τούτων ἁπάντων δῆλός ἐστιν ἀνὴρ πρῶτος ἐπιτετηδευκὼς ταύτην τὴν ἑρμηνείαν, ἵνα διαλλάξῃ τοὺς ἄλλους συγγραφεῖς. ὅταν μὲν οὖν τεταμιευμένως αὐτῇ χρήσηται καὶ μετρίως, θαυμαστός ἐστι καὶ οὐδενὶ συγκριτὸς[1] οὐδ' ἑτέρῳ· ὅταν δὲ κατακόρως καὶ ἀπειροκάλως, μήτε τοὺς καιροὺς διορίζων μήτε τὴν ποσότητα ὁρῶν, μεμπτός. ἐγὼ δὲ οὔτε αὐχμηρὰν καὶ ἀκόσμητον καὶ ἰδιωτικὴν τὴν ἱστορικὴν εἶναι πραγματείαν ἀξιώσαιμ' ἄν, ἀλλ' ἔχουσάν τι καὶ ποιητικόν· οὔτε παντάπασι ποιητικήν, ἀλλ' ἐπ' ὀλίγον ἐκβεβηκυῖαν τῆς ἐν ἔθει· ἀνιαρὸν γὰρ ὁ κόρος καὶ τῶν πάνυ ἡδέων,[2] ἡ δὲ συμμετρία πανταχῇ χρήσιμον.

52 Εἷς ἔτι μοι καταλείπεται λόγος ⟨ὃ⟩[3] περὶ τῶν μιμησαμένων τὸν ἄνδρα ῥητόρων τε καὶ συγγραφέων, ⟨ἀναγκαῖος μὲν ὤν⟩,[4] ὥςπέρ τις καὶ ἄλλος, εἰς τὴν συντέλειαν τῆς ὑποθέσεως, ὄκνον δέ τινα καὶ πολλὴν εὐλάβειαν ἡμῖν παρέχων, μή τινα παράσχωμεν ἀφορμὴν διαβολῆς τοῖς πάντα συκοφαντεῖν εἰωθόσιν ἀλλοτρίαν τῆς ἐπιεικείας, ᾗ κεχρήμεθα καὶ περὶ τοὺς λόγους καὶ περὶ τὰ ἤθη·

[1] συγκριτὸς Sylburg: συγκριτικὸς codd.
[2] ἡδέων Krüger: ἀηδῶν codd.
[3] ὃ inseruit Sadée.
[4] ἀναγκαῖος μὲν ὢν addidit Reiske.

---

[1] See note 4, p. 229.
[2] *c.* 455–360 B.C. Disciple of Socrates and founder of the Cynic sect.

Critias,[1] Antisthenes,[2] Xenophon[3] and the other companions of Socrates. It is clear from all these facts that Thucydides was the first to write in this style, and that he did so in order to be different from the other historians. Whenever he uses it with controlled moderation he is superb and in a class of his own; but when he uses it excessively and in breach of good taste, without discrimination of circumstances or regard for the degree required, he deserves censure. My own view would be that history should not be written in an arid, unadorned and commonplace style: it should contain an element of artistry; and yet it should not be entirely artificial, but should be just a step removed from everyday language.[4] Excess is an abomination even in quite pleasant things, whereas moderation is everywhere desirable.

There still remains one subject for me to discuss, 52
that of Thucydides's imitators among the orators and the historians. It is as essential a topic as any for the completion of my purpose; but I approach it with a certain misgiving and great caution, since I do not wish to present those men who make indiscriminate slander their profession with an opportunity to make a sweeping indictment, by saying something which would ill accord with the spirit of fairness in which I have conducted my discussion of literature and the character ⟨of writers⟩. These critics may think me

[3] *c.* 426–355 B.C. Author of the *Anabasis*, the *Hellenica*, the *Cyropaedia*, the *Oeconomicus*, the *Memorabilia of Socrates* and some minor works; but hardly a typical representative of Attic prose style of the late 5th century, since most of his large output is to be assigned to the years 390–355 B.C., during much of which time he was living in exile: a fact which is reflected in many deviations from Attic usage.

[4] See note 1, p. 305.

οἷς τάχα βάσκανόν τι καὶ κακόηθες πρᾶγμα δόξομεν, εἰ τοὺς μὴ καλῶς τῇ μιμήσει χρησαμένους παράγομεν καὶ παρεχόμεθα τὰς γραφὰς αὐτῶν, ἐφ' αἷς μέγιστον ἐφρόνουν ἐκεῖνοι καὶ δι' ἃς πλούτους τε μεγάλους ἐκτήσαντο καὶ δόξης λαμπρᾶς κατηξιώθησαν. ἵνα δὲ μηδεμία ὑποψία καθ' ἡμῶν τοιαύτη γένηται, τὸ μὲν ἐπιτιμᾶν τισι καὶ μεμνῆσθαι τῶν ἡμαρτημένων αὐτοῖς ἐάσομεν· περὶ δὲ τῶν κατορθωσάντων ἐν τῇ μιμήσει μικρὰ προσθέντες ἔτι καταπαύσομεν αὐτοῦ τὸν λόγον. συγγραφέων μὲν οὖν ἀρχαίων, ὅσα κἀμὲ εἰδέναι, Θουκυδίδου μιμητὴς οὐδεὶς ἐγένετο κατὰ ταῦτά γε, καθ' ἃ δοκεῖ μάλιστα τῶν ἄλλων διαφέρειν, κατὰ τὴν γλωσσηματικὴν καὶ ἀπηρχαιωμένην καὶ ποιητικὴν καὶ ξένην λέξιν, καὶ κατὰ τὰς ὑπερβατοὺς καὶ πολυπλόκους καὶ ἐξ ἀποκοπῆς πολλὰ σημαίνειν πράγματα βουλομένας καὶ διὰ μακροῦ τὰς ἀποδόσεις λαμβανούσας νοήσεις, καὶ ἔτι πρὸς τούτοις κατὰ τοὺς σκαιοὺς καὶ πεπλανημένους ἐκ τῆς κατὰ φύσιν συζυγίας καὶ οὐδ' ἐν ἁπάσῃ ποιητικῇ χώραν ἔχοντας σχηματισμούς, ἐξ ὧν ἡ πάντα λυμαινομένη τὰ καλὰ καὶ σκότον παρέχουσα ταῖς ἀρεταῖς ἀσάφεια παρῆλθεν εἰς τοὺς λόγους.

53 Ῥητόρων δὲ Δημοσθένης μόνος, ὥσπερ τῶν ἄλλων ὅσοι μέγα τι καὶ λαμπρὸν ἔδοξαν ποιεῖν ἐν λόγοις, οὕτω καὶ Θουκυδίδου ζηλωτὴς ἐγένετο κατὰ πολλὰ καὶ προσέθηκε τοῖς πολιτικοῖς λόγοις παρ' ἐκείνου λαβών, ἃς οὔτε Ἀντιφῶν οὔτε Λυσίας οὔτε Ἰσοκράτης οἱ πρωτεύσαντες τῶν τότε ῥητόρων ἔσχον ἀρετάς, τὰ τάχη λέγω καὶ τὰς συστροφὰς καὶ τοὺς τόνους καὶ τὸ πικρὸν καὶ τὸ

carping and malicious if I introduce authors who did not imitate him well, and quote from them passages of which they themselves were very proud and which won for them great wealth and distinction. In order to allay any such suspicion of sinister intentions, I shall refrain from any specific criticisms of such authors, and shall not refer to any faults. But I shall append some brief examples of successful imitation and then conclude my discussion. No historian, so far as I know, of the older generation has imitated the most distinctive qualities of Thucydides's style—his recondite, archaic, artificial, exotic language, his suspended, involved sentences and distorted phrases, which are designed to convey several ideas in an elliptical manner, and whose conclusions are delayed for a long time; and in addition, his awkward and waywardly unnatural collocations of words, and his use of certain figures which would not even find a place in any kind of poetry: features which have produced that obscurity which mars all his fine qualities and overshadows his real merits.

Demosthenes, alone among the orators, imitated 53
Thucydides in many ways, just as he did all who seemed to him to have achieved greatness and distinction in their field; and he added to his political speeches many virtues that he derived from Thucydides, and which neither Antiphon, nor Lysias, nor Isocrates, the leading orators of the day, had acquired: I mean rapid movement, conciseness, intensity, pun-

στριφνὸν καὶ τὴν ἐξεγείρουσαν τὰ πάθη δεινότητα· τὸ δὲ κατάγλωσσον τῆς λέξεως καὶ ξένον καὶ ποιητικὸν οὐχ ἡγησάμενος ἐπιτήδεια τοῖς ἀληθινοῖς ἀγῶσι παρέλιπε, καὶ οὐδὲ τῶν σχημάτων τὸ πεπλανημένον ἐκ τῆς κατὰ φύσιν ἀκολουθίας καὶ τὸ σολοικοφανὲς ἠγάπησεν, ἀλλ' ἐν τοῖς συνήθεσιν ἔμεινε, ταῖς μεταβολαῖς καὶ τῇ ποικιλίᾳ καὶ τῷ μηδὲν ἁπλῶς ἀσχημάτιστον ἐκφέρειν νόημα κοσμῶν τὴν φράσιν. τὰς δὲ πολυπλόκους νοήσεις καὶ πολλὰ δηλούσας ἐν ὀλίγοις καὶ διὰ μακροῦ κομιζομένας τὴν ἀκολουθίαν καὶ ἐκ παραδόξου τὰ ἐνθυμήματα φερούσας ἐζήλωσέν τε καὶ προσέθηκε τοῖς τε δημηγορικοῖς καὶ τοῖς δικανικοῖς λόγοις, ἧττον μὲν ἐπὶ τῶν ἰδιωτικῶν, δαψιλέστερον δὲ ἐπὶ τῶν δημοσίων ἀγώνων.

54 Θήσω δ' ἐξ ἀμφοτέρων παραδείγματα, πολλῶν ὄντων ὀλίγα καὶ τοῖς ἀνεγνωκόσι τὸν ἄνδρα ἀρκοῦντα. ἔστι δή τις αὐτῷ δημηγορία τὴν μὲν ὑπόθεσιν ἔχουσα περὶ τοῦ πρὸς βασιλέα πολέμου, παρακαλοῦσα δὲ τοὺς Ἀθηναίους μὴ προχείρως αὐτὸν ἄρασθαι, ὡς οὔτε τῆς οἰκείας αὐτῶν δυνάμεως ἀξιομάχου πρὸς τὴν τοῦ βασιλέως ὑπαρχούσης οὔτε τῆς συμμαχικῆς πιστῶς καὶ βεβαίως τῶν κινδύνων ἀντιληψομένης· παρακαλεῖ τε αὐτοὺς παρασκευασαμένους τὴν ἑαυτῶν δύναμιν φανεροὺς εἶναι τοῖς Ἕλλησιν, ὅτι τὸν ὑπὲρ τῆς ἁπάντων ἐλευθερίας κίνδυνον ὑπομενοῦσιν, ἐάν τις ἐπ' αὐτοὺς ἴῃ· πρὸ δὲ τοῦ παρασκευάσασθαι πρέσβεις οὐκ ἐᾷ πρὸς τοὺς Ἕλληνας ἀποστέλλειν τοὺς καλέσοντας αὐτοὺς ἐπὶ τὸν πόλεμον, ὡς οὐχ ὑπακουσομένους. τοῦτο λαβὼν τὸ νόημα κατε-

gency, concentration and the rhetorical power that arouses emotion. On the other hand he passed over his use of bizarre, strange and artificial language, considering these unsuitable for practical oratory. Nor did he approve of Thucydides's use of figures of speech which strayed from the natural sequence of the thought and had an air of solecism. He adhered to normal usage, while embellishing his speech by means of substitutions and variation, and by never expressing any idea in an absolutely straightforward way Demosthenes imitated his intricate sentences, which reveal much in a few words, extend the grammatical sequence over a long distance and convey the thought in an unexpected way. He introduced these features into his political and forensic speeches, using them less in the private, more lavishly in the public suits.

I shall quote a few examples from the large 54
number of both kinds available: these will be sufficient for those who have read his works. One of his political speeches concerns a proposed war against the Great King. In it he warns the Athenians not to 354 B.C.
start the war precipitately, because their available resources are no match for those of the Great King, and they cannot rely on their allies to stand by them and share the danger. He further urges them to make their own forces ready for war and to advertise to the rest of Greece their intention to risk their own security in defence of the freedom of all if anyone should attack them. But he advises them against sending ambassadors to the other Greeks to summon them to join the war before such preparations have been made, on the ground that they will not comply.

σκευάκέν τε καὶ ἐσχημάτικεν οὕτως· "Τότε δέ, ἐὰν ἄρα ἃ νῦν οἰόμεθα ἡμεῖς πράττητε, οὐδεὶς δήπου τῶν πάντων Ἑλλήνων τηλικοῦτον ἐφ' ἑαυτῷ φρονεῖ, ὅστις ὁρῶν χιλίους ἱππέας, ὁπλίτας δὲ ὅσους ἂν ἐθέλῃ τις, ναῦς δὲ τριακοσίας οὐχ ἥξει καὶ δεήσεται, μετὰ τούτων ἀσφαλέστατ' ἂν ἡγούμενος σωθῆναι· οὐκοῦν ἐκ μὲν τοῦ καλεῖν ἤδη τὸ δεῖσθαι κἂν μὴ τύχητε ἐφαμαρτεῖν, ἐκ δὲ τοῦ μετὰ τοῦ παρασκευάσασθαι τὰ ὑμέτερα αὐτῶν ἐπισχεῖν δεομένους σῴζειν καὶ εὖ εἰδέναι πάντας ἥξοντας ἔστι." ταῦτα ἐξήλλακται μὲν ἐκ τῆς πολιτικῆς καὶ συνήθους τοῖς πολλοῖς ἀπαγγελίας, καὶ κρείττονά ἐστιν ἢ κατὰ τὸν ἰδιώτην· οὐ μὴν ἐσκότισταί γε οὐδὲ ἀσαφῆ γέγονεν ὥστε ἐξηγήσεως δεῖσθαι. ἀρξάμενός τε ὑπὲρ τῆς παρασκευῆς λέγειν ταῦτα ἐπιτίθησιν· "ἔστι δὲ πρῶτον τῆς παρασκευῆς, ὦ ἄνδρες Ἀθηναῖοι, καὶ μέγιστον, οὕτω διακεῖσθαι τὰς γνώμας ὑμᾶς, ὡς ἕκαστον ἑκόντα προθύμως ὅ τι ἂν δέῃ ποιήσοντα. ὁρᾶτε γάρ, ὦ ἄνδρες Ἀθηναῖοι, ὅτι ὅσα μὲν πώποτε ἐβουλήθητε καὶ μετὰ ταῦτα τὸ πράττειν αὐτὸς ἕκαστος ἑαυτῷ προσήκειν ἡγήσατο, οὐδὲν πώποτε ὑμᾶς ἐξέφυγεν· ὅσα δ' ἐβουλήθητε μέν, μετὰ ταῦτα δὲ ἀπεβλέψατε εἰς ἀλλήλους, ὡς αὐτὸς μὲν οὐ ποιήσων, τὸν δὲ πλησίον τὰ δέοντα πράξοντα, οὐδὲν πώποτε ὑμῖν ἐγένετο." καὶ γὰρ ἐνταῦθα πέπλεκται μὲν ἡ διάνοια πολυπλόκως, λέλεκται δ' ἐκ τῆς κοινότητος εἰς τὴν ἀσυνήθη φράσιν ἐκβεβη-

---

[1] xiv. 13.
[2] xiv. 14.

This is how Demosthenes has presented and elaborated this theme:[1]

"But when the time comes, if you actually do what we now think you intend, I fancy none of the Greek communities rates itself so highly that, when they see a thousand cavalry, as many infantry as you like and three hundred ships, they will not come cap in hand, regarding such aid as their surest hope of deliverance. The position is that by inviting them now you are suppliants, and if your petition fails you also miss your objective; whereas, by biding your time and completing your preparations, you become their saviours at their request, and can be sure that they will all come over to you."

This is far from the manner of most political debate with which most people are familiar, and would be beyond the capabilities of an ordinary speaker. But it has not become befogged and obscure to the point of requiring elucidation. Having begun to discuss the subject of preparations, he continues:[2]

"The first and most important factor in preparation is that you should have your minds made up that each one of you is going to do his duty, whatever it may be, not only willingly but enthusiastically. You can see, Athenians, that whenever a common resolution of yours has been followed by an acceptance of responsibility for action by every man, none of your objectives has ever eluded you, but that you have never been successful when, after resolving to do something, you have looked to one another, each man intending to do nothing while his neighbour did the work."

Here the thought has been intricately interwoven, and normal language has been avoided in favour of unfamiliar expression; but the danger of excess is

κότα, φυλάττεται δὲ τὸ περιττὸν αὐτῶν ἐν τῷ σαφεῖ. Ἐν δὲ τῇ μεγίστῃ τῶν κατὰ Φιλίππου δημηγοριῶν καὶ τὴν ἀρχὴν εὐθὺς οὕτως κατεσκεύακεν· "Πολλῶν, ὦ ἄνδρες Ἀθηναῖοι, λόγων γιγνομένων ὀλίγου δεῖν καθ' ἑκάστην ἐκκλησίαν, περὶ ὧν Φίλιππος ἀφ' οὗ τὴν εἰρήνην ἐποιήσατο οὐ μόνον ὑμᾶς, ἀλλὰ καὶ τοὺς ἄλλους ἀδικεῖ· καὶ πάντων οἶδ' ὅτι φησάντων γ' ἄν, εἰ μὴ καὶ ποιοῦσι τοῦτο, καὶ λέγειν καὶ πράττειν, ὅπως ἐκεῖνος παύσεται τῆς ὕβρεως καὶ δίκην δώσει, εἰς τοῦτο ὑπηγμένα πάντα τὰ πράγματα καὶ προειμένα ὁρῶ, ὥστε δέδοικα μὴ βλάσφημον μὲν εἰπεῖν, ἀληθὲς δέ· εἰ καὶ λέγειν ἅπαντες ἐβούλονθ' οἱ παριόντες καὶ χειροτονεῖν ὑμεῖς ἐξ ὧν ὡς φαυλότατα ἔμελλε τὰ πράγματα ἕξειν, οὐκ ἂν ἡγοῦμαι δύνασθαι χεῖρον ἢ νῦν διατεθῆναι." ὅμοια δὲ τούτοις ἐστὶ κἀκεῖνα· "εἶτ' οἴεσθε, εἰ μὲν αὐτὸν μηδὲν ἐποίησαν κακόν, μὴ παθεῖν δὲ φυλάξαιντο ἴσως, τούτους μὲν ἐξαπατᾶν αἱρεῖσθαι μᾶλλον ἢ προλέγοντα βιάζεσθαι, ὑμῖν δ' ἐκ προρρήσεως πολεμήσειν, καὶ ταῦθ' ἕως ἂν ⟨ἑκόντες⟩ ἐξαπατᾶσθε;" Ἐν δὲ τῷ κρατίστῃ τῶν δικανικῶν, τῷ περὶ τοῦ στεφάνου γραφέντι λόγῳ τῆς Φιλίππου δεινότητος, ᾗ κατεστρατηγήκει τὰς πόλεις, μνησθεὶς οὕτω τὴν διάνοιαν ἐσχημάτικεν· "καὶ οὐκέτι προστίθημι, ὅτι τῆς μὲν ὠμότητος, ἣν ἐν οἷς καθάπαξ τινῶν κατέστη κύριος ὁ Φίλιππος ἔστιν

---

[1] *Phil.* iii. 1.
[2] *Phil.* iii. 13.
[3] *De Corona,* 231. Feigned omission was a recognised

guarded against by the fact that the meaning is clear. In the greatest of his political speeches against Philip, right at the outset he arranges the very first sentence in the following way:[1] 341 B.C.

"Although many speeches have been made, Athenians, in almost every meeting of the Assembly about the offences which Philip has committed since he signed the treaty of peace, not only against you but against all other states; and although everyone, I am sure, would say, if they do not actually say, that our counsels and our actions should be directed to curbing his insolence and bringing him to book, nevertheless I observe that all our affairs have reached such a pass through negligence that—I am afraid that this, though offensive to say, is true—if all the orators had wanted to come forward with proposals, and you to vote for those which would be most disastrous for your interests, I do not think they could have been reduced to a worse state than they are in today."

What follows later is in a similar vein:[2]

"Do you then suppose that, although he chose to deceive people who did not harm him, but might perhaps have defended themselves, rather than attack them after due warning, he will declare war upon you before attacking, especially while you are still willing to be deceived?"

And in his most powerful forensic oration, the speech *On the Crown*, after mentioning Philip's cleverness in outgeneralling the cities, he expresses his thought in the following figure:[3] 330 B.C.

"I refrain from adding the fact that others have experienced the cruelty of Philip, which can be seen

figure of thought, εἰρώνεια, παράλειψις, Latin *occultatio*, *praeteritio*.

ἰδεῖν, ἑτέροις πειραθῆναι συνέβη, τῆς δὲ φιλανθρωπίας, ἣν τὰ λοιπὰ τῶν πραγμάτων ἐκεῖνος περιβαλλόμενος πρὸς ὑμᾶς ἐπλάττετο, ὑμεῖς καλῶς ποιοῦντες τοὺς καρποὺς ἐκομίσασθε." καὶ ἐν οἷς τοὺς προδιδόντας τῷ Φιλίππῳ τὰ πράγματα πάντων αἰτίους ἀποφαίνει τῶν συμβεβηκότων τοῖς Ἕλλησι κακῶν, κατὰ λέξιν οὕτως γράφει·[1] "καίτοι νὴ τὸν Ἡρακλέα καὶ πάντας θεούς, εἴ γ' ἐπ' ἀληθείας δέοι σκοπεῖσθαι ἢ τὸ καταψεύδεσθαι καὶ δι' ἔχθραν τι λέγειν ἀνελόντας ἐκ μέσου, τίνες ὡς ἀληθῶς ἦσαν οἷς ἂν εἰκότως καὶ δικαίως τὴν τῶν γεγενημένων αἰτίαν ἐπὶ τὴν κεφαλὴν ἀναθεῖεν ἅπαντες, τοὺς ὁμοίους τούτῳ παρ' ἑκάστῃ τῶν πόλεων εὕροιτ' ἄν, οὐχὶ τοὺς ἐμοί· οἳ ὅτ' ἦν ἀσθενῆ τὰ Φιλίππου πράγματα καὶ κομιδῇ μικρά, πολλάκις προλεγόντων ἡμῶν καὶ παρακαλούντων καὶ διδασκόντων τὰ βέλτιστα, τῆς ἰδίας ἕνεκ' αἰσχροκερδείας τὰ κοινῇ συμφέροντα προΐεντο, τοὺς ὑπάρχοντας ἑκάστοις πολίτας ἐξαπατῶντες καὶ διαφθείροντες, ἕως δούλους ἐποίησαν."

55 Μυρία παραδείγματα φέρειν δυναίμην ἂν ἐκ τῶν τοῦ Δημοσθένους λόγων τῶν τε δημηγορικῶν καὶ τῶν δικανικῶν, ἃ παρὰ τὸν Θουκυδίδου κατεσκεύασται χαρακτῆρα τὸν ἐν τῇ κοινῇ καὶ συνήθει διαλέκτῳ τὴν ἐξαλλαγὴν ἔχοντα. ἀλλ' ἵνα μὴ μακρότερος τοῦ δέοντος ὁ λόγος γένοιτό μοι, τούτοις ἀρκεσθεὶς ἱκανοῖς οὖσι βεβαιῶσαι τὸ προκείμενον οὐκ ἂν ὀκνήσαιμι τοῖς ἀσκοῦσι τοὺς πολιτικοὺς λόγους ὑποτίθεσθαι τοῖς γε δὴ τὰς

[1] γράφει Sadée: γράφων codd.

in the case of those whom he has once got completely into his hands; while of the generosity which he has feigned towards you while securing the rest of his objectives, you have been fortunate to enjoy the fruits."

And in the passage where he is accusing those who betrayed the cause of Greece to Philip of responsibility for all her misfortunes, he writes the following words:[1]

"But, by Heracles and all the gods, if one had examined the question sincerely, discarding all falsehood and malice, who the men really are, on whom the blame for what has happened may by common consent fairly and justly be thrown, you would find that they are the politicians in the several states who are like Aeschines here, not those like me—men who, when Philip's power was weak and quite insignificant, and we were constantly warning you, advising you and instructing you in the best policies, sacrificed the state's interests to gratify their shameful greed, deceiving and corrupting their respective countrymen until they made them slaves."

I could furnish countless examples from the poli- 55
tical and forensic speeches of Demosthenes which are composed in a style like that with which Thucydides succeeds in being different while using ordinary and familiar language. But in order that my treatise should not become unnecessarily long, I shall content myself with these examples, which are sufficient to prove my thesis. I should not hesitate to suggest to students of political oratory—those, at least, who still try to keep their critical faculties unprejudiced—that

[1] *De Corona*, 294.

κρίσεις ἀδιαστρόφους ἔτι φυλάσσουσι, Δημοσθένει συμβούλῳ χρησαμένους, ὃν ἁπάντων ῥητόρων κράτιστον γεγενῆσθαι πειθόμεθα, ταύτας μιμεῖσθαι τὰς κατασκευάς, ἐν αἷς ἥ τε βραχύτης καὶ ἡ δεινότης καὶ ἡ ἰσχὺς καὶ ὁ τόνος καὶ ἡ μεγαλοπρέπεια καὶ αἱ συγγενεῖς ταύταις ἀρεταὶ πᾶσιν ἀνθρώποις εἰσὶ φανεραί· τὰς δὲ αἰνιγματώδεις καὶ δυσκαταμαθήτους καὶ γραμματικῶν ἐξηγήσεων δεομένας καὶ πολὺ τὸ βεβασανισμένον καὶ τὸ σολοικοφανὲς ἐν τοῖς σχηματισμοῖς ἐχούσας μήτε θαυμάζειν μήτε μιμεῖσθαι. ἵνα δὲ συνελὼν εἴπω, ἀμφότερα μὲν ἐπ' ἴσης ζηλωτὰ εἶναι, τά τε μὴ σαφῶς εἰρημένα ὑπὸ τοῦ συγγραφέως καὶ τὰ προσειληφότα σὺν ταῖς ἄλλαις ἀρεταῖς τὴν σαφήνειαν, οὐκ ἔχει λόγον· ἀνάγκη δὲ ὁμολογεῖν κρείττονα τῶν ἀτελεστέρων εἶναι τὰ τελειότερα καὶ τῶν ἀφανεστέρων τά γ' ἐμφανέστερα. τί οὖν μαθόντες ἅπασαν τὴν διάλεκτον τοῦ συγγραφέως ἐπαινοῦμεν καὶ βιαζόμεθα λέγειν, ὅτι τοῖς καθ' ἑαυτὸν οὖσιν ἀνθρώποις αὐτὰ ὁ Θουκυδίδης ἔγραψε συνήθη πᾶσι καὶ γνώριμα ὄντα, ἡμῶν δὲ λόγος αὐτῷ τῶν ὕστερον ἐσομένων οὐκ ἦν, οἳ δ' ἐκβάλλομεν ἐκ τῶν δικαστηρίων καὶ τῶν ἐκκλησιῶν ἅπασαν τὴν Θουκυδίδου λέξιν ὡς ἄχρηστον, ἀλλ' οὐχ ὁμολογοῦμεν τὸ διηγηματικὸν μέρος αὐτῆς πλὴν ὀλίγων πάνυ θαυμαστῶς ἔχειν καὶ εἰς πάσας εἶναι τὰς χρείας εὔθετον, τὸ δὲ δημηγορικὸν οὐχ ἅπαν εἰς μίμησιν ἐπιτήδειον εἶναι, ἀλλ' ὅσον ἐστὶν αὐτοῦ μέρος γνωσθῆναι μὲν ἅπασιν ἀνθρώποις εὔπορον, κατασκευασθῆναι δ' οὐχ ἅπασι δυνατόν;

they should take Demosthenes as their guide, as I am persuaded that he was the finest of the orators.[1] They should imitate those specimens of his composition in which his brevity, rhetorical power, force, intensity, impressiveness and other related virtues are plain for all men to see; while those which are allusive and difficult to follow, and require a commentary, and those which are full of tortured and apparently ungrammatical constructions deserve neither to be admired nor imitated. To sum up, it does not make sense for us to admire equally the passages in Thucydides which lack clarity and those which possess clarity in addition to his other virtues; for it must be admitted that perfection is better than imperfection, and clarity is better than obscurity. What reasoning, therefore, has led some of us to praise Thucydides's style as a whole, and to insist on asserting that he wrote his history for his contemporaries, and that the language in which it was written was familiar and comprehensible to all of them, but that he took no thought for us, his future readers; while others of us banish all his work from our law-courts and assemblies as being worthless, instead of agreeing that the narrative portions of it, except for very few passages, deserve to be admired and used for every sort of purpose, while the speeches, though they are not all suitable for imitation, contain a good proportion of passages which all men can easily understand, though they cannot all compose in the same style?

[1] See note 2, p. 373. From the inclusion of "brevity" in the following list it is evident that Dionysius is thinking of historical narrative as well as speeches; which makes sense of his recommendation that Demosthenes should be the model for historians as well as for orators.

Τούτων ἡδίω μὲν εἶχόν σοι περὶ Θουκυδίδου γράφειν, ὦ βέλτιστε Κόιντε Αἴλιε Τουβέρων, οὐ μὴν ἀληθέστερα.

THUCYDIDES

I could have written an essay on Thucydides which would have given you more pleasure than this one does, my good Quintus Aelius Tubero, but not one which was more in accordance with the facts.

INDEX

INDEX

(The numbers refer to pages)

INDEX

INDEX

INDEX